Comparative Perspectives on Global Corporate Social Responsibility

Dima Jamali
American University of Beirut, Lebanon

A volume in the Advances in Business Strategy and Competitive Advantage (ABSCA) Book Series

IGI Global
DISSEMINATOR OF KNOWLEDGE

www.igi-global.com

Published in the United States of America by
IGI Global
Business Science Reference (an imprint of IGI Global)
701 E. Chocolate Avenue
Hershey PA, USA 17033
Tel: 717-533-8845
Fax: 717-533-8661
E-mail: cust@igi-global.com
Web site: http://www.igi-global.com

Library of Congress Cataloging-in-Publication Data

Names: Jamali, Dima, editor.
Title: Comparative perspectives on global corporate social responsibility / Dima Jamali, editor.
Description: Hershey : Business Science Reference, 2016. | Series: Advances in business strategy and competitive advantage | Includes bibliographical references and index.
Identifiers: LCCN 2016023677| ISBN 9781522507208 (hardcover) | ISBN 9781522507215 (ebook)
Subjects: LCSH: Social responsibility of business.
Classification: LCC HD60 .C596 2016 | DDC 658.4/08--dc23 LC record available at https://lccn.loc.gov/2016023677

This book is published in the IGI Global book series Advances in Business Strategy and Competitive Advantage (ABSCA) (ISSN: 2327-3429; eISSN: 2327-3437)

British Cataloguing in Publication Data
A Cataloguing in Publication record for this book is available from the British Library.

For electronic access to this publication, please contact: eresources@igi-global.com.

Advances in Business Strategy and Competitive Advantage (ABSCA) Book Series

Patricia Ordóñez de Pablos
Universidad de Oviedo, Spain

ISSN: 2327-3429
EISSN: 2327-3437

Mission

Business entities are constantly seeking new ways through which to gain advantage over their competitors and strengthen their position within the business environment. With competition at an all-time high due to technological advancements allowing for competition on a global scale, firms continue to seek new ways through which to improve and strengthen their business processes, procedures, and profitability.

The **Advances in Business Strategy and Competitive Advantage (ABSCA) Book Series** is a timely series responding to the high demand for state-of-the-art research on how business strategies are created, implemented and re-designed to meet the demands of globalized competitive markets. With a focus on local and global challenges, business opportunities and the needs of society, the **ABSCA** encourages scientific discourse on doing business and managing information technologies for the creation of sustainable competitive advantage.

Coverage

- Competitive Strategy
- Strategy Performance Management
- Adaptive Enterprise
- Globalization
- Joint Ventures
- Tacit Knowledge
- Ethics and Business Strategy
- Innovation Strategy
- Small and Medium Enterprises
- Co-operative Strategies

IGI Global is currently accepting manuscripts for publication within this series. To submit a proposal for a volume in this series, please contact our Acquisition Editors at Acquisitions@igi-global.com or visit: http://www.igi-global.com/publish/.

The Advances in Business Strategy and Competitive Advantage (ABSCA) Book Series (ISSN 2327-3429) is published by IGI Global, 701 E. Chocolate Avenue, Hershey, PA 17033-1240, USA, www.igi-global.com. This series is composed of titles available for purchase individually; each title is edited to be contextually exclusive from any other title within the series. For pricing and ordering information please visit http://www.igi-global.com/book-series/advances-business-strategy-competitive-advantage/73672. Postmaster: Send all address changes to above address.

Titles in this Series

For a list of additional titles in this series, please visit: www.igi-global.com

Crowdfunding for Sustainable Entrepreneurship and Innovation
Walter Vassallo (MC Shareable, Monaco)
Business Science Reference • copyright 2017 • 335pp • H/C (ISBN: 9781522505686) • US $205.00 (our price)

Analyzing the Relationship between Corporate Social Responsibility and Foreign Direct Investment
Marianne Ojo (North West University, South Africa)
Business Science Reference • copyright 2016 • 253pp • H/C (ISBN: 9781522503057) • US $185.00 (our price)

Handbook of Research on Driving Competitive Advantage through Sustainable, Lean, and Disruptive Innovation
Latif Al-Hakim (University of Southern Queensland, Australia) Xiaobo Wu (Zhejiang University, China) Andy Koronios (University of South Australia, Australia) and Yongyi Shou (Zhejiang University, China)
Business Science Reference • copyright 2016 • 743pp • H/C (ISBN: 9781522501350) • US $365.00 (our price)

Ethical and Social Perspectives on Global Business Interaction in Emerging Markets
Minwir Al-Shammari (University of Bahrain, Bahrain) and Hatem Masri (University of Bahrain, Bahrain)
Business Science Reference • copyright 2016 • 372pp • H/C (ISBN: 9781466698642) • US $185.00 (our price)

Strategic Approaches to Successful Crowdfunding
Djamchid Assadi (Burgundy School of Business, France)
Business Science Reference • copyright 2016 • 378pp • H/C (ISBN: 9781466696044) • US $205.00 (our price)

Handbook of Research on Entrepreneurship in the Contemporary Knowledge-Based Global Economy
Neeta Baporikar (University of Pune, India)
Business Science Reference • copyright 2016 • 607pp • H/C (ISBN: 9781466687981) • US $345.00 (our price)

Competitive Strategies for Academic Entrepreneurship Commercialization of Research-Based Products
Anna Szopa (Jagiellonian University, Poland) Waldemar Karwowski (University of Central Florida, USA) and David Barbe (University of Maryland, College Park, USA)
Business Science Reference • copyright 2015 • 317pp • H/C (ISBN: 9781466684874) • US $195.00 (our price)

Incorporating Business Models and Strategies into Social Entrepreneurship
Ziska Fields (University of KwaZulu-Natal, South Africa)
Business Science Reference • copyright 2016 • 362pp • H/C (ISBN: 9781466687486) • US $190.00 (our price)

IGI GLOBAL
DISSEMINATOR OF KNOWLEDGE
www.igi-global.com

701 E. Chocolate Ave., Hershey, PA 17033
Order online at www.igi-global.com or call 717-533-8845 x100
To place a standing order for titles released in this series, contact: cust@igi-global.com
Mon-Fri 8:00 am - 5:00 pm (est) or fax 24 hours a day 717-533-8661

Table of Contents

Detailed Table of Contents

This chapter proposes a conceptual framework for comparing enterprise and governmental approaches to corporate social responsibility (CSR) for developed and developing countries. An enterprise approach is voluntary. A governmental approach provides either requirements or guidance, strong or weak, for enterprise CSR. Focus is on multinational enterprises (MNEs), for two reasons. First, MNEs may operate across quite different conditions. Second, a major MNE concern has to do with fair trade and sustainable development supply chains. The chapter considers three approaches found in the extant literature. One approach asserts autonomy of developing countries from developed countries, and thus divergence of enterprise and governmental CSR by type of context. A second approach examines global convergence as highly context path-dependent and perhaps cosmetic. A third approach emphasizes "glocality" combining global thinking with local action. The author proposes an alternative understanding of how to compare CSR for developed and developing countries using theory versus context.

Despite a growing recognition of national contexts in predicting the dynamics of corporate social responsibility (CSR), the limited prior research has failed to disaggregate national institutions to specify the mechanisms between aspects of national institutional contexts and elements of CSR practices. In this paper we offer a framework for analyzing the nature and status of CSR, which is made up of eight elements: history, religions/ideologies, social norms, geography, political structures, the level of economic development, civil society institutions, and the country's "safety net" provisions. We apply the framework to explain how and why China's understanding of CSR differs from that in Western countries.

This chapter applies Hofstede's cultural dimensions to compare how companies located in Western and Eastern regions present their corporate sustainability strategies to their stakeholders. We compare ten pairs of West-East companies and find that differences in the corporate sustainability strategies they report can be related to geo-political and socio-cultural differences as described by Hofstede. Our findings can serve as a tool for companies in both regions to gain a better understanding about which sustainability initiatives are of more concern, depending on the region they operate.

From the days corporate social responsibility (CSR) became a topic of discussion, extensive amount of research is conducted on CSR in Western countries but still there is relatively little focus on some developed and developing countries. Moreover, relatively little research has compared cross-country and cross-sector CSR variations. Starting from this point, this article investigates the extent of CSR variations of a highly developed (the United States), a developed (South Korea) and a developing country (Turkey) through a detailed comparative analysis of CSR information disclosure on corporate websites of 50 CSR active companies listed in stock exchange markets of each country. For cross-sector comparison, these target corporations are selected from five different industries including consumer electronics & telecommunication services, automobile & component manufacturers, food & beverages, retail stores, and major banks. The research opens the door for more in-depth empirical study on why there are cross-country and cross-sector variations in CSR.

This chapter examines how public banks operating in Egypt and the UAE respond to stakeholders' needs. It uses content analysis to explore the volume, nature, and quality of social information presented on the websites of these banks and the way in which these banks use web technology to report such information. The results indicate that public banks in both countries made more disclosures about corporate social responsibility (CSR) and community issues. Nevertheless, they lag behind stakeholders' expectations in regard to information about employees and cultural issues. Furthermore, the UAE banks tend to offer better stakeholders access to social information than Egyptian banks. However, both have a long way to go in better facilitating interaction with stakeholders. There is evidence to suggest that social reporting by public banks' in both countries is still below the expectations of the Muslim and global communities.

Mining is impact intensive regardless of commodity and scale. A socially responsible mining company, at a minimum, does not knowingly irreparably harm the community's ability to sustain itself after the mine closes. This chapter examines the mining sector in the Philippines: the public concerns, CSR responses and the challenges mining companies face in the country. Information was gathered through a review of academic and grey literature, key informant interviews and content analysis of Sustainability / CSR Reports. Many of the companies invest in the community as well as minimise their environmental impacts. A few invest in the community but appear to ignore people's right to a healthy environment. The chapter argues that mining can become an instrument for inclusive growth in the Philippines only if there is social peace, and that a streamlined and transparent mining policy regime, equitable benefits sharing and demilitarisation of mining areas will help bring this about.

This book chapter focuses on the developmental-oriented perspective of CSR which views corporate involvement as a 'support-aid' for meeting triple bottom-line development in Nigeria. Arising from the literature, the stakeholder, legitimacy and social contract theories provide the required theoretical grounding for the discourse. The qualitative research method was found appropriate for this discourse. From the list of 25 registered telecommunication companies in Nigeria, a sample of 8 functional companies was selected using purposive sampling technique. The data extracted from the annual reports and websites of these companies were analysed using the content analysis. The findings indicate that the telecommunication companies are practically leveraging their CSR initiatives for social, economic and environmental wellness in Nigeria through a number of developmental programmes. The chapter explicates the fact that CSR as a private sector development model can be a potent tool for bridging governance gap environment instead of leaving all social problems to governments.

Corporate social responsibility (CSR) involves multi-faceted concerns and interested parties. The theoretical paper argues that pursuing CSR policies creates value for sustainable economic prosperity for the pulp and paper sector. The pulp and paper industry is one of the largest industrial sectors worldwide and plays a critical role in global development. As the fourth largest energy user and CO2 emitter, the industry is subject to the vicissitudes of global society and environment. Irresponsible pulp and paper operations are now shunned by various stakeholders, which ultimately affect their economic bottom lines. Sustainable operations bring continuity and competitiveness along with innovation, efficiency and social recognition to the industry. Using the criteria of the triple-bottom-line theory (economic, environmental and social), this paper demonstrates that a strong CSR framework and proactive initiatives add value to the pulp and paper business.

In this chapter, we make a contribution to the literature on corporate social responsibility in global value chains that link dispersed consumers and importers in developed countries with local manufacturers, workers, and communities in developing countries. We create an integrated analytical framework and a methodology that can guide master-level and Ph.D. students as well as practitioners on how they may map the governance processes through which multi-stakeholder initiatives (MSIs) in global value chains are formulated, implemented, monitored as well as the impact that MSI standards have on the work conditions of those laboring at the base of global value chains. We use a stylized case study of fair trade in the football manufacturing industry in Pakistan to illustrate how the framework and the methodology might be applied to the empirical analysis of MSI governance processes and their impacts on workers' conditions in export-oriented industries in the South.

This chapter presents challenges in China's governance outlook within a Corporate Social Responsibility (CSR) analysis of China's social, environmental and economic resources and potential impacts in other countries. The purpose of this article sheds light of how CSR in China is emerging as a doorway to a) promote understanding of changes in firm governance for general managers through state and corporate socially responsible practices and b) to explain that preserving the environment and preventing pollution is necessary if China would like to trade with the West and enter global markets with other countries that place importance of governance and CSR principles.

Global systemic risks of climate change, over-indebtedness in the aftermath of the 2008/09 World Financial Crisis and the need for pension reform in the wake of an aging Western world population, currently raise attention for inter-generational fairness. Pressing social dilemmas beyond the control of singular nation states call for corporate social activities to back governmental regulation in crisis mitigation. The following chapter therefore promotes the idea of inter-generational equity in the corporate world to find an inclusive solution comprised by the public and private sectors. In the given literature on global

Preface

This edited volume was launched with the idea to enhance our understanding of Comparative Corporate Social Responsibility (CSR). Comparative studies of CSR are relatively scant, certainly when compared to other fields of study, such as Corporate Governance, where cross-cultural comparative work has made significant progress in recent years. There are many potential explanations for this, including the fact that CSR is still considered an emerging field (Jamali and Karam, forthcoming), and there is still no agreed upon definition of the term CSR itself, which has been described as a tortured and contested concept (Bryan, Jamali and Saffar, 2015; Godfrey and Hatch, 2007), that can mean different things to different people at different times (Caroll, 1999; Rivoli and Waddock, 2011). Comparative work is also invariably tedious, requiring theorizing and collecting and comparing empirical insights across institutional contexts, which is known to be complicated in view of institutional intricacies and their implications for CSR (Jamali and Neville, 2011; Matten and Moon, 2008).

Keeping the above in mind, this edited volume was initiated with the intention to encourage comparative research in the domain of CSR, particularly, comparative work across developed and developing country contexts. The volume ended up collating an interesting mix of contributions, spanning a wide spectrum of country contexts, including USA, Canada, Australia, China, Japan, Korea, South Korea, Tunis, Egypt, United Arab Emirates (UAE), Philippines, Pakistan, Nigeria, and broad geographical areas including, North America, Asia, Latin America and the Arab Region. The chapters also addressed a wide range of industries including, food and beverages, consumer electronics and telecommunications services, automobile and component manufacturers, pulp and paper, mining, oil and gas, retail and banking Although the comparative dimension was not always as accentuated as intended, each chapter presented some valuable contributions that will enhance our understanding of CSR in context, and all chapters make interesting remarks pertaining to future comparative work on CSR.

This edited volume thus makes clear that CSR is alive and well, and the discourse about CSR has picked up momentum across the globe. The volume also makes clear that institutions and institutional constellations still exert a considerable influence on the expressions of CSR around the globe. Windsor in Chapter 1 clarifies how CSR practices are likely to be different in developed and developing countries, because the institutions and social constellations vary significantly highlighting how context certainly matters in analyzing CSR. Also accentuating the important role of national institutions, Davidson and Yin in Chapter 2 compile a framework for analyzing the nature and status of CSR in context, consisting of eight elements, including history, religions/ideologies, social norms, geography, political structures, level of economic development, civil society institutions, and the country's safety net provisions. They also demonstrate an application of this framework in the Chinese context, distilling contextual peculiarities that help differentiate Chinese approaches to CSR from what is commonly observed in Western contexts.

Also dwelling on the importance of context, Kaplan and Montiel (Chapter 3) examine cross-cultural variation in CSR by screening the CSR reports of 10 pairs of companies operating across China, Japan and Korea on one hand versus Canada and the USA on the other hand. They demonstrate intricate differences in CSR themes and disclosures across what they refer to as Eastern versus Western contexts. For example, Eastern-based companies are keen to promote family related CSR programs and more detailed ethical guidance through codes of conduct coupled with more emphasis on risk management and environmental protection, versus Western based companies that emphasize transparency, and innovation related CSR programs. Their analysis of differences along the Hofstede dimensions offers important insights into how culture and cultural differences affect CSR and CSR expressions across contexts.

In Chapter 4, Dikeç, Kane and Çapar also compare CSR disclosures of 50 companies listed on the stock exchange in the US, South Korea and Turkey. They note that CSR disclosures have picked up momentum across South Korea and Turkey but subtle differences are noted across contexts, with the US still leading the way in CSR disclosures particularly those pertaining to codes of conduct, employee diversity, human rights and anti-corruption for example followed by South Korea and Turkey. Also the US is leading the way in terms of environmental disclosures (environmental management systems, energy conservation, waste reduction, and renewable energy) and responsible supply chain related disclosures; the latter seems conspicuously absent in the context of Turkish companies. They note however that Turkish companies are stronger in terms of governance related disclosures, while South Korean companies are particularly strong in terms of employee benefits and career development related disclosures. All in all, their study highlights important variation in CSR disclosures across contexts, which they relate in turn to institutional and cultural contextual factors.

Similarly, in Chapter 5, Osman compares patterns and content of CSR disclosures across banks in two Arab Middle Eastern contexts, the UAE and Egypt, noting more institutionalization of CSR disclosures and reporting among banks based in the UAE, and more Islamic flavors and connotations to the content of their reporting. They also note titled attention to employee issues across both contexts (particularly training and development), and the predominance of reporting on philanthropy across both contexts particularly targeting health and educational issues. In Chapter 6 Ben Rejeb similarly compares CSR disclosures across Tunis and Egypt, noting that firms in Egypt and in Tunisia are increasingly interested in CSR and disclose information about it but that disclosures often remain at the discretion of shareholders and top management. Therefore good governance has a positive influence on disclosures in both contexts, particularly the presence of independent directors, the presence of foreign directors, and the absence of CEO duality, which should be accorded close attention in future research.

The remaining chapters have helped shed light on particular industry specificity and dynamics, which are also important to probe further to advance comparative CSR work. For example in Chapter 7, de-Burgh Woodman, Bressan and Torrisi compare CSR across two important industries/sectors in Australia, namely banking and mining. Using a stakeholder lens, they analyze the CSR disclosures of the four largest banks, and four largest mining firms in Australia from 2012 to 2014 and note important differences across both industries, with the disclosures in the mining sector focusing on environmental management and community development, whereas banks emphasized stakeholder engagement more broadly, with a focus on customers and employees. While these differences are expected, they also note the general strategic appropriation of CSR as a reputational management tool, and its emptying out of ethical and moral underpinnings and foundations.

Other chapters dwell on voluntary disclosure activities of specific controversial industries or sectors, highlighting salient issues that need to be accounted for in future comparative work on CSR. In Chapter

8 for example, Haro-de-Rosario, Del Mar Galvez-Rodriguez and del Carmen Caba-Perez develop an index to analyze the content of CSR reports and use it to analyze the CSR disclosures of the 29 largest Oil and Gas companies in Latin America. They confirm that privately owned, larger and more profitable oil and gas companies are doing better in terms of CSR disclosures, but that the sector as a whole needs to exert more effort to attenuate its negative externalities and increase its positive externalities in the context of CSR. In Chapter 9, Yap and Ground examine the mining sector in the Philippines, and the CSR disclosures of some of the largest mining companies, noting problems pertaining to evading mining regulations, not enforcing procedural guidelines, and potential problems of exacerbating corruption despite the positive disclosures generally shared with the public. They thus note a discrepancy between the CSR rhetoric (what is shared in reports) and anti-CSR behavior on the ground as known and reported in local communities. In contrast, in Chapter 10, Raimi looking at CSR disclosures in the Nigerian telecommunications sector, notes visible improvement in their disclosures across the Triple Bottom Line, with these companies focusing on health, education, sports, capacity building and infrastructure development in host communities, and hence assuming a positive and effective developmental role. In Chapter 11, Hack-Polay and Qiu consider conceptually rather than empirically the advantages of greater attention to CSR in the Pulp and Paper sector in Asia and provide some insights into the urgent need for a more sustainably oriented pulp and paper industry and the need for more governmental monitoring and enforcement in this sector.

Chapters 12-15 offer unique complementary perspectives relevant to the theme of this book. Chapter 12 by Hassan and Lund-Thomsen presents an analytical framework to map the governance processes through which multi-stakeholder initiatives in global value chains are created, and their potential impact on the ground. They accord attention to the important role that institutional contexts play in shaping such multi-stakeholder initiatives which in turn amplify or undermine their effectiveness in catalyzing change in developing countries. Chapter 13 by Wolf and Thiel sheds light on the paramount importance of more emphasis on ecological preservation in the context of the ascendancy of CSR and China's penetration of global markets. Chapter 14 by Puaschunder examines the important notion of inter-generational equity in the context of the ascendancy of CSR models and frameworks and the practical implications of financing an intergenerational harmonious solution to climate change. Finally in Chapter 15, Issa and Pick direct attention to the importance of business ethics teaching, and present an innovative method for teaching business ethics that has the potential to facilitate the mainstreaming of ethics and CSR topics within the context of business schools.

Taken together, the chapters present an interesting mix of contributions and perspectives that are likely to advance our understanding of future comparative work on CSR. Without doubt, managers across the world are increasingly faced with the challenges of CSR and sustainability reporting and are tailoring appropriate responses and communications that are often informed by the realities of the context in question. One basic insight that is validated through the contributions to this edited volume is the paramount importance of accounting for how context and national institutions influence the expressions of CSR given that they shape the boundary conditions and the rules of the game within which business operates (Bruton, Ahlstrom, & Puky, 2009; Gerard 2014). The contributions to this volume begin to capture interesting variation in the themes and approaches adopted in CSR across contexts, but also interesting industry dynamics and peculiarities that deserve closer attention in future comparative work on CSR. We hope that future scholarship will further elucidate these points, focusing less on CSR disclosures and more on the difficult task of comparing country institutions, inspired by the interesting frameworks compiled and presented in this book (e.g. Windsor; Davidson and Yin in this book) and others (e.g. Matten and Moon, 2008; Kang and Moon, 2012; Jamali, Karam and Blowfield, 2015) that have been advanced in recent CSR literature. Such efforts are extremely worthwhile and important to help us trace variations in CSR across contexts in relation to the larger economic, political, cultural and historical determinants of the role of business in society.

Dima Jamali
American University of Beirut, Lebanon

REFERENCES

Bruton, G. D., Ahlstrom, D., & Puky, T. (2009). Institutional differences and the development of entrepreneurial ventures: A comparison of the venture capital industries in Latin American and Asia. *Journal of International Business Studies*, *40*(5), 762–778. doi:10.1057/jibs.2009.3

Bryan, H., Jamali, D., & Saffar, W. (forthcoming). Near and dear? The role of location in CSR engagement. *Strategic Management Journal*.

Carroll, A. B. (1999). Corporate social responsibility evolution of a definitional construct. *Business & Society*, *38*(3), 268–295. doi:10.1177/000765039903800303

Gerard, G. (2014). Rethinking management scholarship. *Academy of Management Journal*, *57*(1), 1–6. doi:10.5465/amj.2014.4001

Godfrey, P. C., & Hatch, N. W. (2007). Researching corporate social responsibility: An agenda for the 21st century. *Journal of Business Ethics*, *70*(1), 87–98. doi:10.1007/s10551-006-9080-y

Jamali, D., & Karam, C. (forthcoming). CSR in developing countries as an emerging field of study. *International Journal of Management Reviews*.

Jamali, D., & Neville, B. (2011). Convergence versus divergence of CSR in developing countries: An embedded multi-layered institutional lens. *Journal of Business Ethics*, *102*(4), 599–621. doi:10.1007/s10551-011-0830-0

Jamali, K., Karam, C., & Blowfield, M. (2015). *Development-Oriented Corporate Social Responsibility*. Sheffield: Greenleaf Publishing.

Kang, N., & Moon, J. (2012). Institutional complementarity between corporate governance and corporate social responsibility: A comparative analysis of three capitalisms. *Socio-economic Review*, *10*(1), 85–108. doi:10.1093/ser/mwr025

Matten, D., & Moon, J. (2008). "Implicit" and "explicit" CSR: A conceptual framework for a comparative understanding of corporate social responsibility. *Academy of Management Review*, *33*(2), 404–424. doi:10.5465/AMR.2008.31193458

Rivoli, P., & Waddock, S. (2011). "First They Ignore You…": The time-context dynamic and corporate responsibility. *California Management Review*, *53*(2), 87–104. doi:10.1525/cmr.2011.53.2.87

Chapter 1
Defining Corporate Social Responsibility for Developing and Developed Countries:
Comparing Proposed Approaches

Duane Windsor
Rice University, USA

ABSTRACT

This chapter proposes a conceptual framework for comparing enterprise and governmental approaches to corporate social responsibility (CSR) for developed and developing countries. An enterprise approach is voluntary. A governmental approach provides either requirements or guidance, strong or weak, for enterprise CSR. Focus is on multinational enterprises (MNEs), for two reasons. First, MNEs may operate across quite different conditions. Second, a major MNE concern has to do with fair trade and sustainable development supply chains. The chapter considers three approaches found in the extant literature. One approach asserts autonomy of developing countries from developed countries, and thus divergence of enterprise and governmental CSR by type of context. A second approach examines global convergence as highly context path-dependent and perhaps cosmetic. A third approach emphasizes "glocality" combining global thinking with local action. The author proposes an alternative understanding of how to compare CSR for developed and developing countries using theory versus context.

INTRODUCTION

This chapter proposes a conceptual framework for comparing enterprise and governmental approaches to corporate social responsibility (CSR) for developed and developing countries. How enterprises and governments can better interact to advance social welfare may differ significantly between the two general categories of countries. The chapter uses these two general categories to make examination of the research question manageable. CSR arguably remains a highly contested idea, the contest fragmenting along several fault lines. The question is not readily resolved theoretically, and the answer may depend

DOI: 10.4018/978-1-5225-0720-8.ch001

greatly on country-specific institutions and conditions. Empirical research on this question, however, remains underdeveloped.

The proposed conceptual framework offers four value-added contributions. First, the framework facilitates comparison and assessment of enterprise and governmental approaches within the varying institutions and social conditions of developed and developing countries. An enterprise approach is one adopted by the business. A governmental approach involves voluntary guidelines or mandatory requirements promoted in public policies of home and host countries. Second, the framework facilitates a comparison and assessment of theoretical and contextual approaches to CSR. Theoretical approaches focus on economic versus altruism conceptions. Contextual approaches focus on whether developing countries require fundamentally different CSR practices, or variations in practices across developed and developing countries may converge globally, or glocality integrating global thinking and local action is the flexible solution. The proposed framework can subsume these various approaches in a more systematic way. Third, the framework – in combining these various considerations – provides a new way of thinking about CSR literature. Fourth, the chapter discusses the research and practice implications of the proposed framework. The conclusion section highlights the importance of future comparative empirical studies of developed and developing countries. The implications for business managers depend on the institutions and social conditions of each country.

The enterprise approach might vary by whether the business is headquartered in a developed or developing country, and whether the business is operating in a developed or developing country. This enterprise approach might be adopted voluntarily, as evidenced by active membership in the United Nations Global Compact for instance; or might be adopted in compliance with governmental guidelines or requirements in home country or host country. The Global Compact endorses ten principles concerning human rights, labor, the environment, and anti-corruption.

Governmental policies in the European Union (EU), in the Nordic countries especially, and India promote CSR (Rahim, 2013). Steurer (2010) studies public policies on CSR in Europe (see Knudsen, Moon, & Slager, 2015), as a basis for explaining why governments do or do not exhibit interest in CSR. Steurer's typology of CSR policies distinguishes among five policy instruments: legal, economic, informational, partnering, and hybrid. Steurer identifies four types of governmental CSR actions: raising awareness, improving transparency, fostering socially responsible investment, and leading by example. That author argues that there has been a shift over time in conceptualization of CSR from voluntary business action intended to help reduce government regulation toward a new approach of societal co-regulation (or co-governance) by businesses and governments acting in concert.

This chapter focuses on multinational enterprises (MNEs), as key sources of foreign direct investment (FDI) in developing countries (Buckley & Ghauri, 2004; Buckley & Strange, 2015; Dunning, 1979). MNEs headquarter typically but not exclusively in developed countries; there are also increasingly MNEs operating from a number of non-developed countries. A developed country MNE is facing reasonably similar conditions when operating in other developed countries. Instances are US or Canadian firms operating in Western Europe, or German firms operating in the US or Canada. A developed country MNE is facing reasonably dissimilar conditions when operating in developing countries. Instances are British or Italian firms operating in Africa, Asia, or Latin America. An MNE headquartered in a non-developed country is operating across reasonably similar conditions in other non-developed countries, but reasonably dissimilar conditions operating in developed countries. Instances are Brazilian or Indian firms operating in North America or Western Europe. A "footloose" or "born global" MNE is one that effectively acknowledges no home country (van Beveren, 2007; Zander, McDougall-Covin, & Rose, 2015).

This chapter focuses primarily on the differences between developed and developing countries as broad categories. For purposes of this chapter, developing and non-developed are reasonably synonymous terms. The focus in this chapter is on economic development considerations, bearing in mind the influences on enterprise and governmental CSR approaches arising in differences among developed, developing, emerging, and transitional countries at a finer grained level of analysis. Some instances noted above – Canada, Germany, Italy, US, and UK – are relatively developed and economically and politically advanced countries. Some instances noted above – Brazil and India – are constitutional democracies politically but are emerging rather than fully developed economies. For certain purposes, non-developed countries as distinguished from developed countries can be subdivided into developing economies, emerging economies, and transitional economies (which may be developing or emerging). The chapter does not draw generally on the categories of emerging economies and transitional countries, except briefly later for Table 1, which concerns perceptions of the bribe paying tendencies of MNEs from developed or emerging economies (including China and Russia which are also transition economies). There are to date no important MNEs headquartered in developing countries which are not yet emerging economies. These differences among non-developed countries have important implications for governmental CSR policies and MNE conduct, but the difference can be subsumed here within the considerable range of conditions occurring across the set of non-developed countries. An emerging economy is one that is becoming much more developed than the typical instance of a developing country (Heakal, 2015; Hoskisson, Eden, Lau, & Wright, 2000). Thus Brazil and India are typically viewed as emerging economies, as is Malaysia or Turkey. China and Russia are typically viewed as emerging economies that are autocratic (one-party) states; China and Russia are also transitional economies. A transitional economy is one shifting from communist central planning toward freer markets (Dawson, 2003). A transitional country is a polity that was formerly dominated by a communist regime or was part of the Soviet Union before its disintegration. Most transitional countries are located in Eastern Europe or the Balkans. Vietnam remains an autocratic (one-party) state (Dawson, 2003).

The chapter assesses three approaches found in the extant literature; and proposes an alternative understanding of how to compare CSR for developed and developing countries. One approach asserts the autonomy of developing countries from developed countries. This approach tends to emphasize advanced country imperialism, recalling the historical condition of European and American colonialism in much of the developing world. The autonomy or divergence approach leads on to policy recommendations that amount to increased host country regulation and taxation of foreign MNEs, through various devices. A second approach predicts global convergence among countries, but typically as highly context path-dependent. This approach tends to emphasize that enterprise CSR, as practiced by foreign MNEs, may be essentially cosmetic in motive and effect. A third approach emphasizes what Visser (2011b) has termed "glocality" which conceptually argues for combining global thinking and local action. The alternative understanding proposed by the present author draws on a juxtaposition of theory and context. This alternative understanding can subsume the other three approaches.

The remainder of the chapter, following this introduction, is organized as follows. The "Background" section which follows next explains the basic issues in CSR affecting interpretation of the three approaches and the author's proposed alternative understanding. The subsequent section explains the

Table 1. Transparency International 2011 Bribe Payers Index (BPI) scores for 28 countries and territories

BPI Score (0 to 10)	Country or Territory	Rank Order of 28 (with ties)
Countries with BPI Score Above 8.0 (Developed Countries Except for Singapore)		
8.8	Netherlands	1 = 2
8.8	Switzerland	1 = 2
8.7	Belgium	3
8.6	Germany	4 = 5
8.6	Japan	4 = 5
8.5	Australia	6 = 7
8.5	Canada	6 = 7
8.3	Singapore (emerging economy)	8 = 9
8.3	United Kingdom	8 = 9
8.1	USA	10
8.0	France	11 = 12
8.0	Spain	11 = 12
Countries with BPI Score Above 7.0 But Below 8.0 (Emerging Countries Except for Italy)		
7.9	South Korea	13
7.7	Brazil	14
7.6	Hong Kong (territory of China)	15 = 16 = 17 = 18
7.6	Italy (developed country)	15 = 16 = 17 = 18
7.6	Malaysia	15 = 16 = 17 = 18
7.6	South Africa	15 = 16 = 17 = 18
7.5	India	19 = 20 = 21
7.5	Taiwan	19 = 20 = 21
7.5	Turkey	19 = 20 = 21
7.4	Saudi Arabia	22
7.3	Argentina	23 = 24
7.3	United Arab Emirates (UAE)	23 = 24
7.1	Indonesia	25
7.0	Mexico	26
Countries with BPI Score Below 7.0 (Transition Countries)		
6.5	China	27
6.1	Russia	28

Notes: Within ties for rank order, countries or territories are in alphabetical order. (The original source reports Taiwan above India; the ordering has been alphabetized here.)

(Transparency International, Bribe Payers Index Report 2011, http://www.transparency.org/bpi2011/results)

three approaches in the extant literature: the North-South divide (or divergence approach); the global convergence approach; and the glocality approach which seeks to bridge convergence and divergence. The next section explains the author's proposed alternative approach and how to subsume the other three approaches. The "Conclusion" summarizes the arguments of the chapter and explains the implications for research and practice.

BACKGROUND

Providing a general and abstract conception of corporate social responsibility (CSR) is not markedly difficult (Carroll, 2015). "The concept of corporate social responsibility (CSR) aims both to examine the role of business in society, and to maximise the positive societal outcomes of business activity" (United Nations, 2007, p. 1). "At its broadest, CSR can be defined as the overall contribution of business to sustainable development — it is in that sense that it is used here" (United Nations, 2007, p. 1).

The broad conception of CSR is also highly abstract with respect to concrete government policies and concrete MNE practices. The profound disagreements about CSR, and multiple definitions of CSR, concern theoretical framing, contexts, and variables, and the detailed content of CSR to be specified under particular theories for particular contexts taking variables into account. The general definitions in the previous paragraph can apply to an anti-CSR position arguing that unregulated markets are the proper role of business and that role maximizes positive societal and sustainable development outcomes. The liberalization school of international trade takes this general view.

The problem lies in detailed specification of the content, minimum requirements, and maximum limits to CSR. At any significant level of detail, CSR becomes complex and controversial. The CSR literature has generated a "bewildering array of conceptualizations and applications" with arguably "unintended consequences" (Bergman, Leisinger, Bergman, & Berger, 2015, p. 1). The Bergman et al. study mapped the academic landscape of CSR by analyzing 120 audio and video recordings or university sponsored or endorsed presentations and other events held between 2010 and 2014 deposited at a media repository (iTunesU). While the sample (deposited at a particular site) and analysis procedures might be criticized, nevertheless the authors provide some reasonable information suggesting complexity and controversy. CSR exposition is not a unified approach or paradigm on this evidence. The UN report cited above addresses CSR detail as follows (see Amaeshi & Adi, 2007):

Defining corporate social responsibility in more detail than this remains a vexed issue. In practice views differ based on two factors. First, the extent to which importance is placed on the centrality of the "financial business case" for responsible business behaviour in defining the scope of CSR practices — i.e. the extent to which tangible benefits to companies must be demonstrable. Secondly, the extent to which government is seen to have a role in framing the agenda — and how. A minimum standard for CSR might be that businesses fulfil their legal obligations or, if laws or enforcement are lacking, that they "do no harm". A median approach goes beyond compliance, calling for businesses to do their best, where a "business case" can be made, to contribute positively to sustainable development by addressing their social and environmental impacts, and potentially also through social or community investments. A maximum standard points toward the active alignment of internal business goals with externally set societal goals (those that support sustainable development) (United Nations, 2007, p. 1).

A principal line of division in the CSR academic literature is between economic and social approaches. In general terms, the economic approach views CSR as a voluntary enterprise action that is inherently unprofitable. The social approach either contributes social benefit or is responsive to stakeholder expectations in some way. For instance, Crifo and Forget (2015) study CSR as a private response to market imperfections for the purpose of satisfying social preferences. The authors classify CSR decisions into three categories: public goods, public bads, and altruism (reflecting interaction with government regulation); imperfect competition; and incomplete contracts. The authors report a disconnection between scholarly understanding of CSR drivers and CSR impacts (or consequences); and a knowledge gap concerning the links among CSR, financial performance, and social and environmental performance.

A major concern for MNEs has to do with fair trade and sustainable development supply chains arising in other countries (Lund-Thomsen & Lindgreen, 2014; Lund-Thomsen & Wad, 2014; Rahim & Wisuttisak, 2013). A multiple-case study finds that firms do not necessarily transfer corporate sustainability agendas into controls on suppliers' sustainability (Schnittfeld & Busch, 2016). The study concludes that sustainability management – within the firm and transfer to suppliers – is affected by a number of factors: the firm's own business case for sustainability, available control mechanisms, trade-offs involved, trust, and degree of market liberalization.

As noted briefly in the "Introduction" section, governments may adopt public policies requiring or guiding CSR in various ways. The Nordic countries are leading in this regard; and this leadership is attracting considerable research interest (Midttun, Gjølberg, Kourula, Sweet, & Vallentin, 2015; Nielsen & Frederiksen, 2015; Strand, Freeman, & Hockerts, 2015). Officially established in September 1961, the Organisation for Economic Co-operation and Development (OECD), still in process of expanding membership, comprised 34 countries in July 2015. While most members presently are developed countries (e.g. Western Europe, Australia, Canada, Finland, Japan, New Zealand, and the US), there are also emerging economies (e.g. Chile, Greece, Israel, Mexico, South Korea, and Turkey) and transitional countries of Eastern Europe (e.g. Czech Republic, Estonia, Hungary, Poland, Slovenia, and Slovak Republic). The OECD Guidelines for Multinational Enterprises, an annex to the OECD Declaration on International Investment and Multinational Enterprises, adopted in 1976 (and subsequently revised several times), provide guidance concerning responsible business conduct. (Some non-OECD countries are also adherents of the guidelines.) In 2000, the OECD guidelines required member countries to establish national contact points (NCPs) charged with promoting effective implementation (Olsen & Sorensen, 2014). Focusing on Denmark, Norway, and the UK, Olsen and Sorensen suggest that the NCP approach may tend to change the guidelines from purely voluntary recommendations (or soft law) toward more binding requirements for MNEs (or hard law). The NCPs can receive complaints. The authors argue that the "very broad and vague terminology in the Guidelines" and vague specification of NCP jurisdiction make enterprise compliance very difficult (Olsen & Sorensen, 2014, p. 9). The authors point to the Danish example as a leading instance of expansive jurisdiction. A survey of 400 fashion companies in the Nordic countries (Denmark, Finland, Iceland, Norway, and Sweden) reveals a diversity of strategic responses to institutional pressures for CSR (Pedersen & Gwozdz, 2014). Pedersen and Gwozdz suggest that inconsistent pressures within (not between) stakeholder groups affect responses, and that increasing pressures stimulate substitution of opportunity-seeking for compliance.

The OECD also has an anti-bribery convention (the Convention on Combating Bribery of Foreign Public Officials in International Business Transactions), in force February 1999. Beasley (2015) is critical of the effectiveness. Some 41 countries had ratified or acceded to this anti-bribery convention by May 2013. The United Nations Convention against Corruption (UNCAC) came into force in December 2005 as an essentially global inter-governmental agreement. Much of reported or suspected corruption occurs in non-developed countries, as Table 1 tends to confirm.

THREE GENERAL APPROACHES IN THE EXTANT LITERATURE

Three general approaches have been proposed in the extant literature for addressing differences in CSR for developed countries and developing countries. These proposals highlight the possibility that CSR is highly contextual and contingent (Athanasopoulou & Selsky, 2015). One approach asserts the autonomy of developing countries from developed countries and their MNEs. This approach emphasizes divergence of CSR by type of context. A second approach examines global convergence as highly context path-dependent and perhaps cosmetic (Jamali & Neville, 2011). A third approach emphasizes "glocality" as "the act of thinking globally, acting locally" (Visser, 2011b). Political processes appear to be important considerations in MNEs (Geppert & Dörrenbächer, 2014). Some degree of universality is supplemented by variable degree of local application.

One consideration in assessing these approaches is the range of variation among MNEs, which can occur at the subsidiary level. A study of 101 British MNE manufacturing and service subsidiaries operating in six South East Asian countries during the period 2003-2007 found that the subsidiaries used regional strategies rather than following a global strategy (Nguyen, 2014). A reason was the strong focus on sales.

Another consideration is the range of variation among developing countries. A study of the determinants of growth in relationship to the effects on poverty reduction over the period 1960-2004 divided a panel data set of 59 developing countries into two subgroups (Belke & Wernet, 2015). In general, investment reduced poverty; and population growth increased poverty. Knowledge import was growth enhancing only in the subgroup characterized as at a relatively higher stage of economic development. The positive growth effect of increasing democratization occurred only in the subgroup characterized as relatively poor developing countries. (Birdsall, 2015, argues out that development of a middle class may not necessarily guarantee good government.) Implications are that knowledge import, as distinct from investment, has little effect in poorer countries; but democratization in such countries may reduce corruption and improve public policies. The base of the pyramid population (Jones Christensen, Siemsen, & Balasubramanian, 2015) and the informal economy (Smith & Thomas, 2015) are particularly prominent in developing countries. Human rights lack protection in corrupt governments, found mostly in developing or transitional countries (Giuliani & Macchi, 2014; Ramasastry, 2015).

These two variables – across MNEs and across developing countries – generate a complexity of possibilities. Researchers de Jong and van Houten (2014) argue that MNE cultural diversity and country cultural diversity are important considerations in how degree of internationalization of the firm affects firm performance. Degree of internationalization is positive for performance for MNEs operating in culturally similar host countries and negative for performance for MNEs operating in culturally diverse or dissimilar host countries.

It is awkward to disentangle illegal corruption and legal lobbying (and related influence) approaches (Rodriguez, Siegel, Hillman, & Eden, 2006). The former is found more in developing and transitional countries; the latter is found more in developed and emerging countries. Kaufmann and Vicente (2011) argue that to a considerable degree the distinction is a matter of legislative declaration, with arguably corrupt or corruptible legislators deciding where to draw the line. In a democratic process, businesses can (and arguably should) undertake to influence public policy domestically and abroad – and generally will do so for self-advantage (Wagner & Anastasiadis, 2014; Windsor, 2007). There is some empirical evidence in support of a thesis that in developing countries where corruption is rampant and law enforcement weaker firms tend to rely on illegal bribery; in advanced countries where there is less corruption and law enforcement is stronger firms tend to switch to legal lobbying (Bennedsen, Feldmann, & Lassen, 2011; Campos & Giovannoni, 2007; Harstad & Svensson, 2011). Organized crime is an important factor in some countries (Vaccaro & Palazzo, 2015), such as Russia for instance.

A fundamental difference between developed and developing countries, including some emerging and transitional countries in the latter for this purpose, is the relative degree and pervasiveness of corruption in government (Khojastehpour, 2015; Rose-Ackerman, 2002). Persistent conflict is an important factor in some countries (Kolk & Lenfant, 2013). Available information suggests that corruption tends to be higher in developing countries in which there is mineral extraction (oil, gas, and mining), Central Asian countries once part of the USSR, Africa, and Latin America. There are empirical studies that draw on firm-level data and surveys to explore what can be discovered about who pays bribes and why (Bennedsen, Feldmann, & Lassen, 2011; Jensen, Li, & Rahman, 2010; Svensson, 2003). While there are some relatively more corrupt countries in the OECD (such as Mexico and the European Union – particularly Italy, Portugal, and Spain), generally developed country members of the OECD are significantly cleaner than many developing countries.

Studies of whether corruption deters or encourages FDI reportedly have yielded somewhat mixed results (Godinez & Liu, 2015), in part because corruption may be high where foreign entry is attractive – as in the extractive industries. Godinez and Liu apply a concept of "corruption distance" between pairs of countries to Latin America, with controls for transaction costs and institutional variables. They find an asymmetrical impact of corruption distance on FDI. Host countries with "positive" corruption distance relative to home countries (meaning the host country is cleaner than the home country) show no significant effects, up or down, on inward FDI levels. Host countries with "negative" corruption distance relative to home countries (meaning the home country is cleaner than the host country) show significantly lower inward FDI levels. The authors' interpretation of these findings is that MNEs from relatively cleaner home countries lack familiarity with the formal and informal institutions of corruption in relatively dirtier host countries. In contrast, MNEs from relatively dirty home countries find no deterrence in high corruption in host countries. These findings suggest that corruption distance is an important determinant of FDI patterns.

Corruption may involve both formal and informal institutions. A study reports that higher levels of formal and informal corruption environments are related to higher levels of corporate social irresponsibility (Keig, Brouthers, & Marshall, 2015). Variable combinations of formal and informal corruption may result in misleading assessments of MNE operating environments. About one-third of the study's sample involved conditions of low formal corruption and high informal corruption.

Transparency International's Bribe Payers Index (BPI), initiated in 1999 and issued periodically since (2002, 2006, 2008, and 2011), ranks the world's largest economies by estimated propensity of their firms to use bribes abroad. The rankings reflect surveys of senior business executives from developed and developing countries, and are reported at a 90% confidence level. The 2011 ranking reported on 28 countries. Table 1 is organized by BPI score in the left column from high to low and rank order (of 28) in the right column from high to low. (Ties among countries are shown in alphabetical order.) The BPI score has a theoretical range from a low of 0 (100% bribery abroad) to a high of 10 (0% bribery abroad). In 2011, the highest score was 8.8 for the Netherlands and Switzerland and the lowest score was 6.1 for Russia. All countries and territories in Table 1 are developed or emerging economies. Hong Kong is a territory of China. Table 1 is subdivided internally using scores above 8.0, between 7.0 and 7.9, and below 7.0 (China and Russia). These divisions are quite revealing, if arguably arbitrary. MNEs from developed countries (with the exception of Italy) are generally less prone to bribe, while MNEs from emerging countries (with the exception of Singapore) are generally more prone to bribe. China and Russia are perceived to be the worst violators in this ranking. China and Russia are transitional as well as emerging economies.

Table 2 provides a basic comparison of the three alternative conceptions of CSR for developing countries. The table provides a working definition and some key implications for each conception. Following the table, three sub-sections discuss in more detail each conception.

The North-South Divide Approach

With respect to the first approach, there is a North-South divide (Knudsen, Moon, & Slager, 2015) over the CSR agenda, in the sense that developing countries may see Western countries and Western MNEs determining the agenda according to their own concerns and priorities (Amaeshi, Adi, Ogbechie, & Amao, 2006). These concerns and priorities are insensitive to host country agendas and arguably can harm sustainable development in host countries (Idemudia, 2011). In the context of Africa, Idemudia proposes research engagement with the role of host country governments, a bottom-up approach to analyzing CSR needs, and an integrated rather than piecemeal research focus. This proposed divide amounts to divergence between developed country CSR and developing country CSR.

In part, the divide approach draws on the imperialism and colonialism conduct of Western countries in which much of Africa and was subjected to foreign political control. In part, there are significant policy disagreements between developed and developing countries (Rolland, 2007). One study applies this perspective to telecommunications deregulation in (Chidozie, Odunayo, & Olutosin, 2015).

One might argue that the Scherer and Palazzo theory of political CSR of MNEs can be regarded as foreign agenda imposition (Scherer & Palazzo, 2011; Scherer, Palazzo, & Matten, 2014; Scherer, Palazzo, & Seidl, 2013). Those authors – supporting democratization in both developed and developing countries – propose that MNE responsibilities increase with governmental incapacity. That is, particularly in developing countries, if governments cannot adequately provide public goods and democratic institutions, MNEs should provide substitutes. From a developing country perspective, this theory might be viewed as a species of imperialism.

Table 2. Comparison of three alternative conceptions of CSR for developing countries

Conception	Working Definition	Some Key Implications
North-South Divide	Divergence between CSR policies and practices in developed (North) and developing (South) countries	• Developed country policies and practices and developed country MNEs tend to be conflated with imperialism and post-colonialism • Developing countries should follow a different CSR path emphasizing national control of resources and taxation of foreign MNEs
Global Convergence	Convergence between CSR policies and practices in developed and developing countries, suggesting a global set of standards	• Developed country policies and practices and developed country MNEs tend to be conflated with the concept of development • National CSR policies and MNEs' CSR practices are likely to be cosmetic and mimetic
"Glocality"	Global thinking (suggestive of policy and strategy convergence) combined with local action (suggestive of institutional and practice divergence)	• Involves a transformation in CSR understanding from first generation (CSR 1.0) to second generation (CSR 2.0) thinking • Involves improved cooperation between enterprises and governments on a country-by-country basis within more global standards (such as the UN Global Compact and ISO 26000, for instance)

At least as important is the developing country perception and likely reality that MNEs from other countries are concerned primarily with profit generation from rather than social benefit contribution to host countries. A comparison of the dividend policies of MNE subsidiaries and domestic firms in South Korea finds that MNE subsidiaries act generally to meet remittance requirements determined by the parent enterprise. These remittance requirements have only weak correlation with local CSR and investment requirements for wealth creation (Kim & Jeon, 2015). The MNE subsidiaries are concerned with profit rather than local social contribution.

This perspective can be carried into MNE tax practices (Adam, Kammas, & Lapatinas, 2015). Taxation is one way in which developing countries might obtain resources from MNE operations (Jenkins & Newell, 2013). One can expect that MNEs will seek to minimize tax liability in all countries of operation. Tax contribution might be viewed as a way of being socially responsible (Jenkins & Newell, 2013).

A study (Attig & Brockman, 2015) finds that CSR initiatives are conditional. Firms are more likely to engage in such initiatives when headquartered where there are large senior citizen populations and a large proportion of the population makes charitable donations. Firms are less likely to engage in such initiatives when headquartered where there are large religiously affiliated groups. The study also finds that CSR initiatives create market value when properly aligned with the prosocial attitudes of local residents.

Extractive industries – exporting minerals, oil, gas, and the like from developing countries – arguably come closest to the model of exploitative foreign MNEs; and this condition has attracted considerable research interest (García-Rodríguez, García-Rodríguez, Castilla-Gutiérrez, & Major, 2013; George, Kuye, & Onokala, 2012; Gilberthorpe & Banks, 2012; Hilson, 2012, Kotilainen, Prokhorova, Sairinen, & Tiainen, 2015). A case study of the Marlin gold mine in Guatemala revealed a sharp contradiction between the rhetoric of commitment to CSR and the reality of absence of actual implementation in developing countries (Slack, 2012).

The Global Convergence Approach

With respect to the second approach, Jamali and Neville (2011) propose a theoretical framework combining a multi-level model of institutional flows and the explicit-implicit CSR model (see Blindheim, 2015). They use this framework to analyze CSR convergence versus divergence in the context of Lebanon. Global convergence may be cosmetic, responding to mimetic pressures. Local divergences suggest that contextualized path-dependent evolution may result in hybrid outcomes.

Global convergence may operate in one of two ways. One path is through the global assertion of CSR and expression of CSR in the form of various international accountability standards and tools (Jamali, Lund-Thomsen, & Khara, 2015). Jamali et al. draw on empirical fieldwork, involving in-depth interviews with a wide range of stakeholders, in the soccer ball manufacturing industry at Jalandhar, in North India. In the context of how local small- and medium-sized enterprises (SMEs) engage in joint CSR initiatives concerning child labor, the authors also find evidence of selective decoupling from CSR in dimensions of humanitarian and labor rights issues. As a result, in the authors' view, the fundamentals of workers' difficulties remain unchanged (see De Neve, 2014). The focus on child labor is essentially cosmetic, from this perspective. Global CSR may be counterproductive (Jamali & Sidani, 2011).

Many factors may affect, directly or indirectly, the relationship between CSR and firm performance (Saeidi, Sofian, Saeidi, Saeidi, & Saaeidi, 2015). The Saeidi et al. study focuses on sustainable competitive advantage, reputation, and customer satisfaction as likely mediators in the relationship between CSR and firm performance. Findings from 205 Iranian manufacturing and consumer product firms support the authors' contention that the relationship between CSR and firm performance is a fully mediated one. CSR has a positive effect on sustainable competitive advantage, reputation, and customer satisfaction. Reputation and competitive advantage, but not customer satisfaction, then mediate the relationship between CSR and firm performance. The authors suggest that CSR indirectly promotes firm performance through positive effects on reputation and competitive advantage, while improving customer satisfaction.

The other path is through adoption of CSR policies by developing countries (Srisuphaolarn, 2013). The Indian Companies Act 2013 is an instance of CSR policy adopted by an emerging country (Ghosh, 2015). A study of 47 top Indian companies estimates effects on level of financial contribution to CSR, the CSR operating system, and the CSR activities undertaken by the companies (Shin, Jung, Khoe, & Chae, 2015). The authors find that many of the companies already contributed profits to CSR activities and have CSR operating systems. The CSR activities are largely in compliance with the statutory requirements. The authors conclude that Indian CSR regulation will create positive developmental conditions for communities without having much negative effect on companies. The basic reason, however, is that the statute captures mostly what is already in place. Another study expresses doubt that investors will want to pay for the CSR requirements of Indian companies (Parinduri & Paul, 2015).

The "Glocality" Approach

With respect to the third approach, Visser (2008) has formulated a second-generation theory of CSR, in which "glocality" is important (Visser, 2011b). Visser (2011b) argues that there is considerable mythology about CSR. The seven myths are that: (1) Economic growth and CSR are incompatible. (2) MNEs are the biggest CSR sinners. (3) MNEs are the biggest CSR saviors. (4) Developing countries are anti-MNE. (5) Developed countries lead on CSR. (6) Codes can ensure CSR in developing countries. (7) CSR is a unitary model for the whole world. The seventh myth is the one most directly related to the purpose of this chapter. "Glocality" is the antidote for this myth in conceptually arguing for combining global thinking and local action. Visser makes an interesting distinction between universal principles (UN Global Compact) and process frameworks (ISO 14001), and local priorities and performance measures. As displayed in Table 3, Visser (2013) uses a five-stage model of evolution of CSR – incorporating sustainability and responsibility. The stages are defensive, charitable, promotional, strategic – and now transformative or systemic CSR. The first four stages constitute CSR 1.0; the fifth stage defines CSR 2.0 as emergent and future practices. Visser (2011a) had identified five principles underlying this fifth stage: creativity, scalability, responsiveness, glocality, and circularity. Complementing the five principles are the four parts of a DNA Model: value creation, good governance, societal contribution, and ecological integrity. This DNA Model is effectively triple bottom line performance (value, social, environmental) combined with good governance.

There is arguably no theoretical consensus on how MNEs prescriptively should implement CSR, for the purpose of building host country legitimacy (Hah & Freeman, 2014). Hah and Freeman argue that addressing this problem will involve theoretical integration of research into business ethics and international business. The authors provide a conceptual framework for this purpose. The idea is to explain theoretically how global CSR strategies can be adapted to more local CSR strategies by MNE subsidiaries intended to build legitimacy. The authors use as a specific setting smaller Asian emerging markets, because growth in the global economy affects such markets more acutely. The framework permits variation in level of ethical pressure across host countries and in degree of how CSR is ingrained in the subsidiary's parent company. That is, the stronger the external ethical pressure on a subsidiary and the

Table 3. Visser's conception of two CSR generations embedding five CSR stages

Time Direction	Generation and Stage	Definitions
	CSR 1.0	**First Generation CSR**
	Stage 1	Defensive
	Stage 2	Charitable
	Stage 3	Promotional
	Stage 4	Strategic
	CSR 2.0	**Second Generation CSR**
	Stage 5	Transformative and Systemic: emergent and future practices
	Five Principles 1. Creativity 2. Scalability 3. Responsiveness 4. Glocality 5. Circularity	
	Four-component DNA Model 1. Value creation 2. Good governance 3. Societal contribution 4. Ecological integrity	

(Visser, 2008, 2011a, 2011b, 2013)

higher the degree of CSR ingrainedness, the more likely the subsidiary will try to establish legitimacy in a host country. In practice, then, global and local pressures operate to shape CSR in a firm (Vigneau & Humphreys, 2014). The Vigneau and Humphreys study compared relations between a head office and two subsidiaries through a three-stage process of framing, negotiation, and dissemination. Subsidiary personnel reframe institutional pressures to fit context.

A PROPOSED ALTERNATIVE APPROACH

The three conceptions discussed above – divergence (North-South divide), convergence, and glocality – focus on (or emphasize) corporate social responsibilities of MNEs operating in developing countries. A fundamental new distinction emerging in the literature is between corporate social responsibility (CSR) and corporate social irresponsibility (CSIR) (George et al., 2012).

Figure 1 , explained in detail in this section, uses CSR as an overarching rubric, with three dimensions: universal business ethics, country-specific legal compliance, and voluntary corporate citizenship. (Windsor, 2013, provides a formal exposition of this approach.) Figure 1 is centered on country-specific institutions including legal compliance and social conditions. As the reader looks at the figure, the left side concerns universal business ethics and the right side concerns voluntary corporate citizenship. So the figure moves, left to right, from universal business ethics through country-specific legal compliance to voluntary corporate citizenship. Irresponsibility is violation of universal business ethics and country-specific legal compliance. Marques and Mintzberg (2015) argue that "the familiar clichés" or "platitudes" of pro-CSR arguments – such as doing well by doing good, developing win-win solutions,

Figure 1. Two intersecting dimensions of the CSR contest: Theory and context

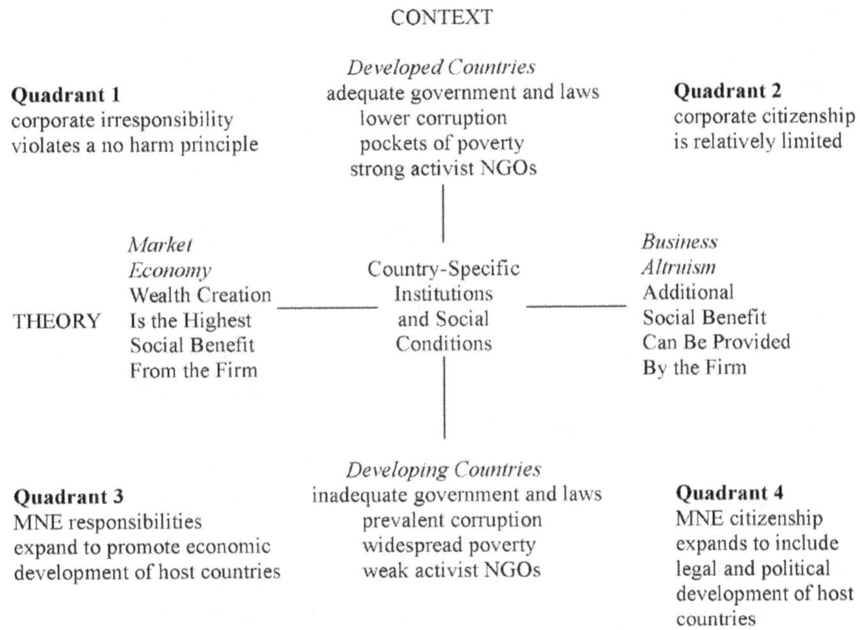

and corporate citizenship – may sometimes encourage irresponsibility. Responsibility can go well beyond not simply avoiding irresponsibility. Strike, Gao, and Bansal (2006) provide evidence – for a sample of 222 US public firms during 1993-2003 – that firms can simultaneously be responsible and irresponsible. There is no obvious weighting scheme for aggregating responsible and irresponsible actions in order to measure something like net responsibility. The relationship between irresponsibility and responsibility differs between developed countries and developing countries.

Figure 1's logical design provides two key value-added contributions. First, it facilitates separation of developed countries and developing countries as general categories, while placing this separation into a framework differentiating among ethics, compliance, and citizenship. Formulated for developed countries, the economics-based anti-CSR argument essentially equates CSR with voluntary corporate citizenship, while assuming relatively limited ethical and legal standards (subject to lobbying efforts aimed to maximizing net benefits to the firm from governmental policies) (Schmitz & Schrader, 2015). The divergence approach reasonably argues that this formulation does not translate adequately to the institutions and conditions of developing countries without invoking overtones of imperialism and post-colonialism (leaving aside here that the overtones may have merit).

Second, the logical design facilitates discussion of controversies in CSR theorizing. Corporate social responsibility is a highly contested term, meaning different things to different academics and practitioners, as well as activists. That the term is contested is widely emphasized. However, a contest can occur for one or both of two reasons: because there is a genuine conceptual problem not yet resolved; or because the topic is convenient for voicing conflicting views.

Bondy, Moon, and Matten (2012) suggest that integrated internationalization strategies do not resolve global and local CSR issues (see Bondy & Starkey, 2015). Rather, integrated internationalization strategies tend to reinforce the outcomes associated with global business strategies, in which those core issues identified by corporate headquarters become legitimated and local issues are marginalized. The authors draw on a study of how foreign national culture and local issues are incorporated into the CSR policy of 37 MNEs. The environments of MNEs are highly complex. Marano and Kostova (2015) examine 710 US MNEs operating in over 100 countries during the period 2007-2011. The authors conclude that salient factors affecting CSR practices are MNE economic dependence on a country, the heterogeneity of institutional forces, degree of exposure to countries with higher CSR templates, and the intensity and commitment of the MNE to particular economic linkages such as whether the MNE emphasizes FDI or trade.

The contest over CSR definition can be simplified for analytical discussion to two intersecting dimensions: theoretical and contextual. Figure 1 depicts this understanding of the contest. The horizontal axis reflects the theoretical dimension. The vertical axis reflects the contextual dimension. The two dimensions intersect in the figure through country-specific institutions and social conditions. The theoretical dimension, captured in the horizontal axis, concerns the relationship between a market economy and business altruism. The horizontal axis simply distinguishes between a market economy, liberalized and globalized in one understanding of international trade, and business altruism occurring in home countries for domestic enterprises and host countries for MNEs. The contextual dimension, captured in the vertical axis, distinguishes between developed countries and developing countries. Institutions and conditions are different in developed countries and developing countries as a generalization about these two categories. (Orientation vertically and horizontally of the figure has no meaning – developing can go above developed; market and altruism can flip.)

There are two basic conditions for CSR. The first condition is adherence to universal business ethics and country-specific legal compliance. There are ethical requirements for a firm in a market economy. (Business ethics is superior to legal compliance, because conditions might occur that require civil disobedience.) The second condition is good citizen policy adopted by a firm (whether for strategic or value reasons) resulting in some altruistic actions. Implementation of these two conditions differs significantly depending on whether the firm is in a developed country or a developing country.

The design of Figure 1 generates four quadrants, which are numbered in the figure one through four for identification. In the first quadrant, defining the market economy in a developed country context, the firm (domestic or MNE) should try to adhere to a no harm principle. Corporate irresponsibility is violation of this no harm principle. In the second quadrant, defining business altruism in a developed country context, the firm (domestic or MNE) should try to be a good citizen by providing additional social benefit as feasible. The need for such provision is relatively limited due to the institutions and conditions in developed countries. In the third quadrant, defining the market economy in a developing country context, the firm (especially an MNE) should go beyond a no harm principle to a greater emphasis on its role in economic development of the country. Corporate responsibility expands beyond simple avoidance of corporate irresponsibility. In the fourth quadrant, defining business altruism in a developing country context, the firm (especially an MNE) should go beyond limited provision of social benefits to accept a good citizen role in helping to build the political and legal institutions of the country. Quadrants one and two treat economic CSR theory as the minimum standard for business operations in developed countries. There institutions and social conditions are consistent with that economic perspective. Quadrants three and four, consistent with political CSR theory (Scherer & Palazzo, 2011; Scherer et al., 2013, 2014), impose greater responsibilities on firms (especially MNEs) for economic, legal, and political development.

The theoretical dimension is the classical distinction between market-oriented economics and normatively-oriented altruism. Lying between these opposed conceptions is the institutional structure –

government and laws – of a specific society. CSR may involve both explicit and implicit dimensions. The economics position is that, given an appropriate competitive, governmental, and legal context (with which the enterprise is compliant), market wealth orientation is the highest social benefit that an enterprise can contribute. That is, an enterprise obeys the law and allocates capital efficiently – thus improving social welfare. In this set of conditions, corporate altruism is an inefficient diversion of enterprise resources. The main argument for altruism-like activities is strategic: a means for aligning stakeholders, including employees, with shareholder wealth goals.

The contextual dimension involves significant variation in institutional and social conditions: the key distinction is between developed countries and developing countries. In the former, institutions – government and laws – more nearly approach the set of conditions posited for the economics position; corruption is much less prevalent, or occurs in legal forms; and poverty persists in isolated pockets rather than being pervasive in the society. In the latter, institutions may be much less adequate (by Western standards); corruption is often pervasive; and poverty is widespread and characteristic of the society. Some developing countries may be conflict ridden.

In consequence, the view of CSR in developed countries tends to focus on the theoretical debate between economic and altruism positions – along the horizontal axis of Figure 1. The reason is that contextually, in Carroll's pyramid of CSR dimensions (see Carroll, 2015), the economic, legal, and ethical dimensions are presumed to work sufficiently well – so that CSR seems to be mostly about voluntary philanthropy. (Spence, 2007, addresses SMEs in developed countries; see Luetkenhorst, 2004, for a direct contrast to SMEs in developing countries). Thus, the European Commission (2011) defines CSR as "a concept whereby companies integrate social and environmental concerns in their business operations and in their interaction with their stakeholders on a voluntary basis." The view of CSR in developing countries tends to focus on institutional structure and social conditions and on how enterprises (domestic and MNE) can contribute to sustainable development through good citizenship. Such contribution will vary greatly in detail country by country – because the conditions vary. What is needed in Ecuador may or may not be what is needed in Mauretania. Thus, there ensues a debate concerning sustainable development, institutional voids, and who should do what and why (Jamali, 2010; Khan & Lund-Thomsen, 2011; Nasrullah & Rahim, 2013; Strike, Gao, & Bansal, 2006).

The economics position aligns with the combination of market economies in developed countries, in the upper left-hand corner of Figure 1. This alignment reduces pressure for business altruism and permits philanthropy to be strategic in content. Criticism of CSR as a Western-oriented construction aligns with the combination of developing country conditions and consequent needs for additional social benefits from businesses, in the lower right-hand corner of Figure 1. A developing country needs to strengthen its market economy and its governmental-legal institutions, and reduce poverty. Amaeshi, Adegbite, and Rajwani (2016) characterize the situation for CSR as one of "challenging and non-enabling institutional contexts." The conditions are challenging for and the institutions are not supportive of CSR. In such conditions, the authors report that CSR practices are adaptive mechanisms forming an institutional buffer.

There are two extensions to this model of alignment. The category of emerging economies – meaning more developed market economies but not necessarily more developed institutional structures – tends to occur in the lower left-hand corner of Figure 1. The category of developing countries with strengthening governmental and legal institutions tends to occur in the upper right-hand corner of Figure 1, where strengthened institutions do not mean automatically marked reduction of poverty (which requires FDI and more developed market economies). Whether market improvements and governmental-legal improvements occur in tandem is an empirical matter; therefore, the two kinds of improvements can occur separately.

The contextual range of market and social conditions and of institutional structures generates correspondingly highly variable definitions for CSR practices (that is to say, for CSR content by country). Bouvain, Baumann, and Lundmark (2013) report distinct brand value – CSR links in a sample of 84 major banks in several East Asia countries and the US. Empirical variability of executive and employee value orientations, country operating conditions and institutional structures, stakeholders, activist NGO attention, corporate social performance (CSP) impacts, and corporate financial performance outcomes is hardly surprising.

A recent instance of NGO activism (Baur & Palazzo, 2011), and home country influence demonstrates the pressures brought to bear on Soco, a UK oil company, not to explore in the Virunga national park in the Democratic Republic of Congo, despite apparent support of the government for exploration (Vidal, 2014). Virunga, home to about half of the world's mountain gorillas, was declared a UN world heritage site in 1979.

Bouvain et al. further conclude that "The study also establishes that CSR is not a universal concept ..." Such a conclusion involves a high degree of nuance in interpretation. The framework proposed here asserts a universal no harm principle and obedience to laws (with a necessary exception for civil disobedience in some local conditions). It is not CSR that is local, but the content of good citizenship. The argument that a firm should be a good citizen is weaker than the arguments that firms should not cause harm and should obey laws. It is citizenship policy that will vary greatly by local circumstances – and understandably so. This variation can be quite strategic. At the same time, sustainable development is an interaction among businesses, governments, and civil society. Businesses may partly drive social change. An Infosys (2013, p. 2) white paper on CSR argues that in financial services "what's beneficial to society can profit the business." Financial services firms "drive socio-economic and environmental change through product innovation and sustainable business solutions." Gupta and Shapiro (2014) provide background information on Infosys.

Figure 1 subsumes the three alternative conceptions of CSR for developing countries – divergence, convergence, and glocality – as follows. There are clearly institutional and conditions differences between developed and developing countries. These contextual differences do not automatically amount to cases for different theories of CSR. Rather, there is considerable divergence now. Convergence can increase as economic, legal, and political development proceeds over time. Glocality asserts a global theory (that is, theoretical convergence rather than divergence) and local action (that is, practical divergence rather than convergence) due to variations in institutions and conditions most pronounced in developing countries presently.

CONCLUSION

An important issue is how to define the corporate social responsibilities of multinational enterprises operating in developing countries (Bardy, Drew, & Kennedy, 2012; Filatotchev & Stahl, 2015). One general view is that CSR is basically the same in developed or developing countries. The competing general view is that CSR is highly context dependent (Ozuem, Howell, & Lancaster, 2014). A key argument in favor of context dependency is that conditions and needs are quite different in developing countries (Millner & Dietz, 2015; Pagliusi, Leite, Datla, Makhoana, Gao, Suhardono, & Homma, 2013; Park, Song, Choe, & Baik, 2015). The difficulty concerns where this key argument leads. One difficulty is continuing controversy over proper definition and application of CSR (Rupp & Mallory, 2015; Rupp, Wright, Aryee, & Luo, 2015).

The extant literature contains three different positions: North-South divide; global convergence; and glocality. The chapter assesses these three approaches. The North-South divide approach asserts autonomy of developing countries, and tends to characterize developed country CSR concepts as either contextually irrelevant or imperialism. The global convergence approach expects that developed and developing country CSR will tend to become similar, but will do so in a highly context path-dependent way. India's CSR statute is cited as an instance. A criticism of global convergence is that CSR will often be essentially cosmetic. The glocality approach of Visser (2011b) argues for combining global thinking and local action.

This chapter proposes an alternative understanding that can subsume these three positions. This alternative understanding draws on a juxtaposition of theory and context. This alternative understanding emphasizes that CSR practices will be different in developed and developing countries, because the institutions and social conditions vary significantly across those categories. In developed countries, firms should emphasize avoidance of corporate irresponsibility, interpreted as violation of a principle of no harm as defined by universal business ethics and country-specific legal compliance. In developed countries, firms face relatively limited requirements and opportunities for corporate citizenship in the form of business altruism. In developing countries, MNEs especially face considerably greater corporate social responsibility for promoting economic development. And corporate citizenship expands to include legal and political development of host countries.

The main lessons or takeaways of the proposed conceptual framework developed in this chapter are as follows. Three proposed approaches to CSR for developing countries contain certain defects. The North-South divide approach tends to be conflated with developing countries independently imposing requirements on MNEs and rejecting developed country experiences and views. The global convergence approach tends to be conflated with developing countries becoming quickly developed, and thus leaving CSR practices by MNEs as largely cosmetic. The glocality approach combines global thinking with local action, and is thus more flexible. However, thus far global thinking remains dominated by developed country experiences and views, while local action is so variable as to make it difficult to formulate a cross-country comparative interpretation. The proposed framework basically guides firms (domestic or MNEs) in developed countries to avoid corporate irresponsibility in conditions which tend to limit corporate citizenship opportunities. The proposed framework expands responsibilities and citizenship opportunities for MNEs especially in developing countries. This approach involves much more judgment by managers and more interaction between enterprises and governments in developing policies and practices contingent on host country institutions and conditions. These main lessons have some implications for research and practice.

Implications for Research

Research concerning CSR in developing countries has tended to focus on three alternative approaches to conceptualization of CSR: desirable autonomy of developing countries; global convergence in the direction of CSR policies and practices of developed countries; or glocality emphasizing global thinking but local action adapting to specific institutions and social conditions in developing countries. Political CSR theory, formulated independently of the debate above, obligates MNEs to substitute partly for developing country governments as necessary and to promote democracy in both developed and developing countries. The key research implication is the need for future comparative studies across countries. The proposed framework of this chapter anchors the theory and context dimensions on country-specific institutions and conditions. The data in Table 1 concerning MNE bribe paying tendencies by country reveal a wide range of differences between developed countries and emerging economies generally, and how much worse China and Russia as transitional emerging economies appear to be. This range on bribe paying tendencies is simply the tip of the iceberg. Detailed studies of developing countries and systematic comparison of CSR policies and practices across developed and developing countries are vitally important in testing the proposed framework as well as the three alternative approaches in the extant literature for how to conceptualize CSR for developing countries.

Implications for Practice

The proposed conceptual framework has important implications for managers. Firms (domestic or MNEs) face different institutions and conditions in developed countries than they do in developing countries (including in this category emerging economies and transitional economies). In practice, firm strategies and values must interact with this variation. In developing countries, managers should emphasize avoidance of corporate irresponsibility defined in terms of a no harm principle. It is far more important that managers do not harm stakeholders and societies. Corporate citizenship requirements and opportunities are relatively limited in developed countries. The situation is quite different for MNEs especially operating in developing countries. Institutions are less advanced and social conditions are worse. The implications for MNEs are that their managers have expanded responsibilities for promoting economic development, and expanded opportunities for corporate citizenship in promoting legal and political development of host countries.

REFERENCES

Adam, A., Kammas, P., & Lapatinas, A. (2015). Income inequality and the tax structure: Evidence from developed and developing countries. *Journal of Comparative Economics*, *43*(1), 138–154.

Amaeshi, K., Adegbite, E., & Rajwani, T. (2016). Corporate social responsibility in challenging and non-enabling institutional contexts: Do institutional voids matter? *Journal of Business Ethics*, *134*(1), 135–153. doi:10.1007/s10551-014-2420-4

Amaeshi, K., Adi, B., Ogbechie, C., & Amao, O. (2006). *Corporate Social Responsibility (CSR) in Nigeria: western mimicry or indigenous influences?* International Centre for Corporate Social Responsibility (ICCSR), Nottingham University Business School, Nottingham, UK. Retrieved from http://www.nottingham.ac.uk/business/ICCSR/assets/researchpapers/39-2006.pdf

Amaeshi, K. M., & Adi, B. (2007). Reconstructing the corporate social responsibility construct in *Utlish. Business Ethics (Oxford, England)*, *16*(1), 3–18. doi:10.1111/j.1467-8608.2006.00465.x

Athanasopoulou, A., & Selsky, J. W. (2015). The social context of corporate social responsibility: Enriching research with multiple perspectives and multiple levels. *Business & Society*, *54*(3), 322–364. doi:10.1177/0007650312449260

Attig, N., & Brockman, P. (2015). The local roots of corporate social responsibility. *Journal of Business Ethics*. doi:10.1007/s10551-015-2757-3

Bardy, R., Drew, S., & Kennedy, T. F. (2012). Foreign investment and ethics: How to contribute to social responsibility by doing business in less-developed countries. *Journal of Business Ethics*, *106*(3), 267–282. doi:10.1007/s10551-011-0994-7

Barkemeyer, R. (2011). Corporate perceptions of sustainability challenges in developed and developing countries: Constituting a CSR divide? *Social Responsibility Journal*, *7*(2), 257–281. doi:10.1108/17471111111141521

Baur, D., & Palazzo, G. (2011). The moral legitimacy of NGOs as partners of corporations. *Business Ethics Quarterly*, *21*(4), 579–604. doi:10.5840/beq201121437

Beasley, M. (2015). Dysfunctional equivalence: Why the OECD Anti-Bribery Convention provides insufficient guidance in the era of multinational corporations. *The George Washington International Law Review*, *47*(1), 191–231.

Belke, A., & Wernet, A. (2015). Poverty reduction through growth and redistribution policies—a panel analysis for 59 developing countries. *Review of Development Economics*, *19*(1), 143–162. doi:10.1111/rode.12131

Bennedsen, M., Feldmann, S. E., & Lassen, D. D. (2011, June 28). Lobbying and bribes - A survey-based analysis of the demand for influence and corruption. CESifo Working Paper Series No. 3496. Retrieved from http://ssrn.com/abstract=1873891

Bergman, M. M., Leisinger, K. M., Bergman, Z., & Berger, L. (2015). An analysis of the conceptual landscape of corporate responsibility in academia. *Business & Professional Ethics Journal*, *34*(2), 165–193. doi:10.5840/bpej20157728

Birdsall, N. (2015). Does the rise of the middle class lock in good government in the developing world? *European Journal of Development Research*, *27*(2), 217–229. doi:10.1057/ejdr.2015.6

Blindheim, B. T. (2015). Institutional models of corporate social responsibility: A proposed refinement of the explicit-implicit framework. *Business & Society*, *54*(1), 52–88. doi:10.1177/0007650312443961

Bondy, K., Moon, J., & Matten, D. (2012). An institution of corporate social responsibility (CSR) in multi-national corporations (MNCs): Form and implications. *Journal of Business Ethics*, *111*(2), 281–299. doi:10.1007/s10551-012-1208-7

Bondy, K., & Starkey, K. (2014). The dilemmas of internationalization: Corporate social responsibility in the multinational corporation. *British Journal of Management*, *25*(1), 4–22. doi:10.1111/j.1467-8551.2012.00840.x

Bouvain, P., Baumann, C., & Lundmark, E. (2013). Corporate social responsibility in financial services: A comparison of Chinese and East Asian banks *vis-à-vis* American banks. *International Journal of Bank Marketing*, *31*(6), 420–439. doi:10.1108/IJBM-05-2012-0054

Buckley, P. J., & Ghauri, P. N. (2004). Globalisation, economic geography and the strategy of multinational enterprises. *Journal of International Business Studies*, *35*(3), 81–98. doi:10.1057/palgrave.jibs.8400076

Buckley, P. J., & Strange, R. (2015). The governance of the global factory: Location and control of world economic activity. *Academy of Management Perspectives*, *29*(2), 237–249. doi:10.5465/amp.2013.0113

Campos, N. F., & Giovannoni, F. (2007). Lobbying, corruption and political influence. *Public Choice*, *131*(1), 1–12. doi:10.1007/s11127-006-9102-4

Carroll, A. B. (2015). Corporate social responsibility: The centerpiece of competing and complementary frameworks. *Organizational Dynamics*, *44*(2), 87–96. doi:10.1016/j.orgdyn.2015.02.002

Chidozie, F. C., Odunayo, L. P., & Olutosin, A. O. (2015). Deregulation of the Nigerian telecommunication sector: Interrogating the nexus between imperialism and development. *Academic Journal of Interdisciplinary Studies*, *4*(1), 173-184. Retrieved from http://www.mcser.org/journal/index.php/ajis/article/view/5968/5739

Crifo, P., & Forget, V. D. (2015). The economics of corporate social responsibility: A firm-level perspective survey. *Journal of Economic Surveys*, *29*(1), 112–130. doi:10.1111/joes.12055

Dawson, T. C. (2003, March 14). *Globalization, the Transition Economies, and the IMF.* International Monetary Fund. Retrieved from https://www.imf.org/external/np/speeches/2003/031403.htm

de Jong, G., & van Houten, J. (2014). The impact of MNE cultural diversity on the internationalization-performance relationship: Theory and evidence from European multinational enterprises. *International Business Review*, *23*(1), 313–326. doi:10.1016/j.ibusrev.2013.05.005

De Neve, G. (2014). Fordism, flexible specialization and CSR: How Indian garment workers critique neoliberal labour regimes. *Ethnography*, *15*(2), 184–207. doi:10.1177/1466138112463801

Dunning, J. H. (1979). Explaining changing patterns of international production: In defense of the eclectic theory. *Oxford Bulletin of Economics and Statistics*, *41*(4), 269–295. doi:10.1111/j.1468-0084.1979.mp41004003.x

European Commission. (2011, October 25). *Communication from the Commission to the European Parliament, the Council, the European Economic and Social Committee and the Committee of the Regions: A renewed EU strategy 2011-14 for Corporate Social Responsibility*. Retrieved from http://ec.europa.eu/enterprise/policies/sustainable-business/files/csr/new-csr/act_en.pdf

Filatotchev, I., & Stahl, G. K. (2015). Towards transnational CSR: Corporate social responsibility approaches and governance solutions for multinational corporations. *Organizational Dynamics*, *44*(2), 121–129. doi:10.1016/j.orgdyn.2015.02.006

García-Rodríguez, F. J., García-Rodríguez, J. L., Castilla-Gutiérrez, C., & Major, S. A. (2013). Corporate social responsibility of oil companies in developing countries: From altruism to business strategy. *Corporate Social Responsibility and Environmental Management*, *20*(6), 371–384. doi:10.1002/csr.1320

George, O. J., Kuye, O. L., & Onokala, U. C. (2012). Corporate social irresponsibility (CSI) a catalyst to the Niger Delta crisis: The case of Nigerian oil multinational companies versus the militants of Niger Delta Region of Nigeria. *Journal of Management Research*, *4*(2), 205–215. doi:10.5296/jmr.v4i2.1186

Geppert, M., & Dörrenbächer, C. (2014). Politics and power within multinational corporations: Mainstream studies, emerging critical approaches and suggestions for future research. *International Journal of Management Reviews*, *16*(2), 226–244. doi:10.1111/ijmr.12018

Ghosh, S. (2015). Is corporate social responsibility in India still in a confused state?—A study of the participation of the private sector companies of India in corporate social responsibility activities. *Global Business Review*, *16*(1), 151–181. doi:10.1177/0972150914553528

Gilberthorpe, E., & Banks, G. (2012). Development on whose terms?: CSR discourse and social realities in Papua New Guinea's extractive industries sector. *Resources Policy*, *37*(2), 185–193. doi:10.1016/j.resourpol.2011.09.005

Giuliani, E., & Macchi, C. (2014). Multinational corporations' economic and human rights impacts on developing countries: A review and research agenda. *Cambridge Journal of Economics*, *38*(2), 479–517. doi:10.1093/cje/bet060

Godinez, J. R., & Liu, L. (2015). Corruption distance and FDI flows into Latin America. *International Business Review*, *24*(1), 33–42. doi:10.1016/j.ibusrev.2014.05.006

Gupta, S., & Shapiro, D. (2014). Building and transforming an emerging market global enterprise: Lessons from the Infosys journey. *Business Horizons*, *57*(2), 169–179. doi:10.1016/j.bushor.2013.10.007

Hah, K., & Freeman, S. (2014). Multinational enterprise subsidiaries and their CSR: A conceptual framework of the management of CSR in smaller emerging economies. *Journal of Business Ethics*, *122*(1), 125–136. doi:10.1007/s10551-013-1753-8

Harstad, B., & Svensson, J. (2011). Bribes, lobbying and development. *The American Political Science Review*, *105*(1), 46–63. doi:10.1017/S0003055410000523

Heakal, R. (2015, December 8). *What Is An Emerging Market Economy?* Retrieved from http://www.investopedia.com/articles/03/073003.asp

Hilson, G. (2012). Corporate Social Responsibility in the extractive industries: Experiences from developing countries. *Resources Policy*, *37*(2), 131–137. doi:10.1016/j.resourpol.2012.01.002

Hoskisson, R. E., Eden, L., Lau, C. M., & Wright, M. (2000). Strategy in emerging economies. *Academy of Management Journal*, *43*(3), 249–267. doi:10.2307/1556394

Idemudia, U. (2011). Corporate social responsibility and developing countries: Moving the critical CSR research agenda in Africa forward. *Progress in Development Studies*, *11*(1), 1–18. doi:10.1177/146499341001100101

Infosys. (2013). *Rethinking Corporate Social Responsibility (CSR) in Financial Services: Making business sense of sustainable CSR*. Bangalore, India: White Paper. Retrieved from http://www.infosys.com/industries/financial-services/white-papers/Documents/corporate-social-responsibility.pdf

Jamali, D. (2010). The CSR of MNC subsidiaries in developing countries: Global, local, substantive or diluted? *Journal of Business Ethics*, *93*(Suppl. 2), 181–200. doi:10.1007/s10551-010-0560-8

Jamali, D., Lund-Thomsen, P., & Khara, N. (2015). CSR institutionalized myths in developing countries: An imminent threat of selective decoupling. *Business & Society*. doi:10.1177/0007650315584303

Jamali, D., & Neville, B. (2011). Convergence versus divergence in CSR in developing countries: An embedded multi-layered institutional lens. *Journal of Business Ethics*, *102*(4), 599–621. doi:10.1007/s10551-011-0830-0

Jamali, D., & Sidani, Y. (2011). Is CSR counterproductive in developing countries: The unheard voices of change. *Journal of Change Management*, *11*(1), 69–71. doi:10.1080/14697017.2011.548940

Jenkins, R., & Newell, P. (2013). CSR, tax and development. *Third World Quarterly*, *34*(3), 378–396. doi:10.1080/01436597.2013.784596

Jensen, N. M., Li, Q., & Rahman, A. (2010). Understanding corruption and firm responses in cross-national firm-level surveys. *Journal of International Business Studies*, *41*(9), 1481–1504. doi:10.1057/jibs.2010.8

Jones Christensen, L., Siemsen, E., & Balasubramanian, S. (2015). Consumer behavior change at the base of the pyramid: Bridging the gap between for-profit and social responsibility strategies. *Strategic Management Journal*, *36*(2), 307–317.

Kaufmann, D., & Vicente, P. C. (2011). Legal corruption. *Economics and Politics*, *23*(2), 195–219. doi:10.1111/j.1468-0343.2010.00377.x

Keig, D. L., Brouthers, L. E., & Marshall, V. B. (2015). Formal and informal corruption environments and multinational enterprise social irresponsibility. *Journal of Management Studies*, *52*(1), 89–116. doi:10.1111/joms.12102

Khan, F. R., & Lund-Thomsen, P. (2011). CSR as imperialism: Towards a phenomenological approach to CSR in the developing world. *Journal of Change Management*, *11*(1), 73–90. doi:10.1080/14697017.2011.548943

Khojastehpour, M. (2015). How does corporate social responsibility avoid the incidence of corruption in international expansion? *European Business Review*, *27*(3), 334–342. doi:10.1108/EBR-01-2015-0002

Kim, J., & Jeon, Y. (2015). Dividend policy and corporate social responsibility: A comparative analysis of multinational enterprise subsidiaries and domestic firms in Korea. *Emerging Markets Finance and Trade*, *51*(2), 306–319. doi:10.1080/1540496X.2015.1021605

Knudsen, J. S., Moon, J., & Slager, R. (2015). Government policies for corporate social responsibility in Europe: A comparative analysis of institutionalisation. *Policy and Politics*, *43*(1), 81–99. doi:10.1332/030557312X656016

Kolk, A., & Lenfant, F. (2013). Multinationals, CSR and partnerships in Central African conflict countries. *Corporate Social Responsibility and Environmental Management*, *20*(1), 43–54. doi:10.1002/csr.1277

Kotilainen, J., Prokhorova, E., Sairinen, R., & Tiainen, H. (2015). Corporate social responsibility of mining companies in Kyrgyzstan and Tajikistan. *Resources Policy*, *45*, 202–209. doi:10.1016/j.resourpol.2015.06.001

Luetkenhorst, W. (2004). Corporate social responsibility and the development agenda: The case for actively involving small and medium enterprises. *Inter Economics*, *39*(3), 157–166. doi:10.1007/BF02933583

Lund-Thomsen, P., & Lindgreen, A. (2014). Corporate social responsibility in global value chains: Where are we now and where are we going? *Journal of Business Ethics*, *123*(1), 11–22. doi:10.1007/s10551-013-1796-x

Lund-Thomsen, P., & Wad, P. (2014). Global value chains, local economic organization and corporate social responsibility in the BRICS countries. *Competition & Change*, *18*(4), 281–290. doi:10.1179/1024529414Z.00000000061

Marano, V., & Kostova, T. (2015). Unpacking the institutional complexity in adoption of CSR practices in multinational enterprises. [online ahead of print]. *Journal of Management Studies*. doi:10.1111/joms.12124

Marques, J. C., & Mintzberg, H. (2015). Why corporate social responsibility isn't a piece of cake. *MIT. Sloan Management Review*, *56*(4), 8–11.

Midttun, A., Gjølberg, M., Kourula, A., Sweet, S., & Vallentin, S. (2015). Public policies for corporate social responsibility in four Nordic countries: Harmony of goals and conflict of means. *Business & Society*, *54*(4), 464–500. doi:10.1177/0007650312450848

Millner, A., & Dietz, S. (2015). Adaptation to climate change and economic growth in developing countries. *Environment and Development Economics*, *20*(3), 380–406. doi:10.1017/S1355770X14000692

Nasrullah, N. M., & Rahim, M. A. (2013). *CSR in private enterprises in developing countries: Evidences from the ready-made garments industry in Bangladesh*. Heidelberg, Germany: Springer.

Nguyen, Q. T. K. (2014). The regional strategies of British multinational subsidiaries in South East Asia. *British Journal of Management*, *25*(Suppl. 1), S60–S76. doi:10.1111/1467-8551.12006

Nielsen, M. E. J., & Frederiksen, C. S. (2015). Political institutions and corporate social responsibility: A Nordic welfare state perspective from Denmark. In S. O. Idowu, R. Schmidpeter, & M. S. Fifka (Eds.), *Corporate social responsibility in Europe* (pp. 197–208). Cham, Switzerland: Springer International Publishing. doi:10.1007/978-3-319-13566-3_11

Olsen, B. E., & Sorensen, K. E. (2014). Strengthening the enforcement of CSR guidelines: Finding a new balance between hard law and soft law. *Legal Issues of Economic Integration*, *41*(1), 9–35.

Ozuem, W., Howell, K., & Lancaster, G. (2014). Corporate social responsibility: Towards a context-specific perspective in developing countries. *Social Responsibility Journal*, *10*(3), 399–415. doi:10.1108/SRJ-04-2012-0086

Pagliusi, S., Leite, L. C., Datla, M., Makhoana, M., Gao, Y., Suhardono, M., & Homma, A. (2013). Developing countries vaccine manufacturers network: Doing good by making high-quality vaccines affordable for all. *Vaccine*, *31*, B176–B183. doi:10.1016/j.vaccine.2012.11.060 PMID:23598479

Parinduri, R., & Paul, S. (2015, January). *Investors are unwilling to pay for corporate social responsibility activities: Evidence from India's Companies Act 2013*. Nottingham University Business School, University of Nottingham, Malaysia Campus, MPRA Paper No. 61360. Retrieved from http://mpra.ub.uni-muenchen.de/61360/

Park, Y. R., Song, S., Choe, S., & Baik, Y. (2015). Corporate social responsibility in international business: Illustrations from Korean and Japanese electronics MNEs in Indonesia. *Journal of Business Ethics, 129*(3), 747–761. doi:10.1007/s10551-014-2212-x

Pedersen, E. R. G., & Gwozdz, W. (2014). From resistance to opportunity-seeking: Strategic responses to institutional pressures for corporate social responsibility in the Nordic fashion industry. *Journal of Business Ethics, 119*(2), 245–264. doi:10.1007/s10551-013-1630-5

Rahim, M. M. (2013). A meta-regulation approach to laws to incorporate CSR principles in corporate self-regulation. In *Legal Regulation of Corporate Social Responsibility* (pp. 129–177). Heidelberg, Germany: Springer. doi:10.1007/978-3-642-40400-9_5

Rahim, M. M., & Wisuttisak, P. (2013). Corporate social responsibility–oriented compliances and SMEs access to global market: Evidence from Bangladesh. *Journal of Asia-Pacific Business, 14*(1), 58–83. doi:10.1080/10599231.2013.741417

Ramasastry, A. (2015). Corporate social responsibility versus business and human rights: Bridging the gap between responsibility and accountability. *Journal of Human Rights, 14*(2), 237–259. doi:10.1080/14754835.2015.1037953

Rodriguez, P., Siegel, D. S., Hillman, A., & Eden, L. (2006). Three lenses on the MNE: Politics, corruption and corporate social responsibility. *Journal of International Business Studies, 37*(6), 733–746. doi:10.1057/palgrave.jibs.8400229

Rolland, S. E. (2007). Developing country coalitions at the WTO: In search of legal support. *Harvard International Law Journal, 48*(2), 483–551.

Rose-Ackerman, S. (2002). "Grand" corruption and the ethics of global business. *Journal of Banking & Finance, 26*(9), 1889–1918. doi:10.1016/S0378-4266(02)00197-8

Rupp, D. E., & Mallory, D. B. (2015). Corporate social responsibility: Psychological, person-centric, and progressing. *Annual Review of Organizational Psychology and Organizational Behavior, 2*(1), 211–236. doi:10.1146/annurev-orgpsych-032414-111505

Rupp, D. E., Wright, P. M., Aryee, S., & Luo, Y. (2015). Organizational justice, behavioral ethics, and corporate social responsibility: Finally the three shall merge. *Management and Organization Review, 11*(1), 15–24. doi:10.1017/mor.2015.8

Saeidi, S. P., Sofian, S., Saeidi, P., Saeidi, S. P., & Saaeidi, S. A. (2015). How does corporate social responsibility contribute to firm financial performance? The mediating role of competitive advantage, reputation, and customer satisfaction. *Journal of Business Research, 68*(2), 341–350. doi:10.1016/j.jbusres.2014.06.024

Scherer, A. G., & Palazzo, G. (2011). The new political role of business in a globalized world: A review of a new perspective on CSR and its implications for the firm, governance, and democracy. *Journal of Management Studies, 48*(4), 899–931. doi:10.1111/j.1467-6486.2010.00950.x

Scherer, A. G., Palazzo, G., & Matten, D. (2014). The business firm as a political actor: A new theory of the firm for a globalized world. *Business & Society, 53*(2), 143–156. doi:10.1177/0007650313511778

Scherer, A. G., Palazzo, G., & Seidl, D. (2013). Managing legitimacy in complex and heterogeneous environments: Sustainable development in a globalized world. *Journal of Management Studies*, *50*(2), 259–284. doi:10.1111/joms.12014

Schmitz, J., & Schrader, J. (2015). Corporate social responsibility: A microeconomic review of the literature. *Journal of Economic Surveys*, *29*(1), 27–45. doi:10.1111/joes.12043

Schnittfeld, N. L., & Busch, T. (2016). Sustainability management within supply chains – A resource dependence view. *Business Strategy and the Environment*, 25(5), 337-354. doi:10.1002/bse.1876

Shin, J. Y., Jung, M., Khoe, K. I., & Chae, M. S. (2015). Effects of government involvement in corporate social responsibility: An analysis of the Indian Companies Act, 2013. *Emerging Markets Finance and Trade*, *51*(2), 377–390. doi:10.1080/1540496X.2015.1021600

Slack, K. (2012). Mission impossible?: Adopting a CSR-based business model for extractive industries in developing countries. *Resources Policy*, *37*(2), 179–184. doi:10.1016/j.resourpol.2011.02.003

Smith, N., & Thomas, E. (2015). Determinants of Russia's informal economy: The impact of corruption and multinational firms. *Journal of East-West Business*, *21*(2), 102–128. doi:10.1080/10669868.2015.1004148

Spence, L. J. (2007). CSR and small business in a European policy context: The five "C"s of CSR and small business research agenda 2007. *Business and Society Review*, *112*(4), 533–552. doi:10.1111/j.1467-8594.2007.00308.x

Srisuphaolarn, P. (2013). From altruistic to strategic CSR: How social value affected CSR development – a case study of Thailand. *Social Responsibility Journal*, *9*(1), 56–77. doi:10.1108/17471111311307813

Steurer, R. (2010). The role of governments in corporate social responsibility: Characterising public policies on CSR in Europe. *Policy Sciences*, *43*(1), 49–72. doi:10.1007/s11077-009-9084-4

Strand, R., Freeman, R. E., & Hockerts, K. (2015). Corporate social responsibility and sustainability in Scandinavia: An overview. *Journal of Business Ethics*, *127*(1), 1–15. doi:10.1007/s10551-014-2224-6

Strike, V., Gao, J., & Bansal, P. (2006). Being good while being bad: Social responsibility and the international diversification of U.S. firms. *Journal of International Business Studies*, *37*(6), 850–862. doi:10.1057/palgrave.jibs.8400226

Svensson, J. (2003). Who must pay bribes and how much? Evidence from a cross section of firms. *The Quarterly Journal of Economics*, *118*(1), 207–230. doi:10.1162/00335530360535180

United Nations Department of Economic and Social Affairs. (2007, February). *CSR and Developing Countries: What scope for government action?* Sustainable Development Innovation Briefs. Retrieved from http://www.un.org/esa/sustdev/publications/innovationbriefs/no1.pdf

Vaccaro, A., & Palazzo, G. (2015). Values against violence: Institutional change in societies dominated by organized crime. *Academy of Management Journal*, 58(4), 1075-1101. doi:10.5465/amj.2012.0865

van Beveren, I. (2007). Footloose multinationals in Belgium? *Review of World Economics. Weltwirtschaftliches Archiv*, *143*(3), 483–507.

Vidal, J. (2014, June 11). Soco halts oil exploration in Africa's Virunga national park: British oil company bows to pressure and abandons drilling in volatile and biodiverse region of Democratic Republic of Congo. Retrieved from http://www.theguardian.com/environment/2014/jun/11/soco-oil-virunga-national-park-congo-wwf

Vigneau, L., & Humphreys, M. (2014, January). Embedding CSR in an MNE: A process model of translation of complex institutional pressures. In Academy of Management Proceedings (Vol. 2014, No. 1, p. 15883). doi:10.5465/AMBPP.2014.15883abstract

Visser, W. (2008). Corporate social responsibility in developing countries. In A. Crane, A. McWilliams, D. Matten, J. Moon, & D. Siegel (Eds.), *The Oxford handbook of corporate social responsibility* (pp. 473–479). Oxford, UK: Oxford University Press.

Visser, W. (2011a). *The age of responsibility: CSR 2.0 and the new DNA of business*. New York: Wiley.

Visser, W. (2011b, December 8). Myths about CSR in developing countries: "Glocality" - the act of thinking globally, acting locally - may be the antidote to CSR myths. Retrieved from http://www.csrwire.com/blog/posts/238-myths-about-csr-in-developing-countries

Visser, W. (2013). *CSR 2.0: Transforming corporate sustainability and responsibility*. New York: Springer.

Wagner, S. M., & Anastasiadis, S. (2014). Do multinational enterprises contribute to sustainable development by engaging in lobbying? The automotive industry and environmental regulations. In R. Van Tulder, A. Verbeke, & R. Strange (Eds.), *International business and sustainable development* (pp. 173–202). Bingley, UK: Emerald Group Publishing Limited. doi:10.1108/S1745-8862(2013)0000008013

Windsor, D. (2007). Toward a global theory of cross-border and multilevel corporate political activity. *Business & Society*, *46*(2), 253–278. doi:10.1177/0007650307301387

Windsor, D. (2013). Corporate social responsibility and irresponsibility: A positive theory approach. *Journal of Business Research*, *66*(10), 1937–1944. doi:10.1016/j.jbusres.2013.02.016

Zander, I., McDougall-Covin, P., & Rose, E. L. (2015). Born globals and international business: Evolution of a field of research. *Journal of International Business Studies*, *46*(1), 27–35. doi:10.1057/jibs.2014.60

KEY TERMS AND DEFINITIONS

Corporate Social Irresponsibility (CSIR): This chapter defines CSIR as a business generating harm to stakeholders by violations of ethical and legal standards. Reducing irresponsibility may contribute more to social welfare than promoting business altruism (or corporate citizenship).

Corporate Social Responsibility (CSR): This chapter defines CSR as a combination of three dimensions. A first dimension is a "do no harm" principle. A second dimension is compliance with laws, except on grounds of morally justifiable civil disobedience. A third dimension – the usual focus of criticisms of voluntary CSR – is business altruism or corporate citizenship.

Developed Country: Characterized by an advanced market economy, adequate government and laws, relatively lower corruption, typically isolated pockets of poverty, and strong activist NGOs.

Developing Country: Characterized by a developing economy, inadequate government and laws, prevalent corruption, widespread poverty, and weak activist NGOs.

Multinational Enterprise (MNE): A business operating in two or more countries. One of these countries is the home country of the enterprise headquarters; any others are host countries for investment and operations.

Chapter 2
Corporate Social Responsibility (CSR) in China
A Contextual Exploration

D. Kirk Davidson
Mount St. Mary's University, USA

Juelin Yin
Xi'an Jiaotong-Liverpool University (XJTLU), China

ABSTRACT

Despite a growing recognition of national contexts in predicting the dynamics of corporate social responsibility (CSR), the limited prior research has failed to disaggregate national institutions to specify the mechanisms between aspects of national institutional contexts and elements of CSR practices. In this paper we offer a framework for analyzing the nature and status of CSR, which is made up of eight elements: history, religions/ideologies, social norms, geography, political structures, the level of economic development, civil society institutions, and the country's "safety net" provisions. We apply the framework to explain how and why China's understanding of CSR differs from that in Western countries.

INTRODUCTION

We, in the West, simply do not know as much as we should about corporate social responsibility (CSR) in other countries and other cultures. It may well be true that over the past forty years the academic world in the West has done the lion's share of theory building in CSR and the related fields of business ethics, business and society, and stakeholder management. And too, managers in the West may well have more experience putting into practice the concepts emerging from those fields. Wang and Juslin (2009) go so far as to say that "…CSR is a term which originated in the West," and the reference lists in the scholarly work of many Asian researchers—for example Yin and Zhang (2012) and Baxi (2013)—would seem to confirm this.

However, we should not assume that all knowledge about CSR resides in North America and Europe. In India the Tata companies were developing their own brand of CSR in the 19th century. In China, although

DOI: 10.4018/978-1-5225-0720-8.ch002

CSR per se is a relatively new phenomenon, as explained below, the historical and philosophical underpinnings for this new development have been in the making for many centuries (Wang & Juslin, 2009).

International trade has increased rapidly since the end of World War II, and business managers have developed increasingly sophisticated tools and management structures to facilitate this. "Globalization" has become a buzzword. The academic world has aligned itself with this development by offering courses in international marketing, international management, and global finance. Many leading business schools are incorporating a mandatory period of travel, work, and study abroad as part of their MBA programs. But the study and practice of CSR (or business ethics, or business and society) has not benefitted in the same way from globalization; there has been too little attention given to a cross-country or cross-cultural comparison of CSR.

This subject has not been ignored entirely; Visser and Tolhurst (2010) edited *The World Guide to CSR*, which is a collection of brief sketches of CSR practice and teaching in fifty-eight nations, but there is no unifying framework. And a number of European scholars have explored the differences of CSR among the countries of Western Europe (Fransen, 2013; Gjolberg, 2009). In this paper we provide what has been missing: a framework for comparative CSR analysis based on national contexts (see Table 1). We suggest that to understand the practice and teaching of CSR in any country or culture – developed or developing, large or small, North or South – one must take into consideration that country or culture's context. And we break down that contextual framework into eight elements: history, religions/ideologies, geography, culture or social norms, political structures, level of economic development, civil society institutions, and the status of its "safety net." We then use this contextual framework to explore and analyze the practice and teaching of CSR in China.

We have chosen China for some obvious reasons. First and foremost is the fact that China has become such a powerful force in the world's economic, geopolitical, and military systems. China now ranks second only to the United States in gross domestic product. No country in the history of mankind has elevated so many of its citizens (hundreds of millions) out of poverty, and it has done so in the extraordinarily brief time span of only thirty to thirty-five years.

Table 1. Contextual elements for understanding a country's CSR

History	1. Liberalism vs. State control 2. Historical involvement with capitalism
Religion/Ideology	1. Embedded beliefs and values
Social Norms	1. Individualism vs. Communitarianism 2. Importance of family structures
Geography	1. Influence of neighboring states 2. History of trade relationships
Political Structures	1. Democratic institutions vs. authoritarian rule 2. Federalist structure
Level of Economic Development	1. Importance of agricultural, industrial, and service 2. Middle class development 3. Overall size of economy influencing importance of international trade
Civil Society Institutions	1. Strength and importance of labor unions 2. Strength, number, and importance of advocacy groups 3. Power and freedom of independent media
Safety Net	1. Degree of government support of the needy

Second, because China's history, culture, and political-economic systems are so different from those of the United States or European countries, it offers some valuable contrasts and comparisons. It only stands to reason that to the extent Western scholars and managers can shed their current strong Western orientation and consider what CSR looks like in other countries, cultures, and circumstances, the better we will understand what CSR really does and should mean.

Third, hardly a week goes by that more managers from the Western countries such as the United States are exposed to CSR (or business ethics or business and society) issues in China, and the same is true for Chinese managers dealing with such issues in the West. In both circumstances it would be better for the long-term interests of the enterprise if the newly-located managers knew what was expected of them by the society in which they now found themselves – if they knew the "CSR territory."

This chapter, then, addresses what Jamali et al (2015) describe as a "limited appreciation of the complexities of context" and contributes to "expanding the analytic lens to include such heterogeneous and irregular contextual factors" so necessary in the deeper understanding of CSR not only as it is known and practiced in the West but as it gains in importance across the global business landscape.

CONTEXTUAL ANALYSIS DEFINED

Let us now look a bit more closely at the eight elements of our contextual analysis framework as described in Table 1. These, we believe, are universal in that they can be used to analyze and understand better the nature of corporate social responsibility in any country. We suggest that a country's political history and its economic development will influence its thinking about CSR. One must ask: what is this country's history with democratic and capitalistic institutions, what Fransen (2013) calls the "strength of corporatist tradition?"

Many scholars in discussing the concept of CSR, and its close associate business ethics, will talk about the values that underlie this concept (Shafer, Fukukawa and Lee, 2007). Gjolberg (2009) emphasizes "the importance of local culture, context and traditions in shaping the perceptions and practice of CSR." Generally, these spring from the country's or the region's religious and cultural heritage, the values and beliefs that are embedded in that country's collective psyche.

In some instances, a country's geographical situation – who are its neighbors, what is the nature of its relationships with them including trade, how powerful and influential those neighbors have been and are – may color that country's understanding and practice of CSR. As shown in Figure 1, these four elements lead to the subject country's beginning concept of CSR.

Corporate social responsibility – how it is conceived and practiced – is not static, however. The concept is a dynamic one; it evolves as the country's political structures and its level of economic development change (Matten and Moon, 2008). How authoritarian or democratic are the country's political institutions? What are the relationship and power differentials between the country's central government and its states, provinces, and cities? To what extent has the country progressed beyond an agricultural economy? How strong is its middle class? How big is the country's economy in terms of gross domestic product? A country's conceptualization and practice of CSR will evolve also as its civil society institutions grow and develop. Here we refer specifically to the quantity and effectiveness of its network of advocacy groups, the power and effectiveness of its labor organizations, and the freedom and coverage of its media. Finally, the concept of CSR will evolve as changes occur in the country's "safety net":

Figure 1. Evolution of CSR

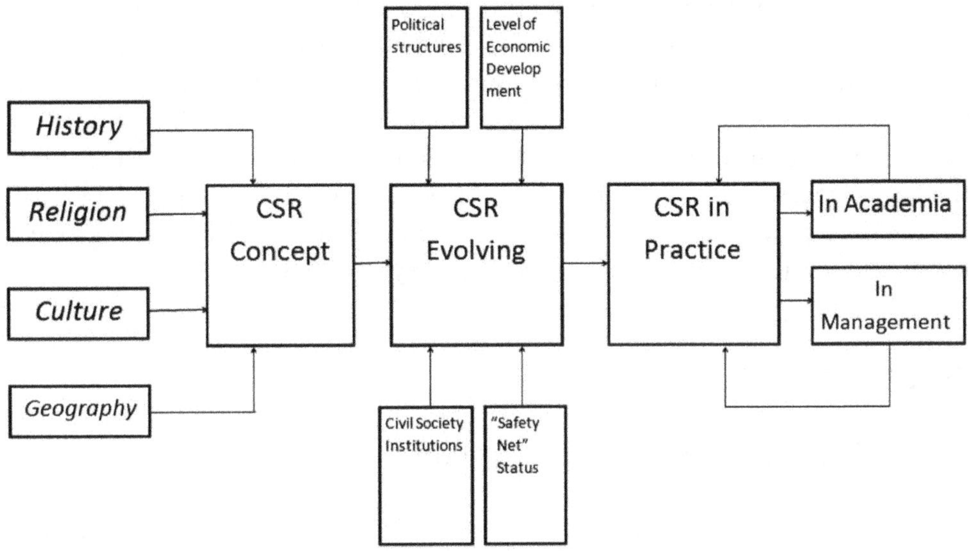

the institutional care provided by the government for its citizens. Arguably, if a government offers very little help to those in need, then it devolves on the business community to provide the bare necessities of life (Fransen, 2013).

We will return to this contextual analysis and a further discussion of the evolution of CSR after first looking at the "status" of CSR in China – how it is practiced and how it is taught.

CSR IN CHINA

The concept of CSR was introduced into China in the late 1990s by a number of multinational companies demanding labor rights protection, better product quality and environmental concerns. This has thrown many Chinese suppliers into the tension between business practices based on profit-maximization and campaigns promoting social standards, best practices, western values and morality (Yin and Zhang, 2012). More recent driving forces come from the Chinese government which has been promoting CSR as a social legitimacy rebuilding lever since 2006. In the intervening years Beijing has advocated for a transition from faster to greener GDP growth, placing "Promote Scientific Development and Harmonious Society" on top of its economic and social policy agenda, and setting energy saving, emission reduction and labor rights protection as national strategies. Also in 2006, the Sixth Plenum of the 16th Communist Party Committee (CPC) Central Committee stated that firms should "conduct extensive activities to build harmony, promote a harmonious situation for all, and focus on enhancing the social responsibility of citizens, enterprises and all kinds of organizations" (Xinhua News, 2006). Thereafter, provincial, city and local government leaders have made significant advancements in promoting CSR. For example, the government of Shanghai Pudong has integrated CSR into the local reform system in the district since 2007 and even issued its own district CSR guidelines and standard as to how local businesses can better implement CSR.

As a result, Chinese managers who have sensed the necessity of CSR act as agents of change by integrating socially responsible practices into daily operations, hoping to gain a potential global competitive edge as well as local legitimacy (Gugler & Shi, 2009). For many state-owned enterprises (SOEs), once their profit motives are unleashed and previous social responsibilities unburdened, they are often associated with social negligence and environmental pollution in the eyes of the public (Shen and Zhou, 2008). As to the export-oriented small-and-medium enterprises (SMEs), many of them are realizing the value of achieving higher social and environmental standards to compete in the global marketplace. A sharp growth of CSR reporting by Chinese firms from 32 in 2006 to 2032 by December 2014 indicates a clear signal of accelerating CSR momentum in China (Syntao, 2015).

CSR IN THE ACADEMY

Prevalence of Courses in Business Programs

Teaching and research into CSR in China began in the 1990s, with a dominant focus on business ethics. By December 2007, of the 95 schools that obtained permission to run MBA programs, only 38.9% had offered business ethics courses, and of those, only 40.5% made it a compulsory requirement for graduation (Zhou, Ou, & Enderle, 2009). Most of the courses adopted the names "Business Ethics" or "Corporate Culture and Business Ethics" instead of "Corporate Social Responsibility". As recently as 2011 the first and only MPA (Master of Public Administration) program with a focus on Social Innovation and CSR was initiated by the School of Social Development and Public Policy in Beijing Normal University, marking an initial attempt for positioning CSR as an independent subject of study in China.

Number of Scholars Growing

The pattern of development in the research field has paralleled the analysis of the origins of CSR practices in China. A meta-analysis throughout the period from 1993 to 2007 by Moon and Shen (2010) indicates a growing salience of CSR issues in China-related research. Specifically, the mid-1990s was a turning point when attention to CSR as a research topic started to grow, exactly the same time as multinational companies began to conduct CSR audits in Chinese factories. Despite the rapid growth in academic attention, the focus of research has represented a lagging trend with a predominant interest on business "doing the right thing" (ethics focus). It was only in 2005 that the research focus shifted towards more specific responsibilities for companies, be it social, environmental or stakeholders (Moon and Shen, 2010).

Academic Organizations

There are over ten institutions that focus on business ethics or CSR research in China, most of which are affiliated with a university and located in major cities such as Beijing and Shanghai (Zhou et al, 2011). While some of them were founded around 2000, more were established very recently, such as the Centre of Corporate Social Responsibility and Corporate Culture established in 2010 by Xiamen University, and the Centre of Responsibility and Social Value under Guanghua School of Management in Peking University in 2012.

Specific Scholarly Journals

To the best of our knowledge, there are no academic journals dedicated to corporate social responsibility within China. However, there are two ethics journals—*Studies in Ethics* and *Morality and Civilization*—which have been publishing academic papers related to ethics and philosophy, and occasionally on business ethics and CSR. There is another business journal—*China Population, Resources and Environment*—which is dedicated to sustainability research in the Chinese context. It is worth mentioning that a growing number of academic journals are paying attention to CSR or sustainability issues with dedicated columns.

Moreover, in the recent decade there emerged some practitioner journals and newspapers which have been promoting CSR research and best practices in China, such as *WTO Tribune*, a pioneering journal transforming itself from a trade journal into a CSR specialist journal since 2003 with the sponsorship of the Ministry of Commerce; and *China Philanthropy Times*, a newspaper under the Ministry of Civil Affairs which is dedicated to philanthropy and social innovation in China since 2001. Meanwhile, many new media tools are also contributing to the spread of CSR ideas and practices, such as *China Dialogue*, a media NGO which has been fostering environmental discussions through a bilingual website; and China CSR Map, a website providing a directory of major CSR organizations and practitioners in China.

From the above, two important points emerge regarding CSR in China's academic community. First, we can see that China still lags behind many Western countries in terms of building CSR platforms, through establishing academic associations and academic journals as an instance. Second, CSR has yet to emerge as an independent field of research in China, but is in a "continuing state of emergence" as described by Lockett, Moon and Visser (2006).

CSR IN MANAGEMENT

Acknowledging CSR in the Business Mindset

The conceptualization of CSR has been a subject of debate for years (e.g., Carroll, 1991; Garriga & Mele, 2004). Exploratory studies have presented some interesting similarities and divergences of CSR understanding between the West and the East. Some common CSR dimensions shared by both the Western and Chinese business leaders include economic responsibility, legal responsibility, customer responsibility, and employee responsibility. However, there are some unique CSR characteristics exhibited in the Chinese context (Lin, 2010).

First, Chinese business leaders attach primary attention to the ethical elements in the understanding of CSR (Yin and Zhang, 2012; Yin, 2015). According to a survey of future Chinese business leaders, they overwhelmingly believe that a well-run company adheres to a strong mission, operates according to its values and a strong code of ethics and adheres to progressive environmental policies (Aspen Institute, 2008). These findings are highly consistent with another large-scale survey conducted by *Fortune China* magazine of Chinese business leaders, which indicates that 89% of the responding managers believe that "complying with business ethics and operating in good faith" were essential to CSR (Zadek & Wickerham, 2009).

Second, CSR is usually aligned with government priorities and initiatives. According to an exploratory study by Xu and Yang, (2010), Chinese businesses emphasize "maintaining employment" (e.g.

increase job opportunities, ease government employment pressure) and "promoting social stability and prosperity" (e.g. ensure social stability and harmony, patriotism, promote national prosperity) as their particular responsibilities towards society, which are in line with the government's various calls for business managers to adopt CSR initiatives (Marquis & Qian, 2014; See, 2009). Thus it is not hard to understand that they see socially responsible business practices primarily as reputational - advancing government, community and employee relations - more than as bottom-line business benefits such as reduced cost and risk or increased revenue (Bunch, Yang, & Xi, 2008).

Third, the implicit focus on ethics and discretionary CSR activities has been partly reflected in the low embeddedness of CSR management in the organizational structure (Yin & Zhang, 2012). Deliberate design and measurement of CSR is virtually non-existent; instead, sporadic donation and philanthropic activities are still the mainstream (Yin & Zhang, 2012). Although firms are most concerned about the financial implications or competitive edges that are derived from CSR, few position themselves with regard to social issues, nor do they design CSR projects in ways that seek to realize competitive advantages.

CSR Organizations and Initiatives

There is a burgeoning group of business associations or elite clubs that are advocating for greater CSR awareness and implementation among leading businesses. The China Business Council for Sustainable Development (CBCSD), jointly established by China Enterprise Confederation (CEC) and World Business Council for Sustainable Development (WBCSD) in October 2003, provides a platform for exchange and cooperation among Chinese and foreign enterprises in the field of sustainable development and CSR. In 2006 the China Entrepreneur Club (CEC) was established consisting of some of the most influential business leaders in China. The mission of the club is to set examples for green transformation in China's business environment and to organize annual China Green Companies Summit since 2008. Some other major private initiatives include "Golden Bee CSR China Honor Roll" which is an annual award aimed at promoting exemplary CSR practices; and Society of Entrepreneurs & Ecology (SEE), a joint initiative among hundreds of leading Chinese entrepreneurs dedicated to sustainability since 2004.

We offer Table 2 to provide a brief comparison of CSR development in China compared to how CSR has developed in the West. To conclude this section, it is useful to consider comments made by Lu Xiaohe (2010), a prominent Chinese business ethicist: "It seems, then, that there are opposite movements in China and the West. If we symbolically represent corporations, governments, and societies as

Table 2. CSR development in China and the West

Dimensions	CSR in the West	CSR in China
Historical tradition	Protestant ethics, high individualism	Confucian ethics, high collectivism,
Penetration	High to medium	Medium to low
Focus	A mix of implicit and explicit; Mainly explicit	Mainly implicit, shifting to more explicit
Mode	Volunteering, partnerships, community involvement	Donation, philanthropy, community involvement
Academic underpinning	Strong	Weak
Legal linkage/foundation	Strong	Weak
Institutionalization	Modest	Weak

three circles, then Westerners are moving from the total separation of the three circles (the past view) to a partial overlapping of the three (current view). The Chinese are moving from the total overlapping of the three circles to a partial separation of them."

CONTEXTUAL ANALYSIS

Let us now return to the eight elements of contextual analysis, as outlined in Table 1, and apply them to corporate social responsibility as it is evolving and developing in China. This helps us understand how and why Chinese CSR is conceived, practiced, and taught the way it is today with some comparisons to CSR in the West (see Table 3).

History

Here it is important to try to pull out from China's long and fascinating history only that which could have some bearing on CSR. For example, over thousands of years the vast majority of China's population served a very small minority of the country – the imperial family itself and a group of wealthy landowners, the elite. Little thought or care was given to the living and working conditions of serfs, and little attention was paid throughout this long, imperial period to such philosophical concepts as human or individual rights.

Table 3. Contextual elements for understanding CSR in China

History	1. Transition from imperial rule to communism to democracy. 2. China's century of "humiliation." 3. From 1949-79 rejection of all things related to West and to capitalism. 4. Only 30+ years of experimentation with capitalism and commercialism.
Religion/Ideology	1. Strong residual influence of Confucianism; mutual responsibilities. 2. Taoist emphasis on harmonious relationship with nature. 3. Harmony ideology
Social Norms	1. Importance of family and village loyalties. 2. Communitarian values.
Geography	1. Proximity to Russia. Influence of Russian political and economic thinking.
Political Structures	1. Authoritarian one-party system. 2. Involvement of party and government in economy through state-owned enterprises. 3. Central government, provincial, village hierarchical structure. 4. Political corruption.
Level of Economic Development	1. Now second largest global economy. Developing or developed country? 2. Still relatively low per capita income. 3. Has managed extraordinarily rapid growth. 4. Transition from agriculture to industry. 5. Environmental issues.
Civil Society Institutions	1. Labor unions do not truly represent the interests of workers. 2. Underdeveloped advocacy groups to put pressure on businesses 3. Very limited free and open media institutions.
Safety Net	1. Loss of the "iron rice bowl." To what extent is the business community expected to take up the responsibility? 2. Adequacy of social security system. 3. Problems exacerbated by aging population.

The 19th century is often referred to as China's "century of humiliation". For the first time the country which had forever thought of itself as the "Middle Kingdom," that is, the center of the world, was forced to pay a price for its long history of inward focus and disdain for all foreigners as "barbarians:" the belief that the rest of the world had nothing of value – tangible or intellectual – to offer. The two Opium Wars led to major concessions by China of territory and rights to the European powers, war with Japan ended badly, and the century closed with the Boxer Rebellion which demonstrated yet again the feebleness of the imperial government. These events all contributed to an even greater resentment of the West and a further rejection of Western ways: economic, political, technological, and cultural.

When the final Qing dynasty lost its last vestiges of power in the early twentieth century there followed several decades of turmoil which included more war with Japan and the struggle between Chiang Kai Shek's Nationalist (Republican) party and Mao Zedong's Communist party. In 1949 the Communists prevailed, with Chiang's forces retreating to the island of Formosa, now Taiwan. Mao established the People's Republic of China and set out to transform the country into a pure form of communism. Influenced by China's experience in the previous century, Western ideas, values, and institutions were systematically rejected. All assets – land, factories, business and commercial enterprises of all kinds – were owned and controlled by the central government. People were assigned jobs. All production was then redistributed by the government to the people in the forms of food, clothing, housing, education, health care, and so on. For the next thirty years – with no corporations and really no business sphere of any kind – there was no opportunity for even the concept of CSR to take root.

A few years after Mao's death in 1976 Deng Xiaoping and the more progressive Chinese leaders were able to seize the reins of power in the Party and the government from the Maoist hard-liners. It was only at this time that China turned from demonizing capitalism and took the first tentative steps toward allowing markets to operate with some degree of freedom from centralized control, the formation of private enterprises, and the welcoming of foreign investment. Since that time there has been a somewhat slow but steady move toward expanding the market-driven sectors of China's economy with an accompanying meteoric rise in China's economic indicators: gross domestic product increasing from roughly $177 billion in 1979 to more than $7.4 trillion in 2011 (Google, 2013), and per capita gross domestic product (on a purchasing power parity basis) rising from less than $250 to more than $8,000 over the same time frame (Indexmundi, 2013). Nevertheless, it is important to note that large swaths of China's economy – for example, the banking, aerospace, and petroleum industries to name a few, are still controlled by the state through SOEs.

Religions/Ideology

A number of scholars have explored the impact of Confucianism on business ethics specifically and, by extension, on CSR (e.g., Ip, 2002; Snell & Tseng, 2003; Whitcomb, Erdener, & Li, 1998). We will leave to others – presumably theologians and perhaps philosophers – to wrangle over whether or not Confucianism is a "religion." Regardless of the outcome of that debate Confucianism is as close as China comes to a dominant religion, and for roughly 2,500 years it has provided the Chinese with a systematic collection of principles on how individuals, families, and larger societal groups should live their lives and conduct their relationships and affairs with one another. Confucius discussed specifically the mutual obligations and responsibilities between master and servant, husband and wife, parent and child, older brother and younger brother, and between friends. Moreover, it upholds five cardinal virtues of human beings (called *Wuchang* in Chinese)—benevolence (Ren), filial conduct (Xiao), trustworthiness (Xin), loyalty (Zhong), and righteousness (Yi)—which are to guide interactions with others within a highly defined hierarchical social order (Lau, 1979). If these proper relationships are realized, the result is a harmonious and productive society. It does not take a great stretch of the imagination to think of this as a very early precursor of what we know today as stakeholder theory. After all, if business executives manage the relationships with their various stakeholders well, and reciprocate those whose interests are affected by the business operations, does that not lead to both a profitable firm and a harmonious society?

Taoism, like Confucianism, has deep roots in Chinese culture and thinking. While Confucian teachings emphasize social harmony based on the duty of social roles and the conformity to external expectations in a social hierarchy, Taoist philosophy respects the nature of everyone in the group and believes that harmony comes from expression of every member and man-nature unity (Lin, Ho, and Lin, 2013). While Tao in Confucianism means "the way of something", Tao in Taoist teachings means a completely independent entity to replace heaven in all its functions (Lau, 2001). Being simple and in harmony with the Tao is the central theme, which implies following the law of nature and benefiting everyone (Davis, 2004). Adherents seek an alignment between their actions, and by extension the actions of society, with the natural processes of the world. Once again, it is a harmonious relationship which is held up as the ideal. Both of these systems of thought are important aspects of the context within which we look at CSR in China.

The concept of harmony has taken on special relevance since 2006 when then-President Hu Jintao called for a "Harmonious Society". The Chinese Harmony approach to CSR underscores respecting nature and loving people, for the first time CSR has been defined in relation to Confucian interpersonal harmony and Taoist harmony between man and nature. See has explored the linkage between President Hu's directive and the spread of CSR in China (See, 2009). Wang and Juslin (2009) point out that the cultural roots explain some of the incompatibilities between Western CSR concept and Chinese interpretation. As a result, we should assume the equivalence of CSR in different cultural contexts with great caution.

Social Norms

Throughout China's long history the family has been a dominant theme in determining the organization of its social structures. Multi-generational living patterns are still widespread; arranged marriages; sons assuming the responsibility for supporting their parents; daughters, when they marry, going off to live in their husbands' households: all these ingrained social patterns have kept the family at the center of social organization in China.

China's dramatic economic growth over the past thirty years has put severe strains on this bedrock feature of the country's culture. Millions of workers have moved from the interior villages to China's manufacturing centers clustered along the southern and eastern coasts, often leaving behind children to be raised by grandparents. The families reunite perhaps once a year over the Chinese New Year celebration, perhaps even less frequently. The situation is made worse by China's *hukou* system which allows Chinese citizens' access to such public services as education and health care only in the village, town, or city of their official residence. Thus, when a man (or woman) leaves an interior village to take a job in a coastal city factory, he gives up his rights to those public services.

As age-old family ties along with inter-family support systems begin to weaken and as migrants can no longer count on the state to provide necessary services, what are the ramifications for the employer-employee relationship? Must employers accept greater responsibilities for their employees under these changing cultural and legal patterns?

Another social norm or Chinese cultural distinction with implications for CSR is the high degree of communitarianism, as opposed to individualism, in the Chinese value system. China's social relationships have been based on network circle differentiation, and different circles imply different moral standards and reciprocity principles (Luo, 2005). Huijser et al (2002), in advising U.S. and Chinese managers about cultural differences between the two countries, note that the United States is more individualistic than any other country in the world, while few countries are lower than the Chinese culture. "A [Chinese] child learns to respect the group to which he or she belongs, usually the family, and to differentiate between in-group members and out-group members (that is, all others outside of the family, regional ethnic group, locale, etc.)" One interpretation of this would be that CSR would fit easily into this Chinese cultural pattern. Because communitarianism is so deeply rooted in Chinese culture, CSR with its concern for human rights/employees, consumer rights, ecological rights, etc. would find a welcoming environment. On the other hand, were managers to think of various stakeholder groups (employees, communities, customers, etc.) as "out-group members," then the environment in China might not be so compatible to CSR. This might be a partial explanation of Lu Xiaohe's assertion (noted earlier in this paper) that Chinese managers lean toward Milton Friedman's rejection of CSR.

Geography

This element from our group of eight elements is probably less important for China than it might be for other countries. However, China's proximity to, and long border with, Russia has without doubt influenced China's political and economic development throughout much of the last one hundred years. While the republic of Mongolia sits between the two countries, (and to a lesser extent Krygystan and Tajikistan also) prior to 1992 it was a Russian satellite state, and so the Chinese-Russian border effectively stretched over more than 6,000 miles.

Shortly after the Russian revolution in 1917 and the founding of the Communist party there under Lenin, China was experiencing its own political and social turmoil with the collapse of the Qing dynasty, the devolution of authority to competing warlords, and then the competition between the Nationalist and the Communist parties. Russia seized the opportunity to send agents to advise and help the fledgling communist cells in China, and once the Communist Party under Mao prevailed in 1949, there began an ongoing relationship – sometimes collaborative, sometimes rocky – between the two countries.

Certainly, Mao's tight control of all economic activity under the central state government and the institution of a series of five-year plans were influenced by what he saw and experienced in his northern neighbor. In contrast, China has very determinedly chosen not to follow Russia's example in more recent years and has maintained far more state control of its economic activity both directly and indirectly through its state-owned enterprises.

These four elements, then – history, religions, social norms, and geography – form the basis of the context in which corporate social responsibility has taken root in China (see Figure 2). We turn now to a brief analysis of China's political structures, its level of economic development, the strength of its civil society institutions, and the condition of its social "safety net," the elements which are influencing the continuing development or evolution of CSR in China.

Political Structures

China's political structures are not only complex but also opaque, and therefore, it is difficult for Westerners to fully understand them. We certainly cannot solve that problem in this paper, but we will call attention to several aspects of those structures that are pertinent to the exploration of CSR in China.

First and foremost is the dominance of the Chinese Communist Party (CCP), for all intents and purposes the only significant party in the country. As such, certainly since it took full political control of the country in 1949, it has controlled not only China's politics but its economic activity as well. Whether we focus on the centralized state planning under Mao, the relaxation of government controls in some sectors under Deng, or the continuing gradual opening up to free market forces under subsequent Party leaders, it is the Communist Party, i.e., the government, which dictates the pace of change or whether, indeed, there will be any change at all.

Westerners tend to focus, perhaps too much, on this "opening up" of China's economy to free market forces and decision-making over the last thirty-five years. But it must not be forgotten that wide swaths of China's economy – for example, banking, aerospace, energy, communications, steel – are still controlled by state owned enterprises. And while these SOEs have become powerful forces in their own right, nevertheless they must ultimately follow the directions handed down by the Party. The combination of these two factors: the dominance of the CCP and the continuing centralized control of much of China's economy, has meant that the movement toward the acceptance of CSR in China has been largely at the instigation of the government.

Li-Wen Lin tells us that China's 1994 Company Law "echoed some aspects of CSR, particularly regarding the rights of employees in a company." However, "[T]he 2006 Company Law gives explicit recognition to CSR." According to Lin, Article 5 of the more recent Company Law states, "[i]n the course of doing business, a company must comply with laws and administrative regulations, conform to social morality and business ethics, act in good faith, subject itself to the government and the public supervision, and undertake social responsibility" (Lin, 2010). The nature and scope of "social responsibility" is left unclear, and Lin goes on to suggest that the government has put considerable emphasis on environmental issues and less so on human rights issues.

In January 2008, the Chinese government, through its State-Owned Assets Supervision and Administration Commission (SASAC), the body which oversees all SOEs, released a "Guide Opinion on the Social Responsibility Implementation for the State-Owned Enterprises Controlled by the Central Government." Lin tells us that SASAC spelled out these implementation guidelines for four reasons: to promote social harmony, to meet public expectations, because they are necessary for sustainable development, and "to participate in the international market and society" (Lin, 2010). Whether it be environmental concerns such as air and water pollution or the safety of products for either foreign or domestic consumption, the push to accommodate these typical CSR issues has been greatly influenced by the Chinese government rather than from the business community or from the civil society. This is quite different from the experience of North American and Western European countries.[1]

Level of Economic Development

China's economic growth over the past thirty years has been nothing short of astounding, rising from $356.9 billion in 1990 to $1,198.5 billion in 2000 to $7,318.5 billion in 2011 (World Bank), at which time it passed Japan to become the world's second largest economy. Never in the history of the world has a country transformed itself so rapidly from an impoverished, developing status to a world power. While the country's per capita GDP is still relatively low – $8,400 vs. $48,100 in the United States and somewhat less than Tunisia and Cuba (CIA, 2012) – nevertheless hundreds of millions of Chinese have been raised out of poverty just in the past few decades.

This rapid growth, and the equally rapid change in the development of China's economy, has several implications for the understanding of CSR in China. First, China's accession to the World Trade Organization (WTO) in 2001, as a result of this growth, has meant that it is subject to the same international expectations regarding CSR issues, especially human rights and environmental issues, as other more developed countries including those in North America and Western Europe.

Second, during this rapid development period from 1979 to the present China has gone from having a surplus of labor to staff its thousands of manufacturing and mining facilities – the widely reported migration from China's interior to the expanding manufacturing centers along its southern and eastern coastal areas – to a labor shortage condition (Chu, 2013). Wages have been rising in excess of ten percent annually over the past decade (LeBeau, 2013), and the "sweatshop" image of China's manufacturing facilities – the human rights issues of withheld wages and bad treatment and unsafe working conditions – has been gradually ameliorating.[2]

Third, during this rapid growth period from 1979 to the present the composition of China's economy has shifted dramatically from primarily agricultural to a quite different composition in 2012 where agriculture accounted for only 10.1% of the economy, manufacturing 45.3%, and the service sector 44.6% (CIA, 2012). Almost by definition, CSR becomes a more important factor as a country's economy transitions from agricultural to industrial, as more businesses are formed, and as those businesses grow in resources and power.

Fourth, China's dramatic economic growth has led to an equally dramatic growth in air quality and water quality issues. This has created a very difficult dynamic between the Chinese government and the business sector. Air pollution problems, in Beijing especially, rose to alarming levels during the winter of 2012-13; sulfur dioxide emissions soared to more than four times government standards, and at one point reached a level that the U.S. Environmental Protection Agency consider so hazardous that people should remain indoors. Nevertheless, one of China's biggest power companies, Huadian, turned off its coal scrubbers to save money, falsified paperwork, and sold its electricity "at a premium rate that the government offers to power plants with low emissions… [So far the government has] lacked the will or the capacity to reduce air pollution on a sustained basis (Mufson, 2013).

The change in China's level of economic development has been so large and it has come so rapidly that there is no historical precedent.[3] There can be no doubt, however, that it has influenced the evolving understanding and practice of CSR in the country.

Civil Society Institutions

The understanding and practice of corporate social responsibility in any country is influenced to a very significant degree by the presence, power, and activity of three important institutions: organized labor, advocacy groups or non-governmental organizations (NGOs), and free media organizations. We will look briefly at each of these institutions in China to help us understand how CSR is evolving there.

Organized Labor

Regarding employee-related issues of all kinds – wages, benefits, working conditions – and especially in the area of human rights, labor organizations can be a major influence on the practice of corporate social responsibility by businesses. Throughout much of the world labor unions can provide a counter-balance to the power of corporations in the ongoing resolution of management-worker issues. And unions are not just an important civil society institution, Michael Hardt (1995) citing Hegel tells us that "a civil society is fundamentally linked to the modern notion of labor."

In exploring the subject of labor unions in China there is an immediate anomaly to be addressed. In a communist state, theoretically, there should be no distinction between the interests of the state and the interests of workers. There should be no need for unions. Indeed, "the party-state [should be] the embodiment of the workers' aspirations." Yet the re-emergence of the All China Federation of Trade Unions (ACFTU) after the death of Mao is "implicit recognition" (Chan, 1995) of the divergent interests in China of the state and workers. Now, unions not only exist in China, they are mandatory.[4]

However, we should not assume from this that workers' rights vis-à-vis their corporate employers are well-protected. Only those unions sanctioned and affiliated with the ACFTU are allowed. According to Lee (2007), "Independent unions are illegal and those who attempt to form autonomous unions have been charged by the government with treason or subversion." Workers do not have the right under Chinese law to form an independent union, nor do they have the right to strike (Costello, Smith, and Brecher, 2007. Chinese unions play a quite different role than do unions throughout most of the rest of the world. They play a mediating role between workers and corporations and in the process become as much an agent of the latter as the former. The unions certainly do not "represent" the workers in trying to gain higher wages, more attractive benefits, and better working conditions. Lee continues, "As market reform has incessantly chipped away at workers' entitlements and tilted the balance of power further toward employers, the weakness of unions as defenders of labor rights is acutely felt" (Lee, 2007). Under these circumstances, labor unions in China bring relatively little pressure to bear on corporations to act in a socially responsible manner; they are ineffectual as a stimulant of CSR.

Advocacy Groups/Non-Government Organizations

In the developed countries of the West we take almost for granted not just the existence of thousands of advocacy groups or non-government organizations (NGOs) but also their power and importance in calling society's attention to the issues and problems created by corporations, whether those issues be environmental, human rights, consumer protection, or governance in nature. Thomas Carothers and William Brandt (1999) tell us that while NGOs are not to be equated with "civil society," they are an important component. The authors go on to state that, "Such groups have been multiplying in recent years, especially in developing countries".

Just as with labor unions, there is in theory no need for non-governmental organizations in a communist state because the state is the only (and a sufficient) provider of social services. Thus in China prior to 1978 the number and the importance of NGOs were minimal. Since the death of Mao, however, there has been a dramatic growth in the number of NGOs and the gradual relaxation of government controls – from 6,000 in 1978 to 142,000 in 2003, 354,000 in 2007, and 460,000 in 2012 (Brundenius, 2005) – but this growth should not be construed as an indication of their influence on CSR which pales in comparison with what is to be found in North America and Western Europe.

Nor do NGOs in China enjoy the independent status that we take for granted in the West. Chinese NGOs must register with either the Ministry of Civil Affairs or with the Bureau of Industry and Commerce. "Those not registered at all are technically considered illegal" (Brundenius, 2005). Ma states that the Chinese central government "remains the most decisive component in the development of NGOs" and notes "the interactive and mutually dependent relations between the government and NGOs" in China (Ma, 2002).

Because of this lack of autonomy and self-governance, China's NGOs and advocacy groups do not exercise the same kind of influence on CSR as do their counterparts in the West.

The Media

Free and active media organizations represent the third critical civil society institution in influencing the development of corporate social responsibility in any country. To a very large extent the central government in China controls the media in the country directly. The principal news agency, Xinhua, is a government body. The state also controls directly the leading newspapers such as *People's Daily*, *Guangming Daily*, *China Daily*, and the major national television station CCTV. Chapter II, Article 35, of China's Constitution specifically grants to the Chinese people freedom of speech and freedom of the press, but as with other freedoms the interests of the state take precedence, and so even with those media not controlled directly, the state exercises indirect control.

Early in 2013, for example, the *Southern Weekend*, an independent newspaper in the southern province of Guangdong, drew the ire of government censors by urging greater respect for constitutional rights in its New Year's editorial. The censors intervened and without even the tacit approval of the paper's editorial staff rewrote the headline and the editorial turning it into a bland New Year's greeting. Surprisingly, a brouhaha ensued during which the journalists on the *Southern Weekend* staff wrote an open letter of protest and threatened to go on strike. Embarrassed when this incident quickly drew international attention, the central government made amends and admitted that the censors had acted too aggressively, all the while urging other publications to criticize the action of *Southern Weekend* (Gao, 2013).

But if the government has had reasonable success censoring the traditional media such as newspapers and the radio and television broadcasters, the problems of controlling news and views flowing over, around, and through the Internet have proven much more difficult in recent years.

China has been edging tentatively away from central economic planning and decision making toward more free market activity, and there is the prospect of further moves along that trajectory. But the Chinese government has shown little inclination to relax its control of the mediaAs noted above, however, free media institutions have a critical influence in establishing social responsibility as an integral part of the role corporations play in a society. How this tension is resolved is an important consideration in the ongoing evolution of establishing CSR in China.

Safety Net

In his more than thirty years as the largely unchallenged supreme leader of China, Mao Zedong established a true communist society in which, in theory at least, all the necessities of life were provided to workers and peasants in exchange for their labor in the fields and factories. Families lived in assigned quarters in the communes; they shared meals together in commune-style eating areas; the state provided clothing, medical care, and education: all in exchange for their labor for the entirety of their working lives. This cradle-to-grave provision of essential services came to be known in China as the "iron rice bowl".

When Deng Xiaoping set in motion the gradual introduction of free market forces – for example the ability of farmers to make small profits from surplus agricultural production and the authorization to form small businesses – this reliance on the state came to an abrupt end. No longer can workers and farmers look to the state to provide their housing, food, and other living essentials, and the transition has been a most difficult one. This dramatic shift raises serious questions as to what extent businesses must take up the slack left by the government. Many of the employers who were criticized for running "sweat shops" provided eating and living facilities for their young, mostly female workers, but this was definitely a significant part of the workers' compensation. At present it is not at all clear just what responsibilities corporations will take on or how the evolving expectations of the Chinese society will impact those corporations.

CONCLUSION

What, then, can we conclude about corporate social responsibility in China, and why does it matter? To answer the second question first, it matters because China matters. China has become such an important factor in the economic workings of the entire world: not just the United States and the rest of North America, but also Western Europe, Africa, and, quite obviously, the east and Southeast Asia regions. It matters because the economies of individual nation states and regions have become so tightly integrated through the process of globalization that Western managers and Western scholars must learn about, and pay attention to, CSR in its various forms in all parts of the world. Because of that tight integration managers in China and in the West must know what is expected of them and of their companies as they seek to become an increasingly important part of foreign cultures.

About the first question, we have described the status of CSR in China at present: how it is conceived and practiced in Chinese businesses, and to what extent it is incorporated into the Chinese academic community. It is clear that the concept and practice of CSR is more deeply embedded in Western management practices than it is in China at this time. And it is equally clear that Chinese managers and scholars, with the strong encouragement of the Chinese government, are moving rapidly to develop the concepts, the processes, and the outcomes of CSR that they believe to be appropriate for China.

We have presented an eight-element framework as an analytical tool to help understand why and how Chinese CSR differs from what we know in the West. Additionally, we have emphasized that CSR, in China especially, is an evolving concept: that it will change and mature as there are changes in China's level of economic development (a continuously declining role for agriculture and the further development of an industrial and service economy), its political structures (for example, a declining role for the state-owned enterprises), the development and strengthening of its civil society institutions (more independence for China's unions, more powerful advocacy groups, freer media institutions), and further changes in the division of "safety net" provisions between government and private corporations. Just as China is developing its own, unique form of economic system, "state capitalism," (Lin, 2010) so too is China certain to develop its own form of corporate social responsibility.

More broadly we offer this eight-element framework for contextual analysis as a contribution toward further research into the complexities of future comparative work on CSR in all its many manifestations across the global business spectrum. Regardless of whether or not CSR is a "largely Western concept" (Mullich, 2011), it behooves scholars, and most definitely business managers as well, to follow how and why CSR is developing in China and most certainly in other countries as well. An insular approach to CSR is no more appropriate and no less dangerous than an inward-focused approach to marketing, finance, human resource management or any of the other functions of business in this economically integrated, "globalized," twenty-first century.

REFERENCES

Aspen Institute Center for Business Education. (2008). Where Will They Lead.

Barboza, D., & Buckley, C. (2013). China plan cuts the state's role in the economy. *The New York Times*, May 25, p. A1.

Baxi, C.V. (2013). *Corporate social responsibility, the Indian experience.*

Beach, S. (2013). Challenged in China. *Committee to Protect Journalists*, March 11.

Brown, J. (2013, March 13). Art, China, and censorship according to Ai Weiwei (Television program). *PBS Newshour*.

Brundenius, P. (2005). *China's emerging civil society: the autonomy of NGOs in China*. Department of Political Science, Lund University.

Bunch, R., Yang, D., & Qi, D. (2008), Where will they lead: China 2008 MBA student attitudes about business & society. The Aspen Institute Centre for Business Education.

Carnogurska, M. (1998). Original ontological roots of ancient Chinese philosophy. *Asian Philosophy*, *8*(3), 203–213. doi:10.1080/09552369808575484

Carothers, T., & Brandt, W. (1999). Civil society. *Foreign Policy*, *117*(117), 18–24, 26–29. doi:10.2307/1149558

Carroll, A. B. (1991). The pyramid of corporate social responsibility: Toward the moral management of organizational stakeholders. *Business Horizons*, *34*(4), 39–48. doi:10.1016/0007-6813(91)90005-G

Chan, A. (1995). The emerging patterns of industrial relations in China and the rise of two new labor movements. China Information, 9(4).

Chao, L. (2012, June 3). Google tips off users in China. *The Wall Street Journal*.

Chapple, W., & Moon, J. (2005). Corporate social responsibility (CSR) in Asia: A seven-country study of CSR web site reporting. *Business & Society*, *44*(4), 415–441. doi:10.1177/0007650305281658

Chu, K. (2013), A billion strong but short on workers. *The Wall Street Journal*, May 2, p. B 1.

CIA. (2012). World Factbook. Retrieved from http://www.photius.com/rankings/economy/gdp_per_capita_2012_0.html

CIA. (n. d.) Retrieved from www.cia.gov

Costello, T., Smith, B. & Brecher, J. (2007). Labor rights in China. *Post-Autistic Economics Review*, issue 41, 34-38.

Davidson, D. K. (2011), The importance of context in understanding CSR: China's lab conditions as a case study. *Paper presented at the annual meeting of the International Association for Business and Society.*

Davis, D. D. (2004). The Tao of leadership in virtual teams. *Organizational Dynamics*, *33*(1), 47–62. doi:10.1016/j.orgdyn.2003.11.004

Denyer, S., & Gu, J. (2015). The end of an era for journalism in China. *The Washington Post*, January 11, A10.

Fransen, L. (2013). The embeddedness of responsible business practice: Exploring the interaction between national-institutional environments and corporate social responsibility. *Journal of Business Ethics*, *115*(2), 213–227. doi:10.1007/s10551-012-1395-2

Gao, H. (2013). A press renaissance? The legacy of China's "Southern Weekend.". *Atlantic (Boston, Mass.)*, (January): 13.

Garriga, E., & Mele, D. (2004). Corporate social responsibility theories: Mapping the territory. *Journal of Business Ethics*, *53*(1/2), 51–71. doi:10.1023/B:BUSI.0000039399.90587.34

Gjolberg, M. (2009). Measuring the immeasurable?: Constructing an index of CSR practices and CSR performance in 20 countries. *Scandinavian Journal of Management*, *25*(1), 1, 10–22. doi:10.1016/j.scaman.2008.10.003

Google. (2013, April). Public Data: China. Retrieved from http://www.google.com/publicdata/explore?ds=d5bncppjof8f9_&met_y=ny_gdp_mktp_cd&idim=country:CHN&dl=en&hl=en&q=gdp%20china

Gugler, P., & Shi, J. Y. J. (2009). Corporate social responsibility for developing country multinational corporations: Lost war in pertaining global competitiveness? *Journal of Business Ethics*, *87*(S1), 3–24. doi:10.1007/s10551-008-9801-5

Hardt, M. (1995). The withering of civil society. *Social Text*, (45): 27–44. doi:10.2307/466673

Huijser, M., Stück, J. M., & Tanaka, L. S. (2002). *Cross-cultural management education in China: from Marx to markets*. CMC/Global Associates/AER.

Indexmundi. (n. d.). Retrieved from www.indexmundi.com/china/gdp_per_capita_(ppp).html

Ip, P. K. (2002). The Weizhi group of Xi'an: A Chinese virtuous corporation. *Journal of Business Ethics*, *35*(1), 15–26. doi:10.1023/A:1012619405545

Jacobs, A. (2013, May 4). Plans to harness Chinese river's power threatens a region. *The New York Times*.

Jamali, D., Karam, C., & Blowfield, M. (2015). Development Oriented CSR. London: Greenfield Press.

Lau, D.-C. (1979). *Analects*. London: Penguin.

Lau, D.-C. (2001). *Tao Te Ching*. Hong Kong: Chinese University Press.

LeBeau, P. (2013, April 18). New study finds China manufacturing costs rising to US level. *CNBC.*

Lee, C. K. (2007). *Against the law: labor protests in China's rustbelt and sunbelt.* Berkeley: University of California Press.

Lin, L. H., Ho, Y., & Lin, W. E. (2013). Confucian and Taoist work values: An exploratory study of the Chinese transformational leadership behavior. *Journal of Business Ethics, 113*(1), 91–103. doi:10.1007/s10551-012-1284-8

Lin, L.-W. (2010). Corporate social responsibility in China: Window dressing or structural change? *Berkeley Journal of International Law, 28*(1), 64–100.

Lin, L.-W. (2010). Corporate social responsibility in China: Window dressing or structural change? *Berkeley Journal of International Law, 28*(1), 64–100.

Lin, N. (2011, March). Capitalism in China: A centrally managed capitalism (CMC) and its future. *Management and Organization Review.*

Lockett, A., Moon, J., & Visser, W. (2006). Corporate social responsibility in management research: Focus, nature, salience and sources of influence. *Journal of Management Studies, 43*(1), 115–135. doi:10.1111/j.1467-6486.2006.00585.x

Lu, X. (2009). A Chinese perspective: Business ethics in China now and in the future. *Journal of Business Ethics, 86*(4), 451–461. doi:10.1007/s10551-008-9857-2

Lu, X. (2010). *Business ethics: a Chinese approach.* Shanghai Academy of Social Sciences Press.

Luo, J. (2005). Particularistic trust and general trust: A network analysis in Chinese organizations. *Management and Organization Review, 1*(3), 437–458. doi:10.1111/j.1740-8784.2005.00022.x

Ma, Q. (2002). The Governance of NGOs in China since 1978: How much autonomy? *Nonprofit and Voluntary Sector Quarterly, 31*(3), 305–328. doi:10.1177/0899764002313001

Marquis, C., & Qian, C. (2014). Corporate Social Responsibility Reporting in China: Symbol or Substance? *Organization Science, 25*(1), 127–148. doi:10.1287/orsc.2013.0837

Matten, D., & Moon, J. (2008). "Implicit" and "explicit" CSR: A conceptual framework for an understanding of corporate social responsibility. *Academy of Management Review, 33*(2), 404–424. doi:10.5465/AMR.2008.31193458

Moon, J., & Shen, X. (2010). CSR in China research: Salience, focus and nature. *Journal of Business Ethics, 94*(4), 613–629. doi:10.1007/s10551-009-0341-4

Mufson, S. (2013, May 12). In China, pollution resists change. *The Washington Post*, p. A12.

Mullich, J. (2011). Corporate social responsibility emerges in China. *The Wall Street Journal.*

Quan, K. (2011, March 18). Presented at the 17th annual Symposium on Corporate Social Responsibility, Mount St. Mary's University.

See, G. (2009). Harmonious society and Chinese CSR: Is there really a link? *Journal of Business Ethics, 89*(1), 1–22. doi:10.1007/s10551-008-9981-z

Shafer, W. E., Fukukawa, K., & Lee, G. M. (2007). Values and the perceived importance of ethics and social responsibility: The U.S. versus China. *Journal of Business Ethics*, *70*(3), 265–284. doi:10.1007/s10551-006-9110-9

Shen, Z. Y., Liu, X. G., & Zhou, X. H. (2008). Research on state-owned enterprise reform: In view of social responsibility[in Chinese]. *China Industrial Economics*, *9*, 141–149.

Snell, R. S., & Tseng, C. S. (2003). Images of the virtuous employee in China's transitional economy. *Asia Pacific Journal of Management*, *20*(3), 307–331. doi:10.1023/A:1024045415888

Spegele, B. (2013, May 6). Chinese protest plans for industrial plants, *The Wall Street Journal*, p. A8.

SynTao. (2015). A Journey to Discover Values: A Study on sustainability reporting in China. Retrieved from http://www.syntao.com

Wang, L., & Juslin, H. (2009). The impact of Chinese culture on corporate social responsibility: The harmony approach. *Journal of Business Ethics*, *88*(S3), 433–451. doi:10.1007/s10551-009-0306-7

Whitcomb, L. L., Erdener, C. B., & Li, C. (1998). Business ethical values in China and the U.S. *Journal of Business Ethics*, *17*(8), 839–852. doi:10.1023/A:1005793424492

World Bank. (n. d.) Retrieved from: www.google.com/publicdata/explore

Xinhua News. (2006). The decisions on the key problems in building socialist harmonious society by Chinese communist party central committee. Retrieved from http://cpc.people.com.cn/GB/64093/64094/4932424.html

Xu, S., & Yang, R. (2010). Indigenous characteristics of Chinese corporate social responsibility conceptual paradigm. *Journal of Business Ethics*, *93*(2), 321–333. doi:10.1007/s10551-009-0224-8

Yin, J. (2015). Institutional Drivers for Corporate Social Responsibility in an Emerging Economy A Mixed-Method Study of Chinese Business Executives. *Business & Society*.

Yin, J., & Zhang, Y. (2012). Institutional dynamics and corporate social responsibility (CSR) in an emerging country context: Evidence from China. *Journal of Business Ethics*, *111*(2), 301–316. doi:10.1007/s10551-012-1243-4

Zadek, S., & Wickerham, J. (2009). Managerial survey on corporate responsibility: China's CSR change makers. *Fortune China*. Retrieved from http://www.accountability.org/home.aspx

Zhang, Y. (2003, June). China's emerging civil society. Center for Northeast Asian Policy Studies, Brookings Institution.

Zhou, Z. (2008). Business ethics education in China's MBA curriculum. *Journal of Business Ethics Education*, *5*, 261–266.

Zhou, Z., Nakano, C., & Luo, B. N. (2011). Business ethics as field of training, teaching, and research in East Asia. *Journal of Business Ethics*, *104*(Suppl. 1), 19–27. doi:10.1007/s10551-012-1259-9

Zhou, Z., Ou, P., & Enderle, G. (2009). Business ethics education for MBA students in China. *Journal of Business Ethics Education*, *6*, 103–118.

ENDNOTES

1 Promoting CSR around environmental issues and at the same time being responsible for economic growth and development can put the central Chinese government in an awkward bind. Beijing's plans to build a series of dams on the Nu River has generated local popular resistance (Jacobs, 2013) as have the plans for an oil refinery and petrochemical development in Kunming, capital of Yunnan province (Spegele, 2013).

2 There is some disagreement on this point. While the reporting of sweatshop issues in China has declined in recent years (Davidson, 2011), Katie Quan, Associate Chair of the UC Berkeley Center for Labor Research and Education, noted in 2011, "After eight years of research I continue to be shocked at just how bad labor conditions in China still are." (Quan, 2011).

3 At the time of this writing there is great concern and scrutiny from countries around the world regarding whether or not China can maintain the pace of its economic growth demonstrated over the past decade. Premier Le Keqiang has recently announced that the Chinese government will relax certain restrictions and open the economy further to free market forces (Barboza and Buckley, 2013). Regardless of how much "opening up" actually takes place, there is general agreement that the Communist Party/state will continue to exercise very significant control of not only macroeconomic but also microeconomic decisions and, therefore, continue to bear the responsibility for the pace of economic development in China.

4 For example, when Walmart arrived in China in 1996, the company hoped to maintain its near-universal anti-union policies. However, the central government ultimately prevailed in insisting that Walmart establish a union under the aegis of the ACFTU.

Chapter 3
East vs. West Approaches to Reporting Corporate Sustainability Strategies to the World:
Corporate Sustainability Reporting: East vs. West

Jensena Kaplan
Loyola Marymount University, USA

Ivan Montiel
Baruch College - City University of New York, USA

ABSTRACT

This chapter applies Hofstede's cultural dimensions to compare how companies located in Western and Eastern regions present their corporate sustainability strategies to their stakeholders. We compare ten pairs of West-East companies and find that differences in the corporate sustainability strategies they report can be related to geo-political and socio-cultural differences as described by Hofstede. Our findings can serve as a tool for companies in both regions to gain a better understanding about which sustainability initiatives are of more concern, depending on the region they operate.

INTRODUCTION

Corporate sustainability (CS) is rapidly becoming a strategic issue for companies in all sectors all over the world. Today, the mainstreaming of sustainability thinking is present in boardrooms and at the top management levels of the most visionary companies. However, it is still not clear what being "sustainable" exactly means, since neither an accepted definition nor a CS systematic measurement system is well established (Montiel & Delgado-Ceballos, 2014). Generally, CS has been defined as a tridimen-

DOI: 10.4018/978-1-5225-0720-8.ch003

sional construct that integrates economic, social, and environmental performance (Bansal, 2005), and there seems to be consensus on these three main dimensions. However, we still do not know precisely what each of these three dimensions entails. For the purpose of this chapter we use as definition of CS those management practices that organizations put in place to deliver simultaneous economic, social, and environmental benefits (Hart & Milstein, 2003).

One of the CS activities that companies devote time to study is CS or corporate social responsibility (CSR) reporting,[1] which has become institutionalized among businesses worldwide (Etzion & Ferraro, 2010). Companies today publish annual CS reports to inform all interested stakeholders (e.g., customers, investors, employees, researchers) on the policies and practices they have adopted toward being a more sustainable organization.

In this chapter we compare the information that companies in both Western (North America) and Eastern (East Asia) regions present to their stakeholders in their CS reports and publications as well as on their corporate websites. It is important to examine the similarities and differences between Western and Eastern companies because, as the world becomes increasingly interconnected, it becomes relevant to understand CS strategies through the lens of differing cultures and environments. This examination enables both shareholders and all interested stakeholders to understand more fully the motivating factors behind certain CS strategies pursued by companies. In addition, this analysis may help companies learn from CS practices undertaken by their other-side-of-the-world counterparts.

The companies studied operate in different industries: technology, automotive, apparel manufacturing, and telecommunications. The primary mechanisms for comparison are the corporate sustainability reports generated by the examined companies, other third party rating agencies, and additional public information disclosed by the companies. These reports are analyzed for any similarities or differences between companies located in Eastern Asia— specifically China, Japan, and Korea—as compared to North American companies in the United States and Canada.

This chapter is organized as follows: first, we conduct a brief literature review on CS and Western versus Eastern approaches to CSR and sustainability. Second, we describe the method used in our comparative study. Third, we elaborate on the differences found between companies in the two regions by organizing them in a set of CSR themes that we classify following to Hofstede's cultural dimensions. Last, we present some general conclusions from our study and propose directions for future research.

EAST VS. WEST APPROACHES TO BUSINESS

Previous research has addressed East-West differences in the way business is conducted. Chung et al. (2008) pointed out differences in ethical perceptions between East and West students, but went further to also identify differences in these perceptions within the three "Confucian" cultures analyzed (i.e., Japan, South Korea, and China) (Chung et al., 2008). Differences regarding moral values and the relationships with nature have also been explored. Miller (2012) stated that fundamental approaches to ethics and morality in both East and West countries are heavily influenced by the concepts of religion, ultimate truth, and the perception of the natural environment.

On the practitioner side, we also find discussions on the main East-West differences in business conduct. Beckman (2013) identified seven cultural traits that Easterners value more than Westerners when conducting business: (i) relationships are emphasized more than the "letter of the law"; (ii) aspiration and intentions matter strongly, not just measurable performance; (iii) the good of the group outweighs the needs of the individual; (iv) face-saving tact is absolute; (v) long past history and achievement matters, often more than recent history; (vi) rewards should be consistent with effort, not just results; and (vii) long-term thinking instead of short-term gains (Beckman, 2013). We expect that these differences will shape the way companies in those regions tackle sustainability.

One of the most commonly used conceptual frameworks to compare nations based on their cultural values was first introduced in 1984 by Geert Hofstede. Hofstede described six dimensions of national culture: (i) power distance, (ii) individualism, (iii) masculinity, (iv) uncertainty avoidance, (v) long term orientation, and (vi) indulgence. Hofstede's cultural dimensions help us to organize the different CSR themes found in the company reports, to understand differences in East-West CS strategies, and to compare how they publicly report their strategies. Table 3 provides the indices for both the West and East countries analyzed in this chapter. Based on this evidence, we also expect to find that CS strategies reported by companies will differ between the West and the East. We anticipate that the primary differences will be due to both geo-political and sociocultural factors which will impact the information companies include in their CS reports.

METHOD

In order to compare how companies on both sides of the world present themselves with respect to the CSR and sustainability practices, we conducted a comparative case study analysis focused on self-reported information. This information takes the form of CS annual reports, codes of conducts, and any other information posted on the companies' websites. Our goal is to ascertain the issues companies identify as important and thus, address in their public documents.

In this study, we identified a set of 10 pairs of companies in different industry sectors that are similar in their activities and leaders in their respective markets. These pairs of companies, being multinationals operating in both the East and the West, may be considered direct competitors. Table 1 lists the pairs of companies analyzed and the rationale for their selection. We compare reports by using a sustainability practices checklist designed by Antolin-Lopez et al (2015) and summarized in Table 2. The checklist includes CS sub-dimensions and items for each of three CS dimensions. These three dimensions are in line with the three aforementioned tridimensional CS construct that integrates economic, social, and environmental performance (Bansal, 2005).

CULTURAL DIMENSIONS AND CS REPORTING

The comparative analysis of CS public information reported by the analyzed companies generated a list of differences between East and West. Most of these differences can be classified under one of the six Hofstede's cultural dimensions. In Table 3 we summarize Hofstede's cultural dimensions along with the indices for the studied countries and a list of CSR themes related to each of the dimensions. The CSR themes emerged after each of the two authors reviewed the CS reports. They identified the CSR themes most closely related to each of the Hofstede's cultural dimensions included in this analysis.

Table 1. Company selection and rationale

Industry/Company	Rationale
Automotive	
Ford Motor Company, United States	Second largest U.S. auto manufacturer after General Motors, but less diversified to comparison is easier across brands
Nissan Motor Co., Japan	Revenues of nearly $98 billion (2014 financial report) comparable to Ford's $144 billion in revenue (2014 financial report)
Brewing	
Anheuser-Busch, United States	US most popular beer as of 2012 and holder of several top 10 brands globally (Tepper, 2012)
Asahi Breweries, Japan	Japan's most popular beer as of 2012 and ranked tenth most popular globally (Tepper, 2012)
Energy	
Barrick Gold, Canada	One of the highest grossing gold mining companies in North America. The mining industry is known for human rights issues
Shenuah Energy, China	One of the top six energy and mining companies in China in 2015 (Carpenter, 2015)
Electronics/Communications	
General Electric, United States	American conglomerate operating in industries such as software development and engineering, home appliances, and pharmaceuticals
LG Corporation, South Korea	South Korean conglomerate in industries such as electronics, chemicals, and telecom products
Technology/Hardware	
Dell Inc., United States	One of the largest technological corporations in the world
NEC Corporation, Japan	One of the top Japanese information technology product and services companies
Manufacturing	
Flextronics, United States	America's largest original design manufacturer
Foxconn, China	Foxconn has several reported cases of human rights abuses, and because of Apple partnership they are often in the spotlight
Kohler, United States	One of the most widely used plumbing brands in the United States and #76 in Forbes Largest Private companies in 2014
Toto Ltd., Japan	Number one toilet brand in Japan and comparable 2015 revenue ($3.5 million) to Kohler ($6 million)
Telecommunications	
AT&T, United States	One of the leading players in the wireless and communications industry in the United States, with revenue of $146 billion in 2015 (2014 financial report)
SK Telecom, South Korea	The largest cell carrier and provider in South Korea (SK telecom financial report)
Textiles/Apparel	
Nike Inc., United States	The largest apparel manufacturers in the United states and globally who sponsors many Olympic athletes (Balfour, 2008)
Li Ning, China	China's top athletic wear maker and sponsor of many Chinese Olympic athletes with prices "comparable to Nike" (Balfour, 2008)
Technology/Sales	
Amazon.com Inc., United States	Largest US e-commerce site and 9th most visited website globally (Peterson, 2014)
Alibaba Group, China	Largest Chinese e-commerce site and 10th most visited website globally (Peterson, 2014)

Table 2. Corporate sustainability strategies checklist

Economic Sub-Dimensions	Examples of Items	Western	Eastern
Profit Generation	Direct Economic Value Generated; Return on Investment		
Efficiency	Input Cost Reduction per Outputs; Waste Management Cost Reduction per Output		
Supplier Relations	Supply Chain Management Requirements; Supplier Development Programs		
Marketing Practices	Marketing Based on Sustainable Practices; Fair marketing practices		
Innovation	R & D Investments; Spin-Off Technologies		
Risk & Crisis Management	Coordinated Risk Management Response; Burma Concern		
Employee Compensation	Caps on Executive Compensation; Cash Profit Sharing		
Government Relations	Collaboration with Government Officials; Political Involvement		
Ethics in Management	Codes of Conduct/Compliance/Corruption & Bribery; Fair Competition		
Social Sub-Dimensions			
Employee Programs	Diversity practices, LGBT policies		
Occupational Health & Safety	Employee Safety Improvements; Healthy Lifestyle Incentives		
Human Rights	Forced Labor Policies; Child Labor Policies		
Philanthropy	Charitable Giving; Funds for Local Community Activities		
Volunteerism	Paid Employee Volunteer Hours; Employee Volunteer Impact Measures		
Local Commitment	Local Sourcing; Indigenous Communities Programs		
Bottom of Pyramid (BoP)	BoP Development Programs; Poverty Alleviation Programs		
Product Responsibility	Product LifeCycle Assessment; Waste Minimization in Packaging		
Quality Management	Quality Control Programs; Quality Data & Reporting for Sustainability		
Consumer Relations Management	Customer Satisfaction Management; Customer Feedback Process		
Sustainable Consumption	Responsible Labeling; Responsible Product Disposal Information		
Environmental Sub-Divisions			
Energy Conservation	Energy Efficiency; Clean Energy		
Materials Management	Low Impact Resources; Renewable Resources		
Water Issues	Water Use; Recycled Water		
Waste Management	Waste Reutilization; Toxic Waste Management		
Climate Change	Climate Change Mitigation; Carbon Reduction Practices		
Pollution	Acid Rain (NOx and Sox Emissions); Runoff; Noise		
Biodiversity	Natural Habitats Restoration; Elimination of Operation in Environmentally Sensitive		
Product Stewardship	Green Products; Packaging Materials		
Environmental Management Systems	ISO 14001; EMAS		
Distribution and Transportation	Low-Emissions Transport Vehicles; Clean Outsourced Fleet		
Green Suppliers	Suppliers Monitoring; Suppliers Screened by Green Criteria		
Environmental Reporting	Environmental/Sustainability Reports; Environmental Communications		
Environmental Compliance	Fines for Non-Compliance with Environmental Regulations; Environmental Laws Obedience		
Environmental Risk	Reduction of Environmental Accidents; Environmental Risks Prevision		

Adapted from Antolin-Lopez, Delgado-Ceballos & Montiel (2016)

Table 3. Hofstede's cultural dimensions and CSR themes

Cultural Dimension	West Indices	East Indices	CSR Themes
Power Distance	40 (USA) 39 (Canada)	54 (Japan) 60 (S. Korea) 80 (China)	• Employee autonomy • Hierarchy
Individualism	91 (USA) 80 (Canada)	46 (Japan) 18 (S. Korea) 20 (China)	• Innovation • Individual entrepreneurship • Family
Uncertainty Avoidance	46 (USA) 48 (Canada)	92 (Japan) 85 (S. Korea) 30 (China)	• Crisis management
Masculinity	62 (USA) 52 (Canada)	95 (Japan) 39 (S. Korea) 66 (China)	• Minority and non-discrimination • Age
Long-Term Orientation	26 (USA) 36 (Canada)	88 (Japan) 100 (S. Korea) 87 (China)	• Population growth • Biodiversity
Indulgence	68 (USA) 68 (Canada)	42 (Japan) 29 (S. Korea) 24 (China)	

Based on Hofstede's (1984) cultural dimensions theory
Indices available at the Hofstede Centre (geert-hofstede.com)

Power Distance

Hofstede's power distance dimension refers to "the degree to which the less powerful members of a society accept and expect that power is distributed unequally" (The Hofstede Centre, 2015). "The fundamental issue here is how a society handles inequalities among people. People in societies exhibiting a large degree of power distance accept a hierarchical order in which everybody has a place and which needs no further justification. In societies with low power distance, people strive to equalize the distribution of power and demand justification for inequalities of power" (The Hofstede Centre, 2015). The countries in our analysis score slightly differently with regard to power distance. Western countries indices (USA=40, Canada=29) are lower than Eastern country indices (Japan=45, South Korea=60 and China=80). We expect these differences in power distance also to surface in the corporate world and in the ways that CS strategies are implemented and reported.

We suggest that power distance relates to the employee autonomy-hierarchy within the company's organizational structure. Hofstede's country indices show lower power distance among Western countries, especially compared to China. Our analysis of CS reports shows some evidence of this difference. For example, the Western company Dell encourages "Employee risk taking because Dell promotes a culture where team members are encouraged to take risks and feel supported, valued and proud to be part of Dell" (Dell, 2015: 17).

Another interesting finding related to power distance relates to the way companies describe their internal communication systems. For example, Shenuah Energy of China states "Under the employee representative committee, four special committees comprising employee representatives have been established for democratic management, protection of rights and interests, safety production and collection of proposals, as an important platform to listen to the voices of employees" (Shenuah, 2012: 55).

In 2012, the employee representative committee collected 113 proposals from employees, which were summarized into 83 proposals covering a range of topics such as corporate development, operation and management, talent teambuilding, and corporate culture. The company "proactively implemented the adopted proposals from employees, and provided positive feedbacks to those that are unable to implement" (Shenuah, 2012: 55). Shenuah's employee representative committees, which are set up to communicate with management, seem hierarchical. They do not show any evidence of employee-manager direct communications, which is consistent with a high power distance index in China. The Western counterpart in our analysis, Barrick Gold, claims that they "Believe that keeping the lines of communication open between management and labour is the most effective way to avoid a work stoppage. In 2013, they experienced one 18-day stop work by employees at the Porgera operation over allegations of a breach of the Code of Conduct" (Barrick, 2013: 95). Barrick Gold's approach reads as more autonomous and based on a less hierarchical system.

Another example of East-West differences can be found in the Flextronics - Foxconn pairing. At Flextronics they "encourage open dialog between employees and managers," which lessens power distance. They describe "special projects and programs to address employee concerns and improve employee engagement: GM Talk2Me, Talk2Me by managers, town halls, lunch & learn, mutual respect training, management workshop (culture intervention), values workshop, leadership skills training(e.g. coaching & mentoring skills workshop, frontline leaders program), recognition programs, team building activities, community involvement projects" (Flextronics. 2013: 54). In comparison, Foxconn mentions employee training and employee health and safety, and an avenue for employees to report health and safety concerns, but does not mention formal ways for employees and managers to engage and communicate with one another. (Flextronics. 2014: 54).

Finally, it is interesting to note that LG claims to foster more employee autonomy: "LG Electronics puts great energy into fashioning a working style unique to LG Electronics and a corporate culture that celebrates creativity and autonomy, which form the foundations of our efforts to achieve leadership in the global market" (LG, 2015: 73). South Korea's power distance index (60) is in between the United States (40) and China (80), which may explain why autonomy is more prevalent in that country compared to China.

Individualism

Hofstede's individualism dimension is defined as "a preference for a loosely-knit social framework in which individuals are expected to take care of only themselves and their immediate families" (The Hofstede Centre, 2015). Its opposite, collectivism, represents a preference for a tightly-knit framework in society in which individuals can expect their relatives or members of a particular in-group to look after them in exchange for unquestioning loyalty. A society's position on this dimension is reflected in whether people's self-image is defined in terms of "I" or "we." (Hofstede Centre, 2015). In our set of countries, we find differences in their Hofstede's indices between Western (USA=91, Canada=80) and Eastern regions (Japan=46, South Korea=18, China=20) that impact how companies address CS strategies related to individualism.

Individualism vs. collectivism traits becomes relevant when we analyze and compare CS reports. Eastern companies report more CSR-related activities targeting employee family members, a sign of collectivism, than Western companies. Interestingly, Western companies tend to report family-oriented CSR activities when they operate in other regions such as Europe or East Asia.

An example of collectivism is found in the Eastern company Nissan, which offers childcare services to employees. They state in their CS report: "The first March Land, at the Technical Center in Atsugi, Kanagawa Prefecture, was followed in fiscal 2012 by daycare facilities at the Global Headquarters and at the Nissan Global Information System Center" (Nissan, 2015: 86). Nissan has also "been recognized by the Japanese government as a corporation actively promoting childcare support, successfully implementing programs to achieve the goals set forth in the action plan of the Ministry of Health, Labor and Welfare based on an April 2005 law outlining measures to support the development of future generations" (Nissan, 2015: 86). Ford, the Western counterpart we analyzed in this study, did offer childcare, but seemed to limit their activities to Europe rather than in their native United States. They claim, "In Europe, we offer a variety of flexible working patterns. In the U.K. and Germany, for example, we support part-time working and telecommuting and, at some locations, offer child-care facilities for the children of our employees." (Ford, 2014: 453).

Another noteworthy example relates to the Eastern company Asahi. Asahi offers family counseling: "In September 2005, mental health counseling by a certified clinical psychologist was introduced for employees and family members. User privacy is strictly protected" (Asahi, 2012: 84). Asahi also offers a childcare leave system which "allows employees to take off 10 days per year per child of pre-junior high school age, up to 20 days. Days off under this system are counted as paid leave until the child turns 3 years old" (Asahi, 2012: 86). The Western counterpart, Anheuser-Busch, introduced a "family talk program in Korea as part of the local Global Be(er) Responsible Day celebration. Family Talk is designed to encourage conversations between parents and children in order to help prevent underage drinking. AB InBev provides free materials that coach parents through tough conversations and encourage direct questions and discussion. With the launch of the program in Korea, Family Talk is now available in all of our key markets worldwide" (Anheuser-Busch, 2014: 11). Interestingly, this program was first introduced by a Western company in a more collectivistic market, in this case, South Korea, which shows how when operating in new foreign markets, a Western/individualistic company may need to adapt to a more collectivist culture to best fit employee needs.

Finally, another example important to highlight comes from the Eastern energy company analyzed, Shenuah Energy. Shenuah "attends to employees' social needs and cares for their physical and mental health. The subsidiaries (branches) vigorously carried out the training on employee health management, allowing employees to work with pleasure. Extending its cares to employees' families, the company took initiatives to create opportunities for young employees to solve marriage concerns" (Shenuah, 2012: 57). In contrast, marital issues do not seem to pose a major concern within Western countries in this study. Western energy company Barrick Gold only mentions family when they address their biometric screening for disease (Barrick, 2013: 102). They also offer family counseling to the Western Shoshone people in Nevada where they operate, but family counseling is not offered globally across the company.

Another theme that can be linked to individualism is whether companies promote individual employees to act as entrepreneurs within their companies. In our analysis, Wester companies seem more likely to promote entrepreneurship among employees than Eastern companies. For example, Ford reports having received awards for fostering entrepreneurship for female employees. Its report states that "Ford earned these awards for developing and driving innovative best practices across our organization that result in productive business partnerships with minority and women entrepreneurs and valuable products and services for their customers" (Ford, 2013: 63). Interestingly, the Eastern counterpart, Nissan, promotes entrepreneurial activities in their American facilities by using "Business Driven Synergy Teams" to foster new ideas. The CS report states, "in the United States, employee-driven Business Synergy Teams

(BSTs) have been launched with management support to leverage diversity to achieve business objectives, expand cross- functional interaction and assist with community outreach. These BSTs are operated from Nissan's North American headquarters in Franklin, Tennessee, R&D facility in Farmington Hills, Michigan, and the Dallas-based Nissan Motor Acceptance Corporation (NMAC), as well as at production facilities in Smyrna and Decherd, Tennessee, and Canton, Mississippi" (Nissan, 2015: 86). Those teams notably were not present in Nissan's Eastern offices. These activities also seem to be focused on group collaboration as a means to foster entrepreneurship as opposed to the individual entrepreneurial efforts reported by Ford.

Another entrepreneurial example is found in NIKE. NIKE fosters entrepreneurship through LAUNCH: "In 2013, NIKE hosted the LAUNCH 2020 Summit. Along with NASA, the US Agency for International Development and the US Department of State, we convened more than 150 materials specialists, designers, academics, manufacturers, entrepreneurs and NGOs to catalyze action around the sustainability of materials and how they are made. Since it was founded in 2010, LAUNCH has successfully introduced and supported initiatives and technologies that are solving challenges facing our society" (NIKE, 2013: 80). In contrast, the Eastern counterpart, Li Ning, states that innovation happens at the company level when employees feel a sense of ownership of the company, reporting that "our staff was also greatly encouraged to project their positive energy and develop a sense of ownership of the Company, which helped them deliver excellent performance, inspire innovation and proactively take part in the corporate reform and transformation" (Li Ning, 2014: 62). This highlights a more collaborative Eastern approach versus Western entrepreneurial ideals.

Uncertainty Avoidance

Hofstede's uncertainty avoidance dimension refers to "the degree to which the members of a society feel uncomfortable with uncertainty and ambiguity" (The Hofstede Centre, 2015). "The fundamental issue here is how a society deals with the fact that the future can never be known. Countries exhibiting strong uncertainty avoidance maintain rigid codes of belief and behavior and are intolerant of unorthodox behavior and ideas. Weak uncertainty avoidance societies maintain a more relaxed attitude in which practice counts more than principles" (Hofstede Centre, 2015). Table 3 also shows considerable differences between Eastern vs. Western indices on this dimension. The Western countries have lower indices (USA=46, Canada=48) while Eastern regions score higher (Japan=92, S. Korea=85) except for China, which scores lower than any of the other regions (China=30). These differences in uncertainty avoidance also appeared in our analysis of CS reports.

One CSR theme that is closely related to uncertainty avoidance is crisis management. We find differences in this CSR theme between East and West firms but mainly between Japan and South Korea versus US and Canada. For instance, the Asahi Group "has prepared various response manuals and conducts maintenance of emergency equipment and supplies and emergency drills to minimize damage and impact on the local environment in the event of a major disaster such as an earthquake" (Asahi, 2012). However, there is only a brief mention of having a World Safety Day at Anheuser-Busch, though no specifics are given. One reason explaining these differences may be that even though Anheuser-Busch has a crisis management program, they do not see the need to report it in detail among their CSR documents as Asahi does in its documents.

Another example is found in the Eastern company LG, where there is a push to adopt the ISO 22301 standard for crisis management. In their CS report we can read: "with environmental and safety related accidents/disasters growing in scale and diversity, a single devastating event could threaten the very foundation of a company or, worse still, force it out of business. In order to fully prepare itself against such unforeseen events and ensure business continuity, LG Electronics implemented the Business Continuity Management (BCM) System for mobile phone production lines in 2008. As part of efforts to better manage the system and promote stakeholder confidence, we began to pursue the ISO 22301 certification at the corporate level in 2014" (LG, 2015: 57). However, General Electric, the Western counterpart, makes mention of "crisis" or "disaster" in their CS report other than protection against cyber attacks (a common concern across the technology sector in both Eastern and Western companies).

The third example refers to the Eastern company Toto. Toto describes in its CSR report how the 2011 Fukushima earthquake affected their business: "In fiscal 2010–2011, the Great East Japan Earthquake of March 2011 had a considerable impact on the TOTO Group's business performance, causing damage to some of our plants', sales sites and distribution centers" (Toto, 2014: 18). They now take risk monitoring very seriously, noting that "to strengthen our capacity to prevent and respond to major risks, we have been carrying out practical risk simulations since 2005. The Great East Japan Earthquake in particular required us to take unanticipated actions, and so using this as motivation, and in order to help us develop more flexible decision-making and executive abilities, we introduced real-time risk simulations (mock disasters) and have been conducting training at each business site. 'Real- time' training has been conducted 54 times in the past three years, and we are planning to offer this training to all manufacturing and sales business sites by fiscal 2014" (Toto, 2014: 32).

Finally, it is worth mentioning that while the Western company AT&T does not mention earthquakes or other natural disasters in their CS report, the Korean counterpart, SK Telecom describes its work with ITC earthquake monitoring along with NEC Japan. SK Telecom also has a whole crisis response center: "Since 2014, SK Telecom has enhanced its risk management system to operate a company-wide crisis response center that immediately handles serious crisis situations" (SK Telecom, 2013: 171).

Some of the emphasis in crisis management, especially in Japan, can be attributed to the recent natural disasters, especially the 2011 earthquake, tsunami, and Fukushima nuclear accident. However, in general, it is safe to say that the higher indices in avoiding uncertainty found in Japan and South Korea extends into the way they design and report their CS strategies. Even though many companies mention disaster relief efforts as part of charitable giving (e.g. Amazon reports a total of nearly $38.5 million donated to disaster relief between 2001-2013), only Japanese and South Korean companies include comprehensive disaster preparedness plans as part of their CS. Finally, as mentioned in the individualism section, the fact that a Western company like Dell encourages team members to take risks demonstrates that they value risk and do not fear uncertainty as much as other companies.

Masculinity

Hofstede's masculinity dimension represents "a preference in society for achievement, heroism, assertiveness and material rewards for success. Society at large is more competitive. Its opposite, femininity, stands for a preference for cooperation, modesty, caring for the weak and quality of life. Society at large is more consensus-oriented. In the business context Masculinity versus Femininity is sometimes also related to as 'tough versus gender' cultures" (Hofstede Centre, 2015). Hofstede's indices show some differences between some Western (USA=62, Canada=52) and Eastern (Japan=95) countries, but interestingly the other two Eastern countries have similar values (China=66) or even lower values (South

Korea=39) than those in the West. Based on these indices, South Korea is the most feminine country in our sample while Japan is the most masculine.

One of the CSR themes that can be closely related to the masculinity-femininity dichotomy is aging. Feminine cultures are described as those that care more about the weak such as the elderly segment of a population. The first example, the BRAVO! Restart program, is found in the Korean company SK Telecom, "which helps retirees start new businesses and identify new growth areas. In 2013, the first round of the program's ten teams launched businesses and several patent rights were obtained" (SK Telecom, 2013: 43). SK Telecom developed the HD laser pico beam technology jointly with Cremotech, one of the supported business start-ups in the BRAVO! Restart program. Another BRAVO! Restart start-up, Hub and Spoke, developed the sales channel of a product called Smart Gym Board, a channel that ultimately included domestic hospitals, schools, and the Chinese market, jointly with the business unit of SK Telecom.

The baby boom generation has been critical to the economic development in South Korea over the last few decades. Unfortunately, this generation now has few opportunities to launch new ventures, or re-enter the job market. More than half of baby boomer entrepreneurs close their business in the first three years (SK Telecom, 2013: 95). ICT and SK Telecom have developed a way to help those baby boomers solve their problems in establishing their businesses. In their 2013 report, SK Telecom claims the company "fosters those who will establish businesses by inviting public participation, investing in physical resources including funds and spaces, transferring its business know-how to turn a business model into reality, providing one-to-one mentoring and educational programs, and providing indirect capital for developments in joint technology, prototype and sales channel, while increasing the chance of the success of the new businesses established" (SK Telecom, 2013: 95). The Western counterpart does not specifically address aging issues in their CS report, although they do advertise a new product, AT&T EverThere, a small wearable device that can detect falls and quickly identify the location of the wearer.

An interesting finding that may contradict Hofstede's masculinity index for Japan is that Japanese companies are the most engaged in helping the elderly. The fact that Japan is facing an aging crisis and below-replacement birth rates may explain why companies there are now emphasizing programs for the older generations. Is Japan becoming a more "feminine" culture based on Hofstede's dimensions? Examples of this shift are found in Nissan, which mentions aging populations several times. "In a society facing issues including aging populations and urban congestion, Autonomous Drive technologies may one day be able to help reduce traffic accidents, thus providing peace of mind to drivers and increasing opportunities for mobility in the daily lives of the rapidly growing number of senior citizens" (Nissan, 2015: 53). They even conduct seminars for employees with aging parents: "given the likely rise in the number of employees who must care for aging parents, a seminar was held in 2015 that offered employees basic knowledge about nursing care and prompted them to think about how they can best balance their work and caring needs by taking advantage of the company's policies and community services" (Nissan, 2015: 86). Nissan also sees autonomous cars as being a solution for the elderly and mobility, noting that "Autonomous Drive technology will also improve mobility for the elderly, allowing them to enjoy personal vehicle mobility much later in life" (Nissan, 2015: 9).

The Western counterpart, Ford, only mentions "impact of an aging workforce" once (Ford, 2014: 44). However, Ford does mention in their "Salute to Dealers" section one particular dealer, Divonsir Cardoso, which "makes significant financial donations to Lar Dos Idosos, a home for the elderly" (Ford, 2014: 469) and "in Venezuela at the Valencia Plant, a group of volunteers visited a retirement home called Mi Viejo Antonio and took essential products such as medicines, food, mattresses, pillows and disposable hygiene products to support the institution, with cares for underprivileged elderly citizens" (Ford, 2014: 546).

Another final example is Asahi Group, which is "hiring more elderly workers" (Asahi, 2012: 81) and where "employees who had left the company due to marriage, childbirth, childcare, care provision for ill or elderly family member are reemployed if certain requirements are met" (Asahi, 2012: 85). However, there is no mention of aging or elderly care in the CS report of Western counterpart Anheuser-Busch. In summary, we find differences in the way the aging issue is addressed. Whereas Eastern companies seem to integrate the aging issue in their vision and competitive strategies, Western companies appear to address the issue from a more philanthropic angle.

Long-Term Orientation and Indulgence

Hofstede's long-term orientation dimension "focuses on the future, a willingness to delay short-term material or social success or even short-term emotional gratification in order to prepare for the future. Short-term orientation focuses on the present or past and considers them more important than the future. If you have a short-term orientation, you value tradition, the current social hierarchy and fulfilling your social obligations. You care more about immediate gratification than long-term fulfillment" (Hofstede Centre, 2015). Hofstede's indices for our regions of analysis are very different. Whereas Western country indices (USA=26, Canada=36) are very low, the Eastern regions' indices (Japan=88, S. Korea=100, China=87) are the highest. These differences also are apparent in the way CS strategies are reported. The long term orientation can be easily related to the long term perspective that the corporate sustainability movement tries to implement. Sustainability embodies the idea that companies need to consider sustainable development while growing and to ensure that future generations will be able to have the same quality of life than of present generations.

Hofstede also included a sixth dimension focused on indulgence and restraint. Indulgence stands for "a society that allows relatively free gratification of basic and natural human drives related to enjoying life and having fun. Restraint stands for a society that suppresses gratification of needs and regulates it by means of strict social norms" (Hofstede Centre, 2015). Hofstede's indices are a bit higher for our Western countries (USA and Canada=68) than for our Eastern ones (Japan=42, S.Korea=29 and China=24). In the context of CS, this dimension seems to also be related to the short versus long term perspective. Societies that emphasize indulgence may be less likely to think long term when they use resources than a more restrained society.

Asahi Group presents their environmental philosophy as follows: "Beer is made from the bounties of nature, such as water, barley and hops. We at the Asahi Group believe we are responsible for ensuring our children inherit a healthier planet. To achieve our goals for protecting this beautiful planet and the people who live on it, we believe our actions must demonstrate both gratitude for the natural bounty the Earth provides us all," which demonstrates both harmony and using resources with restraint (Asahi, 2012: 26).

Two of the main CSR themes that can be related to this long term orientation are biodiversity and deforestation, which are, in fact, interconnected. In continuing our analysis of Asahi, we find this company very committed to preservation of biodiversity for future generations, with a comprehensive "Declaration on Biodiversity" composed of three main policies and nine action guidelines. The first policy encompasses the natural environment: "Protect nature, which serves as the home of living things and includes three action guidelines: (i) protect the rich rivers and seas where species live; (ii) protect and nurture the rich forests where species live; and (iii) create rich environments around our factories for living things to flourish" (Asahi, 2012: 46). The second policy guides the use of nature: "Use the gifts of nature with care, with three accompanying action guidelines: (i) properly use the gifts of nature; (ii) use the gifts of nature more effectively; and (iii) study the relationships within nature, and undertake research and development to make use of them well" (Asahi, 2012: 46). The third policy is: "Take action with people around the world, and (i) share this Declaration throughout the Asahi Group and put in efforts with our employees; (ii) make use of our products and services to clearly convey the importance of nature's gifts; and (iii) take action globally and in cooperation with our business partners" (Asahi, 2012: 46). Asahi also reports owning the Asahi Forest, managed by Asahi Breweries since 1941, which spans a total of 2,165 hectares and absorbs 12,200 tons of CO2 each year. The Asahi Forest received FSC certification in 2001 (Asahi, 2012).

The Western counterpart in our sample, Anheuser-Busch, also includes a couple of initiatives related to biodiversity but not a comprehensive declaration to protect nature. One example is from their brewery in Guarulhos (São Paulo) Brazil, where they work with the local Department of Environment to catalog wild animals and rehabilitating animal species within the boundaries before re-integrating them into the forest (Anheuser-Busch, 2014). In the United States, Anheuser-Busch also lists a couple of projects related to biodiversity, such as one in their Cartersville, Georgia brewery, where they have developed habitat projects in cooperation with conservation groups and governmental agencies. They also report that they own an eight-acre natural area around their Fort Collins brewery in Colorado, where they "keep inventory of resident species, place nesting boxes and ensure that the structures are inhabited by the intended wildlife" (Anheuser-Busch, 2014). This emphasizes how biodiversity is integral to Eastern, but seen as small part of Western sustainability philosophies in this study.

Table 4 summarizes key examples that illustrate East-West differences along the five Hofstede's dimensions analyzed in this chapter.

Table 4. Examples of East vs. West reporting differences and Hofstede's cultural dimensions

Cultural Dimension	Examples of West-East Reporting Differences
Power Distance	• Barrick Gold's (Canada) open communication strategy which encourages employee and manager interaction. • Shenuah Energy's (China) employee committee that reviews employee suggestions, acts as a liaison, and keeps direct employee manager interaction to a minimum.
Individualism	• Ford Motors' (United States) emphasis on intra-company entrepreneurship fosters individualism, giving employee autonomy to work on side projects. • Li Ning (China) emphasizes team work and working toward shared goals as a way to foster employee loyalty and ownership of the company.
Uncertainty Avoidance	• Dell (United States) encourages employees to "take risks" and innovate; no western company's CSR reports reviewed in this study mentioned natural disaster preparedness. • Asahi and Toto (Japan) who both specifically mention earthquake safety and preparedness.
Masculinity	• Ford (United States) takes a more philanthropic approach to caring for the elderly. • SK Telecom's (S. Korea) BRAVO! Restart program which helps retirees start new businesses, shows care for the elderly and community (a feminine trait according to Hofstede).
Long-Term Orientation & Indulgence	• Anheuser-Busch's (United States) approach of relocating wildlife when it is close to company property/ operations; the omission of biodiversity issues by many Western CSR reports. • Asahi's purchase and protection of the Asahi national forest helps to ensure there will be biodiversity for future generations.

Corporate Sustainability through Art

In addition to the East-West differences that can be linked to the six Hofstede's cultural dimensions, it is notable that art is considered a relevant theme in Eastern company CS reports but not so much part of Western CS activities and reports. This study adds CS through art as an additional dimension. For example, art is a big part of TOTO's philanthropy. The TOTO gallery focuses on architecture and design, showcasing works of artists from Japan and throughout the world. TOTO sponsors printing books showcasing "unique viewpoints on such themes as architecture, design, lifestyle and culture, thereby also helping to educate the next generation" (Toto, 2014: 36). TOTO also supports the Kitakyushu International Music Festival sin the city of culture in Kitakyushu, where the TOTO headquarters are located (Toto, 2014: 36). In their 2014 report TOTO claims the company is "nurturing a spirit of enjoying sport, such as through track and field clinics run by members of the TOTO Athletics Club at elementary schools, and through the Kids Challenge Sports Meet, which is organized by TOTO" (TOTO, 2014: 36).

Another example is the Asahi Group, which utilizes its assets "to support artistic and cultural activities based on these keywords offering many people the opportunity to come into contact with art so that a highly creative and diversified culture takes root in daily life: the future, citizens and local communities" (Asahi, 2012: 87). In addition, "An arts festival for bringing energy to the community through discovery of its distinctive regional appeal and creating a future culture using the power of art, based on a citizen's planning and organization initiative. This annual summer festival has been held every year since 2002 in collaboration with art-related Non-profit organizations (NPOs) and citizen groups nationwide" (Asahi, 2012: 88). Asahi also subsidizes the arts through the Asahi Beer Arts Foundation: "We provide subsidies for the multifaceted development of Japanese arts and culture to assist in the development of regional communities through the creation of future culture and by offering opportunities for citizens to experience the arts in collaboration with art-related NPOs" (Asahi, 2012:88). Finally, "Asahi sponsored the Asahi Beer Oyamazaki Villa Museum of Art Sponsored by the Asahi Beer Arts Foundation "A villa built on the side of Mount Tenno in Kyoto during the Taisho and Showa eras by businessman Shotaro Kaga was renovated and reopened as a museum, which includes an annex designed by architect Tadao Ando. In addition to exhibiting its main collection of folk craft and Monet paintings, the museum features exhibitions planned by modern artists. The grand opening was held in May 2012 after completion of a new wing and full access ramps for those with disabilities" (Asahi, 2012: 89).

Anhauser-Busch, on the other hand, has "chalices (that) feature artwork inspired by traditional handcrafted objects from three developing countries, including textiles from India, baskets from Ethiopia and pottery from Honduras" to support their "Buy a Lady a Drink Campaign in partnership with Water.org which with the purchase of these chalices will donate 5 years of clean drinking water for one person in the developing world" (Anheuser-Busch, 2014: 25). Finally, Shenuah Energy presents art exhibitions for employees. Their report states that "the company actively creates the conditions for employees to enrich their spare time and refresh their minds. To this end, the production units have established libraries, gymnasiums, cinemas, karaoke rooms and other cultural facilities. In 2012, the Company's labor union organized a series of events including table tennis games, the 'Shenuah Cup' calligraphy and art exhibition" (Shenuah, 2012: 57). Because art is mentioned in only one Western but three Eastern companies, it could be inferred that art is of greater importance in Eastern CS reporting.

Similarities

Although the primary goal of this study was to examine the differences between Western and Eastern CS reporting, several key similarities were also found. One CSR theme present in all of the 20 reviewed reports is employee health and safety (EHS) issues. Flextronics' sustainability report states "Flextronics' Health and Safety management approach aims to ensure that all of our employees and contractors have a safe and healthful work environment. The foundation of their system is to identify risky activities and tasks and to implement measures intended to avoid and mitigate negative impacts" (Flextronics, 2013: 71). The Chinese company used for comparison to Flextronics, Foxconn, states "We place a high priority on ensuring the health, safety, and well-being of all our employees across all of our global operations, and our employee health and safety policies and standards meet all relevant international and local laws and regulations. Foxconn supports a number of measures to provide for employee health care needs and ensure workplace safety" (Foxconn, 2014: 6). The reason this information is included in all reports is that in both North American and Asian countries, laws exist outlining EHS standards.

DISCUSSION AND CONCLUSION

In the previous sections we have provided a list of examples that illustrate how companies in the same industry but in different regions present and emphasize varying CS strategies in their public documents on sustainability. We posit that some of these differences are related to cultural differences that can be matched with Hofstede's cultural dimensions. First, we describe how differences in power distance are evident in how companies in the West describe more open and across the board approaches to CS management, as opposed to the more hierarchical approaches that East companies seem to undertake. Secondly, we present some evidence for the individualism dimension by showing a major emphasis on family matters among Eastern companies compared to Western companies. Companies in the East are keener to provide family CSR programs compared to those in the West. Individualism can also affect how companies value individual entrepreneurial initiatives among their employees. Our analysis shows that the West provides more opportunities for individuals to innovate, develop their own initiatives, and propose changes than the East. Third, we illustrate how Eastern companies are more prone to avoid uncertainty than Western companies. Eastern businesses present more detailed codes of conduct and a emphasize risk and crisis management. Fourth, we present parallels between Hofstede's masculinity dimension and the ways that companies deal with aging. We found that most feminine societies show more concerns about the weakest segments of the population, i.e., senior citizens. However, interestingly, the most masculine of the five regions analyzed according to Hofstede, Japan, also strongly emphasizes programs to help older citizens. This finding may be easily explained by the aging crisis and below-replacement birth rates that the country is currently suffering. Fifth, we compare Hofstede's long term orientation and indulgence dimensions with how companies deal with biodiversity and deforestation issues. We find that Eastern companies are reporting more information describing efforts to mitigate biodiversity loss and deforestation issues than the Western counterparts. Lastly, we found interesting differences between East and West in how they integrate art and art preservation as an additional CS component.

Lessons Learned: East to West and West to East

Increasing globalization has led to growing visibility of companies and the need to report their sustainability strategies. This has created an opportunity for both Eastern and Western companies alike to learn from one another's sustainability efforts. A key example of CS strategies that seem to have crossed over includes the Japanese Kaizen program and American intra-company entrepreneurial efforts.

An example of an American company adopting Eastern CS practices is Amazon.com Inc., which is taking the Japanese Kaizen principle and using it to implement cost saving and environmental and energy initiatives in many parts of the company. Kaizen is not a new philosophy, with origins in the mid-twentieth century, as illustrated by Masaaki Imai and his book entitled *Kaizen: The Key to Japanese Competitive Advantage*. The Kaizen term is thought to possibly have origins in Toyota Motor with key principles including: customer focus, continuous improvements, open acknowledgment of the problem, creation of work teams, development of self-discipline, provision of constant feedback to employees, and promotion of employee development (García et al., 2014). All of these key principles can be applied to CS initiatives such as waste reduction and employee innovation, as seen in companies such as Amazon.com.

On its website, Amazon states that "the power of the Kaizen projects comes from the cumulative impact of many people participating in a large number of focused projects, each delivering reductions in energy consumption and waste. The energy savings from a single Kaizen project may not seem significant, but shared across our global network, it can produce meaningful results" (Amazon.com, 2016). Amazon gives examples of several locations that have successfully implemented the Kaizen program, including the creation of a system to reuse pallets traveling between the Hazleton and Breinigsville fulfillment centers, eliminating hundreds of discarded pallets each week and saving more than $100,000 annually. Amazon also works with vendors in Gourock, Scotland to deliver products in reusable totes rather than cardboard boxes, eliminating waste for both parties. They have also implemented a timer system on the conveyer belt in Coffeyville, Kansas that saves around 30% kilowatt-hours of electricity (Amazon.com, 2016). Several additional US companies such as Great Western Bank, The Ford Motor Company, Herman Miller, and Lockheed Martin have also successfully implemented Kaizen principles (Flory, 2014). At Lockheed Martin, "In 2010, while developing its Joint Air-to-Ground Missile (JAGM) system, Lockheed Martin held multiple Kaizen events at plants in Florida and Alabama to help improve the way that the JAGM is manufactured. Lockheed Martin's use of Kaizen shows how the concept can help businesses launch a new product or service" (Flory, 2014). To implement Kaizen effectively and successfully, "Management commitment and education and training" are paramount (Garcia et al, 2014). As seen through the effective use of Kaizen in many companies throughout the world, this Japanese philosophy can be used and adapted globally, and has a far reaching impact beyond Japan's borders.

One way companies can learn from one another is by the disclosure of mistakes, such as the labor issues encountered by Nike. In the sustainability report Nike acknowledges past labor risks in citing a Harvard Business School case study which "describes how we (Nike) transformed from a company that reacted to external pressures while working to minimize reputational risks to one that views sustainability as among our leading innovation opportunities" (Nike, 2013: 22). They also cite another case study published by Stanford Graduate School of Business that "highlights (Nike's) long-term journey of sustainability and labor" (Nike, 2013: 22). By disclosing missteps and critical incidents, especially in the form of HBR cases, both companies and academics alike can think critically about the issues described, and take appropriate steps to mitigate the chances that these mistakes will be made by others.

Contribution and Further Research

This study not only provides reason for companies to learn from CSR reporting in other cultures, but gives relevant stakeholders a lens through which to better understand company CS reports. It is critical for all stakeholders such as academics, customers, and investors to be able to read and understand these reports when choosing to study, purchase from, or invest in these large multinational companies. This study may assist them in identifying what CSR issues are important to the company, provide a checklist (see Table 2) to determine how many CSR strategies a company is engaged in, and also help them to identify core company values. Having a deeper level of cultural understanding through Hofstede's dimensions helps to analyze these CS reports more objectively and be aware of their own cultural biases.

Further research could be done to identify any "greenwashing" found within these reports. This study assumed truthfulness in all reports in order to make direct comparisons. However, a follow up study may determine if there should be weighted comparisons based on a company's history or likelihood to engage in greenwashing.

Lastly, further research should be done comparing CSR reporting practices from other geographic regions to see if those are consistent with our framework as well as Hofstede's cultural dimensions. Such an analysis can help understand the role that cultural dimensions have on corporate culture, company values, and ultimately the way a company approaches the topics of corporate social responsibility and sustainability.

CONCLUSION

In this chapter, we first provided an overview on how companies in different cultural environments differ in the CS strategies that they report to their stakeholders. Our findings are aligned with previous research pointing out variations in CSR strategies across differing national cultures and institutional realities (Jamali, Sidani & El-Asmar, 2009). Companies from both regions have an opportunity to learn from each other in order to achieve sustainable outcomes more effectively. Future research may consider performing a more in-depth analysis of CS strategies in different regions. This data collection would include a larger number of companies, not only from large multinationals such as in this analysis, but also from smaller domestic firms.

There is little doubt that the exponential development of technology has had an enormous impact on how sustainability and CSR are managed. The increased availability of information of CS initiatives, and the increasing demand by stakeholders for CSR disclosure have fundamentally changed how companies, particularly large global companies, manage sustainability. Amazon.com hired their first sustainability executive Kara Hurst; Apple hired Lisa Jackson, a former EPA chief to lead companywide sustainability efforts; and their CEO Tim Cook has been more outspoken on sustainability than former CEO Steve Jobs (Makower, 2014). As found in many CS reports discussed here, large companies in both the East and the West are making CS strategies part of their competitive strategy, and are successfully creating profit through CS.

REFERENCES

Amazon.com. (n. d.) *Amazon and the Planet.* Retrieved from http://www.amazon.com/p/feature/tdfn6a3sn2bg5xg?ref_=aa_bx_7&pf_rd_r=18RQAVEGVEVFC5SZDZT8&pf_rd_p=d4e53df4-3f1f-4d63-b9c4-eb3f5a5db605

Anheuser-Busch. (2014). *Bringing People Together for a Better World.* Anheuser-Busch InBev /2014 Global Citizenship Report. Retrieved from http://www.ab-inbev.com/content/dam/universaltemplate/abinbev/pdf/media/press-kit/2014/ABInBev_AR_14_EN_Narrative.pdf

Antolin-Lopez, R., Delgado-Ceballos, J., & Montiel, I. (2016). (Forthcoming). Deconstructing Corporate Sustainability: A Review of Stakeholder Metrics. *Journal of Cleaner Production.* doi:10.1016/j.jclepro.2016.01.111

Asahi, (2012) *Asahi Group CSR activities*. Retrieved from http://www.asahigroup-holdings.com/en/csr/pdf/summary12_e_all.pdf

Balfour, F. (2008) *China's Li Ning Toe-to-Toe Against Nike and Adidas* Bloomberg Business, Retrieved from http://www.bloomberg.com/bw/stories/2008-04-30/chinas-li-ning-toe-to-toe-against-nike-and-adidas

Bansal, P. (2005). Evolving sustainably: A longitudinal study of corporate sustainable development. *Strategic Management Journal, 26*(3), 197–218. doi:10.1002/smj.441

Barrick, (2013) *Responsible Mining. Responsibility report 2013.* Retrieved fro: http://www.barrick.com/files/responsibility-report/2013/Barrick-2013-Corporate-Responsibility-Report.pdf

Beckman, Z. (2013). *7 ways Western and Eastern business relationships differ*. Hyrax International, LLC.

Chung, K. Y., Eichenseher, J., & Taniguchi, T. (2008). Ethical perceptions of business students: Differences between East Asia and the USA and among "Confucian" cultures. *Journal of Business Ethics, 79*(1-2), 121–132. doi:10.1007/s10551-007-9391-7

Dell, (2015). *An annual update of our 2020 Legacy of Good Plan. FY15 Corporate Social Responsibility Report.* Retrieved from http://i.dell.com/sites/doccontent/corporate/corp-comm/en/Documents/fy15-cr-report.pdf

Etzion, D., & Ferraro, F. (2010). The role of analogy in the institutionalization of sustainability reporting. *Organization Science, 21*(5), 1092–1107. doi:10.1287/orsc.1090.0494

Flextronics. (2013). Corporate Sustainability Report 2012-13. Retrieved from http://www.flextronics.com/sites/default/files/component_b2/FLEXTRONICS%2520Corporate-Sustainability-Report-2012-2013.pdf

Flory, L. (2014). How 5 companies used Kaizen effectively. Effex Management Solutions Blog. Retrieved from http://blog.effexms.com/how-5-companies-used-kaizen-effectively

Ford. (2014). *Go Further. Sustainability Report 2013/14.* Retrieved from http://corporate.ford.com/microsites/sustainability-report-2013-14/doc/sr13.pdf

Foxconn. (2014). Social and Environmental Sustainability Report. Retrieved from http://www.foxconn.com/Files/index/Foxconn_SER_Report_EN.pdf

Garcia, J. L., Maldonado, A., Alvarado, A., & Rivera, D. (2014). Human critical success factors for kaizen and its impacts in industrial performance. *International Journal of Advanced Manufacturing Technology, 70*(9-12), 2187–2198. doi:10.1007/s00170-013-5445-4

Hart, S., & Milstein, M. (2003). Creating sustainable value. *The Academy of Management Executive, 17*(2), 56–67. doi:10.5465/AME.2003.10025194

Hofstede, G. (1984). *Culture's consequences: International differences in work-related values* (Vol. 5). Sage publications.

Hofstede Centre. (2015). Retrieved from http://geert-hofstede.com/

Jamali, D., Sidani, Y., & El-Asmar, K. (2009). A three country comparative analysis of managerial CSR perspectives: Insights from Lebanon, Syria and Jordan. *Journal of Business Ethics, 85*(2), 173–192. doi:10.1007/s10551-008-9755-7

LG. (2015). *Life's Good with LG. 2014-2015 LG Electronics Sustainability Report.* Retrieved from http://www.lg.com/global/sustainability/communications/sustainability-reports

Li Ning. (2014). *Environmental, Social and Governance Report. Li Ning Company Limited 2014.* Retrieved from http://ir.lining.com/eng/csr/csr_reports/csr_report_2014.pdf

Makower, J. (2014). Kara Hurst named Amazon's first sustainability executive. Retrieved from http://www.greenbiz.com/blog/2014/08/15/kara-hurst-named-amazons-first-sustainability-executive

Miller, J. (2013). Authenticity, sincerity and spontaneity: The mutual implication of nature and religion in China and the West. *Method & Theory in the Study of Religion, 25*(3), 283–307. doi:10.1163/15700682-12341259

Montiel, I. (2008). Corporate social responsibility and corporate sustainability: Separate pasts, common futures. *Organization & Environment, 21*(2), 245–269. doi:10.1177/1086026608321329

Montiel, I., & Delgado-Ceballos, J. (2014). Defining and measuring corporate sustainability: Are we there yet? *Organization & Environment, 27*(2), 113–139. doi:10.1177/1086026614526413

Nike. (2013). *Sustainable Business Performance Summary. Nike, Inc. FY12/13.* Retrieved from http://www.nikeresponsibility.com/report/uploads/files/FY12-13_NIKE_Inc_CR_Report.pdf

Nissan. (2015). *Nissan Sustainability Report, 2015.* Retrieved from http://www.nissan-global.com/EN/CSR/SR/2015/

Peterson, H. (2014). *The Key Differences Between Alibaba and Amazon in One Chart.* Retrieved from www.businessinsider.com/alibaba-versus-amazon-2014-9

Shenuah. (2012). *CSR Report 2012.* Retrieved from http://www.shenhuachina.com/cs/sh_china_en/PAGE1382683238892/sh_china_en_ED.html

Telecom, S. K. (2013). *Partner for New Possibilities.*www. SK*Telecom Annual Report 2013.* Retrieved from http://www.sktelecom.com/en/social/list_persist_report.do

Tepper, R. (2012). *World's Most Popular Beers: 'The Drinks Business' Names Top 10 Biggest Brands Of 2011* Retrieved from http://www.huffingtonpost.com/2012/09/26/worlds-most-popular-beer_n_1914327.html

Toto. (2014). *Toto Corporate Report 2014.* Retrieved from http://www.toto.co.jp/company/profile/library/pdf/report2014_en.pdf

ENDNOTE

1 Even though there are some definitional differences between CS and CSR (Montiel, 2008) for the purpose of our study we refer to these types of social and environmental sustainability reports with the term "CS reports".

Chapter 4
Cross-Country and Cross-Sector CSR Variations:
A Comparative Analysis of CSR Reporting in the U.S., South Korea, and Turkey

Altay Dikeç
Melikşah University, Turkey

Victor Kane
University of the West USA

Nejat Çapar
Melikşah University, Turkey

ABSTRACT

From the days corporate social responsibility (CSR) became a topic of discussion, extensive amount of research is conducted on CSR in Western countries but still there is relatively little focus on some developed and developing countries. Moreover, relatively little research has compared cross-country and cross-sector CSR variations. Starting from this point, this article investigates the extent of CSR variations of a highly developed (the United States), a developed (South Korea) and a developing country (Turkey) through a detailed comparative analysis of CSR information disclosure on corporate websites of 50 CSR active companies listed in stock exchange markets of each country. For cross-sector comparison, these target corporations are selected from five different industries including consumer electronics & telecommunication services, automobile & component manufacturers, food & beverages, retail stores, and major banks. The research opens the door for more in-depth empirical study on why there are cross-country and cross-sector variations in CSR.

DOI: 10.4018/978-1-5225-0720-8.ch004

INTRODUCTION

With the force of globalization shaping business practices worldwide, there has been a strong push to incorporate the values and principles of corporate social responsibility (CSR) into the strategic and operational processes of many local and multinational corporations. A myriad of forces has propelled companies to adopt a strategic CSR mindset and to develop a set of related programs to make CSR a practical reality. Some of these forces include industry and country-specific regulatory initiatives, calls from international organizations such as the World Bank, OECD, IMF and the United Nations (Jenkins, 2005; Hafsi & Farashahi, 2005), a rise in socially responsible investing and 'standard-setting' institutions for CSR reporting (e.g., SRI index, Global Reporting Initiative), and increasing pressure from governments, consumer watchdog groups, NGOs, and concerned citizens (Aaronson, 2003; Fombrun, 2005). Fundamentally, CSR has strongly entrenched in the corporate mindset of Anglo-American corporations (Robertson, 2009), however with the increasing presence of multinational companies across the world - many of them originating in the Western industrialized countries - has led to the adoption of many CSR practices in other developed and developing countries.

Despite the global push toward CSR, the degree of commitment to which companies in different countries embrace the CSR concept and its practices is strongly influenced by national context - namely, the confluence of economic (Chapple & Moon, 2005; Robertson, 2009), social (Baughn et al., 2007), cultural (Welford, 2004, 2005), political-legal (institutional) (Campbell, 2007; Matten & Moon, 2008), and religious (Agle & Van Buren, 1999) forces impacting local business practices (Jamali & Mirshak, 2006).

This global push toward social responsibility makes corporations practice CSR at some level and since messages regarding corporate ethics and social initiatives have the power to evoke strong positive reactions among stakeholders (Morsing & Schultz, 2006), companies share this information through corporate websites. Hence, corporate websites have become important tools for understanding the difference between countries and industries in the degree of commitment to CSR since they provide official perspective regarding CSR within the corporation for all its stakeholders (Wanderley et al., 2008).

Although a great deal of research has been conducted on CSR in Western economies, there is relatively little focus on Asian countries (but see Baughn et al., 2007; Chapple & Moon, 2005; Welford, 2004, 2005) and even less focus on countries in the Middle East (but see Jamali & Mirshak, 2006; Kusku & Fraser, 2004). Moreover, there are very few comparative studies focusing on different stages of economic development countext (but see Robertson, 2009). Therefore, the U.S., South Korea and Turkey were selected as the focus of this research. These three countries are representative of a highly-developed economy (U.S.), a developed economy (South Korea) and a rapidly developing economy (Turkey) and they present opportunities for analysis on CSR website reporting.

This article investigates the extent of CSR variations of the largest corporations from these three countries – the U.S., South Korea, and Turkey – through analysis of website reporting of CSR by the top 50 companies of each country. The article addresses the following three research questions:

- To what extent does CSR vary between the U.S., South Korea, and Turkey?
- To what extent does CSR vary in different industries within the same country in focus?
- To what extent does CSR in the same industry vary across different countries in focus?

LITERATURE REVIEW

CSR Information Disclosure and the Internet

Before websites, other types of corporate materials such as speeches and annual reports were subjected to empirical studies including content analysis (Paul, 2008). However, recent studies (Wanderley et al., 2008) demonstrate that the Internet is increasingly becoming one of the main tools for CSR information disclosure, as it allows companies to publicize more up-to-date information less expensively with the added benefit of being able to communicate with the firm's stakeholders and obtain feedback (Bondy et al., 2004). A single website can have multiple pages, each directed at a different stakeholder group (Esrock & Leichty, 2000). In addition, the information remains permanently available on the web, often times in web archives, allowing the Internet user to choose which subjects he/she wants to access and as often as he/she wishes (Wanderley et.al, 2008). Hunter and Bansal (2007) argue that websites are even superior to annual reports, as the reporting cycle of annual reports makes the information less timely.

The increasing prevalence of web-based CSR information has been noted in the research literature. According to Esrock and Leichty (1998), 90 percent of companies in the Fortune 500 addressed at least one CSR issue in 1998, such as community involvement, education and the environment. In 2000, another study by the same authors demonstrated that this percentage had risen to 95% (Esrock & Leichty, 2000). Another study using the Fortune Global 200 found considerable amounts of environmental information among companies active in environmentally sensitive industries such as automotive, and oil and gas (Jose & Lee, 2007).

It could be argued that CSR communication or CSR reporting does not necessarily demonstrate CSR activity and actual level of CSR activity can be different than the level of communication. Additionally, absence of communication does not necessarily indicate lack of CSR activity. However, from the assumption of reporting, transparency and accountability are an important part of CSR, thus there is no reason for expecting an increasing gap between communication and action (Fukukawa & Moon, 2004). Moreover, in today's business environment of close stakeholder and media scrutiny of business claims and practice, corporations would hesitate to exaggerate CSR practice and performance reported on their website because of the reputational damage they would face (Chapple & Moon, 2005). One obvious problem that can be faced in CSR website reporting studies is that some companies may 'cherry pick' the activities on which they can report favorably, while ignoring those issues which criticism can be directed. Additionally, many companies report on various issues that come within a broad corporate responsibility remit, while failing to address major issues at the core of the business activity (Blowfield & Murray, 2008). A solution to this problem has come from standard-setting third parties such as the 'Global Reporting Initiative' (GRI)'s G3, United Nation's Global Compact's COP, and the ISO 26000 – Social Responsibility Standards (Tschopp & Nastanski, 2014). They classified social responsibility into five dimensions including *corporate governance*, *ethics and integrity*, *economic*, *environmental* and *social* (GRI G4, ISO 26000). DJSI, FTSE4Good and AccountAbility 1000 are also some other institutions setting CSR reporting standards. By monitoring and approving social responsibility reports of the corporations they greatly minimized any attempt for companies to 'cherry pick' or avoid to address the major issues at the core of their business activity.

Dimensions and Indicators of CSR

Previous studies also worked on defining the dimensions of CSR and used these dimensions to measure social responsibility related information on corporate websites. Among these, in their study on a Japanese model of CSR, Fukukawa and Moon (2005) identified environmental responsibility, community involvement, employment relations, consumer-related issues, and supply chain as core CSR dimensions. In his comparative CSR studies, Welford (2004, 2005) classified CSR dimensions (elements) as internal aspects, external aspects, accountability, and citizenship. Titles for the dimensions were quite different but the content of them were pretty much similar since by internal aspects Welford was emphasizing workplace related issues, and by external aspects he meant environmental aspects, local community protection and engagement. Chapple and Moon (2005) also used community involvement, responsible production processes, and employee relations as CSR dimensions.

Some other dimensions identified by various scholars are: maintaining *fair and honest business practices* or in other words *decent work* (Esrock & Leichty, 1998; Gildea, 1995), *product responsibility* (Esrock & Leichty, 1998; Gildea, 1995; Epstein, 1993), *labor practices* (Epstein, 1993; Esrock & Leichty, 1998; Gildea, 1995; Lindgreen, Swaen & Johnston, 2008; Stanwick & Stanwick, 2001), *responsible environmental practices* (Epstein, 1993; Esrock & Leichty, 1998; Gildea, 1995; Lindgreen *et al.*, 2008; Stanwick & Stanwick, 2001), *economic performance*, (Epstein, 1993; Lindgreen *et al.*, 2008; Stanwick & Stanwick, 2001), *society* (Paul, 2008; Lindgreen *et al.*, 2008; Gildea, 1995; Esrock & Leichty, 1998), *human rights* (Welford, 2004, 2005), *ethics and integrity* (Wanderley *et al.*, 2008; Esrock & Leichty, 1998) and responsible practices on *corporate governance* (Wanderley *et al.*, 2008; Stanwick & Stanwick, 2001).

Ethics and integrity codes, corporate governance, workplace and personnel related issues, responsible supply chain practices, environmental practices, and community development efforts are the dimensions identified and used in our research. 'CSR indicators' are commonly used to reflect CSR dimensions. Most common CSR indicators that are identified and used by these studies are also used in this study. These indicators are used to measure CSR information and reporting published on the corporate websites examined in this study. A detailed list of CSR indicators and their references are provided in Table 1 in the appendix.

Cross-Country Studies

As CSR is diffused globally, corporate managers embracing its tenets have to meet different societal expectations (Campbell, 2007; Husted & Allen, 2006). Firms and their CSR advocates now face different motivational factors, value systems, and commitments to different agendas internationally (Doh & Guay, 2006). Several studies show that the nature and depth of CSR reporting vary across regions and countries of the world. In highly mature and developed economies, such as those in the United States, UK and Japan, corporate communications are often used for various purposes: namely, to highlight corporate commitments to CSR (Esrock & Leichty, 1998; Hooghiemstra, 2006), to enhance marketing efforts, and to legitimize a given company's corporate image in the eyes of its various stakeholders (Birch & Moon, 2004; Morsing & Schultz, 2006; Ringov & Zollo, 2007).

KPMG has been surveying CSR reporting trends around the world since 1993 in its annual KPMG International Survey of Corporate Responsibility Reporting. According to its most recent survey (KPMG,

2011), which represents the largest and most comprehensive survey of CSR reporting trends ever published (encompassing 3,400 companies globally – including the world's 250 largest companies), it was noted that Japan and the UK are the dominant leaders in CSR reporting with 'near-unanimous adherence' (99 percent and 100 percent, respectively). As a whole, European companies continued to lead the pack in the survey, with 71 percent of companies reporting on CSR. The survey also found that a number of Central and Eastern Europe countries, such as Romania, Bulgaria and Hungary, have been slower in adopting CR reporting compared to their global peers. China, which was new to the KPMG survey in 2011, is catching up to traditional leaders in this field. Almost 60 percent of China's largest companies reported on corporate responsibility metrics, bringing the country on par with where Spain, Italy and the Netherlands were just three years ago in the survey.

Welford (2005) found that the incidence of CSR policies was consistently higher in Canada than in the USA. Mexico generally had far fewer CSR policies than did Canada or the US. The incidence of policy reporting in North America was low relative to that found in Europe, while the level of philanthropy was found to be higher in North America. US firms tend to emphasize giving resources to the community with philanthropic programs and volunteerism. The Dutch and French firms, on the other hand, tend to emphasize their commitment to environmental management. Welford's (2004, 2005) studies of comparative CSR were based on surveys dealing with the existence of firms' written policies. He found that there tended to be more activity in Northern Europe than Southern Europe. In Europe, the most philanthropic companies were found in Norway, the least in Spain. CSR reporting was most common in Germany, Norway and the UK. Chauvey *et al.* (2015) also mentions an increase of 81 publicly traded companies in CSR disclosure from 2004 to 2010.

The relatively high level of reporting in Europe can be explained in large part by the development of the standard-setting and regulatory environment in this region. Forceful regulatory action by European countries and pan-European bodies differs from the more voluntary forms of CSR favored in the US. The regulatory framework in European nations includes such country initiatives as annual reporting requirements for social and environmental performance of companies listed on the French stock exchange, requirements for environmental reporting for Norwegian and Swedish firms, and Germany's Corporate Governance Code, which requires companies to provide information regarding how social and environmental policies are being integrated. The European Parliament has also established directives allowing reliance on CSR criteria when selecting companies to receive government contracts (Fombrun, 2005).

CSR policies and practices in Asia have often been compared unfavorably with those in the US, Europe and Australia. On many of the 20 CSR elements assessed in Welford's (2004) study of company policies, Asian firms appeared to be doing less than European firms. There were stark contrasts between European and Asian firms in regard to policies regarding fair wages, freedom of association and equal opportunities for employees. In a follow-up survey, Welford (2005) found that policies regarding philanthropy were most prevalent in North America, significantly lower in Europe, and even lower in Asia.

There is also substantial variance in CSR reporting among Asian countries (Chapple & Moon, 2005; Welford, 2005). Japanese companies, for example, are noteworthy for their reporting of CSR performance (Fukukawa & Moon, 2005). The author also notes that while the most established form of CSR in the Asian region involves traditional community involvement, newer forms – including socially responsible products and processes and socially responsible employee relations – are emerging. While Japanese companies are more likely to focus their CSR disclosure on environmental programs and policies rather than social issues, the perceived importance of CSR among firms in the country is quite high (Tanimoto

& Suzuki, 2005). Welford's (2005) survey found that 62 percent of companies in Japan and 50 percent of the surveyed firms in Korea had policies on CSR and/or sustainable development reporting. This was substantially higher than the average for the other Asian countries (Thailand, Malaysia, Singapore and Hong Kong) in his study.

Serious shortcomings in adopting best practices in corporate governance have been noted in China (Kimber & Lipton, 2005). Ang and Leong (2000) suggest that values associated with Asian business, such as the cultivation of special relationships and a substantial distinction between 'insiders' versus 'outsiders', may contribute to less ethical and socially responsible business practices in the region. Moreover, it has been argued that the lack of codification of CSR policies in Asian firms is related to the inherent modesty in Asian cultures to tout one's success in activities such as CSR (Welford, 2005), and therefore some activities may not be as readily discerned by outside observers. Americans tend to codify social relations with rules, while Asian firms may rely more on cultural mechanisms such as philosophy and guiding principles (Tanimoto & Suzuki, 2005; Weaver, 2001).

Research has also found that there is a stronger emphasis on philanthropy and community development in developing countries than on environmental, ethical, or stakeholder issues which are more prominent concerns in the developed nations (Baskin, 2006; Chambers, E., Chapple, W., Moon, J., & Sullivan M. 2003; Mohan, 2001; Moon, 2002; Schmidheiny, 2006). In Baskin's (2006) research on the reported corporate responsibility behavior of 127 leading companies from 21 emerging markets across Asia, Africa, Latin America, and Central and Eastern Europe, which he compares with over 1700 leading companies in developed countries, the authors noted that: 'Corporate responsibility in emerging markets, while more extensive than commonly believed, is less embedded in corporate strategies, less pervasive and less politically rooted than in most high-income countries from the Organization for Economic Cooperation and Development (OECD)'.

Thus, it can be reasonably argued that a number of factors prevent the development of CSR in developing countries, among them: civil society is not well organized; the government does not strongly promote CSR; companies do not face strong, constant pressure; and the press has yet to assume the role of watchdog. In addition, standards and systems – which are the foundation of CSR in Europe and the U.S. – are comparatively weak in developing nations (Kemp, 2001). Henceforth, corporations in developing nations may not see any reason to behave in socially responsible ways because of various institutional weaknesses (Campbell, 2007).

As the literature review indicates, cross-regional and cross-country CSR analysis has been pursued by a number of scholars and organizations. However, there is relatively little focus on CSR in South Korea (but see Baughn et al., 2007; Chapple & Moon, 2005; Welford, 2004, 2005) and even less focus on Turkey (but see Kusku & Fraser, 2004; Ararat & Gocenoglu, 2006; Basar & Basar, 2006) and additionally, there are very few comparative studies of CSR focusing on different stages of economic development (but see Robertson, 2009) and extremely few cross-sector comparison studies.

Wayne Visser emphasizes this gap in research in the 'Oxford Handbook of Corporate Social Responsibility' (2008) with these words:

There is a dearth of international research which surveys the nature and extent of CSR in developing countries, as compared with developed countries. Next to this need for more data in general, there is need for more comparative work which analyses CSR between regions (e.g. Africa, Latin America, Asia) and between countries within regions... Alongside these efforts there seems to be a specific need for more sectoral research on CSR codes and practices, especially for the lesser covered industries like chemicals, financial services, infrastructure (including construction), manufacturing (including motor), media, retail, telecommunications, and travel and leisure.

Our research attempts to close this gap and add to our understanding of cross-country and cross-industry research on CSR by looking at CSR web disclosure in three countries – the U.S., South Korea and Turkey – which represent different levels of economic development. Through cross-sectoral comparison of five less focused industries – automotive and component manufacturers, consumer electronics and telecommunications services, food and beverages, retail stores and major banks – researchers aimed to closed the sectoral research gap in the literature.

METHODOLOGY

As the main sources, the U.S., South Korea and Turkey were selected as the target countries, and companies listed in the stock exchange markets of these countries were selected as target companies for analysis. These three countries were chosen because they are good examples of a highly developed economy (U.S.), a developed economy (South Korea) and a rapidly developing economy (Turkey), and therefore provide an opportunity to explore variations in depth and types of CSR reporting across different countries of varying economic development.

The U.S., South Korea and Turkey's stock exchange market lists from NYSE and NASDAQ, KOSPI and KOSDAQ, 1st National Market and 2nd National Market were combined within each country which produced an unduplicated list of approximately 4800 (US), 1800 (Korea), and 300 (Turkey) companies for each corresponding country. For cross-sector CSR variation comparison purpose the samples were further broken down by five industry types: consumer electronics and telecommunication services; automobile and component manufacturers; food and beverages; retail stores; major banks and financial services. Among the leading companies ranked at the top of the stock exchange market lists, by selecting only 'CSR active' companies (Welford, 2004) (i.e. companies we observed having some mention of program or activity about CSR on their corporate website), the sample included 50 CSR active companies for each country and 150 CSR active companies in total.

As mentioned in the review of previous studies, a set of indicators for CSR information disclosure was used drawing from previous research in this area (Fukokawa & Moon, 2005; Chapple & Moon, 2005; Wanderley et al., 2007; Welford, 2004, 2005). Each of the 150 corporate websites (50 per country) was analyzed via a questionnaire (composed of CSR dimensions and indicators listed below) to code the presence in the following six indicator domains:

- Ethics and Integrity Codes (e.g., employee code of conduct, employee diversity policy, human rights principles, anti-corruption codes, conflict of interest codes, anti-trust/fair competition policies, confidentiality/privacy policy, supplier code of conduct, supplier diversity policy, political donations policies)
- Corporate Governance (e.g., mission or values statement, composition of board, independent directors, BOD guidelines, board compensation, governance status reports)
- Workplace & Personnel (e.g., training on employee code of conduct, health and safety training, employee diversity, employee turnover rates, equal employment opportunity, employee network-

ing groups, process for formal complaints, harassment policies, employee benefits and compensation, work/life balance programs, learning and career development, objectives and targets for workplace performance)
- Supply Chain (e.g., supplier vision/standards/guidelines, supplier diversity policy, supplier training in social and/or environmental accountability, supplier registration or certification, supplier assessment or audit)
- Environmental (e.g., environmental management system, energy/water conservation initiatives, waste reduction/recycling initiatives, renewable energy initiatives)
- Community Development (e.g., agriculture, arts and culture, education and training, local economic/community development, overseas economic/community development, environment and conservation, health and safety, housing, religion, sport, poverty, emergency/disaster relief, youth and children related)

FINDINGS AND DISCUSSION

Ethics and Integrity Codes

The institutionalization of CSR is often expressed through its corporate codes and policies. This codification process enables the organization to formally communicate its values and standards of business conduct to its key stakeholders, both within and outside the organization. Figure 1 gives us important clues about the differences in codes and policies among the three countries – at least in how these companies show how transparent they are with respect to these codes and policies.

As shown in Figure 1, the US leads in all areas of codes and policies showing the highest levels of disclosure. Furthermore, the vast majority (i.e., in excess of 80%) of all US companies have reported ethics and integrity codes in all areas. The only exception is in the human rights area, with less 50%. This is probably due to the fact that most rights are already covered by employment laws that companies must strictly obey.

The areas that show the greatest divergence from South Korea and Turkey are in supplier diversity, equal employment opportunity, employee diversity, fair competition, and confidentiality. While about 8 out of 10 (82%) companies in South Korea report a Code of Conduct or a Code of Ethics, under half of the companies report codes and policies in the other areas, with especially low levels of reporting in employee diversity (14%) and supplier diversity (0%). The low level of employee diversity policy and supplier diversity in South Korea is not surprising given the high level of homogeneity in the society making up the workforce and businesses. This stands in sharp contrast to most large U.S. corporations made up of diverse, multiethnic workforces. In short, being an ethnically homogenous 'nation-state' makes codes like employee and supplier diversity most likely less important and relevant for South Korean companies.

Turkey is below the U.S. and South Korea in all categories except being slightly higher than South Korea in human rights. This is perhaps a reflection of the fact that Turkey is still a developing nation where ethics and integrity codes have yet to be perceived as an important issue by companies as well as the society in general. Turkey is still a male dominant country and the rate of female presence in society is low in comparison with the other two countries. Except for only a few large companies, it is hard to

Figure 1. Cross-country variations on ethics and integrity codes

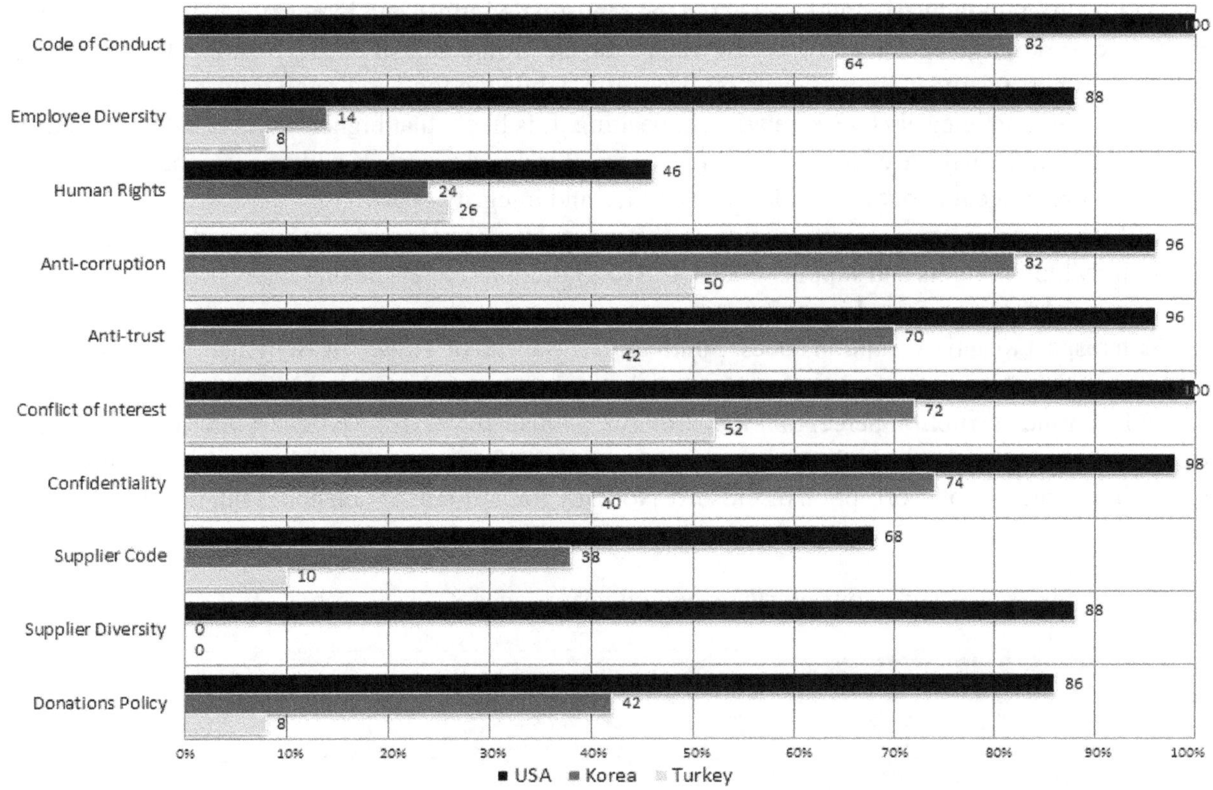

see female directors in Turkish companies. Thus in Turkey, male dominance might be the reason for not having employee diversity policies as expressed in its company codes.

The majority of the firms in all three countries have anti-corruption, fair competition and conflict of interest codes. This is most likely due to the high level of awareness about corporate corruption related scandals in society. More and more, external stakeholders are putting pressure on companies to develop policies that regulate codes of conduct and ensure that corporate scandals are avoided. The highly publicized corporate and accounting scandals in the U.S., such as Enron, Tyco International and Adelphia, have raised the awareness of corporate misconduct throughout the world.

Three other areas that show marked differences between the U.S. and its South Korean and Turkish company counterparts are in political donations, supplier diversity, and supplier code of conduct. Over 80 percent (88%) of the U.S. companies disclose policies about political donations. Like NGOs, it is common for U.S. companies to advocate policies that are within their stakeholders' interests and benefits. With its civil movements, NGOs, and many corporate watchdog organizations, American corporations are hightly aware of and sensitive to political and public policy issues and are not hesitant to get involved in politics within the limits of laws and regulations. By comparison, companies in South Korea and Turkey try to keep themselves out of politics, at least publicly.

With respect to supplier codes and policies, the U.S. outranks South Korea and Turkey in disclosing supplier diversity policies and supplier codes of conduct. Holding suppliers accountable for their business conduct is very important to U.S. companies and ultimately reflects the moral and ethical principles of the latter.

What is also interesting to observe is that both in South Korea and Turkey, there is more variation among the different industries with respect to the reporting of ethics and integrity codes. Both in South Korea and Turkey, the banking industry as well as the electronic industries and to some degree the auto industries report relatively higher levels of disclosure, while the food and retail industries report lower levels of ethics and integrity codes, relatively speaking. It is likely that higher levels of internationalization and regulation may have increased the awareness of industries such as banking, electronics and auto in being more diligent about the disclosure of ethics and integrity codes.

All five sectors in the U.S. are leading in the presence of ethics and integrity code related topics, particularly human rights and supplier codes. U.S. corporations are disclosing many more ethics related codes, as can been seen from Figure 2.

With respect to anti-corruption codes, South Korea is ahead of Turkey in all industries except for the banking sector. Notably, in Turkey there are tough regulations by the Capital Markets Board of Turkey (CMBT). In the corruption perception index that is published by "Transparency International" South Korea is ranked as 45th and Turkey is ranked 54 for year 2012 which is parallel with the findings of this research in terms of anti-corruption disclosure. Not only for anti-corruption codes but also for anti-trust

Figure 2. Cross-sector variations on ethics and integrity codes

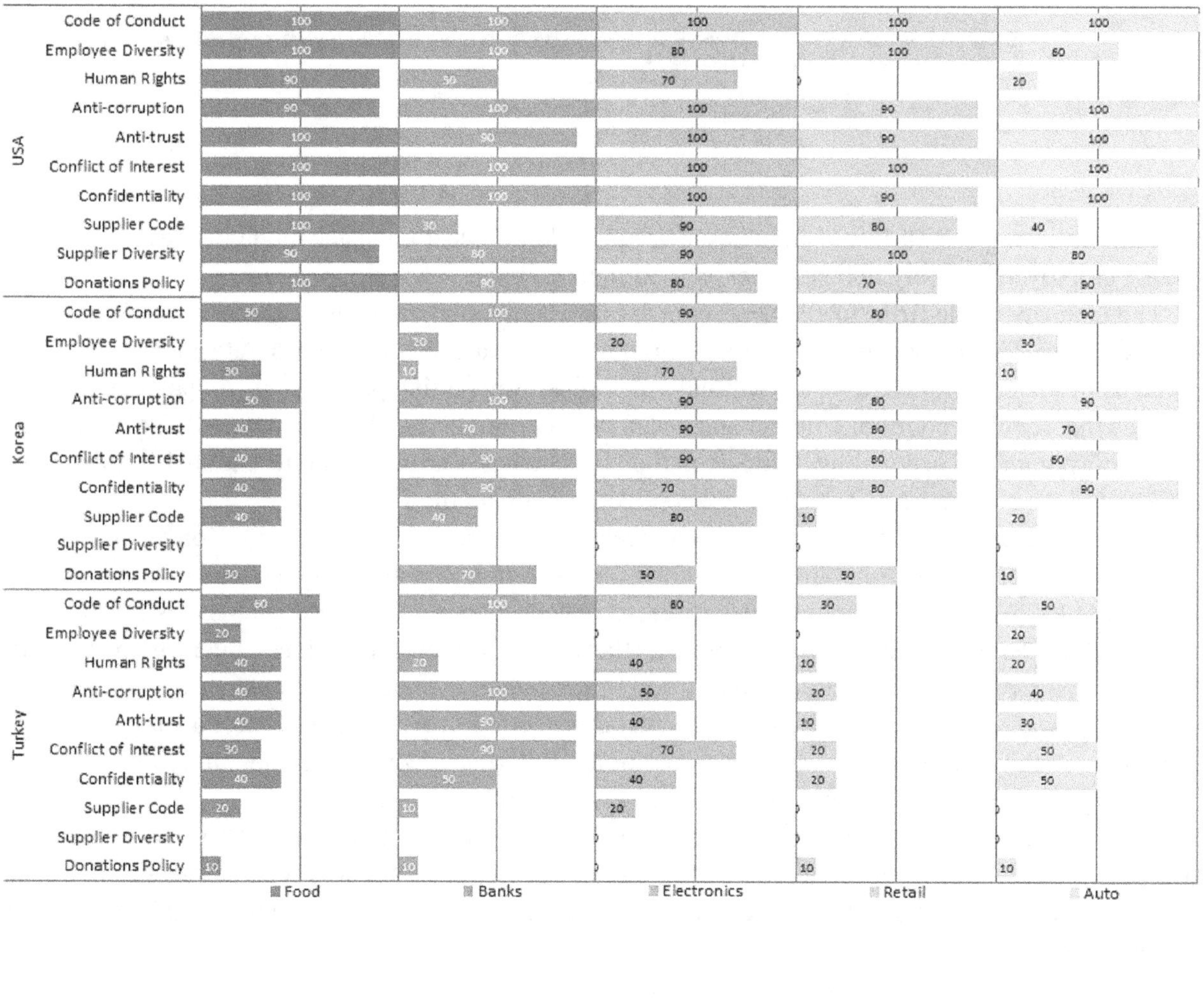

and conflict of interest codes which are published by more than 90 percent of major banks in Turkey, most likely because of the tough regulations of CMBT. In the case of Turkey, the retail industry shows the lowest level of disclosure in ethics and integrity codes.

We conclude this section by saying that as the country's level of development increases (from Turkey to the U.S.), the major pattern for ethics and integrity code disclosure also increases in each industry except for the few specific cases mentioned above.

Corporate Governance

Differences in governance structure and practices are quite revealing for the three countries. As Figure 3 above shows, the U.S. dominates the three countries in terms of disclosing the composition of their board of directors (including number of independent directors) and compensation. This is not surprising given the requirements for such transparency promulgated by the Sarbanes-Oxley Act of 2002 set in motion in the aftermath of the Enron scandal. Noteworthy are the high levels of governance mission, diversity, compensation, guidelines and status reporting among the Turkish companies, virtually on par with the U.S. The reason for this becomes clear given the recent changes in stock exchange reporting requirements in Turkey. Turkish stock exchange companies are forced by the so called Capital Markets Board of Turkey to catch up with the requirements that the board requests from the companies and publish an annual corporate governance compliance report accordingly. Hence, Turkish companies are highly concentrated on corporate governance related issues and show this transparency on their corporate websites.

Figure 3. Cross-country variations on CSR related corporate governance practices

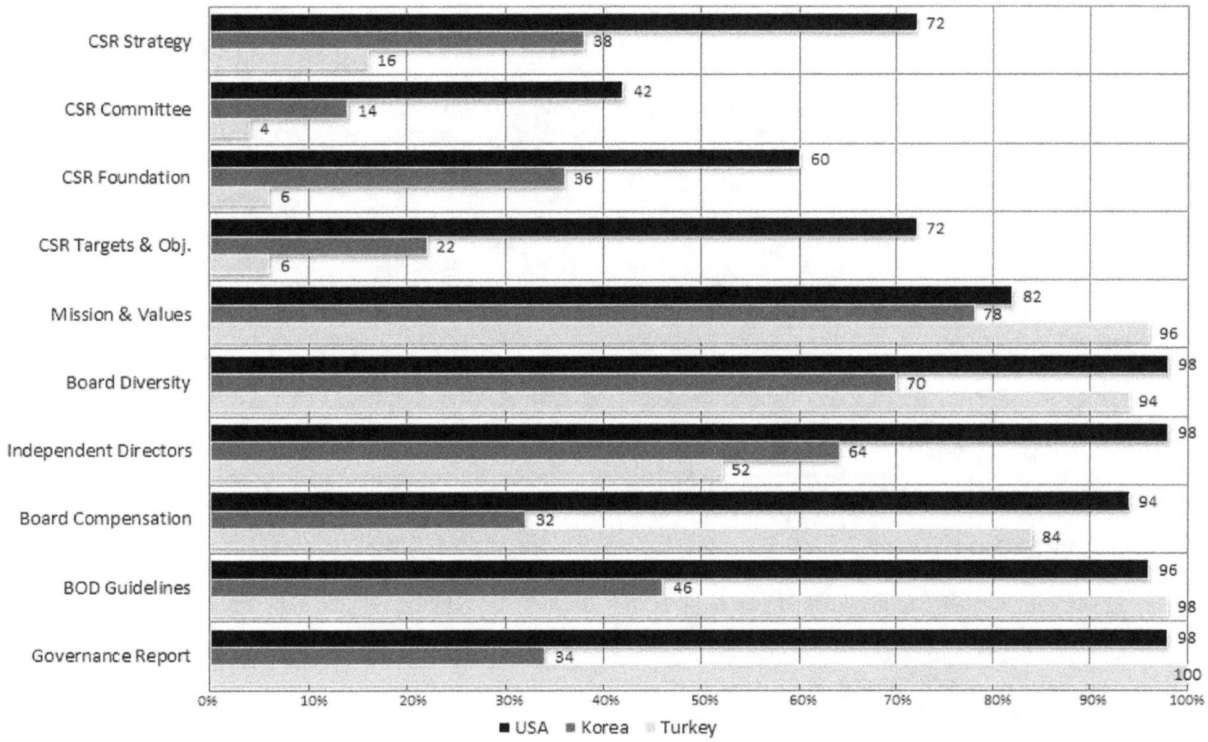

Recruiting independent directors to participate on corporate boards has only recently become a hot issue in South Korea and Turkey. As such, there is still a huge gap between the U.S. and the other two countries in the percentage reporting the number of independent directors on the board. On the other hand, reporting by Turkish companies related to CSR strategies and structures are almost non-existent. This stands in stark contrast to the reporting on corporate governance issues. In comparison, both US and South Korean companies show a more balanced picture with regards to reporting their CSR strategies and structures.

In the U.S. all the industries show similar disclosure patterns with more than 90% disclosing board diversity, independent directors, board compensation, board of directors (BOD) guidelines and governance report topics (Figure 4). The automobile and component electronics industries show relatively lower levels of interest in disclosing mission and values and that might be because the majority of the companies listed in these sectors is composed of SMEs (see Appendix, Table 2 for the complete list of companies). As a pattern, the retail and automobile manufacturing sectors show lower levels of disclosure in the areas of CSR strategy, CSR committee, CSR foundation, and CSR targets & objectives.

In South Korea, the Food & Beverages industry shows nearly no interest (except for mission & values statement) in disclosing CSR related corporate governance practices. Major banks and consumer

Figure 4. Cross-sector variations on CSR related corporate governance practices

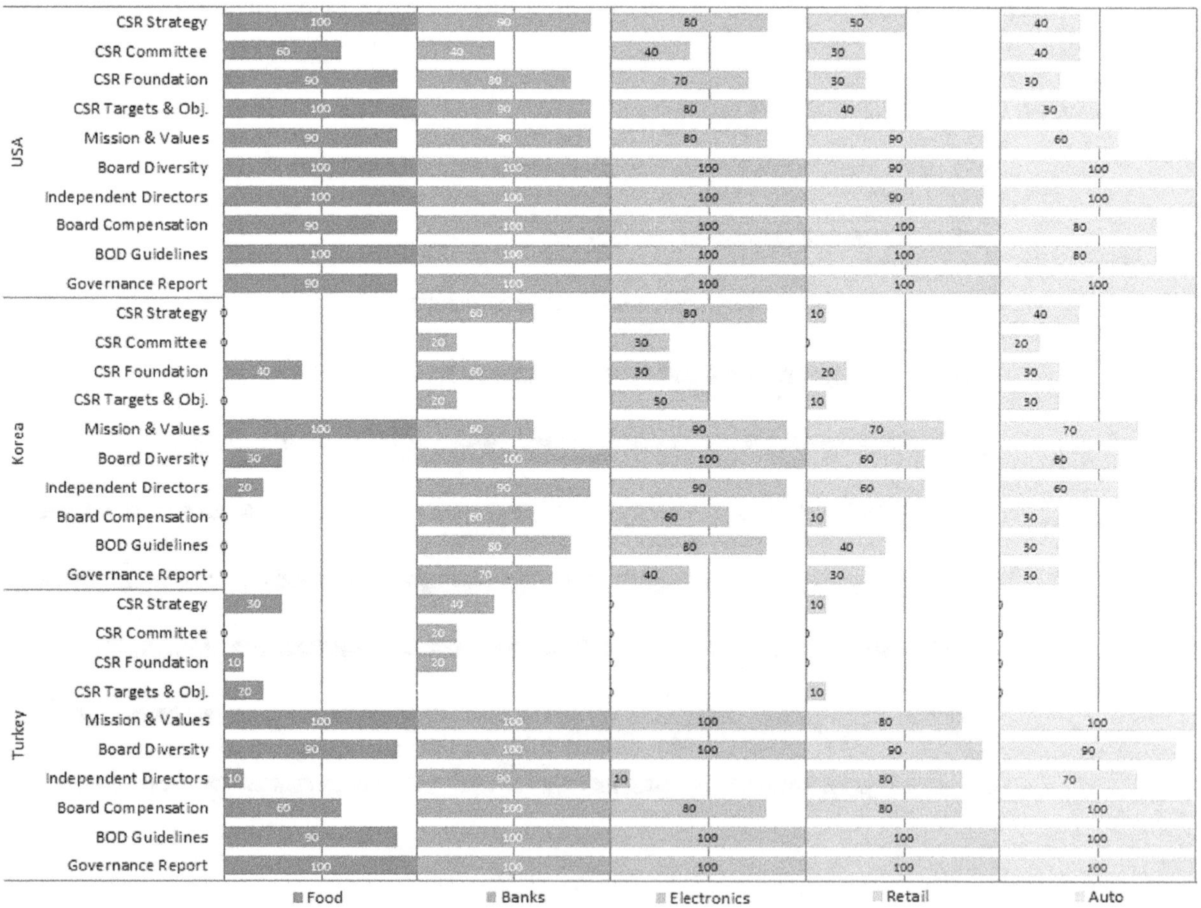

electronics and telecommunication services are the leading industries in South Korea in disclosing corporate governance practices in the areas of CSR strategy, board diversity, independent directors and BOD guidelines. Commonly, CSR committee and CSR targets and objectives topics are the least disclosed topics among all industries.

In Turkey, all the industry sectors show nearly no interest in disclosing CSR strategy, CSR committee, CSR foundation, and CSR targets and objectives (except food & beverages and major banks sectors disclosing CSR strategy with a percentage of 30% and 40%, respectively). As was mentioned in the ethics and integrity codes section, with the institutional effect of the Capital Markets Board of Turkey, each of the industry sectors show high disclosure in the areas of corporate mission and values, board diversity, board compensation, BOD guidelines and governance report. The food and beverages and consumer electronics and telecommunication sectors show low disclosure of independent directors on the board (only 10% of these industry sectors disclosing that the board has independent directors).

Workplace and Personnel

As employees are considered by most companies to be one of the key primary stakeholder groups of the organization, workplace policies and procedures are critical to sound employee stakeholder relations. As shown in Figure 5, U.S. companies rank high (over 50%) in disclosing information about making formal complaints, learning and career development, employee benefits, and employee networks. This is not

Figure 5. Cross-country variations on CSR related workplace practices

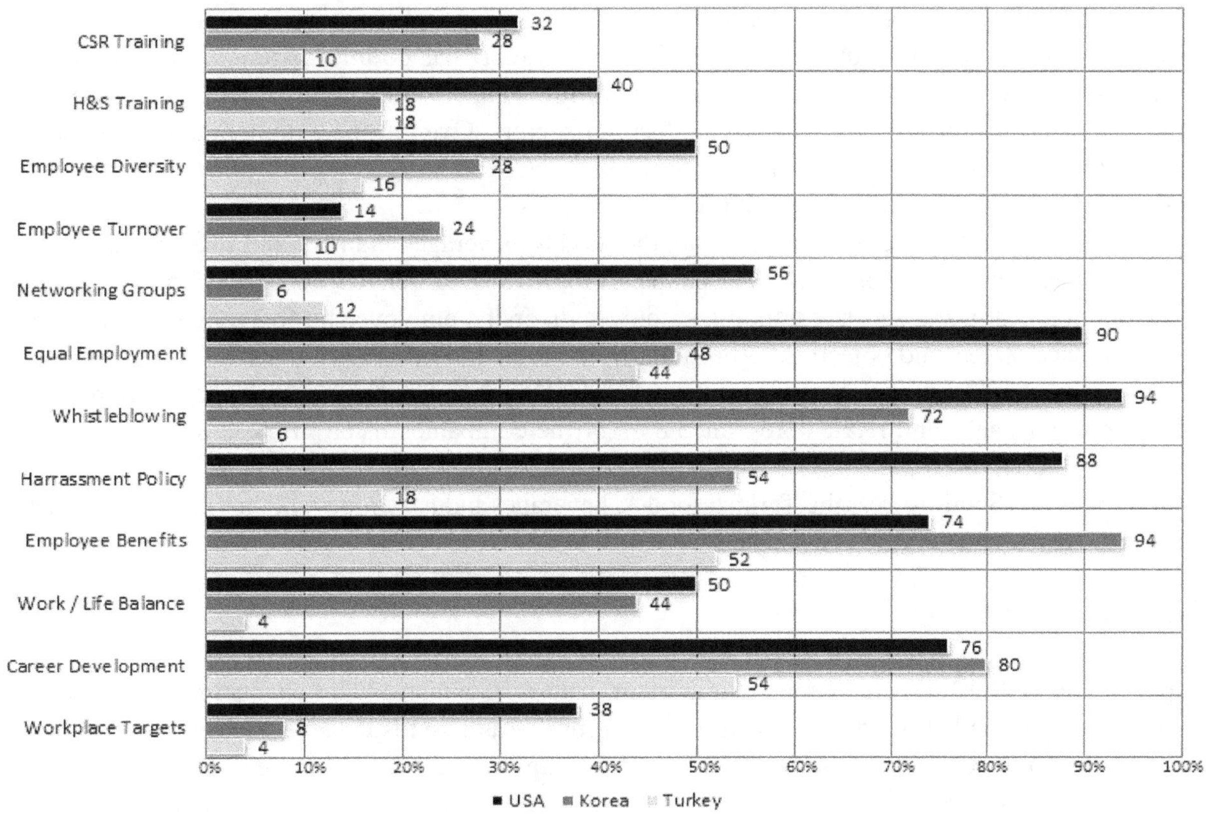

surprising given the importance of encouraging whistleblowing to report misconduct, and attracting and retaining employees through career development and special employee groups or networks, including minority and women networks.

South Korea also ranks high in disclosing policies and procedures for making formal complaints as well as disclosing information about learning and career development and employee benefits. The remaining areas of workplace and personnel reporting in South Korea are relatively lower when compared to whistleblowing, employee benefits and career development. The overall pattern of reporting is quite similar between the U.S. and South Korea. Turkey, on the other hand, falls well below the other two countries in all areas of reporting workplace policies and practices with only two areas with rates slightly over 50 percent (employee benefits and learning/career development). Besides employee benefit and career development, the remaining areas of workplace and personnel reporting show negligible levels among most Turkish companies. This clearly indicates that Turkish companies have a long way to go in establishing more detailed and refined policies about various aspects related to employment.

All five industries in the U.S. show high levels of disclosure in reporting CSR related workplace practices such as equal employment, harassment policy, whistleblowing, and career development (Figure 6). As was mentioned in disclosure of ethics and integrity codes, whistleblowing policies are prevalent in the U.S. companies, given the requirements for such transparency promulgated by the Sarbanes-Oxley Act of 2002 set in motion in the aftermath of the Enron debacle. The consumer electronics industry sector reported the highest level of disclosure (40%) of employee turnover rates with the other sectors reporting relatively low levels of disclosure of employee turnover rates. Low levels of reporting of employee turnover may be related to the notion that reporting on employee turnover would reflect badly on the company's ability to retain employees and deter interest in joining the firm among talented prospective employees. While all the other industries disclose CSR training and employee diversity topics with an average of 50% to 60%, the automobile manufacturing sectorr has no information disclosure on these topics. Furthermore, low rates of disclosure in work/life balance and employee networking is evident among the automobile and component manufacturer sectors. Overall, the automobile and component manufacturers sectors' level of information disclosure on CSR related workplace practices is the lowest among all five industry sectors in this study.

Interestingly, in the case of South Korean, the food & beverages industry and retail industry show very low rates of disclosure on (only 10%) on the six topics of CSR related workplace practices, namely CSR training, health and security training, employee diversity, employee turnover, networking groups and workplace targets and objectives. Additionally, the food and beverages industry shows low rate of disclosure on equal employment opportunity statement. Notably, harassment seems to be an important issue for major banks and retail stores since 80% of the companies listed in those industries publish information about this topic.

In contrast to South Korea, the Turkish food & beverages industry report higher rates of disclosure (from 10% to 70%) on all the CSR related workpace topics.

Supply Chain

Supply chain CSR efforts are extremely important matters. Companies that encourage or require their suppliers to be socially responsible may ultimately promote a more responsible business environment – particularly in relation to doing business with overseas suppliers. As suppliers are an integral part of the value chain of corporations, it would be difficult to maintain high CSR standards without the involment

Figure 6. Cross-sector variations on CSR related workplace practices

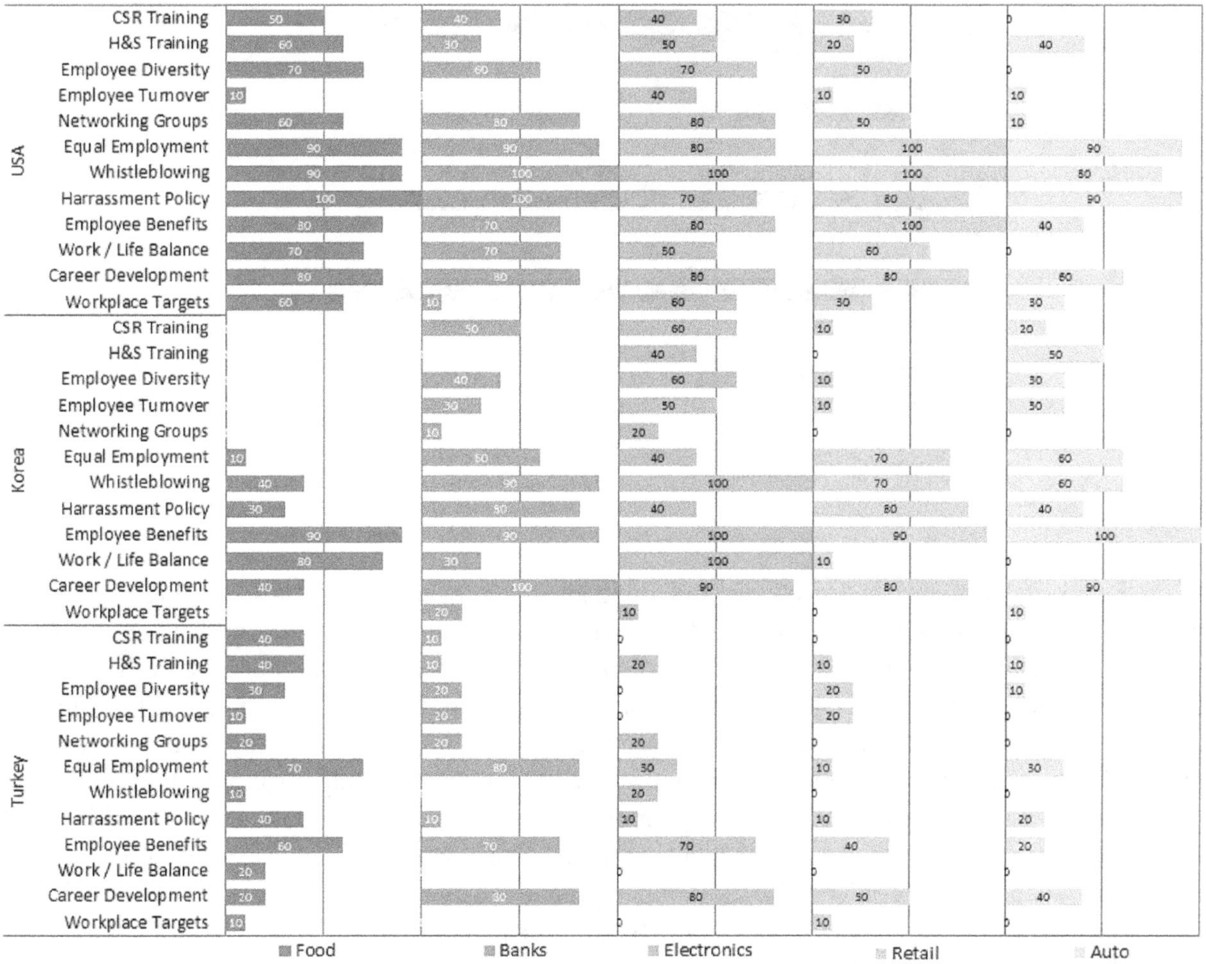

of suppliers. As such, if companies target effective levels of CSR practices, they need to integrate their suppliers into their own CSR efforts and expect the same standards of compliance by their suppliers. As Figure 7 demonstrates, U.S. companies hold the leading position in supply chain CSR practices as evidenced by the higher rate of disclosure of supplier mission/guidelines, supplier assessment, and supplier accreditation. While ranking the lowest among the measures of supply chain CSR practices, supplier training in CSR was still the highest among the U.S. companies. Turkey ranks the lowest in all areas of CSR supplier disclosure, where disclosure is almost non-existent. This suggests that Turkish companies need to raise awareness of CSR among its suppliers and other business partners. As mentioned above, this is essential if Turkish companies want to be more effective in their overall CSR efforts.

Sooth Korea's situation, on the other hand, is somewhere between the U.S .and Turkey. About 30% of South Korean companies have CSR disclosure policies with respect to their suppliers. However, this finding is not uniform across the different industries. Disclosure on suppliers CSR guidelines is only present in the electonics, retail and auto industries, while it is nonexistent in the food and beverages and banking industries.

Figure 7. Cross-country variations on responsible supply chain practices

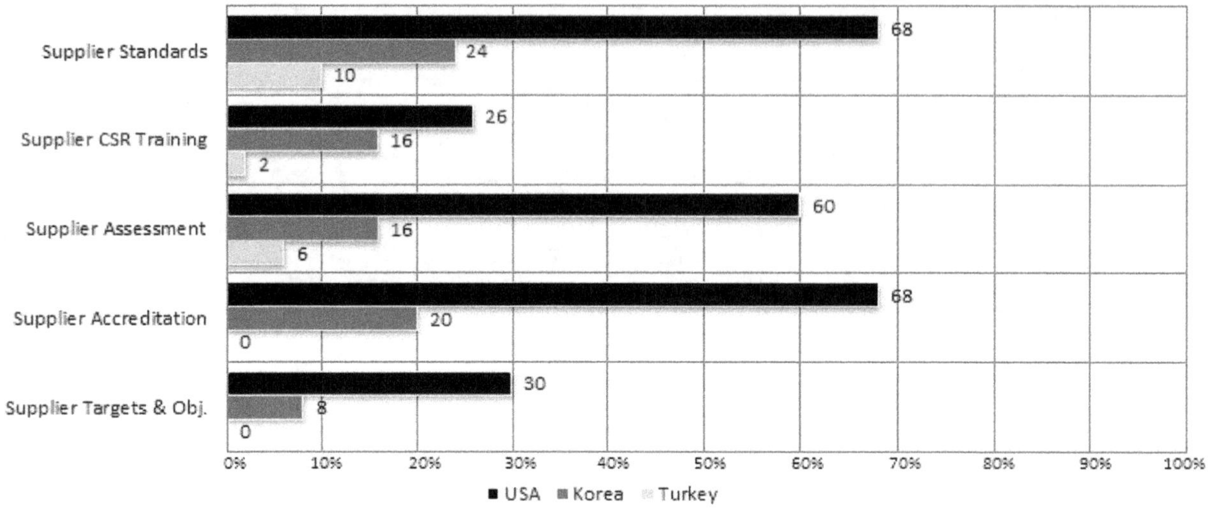

As mentioned in earlier sections, expecting a high level of information disclosure among major banks in the area of responsible supply chain practices is not expected given that their suppliers tend to be no more than consulting companies, hardware and software producers, and stationary stores (Figure 8). In the U.S., except for major banks, the other sectors report more frequently on topics such as supplier standards, supplier assessment, and supplier accreditation. Turkey is virtually nonexistent in reporing on supply chain practices, except for some disclosure on supplier standards. Notably, the food industry in Turkey is slightly more active on supplier assessment. Among the industries analyzed in South Korea, consumer electronics, retail stores and automobile manufacturers are more active on disclosing responsible supply chain practices. The most important point to mention here is on supplier accreditation programs wherein the consumer electronics industry shows higher rates of disclosing (70%). It would be worth doing a special research on "why consumer electronics sector is specially interested in supplier accreditation while all other industries are not interested at all?".

Figure 8. Cross-sector variations on responsible supply chain practices

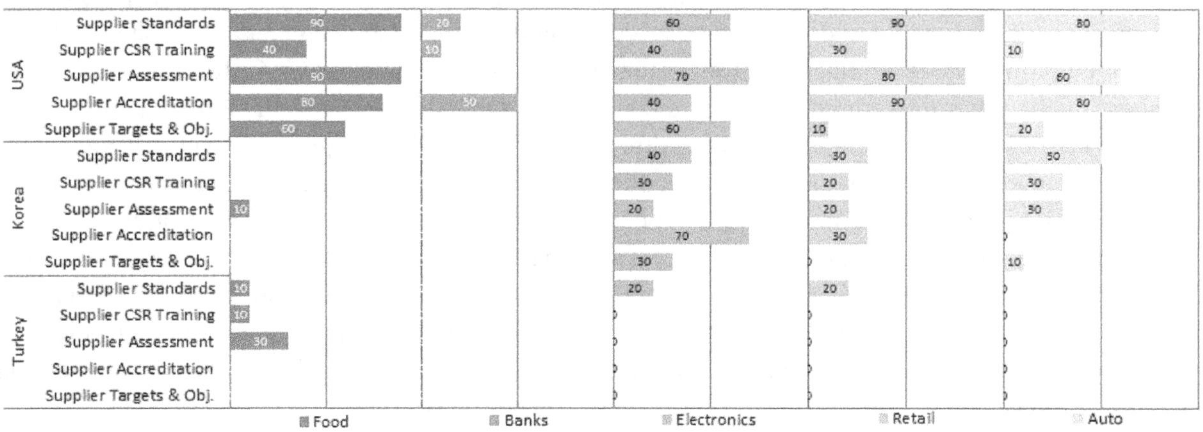

Environment

Environmental issues have become an increasingly important area of corporate responsibility as more and more companies want to demonstrate their environmental stewardship by minimizing their environmental impacts and promoting sustainability. To be sure, environmental impact has become a core part of sustainability reports worldwide. Figure 9 illustrates the differences in environmental practices across the three countries. The U.S. leads in reporting on an energy management system (EMS), energy/water conservation programs, and renewable energy programs (over 50% of the companies). Furthermore, many US companies do not only have environmental policies but they also have set specific targets and objectives in achieving them. South Korea is in second place, and Turkey has the lowest rate of disclosure of renewable energy programs (or initiatives) (under 5%). The reporting is higher in the electronics and auto industries compared to the other three industries. In contrast, the reporting on specific targets and objectives is much lower than the reporting on policies about the environment. Turkey's position as a developing economy is consistent with its low levels of environmental practices (particularly in renewable energy programs) relative the more mature economies of the U.S. and South Korea.

Manufacturing industries (consumer electronics, automobile manufacturers) are slightly ahead of the remaining three industries in the U.S and renewable energy is used in relatively lower levels at automobile and food sectors. In terms of environmental targets and objectives, major banks and automobile manufacturers have less information disclosure than the other industries. Additionally, in all industries, companies have less targets and objectives on renewable energy (Figure 10).

In South Korea, just like in the U.S., consumer electronics and automobile manufacturers are disclosing more information than other industries about EMS, energy/water conservation, and waste reduction/recycling, which is reasonable as they have more impact on the environment. Notable, renewable energy and environment related targets/objectives are not disclosed at a high rate for any specific South Korean industry.

Figure 9. Cross-country variations on environmental practices

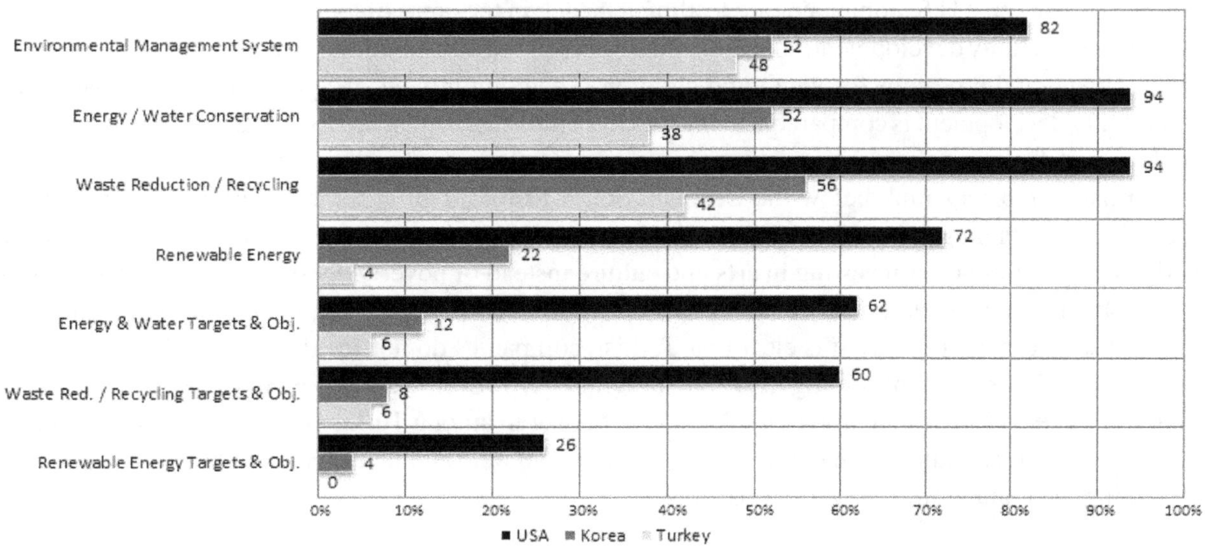

Figure 10. Cross-sector variations on environmental practices

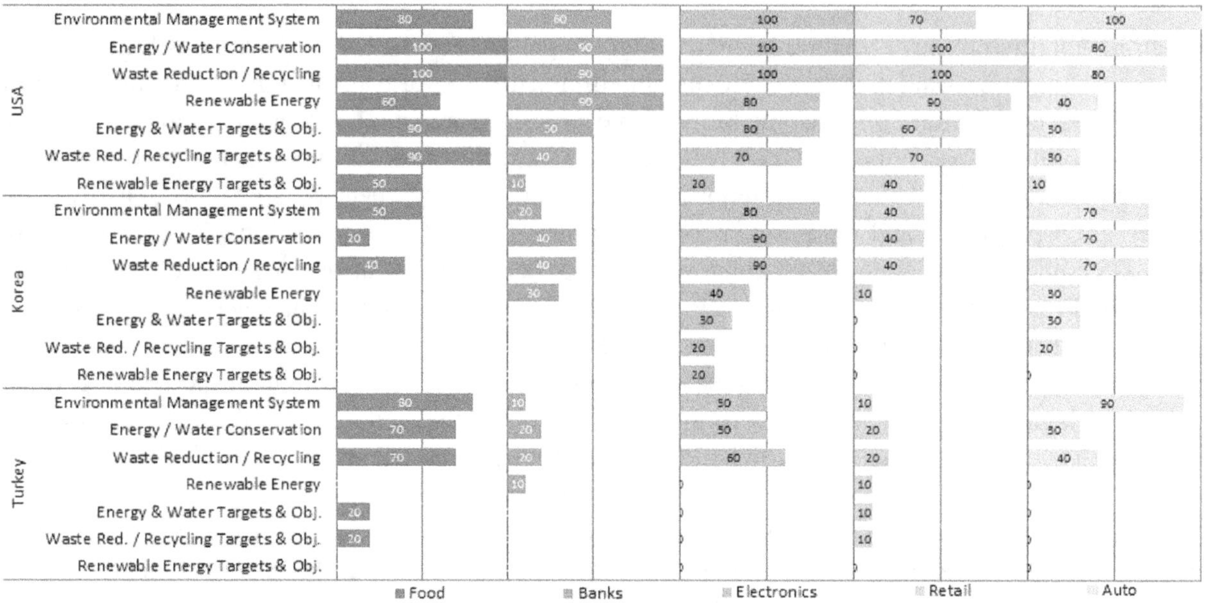

Not surprisingly, consumer electronics and automobile manufacturers in Turkey are fairly active in disclosing information on EMS, energy/water conservation, and waste reduction/recycling. However there is a different point of difference from South Korea. The food and beverages sector is surprisingly very active in Turkey. Hence, it would be meaningful starting point for conducting further research into *why the food & beverages industry in Turkey is highly active in environmental practices.*

Community Development

Investment in community development programs is a core part of being a socially responsible company. Figure 11 shows that U.S. companies are leading the pack in the areas of local community development, overseas community development, education and training programs, health and safety programs, housing development, and programs for youth and children. The commitment of South Korean companies on community development is comparable to that of US companies in general. In fact, South Korea outranks the U.S. and Turkey in the areas of agriculture, arts and culture, and welfare programs.

Turkish companies rank below the U.S. and South Korea in all areas, but within its own country education and training, youth and children, and arts and culture programs are most often mentioned. Turkish companies prefer investing in arts and culture instead of poverty. Despite having a serious poverty problem in many parts of the country as well as in lower income groups throuout the country, its east and southeastern regions, it is clear that Turkish companies do not see their role as being a central player in developing or contributing to welfare programs. However, we still see a considerable amount of support in selected areas for community development overall among Turkish companies. As the firms in Turkey grow larger and become more successful in time, they could be expected to be more supportive of helping the communities in various aspects.

Figure 11. Cross-country variations on community development efforts

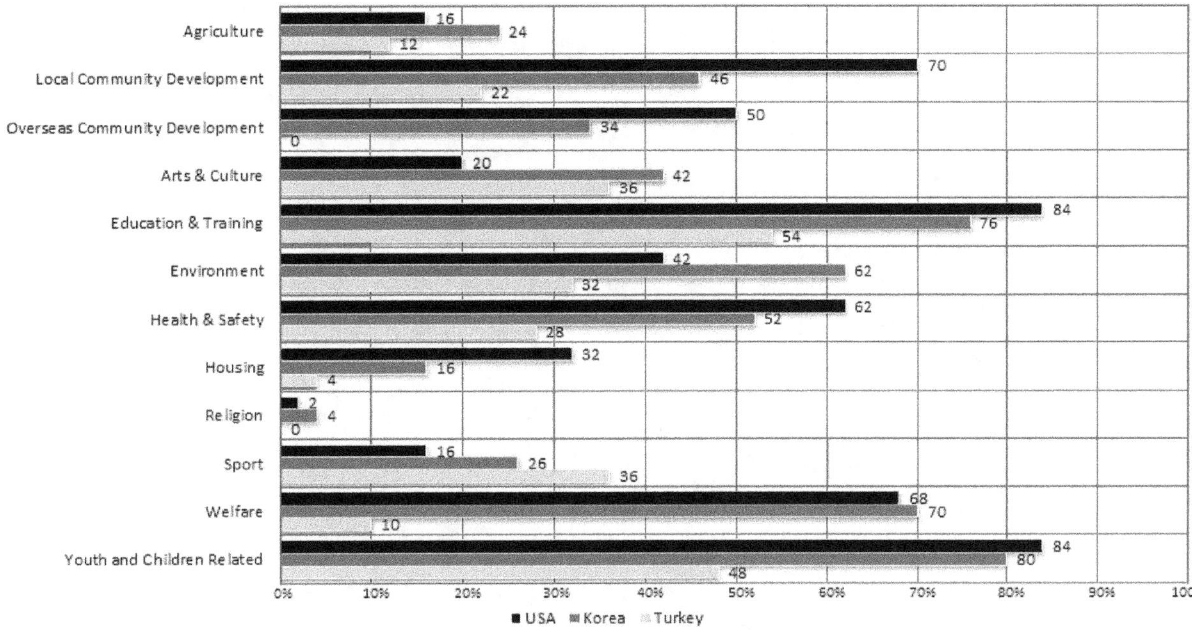

In cross-sector comparison shown in Figure 12, regardless of the country of origin, it is not surprising in all three countries that except for the food and beverages industry, no other industry is interested in investing in agricultural community development efforts since agriculture is the biggest supplier of food industry. The banks and retail sectors are much more interested in developing the local communities than the other two. Also, interestingly, the consumer electronics industry seems to be more interested in investing in overseas community development programs than local community development programs since the ratio is 70% to 50%. Representatively, major banks are very interested in housing programs since they provide mortgage credit for consumers, and the food and beverage industry is very interested in health and safety related programs since food is very related to health.

Interestingly, in South Korea the consumer electronics industry is disclosing a lot of information on overseas community development programs than the other industries. Similar to the U.S., the food and beverage industry is expected to disclose more information on health and safety related CSR activities; however only 10% of the companies disclose such information. Another surprising point is about environment related community development programs. Consumer electronics and automobile manufacturers industries in South Korea are much more concerned than their U.S. competitors with 60% and 90% information disclosure, respectively.

The Turkish food and beverage industry is showing more interest in agriculture related community development programs than the South Korean food and beverage industry with a disclosure rate of 40% to 30%, respecitively. Agriculture is one of the major economic activities in Turkey with huge employment rate (20% of the overall employment in Turkey) which is contrast to South Korea (6% of the overall employemtn in South Korea) (World Bank, 2014). Turkish and South Korean industries are interested in arts and culture and sports related community development activities more than their competitors in the U.S. This raises an interesting question as to "why Turkish and South Korean industries are more interested in arts & culture and sports related community development activities than the U.S. industries?".

Figure 12. Cross-sector variations on community development efforts

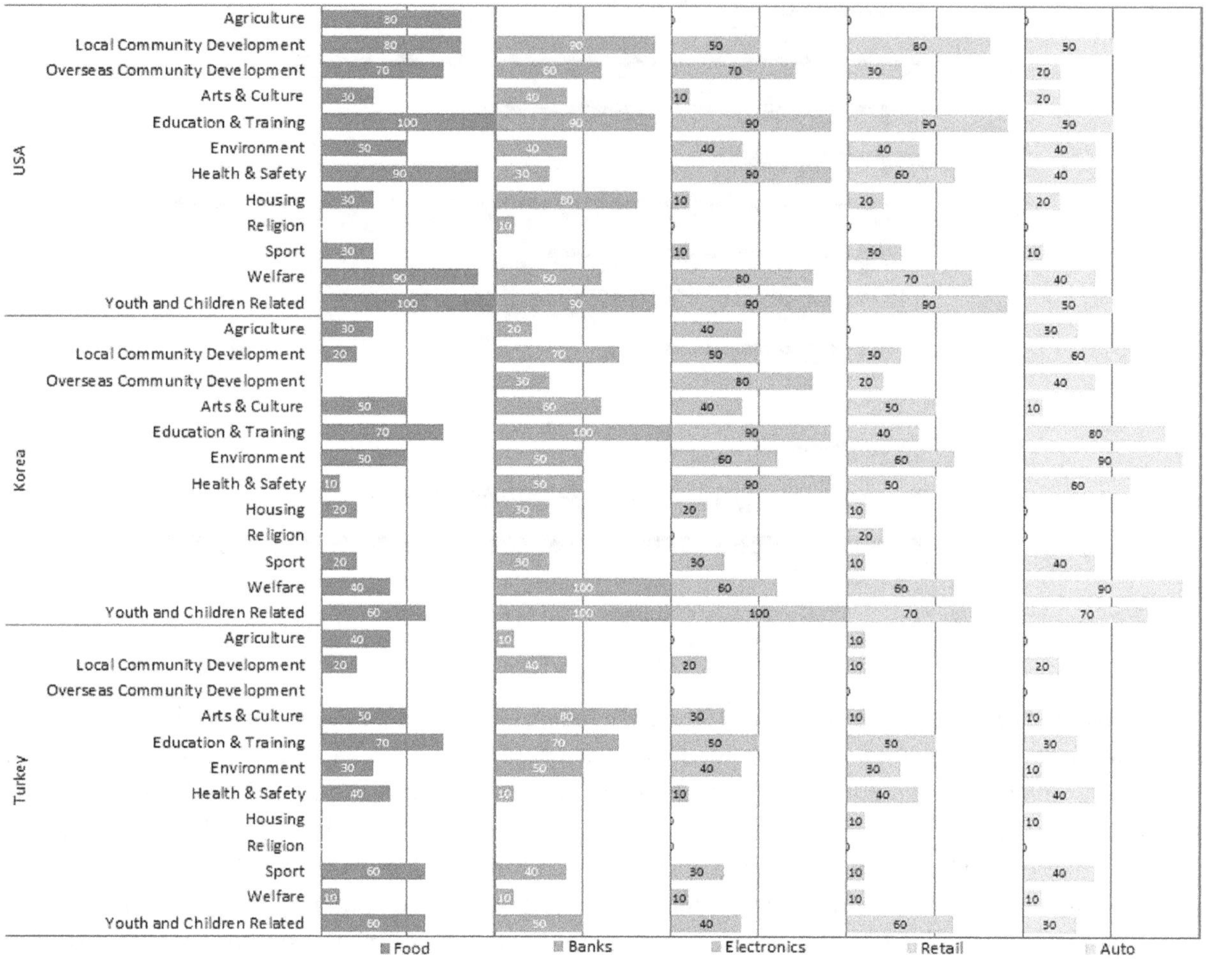

CONCLUSION

We have argued that U.S.-style CSR has been embedded in a system that leaves more incentive and opportunity for corporations to exhibit and disclose higher levels of explicit SCR. By "explicit CSR" we mean corporate policies that assume and articulate responsibility for related to societal interests. They normally consist of voluntary programs and strategies by corporations that combine social and business value and address issues perceived as being part of the social responsibility of the company. The guiding assumption in this study was that CSR is largely a western phenomenon and hence one would expect to find higher rates of CSR information disclosure on corporate websites among U.S. companies compared to South Korea and Turkey. This assumption is predicated on the notion (and supported by the research literature) that CSR strategy and programming is highly country-context based, shaped by a confluence of social-political, legal-regulatory, and economic forces impacting business practices. The CSR research literature and its conceptual underpinnings indeed suggest that there are numerous obstacles to achieving corporate responsibility, particularly in many developing countries where the institutions, standards and regulatory systems, which have supported CSR in North America and Europe, are relatively weak. Lending further insight into this argument is the notion that civil society in western countries stimulates CSR by imposing greater societal demands and expectations of business responsibility from consumers, social advocacy organizations (NGOs and corporate watchdog organizations), socially responsible investors, industry trade associations, and government laws and regulations.

The findings from this study are consistent with prior research on cross-country differences in CSR Web reporting. Namely, that the U.S., like other developed countries in the western world, exhibit higher levels of CSR transparency as evidenced by higher levels of CSR reporting, codification of CSR principles, institutional embeddedness (such as dedicated CSR departments and personnel), corporate social programs, supply chain practices, workplace culture and practices, and overall stakeholder engagement. It is interesting to note that while South Korea descriptively showed higher levels of CSR disclosure across many of the indicators, overall CSR was not significantly higher than that shown collectively among companies in Turkey.

To be sure, the fast changing global economy, combined with government, institutional and societal pressures for greater social accountability, will most certainly require firms in both developed and developing economies to adopt and adapt their strategic CSR mindsets.

With respect to South Korea, despite an increased sensitivity and mindset to CSR, one of the main criticisms of Korean companies lies in the lack of CSR reporting among the nation's businesses. Similar to the U.S., the South Korean government does not regulate CSR reporting and therefore it remains a voluntary activity among the nation's private-sector businesses. As a result, there have been an insufficient number of Korean companies that have proved to effectively implement CSR activities. Powerhouse conglomerates, such as Hyundai-Kia Motor Group, Posco, SK Energy, LG Group and Samsung, have adopted socially responsible activities, yet only two percent of their profits is spent on CSR activities, according to the Federation of Korean Industries (FKI) (Samsung Sustainability Report, 2012). This may be related to the corporate culture of many Korean companies that do not view themselves as the primary players in advancing social causes outside of their responsibility as being good stewards of the environment and promoting environmental sustainability. In addition, the 'implicit' nature of many Asian cultures (including South Korea) compared to the more 'explicit' nature of countries in the Western world may be a contributing factor to the lower level of social responsibility reporting among the South Korean companies.

As Turkey is still a developing economy, it is not surprising to see its CSR programs and reporting lagging behind the more advanced economies of the U.S. and South Korea. Similar to other emerging economies, Turkey has yet to rise to the level of its counterparts in the developed world in embedding social responsibility into its corporate culture and ethos. This may be the result of several key factors including the role that Turkish companies view themselves in promulgating CSR policies and initiatives, the lack of pressure on Turkish companies from its civilians and civil watchdog organizations, the government's inability to proactively advance CSR laws and regulations, and the lack of CSR standards and reporting protocols among Turkish-based industry associations and publicly traded stock exchanges.

To be sure, the fast changing global economy, combined with government, institutional and societal pressures for greater social accountability, will most certainly require firms in both developed and developing economies to adopt and adapt their strategic CSR mindsets. It would be wrong to conclude that corporations in the U.S. are always ahead of South Korean and Turkish companies, although this usually appears to be generally the case in our findings. On certain aspects both South Korea and Turkey were ahead of the U.S. as well. This indicates that companies can certainly learn a lot from each other and about their different practices and priorities. This paper provides the first steps toward understanding the differences in reporting and priorities for CSR across developed and developing nations.

ACKNOWLEDGMENT

The authors would like to thank *Jin Yong Park, Ph.D.*, *Abdullah Yuvacı, Ph.D.* and *Dima Jamali, Ph.D.* for their helpful and guiding comments.

REFERENCES

Aaronson, S. A. (2003). Corporate Responsibility in the Global Village: The British Role Model and the American Laggard. *Business and Society Review*, *108*(3), 309–338. doi:10.1111/1467-8594.00167

Agle, B. R., & Van Buren, H. J. (1999). God and Mammon: The modern relationship. *Business Ethics Quarterly*, *9*(4), 563–582. doi:10.2307/3857935

Ararat, M. & C. Gocenoglu (2006). Drivers for sustainable corporate responsibility: Case of Turkey. *Report for MDF 5*.

Basar, A.B. & M. Basar (2006). Social Responsibility Reporting: The Case of Turkey. *Sosyal Bilimler Dergisi*, 2.

Baughn, C. C., Bodie, N. L., & McIntosh, J. C. (2007). Corporate Social and Environmental Responsibility in Asian Countries and Other Geographical Regions. *Corporate Social Responsibility and Environmental Management*, *14*, 189–205. doi:10.1002/csr.160

Bondy, K., Matten, D., & Moon, J. (2004). The Adoption of Voluntary Codes of Conduct in MNCs: A Three-Country Comparative Study. *Business and Society Review*, *109*(4), 449–477. doi:10.1111/j.0045-3609.2004.00205.x

Bowen, H. R. (1953). *Social Responsibility of the Businessman*. New York: Harper & Row.

Campbell, J. L. (2007). Why Would Corporations Behave in Socially Responsible Ways? An Institutional Theory of Corporate Social Responsibility. *Academy of Management Review*, *32*(3), 946–967. doi:10.5465/AMR.2007.25275684

Carroll, A. B. (1979). A Three-Dimensional Conceptual Model of Corporate Performance. *Academy of Management Review*, *4*(4), 497–505.

Chapple, W., & Moon, J. (2005). Corporate Social Responsibility (CSR) in Asia: A Seven-Country Study of CSR Web Site Reporting. *Business & Society*, *44*(4), 415–441. doi:10.1177/0007650305281658

Chaudhri, V., & Wang, J. (2007). Communicating Corporate Social Responsibility on the Internet A Case Study of the Top 100 Information Technology Companies in India. *Management Communication Quarterly*, *21*(2), 232–247. doi:10.1177/0893318907308746

Chauvey, J. N., Giordano-Spring, S., Cho, C. H., & Patten, D. M. (2015). The Normativity and Legitimacy of CSR Disclosure: Evidence from France. *Journal of Business Ethics*, *130*(4), 789–803. doi:10.1007/s10551-014-2114-y

Epstein, M.J. (1993). The Fall of Corporate Charitable Contributions. *Public RelationsQuarterly*, 1993, 37-39.

Esrock, S. L., & Leichty, G. B. (1998). Corporate World Wide Web pages: Serving the news media and other publics. *Journalism & Mass Communication Quarterly*, *76*(3), 456–467. doi:10.1177/107769909907600304

Fombrun, C. J. (2005). Building Corporate Reputation through CSR Initiatives: Evolving Standards. *Corporate Reputation Review*, *8*(1), 7–11. doi:10.1057/palgrave.crr.1540235

Freeman, R. E. (1984). *Strategic Management: A Stakeholder Approach*. Boston: Pitman.

Fukukawa, K., & Moon, J. (2004). A Japanese model of corporate social responsibility: A study of website reporting. *Journal of Corporate Citizenship*, *16*(16), 45–59. doi:10.9774/GLEAF.4700.2004.wi.00008

Gildea, R.L. (1995). Consumer Survey Confirms Corporate Social Action Affects Buying Decisions. *Public Relations Quarterly,* 1995, 20-21.

Gray, R., Owen, D., & Maunders, K. (1987). *Corporate Social Reporting - Accounting & Accountability*. Hemel Hempstead: Prentice-Hall.

Hafsi, T., & Farashahi, M. (2005). Applicability of Management Theories to Developing Countries: A Synthesis. *Management International Review*, *45*(4), 483–511.

Hunter, T., & Bansal, P. (2007). How standard is standardized MNC global environmental communication? *Journal of Business Ethics*, *71*(2), 135–147. doi:10.1007/s10551-006-9130-5

Jamali, D., & Mirshak, R. (2006). Corporate Social Responsibility (CSR): Theory and Practice in a Developing Country Context. *Journal of Business Ethics*, *72*(3), 243–262. doi:10.1007/s10551-006-9168-4

Jenkins, R. (2005). Globalization, corporate social responsibility and poverty. *International Affairs*, *81*(3), 525–540. doi:10.1111/j.1468-2346.2005.00467.x

Jose, A., & Lee, S. M. (2007). Environmental Reporting of Global Corporations: A Content Analysis based on Website Disclosures. *Journal of Business Ethics*, *72*(4), 307–321. doi:10.1007/s10551-006-9172-8

Kotler, P., & Lee, N. (2005). *Corporate Social Responsibility: Doing the Most Good for Your Company and Cause*. New Jersey: John Wiley & Sons.

KPMG. (1999). *The KPMG Survey of Corporate Responsibility Reporting 1999*. Netherlands: KPMG International.

Kusku, F., & Frazer, A. Z. (2004). An Empirical Investigation of Corporate Citizenship in Australia and Turkey. *British Journal of Management*, *15*(1), 57–72. doi:10.1111/j.1467-8551.2004.t01-1-00400.x

Lindgreen, A., Swaen, V., & Johnston, W. J. (2008). Corporate Social Responsibility: An Empirical Investigation of U.S. Organizations. *Journal of Business Ethics*, *85*(Suppl. 2), 303–323. doi:10.1007/s10551-008-9738-8

Maignan, I., & Ralston, D. A. (2002). Corporate Social Responsibility in Europe and the US: Insights from businesses' self-presentations. *Journal of International Business Studies*, *33*(3), 497–514. doi:10.1057/palgrave.jibs.8491028

Morsing, M., & Schultz, M. (2006). Corporate Social Responsibility Communication: Stakeholder Information, Response and Involvement Strategies. *Business Ethics (Oxford, England)*, *15*(4), 323–338. doi:10.1111/j.1467-8608.2006.00460.x

Paul, K. (2008). Corporate Sustainability, Citizenship and Social Responsibility Reporting. *Journal of Corporate Citizenship*, *32*(32), 63–78. doi:10.9774/GLEAF.4700.2008.wi.00007

Robertson, D. C. (2009). Corporate Social Responsibility and Different Stages of Economic Development: Singapore, Turkey, & Ethiopia. *Journal of Business Ethics*, *88*(Suppl. 4), 617–633. doi:10.1007/s10551-009-0311-x

Stanwick, P.A. & S.D. Stanwick (2001). The Determinants of Corporate Social Performance: An Empirical Examination. *American Business Review*, 2001, 86-93.

Thompson, P., & Zakariya, Z. (2004). Corporate Social Responsibility Reporting in Malaysia: Progress and Prospects. *Journal of Corporate Citizenship*, *13*(Spring), 125–136. doi:10.9774/GLEAF.4700.2004.sp.000014

Tschopp, D., & Nastanski, M. (2014). The Harmonization and Convergence of Corporate Social Responsibility Reporting Standards. *Journal of Business Ethics*, *125*(1), 147–162. doi:10.1007/s10551-013-1906-9

Visser, W. (2008). *"Corporate Social Responsibility in developing countries", The Oxford Handbook of Corporate Social Responsibility* (pp. 473–499). Oxford University Press.

Wanderley, L. S. O., Rafael, L., Francisca, F., & Sousa Filho, J. M. (2008). CSR Information Disclosure on the Web: A Context-Based Approach Analyzing the Influence of Country of Origin and Industry Sector. *Journal of Business Ethics*, *82*(2), 369–378. doi:10.1007/s10551-008-9892-z

Welford, R. (2004). Corporate Social Responsibility in Europe and Asia: Critical Elements and Best Practice. *Journal of Corporate Citizenship*, *13*(13), 31–47. doi:10.9774/GLEAF.4700.2004.sp.00007

Welford, R. (2005). Corporate Social Responsibility in Europe, North America and Asia: 2004 Survey Results. *Journal of Corporate Citizenship*, *17*(17), 33–52. doi:10.9774/GLEAF.4700.2005.sp.00007

APPENDIX

Table 1. Full list of indicators used in the literature and reporting standard-setting institutions

CSR Dimensions	Academic Reference	CSR Indicators	Practical Reference
Corporate Governance	Chapple and Moon, 2005; Stanwick and Stanwick, 2001; Wanderley, 2007	• Governance Structure and Composition • Governance purpose, values, strategy • Economic, Environmental and Social Performance Evaluation • Role in sustainability reporting • Remuneration and Incentives	GRI G4, ISO 26000, AA1000, FTSE4Good, DJSI
Ethics and Integrity	Wanderley *et al.*, 2007; Esrock and Leichty, 1998	• Corporate values, principles, standards and norms • Internal and external mechanisms for seeking advice on ethical and lawful behavior • Codes of Conduct	GRI G4
Economic	Epstein, 1993; Lindgreen, 2009; Stanwick and Stanwick, 2001	• Economic Performance • Market Presence • Indirect Economic Impacts • Procurement Practices	GRI G4, AA1000, DJSI
Environmental	Lindgreen, 2009; Stanwick and Stanwick, 2001; Welford, 2004, 2005; Chapple and Moon, 2005; Esrock and Leichty, 1998; Gildea, 1995; Epstein, 1993	• Materials • Energy Consumption • Water Conservation • Biodiversity • Gas Emissions • Recycling and Waste Reduction • Products and Services • Compliance • Transport • Supplier Environmental Assessment • Environmental Management Systems & Policies	GRI G4, ISO 14031, ISO 26000, FTSE4Good, DJSI
Social	Lindgreen, 2009; Stanwick and Stanwick, 2001; Paul, 2008; Welford, 2004, 2005; Chapple and Moon, 2005; Wanderley *et al.*, 2007; Esrock and Leichty, 1998; Gildea, 1995; Epstein, 1993	**Labor Practices and Decent Work** • Employment • Labor / Management Relations • Occupational Health and Safety • Training and Education • Diversity and Equal Opportunity • Equal Remuneration for Women and Men • Supplier Assessment for Labor Practices • Labor Practices Grievance Mechanisms **Human Rights** • Investment • Non-discrimination • Freedom of Association and Collective Bargaining • Child Labor • Forced or Compulsory labor • Security Practices • Indigenous Rights • Assessment • Supplier Human Rights Assessment • Human Rights Grievance Mechanisms **Society** • Local Community Involvement and Development • Anti-corruption • Public Policy • Anti-competitive Behavior • Complience • Supplier Assessment for Impacts on Society • Grievance Mechanisms for Impacts on Society **Product Responsibility** • Customer Health and Safety • Product and Service Labeling • Marketing Communications • Consumer Data Protection and Privacy • Compliance	GRI G4, ISO 26000, FTSE4Good, DJSI

Table 2. List of corporations used in the study. 150 Corporations listed in the stock exchange markets of the U.S., South Korea, and Turkey. Classified according to their industries.

The United States	
ACM	Ford Motor Comp. Honeywell Intl. General Motors Comp. Paccar Inc. Harley-Davidson, Inc. BorgWarner Inc. Lear Corporation TRW Automotive LKQ Corporation Gentex Corporation
CETS	AT&T Inc. General Electric Comp. Verizon Communications Emerson Electric Comp. DirecTV American Tower Corp. Corning Incorporated CenturyLink, Inc. Crown Castle Intl. Sprint Nextel Corp.
FB	Coca-Cola Company Pepsico, Inc. McDonald's Corp. Kraft Foods Inc. Starbucks Corp. General Mills, Inc. Yum! Brands, Inc. Kellogg Company ADM H.J. Heinz Company
RS	Wal-Mart Stores, Inc. Home Depot, Inc. CVS Corporation Costco Wholesale Target Corporation Walgreen Co. Lowe's Companies, Inc. TJX Companies, Inc. Kohl's Corporation Macy's Inc
MB	J.P. Morgan Chase & Co. Citigroup Inc. Bank of America American Express Goldman Sachs Group U.S. Bancorp Morgan Stanley BlackRock, Inc. PNC Financial Services Bank of New York Mellon

continued in next column

Table 2. Continued

South Korea	
ACM	Hyundai Motor Hyundai Mobis Kia Motor Hankook Tire Hyundai Wia Mando Nexen Tire Kumho Tire SL Corporation SW Hitech
CETS	Samsung Electronics SK Telecom LG Electronics KT LG Display Samsung Electromech. Samsung SDI LG Uplus Samsung Techwin Daum
FB	CJ Cheil Jedang Orion Lotte Confectionery Hite Jinro Lotte Chilsung Nongshim Samyang Corporation Namyang Dairy Dongwon Industries Binggrae
RS	Lotte Shopping E-Mart Hyundai Dept. Store Shinsegae HiMart Hyundai Greenfood Lotte Midopa Daegu Dept. Store Hanwha Timeworld SaveZone
MB	Shinhan Group KB Financial Group Hana Financial Group Woori Finance IBK Samsung Card Korea Exchange Bank Busan Financial Group Korea Investment Holdings DGB Financial Group

continued on following page

Table 2. Continued

Turkey	
ACM	Ford Otomotiv TOFAŞ Türk Türk Traktör Brisa Bridgestone Otokar Otomotiv Goodyear Lastikleri Bosch Fren Sistemleri Karsan Otomotiv Mutlu Akü Anadolu Isuzu
CETS	Türk Telekom Turkcell İletişim Arçelik A.Ş. Bsh Ev Aletleri Aselsan Elektronik Netaş Telekomünikasyon Vestel Elektronik Demir Döküm Vestel Beyaz Eşya Alcatel Lucent Teletaş
FB	Anadolu Efes Coca-Cola İçecek A.Ş. Kent Gıda Ülker Bisküvi Pınar Süt Tat Konserve T.Tuborg Bira Banvit Kerevitaş Gıda Tukaş Gıda
RS	BİM Birleşik Mağazalar Migros Ticaret Tesco Kipa Carrefoursa Doğuş Otomotiv Bizim Toptan Satış Kiler Alışveriş Boyner Adese Alışveriş Uyum
MB	T.Garanti Bankası Akbank T.İş Bankası Yapı ve Kredi Bankası Türkiye Halk Bankası Finansbank Denizbank Türkiye Vakıflar Bankası Türk Ekonomi Bankası Asya Katılım Bankası

ACM: Automotive & Component Manufacturers,
CETS: Consumer Electronics & Telecommunication Services,
FB: Food & Beverages,
RS: Retail Stores,
MB: Major Banks

Chapter 5
Internet-Based Social Reporting in Emerging Economies:
Insights from Public Banks in Egypt and the UAE

Mohamed Nagy Osman
Benha University, Egypt

ABSTRACT

This chapter examines how public banks operating in Egypt and the UAE respond to stakeholders' needs. It uses content analysis to explore the volume, nature, and quality of social information presented on the websites of these banks and the way in which these banks use web technology to report such information. The results indicate that public banks in both countries made more disclosures about corporate social responsibility (CSR) and community issues. Nevertheless, they lag behind stakeholders' expectations in regard to information about employees and cultural issues. Furthermore, the UAE banks tend to offer better stakeholders access to social information than Egyptian banks. However, both have a long way to go in better facilitating interaction with stakeholders. There is evidence to suggest that social reporting by public banks' in both countries is still below the expectations of the Muslim and global communities.

INTRODUCTION

Across the world, organizations have shown growing awareness of social responsibility. As a result, academic interest in the voluntary reporting of social responsibility information has greatly increased. Corporate Social Responsibility (CSR) has been defined as "the process of communicating the social and environmental effects of an organization's economic action to a particular interest grouping within society and to society at large" (Gray et al., 1987, p.9). It is noticeable that most of the studies on social reporting are dominated by studies from Anglo-Saxon and Western countries and by international comparative studies that focus on interpreting the differences and similarities of reporting practices in these countries (Fifka, 2013). It is not fair to generalize the findings of these studies to emerging economies, because their development is different, as well as cultural differences affect the disclosure practices in

DOI: 10.4018/978-1-5225-0720-8.ch005

general, and social reporting in particular (Mathews, 1993; Perper & Mathews, 1990). At the same time, in the era of globalization, the internet has shown itself to be important in the 21th century business communication revolution. During this time, internet access started to increase in developing countries and in the Arab region in particular. Most of Arab Spring revolutions in Egypt and other Arab countries used internet to help countries to communicate with each other. In Egypt, the revolution of 25th January, 2011 was called the "Facebook Revolution" (West, 2013). Meanwhile, the use of the internet as a communication medium has increased day by day, particularly in less developed countries. The main advantages of the internet are these: it is accessible 24 hours a day; its search option help users to highlight relevant documents; its information can be promptly updated; it can provide presentation options (text graphs, 3D simulations, for example); it is relatively undamaging to the environment, and its interactive feedback is easy via e-mails, feedback forms and video conferencing (Adams and Frost, 2004). These advantages reflect changes in the way that companies communicate with different stakeholders (Rikhardsson Et al., 2002). With this in mind, this research investigates how public banks in the Arab Middle East Countries (AMEC) respond to stakeholders' needs by exploring the volume, nature, and quality of the social information represented on the websites of public banks operating in Egypt and the UAE. It also explores the way in which these banks use web technology to report such information. This study contributes to the literature in two ways: it is the first study to explore the social reporting on the web in Arab Middle East Countries (AMEC), and the disclosure index adopted in this research is based on the literature and cultural/Islamic issues presented on the websites such as quard hassan, and zakat fund. The reminder of the chapter is organized as follows. The next section reviews the literature and socio-economic context of Egypt and the UAE. The results are then reported, and the final sections present discussions and conclusions.

LITERATURE REVIEW

Different sectors in the business field have various social responsibility priorities (Branco & Rodrigues, 2008). It is argued that "customer oriented "sectors are seen as having a lower direct environmental impact (Jeucken & Buma, 1999). They offer goods and services that are considered indispensable by the general public (Miles, 1987); this is evidenced from a wide array of stakeholder groups who have direct and indirect stakes in the business activities. This resembles the case in banking industries whose stakeholders are varied and need a variety of social responsibility reporting (Branco & Rodrigues, 2008).

The banking sector is considered to have high public visibility, with activities and policies closely linked to the public interest (Miles, 1987). In addition, the banking sector has through its lending decisions a great impact on social and environmental strategies. Simpson and Khoers (2002) note that banks bear legal and social responsibility in that they make loans to companies that pollute or produce unsafe products. Only a relatively small number of studies address the social reporting by financial institutions (Hamid, 2004; Douglas, 2004; Branco & Rodrigues, 2006; Day & Roberts, 2009; Menassa, 2010; Khan et al., 2011).

Hamid (2004) investigated the social reporting practices in the banking and finance companies' annual reports and revealed that reporting on product/service predominates over other topics. Further, there is a positive association between a bank's size, listing status, and age and its level of social disclosure. Douglas et al. (2004) examined the social responsibility reporting on websites and annual reports of six

Irish banks and four international banks. The results suggest that Irish banks disclose more information than international ones. The most frequently reported information concerns corporate governance and human resources. Reporting is more common on websites than in annual reports.

Branco and Rodrigues (2006) considered social responsibility reporting by Portuguese banks in annual reports and on the web, comparing 2004 with 2003. The findings emphasize that banks with high visibility among consumers show great interest in developing their corporate image through social reporting. Moreover, the results support the use of legitimacy theory as an interpretation of social disclosure by Portuguese banks.

Day and Woodward (2009) attempted to explore the extent to which Corporate Social Responsibility (CSR) reporting in the paper reports of the UK's financial sector complies with the CSR guidelines for this sector. Content analysis is applied to annual reports and stand-alone reports of the financial sector. It is observed that the level of disclosures is low across the sector, with the possibility that the level of compliance is related to size.

Khan (2010) investigated the frequencies of sustainability reporting by major commercial banks in Bangladesh in comparison with the global sustainability reporting indicators manifested in the GRI framework. This research used the content analysis method on 2008/2009 annual reports in five broad areas (1). The findings showed that information on society was the most extensively disclosed, followed by disclosures on labor practices and environmental matters. Disclosures about product responsibility and human rights were scarce.

In the Arab Middle East Countries (AMEC), Menassa (2010) highlighted the type, quality and extent of social disclosures by Lebanese banks and pointed out the association between this reporting and the bank's size, financial performance, age, international exposure, and ownership. This research used content analysis to examine 24 annual reports from Lebanese commercial banks. The findings showed the prevalence of disclosures about human resources, products & customer concerns. Environmental reporting was comparatively low. Moreover, there was a positive relationship between social reporting and size and financial performance variables.

Only two studies included the banking sector in their sample (Kamla, 2007; Abu-Baker & Nasr, 2000). Abu-Baker and Nasr (2000) revealed that all banking and insurance companies reported human resources and community involvement information. Kamla (2007), however, discovered that most banking institutions in most economically significant Arab countries took a "repressive/counter radical" position in their social reporting. Meanwhile, Belal and Momin, (2009) and Belal et al. (2013) have called for more research about social and environmental issues in emerging economies, highlighting the current status of social disclosure on the public banks websites in Egypt and the UAE. The next section explores the socio-economic context of these two countries.

The Socio-Economic Context

Egypt and the UAE are both Arab Middle East Countries (AMEC), and were, at one time, British colonies. Although they achieved independence, they are still affected by British models and laws. For instance, the company law in Egypt, its disclosure and financial reporting standards on British regulations (Samuels & Oliga, 1982). The same applies to the UAE, where the Accountants and Auditors Association asked the profession to follow international accounting standards, because no national accounting standards exist (IFRS UAE, 2015).

The Egyptian economy began to follow liberal and privatization programs in 1970 (Mckee et al., 1999). Similarly, the UAE economy started to flourish in 1970s, thanks to its oil and gas exports. UAE oil reserves are considered to be the seventh largest in the world (CIA, 2015). Although the UAE economy is the largest diversified economy among the Gulf Cooperation Council (GCC) countries, it still relies on oil and gas exports (Hvidt, 2013) (2). The Egyptian economy, however, is more diversified, with agricultural exports, income from Suez Canal, tourism, taxes, oil exports and remittances from Egyptian workers in the Arab gulf countries to depend on. Nevertheless, the state of the economy led, in part to revolution of 25th January 2011 (State Information Service, 2015).

Both countries have the same language (Arabic) and the same religion (Islam), which is the faith of more than 90 percent of both populations. Islamic Shar'ia is the main basis of legislation in both countries. In Western countries, religion is considered a private issue, but in Muslim countries, Islam is reflected in all aspects of life (Rice, 1999). The impact of Islam on everyday business activities is articulated in the *Qur'an* and *Sunnah*. Islam provides guidance on the ethical values that should be adopted when engaging in business (Graafland et al., 2006). Islamic values are considered part of (CSR). For instance, freedom and justice are the core values of both business life and Islam. The target of Islam is to build a socio-economic order founded on justice that takes economic activities into account (Ebrahim & Joo, 2001). Islam depends on a clear system of law, which expects Muslim to be fair among themselves and with others (Williams & Zinkin, 2010). Social responsibility in Islam stresses brotherhood/sisterhood and equality. The concept of unity (*Tawhid*) to God implies that God is the only creator of the world and human beings are equal partners (Rice, 1999). Furthermore, underlying the concept of the *Khalafah* (vicegerent), the individual is seen as a trustee of the earth on behalf of God. Every individual is accountable to God for their actions and is happy to take up his great responsibility in a covenant with God (Hamid et al., 1993; Lewis, 2001). Resources should be disposed of in such a way as to protect human life. Nobody is allowed to destroy God-given resources. The idea of trusteeship is similar to the concept of sustainable development in Western economies (Rice, 1999).

One of the main pillars of Islam and one that has a close affinity to social responsibility is the payment of zakat (obligatory charity). Zakat is considered to be a redistribution of wealth. In any Islamic community, zakat is collected from Muslim businesses and individuals and paid to poor people to further the welfare of the community (Lewis, 2001; Rice, 1999). Zakat is the most common practice of organizations and individuals in Egypt and the UAE. Various companies donate generous funds to a range of charities. Corporate philanthropy is the prevalent conduct of CSR in Egypt, dating back to the 11th century and known as "awqaf" (Osman, 2013).

In addition to protecting human lives, Islam encourages the prohibition of specific kinds of business activities such as trading in alcohol, tobacco, and armaments, and gambling. Moreover, Islam prohibits usury or interest. Most Islamic scholars agree that the prohibition of interest in Islam is based on enhancing the moral, social and economic well-being of society. Interest depends on creating profit without work and involves no sharing of risk (Al-Qaradawi, 1985).

Islam is more concerned than other faiths to safeguarding the environment. Man is considered the steward of the natural environment, playing the role of Allah's vicegerent, and man's responsibility is to protect the environment. Individual is responsible to Allah for their stewardship and will be punished if they abuse this role (Williams & Zinkin, 2010). The Prophet Muhamed emphasized this interest in protecting the environment by creating special areas that were inviolable, known as haram. *Haram* areas were "often drawn up around wells and springs to protect the water table from depletion" (Ziaudin, 1990 cited in Willaims & Zinkin, 2010, p. 528). In the same way, environmental protection is given explicit attention in Islamic laws and Shar'ia (Kamla et al., 2006). Finally, Williams and Zinkin (2010) suggested that Islamic teaching principles have affinity with the ten principles of the UN global compact, but exceeds its requirements in different ways. Firstly, they seem to be wider in scope. Secondly, they clearly define what *haram* is. And Thirdly, Islam has an obvious obligation mechanism in *Shar'ia* and in society's obligations.

Egypt and the UAE, like most countries of the Arab world, have high percentages of young people in their demography. In the UAE, about 45 percent of the national population is under 15 years of age and alarm has been expressed about high unemployment among UAE nationals. The UAE government has reacted to this prospect by issuing an "emiratization" program for all kinds of businesses working in the UAE (Katsioloudes & Brodtkorb, 2007). The case is worse in Egypt. Here, the percentage of nationals of working age (15 to 64) has increased since 1980, and is expected to reach 66.9 percent by 2040. Unemployment is considered the main challenge for the Egyptian economy. In 2010/201, unemployment reached 12.4 percent (24 percent for women). Almost 60 percent of the unemployment in Egypt comprises of new entrants to the labor force (UNDP, 2010; 2012).

Most Arab countries suffer from social and environmental problems such as population pressures, demographics pressures, desertification, water scarcity and pollution, climate change, unemployment, poverty, legal restrictions, and violence against women, all of which represents threats to human security (UNDP, 2009). Hence, it is interesting to explore how public banks respond to stakeholders' needs in Egypt and the UAE by examining the social reporting practices of these banks on their websites. The next section explains the research methods used in this study.

RESEARCH METHODS

This research is based on the websites of public banks operating in two Arab Middle East Countries (AMEC). This study focuses on websites rather than paper reports, as websites enable more information to be communicated to different stakeholders at less expense and more promptly, with good interactive feature (Branco & Rodrigues, 2006). Esrock and Leichty (2000) suggest that "unlike traditional mass channels, a single web can have multiple sections, each targeted to a different audience" (p.328).

This research focuses on Egypt and the UAE, two countries with the same cultural, social and environmental problems. Furthermore, the governments of both countries use the public banks to implement their policies. The initial sample of this study was obtained from the central bank website of Egypt and the UAE. Egypt has only five national banks, while the UAE has 23. The five UAE banks that disclose the most about social issues on their websites were selected for the purpose of this research. The totals of 10 banks are included in Table 1. The websites were examined during June 2015 to produce a picture of the current status of the banks' social reporting practices.

Content analysis was used to examine the volume and quality of social information reported on their websites and the way in which the banks use the websites' functions to disclose this information. This same method has been used in several social reporting studies (e.g. Guthrie and Parker, 1990; Roberts, 1991; Adams et al., 1995; Adams et al., 1998; Campbell, 2000). The technique involves codifying the detail of a text/piece of writing into various groups (or categories) according to specific criteria (Weber, 1998). In addition, this method supports the "structuring of essentially unstructured documents in order to highlight matters that many stakeholders will not have necessarily been so consciously aware of "(Hines, 1998 cited in Unerman, 1999, p.311). A number of studies have used content analysis to explore social

Table 1. List of public banks investigated in the UAE and Egypt

The UAE	Egypt
National Bank of Abu Dhabi	National Bank of Egypt
Abu Dhabi Commercial Bank	Bank Misr
Al Mashreq Bank	Banque Du Caire
Dubai Islamic Bank	Principal Bank for Development and Agricultural Credit
Emirates NBD Bank	Egyptian Arab Land Bank

reporting on websites (Williams & Pei, 1999; Maignan & Ralston, 2002; Patten, 2002; Cooper, 2003; Campbell & Beck, 2004; Douglas et al., 2004). The critical component of content analysis is a disclosure index that develops major categories and divides these into sub-categories. This disclosure index can be weighted or un-weighted (Khan, 2010). This research uses the un-weighted disclosure index, which means that if the item exists, it will be valued at 1; if not, it will be defined as 0.

The main categories and sub-categories of this disclosure index are adopted from the literature (Aribi & Gao, 2010; Belal, 2001; Kamal, 2007) with an additional category called cultural which is chosen to reflect the Arab/Islamic context. The main categories represented in this research are employee, community, cultural, and CSR. The sub-categories under each main category are highlighted in Table 2. The sub-categories under the main category "cultural" are adopted from pilot research on the websites of public banks in the two countries. The sub-categories under this main category comprise issues that represent the cultural/Islamic context of two countries; such as adopting government requirements/vision, having a *Shar'ia* Supervisory Board (SSB), adhering to *Shar'ia*, promoting Arab/Islamic culture, and the zakat fund.

The nature of reporting in this study has been analyzed by allocating information to the following categories: qualitative, quantitative, monetary, pictures, videos, and charts/graphs/tables. Various studies have used this approach to describe the nature of disclosures (Williams & Pei, 1999; Zeghal & Ahmed, 1990). To these, the researcher added video to better reflect nature of the web.

Similarly, the quality of disclosure was assessed by classifying information into good, bad, and neutral news. This research also investigated how banks used their website to present social information through examining the forms of interaction and navigation and information access tools. The investigation index was adopted from the literature (Rikhardsson et al., 2002) and observation of the options available on the websites. The following section represents the findings of this research.

FINDINGS

This section presents the results of the content analysis. Descriptions of social reporting practices are presented, with reflections on these disclosures. Table 2 sheds light on the level of reporting under each category. The results demonstrate that all banks in the sample, except for one bank in Egypt reported on social issues. As indicated in Table 2, the level of social reporting by the UAE banks is greater than those in Egypt in four categories of disclosure. The following sub-sections deal with each category in more details.

Table 2. Level of Social Reporting of Public Banks in Egypt and the UAE

	The UAE		Egypt	
	No. of Banks Disclosures	%	No. of Banks Disclosures	%
CSR				
Commitment to Social Responsibility/ Sustainability	**5**	%100	**3**	60%
Awards	**5**	%100	**0**	0%
Employees				
Training and development	5	%100	2	40%
Employee consultation	1	%20	2	40%
Employee localization	5	%100	0	0%
Equal opportunities	2	%40	1	20%
Employee benefits	2	%40	0	0%
Workforce environment	2	%40	1	20%
Appreciation and thanks	0	%0	0	0%
Others	2	%40	0	0%
Community				
Donations	5	%100	4	80%
Sponsorship	5	%100	3	60%
Customer relations	3	%60	1	20%
Others	2	%40	2	40%
Cultural				
Islamic values	1	%20	0	0%
Quard hassan	1	%20	0	0%
Adapting to government requirements/ vision	2	%40	4	80%
SSBR	4	%80	1	20%
Adherence to Shar'ia	4	%80	1	20%
Promoting Arab/Islamic Culture	5	%100	4	80%
Zakat fund	2	%40	1	20%

Corporate Social Responsibility (CSR)

This section touches on the issues that are related to social information, such as commitment to corporate social responsibility (CSR)/sustainability and awards. Table 2 indicates that banks in the UAE disclose more information about these issues than those in Egypt. All banks in the UAE show commitment to CSR, while only three banks in Egypt disclose information about it. The Al Mashreq Bank emphasizes that CSR is a kind of corporate self-regulation integrated into a business model and comments that "Mashreq Bank has been actively involved in many activities that give back to the community; it operates across all its regional offices of the UAE, Qatar, Bahrain, Kuwait, and Egypt. The Mashreq Bank prides itself in demonstrating socially responsible actions which positively impact the community" (Mashreq Bank website, 2015). This bank defines its CSR philosophy as "the integration of stakeholders and customer, society, community and environment into a company's business operations". Through this definition, the bank shows its commitment to stakeholders and the community. The Banque Misr also states that "Corporate Social Responsibility at Banque Misr is an integral part of how we operate, and acts well as a key to our success in maintaining sustainability. Through responsible business, we aim to create value for society and strive for economic achievement" (Banque Misr website, 2015).

In the same vein, Islamic banks according to *Shar'ia* are committed to CSR/sustainability. The Dubai Islamic Bank observes that since the concept of giving back to the community is an essential constituent of the Islamic religion, "CSR is considered an essential part of the bank's philosophy and principles" (Dubai Islamic Bank Website, 2015). This bank discloses its commitment to CSR on its website to show its compliance with *Shar'ia* and Islamic principles. Again, although public banks in Egypt disclose nothing about CSR awards, all public banks operating in the UAE claim some awards for their CSR. For instance, the National Bank of Abu Dhabi has been awarded the Dubai Chamber CSR mark and ranked top bank on the S&P Hawkamah ESG Pan-Arab Index. Moreover, Emirates NBD bank has been named the best bank in the UAE for philanthropy and social impact. In this category, all news is neutral, with the kind of commitments and awards attesting to its quality. Furthermore, the nature of information under this category is qualitative and includes some pictures. The next section discusses the category of employees.

Employees

The results of this research show that benefits conferred by companies in less developed countries are more likely to be in this category (Andrew et al., 1989). Table 2 makes it clear that banks in the UAE disclose more information about employees than banks in Egypt. Disclosing banks tended to focus mainly on training, development, and employee localization. There are few disclosures about equal opportunities or workplace conditions. Moreover, little is said about appreciation and thanks by either country. The highest number of banks (five banks in the UAE and two banks in Egypt) reporting in the employee category in both countries were found in the sub-category of training and development. Banks in the UAE provided some sort of quantitative information regarding training delivery days, number of employees trained, number of employees trained on anti-money laundering and, number of employees trained on sustainability awareness e-learning programs. There are also some charts about average length of training per employee category (in hours), and average length of training per gender. Qualitative information is available about the kinds of courses available. Only one bank used a video by one of its employees expressing his happiness about the available training and development facilities offered by his bank and encouraging young Emirati people to apply for jobs there. Typical examples of disclosures are elaborated below.

The National Bank of Abu Dhabi mentions the following on its website:

We are committed to providing support for learning, education and growth by our people. As such we continue to invest significant resources in our learning and development activities.

NBAD has created a structured career plan to help every employee reach his or her potential. The NBAD Academy delivers high-level financial education and cutting-edge training and skills development to support the Bank's 'learning culture' and its long-term business success as well as individual career aspirations (National Bank of Abu Dhabi website, 2015).

Egyptian banks stressed in a qualitative statement that they give great importance to the training and development of their staff. At the same time, all banks in the UAE comment on "employee localization". For instance, Dubai Islamic Bank highlights the following in a clear box on its website:

- To counsel, development, awareness and retention of UAE Nationals within and outside the organization which will help in driving UAE Nationals to the highest performance.
- To recruit, develop, reward and retain excellent UAE staff from various development programs.
- Proactively interact with external institutes and government bodies to attract UAE Nationals to DIB.
- Identify the training and development needs of UAE National employees by proactively interacting with them and their respective managers to ensure that their training needs are fulfilled.
- Establish an effective mentoring system to guide UAE National employees in their careers and to educate them in the various opportunities for learning and self-development (Dubai Islamic bank website, 2015).

The UAE banks, knowing that only 20 percent of the population in the UAE is made up of citizens (Emaratalyoum, 2015), disclose more information about training & development and employee localization. This gives importance to the issue of educating and nationalizing working people (Mckee et al., 1999). So, banks strive to portray themselves as patriotic by offering more training courses to the young citizens encouraging them to work in the banking sector with a view to taking over from foreign experts. This is, however, not the case in the Egyptian banking sector as most members of the workforce are Egyptians and there is not the same need for localization. Additionally, the quality of information reported under "Employee" category is good and neutral, with an absence of bad news.

Only two banks are found to offer employee financial benefits in a monetary form that would encourage talented candidates to apply for a job. The UAE banks report other issues such as the percentage of women in the workforce and the child labor. In fact, all disclosures under the "employee" main heading are good news. The following section discusses community issues.

Community

As highlighted in Table 2, all banks in the UAE mention community issues, but only four banks in Egypt do the same. The predominant disclosures under this category are around types and amounts of donations, and sponsorship of health and educational events. In Egypt, most of these go to healthcare, education and development projects. The National Bank of Egypt commented on its website that:

NBE continued to boost its role in social responsibility by making donations to the amount of EGP 150 MM. in FY 2013/14, mainly directed to health care, education, combating poverty and slums development. Accordingly, NBE's donations over the last five years totaled EGP 480 MM (National Bank of Egypt website, 2015).

In the UAE, banks go beyond donations by participating in fund raising for various events. This is evident in the Abu Dhabi Commercial Bank's website; the bank partners with and raises funds for Al Jalila Education through various initiatives. In addition, the NBD Emirates Bank seeks to enhance financial literacy by sponsoring various educational programs such as Folosy. Throughout the analysis, it was observed that banks in both countries put more emphasis on donations for education. This is due to the high illiteracy rates, high growth rate, and the high percentage of young people in the population (UNDP, 2009).Therefore, education is considered integral to the development of society in both countries.

Since banking is a service industry, it can be expected to take more interest in customers. Three banks in the UAE discuss relations with customers. Banks in the UAE stress that they are keen to integrate with stakeholders (including customers) and to add value for them. The Mahreq Bank emphasized on its website that:

Mashreq's Corporate Social Responsibility philosophy is "the integration of stakeholders' and customer's society, community and environment into a company's business operations" (Mashreq Bank website, 2015).

The National Bank of Abu Dhabi conducted a customer satisfaction survey in 2014, finding that it achieved the international average benchmark for customer satisfaction in relation to its line of business. Furthermore, the bank is keen to be responsive to its customers:

Our customers are at the heart of everything we do. We recognize that, at its very core, banking has and continue to be a people-to-people business (National Bank of Abu Dhabi website, 2015).

In Egypt, only the Bank Misr has shown an interest in customer service and getting feedback from customers to enhance its performance. It is apparent that banks in the UAE treat customer relations more carefully than banks in Egypt, and they hire foreign experts to help them increase customer satisfaction. Other issues that are related to the community but not highlighted in the above sub-categories are as follows: certain banks in both countries collaborate with NGOs to facilitate the collection of donations and disclose the account numbers for donations. Banks show commitment to providing financial services to low income customers in both countries.

In relation to the quality, of information reported in the community category, all the news is good. The nature of the information reported under this heading is monetary representing the amounts of donations, as well as qualitative and quantitative information describing the nature of customer relations, community involvement, donations and sponsorship. Additionally, the National Bank of Abu Dhabi uses charts on its website to illustrate the increase in donations from 2013 to 2014, and most of the UAE banks use pictures in the community section of their website to show donations to poor communities in Africa and to Syrian refugees, along with photographs of employees and customers. The following section discuses cultural issues.

Cultural

The cultural category relates to the social characteristics of Egyptian and UAE bank's websites that are not highlighted in other categories. It can be seen that five banks in the UAE and four in Egypt mention these issues. Sub-categories are: Islamic values, qurad hassan, Adapting to government requirements/ vision, Shar'ia Supervisory Board Report (SSBR), Adherence to Shar'ia, Promoting Arab/Islamic culture, and zakat fund. All banks in the UAE and Egypt promote Arab/Islamic culture by sponsoring various cultural initiatives and offering Islamic products and services that satisfy the needs of the Islamic community in their countries. For example, the Abu Dhabi Commercial Bank sponsors the "Sheik Zayed Heritage Festival" with AED 1.5m and honors the rulers of seven Emirates. The bank also "attracts and develops UAE national talent through numerous initiatives including targeted recruiting through Washington career fairs and active contribution to the Ministry of Presidential Affairs"Absher initiative" (Abu Dhabi Commercial Bank website, 2015).

In Egypt, the National Bank of Egypt sponsors other activities that celebrate Arabic culture such as the annual competition of Arabic language teachers held by the Ministry of Education, and grants "awards to winners and cultural festivals organized by the education, scientific research and youth committee in the Shoura council" (National Bank of Egypt, 2015). Banks in both countries also promote Islamic culture by offering Islamic products/services.

Four banks in the UAE (but only one in Egypt) provide a Shar'ia Supervisory Board Report (SSBR), with the names and CVs of the members. These banks of course adhere to Shar'ia. Moreover, the Abu Dhabi Commercial Bank and Dubai Islamic Bank display on their websites a stamp to show that all their Islamic products and services are approved by *Fatwa* and Shar'ia Supervisory Board (SSB) members. In the same way, the findings highlight that one bank in Egypt and two banks in the UAE have zakat funds, to support the Islamic communities in both countries. It is noted that no details are disclosed about the resources, amounts spent, or activities of these funds.

Surprisingly, no disclosure is made about quard hassan in Egypt and only one bank (the Dubai Islamic Bank) in the UAE comments on its website that the bank offers quard hassan as recommended in Islamic Jurisprudence to help customers solve their financial problems. The bank confirms that it makes no financial gains from this service, which promotes Islamic social justice by making the lives of Muslims easier. Furthermore, this bank mentions on the resources and amount of its fund, and who may be eligible to share it, offering a hyperlink. Islamic values seem not to be presented by the banks in either country, apart from the Mashreq Bank in the UAE which asserts on its website "we work closely with the Shar'ia Supervisory Board, in-house governance department and external auditors to ensure all our transactions are carried out in strict compliance with Islamic financial principles". The same bank stresses on its website that it treats customers and colleagues with fairness, respect, and trust (Mashreq Bank website, 2015). The bank makes this claim about being committed to Islamic values to portray itself as a good member of the Islamic community.

The most important sub-category in the cultural dimension is that "adapting to the government's vision/requirements". The results of the survey indicate that only two banks in the UAE (the National Bank of Abu Dhabi and the Abu Dhabi Commercial Bank), but all banks in Egypt are committed to working according to the government vision/strategy because they are public banks. For instance, the National Bank of Abu Dhabi specifies that it sustains Abu Dhabi's economic vision:

We continue to finance transportation, infrastructure and power projects in the region, which supports the Abu Dhabi Economic vision 2030 (The Nation Bank of Abu Dhabi website, 2015).

Furthermore, the National Bank of Egypt supports the Egyptian economy, stating:

NBE has further provided a set of a distinguished finance schemes that meet the needs of key economic sectors. The total retail loan portfolio reached EGP 26.2 bn as at the end of June 2014.

NBE also assumed an active role in funding key strategic economic sectors including oil, power, electricity, gas, telecommunications, air transportation, tourism and contracting. Total large corporate loan portfolio surged 3% to reach EGP 85 bn as at June 2013 (National Bank of Egypt website, 2015).

It is apparent from the evidence that almost all banks in Egypt claim some activity in this sub-category to present themselves favorably to the Egyptian government/community. These banks have supported the national economy in many areas since the revolution of 25th January, 2011. All the information disclosed under the cultural heading is good news. The prevalent nature of the information reported is qualitative on websites depicting cultural activities, with some monetary information about the zakat fund, quard hassan, and the way in which banks support the national economy. The public banks in the UAE such as the Mashreq Bank and the Dubai Islamic Bank go a step further by publishing pictures of SSB members. The next section reports about how banks in both countries use the internet to disclose social information.

How Banks use the Internet to Present the Social Information

On the bank websites, it takes two to three hyperlink clicks from the homepage to access the social information sections. In the UAE, three banks have clear boxes on the homepage (for sustainability, community service, and CSR). For Egyptian public banks, in contrast, the link is made through the "About Us" box. Thus, social information is comparatively easy to find on the banks' webpages.

Table 3 demonstrates that banks in the UAE and Egypt use a "specific navigation panel" and only banks in the UAE use "hyperlinks" to access the contents of the social information. Surprisingly, only one bank in the UAE uses a "specific search engine", "links to external sites from the social information section", and "printer friendly formats for social information". Egyptian public banks do not use these navigation options at all. Only one bank, Banque Du Caire, uses the frequently asked questions "FAQ" for social section. It seems from the analysis that the public banks in the UAE use the navigation tools far better than the public banks in Egypt do, having more foreign technological experts and global stakeholders.

Table 3. Navigation and information access tools by banks in Egypt and the UAE

	The UAE		Egypt	
	No. of Banks Disclose	**%**	**No. of Banks Disclose**	**%**
Specific navigation panel	5	100%	3	60%
Specific search engine	1	20%	0	0%
Hyperlinks to the social information section	4	80%	0	0%
Links to external sites from social section	1	20%	0	0%
Printer friendly formats for social sections	1	20%	0	0%
FAQ for social information section	0	0%	1	20%

Regarding the availability and format of the social information published on the websites of public banks in the UAE and Egypt, Table 4 shows that three public banks in the UAE issue sustainability reports with social information in PDF format. Banks in the UAE use their foreign expertise to adapt to international guidelines and satisfy their international stakeholders. No bank in Egypt uses the PDF format for its social information. All banks in both countries use HTML to report their social information. Only, one bank in the UAE uses multimedia.

Disclosure on the web offers the potential to interact with the stakeholders who access information. Table 5 shows that the most common way of interacting with stakeholders through websites is by e-mail comments and by providing the contact addresses of the officers responsible for social reporting. Unfortunately, no bank in either country provides the contact addresses of such officers, or a mailing list. Nevertheless, most of banks in both countries offer e-mails addresses, via which stakeholders can make comments in the "Contact Us" section. All banks also provide additional Arabic websites to facilitate communication with Arab communities all over the world.

Table 4. The availability and format of social information

	The UAE		Egypt	
	No. of Banks Disclose	**%**	**No. of Banks Disclose**	**%**
All Social Information provided in PDF format	3	60%	0	0%
All Social Information provided in HTML	5	100%	4	80%
All social information provided in other formats	1	20%	0	0%

Table 5. Interaction with stakeholders

Forms of Interaction	**The UAE**		**Egypt**	
	No. of Banks disclose	**%**	**No. of banks disclose**	**%**
Provision of contact addresses of relevant officers	0	0%	0	0%
Provision of option to make comments by e-mail	5	100%	4	80%
Provision of a discussion forum	1	20%	0	0%
Availability of a mailing list	0	0%	0	0%
Availability of Arabic website	5	100%	5	100%

DISCUSSION

This research investigated how public banks in the UAE and Egypt respond to stakeholders' needs. It explored the volume, quality and quantity of social information disclosed on the websites of these banks. This study used a disclosure index that employs CSR, employee, community, cultural as categories to examine the above topic.

In the CSR category, the results show that all UAE banks disclose their commitment to social responsibility, while only three Egyptian banks do so. This is consistent with Kamla's finding (2007), that 51 percent of the Arab companies investigated claimed their commitment to social responsibility. Furthermore, all UAE banks stated that they had received various awards, whereas no Egyptian bank mentioned them. It can be noted that all UAE banks seek to demonstrate their public spiritedness in the eyes of regional and global stakeholders by mentioning these issues. Egyptian banks, however, lack this method of impressing stakeholders as they do not have Western expertise to help them in developing their reporting strategies.

In the employee main category, the findings indicate that the UAE and Egyptian banks made most disclosures in the sub-category of training and development because they were keen to attract talented candidates. Therefore, they portray themselves as benevolent employers to their prospective employees and stakeholders. Additionally, only the UAE banks write anything about employee localization, since it is part of the UAE vision to replace foreign workers with UAE recruits as a step towards nationalization. This is not the case in Egypt. These results recall a survey of annual reports from 2005, which highlighted that 53 percent of Arab companies disclosed information about "training and education" and 40 percent of companies from the same sample disclosed information about nationalization of employees (Kamla, 2007). Conversely, disclosures about equal opportunities, the workforce environment, and employee consultations are few in number. This is similar to the findings from Lebanese banks (Menessa, 2010). It is perhaps surprising that there is silence from both countries about appreciation and thanks, but this may be these being sensitive issues in Arab communities (Dahawy et al., 2002). The study indicates that public banks in both countries fail to meet the needs of regional and global stakeholders in various employee categories.

In the community main category, the findings show that most public banks in the UAE and Egypt give considerable attention to donations and the sponsorship of health and educational events. This is similar to the situation of Lebanese commercial banks, 29% of Lebanese banks surveyed published details of sponsorship, education, health and charity events (Menessa, 2010). These activities are needed to remedy the high rates of illiteracy, demographic growth, and the high proportion of unemployment of young people in the Arab population (UNDP, 2009). UAE and Egyptian public banks give prominence to these issues on their websites to show their merit to Arab communities and to satisfy the needs of regional stakeholders by supporting the education and health of Arab people.

In the cultural main category, it is clear from the analysis that UAE banks disclose more information than Egyptian ones, in particular in SSBR, Adherence to *Shar'ai*, promoting Arab /Islamic culture. The reason is that, Islam is more institutionalized in the UAE and its rulers adhere keenly to Islamic teachings. Although Egypt is a Muslim country, its dominant ideology is not Islam. It is a secular state with a mix of feudalism, capitalism, and socialism (Rice, 1999). It is noticeable, moreover, that there are few disclosures about Islamic values, quard hassan, and zakat fund. This contradicts with Kamla's results (2007), in which 53 percent of Arab companies gave information about cultural issues. This may be due to the "dual identity" (3) of all Muslim countries including Egypt and the UAE. Furthermore, Islamic cultural values in some Muslim countries are suppressed by Western values, institutions, and practices

(Rice, 1999). Thus, banks in both countries, Egypt in particular, lag behind the needs of stakeholders on some cultural issues. It is interesting to see Egyptian public banks stating their commitment to adapting to the government's vision in particular after the 25th January 2011 revolution, as a way of showing patriotism by supporting the government in carrying out its mission in the eyes of both global and local stakeholders. It is no wonder that all news is good or neutral and no bad news is published, since all Arab communities have a high level of secrecy (e.g. Dahawy et al., 2002). All banks use quantitative, qualitative, monetary, pictures, charts and graphs to present social information. Only two UAE banks use video to report the same information, which may be because they have Western expertise to help them use these functions.

In the web reporting section, it is obvious that UAE banks offer a better platform than Egyptian banks for stakeholders to access social information. The UAE banks provide clear boxes on the homepage as British banks do, with at least two options on the homepage to access social and environmental information (Coupland, 2006). The UAE banks have this advantage thanks to Western technology and to the fact that most of workforce and board of directors in UAE banks are foreigners from the West. Thus, the practices of UAE banks feel the impact of Western styles of communication. What is more, UAE banks have better navigation and information access tools than Egyptian ones and seek to increase the accessibility of social information for global/regional stakeholders by providing a specific navigation panel, and hyperlinks to the social information section. In the same way, UAE banks provide social information not only in PDF format but also in HTML and other formats in their effort to satisfy the needs of stakeholders. These results are close to the practices of Global Fortune 500 companies (Rikhardsson et al., 2002).

The most important function of the web is to facilitate interaction with stakeholders. The results reveal that banks in both countries provide only e-mail as a channel for comments but they do provide Arabic websites to give a voice to Arab/Islamic communities. These results contrast with the practices of Global Fortune companies, which provide discussion forms, the contact addresses of relevant officers, and a mailing list to facilitate interaction with various stakeholders (Rikhardsson et al., 2002). Table 6 summarizes the similarities and differences between the UAE and Egyptian banks.

Table 6. Similarities and differences between banks in Egypt and UAE in relation to social reporting

Dimensions of Comparison	Social Reporting	
	Similarities	**Differences**
CSR	• Commitment to social responsibility/sustainability.	• Only UAE banks make disclosure about awards.
Employees	• Focus on training and development. • No/few disclosure about workplace conditions, equal opportunities, appreciation and thanks.	• Only UAE banks disclose anything about localization.
Community	• Bank in both countries have the same attitudes in all community sub-categories.	
Cultural	• Banks in both countries promote Arab/Islamic culture. • Few/no disclosures about Islamic values, Quard Hassan, zakat fund.	• UAE banks have more disclosure about SSBR, and adherence to Shar'ia.
Nature of Information disclosed.	• Banks in both countries disclose information as quantitative, qualitative, monetary, charts, graphs and tables.	• Some UAE banks use video in addition to other kinds of information.
Quality of information disclosed	• All information disclosed is good and neutral news.	

CONCLUSION

The recent research attempt to fill the gap in the literature of social reporting by addressing how public banks in two countries in the Arab Middle East region (namely, Egypt and the UAE) respond to stakeholders' needs by exploring the volume, nature, and quality of social information reported on the websites of these banks. The social information reported has been examined using a disclosure index in which main categories of CSR, "employees", "community", "cultural".

The analysis shows that public banks in both countries have a commitment to social responsibility/sustainability, focused on training and education of employees, and report on their own donations and sponsorship programs, and on their promotion of Arab/Islamic culture. Nevertheless, public banks in UAE disclose only news about awards, localization, SSBR, and adherence to Shar'ia. Furthermore, the public banks in both countries disclose social information in quantitative, qualitative, monetary, charts, graphs and tables form. They report only good and neutral news. Only two banks in the UAE use videos. These results show how public banks in this region seek to portray themselves in a favorable light for regional/global stakeholders. However, public banks in both countries lag behind stakeholders' needs in some employee and cultural sub-categories.

The results of this research may have practical implications for managers of public banks in this region. This study encourages advice to the top management of such banks to disclose more about such important employee issues as "equal opportunities", "workplace conditions", "appreciation and thanks", and "employee consultation" to satisfy the needs of different stakeholders. What may be stressed even more is more disclosure about "Islamic Values", "Quard Hassan", and "Zakat Fund" to challenge the Western Capitalistic system and give a voice to Islamic/Arab culture, as well as satisfying the needs of Muslim stakeholders. Similarly, in web reporting, this research may encourage top management to lead the way to developing their websites in order to facilitate interaction with stakeholders by providing the contact addresses of responsible officers, a discussion form, and mailing list. Moreover, it is apparent from the analysis that Egyptian banks lag behind the UAE banks in disclosing social information and using the available web functions. Thus, it is important for mangers of Egyptian banks to develop reporting strategies (content and form) to facilitate interaction with different stakeholders to a satisfactory degree.

This research is important for future comparative work on CSR as it provides updated evidence on social reporting practices on the websites of public banks in two Arab Middle East Countries (namely, Egypt and the UAE). It would be valuable to compare CSR reporting practices on websites and in paper reports with those of foreign/multinational banks operating in the Arab region and to investigate to what extent foreign banks satisfy the needs of Arab/Muslim stakeholders.

REFERENCES

Abu-Baker, N., & Naser, K. (2000). Empirical Evidence on Corporate Social Disclosure (CSD) practices in Jordan. *International Journal of Commerce and Management*, *10*(3/4), 18–34. doi:10.1108/eb047406

Adams, C., Coutts, A., & Harte, G. (1995). Corporate Equal Opportunities (non-) Disclosure. *The British Accounting Review*, *27*(2), 87–108. doi:10.1006/bare.1994.0005

Adams, C., & Frost, G. (2004). *The Development of Corporate Web-sites and Implications for Ethical, Social and Environmental Reporting Through these Media*. Edinburgh, UK: The Institute of Chartered Accountants of Scotland.

Adams, C., Hill, Y., & Roberts, C. (1998). Corporate Social Reporting Practices in Western Europe: Legitimating Corporate Behavior? *The British Accounting Review*, *30*(1), 1–21. doi:10.1006/bare.1997.0060

Al-Qaradawi, Y. (1985). *The Lawful and The Prohibited in Islam*. Kuala Lumpur: Islamic Book Trust.

Andrew, B., Gul, F., Guthrie, J., & Teoh, H. (1989). A Note on Corporate Social Disclosure Practices in Developing Countries: The Case of Malaysia and Singapore. *The British Accounting Review*, *21*(4), 371–376. doi:10.1016/0890-8389(89)90034-6

Aribi, Z., & Gao, S. (2010). Corporate Social Responsibility Disclosure: A Comparison between Islamic and Conventional Financial Institutions. *Journal of Financial Reporting and Accounting*, *8*(2), 72–91. doi:10.1108/19852511011088352

Belal, A. (2001). A Study of Corporate Social Disclosures in Bangladesh. *Managerial Auditing Journal*, *16*(5), 274–289. doi:10.1108/02686900110392922

Belal, A., Cooper, S., & Roberts, R. (2013). Vulnerable and Exploitable: The Need For Organizational Accountability and Transparency in Emerging Less Developed Economies. *Accounting Forum*, *37*(2), 81–91. doi:10.1016/j.accfor.2013.04.001

Belal, A., & Momin, M. (2009). Corporate Social Reporting (CSR) in Emerging Economies: A Review and Future Directions. *Research in Accounting in Emerging Economies.*, *9*, 119–143.

Branco, M., & Rodrigues, L. (2006). Communication of Corporate Social Responsibility by Portuguese Banks. *Corporate Communication: An International Journal*, *11*(3), 232–248. doi:10.1108/13563280610680821

Branco, M., & Rodrigues, L. (2008). Social Responsibility Disclosure: A Study of Proxies for the public Visibility of Portuguese Banks. *The British Accounting Review*, *49*(2), 161–181. doi:10.1016/j.bar.2008.02.004

Campbell, D. (2000). Legitimacy Theory or Mangerial Reality Construction? Corporate Social Disclosure in Marks and Spencer Plc Corporate Reports 1969 - 1997. *Accounting Forum*, *24*(1), 80–100. doi:10.1111/1467-6303.00030

Campbell, D., & Beck, A. (2004). Answering Allegations: The Use of The Corporate Websites for Restorative Ethical and Social Disclosure. *Business Ethics: European Review*, *13*(2/3), 100–116. doi:10.1111/j.1467-8608.2004.00357.x

CIA. (2015). Fact Book. Retrieved from https://www.cia.gov/library/publications/the-world-factbook/geos/eg.html

Cooper, S. (2003). Stakeholder Communication and The Internet in UK Electricity Companies. *Managerial Auditing Journal*, *18*(3), 232–243. doi:10.1108/02686900310469925

Coupland, C. (2006). Corporate Social and Environmental Responsibility in Web-based Reports: Currency in the banking sector? *Critical Perspectives on Accounting*, *17*(7), 865–881. doi:10.1016/j.cpa.2005.01.001

Dahawy, K., Merino, B., & Conovort, T. (2002). The Conflict between IAS Disclosure Requirements and The Secretive Culture in Egypt. *Advances in International Accounting*, *15*, 203–228. doi:10.1016/S0897-3660(02)15024-0

Day, R., & Woodward, T. (2009). CSR Reporting and the UK Financial Services Sector. *Journal of Applied Accounting Reserach*, *10*(3), 159–175. doi:10.1108/09675420911006398

Deegan, C., Rankin, M., & Vought, P. (2000). Firms' Disclosure Reactions to Major Social Incidents: Australian Evidence. *Accounting Forum*, *24*(1), 101–130. doi:10.1111/1467-6303.00031

Douglas, A., Doris, J., & Johnson, B. (2004). Corporate Social Reporting In Irish Financial Institutions. *The TQM Magazine*, *16*(6), 387–395. doi:10.1108/09544780410563301

Ebrahim, M., & Joo, T. (2001). Islamic Banking in Brunei. *International Journal of Social Economics*, *28*(4), 314–337. doi:10.1108/03068290110357708

Esrock, S., & Leichty, G. (2000). Organization of Corporate Web Pages: Publics and Functions. *Public Relations Review*, *26*(3), 327–344. doi:10.1016/S0363-8111(00)00051-5

Fifka, M. (2013). Corporate Responsibility Reporting and Its Determinants in Comparative Perspective: A Review of the Empirical Literature and a Meta-analysis. *Business Strategy and the Environment*, *22*(1), 1–35. doi:10.1002/bse.729

Graafland, J., Mazereuw, C., & Yahia, A. (2006). Islam and Socially Responsible Business Conduct: An Empirical Study of Dutch Entrepreneurs. *Business Ethics (Oxford, England)*, *15*(4), 390–406. doi:10.1111/j.1467-8608.2006.00458.x

Gray, R., Owen, D., & Maunders, K. (1987). *Accounting and Accountability: Changes and Challenges in Corporate Social and Environmental Reporting*. London, UK: Prentice Hall.

Guthrie, J., & Parker, L. (1990). Corporate Social Disclosure Practice: A Comparative International Analysis. *Advances in Public Interest Accounting*, *3*, 251–176.

Hamid, F. (2004). Corporate Social Disclosure by Banks and Finance Companies: Malaysian Evidence. *Corporate Ownership and Control*, *1*(4), 118–130.

Hamid, S., Craig, R., & Clarke, F. (1993). Religion: A Confounding Cultural Element In The International Harmonization of Accounting? *Abacus*, *29*(2), 131–148. doi:10.1111/j.1467-6281.1993.tb00427.x

Hvidt, M. (2013). Economic Diversification in GCC countries: Past Record and Future Trends. Kuwait Programme on Development, Governance and Globalization in The Gulf States.

IFRS UAE. (2015). *IFRS Jurisdictional profile*. United Arab Emirates: IFRS Foundation.

Jeucken, M., & Bouma, J. (1999). The Changing Environment of Banks. *Greener Management International*, *27*, 21–35.

Kamla, R. (2007). Critically Appreciating Social Accounting and Reporting in The Arab Middle East: A Postcolonial Perspective. *Advances in International Accounting*, *20*, 105–177. doi:10.1016/S0897-3660(07)20005-4

Kamla, R., Gallhofer, S., & Haslam, J. (2006). Islam, Nature and Accounting: Islamic Principles and the Notion of Accounting for The Environment. *Accounting Forum*, *39*(3), 245–265. doi:10.1016/j.accfor.2006.05.003

Katsioloudes, M., & Brodtkorb, T. (2007). Corporate Social Responsibility: An Exploratory Study in The United Arab Emirates. *SAM Advanced Management Journal*, Autumn, 9-20.

Khan, M. (2010). The Effect of Corporate Governance Elements on Corporate Social Responsibility (CSR) Reporting. *International Journal of Commerce and Management*, *52*(2), 82–109.

Lewis, M. (2001). Islam and Accounting. *Accounting Forum*, *25*(2), 103–127. doi:10.1111/1467-6303.00058

Maignan, I., & Ralson, D. (2002). Corporate Social Responsibility in Europe and the US: Insights from Business' Self-Presentations. *Journal of International Business Studies*, *33*(3), 497–514. doi:10.1057/palgrave.jibs.8491028

Mathews, M. (1993). *Socially Responsible Accounting*. London: Chapman & Hall.

Mckee, D., Garner, D., & Mckee, Y. (1999). *Accounting Services, The Islamic Middle East and The Global Economy*. Westport, CT: Quorum Books.

Menassa, E. (2010). Corporate Social Responsibility: An Exploration Study of the Quality and Extent of Social Disclosures by Lebanese Commercial Banks. *Journal of Applied Accounting Research*, *11*(1), 4–23. doi:10.1108/09675421011050009

Miles, M. (1987). *Managing the Corporate Social Environment*. NJ, USA: Prentice- Hall.

Osman, M. (2013). *Corporate Social Responsibility (CSR) of Egyptian Banking Sector: A Critical and Postcolonial Perspective* [PhD Thesis]. Queen Mary, University of London, UK.

Patten, D. (2002). Give or Take on the Internet: An Examination of the Disclosure Practices of Insurance Firm Web Innovators. *Journal of Business Ethics*, *36*(3), 247–259. doi:10.1023/A:1014009229437

Perera, M., & Mathews, M. (1990). The Cultural Relativity of Accounting and International Patterns of Social Accounting. *Advances in International Accounting*, *13*, 215–251.

Rice, G. (1999). Islamic Ethics and the Implications for Business. *Journal of Business Ethics*, *18*(4), 345–358. doi:10.1023/A:1005711414306

Rikhardsson, P., Andersen, A., & Bang, H. (2002). Sustainability Reporting on the Internet: A Study of Global Fortune 500. *Greener Management International,* Winter, 57-75.

Roberts, C. (1991). Environmental Disclosure: A Note on Reporting Practices in Mainland Europe. *Accounting, Auditing & Accountability Journal*, *4*(3), 62–71. doi:10.1108/09513579110005536

Samuels, J., & Oliga, J. (1982). Accounting Standards in Developing Countries. *The International Journal of Accounting*, *18*(1), 69–88.

Simpson, W., & Kohers, T. (2002). the Link between Corporate Social and Financial Performance: Evidence from the Banking Industry. *Journal of Business Ethics*, *35*(2), 97–109. doi:10.1023/A:1013082525900

SIS. (2015). State Information Service, Egypt. Retrieved from http://www.sis.gov.eg/en/

UNDP. (2009). Arab Human Development Report: Challenges to Human Security in The Arab Countries. New York, USA: United Nations Development Programme: Regional Bureau for Arab States.

UNDP. (2010). *Youth in Egypt: Building our Future*. Egypt: United Nations Development Programme & the Institute of National Planning.

UNDP. (2012). *Assessment of Development Results: Evaluation of UNDP Contribution in Egypt*. Egypt: United Nations Development Programme.

Unerman, J. (1999). A Critique of Content Analysis as A Research Method for Corporate Social Reporting. *Paper presented atCritical Perspectives on Accounting Conference.*

Weber, R. (1988). *Basic Content Analysis*. Beverly Hills, CA: Sage Publications.

West, J. (2013). Social Media Ignited the Arab Spring. In M. Haerens & L. Zott (Eds.), *The Arab Spring*. USA: Greenhaven Press.

ENDNOTES

1. The five areas are environment, labor practices and working conditions, product responsibility, human rights and society.
2. UAE economy is stronger than Egyptian economy as it is dependent on oil reserves and exports.
3. This dual identity is due to colonialism and artificial division into nation-states (Rice, 1999).

Chapter 6
Empirical Evidence on Corporate Governance Impact on CSR Disclosure in Developing Economies:
The Tunisian and Egyptian Contexts

Wajdi Ben Rejeb
National Institute of Applied Sciences & Technology, Tunisia

ABSTRACT

This chapter investigates the influence of the board composition and leadership on Corporate Social Responsibility (CSR) disclosure. The empirical study of 68 Tunisian listed companies and 100 Egyptian listed companies reveals that board independence, foreign directorship, female directorship and state directorship, influence positively CSR disclosure. However, these findings indicate that CEO duality has a negative impact on CSR disclosure. Overall, the findings are consistent with the agency theory as well as the stakeholders theory and suggest that CSR disclosure seems to result from the willingness to meet shareholders' expectations in terms of transparency and voluntary disclosure of non-financial information.

INTRODUCTION

The issue of CSR has gained importance recently with the growing awareness for sustainable development but also due to several financial crises, food scandals and ecological problems orienting the debate towards the role of business in society beyond its classic economic purpose (Deegan & Gordon, 1996; Gray et al., 1995; Hooghiemstra, 2000; Kolk, 2003). There is no universal definition of CSR (Godfrey & Hatch, 2007) but most definitions describe CSR as the voluntary integration by companies of social and environmental concerns in their activities and through their relations with their stakeholders. The arising of the CSR issues is reflected through the growing number of CSR and sustainability reports, as well as through institutional communication of information in relation with CSR (Gray et al., 2001; Kolk 2005).

DOI: 10.4018/978-1-5225-0720-8.ch006

CSR Disclosure can be defined as the information that the company disclose, in relation with the impact of its activities on the environment as well as its relationship with its stakeholders, through relevant communication channels (Campbell, 2004; Gray et al., 2001). The stakeholder theory suggests that CSR disclosure is part of a dialogue between the company and its stakeholders through which the company provides information on its activities to legitimize its behavior, to educate, to inform and to change the perceptions of its stakeholders (Adams & Larrinaga-González, 2007; Adams & McNicholas, 2007; Gray et al., 1995). Literature review shows that the impact of corporate governance on financial disclosure has received considerable attention (Anderson et al., 2004), unlike the effect of corporate governance mechanisms on non-financial voluntary disclosure (Haniffa & Cooke, 2005). Indeed, previous studies have concluded that disclosure policies emanate from the Board of Directors (Cerbioni & Parbonetti, 2007; Fernandez-Feijoo et al., 2012; Gul & Leung, 2004; Haniffa & Cooke, 2005; Ho & Wong, 2001).

The objective of this chapter is to investigate the impact of board characteristics and leadership on the CSR disclosure in Tunisian and Egyptian listed companies. This chapter deals with three sections: literature review, methodology, and findings.

BACKGROUND

The purpose of this section is to provide an overview of CSR disclosure within the Tunisian and Egyptian contexts in Tunisia and Egypt. The review of institutional arrangements and previous researches in this field in relation with the previously mentioned countries will be also examined in this section.

Context of CSR Disclosure in Tunisia

The implementation of reports on the CSR disclosure by Tunisian companies is relatively a new concern and has become a popular topic since late 90'. In fact, Koleva and Gherib (2012) demonstrate that the interaction between specific features of Tunisian capitalism which is characterized by state capitalism and the dominance of small and family-owned companies as well as the influence of globalization and the economic relationship with the EU, has shaped the perception and the involvement of Tunisian companies in CSR orientations. According to Koleva and Gherib (2012), the search for differentiation and the enhancement of the brand image are the most important motivations for the CSR orientation, especially as far as large Tunisian industrial companies are concerned. Tunisian firms from industries with higher sensitivity to the environment tend to provide more CSR disclosure than firms from less environmentally sensitive industries. This is also supported by Belhaj and Damak-Ayadi (2011) who reported that out of 500 largest Tunisian firms, only 53 have published environmental information in their annual reports or in their websites.

Concerning the institutional aspect of CSR disclosure, the Financial Market Council imposes to listed companies on the Tunis Stock Exchange (BVMT) an obligation of regular information disclosure with regards to its financial performance, governance structure as well as Top - Management compensation. In this respect, CSR disclosure is not mandatory and remains at the discretion of companies and their shareholders.

Moreover, the Tunisian accounting conceptual framework provides information on the social and environmental corporate disclosure as a supplement to conventional reporting of financial information.

Furthermore, the effort of the Tunisian legislator, who insists on the philanthropic orientation of CSR, focuses on the principles of environmental and social actions.

However, communication of information in the annual report is a form of disclosure which is not yet strictly regulated in Tunisia. Some institutional initiatives aim to enhance the voluntary disclosure with the publication by the Arab Institute of Business Managers in 2008 of a Guide of Good Corporate Governance Practices and as well as a Guide of Annual Report of the Tunisian Companies.

Ben Othman and Zeghal (2010) who have studied the determinants of transparency and disclosure in the MENA region companies, estimate that companies from countries having historical links with Britain show better scores of disclosure in comparison with countries that were former French colonies. Indeed, the Tunisian accounting regulations and practices have been governed since 1968 by a French style macroeconomic oriented accounting system. Mattoussi, Karaa and Maghraoui (2004) note that Tunisian companies reporting policies are in line with the policy of its former French colonizer. Therefore, the issue of CSR disclosure in Tunisia is relatively new and not widespread among Tunisian companies that are generally characterized by a low level of CSR disclosure since these companies have significant discretion regarding disclosure of non-financial information with the absence of an appropriate regulatory framework as well as an audit standards governing social communication.

Context of CSR Disclosure in Egypt

In this chapter, Egypt as a developing country is considered as an interesting case study in the context of CSR disclosure. This case study is selected for several reasons. First, Egypt has historical links with Britain and may show better scores of disclosure in comparison with countries that were former French colonies (Ben Othman & Zeghal, 2010). This historical background may provide additional insights if it is compared to the Tunisian context. Second, Egypt represents a large market where stakeholders and media awareness of the business's role in the Egyptian society are growing (Salama, 2009). Third, Egypt is one of the most attractive countries for foreign direct investments in Africa because of the rapid growth of its economy in comparison with other African economies (E&Y, 2015). Finally, the Egyptian stock Exchange is well established and developed with a large number of listed companies. Therefore, Egyptian listed companies are more likely to disclose CSR information in order to attract more foreign investors.

In Egypt, even though the philanthropic side of CSR has always existed due to the religious beliefs of the Egyptian society and public concerns for the disadvantaged, the institutional efforts to improve and to implement CSR practices as well as CSR disclosure are relatively recent. Several recent initiatives have been conducted in order to enhance the profile of CSR practices in Egyptian listed companies. The Egyptian Ministry of State and Environment Affairs has focused on defining environmental policies, setting priorities and implementing initiatives within a context of sustainable development. In this perspective, the Egyptian government recently created the Egyptian Corporate Responsibility Center (ECRC) to promote awareness of CSR issues. In 2008, ECRC published the "Sustainability Report guidelines" in collaboration with the UN Development Program. Moreover, the Egyptian stock exchange (EGX) established an annual index "ESG 30" in collaboration with rating agencies specialized in environmental and social performance, and corporate governance.

Due to the growing and global awareness of companies' role within societies, many Egyptian companies use CSR orientation and disclosure as a marketing or public relations (PR) tool to gain stakeholders approval, support and endorsement. This argument allows such companies to expand and compete on the international market with their environmentally-friendly products. However, the levels of CSR disclosure by Egyptian companies are still lower than expected (Rizk, et al., 2008). Effectively, Rizk et al. (2008) have conducted a survey of the CSR disclosure practices in the Egyptian context, which is using a 34-point disclosure index and is including 4 components namely the customers, employees, environment and community. In this survey, the disclosed CSR information is relatively modest. Following the same perspective, the study of internet voluntary disclosure of social reporting and stakeholders' requirements, Salama (2009) concludes that the CSR disclosure in Egyptian companies is still far beyond the community stakeholder expectations.

LITERATURE REVIEW AND RESEARCH HYPOTHESES

The objective of this section is to review the theoretical as well as the empirical literature on the effect of board composition and leadership in relation with CSR disclosure in order to formulate a set of hypotheses.

Family Directors and CSR Disclosure

The majority of Tunisian companies and Egyptian companies starts as a family business, develops gradually over time to form corporate groups which decide afterward to list a part of the capital of the flagship company on the stock market to allow owners to raise funds. However, these listed companies do not open the major part of their capital to the public, which is reflected by boards often dominated by family members. These latter can use their power to directly obtain various information from the management of the company who will have no incentive to voluntarily disclose information related to CSR given its proximity to family directors and the low power of external shareholders. Moreover, as soon as the family controls both the top management and the board, it may adopt opportunistic behavior given the traditional conflict of interests between majority and minority shareholders (Shleifer & Vishny, 1997).

Ho and Wong (2001) have found a very low level of voluntary disclosure in family businesses and suggest that the family shareholders may undermine the interests of minority shareholders in order to enrich themselves by amplifying information asymmetry and engaging related party transactions. Moreover, family businesses tend to be less committed to CSR than non-family businesses and to disclose less information about their CSR practices to avoid the costs from the use of this information by users (employees, competitors, etc.) that can damage the image of the company, generating significant competitive disadvantages (Elliott & Jacobson, 1994).

In the Tunisian context, Fekih Ahmed (2007) has reported a negative and significant effect of family ownership on the level of voluntary disclosure of 62 Tunisian companies in his sample. On the basis of these arguments, together with an opacity culture in family firms that reduces transparency and accountability (Eng & Mak, 2003; Ho & Wong, 2001), the following hypothesis is advanced:

Hypothesis 1: CSR disclosure is negatively related to the proportion of family directors on the board.

Board Independence and CSR Disclosure

Mainstream thinking in corporate governance considers that the director's independence is a key condition of boards of directors efficiency given that independent directors are detached from management influence and ensure diligence in dealing with minority shareholders rights as well as stakeholders interests (Petra, 2005).

Concerned about their reputation and their value on the director's market, the independent directors seek to increase the company's transparency and to foster communication of any type of information to enhance the perception of their independence from management. Tricker (1984) considers the independent directors as "additional windows on the world" (Tricker, 1984, p. 171). In addition, the resources dependency theory assumes that independent boards are more effective in terms of improving company image and stakeholder's management (Coffey & Wang, 1998; Dunn & Sainty, 2009; Ibrahim & Angelidis, 1995; Johnson & Greening, 1999).

Several studies have found a positive relationship between board independence and voluntary disclosure of non-mandatory information. Researchers have reported a positive relationship between the proportion of independent directors and CSR disclosure (Gul & Leung, 2004; Htay et al, 2012; Mohd Nasir Abdullah 2004). Within a developing economy context, an independent director is a fairly recent notion that is not prevalent. It should be noted, however, that it is only since 2011 that the Tunisian Central Bank has required the independence of credit institutions boards. Hence, these boards are compelled to include at least two independent members and at most an executive member. Non-financial companies have no regulatory obligation to establish independence within their boards and the decision to hire independent directors is left to the entire discretion of the main shareholders. In the Egyptian context, Ezat and El-Masry (2008) and Samaha and Dahawy (2011) have reported a positive association between board independence and voluntary disclosure in Egypt.

The analysis of the relationship between board independence and CSR disclosure infers the following hypothesis:

Hypothesis 2: CSR disclosure is positively related to the proportion of independent directors on the board.

State Directors and CSR Disclosure

State capitalism has been practiced in Tunisia since the country independence. The Tunisian state holds parts of the capital of certain companies operating in strategic areas as well as in public services as transport, finance, energy, etc. Through public enterprises and companies where he is a shareholder, the state acts both as an investor and a stakeholder. Therefore, it is in the State interests that the companies in which it holds shares follow its policies which often benefit to the society as a whole.

The stakeholder theory suggests that state-controlled companies disclose more information than other businesses to facilitate the management of the interests of all stakeholders in relation with the state and serve as an example for private companies (Eng & Mak, 2003).

Studies have found a higher social and environmental disclosure in companies controlled by the government (Eng & Mak, 2003; Mohd Nasir Abdullah 2004). Therefore, the following hypothesis is formulated:

Hypothesis 3: CSR disclosure is positively related to the proportion of state directors on the board.

Gender Differences and CSR Disclosure

The impact of gender on business performance is a subject that generates debate in the management literature. The researchers suggest that gender is manifested through a difference in values and moral reasoning (Gilligan, 1982). Studies have reported that the directorship of women has a positive effect on non-financial performance and especially on CSR (Bernardi & Threadgill, 2010; Stanwick & Stanwick, 1998; Williams, 2003).

Furthermore, the authors suggest that the presence of women on the board shows that the company's concern for equality and diversity improves its reputation (Bernardi et al., 2006; Brammer et al. 2009). According to Ibrahim and Angelidis (2011), women directors have a higher orientation towards the discretionary component of CSR as their male counterparts; the latter being more focused on economic performance. Williams (2003) has found a positive relationship between the presence of women directors and corporate philanthropy.

In the same vein, Bear's et al. (2010) study has reported a positive relationship between CSR and the number of women serving on the board. The authors have identified two main contributions related to female directorship: more sensitivity and more participatory decision making style. Kruger (2010) has found that companies whose boards have several female members are more socially responsible than others, and show more generosity to the community and more attention to the welfare of stakeholders. Finally, Fernandez-Feijoo et al. (2012) have found that the presence of at least three women on the board is positively related to CSR disclosure.

The Scandinavian countries constrain listed companies to have at least 40% female directors in their organizations. However, in developing economies such as Tunisia and Egypt, there is no government policy which is adopted to compel the appointment of specific percentage of females on the boards of directors. It is worth noting that gender equality is considered as an established concept in Tunisia. Therefore, the following hypothesis is proposed:

Hypothesis 4: CSR disclosure is positively related to the proportion of women directors on the board.

Foreign Directors and CSR Disclosure

Some Tunisian companies are partly controlled by foreign shareholders which is due to historical factors, privatization and partnership strategies. This situation has led to the presence of foreign directors in the governing bodies of these companies.

The presence of foreign directors may influence the management and strategic direction of the business. Indeed, institutional, cultural and political factors influence the background of the directors and therefore the perception of the issues related to CSR (Hofstede, 1983). It is worth noting that the development of environmental regulations in the European Union was due to the rise in power of Green parties in several countries but also in relation to the societal culture of many central and northern European countries (Harris, 2002; Mair, 2001; Vogel, 2007). In addition, people from different cultures have access to different information and adhere to different values in relation to environmental and social issues (Bechtel et al., 1999; Schwartz & Bardi, 2001).

Several studies have shown that cultural factors influence the CSR orientation (Mair, 2001; Vogel, 2007; Waldman et al., 2006). Ayuso and Argandona (2009) suggest that foreign directors play a key role in promoting CSR reporting strategies to show that they behave as good citizens in the countries in which they serve.

Moreover, Post et al. (2011) have found that the number of directors who have completed their studies in Europe is positively related to CSR orientation. Therefore, a positive relationship between the presence of foreign directors and CSR disclosure is expected and expressed through this hypothesis:

Hypothesis 5: CSR disclosure is positively related to the proportion of foreign directors on the board.

CEO Duality and CSR Disclosure

Duality means that the responsibilities of the board of directors chair and the executive manager are exercised by the same person. Corporate governance theories are divided over the impact of duality on performance.

The agency theory considers that duality may negatively affect the firm performance because it reduces the effectiveness of the control exerted by the board of directors (Donaldson & Davis, 1991), while the stewardship theory considers that duality improves performance by strengthening leadership at the top of the company (Kiel & Nicholson, 2003).

In addition to the impact on financial performance, several studies have found a positive effect of the separation of management and control functions on voluntary disclosure (Gul & Leung, 2004; Huafang & Jianguo, 2007). However, few studies have investigated the effect of duality on CSR disclosure. Al-Arusi et al. (2009) have found a positive association between the absence of duality, voluntary financial disclosure and voluntary environmental disclosure in Malaysian companies.

In the Egyptian context, Ezat and El-Masry (2008) have found that CEO duality is negatively linked to levels of corporate voluntary disclosures. Based on a stakeholder approach, it is expected that the duality is not favorable to the interests of all stakeholders which will result in less disclosure of information about CSR practices. Therefore, the sixth hypothesis is set as follow:

Hypothesis 6: CSR disclosure is negatively related to CEO duality.

METHODOLOGY AND FINDINGS

In this section, the impact of board characteristics on CSR disclosure is analyzed by introducing the sample and the explanatory model. The results of the multivariate analysis are then presented and interpreted.

The Sample

Given the nature of the research problem, listed companies in the BVMT are chosen to be investigated. Compared to other Tunisian companies, listed companies have relatively advanced corporate governance practices and comply with the transparency requirements in relation to the regulations which they were subjected. According to the BVMT website, which was consulted in September 2014, there are 74 Tunisian listed companies. However, six companies newly listed do not provide any accessible information. For the remaining companies, the information on corporate governance and CSR are collected through a content analysis based on the annual reports dating from 2014 and 2013 as well as from company web sites (Milne & Adler, 1999; Parker, 2005).

The same data collection methodology was adopted for the Egyptian sample. The sample consists of the top 100 Egyptian companies (EGX 100) listed in the Egyptian Exchange (EGX), which mixes the constituents of the other two main indices of the exchange, EGX 30 and EGX 70. EGX 100 is selected because it includes the biggest listed companies in the Egyptian securities and the leading of that market as well. Therefore, it is expected that these companies are more likely to disclose CSR practices than other listed companies. The reason behind this expectation can be explained by the presence of larger companies, more active trading, stronger investor orientation and greater assets.

The Regression Model

The multiple regression analysis is appropriate for the purposes of this study since this method allows to determine the effect of several independent variables on a dependent variable. Furthermore, the regression seems appropriate compared to other techniques given the size of the sample (Hair et al., 2006).

The methodology is to estimate a multiple regression in which the dependent variable is CSR disclosure. This latter is assessed both in terms of quantity and quality. CSR disclosure quantity can be measured in different ways: number of words, phrases, characters, paragraphs, graphics, pages, pages proportions in relation to CSR in annual reports, official documents and company website (Hackston & Milne, 1996; Milne & Adler, 1999; Unerman, 2000). Hackstone and Milne (1996) have demonstrated, through several models testing, that the proportion of pages devoted to CSR in relation to the total volume of information disclosed by the company is the most appropriate measure of CSR disclosure quantity. According to Haron et al. (2006), the proportion of pages devoted to CSR are determined by apportioning an annual report page to the nearest hundredth of a page.

CSR disclosure quality is appreciated throughout the depth of the reporting and the number of components discussed in relation to CSR. Thirty items, inspired from previous works, are chosen to measure the disclosure of information in relation with employees, customers, product, environment, community and corporate governance (Barako & Brown, 2008; Gray et al.,1995; Hackston & Milne, 1996; Haniffa & Cooke, 2005). The quality of CSR disclosure score is calculated based on an unweighted method meaning that all information has an equal value regardless of their importance to a particular group of users (Chau & Gray, 2002; Cooke, 1989). A value of "1" is assigned to a given item if it is disclosed by the company and "0" otherwise. The score of CSR disclosure quality is obtained by calculating a ratio of the total points obtained by the company divided by the maximum score obtainable namely 30 points.

The explanatory variables in the model are the proportion of family directors, independent directors, state directors, female directors, foreign directors and CEO duality.

Directors' proportion is a ratio of the number of directors having a given profile over the total board size while CEO duality is a dummy variable that equals "1" if the chairman of the board is also the CEO and, "zero" otherwise. In addition, two control variables are taken into account. They are the company age and the industrial activity (Huse, 2005; Johnson, 1997; Lynall et al., 2003). Over time, business behavior tends to be more institutionalized and companies are more and more concerned with their public image. Indeed, stakeholders have more expectations towards well-established companies in comparison to small and young firms (Drawbaugh, 2001). Companies operating in manufacturing activities which may have an environmental impact, are more inclined to manage their reputation and image vis-à-vis their customers through CSR disclosure practices (Cowen, Ferreri & Parker, 1987). Table 1 provides a summary of all the variables.

Results of the Descriptive Statistics

Descriptive statistics which is concerned with quality in CSR disclosure are analyzed in Table 2. It shows that the most disclosed items by Tunisian listed firms are related to the shareholding structure, employee profile, employee training and product quality. Regarding the Egyptian sample, the descriptive statistics show the dominance of corporate governance information, then the community information and the workplace information, and finally the environment information.

However, Tunisian listed companies as well as Egyptian listed companies do not provide much disclosure in relation with employee morale, employment of minorities, product and social contribution activities and the conservation of the natural environment and biodiversity.

From a comparative perspective, it appears that quality in CSR disclosure is slightly higher in Egypt than in Tunisia. Egyptian companies show a higher disclosure rate in 16 items while Tunisian firms obtained a higher percentage in 11 items. Tunisian firms are more likely than their Egyptian counterparts to disclose information in relation with Human Resources Management and Corporate Governance structure which fall under mandatory disclosure required by the Financial Market Commission. In contrast, Egyptian companies are more likely than their Tunisian counterparts to disclose information relating to donations and community services.

Table 1. Variable definition

Variables	Description
QUANCSR	Quantity of CSR disclosure (proportions of annual report page devoted to CSR to the nearest hundredth of a page).
QUALCSR	Quality of CSR disclosure $\sum_{t=1}^{nj} Xij / nj$; nj = total items, Xij = 1 if the item is disclosed and zero otherwise.
FAMDIR	Proportion of family directors on the board.
STADIR	Proportion of state directors on the board.
INDIR	Proportion of independent directors on the board.
FEMDIR	Proportion of women directors on the board.
FORDIR	Proportion of foreign directors on the board.
DUAL	Dummy variable that equals 1if the chairman of the board is also the CEO and, zero otherwise.
IF	Dummy variable that equals 1 for industrial company and, zero otherwise.
AGE	Age of the company (1 if the firm is under the age of 30, 2 if aged between 30 and 60 years and 3 if aged more than 60 years).

Table 2. Descriptive statistics of CSR disclosure quality in Tunisia and Egypt

Disclosure Items	Proportion of Companies Disclosing the Item (%)	
	Tunisian Listed Companies	Egyptian Listed Companies
Workplace		
1. Employee profiles	44	21
2. Employee Recognition and Appreciation	25	9
3. Employee training	38	24
4. Employee morale	1	5
5. Employment of minorities/diversity/disabled	2	3
6. Employees' welfare and benefits	9	13
7. Employee Health and Safety	10	16
Product and Marketplace		
8. Product development	13	4
9. Product quality	35	32
10. Product safety	12	16
11. Customer service improvement and awards	3	8
12. Product and social contribution activities	4	2
13. Ethical principles	24	13
Environment		
14. Commitment to minimize environmental pollution	18	18
15. Commitment to safeguarding the environment aesthetics	4	2
16. Environmental impact studies/monitoring program	3	1
17. Conservation of natural environment & biodiversity	2	3
18. Environmental management program/system	10	10
19. Commitment to energy management policy	4	8
Community		
20. Donations cash/products/employee services	13	25
21. Participation in social campaign	12	24
22. Commitment/sponsoring public health project	4	26
23. Sponsoring educational related project	9	24
24. Sponsoring sports project	7	7
Corporate Governance		
25. Corporate governance philosophy	18	13
26. Board and committees code of conduct	19	17
27. Ownership and governance structure	56	85
28. Stakeholder engagement	3	9
Certifications and Labels		
29. CSR Certification	15	21
30. CSR Reporting (GRI)	3	4

The interpretation of these findings can be explained by different reasons. First, Egypt has historical links with Britain. In this regard, the Anglo-Saxon countries have more developed disclosure traditions compared to Latin countries (Ben Othman & Zeghal, 2010). Second, the Egyptian culture is more conducive to the disclosure of CSR information than Tunisian counterparts. In this respect, previous studies have found that cultural characteristics affect CSR disclosure in different countries (Orij, 2010; Vachon, 2010; Van der Laan Smith et al., 2005) especially through Hofstede's national culture dimensions. Although that Tunisia and Egypt are often assigned to the same cultural cluster, there are differences between their respective national cultures. Tunisian and Egyptian national cultures are characterized by an inclination for avoiding uncertainty as well as a long power distance. However, Tunisian culture leans lightly towards masculinity while Egypt is described as a feminine society. Furthermore, the collectivist orientation is higher in Egypt than in Tunisia.

Egypt is considered as a collectivist society. Collectivism increases the likelihood of CSR disclosure because it requires a higher level of commitment to society, and behaving as a group member, rather than as an individual economic unit (Hofstede, 1983). Moreover, Egypt is considered a relatively feminine society where managers strive for consensus, people value equality, solidarity and quality in their working lives (Hofstede, 1983). Most feminine societies tend to be increasingly open to disclose social information.

To sum up, the descriptive statistics reveal that the patterns of CSR disclosure are similar in the two countries. It seems that in Egypt as well as in Tunisia, regardless of culture specificities and disclosure backgrounds, CSR disclosure falls under a logic of compliance to corporate governance and workplace information. These patterns are also used as a marketing and PR tool to gain customers' and investors' sympathy which is performed through the communication of community actions.

The descriptive statistics which are related to the board characteristics are shown in Table 3. It appears that Tunisian firms are more likely than their Egyptian counterparts to have family board members as well as state directors in their board with state capitalism and the dominance of family-owned companies especially within Tunisian economy. Moreover, foreign ownership and gender equality make that Tunisian firms are more likely than their Egyptian counterparts to have foreign directors as well as female directors in their board of directors. However, CEO duality is more current in Egyptian listed companies. Board independence is relatively weak in Tunisia as well as in Egypt.

Table 3. Descriptive statistics of board of directors characteristics in Tunisia and Egypt

Board Characteristics	Tunisia	Egypt
% of companies with at least one family director on the board of directors	44	22
% of companies with at least one state director on the board of directors	19	12
% of companies with at least one independent director on the board of directors	25	24
% of companies with at least one foreign director on the board of directors	37	25
% of companies with at least one female director on the board of directors	51	37
% of companies with a CEO duality	57	66

Multivariate Analysis Results

The results of multivariate analysis are presented by country beginning with the Tunisian sample.

As shown in Table 4, the results of the correlations analysis for the Tunisian sample are significant in suggesting a possible causal association between the studied variables consistent with the hypotheses. Besides, the results do not show the existence of correlations between independent variables above 0.7, confirming the absence of multi-colinearity problem (Tabachnick & Fidell, 2001).

The numbers listed horizontally across the top row correspond to the numbers of the variables listed vertically on the table.

*p .05, ** p 0.01 ; N=68

The results of the regression analysis are presented in Table 5. Two regressions were performed: The first regression (model 1) examines the effect of the board characteristics on CSR disclosure quantity while the second regression (Model 2) explains the impact of board characteristics on CSR disclosure quality.

For both regressions, R -squared (statistically significant at the 1% level) are around 38% for Model 1 and 46% for Model 2. With regard to the board composition, CSR disclosure quantity is more practiced in companies with an important proportion of foreign directors (β=.381, p = .004) and independent directors (β=.206, p = .09). With reference to the board leadership, the results reveal that companies where the CEO holds also the position of the chairman of the board disclose less in terms of quantity of the CSR disclosure (β=−.255, p = .027). When considering the others independents variable, neither the proportion of family directors, nor the proportion of State directors and female directorship demonstrate any relation with the quantity of the CSR disclosure. The same conclusion is also relevant to the control variables.

Companies present a better quality of CSR disclosure when foreign directors are well represented in the board (β=.347, p = .005). Further, the proportion of state directors and the extent of the board independence are positively associated with the CSR disclosure quality (β=.290, p = .025 ; β=.206,

Table 4. Results of correlation analysis for Tunisian listed Companies

Variable	1	2	3	4	5	6	7	8	9	10
1. EXTCSR	1									
2. QUALCSR	,820**	1								
3. FAMDIR	-,281*	-,351**	1							
4. STADIR	-,004	,228	-,348**	1						
5. INDIR	,304*	,253*	-,343**	-,062	1					
6. FORDIR	,518**	,461**	-,295*	-,152	,268*	1				
7. FEMDIR	,050	,187	-,042	,341**	-,035	,033	1			
8. DUAL	-,328**	-,303*	-,086	,284*	-,082	-,245*	-,082	1		
9. AGE	-,075	,026	,160	,049	-,414**	-,186	-,011	,102	1	
10. IF	,253*	,310*	-,152	,192	-,082	,331**	-,036	-,099	,102	1

Table 5. Results of regression analysis for Tunisian listed companies

	Expected Sign	Model 1: QUANCSR		Model 2: QUALCSR	
		Beta	T-Value	Beta	T-Value
Constant		0.022	1,343	0.085†	1,764
Family directors (FAMDIR)	-	-,095	-,756	-,119	-1,003
State directors (STADIR)	+	,089	,662	**,290†**	2,301
Independent directors (INDIR)	+	**,206†**	1,687	**,206†**	1,802
Foreign directors (FORDIR)	+	**,381***	3,020	**,347***	2,928
Women directors (FEMDIR)	+	-,007	-,061	,060	,560
Duality (DUAL)	-	**-,255***	-2,265	**-,301***	-2,848
Industrial firm (IF)	+	,110	,968	**,203†**	1,898
Firm age (AGE)	+	,076	,643	,090	,815
R^2		0.38		0.46	
F-test		4.54***		6.17***	
Durbin Watson		2.07		1.95	

† p .10, * p .05, ** p .01, *** p .001; N=68

p = .077 respectively). With regard to board leadership, the results reveal that CEO duality is negatively associated with the quality of CSR disclosure (β=–.255, p = .027). Concerning the effect of the control variable, companies operating in industrial sector have a better quality of CSR disclosure (β=.203, p = .063). However, the other independent variables, namely the proportion of family directors and female directors as well as the control variable "firm age" are not significantly related to the quality of CSR disclosure.

Table 6. shows the results of the correlation analysis for the Egyptian sample. All the correlations coefficients between the independent variables are below 0.7, confirming the absence of multi-colinearity problem (Tabachnick and Fidell, 2001).

Table 6. Results of correlation analysis for Egyptian listed companies

Variable	1	2	3	4	5	6	7	8	9	10
1. EXTCSR	1									
2. QUALCSR	,855**	1								
3. FAMDIR	-,023	-,014	1							
4. STADIR	,002	,079	-,135	1						
5. INDIR	,114	,190*	,091	,026	1					
6. FORDIR	,377**	,410**	-,047	-,158	-,073	1				
7. FEMDIR	,174	,193*	,161	,066	,045	,025	1			
8. DUAL	-,167	-,160	,091	,101	-,048	-,195*	,170	1		
9. AGE	-,145	-,131	-,040	-,084	,039	-,195*	-,173	,143	1	
10. IF	-,122	-,089	-,201*	,111	,228**	-,223*	-,110	,113	,235**	1

*p .05, ** p 0.01 ; N=100

Table 7 provides the results of the regression analysis of the Egyptian sample. Two regressions are performed: The first regression (model 1) considers CSR quantity as independent variable while the second regression (Model 2) explains the effect of board characteristics on CSR disclosure quality.

For both regressions, R -squared (statistically significant at the 1% level) are around 36% for Model 1 and 38% for Model 2. The results show that the proportion of foreign directors, the board independence and the proportion of female directors are positively associated with the scope of CSR disclosure (β=.553, p = .000; β=.170, p = .030; β=.160, p = .042 respectively). However, the others independents variables namely the proportion of family directors and the proportion of State directors are not significantly related to the quantity of the CSR disclosure. The same conclusions are found for the control variables.

Regarding CSR disclosure quality, the results reveal that this latter is more practiced in companies having boards composed by an important proportion of: foreign directors (β=.552, p = .000), independent directors (β=.239, p = .002), female directors (β=.174, p = .024) and state directors (β=.157, p = .040). Concerning board leadership, the results did not reveal a significant effect of CEO duality and CSR disclosure quality. Finally, the results did not reveal significant associations of control variables on the two models explaining CSR disclosure in Egypt.

To sum up, the common factors explaining the two dimensions of the CSR disclosure both in Tunisia and in Egypt are independent directors and foreign directors. It was also found that state directorship affect positively the quality of CSR disclosure both in Tunisia and in Egypt. The results confirm the expected positive effect of female directorship on CSR disclosure only in the Egyptian sample. Furthermore, it is found that CEO duality is negatively associated with the two dimensions of the CSR disclosure only in the Tunisian context. However, the results do not report a significant effect of family directors on

Table 7. Results of regression analysis for Egyptian listed companies

	Expected Sign	Model 1: QUANCSR		Model 2: QUALCSR	
		Beta	T-Value	Beta	T-Value
Constant		,011	,501	,078	1,572
Family directors (FAMDIR)	-	,014	,173	,028	,360
State directors (STADIR)	+	,080	1,040	**,157***	2,081
Independent directors (INDIR)	+	**,170***	2,192	**,239****	3,151
Foreign directors (FORDIR)	+	**,553*****	6,865	**,552*****	7,024
Women directors (FEMDIR)	+	**,160***	2,055	**,174***	2,279
Duality (DUAL)	-	-,074	-,933	-,079	-1,020
Industrial firm (IF)	+	,022	,277	,042	,540
Firm age (AGE)	+	-,026	-,313	-,017	-,208
R^2		0.36		0.38	
F-test		8.17***		9.17***	
Durbin Watson		1.83		1.98	

† p .10, * p .05, ** p .01, *** p .001; N=100

the CSR disclosure in Tunisia as well as in Egypt. So, the hypotheses H1 could not be proved. Regarding the control variables, a positive and significant effect of industrial activity on the quality of CSR disclosure is found only in the Tunisian context. Both in Tunisia and in Egypt the results do not reveal any significant effect of firm age on CSR disclosure. The results and the hypotheses validation are summarized in Table 8.

DISCUSSION

At the end of this study, several conclusions emerge. First, the board's independence is a key factor for CSR disclosure. In fact, the agency theory stipulates that independent directors may exercise a strict control over the management and request more transparency and disclosure (Jensen & Meckling, 1976). In Tunisia as well as in Egypt, independent directors are often chosen from retired politicians, university professors or members of professional organizations. The concern with public reputation has led independent directors to encourage comments on issues which are related to CSR in the board of directors' agenda (Wiedemann-Goiran et al., 2003; Markarian & Parbonetti, 2007).

In addition, the results reveal that the presence of foreign directors is critical to CSR disclosure. These directors often operate in subsidiaries or partners of multinational companies. The annual reports might provide foreign directors a significant opportunity to influence CSR disclosure in order to reduce information asymmetry caused by the geographical separation between foreign shareholders and local management. These directors also ensure the alignment of the annual reports with the disclosure practices in their countries. For example, Dhouibi and Mamoghli (2013) have found a positive relationship between foreign ownership and voluntary disclosure in Tunisian banks. Moreover, these results are in consensus with the study of Soliman et al. (2012) who have reported a significant positive relationship between CSR rating and ownership by institutional and foreign investors in Egypt.

Previous research has discovered a positive effect of state directors on the quality of CSR disclosure, which is in accordance with the stakeholder theory assumptions. CSR disclosure has permitted the state to gain legitimacy with regard to its stakeholders but also to set an example for private companies (Cho & Patten, 2007; Eng & Mak, 2003).

Although in Tunisia the proportion of listed companies that include female directors in their board is higher than in Egypt, no significant relationship between gender and CSR disclosure is found in the

Table 8. Results summary and hypotheses validation

Variable	Expected Sign	Confirmed Hypothesis	Unconfirmed Hypothesis
H1: Family Directors	-		Tunisia, Egypt
H2: State Directors	+	Tunisia, Egypt	
H3: Independent Directors	+	Tunisia, Egypt	
H4: Foreign Directors	+	Tunisia, Egypt	
H5: Female Directors	+	Egypt	Tunisia
H6: CEO Duality	-	Tunisia	Egypt

Tunisian context. The findings also suggest that gender diversity in the board affect positively CSR disclosure, which is noticed only in Egypt. It is shown that the representation of women in boards can moderate the effect of masculinity as well as individualism (Fernandez-Feijoo et al., 2012). Therefore, the inclusion of women in boards can boost feminine characteristics within the national culture. Countries with a feminist culture are more committed societies and tend to be more open minded especially for socially related information (Orij, 2010). The results of Egypt analysis concord with several studies assuming that women directors tend to be less business-oriented, more sensitive to CSR issues and considerate for the welfare of diverse stakeholders (Bear et al., 2010; Wang & Coffey, 1992).

Finally, a negative relationship between CEO duality and CSR disclosure is determined only in the Tunisian context. This result is in agreement with the assumptions of agency theory suggesting that the absence of CEO duality improves the transparency and the disclosure (Forker, 1992; Jensen, 1993). Moreover, the results are consistent with the findings of Nekhili and Fakhfakh (2006) who have studied two Tunisian listed companies and have found that the voluntary disclosure is associated with the absence of CEO duality. This can be explained by the fact that in Tunisia, the person serving simultaneously as CEO and chairperson of the board is usually a substantial shareholder, which reduces the interest of voluntary disclosure of information relating to CSR.

Regarding the control variables, the results show a significant influence of the industry on the quality of CSR disclosure only in Tunisia. Industrial companies, whose activities may have negative externalities, are more exposed than others to social and environmental risks and are subject to special attention in terms of quality of the disseminated information. Thus, industrial companies try to reassure shareholders and stakeholders through CSR disclosure.

CONCLUSION

Increasingly firms in Tunisia as well as in Egypt are interested in improving CSR practices and disclose information for this purpose. However, CSR disclosure is often allowed at the discretion of the principal shareholders and the top management. In this context, the objective of this chapter is to determine the impact of the board characteristics and leadership on the CSR disclosure in Tunisian listed companies as well as in Egyptian listed companies. At the end of the empirical study, the findings reveal a positive influence of independent directors, foreign directors, female directors and state directors on CSR disclosure.

Furthermore, it is shown that Tunisian companies disclose less on CSR when the same person holds the functions of CEO and Chairman. CSR disclosure is also influenced by the belonging of the company to an industry generating more social and environmental externalities than other sectors. However, the results do not confirm the expected effect of family directorship on CSR disclosure.

The results of this study highlight that CSR disclosure depends partially on the composition and leadership structure of the board. Thus, based on the professional profiles of influential directors as determined by the results, it can be concluded that CSR disclosure appears to result from the willingness to meet shareholders' expectations in terms of transparency and voluntary disclosure of non-financial information.

It is worth mentioning that the findings of this chapter include a set of restraints due to the following reasons. First, CSR disclosure is relatively a new concept in Tunisia and often confused with social marketing. This voluntary information does not necessarily meet the reporting standards. Then, the scope of this chapter which is exclusively concerned with the board's characteristics does not refer to three important notions namely the organizational culture, the information systems and the managers' background. These notions may affect the company's CSR orientation and its disclosure policy. Other criteria such as the different roles that can be played by the board of directors and influenced by the director's profiles, ages, experience, qualifications and ownership as well as cognitive dynamics within the board room are not examined in this chapter. Finally, the study results are derived from a sample relatively small, it would be appropriate to extend the sample and to consider the study of SMEs and unlisted companies especially as the fabric of businesses in Tunisia and Egypt are dominated by small family businesses. The expansion of the empirical study field will permit to generalize the results and to assess the validity of corporate governance theories within the context of developing economies.

This research is a contribution to the field of comparative studies on CSR and particularly those conducted in developing countries. By determining the effect of state capitalism, foreign ownership, board independence, culture and gender diversity traditions, this research provides evidence in favor of the institutional theory that shows that the quality and volume of CSR disclosure may be different in two countries that researchers tend to assign to the same cultural, economic and geographical cluster. This research opens new perspectives of research for future comparative work on CSR to the extent that the results can serve as a basis for studying the way in which national corporate governance systems and internal governing bodies affect corporate CSR behavior. It is worth noting that extensive intercultural research must be conducted in focusing on social and institutional frameworks' characteristics that influence corporate governance practices, CSR orientation as well as motivations related to CSR disclosure.

REFERENCES

Abdullah, S. N., & Nasir, N. M. (2004). Accrual management and the independence of the boards of directors and audit committees. *International Journal of Economics, Management and Accounting, 12*(1).

Adams, C. A., & Larrinaga-González, C. (2007). Engaging with organisations in pursuit of improved sustainability accounting and performance. *Accounting, Auditing & Accountability Journal, 20*(3), 333–355. doi:10.1108/09513570710748535

Adams, C. A., & McNicholas, P. (2007). Making a difference: Sustainability reporting, accountability and organisational change. *Accounting, Auditing & Accountability Journal, 20*(3), 382–402. doi:10.1108/09513570710748553

Anderson, R. C., Mansi, S. A., & Reeb, D. M. (2004). Board characteristics, accounting report integrity, and the cost of debt. *Journal of Accounting and Economics, 37*(3), 315–342. doi:10.1016/j.jacceco.2004.01.004

Ayuso, S., & Argandona, A. (2009). Responsible corporate governance: Towards a stakeholder board of directors? *Corporate Ownership & Control, 6*(4), 9–19.

Barako, D. G., & Brown, A. M. (2008). Corporate social reporting and board representation: Evidence from the Kenyan banking sector. *Journal of Management & Governance, 12*(4), 309–324. doi:10.1007/s10997-008-9053-x

Bear, S., Rahman, N., & Post, C. (2010). The impact of board diversity and gender composition on corporate social responsibility and firm reputation. *Journal of Business Ethics*, *97*(2), 207–221. doi:10.1007/s10551-010-0505-2

Bechtel, R. B., Verdugo, V. C., & de Queiroz Pinheiro, J. (1999). Environmental Belief Systems United States, Brazil, and Mexico. *Journal of Cross-Cultural Psychology*, *30*(1), 122–128. doi:10.1177/0022022199030001008

Belhaj, M., & Damak-Ayadi, S. (2011). Financial performance, environmental performance and environmental disclosure: The case of Tunisian firms. *Afro-Asian Journal of Finance and Accounting*, *2*(3), 248–269. doi:10.1504/AAJFA.2011.041632

Bernardi, R. A., Bosco, S. M., & Vassill, K. M. (2006). Does Female Representation on Boards of Directors Associate With Fortune's "100 Best Companies to Work For" List? *Business & Society*, *45*(2), 235–248. doi:10.1177/0007650305283332

Brammer, S., & Millington, A. (2006). Firm size, organizational visibility and corporate philanthropy: An empirical analysis. *Business Ethics (Oxford, England)*, *15*(1), 6–18. doi:10.1111/j.1467-8608.2006.00424.x

Campbell, J. L. (2004). *Institutional change and globalization*. Princeton, NJ: Princeton University Press.

Cerbioni, F., & Parbonetti, A. (2007). Exploring the effects of corporate governance on intellectual capital disclosure: An analysis of European biotechnology companies. *European Accounting Review*, *16*(4), 791–826. doi:10.1080/09638180701707011

Cho, C. H., & Patten, D. M. (2007). The role of environmental disclosures as tools of legitimacy: A research note. *Accounting, Organizations and Society*, *32*(7), 639–647. doi:10.1016/j.aos.2006.09.009

Coffey, B. S., & Wang, J. (1998). Board diversity and managerial control as predictors of corporate social performance. *Journal of Business Ethics*, *17*(14), 1595–1603. doi:10.1023/A:1005748230228

Cowen, S. S., Ferreri, L. B., & Parker, L. D. (1987). The impact of corporate characteristics on social responsibility disclosure: A typology and frequency-based analysis. *Accounting, Organizations and Society*, *12*(2), 111–122. doi:10.1016/0361-3682(87)90001-8

Deegan, C., & Gordon, B. (1996). A study of the environmental disclosure practices of Australian corporations. *Accounting and Business Review*, *26*(3), 187–199. doi:10.1080/00014788.1996.9729510

Dhouibi, R., & Mamoghli, C. (2013). Determinants of voluntary disclosure in Tunisian bank's reports. *Research Journal of Finance and Accounting*, *4*(5), 80–94.

Donaldson, L., & Davis, J. H. (1991). Stewardship theory or agency theory: CEO governance and shareholder returns. *Australian. Journal of Management*, *16*(1), 49–64.

Dunn, P., & Sainty, B. (2009). The relationship among board of director characteristics, corporate social performance and corporate financial performance. *International Journal of Managerial Finance*, *5*(4), 407–423. doi:10.1108/17439130910987558

Elliott, R. K., & Jacobson, P. D. (1994). Costs and Benefits of Business information. *Accounting Horizons*, *8*(4), 80–96.

Eng, L. L., & Mak, Y. T. (2003). Corporate governance and voluntary disclosure. *Journal of Accounting and Public Policy*, *22*(4), 325–345. doi:10.1016/S0278-4254(03)00037-1

Ezat, A., & El-Masry, A. (2008). The impact of corporate governance on the timeliness of corporate internet reporting by Egyptian listed companies. *Managerial Finance*, *34*(12), 848–867. doi:10.1108/03074350810915815

Fernandez-Feijoo, B., Romero, S., & Ruiz, S. (2012). Does board gender composition affect corporate social responsibility reporting. *International Journal of Business and Social Science*, *3*(1), 31–38.

Fields, M. A., & Keys, P. Y. (2003). The emergence of corporate governance from Wall St. to Main St.: Outside directors, board diversity, earnings management, and managerial incentives to bear risk. *Financial Review*, *38*(1), 1–24. doi:10.1111/1540-6288.00032

Forker, J. J. (1992). Corporate governance and disclosure quality. *Accounting and Business Review*, *22*(86), 111–124. doi:10.1080/00014788.1992.9729426

Gilligan, C. (1982). *In a different voice*. Cambridge, MA: Harvard University Press.

Godfrey, P. C., & Hatch, N. W. (2006). Researching corporate social responsibility: An agenda for the 21st century. *Journal of Business Ethics*, *70*(1), 87–98. doi:10.1007/s10551-006-9080-y

Gray, R., Javad, M., Power, D. M., & Sinclair, C. D. (2001). Social and environmental disclosure and corporate characteristics: A research note and extension. *Journal of Business Finance & Accounting*, *28*(3-4), 327–356. doi:10.1111/1468-5957.00376

Gray, R., Walters, D., Bebbington, J., & Thompson, I. (1995). The greening of enterprise: An exploration of the (non) role of environmental accounting and environmental accountants in organizational change. *Critical Perspectives on Accounting*, *6*(3), 211–239. doi:10.1006/cpac.1995.1021

Gul, F. A., & Leung, S. (2004). Board leadership, outside directors' expertise and voluntary corporate disclosures. *Journal of Accounting and Public Policy*, *23*(5), 351–379. doi:10.1016/j.jaccpubpol.2004.07.001

Hackston, D., & Milne, M. J. (1996). Some determinants of social and environmental disclosures in New Zealand companies. *Accounting, Auditing & Accountability Journal*, *9*(1), 77–108. doi:10.1108/09513579610109987

Hair, J. F., Black, W. C., Babin, B. J., Anderson, R. E., & Tatham, R. L. (2006). *Multivariate data analysis* (Vol. 6). Upper Saddle River, NJ: Pearson Prentice Hall.

Haniffa, R. M., & Cooke, T. E. (2005). The impact of culture and governance on corporate social reporting. *Journal of Accounting and Public Policy*, *24*(5), 391–430. doi:10.1016/j.jaccpubpol.2005.06.001

Ho, S. S., & Wong, K. S. (2001). A study of the relationship between corporate governance structures and the extent of voluntary disclosure. *Journal of International Accounting, Auditing & Taxation*, *10*(2), 139–156. doi:10.1016/S1061-9518(01)00041-6

Hofstede, G. (1983). The cultural relativity of organizational practices and theories. *Journal of International Business Studies*, 1983, 75–89.

Hooghiemstra, R. (2000). Corporate communication and impression management-new perspectives why companies engage in corporate social reporting. *Journal of Business Ethics*, *27*(1/2), 55–68. doi:10.1023/A:1006400707757

Htay, S. N. N., Rashid, H. M. A., Adnan, M. A., & Meera, A. K. M. (2012). Impact of corporate governance on social and environmental information disclosure of Malaysian listed banks: Panel data analysis. *Asian Journal of Finance & Accounting*, *4*(1), 1–24. doi:10.5296/ajfa.v4i1.810

Huafang, X., & Jianguo, Y. (2007). Ownership structure, board composition and corporate voluntary disclosure: Evidence from listed companies in China. *Managerial Auditing Journal*, *22*(6), 604–619. doi:10.1108/02686900710759406

Ibrahim, N. A., & Angelidis, J. P. (1995). The corporate social responsiveness orientation of board members: Are there differences between inside and outside directors? *Journal of Business Ethics*, *14*(5), 405–410. doi:10.1007/BF00872102

Ibrahim, N. A., & Angelidis, J. P. (2011). Effect of board members' gender on corporate social responsiveness orientation. *Journal of Applied Business Research*, *10*(1), 35–40. doi:10.19030/jabr.v10i1.5961

Jensen, M. C. (1993). The modern industrial revolution, exit, and the failure of internal control systems. *the Journal of Finance, 48*(3), 831-880.

Jensen, M. C., & Meckling, W. H. (1976). Theory of the firm: Managerial behavior, agency costs and ownership structure. *Journal of Financial Economics*, *3*(4), 305–360. doi:10.1016/0304-405X(76)90026-X

Jo, H., & Harjoto, M. A. (2011). Corporate governance and firm value: The impact of corporate social responsibility. *Journal of Business Ethics*, *103*(3), 351–383. doi:10.1007/s10551-011-0869-y

Johnson, R. A., & Greening, D. W. (1999). The effects of corporate governance and institutional ownership types on corporate social performance. *Academy of Management Journal*, *42*(5), 564–576. doi:10.2307/256977

Kaymak, T., & Bektas, E. (2008). East meets west? Board characteristics in an emerging market: Evidence from Turkish banks. *Corporate Governance: An International Review*, *16*(6), 550–561. doi:10.1111/j.1467-8683.2008.00713.x

Kiel, G. C., & Nicholson, G. J. (2003). Board composition and corporate performance: How the Australian experience informs contrasting theories of corporate governance. *Corporate Governance: An International Review*, *11*(3), 189–205. doi:10.1111/1467-8683.00318

Koleva, P., & Gherib, J. (2012). La responsabilité sociale des entreprises en Tunisie: Une lecture institutionnaliste. *Revue Tiers Monde*, *212*(4), 83–99. doi:10.3917/rtm.212.0083

Kolk, A. (2003). Trends in sustainability reporting by the Fortune Global 250. *Business Strategy and the Environment*, *12*(5), 279–291. doi:10.1002/bse.370

Kolk, A. (2005). Environmental reporting by multinationals from the Triad: Convergence or divergence? *Management International Review*, 2005, 145–166.

Krüger, P. (2009). *Corporate social responsibility and the board of directors. Job Market Paper*. France: Toulouse School of Economics.

Markarian, G., Parbonetti, A., & Previts, G. J. (2007). The Convergence of Disclosure and Governance Practices in the World's Largest Firms. *Corporate Governance: An International Review*, *15*(2), 294–310. doi:10.1111/j.1467-8683.2007.00561.x

Matoussi, H., Karaa, A., & Maghraoui, R. (2004). Information asymmetry, disclosure level and securities liquidity in the BVMT. *Finance India*, *18*, 547–558.

Milne, M. J., & Adler, R. W. (1999). Exploring the reliability of social and environmental disclosures content analysis. *Accounting, Auditing & Accountability Journal*, *12*(2), 237–256. doi:10.1108/09513579910270138

Nahar Abdullah, S. (2006). Board structure and ownership in Malaysia: the case of distressed listed companies. Corporate Governance: *The international journal of business in society, 6*(5), 582-594.

Nekhili, M., & Fakhfakh, I. (2006). Les relations entre les mécanismes de gouvernement et l'indice de divulgation volontaire d'informations: étude clinique de deux entreprises tunisiennes. *Paper presented at the 27th conference of AFC on Comptabilité, Contrôle,* Audit et Institution(s). Tunis, Tunisia.

Orij, R. (2010). Corporate social disclosures in the context of national cultures and stakeholder theory. *Accounting, Auditing & Accountability Journal*, *23*(7), 868–889. doi:10.1108/09513571011080162

Parker, L. D. (2005). Social and environmental accountability research: A view from the commentary box. *Accounting, Auditing & Accountability Journal*, *18*(6), 842–860. doi:10.1108/09513570510627739

Petra, S. T. (2005). Do outside independent directors strengthen corporate boards?. *Corporate Governance: The international journal of business in society, 5*(1), 55-64.

Post, C., Rahman, N., & Rubow, E. (2011). Green governance: Boards of directors' composition and environmental corporate social responsibility. *Business & Society*, *50*(1), 189–223. doi:10.1177/0007650310394642

Rizk, R., Dixon, R., & Woodhead, A. (2008). Corporate social and environmental reporting: A survey of disclosure practices in Egypt. *Social Responsibility Journal*, *4*(3), 306–323. doi:10.1108/17471110810892839

Salama, A. (2009). Egypt: Social responsibility disclosure practices. In S. O. Idowu & W. L. Filho (Eds.), *Global Practices of Corporate Social Responsibility* (pp. 325–342). Berlin, Heidelberg: Springer. doi:10.1007/978-3-540-68815-0_16

Saleh Al Arussi, A., Hisyam Selamat, M., & Mohd Hanefah, M. (2009). Determinants of financial and environmental disclosures through the internet by Malaysian companies. *Asian Review of Accounting*, *17*(1), 59–76. doi:10.1108/13217340910956513

Samaha, K., & Dahawy, K. (2010). An empirical analysis of corporate governance structures and voluntary corporate disclosure in volatile capital markets: The Egyptian experience. *International Journal of Accounting. Auditing and Performance Evaluation*, *7*(1-2), 61–93.

Schwartz, S. H., & Bardi, A. (2001). Value hierarchies across cultures taking a similarities perspective. *Journal of Cross-Cultural Psychology*, *32*(3), 268–290. doi:10.1177/0022022101032003002

Shleifer, A., & Vishny, R. W. (1997). A survey of corporate governance. *The Journal of Finance*, *52*(2), 737–783. doi:10.1111/j.1540-6261.1997.tb04820.x

Siciliano, J. I. (1996). The relationship of board member diversity to organizational performance. *Journal of Business Ethics*, *15*(12), 1313–1320. doi:10.1007/BF00411816

Stanwick, P. A., & Stanwick, S. D. (1998). The determinants of corporate social performance: An empirical examination. *American Business Review*, *16*(1), 86.

Tabachnick, B. G., & Fidell, L. S. (2001). *Using multivariate analysis. California State University Northridge*. Harper Collins College Publishers.

Tricker, R. I. (1984). *Corporate governance: Practices, procedures, and powers in British companies and their boards of directors*. Aldershot: Gower Pub Co.

Unerman, J. (2000). Methodological issues-reflections on quantification in corporate social reporting content analysis. *Accounting, Auditing & Accountability Journal*, *13*(5), 667–681. doi:10.1108/09513570010353756

Vachon, S. (2010). International operations and sustainable development: Should national culture matter? *Sustainable Development*, *18*(6), 350–361. doi:10.1002/sd.398

Van der Laan Smith, J., Adhikari, A., & Tondkar, R. H. (2005). Exploring differences in social disclosures internationally: A stakeholder perspective. *Journal of Accounting and Public Policy*, *24*(2), 123–151. doi:10.1016/j.jaccpubpol.2004.12.007

Vogel, D. (2007). *The market for virtue: The potential and limits of corporate social responsibility*. Washington, DC: Brookings Institution Press.

Waldman, D. A., de Luque, M. S., Washburn, N., House, R. J., Adetoun, B., Barrasa, A., & Wilderom, C. P. (2006). Cultural and leadership predictors of corporate social responsibility values of top management: A GLOBE study of 15 countries. *Journal of International Business Studies*, *37*(6), 823–837. doi:10.1057/palgrave.jibs.8400230

Wiedemann-Goiran, T., Perier, F., Lépineux, F., & Tiberghien, F. (2003). *Développement durable et gouvernement d'entreprise: un dialogue prometteur*. Paris: Éditions d'Organisation.

Williams, R. J. (2003). Women on corporate boards of directors and their influence on corporate philanthropy. *Journal of Business Ethics*, *42*(1), 1–10. doi:10.1023/A:1021626024014

Chapter 7
An Evaluation of the State of the CSR Field in Australia:
Perspectives from the Banking and Mining Sectors

Hélène de Burgh-Woodman
The University of Notre Dame, Australia

Alessandro Bressan
The University of Notre Dame, Australia

Angela Torrisi
The University of Notre Dame, Australia

ABSTRACT

While Corporate Social Responsibility (CSR) has become established in the managerial lexicon, its meaning and application varies according to geographical and sector contexts. In this chapter, we focus on the application of CSR across the banking and mining sectors in Australia to analyse the ways in which this managerial mechanism, with its theoretical underpinnings of social, environmental and economic balance, has been strategically appropriated and applied. We pose the key questions of how has CSR been implemented in Australia's largest industries and, secondarily, why has CSR not been more effective in transforming business practice in Australia? To demonstrate the alternative purposes to which CSR has been put, we use two case studies drawn from Australia's two most visible industries. The purpose of these case studies is to illustrate the larger conceptual ambiguity or fragmentation endemic to CSR and how this ambiguity affects its application – and therefore effectiveness – across different contexts.

DOI: 10.4018/978-1-5225-0720-8.ch007

INTRODUCTION

In the same vein that Corporate Social Responsibility (CSR) has become a mainstream global practice (De Bakker, Gronenewegen & Den Hond, 2005; Carroll, 1991; Carson, 1993; Zu, 2009), CSR is an established mechanism in the Australian business landscape with most large organisations engaging in CSR related initiatives. As in most contexts across the world, the concept remains essentially fragmented and applied to divergent purposes, covering such areas as financial performance (Peloza, 2009), implementation (Carroll, 1999; Waddock, 2004), measurement (Wood, 2010) and stakeholder value creation (Peloza & Shang, 2011). CSR has also been used in human contexts such as organisational life, industrial and organisational psychology (Aguinis, 2011) and operations (Hoejmose, Brammer & Millington, 2011).

The effect of this definitional, and applied, fragmentation of the CSR concept has been a "cherry-picking" approach to its adoption. In this chapter, we suggest that, despite Jin et al.'s (2013) observation that CSR should strengthen "professional ethical thinking and consciousness" (p.17), there is little evidence to suggest that the uptake of CSR initiatives in Australia has led to substantively more ethical business practice or better outcomes for people and planet (Carroll, 1991). In focusing on Australia, it also alerts us to the larger questions of the extent to which CSR has resonance across different socio-economic environments (Zhang & Han, 2008). We further observe that CSR has often become a mechanism for strengthening reputational capital (Du & Vieria, 2012) and a vehicle for masking questionable professional conduct (Banerjee, 2007). Therefore, we pose the key research questions of how has CSR been implemented in Australia's largest industries and, secondarily, why has CSR not been more effective in transforming business practice in Australia? In order to demonstrate the alternative purposes to which CSR has been put in Australia and the problems associated with its application, we use two case studies drawn from Australia's two most visible industries - mining and banking. The purpose of these case studies is to illustrate the conceptual ambiguity or fragmentation lent to CSR generally and how this ambiguity has significant consequences for its application. In order to conduct our comparative analysis, we use stakeholder theory (Buchholz & Rosenthal, 2005; Donaldson & Preston 1995; Freeman 1984; Jones & Wicks, 1999) as our conceptual base.

The first case study from the banking sector illustrates the complexities associated with the uptake of CSR as a philanthropic framework (Balmer et al., 2007). The second case study devoted to the mining sector focuses on the use of CSR as a mechanism for narrating apparent organisational commitment to environmental sustainability (Harris & Crane, 2002; Pane-Haden, Oyler, & Humphreys, 2009; Preuss, 2005; Purser et al., 1995). The use of stakeholder theory as a conceptual frame enables us to compare and contrast the methods by which two prominent industries have utilised CSR to better position their organisations, buffer against criticism of their operations and enhance their image among consumers.

In visiting these cases, the aim of the present chapter is to re-visit CSR as a practical framework for the implementation of business ethics (de Burgh-Woodman et al., 2014), asking firstly whether the definitional fragmentation of CSR is hindering its implementation and secondly why this may be occurring. The second aim of the chapter is to look at how major industries in Australia are adopting CSR and what the real outcomes of these initiatives are. Finally, the chapter discusses the theoretical and practical implications of the case study findings. While the dynamics of the case studies emerge from the Australian context, the discussion takes account of broader theoretical and practical implications.

BACKGROUND

The following framework focuses on CSR literature in order to establish the extent to which this concept remains fragmented and therefore open to ambiguity at the level of implementation. We then review the state of the field in the Australian context, focusing in particular on the industries that form the basis of our case studies in this chapter. Lee (2008) notes that CSR has shifted from a relatively marginalised idea to one of the most widely accepted concepts in the academic and business world in the past 20 years. The impetus behind the evolution of CSR has been principally social to the extent that shifting social and cultural values have seen the uptake of discourses around environmental degradation, social equity and corporate citizenship. Currently, CSR literature has not stipulated a clear and holistic understanding of the conceptualisation of CSR at the level of application (Crane, McWilliam, Matten, Moon & Seigel, 2008; Garriga & Mele, 2004; Carroll, 2008). This conceptual framework will thus explore the fragmentation and ambiguity of CSR and the implications for practical uptake among corporations in Australia.

Defining Corporate Social Responsibility (CSR)

CSR has experienced a unique evolution in the management literature (Luo & Bhattacharya, 2009). The focus of CSR research has gravitated towards strategy and its rise to prominence in the 1990s and 2000s suggests that it is a relatively new area of scholarly research (Porter & Kramer, 2006). However, the scholarly literature dates back to the 1950s when Bowen (1953) first flagged the responsibilities of business. The concept and practice of CSR has since proliferated at a rapid rate causing a multi-stranded, and often fragmented, concept to emerge. However, while this has led to multiple (and often contradictory) conceptual understandings of CSR, it is still important to make sense of the multidimensional reality of CSR in the corporate world and its benefits or consequences for its application (Crane et al., 2008). Hence, as distinct from the evolution of the CSR concept, there are noticeably four dominant theoretical bases informing CSR practice today (Cetindamar & Husoy, 2007; Garriga & Mele, 2004). These theories include Corporate Social Performance (Clarkson, 1995), Shareholder Value Theory (Lazonick & O'Sullivan, 2000; Rappaport, 1986), Stakeholder Value Theory (Freeman, 1984; Donaldson & Preston, 1995) and Corporate Citizenship (Matten et al., 2003; Valor, 2005; Waddell, 2000). Furthermore, it is important to note that there is no 'one' collaborative definition or theory that depicts CSR (Valor, 2005), but these four different theories illuminate its practice within business management (Carroll, 2008).

Dahlsrud (2008) recognises the variety of definitions, suggesting that 'the existing definitions are to a large degree congruent' (Dahlsrud, 2008, p. 1). Through a content analysis of existing CSR definitions, Dahlsrud reasoned that all of the definitions consistently referred to five dimensions; these being the environmental dimension, the social dimension, the economic dimension, the stakeholder dimension and the voluntariness dimension. These findings coincide with Garriga and Mele's (2004) frame which refers to the instrumental, political, integrative and ethical perspectives given to CSR. Therefore, the ambiguity surrounding CSR is not so much about how CSR is defined but rather how CSR is constructed and practiced in a specific context (Dahlsrud, 2008, p. 1). Similarly, in looking at the origins of CSR, Gjølberg (2009) indicates that CSR cannot be separated from the contextual factors of the nation in which it is practiced. This insight draws attention to the need for research that takes account of specific national and industry contexts such as the case studies discussed here.

As noted by Brine, Brown & Hackett (2007) the practicality of CSR for corporations should not be an 'add-on' or just obeying the law but essentially embedded within the 'core business operations'

(Brine, Brown & Hackett, 2007). Hence, one of the most applicable, and frequently used, definitions is McWilliams and Siegel's (2001) interpretation of CSR as 'actions that appear to further some social good, beyond the interest of the firm and that which is required by law' (McWilliams & Siegel, 2001, p. 117; see also Tsoutsoura, 2004; Kristoffersen, Gerrans, Clarke-Murphy, 2005; McWilliams, Siegel, & Wright, 2006). Again, we see the same emphases on social, environmental and legal impacts that underpin most CSR definitions.

CSR as an Ambiguous Concept

CSR is a complex term that has many layers of meaning (Shanahan, 2001) and contextual characteristics (Vidal & Kozak, 2008). Despite the relative maturity of the field, researchers and practitioners alike have nevertheless still to agree on a definition and understanding of its very core object of analysis (Carroll, 1999; Lockett, Moon, & Visser, 2006). Equally, practitioners need to form a cohesive understanding of CSR, so practical implementation within corporations can be congruent, relevant and beneficial (Truscott, Bartlett, & Tywoniak; 2009). Moreover, CSR literature is deeply divided about the very status of CSR itself, dominated by either proponents of corporate social engagement or critics who believe that such initiatives use corporate resources misguidedly. As noted by Waddock (2004), 'parallel and sometimes confusing universes exist' (pg. 5), leading to Mazurkiewicz's (2004) pondering as to whether a common CSR framework is even possible. One reason for this fragmentation is that CSR has evolved through different disciplinary and conceptual lenses (Carroll, 1999; Waddock, 2004). A further dimension is that, as Mazurkiewicz (2004) points out, around the world "so far there have been over 300 CSR codes, principles, performance standards, management standards developed by governments, business associations, or academia, not mentioning a huge number of individual companies' codes of conduct or reporting initiatives" (pg. 6).

As CSR is therefore contextual and complex, scholars and corporations alike have been able to define and interpret CSR as best fits their purposes – which has resulted in definitions or interpretations that generate further subjectivities or reflect fundamental ideologies (Clark-Murphy et al., 2005). Garriga and Mele (2004) make the important point that it is vital when conceptualising CSR that what is practiced is business *in* society, not business and society – a point that comes into question when focusing on how corporation use the CSR concept. While Kotler and Lee (2005) reference the purpose of CSR as 'a commitment to improve societal well-being through discretionary business practices and contribution of corporate resources', the drivers for this so-called social well-being endeavour remain essentially commercially focused. Although the distinctive features of CSR are to positively engage the 'business world' with the surrounding 'environment and society' (Corbett & Kappagoda, 2013), this would appear to emerge from corporations responding to risks such as reputation, compliance failure or community pressure (Table 1).

As indicated by the drivers identified above, CSR today has become a powerful strategic instrument that can "enhance a firm's competitiveness and reputation' (Hill, 2007, p.6) and while there should be an omnipresence of CSR's impact on the business interface (Porter & Kramer, 2006; Isaksson, 2012), this often manifests at the level of reputational or strategic mechanism rather than philosophical commitment.

Table 1. Summary of principle drivers for CSR uptake

Economic Drivers	Social Drivers	Political Drivers
• Company image/reputation • Improved risk management • Competitive advantage • Pressure from business partners • Pressure from consumers • Pressure from investors • Competitiveness	• Pressure from NGOs/CSOs • License to operate • Pressure from local communities • Research	• Improved standing with Government • Legal, regulatory drivers • Political pressure • License to operate

Mazurkiewicz (2004, pg. 9)

The Concept of CSR in the Australia Context

As in other developed countries, CSR has become a relevant phenomenon among Australian companies (Truscott, 2007). However, as noted by Gustavson (2009) 'there is no clear consensus in Australia of what CSR is' (pg. 463) and as indicated in a recent report conducted by the Australian Centre for Social Responsibility (ACCSR) 'CSR is still an emerging concept and practices in the last 10 years have been slow and insufficient' (ACCSR, 2014, p. 6).

Certain sectors have led CSR initiatives in the Australian business landscape. This active role is emerging particularly in the financial and mining sectors, both key industries in the context of the Australian economy. Australian Bureau of Statistics (ABS) data indicate that the main industries contributing to the 2013-14 GVA growth of 2.5% were mining (9.5%) and financial and insurance services (5.3%) making these two industries amongst the most important in Australia. For context, in 2014 the mining industry employed directly 267,700 workers, almost 2.3% of the overall Australian workforce (Industry Outlook, Mining, Department of Employment, Australian Government, 2014). Similarly, the financial sector employs approximately 400,000 workers, 3.6% of the Australian work force (Australia Benchmark Report, 2015, ABS, 2014).

Most large mining and banking companies report their CSR activities covering various dimensions as social and environmental performance, health and safety issues and ethics. These two sectors represent the most active industries in Australia with respect to CSR. The 2013 KPMG Survey on global trends in corporate responsibility (CR) reporting found that almost 85% of the top 100 companies in Australia by revenue report on CSR, compared to 57% in 2011 and the large majority are in the mining and banking sectors. Further, among the 150 largest Australian companies signatory of the Global Reporting Initiative (GRI), 18 were in the mining sector and 16 in the financial service sector. Equally, at May 2015 four of the major financial Australian institutions out of 33 Australian companies signed the UN Global Compact while only 2 were mining firms. All four Australian largest banks have also signed for the Equator principles. Table 2 provides an overview of the main CSR signatures undertaken in 2014 by the eight largest Australian companies in the financial and mining sectors.

The assessment and measurement of CSR practices is well established in the literature on corporations. For example, Porter and Kramer (2006) reported that large organisations embraced CSR for strategic gain and to enhance their competitive advantage. Galbreath (2010) found that positive strategic and reputational advantages were achieved through CSR practices among large firms in Australia. He was able to quantify the positive relationship between a firm's implementation of CSR and a reduction in employee turnover, as well as measure increased reputational capital among consumers and other stakeholders.

Table 2. Australian largest mining and banks companies andCSR Signatory

Company	Sector	CSR signatory
Australian and New Zealand Banking Group (ANZ)	Financial service	- Equator-principles - Global Reporting Initiative (GRI) - UN Global Compact - OECD Guidelines for Multinational Enterprises
BHP Billiton (BHP)	Mining	- UN Global Compact - Extractive Industries Transparency Initiative (EITI) - Global Reporting Initiative (GRI) - International Council on Mining and Metals - Extractive Industries Transparency Initiative - UN Declaration of Human Rights and Voluntary Principles on Security and Human Rights - World Resources Institute/World Business Council for Sustainable Development Greenhouse Gas Protocol (WRI/WBCSD GHG Protocol) - International Standards on Auditing and Assurance Engagements - Socially Responsible Investment (SRI) Index
Commonwealth Bank of Australia (CBA)	Financial service	- Equator-principles - Global Reporting Initiative (GRI) - United Nations Global Compact
Fortescue Metals Group Limited (FMG)	Mining	- UN Global Compact
National Australia Bank (NAB)	Financial service	- Equator-principles - Global Reporting Initiative (GRI)
Newcrest Mining Limited (NCM)	Mining	- Environmental project report
Rio Tinto Limited (RIO)	Mining	- UN Global Compact - Extractive Industries Transparency Initiative (EITI) - Global Reporting Initiative (GRI) - Implemented a corporate approach to Indigenous communities' free, prior, informed consent (FPIC) which has been recognised as best practice by non-governmental organisations. - Procurement Academy as part of the Rio Tinto College - Sustainable development principles of the International Council on Mining and Metals (ICMM) - Voluntary Principles on Security and Human Rights (VPSHR) - United Nations Universal Declaration of Human Rights - UN Guiding Principles on Business and Human Rights - Principles on Security and Human Rights - 2012 International Finance Corporation Performance Standard 7 and supporting guidance
Westpac Bank (WBC)	Financial service	- Equator-principles - Global Reporting Initiative (GRI) - UN Global Compact - Declaration on Human Rights

Conversely, Gustavson (2009) is of the view that the principle drivers for Australian companies to embrace CSR are mostly in response to 'risk management' (e.g. see the changes in terms of Exchange Corporate Governance Principles) and the growing influence of institutional investors. His view is consistent with the stakeholder view of CSR (Peloza & Shang, 2011) that notes the increasing emphasis placed on CSR by stakeholders. Indeed, the increased participation of institutional shareholders within the organisation is becoming an important driver for CSR (Mazurkiewicz, 2004). However, the recent (2014) repeal of the carbon tax law (Department of the Environment, 2014) by the Australian Senate, and the future actions in the Direct Action Plan Policies on environmental issues at the federal level, undermine the internal drive for CSR in failing to provide clear policy direction relative to environmental and social responsibility. This situation is not only destabilising for the organisations affected by these laws, but it diminishes their enthusiasm, motivation and commitment to substantive CSR practices. Equally, when looking at the mining and banking sector in Australia, CSR philosophies and practices reveal a lack of consistency where "lack of a universally accepted definition allows for too much leeway to pick and choose practices that best suit their corporate agendas" (Smith, 2011, p. 9). There is not only a great deal of murkiness in terminology and definitions of the concept, but also there is no clarity on what can be regarded as socially irresponsible behaviour (Shinde et.al., 2011).

As noted by Pomering and Dolnicar (2009), the Australian banking industry has faced 'consumer disaffection' where banks have used CSR as a 'suitable avenue to re-engage with communities and improve their corporate images' (pg. 286). The essential observation of CSR in the banking context is that CSR serves as a reputational mechanism to enhance consumer satisfaction. Equally, the mining industry faces significant environmental and social challenges from pollution to community issues. Jenkins and Yakovlena (2006) noted that CSR, for the mining sector, is about balancing the diverse demands of communities, the environment and the need to make profit. Mining companies have responded to these challenges by developing CSR policies and are amongst the most prolific in providing social and environmental information (Jenkins & Yakovleva, 2006). Again, the observation of how CSR is used in this sector is that it serves to mitigate or obscure the core activities of the industry, which is, by definition, environmentally and socially destructive. Therefore, while both these sectors are highly engaged in apparent CSR initiatives, the approach taken and the drivers behind these activities are open to further scrutiny.

Stakeholder Theory in the CSR Context

While the above literature review traces the conceptual ambiguity of CSR and its varying application in the Australian context, it is important to visit the foundations of stakeholder theory as some of the theoretical development in this field gives much explanatory force to both of the ensuing case studies. As the following cases will demonstrate, CSR practice is fundamentally driven by stakeholder-based interests.

Like the notion of CSR, since Freeman's (1984) landmark work, stakeholder theory has enjoyed a degree of conceptual ambiguity (Donaldson & Preston, 1995), drawing from differing standpoints such as normative (Burton & Dunn, 1996; Donaldson & Dunfee, 1999) instrumental (Egels-Zandén & Sandberg, 2010; Jones & Wicks 1999) and descriptive (Egels-Zandén & Sandberg, 2010).

The *normative* thesis involves the acceptance of two main ideas: a) stakeholders, as groups or individuals, have legitimate interests; these interests can be substantive or procedural elements of corporate activity. b) "The interests of all stakeholders are of intrinsic value" (Donaldson & Preston, 1995, pg. 67); thus, all groups of stakeholders merit consideration for their own sake. The *instrumental* aspect of Stakeholder theory refers to the framework for exploring links between achieving several corporate performance goals, such as growth or profitability, and practicing stakeholder management (Donaldson & Preston, 1995); that is a combination of recommended structures, practices, or attitudes (Donaldson & Preston, 1995). Finally, the *descriptive* thesis describes the corporation, including specific behaviours or corporate characteristics. Based on this thesis, the corporation is a constellation of competitive and comparative interests that have intrinsic value (Donaldson & Preston, 1995).

Donaldson and Preston traced this tripartite taxonomy but argued that all stakeholder theory could be seen to be essentially normative – a position that has been subsequently challenged. While this has led to the observation that other stakeholder perspectives such as instrumental and descriptive have been somewhat ignored in the literature (Butterfield et al., 2004; Jones & Wicks, 1999; Jawahar & McLaughlin, 2001; Trevino & Weaver, 1999), more recent evolutions in stakeholder theory have sought to explore alternative views (Egels-Zandén & Sandberg, 2010) and to engage emergent developments such as the broad instrumental position.

The instrumental strain of stakeholder theory (Donaldson & Preston, 1995) is salient for the present study since we see the balancing of financial and stakeholder imperatives at play in both contexts – albeit for different reasons. As such, we use the instrumental stakeholder view as a way to interpret the findings from the two case studies.

CSR IN AUSTRALIA: TWO CASE STUDIES

We adopt a case study method (Eisenhardt, 1989; Gibbert et al., 2008; Mallin, 2009; Voss et al., 2002) to look at the two sectors. The case study method has been used widely in research focused the uptake of CSR in SME (Castka et al., 2004; Nielsen & Thomsen, 2009), emerging (Chaudry & Wang, 2007; Wiig & Kolstad, 2010) and commercial (Bowd et al., 2006; Weber, 2008) contexts. This study extends on this significant body of work by extending the case study method to the commercial environment in Australia.

We follow Eisenhardt and Graebner's (2007) observation that "the central notion is to use cases as the basis from which to develop theory inductively. The theory is emergent in the sense that it is situated in and developed by recognizing patterns of relationships among constructs within and across cases and their underlying logical arguments" (p. 25). The objective of the case study presented here is to focus on two of Australia's largest sectors and sample across the dominant organisations within the sectors in order to trace the patterns of how CSR is being used, why certain practices emerge as industry norms and what the state of CSR uptake in major Australian industries actually is. In this respect, we adopt a theoretical sampling approach (Yin, 1994) to the case study selection (Eisenhardt & Graebner, 2007) where "cases are selected because they are particularly suitable for illuminating and extending relationships and logic among constructs" (p. 27).

The two sectors have been selected both for their size or scale and for their reputation as leaders in CSR uptake. By focusing on these two sectors, we are able to focus on so-called "best practice" in Australian CSR and how this concept has been used in some of Australia's largest corporations. The value of this is that in looking at best practice, we are able to assess the best of CSR uptake in Australia and the ways in which this framework has been used in large, influential industries.

Case Study 1: CSR in the Australian Banking Sector

Australia is ranked amongst the top five leading financial systems in the World (World Economic Forum, 2012) and banks play a central role within the Australian financial system by managing the large majority of financial system assets (Reserve Bank of Australia, 2012). Furthermore, the financial sector is a significant contributor to the Australian economy, with almost 6% of the 2013-14 GVA growth flowing from the financial and insurance industries.

This study analyses the four largest domestic banks (the "four pillars") by market capitalisation which represent almost 80% of the entire Australian market: Australia and New Zealand Bank (ANZ), Commonwealth Bank of Australia (CBA), National Australia Bank (NAB), and Westpac Banking Corporation (WBC). In the last decade, these organisations have positioned as the main protagonists and committed participants in the CSR arena, leading to recognition as being amongst the world leaders in their sectors for CSR practices. For instance, WBC has been included in the Global 100 Index compiled by Corporate Knights for 9 of the last 10 years, including being ranked in the first position in 2014. WBC was recognized as the global bank industry leader in the 2014 Dow Jones Sustainability Indices (DJSI).

In order to explore the research questions, this study analysed the annual reports and sustainability reports of the four major banks in Australia for the years 2012-2014. Reporting has been accepted as a rich context for study in looking at CSR practices (Golob & Bartlett, 2007). As noted by Wickham et al. (2011), companies use reports to formally and regularly communicate with their stakeholders about the company CSR commitment and practices. Thus, by analysing their sustainability reports, it is possible to track and evaluate the organisation's environmental and social responsibility activities.

To manage the data, NVivo 10 was used. In line with established research practice (Bennett & Robson, 2005; Hsieh & Shannon, 2005), content analysis was used to identify the themes and practices that emerged from the reports. As noted by various scholars (e.g. Bennett & Robson 2005; Hsieh & Shannon, 2005), content analysis is a research method used for the (subjective) interpretation of content data within the document investigated. This method therefore enabled the isolation of present themes, trends and practices both within and across corporations in order to give an accurate account of what constitutes CSR activity in the Australian banking sector.

Analysis

The first theme to emerge from the content analysis was the language used by the banks to describe their socially and environmentally responsible practices. Despite the academic lexicon that still favours CSR, none of the four banks use the term "corporate social responsibility" to describe their activities. Instead, NAB uses the term "corporate responsibility" (CR) to mean 'getting the fundamentals right for our customers being a good employer and addressing our broader responsibility to society' (NAB, Annual review 2013, pg. 2) and the term "sustainability" has been adopted by ANZ, WBC and CBA. CBA defines sustainability as 'building a successful business today, while creating enduring value for the Group's customers, people, shareholders and the broader community' (Commonwealth Bank of Australia, Annual Report, 2014). In other words, sustainability is literally about the long-term resilience of the firm, not about social, ethical and environmental actions that enhance the future for everyone. At ANZ, sustainability 'is about ensuring our business is managed to take account of social, environmental and economic risks and opportunities' (ANZ, 2014, pg. 17). In this respect, we see overtones of a traditional CSR intent in ANZ's definition with its acknowledgement of social, environmental and economic factors – although these are positioned as risks and opportunities rather than ethical obligations.

The emphasis on stakeholder engagement and satisfaction emerged as the second dominant theme from the content analysis. Shareholders, customers, employees and community emerged to be the main stakeholders in all four banks. Despite shareholders playing a relevant role within a publicly listed organisation, only customers, employees and community are analysed here since these three stakeholder groups were amongst the top 25 most frequently recurrent terms in the reports. "Customers", in the stakeholder context, was the foremost word adopted in the reports, thus providing an indication of how banks use sustainability initiatives as a reputational mechanism to enhance consumer satisfaction (Rae 2013) and to improve and consolidate the organisation's reputation (Du & Vieria, 2012). Customers are the primary source of income, positioning them 'at the heart of our strategy and central to our success'

(WBC, 2014, p. 10). There is no doubt that providing a good service is part of the core business activity, where 'what is good for our customers is also good for business' (ANZ, 2013, p. 2). Thus, an intriguing conflating between core business activity and CSR starts to emerge. The ethical intent that underpins CSR as a theoretical and philosophical construct starts to give way to core business function at the point of actual application. For example, WBC's strategic approach to customer satisfaction is that "our strategy is centred around customers, helping them to prosper and grow… Supporting customers is at the heart of our strategy and central to our success" (WBC, 2014, pg. 6 – 10). Similarly, the approach of NAB aims "to make a positive and sustainable impact in the lives of our customers… This underpins a strong and sustainable business for our shareholders and creates shared value for stakeholders" (NAB, 2014, p. 3). In all cases, the traditional language of CSR is used to describe profit-seeking, core business activity.

Employees emerged as another important stakeholder for the four Australian banking firms. Employees occupy the cold face of the business, linking the business with the customers and act as the key resource to achieve core business objectives. On their site, CBA claims to ensure that their "52,000 employees around the world are engaged, motivated and passionate advocates for the Group" (CBA, 2014). For NAB, 'engaged employees are considered to be more productive, foster greater customer loyalty and drive profitability. They also tend to stay for longer' (NAB, 2014, p. 34). Furthermore, the CR approach at NAB is expressed in terms of 'being a good employer, through investing in the skills and capabilities of our employees' (NAB, 2014, p. 3).

In line with this view of employees as stakeholders, analysis showed attention given to training and development. Training and development were emphasised as principal forms of engagement between firm and employees in all four banks. Again, while all four banks reported on their professional development programs as "sustainability initiatives", they represented basic professional development to enhance core business function. For instance, at NAB, every employee in the Australian region 'participated in an average of more than four days of formal training including training in products and services, credit risk and regulatory change and leadership development ensuring we develop the right skills to realise business benefits' (NAB, 2014, p. 37). At WBC, training and development aimed to 'strengthen our customer-centred, high performance culture' (WBC, 2014, p. 21). Almost 2,000 employees (5% of the total employees) completed professional qualifications or accreditation and 7,500 employees (20% of the total employees) completed training to support the implementation of the future of financial advice reforms. Furthermore, WBC introduced Prime of Life, a program with the aim to embrace and retain employees over 50 years old (almost 21% of the whole WBC workforce) and training and coaching to implement career transition priorities (WBC, 2014 p. 21).

Despite the evidence of training and development among the four banks, there was virtually no sign of any courses, workshops or seminars related to environmental and social responsibility. Most of the training and development implemented by the organisations was in a strategic direction 'ensuring we develop the right skills to realise business benefits' (NAB, 2014 p. 37). Only ANZ emerged to be the bank that, in 2014, provided training on 'environmental and social risk training issues' to more than 1,300 (2.6% of full time equivalent employees) and participation in a sustainability leadership program (ANZ, 2014). The comparatively insignificant number of employees who undertook this training (2.6% of the total organisation) would prompt further questions about how effective this training is as far as achieving overall organisational awareness and performance is concerned.

The last theme to emerge as a dominant aspect of the reports was community engagement. All four banks analysed demonstrated engagement with charities, sporting organisations and communities across Australia. Again, this engagement was given strategic, rather than ethical, emphasis. For instance, at

ANZ, 'earning community trust is fundamental to building our reputation in the region and maintaining our social license to operate' (ANZ, 2014, p. 63). ANZ provides a community contribution by 'including local employment, use of local suppliers, direct economic contribution through payment of taxes and employee contributions through volunteering and workplace giving' (ANZ, 2014, p.63). The emphasis is on undertaking socially beneficial activities in order to maintain reputational and economic capital rather than aiding and building communities. At CBA, community engagement was achieved 'through a combination of financial contribution and staff freely giving their time' (CBA, 2014 p. 6). CBA has been involved in sponsoring cricket, fundraising activities to Breast Cancer Institute Australia, Prostate Cancer Foundation and partnerships with Opera Australia, the Australian Chamber Orchestra and Bangarra Dance Theatre, as well as supports the Great Barrier Reef Foundation.

All four banks engaged in some form of community involvement yet the way in which the outcomes were reported suggests that community engagement is seen as a key strategic tool to enhance consumer retention, build brand loyalty and enhance profitability. The way in which community engagement is reported by all four banks would suggest that a case of "give a little, get a lot" is at play.

Findings

The results of the analysis suggest there is a missing link between CSR activities and the moral approach/ethical corporate behaviour (Jutterstrom & Norberg, 2013) required for a holistic CSR approach that can have enduring, positive effect. From the analysis of the definitions used by banks to describe their sustainability and corporate responsibility, it emerges that "social responsibility" has been altogether abandoned with a newfound emphasis on "sustainability" giving impetus to the long-term endurance of the firm. The definitions offered by the banks further confirm this movement away from an outward sense of social responsibility to an inward sense of survival with their articulation of financial gain and risk mitigation situated at the heart of their sustainability agenda. It becomes clear that "sustainability" just means the buoyancy of the bank - not the people and planet around it. This approach confirms what Hill (2007) sees in CSR where it becomes an instrument that can "enhance a firm's competitiveness and reputation' (Hill, 2007 p. 6).

Banks disclose information about their business success, achieved by offering new products and services, and the consequent business profitability rather than reporting on their ethical conduct. Despite the fact that CSR is embedded in a discourse of ethical conduct, it is clear that in the Australia banking sector that CR or sustainability reporting is about reporting the activities that have made the institution wealthier and their customers happier. Investigated banks demonstrated a scarce amount of training and development in terms of culture and knowledge on social and environmental responsibility amongst employees and do not engage in any ethical conduct dialogue with their consumers. Only one bank indicated training outcomes related to social and environmental issues and this was offered to 2.6% of full time employees. All four banks have been involved in some sort of community engagement, mostly linked with sponsorship and fundraising. This is in line with the 'consumer disaffection' found by Pomering and Dolnicar (2009) where banks have mostly used CSR as a reputational mechanism to enhance consumer satisfaction rather than to achieve ethical business practices or better outcomes for people and planet as suggested by Carroll (1991).

The sustainability reports analysed seem to be primarily used by banks as an instrumental and reputational tool, bypassing its main purpose to communicate with stakeholders about the company CSR commitment and practices (Mole, et al. 2011).

Case Study 2: CSR in the Australian Mining Sector

The mining industry has been part of the Australian's socio-economic development since the 19th century. Australia is home of three of the top 40 mining companies in the world in terms of market capitalisation (Mine 2014, PWC, 2014) with the mineral extraction industry being a relevant driver for economic and social growth, both in terms of employment and GDP. In 2014, the mining industry employed close to 270,000 workers, almost 2.5% of the overall Australian workforce (Industry Outlook, Mining, Department of Employment, Australian Government, 2014) and contributed to approximately 10% of the Australian's GDP (ABS, 2014).

However, this economic prosperity has not been without some environmental and social costs. CSR has been used by the mining sector to balance the demands from communities, the environment and profit seeking (Jenkins & Yakovleva, 2006). According to the Mineral Council of Australia, 'Australia's minerals industry has a strong, practical commitment to corporate social responsibility and environmental sustainability'. Thus, this study scrutinises the environmental social responsibility activities reported by the four highest value Australian mining companies: BHP Billiton Limited (BHP), Fortescue Metals Group Limited (FMG), Newcrest Mining Limited (NCM) and Rio Tinto Limited (RIO).

As with the analysis of the banking sector, this study analysed the annual reports and sustainability reports of the four largest mining firms for the years 2012-2014. NVivo 10 was used to manage and classify the data. Content analysis was then used to isolate the dominant themes that emerged from the reports (Bennett & Robson, 2005; Hsieh & Shannon, 2005).

Analysis

All four companies have been reporting their environmental and social sustainability strategy for over a decade, and frequently appear in global reporting indexes. Sustainability reports, documents and website information have been used by the four companies to maintain communication with their stakeholders. For instance, BHP sees the sustainability report as 'an approach to stakeholder engagement, accountability and transparency' (BHP, 2014, pg. 4) in which the company describes their responsibility to and actions towards environmental sustainability and stakeholder commitment. Equally, in their report, NCM aims to 'inform our stakeholders of our environmental, social and financial management and performance enabling a public review of our performance' (NCM, 2014, pg. 2).

The first theme to emerge from the analysis was, again, the language in which mining firms couch their CSR activities. The four firms recurrently used expressions such as 'sustainable development', 'stakeholder engagement' and 'license to operate' to describe their approach to environmental and social sustainability. None of these terms carry any ethical inflection but rather describe the access granted to conduct core business activities. For instance, RIO placed emphasis on sustainability development and stakeholder relationship as tools to support 'our license to operate and ensuring access to mineral resources, people and capital needed to execute the business strategy' (RIO, 2013, pg. 2). Similarly, NCM refers to sustainability both in terms of stakeholder engagement 'to maintain our social license to operate' and as a business approach 'to manage all-in sustaining costs of the business to be able to respond to changes in market conditions and progress growth opportunities' (NCM, 2014, pg. 1). BHP goes further in stating that sustaining the license to operate amongst stakeholders is strategically relevant in order to 'gaining access to natural resources and ensuring we build long-term relationships with our shareholders, employees, contractors, communities, customers and suppliers' (BHP, 2014, pg. 3).

The second, and perhaps the most striking theme to emerge from the analysis, was the persistent emphasis on environmental management. By definition, mining involves resource extraction and processing as the core business. In turn, their activities have a high and permanent impact on the biodiversity and ecosystem where operations are conducted. Some of the short and long-term impacts, (such as topographic modification, air quality reduction, surface and groundwater impacts), may be permanent leaving a direct effect on local fauna and flora. All four mining firms stated their commitment to environmental sustainability and took particular care to position environmental sympathy at the forefront of their positioning statement. For Mr. Biswas, CEO of NCM, 'minimising our impact on the environment is important' (NCM Sustainability Report, 2014, p. 1). Likewise, Mr. Mackenzie, CEO of BHP, noted that 'as a significant user of energy and water, we seek to minimise the environmental footprint of our operations (BHP, 2014). Environmental policies, management plans and rehabilitation procedures were reported by all firms as a means to prevent, control and balance the impact on biodiversity and ecosystem surrounding the mining sites. For instance, RIO reported on its biodiversity actions taken for the realisation of the Mount Pleasant open cut coal mine. The company was granted permission to clear almost 3,000 hectares of native vegetation housing various bird species of high conservation value. To compensate for the land taken, an offsets plan consisting of 15,500 hectares was enacted and the conditions conducive to bird restoration was created. In 2014, RIO performance data indicated that almost 14% of the land disturbed was rehabilitated (RIO, 2014, p. 108).

Furthermore, from the analysis, it emerged that mine closure represents a critical phase in terms of environmental and social risks. Although rehabilitation is expected from regulators and stakeholders as a basic matter of course, all of the mining firms positioned their expected rehabilitation activities as instead reflective of their good intentions

We firmly believe that when we close an operation, the land should be left in a condition capable of being used by others and that is at least compatible with the natural landscape (RIO, 2013, p. 6).

However, the mining process is an 'invasive and destructive' activity for the environment and, despite the strong commitment and good intention of the mines, it is questionable that a rehabilitation program/project can dismiss the damages created by the mining operation. The potential fallacy of rehabilitation programs has been recently highlighted as the world's third largest open cut zinc mine (owned by MMG Limited) located in Australia is closing in 2016. As noted by the mine closure planning superintendent, Matt Lord:

rehabilitating the site to its pre-mining state will occur over a 30-year period after operations cease and the 340 metre hole may never completely disappear and could take up to 120 years to fill with water (ABC News, September 19 2013).

In their reporting, the four mining firms are reluctant to engage in this dialogue and elect to emphasise their good intentions rather than negative impacts. For instance, RIO, in 2013 and 2014, counted respectively 15 and 12 'significant environmental incidents' which doubled from 2012 (RIO, 2013, p. 104, 2014 p. 108). Despite these incident flags appearing in the table of the environmental data performance at the end of RIO's sustainability report, no description or acknowledgement of the events occurred within the reports themselves. Thus, while the firms are keen to represent basic business activities such as rehabilitation as their own "good works" and narrate their environmental consideration, the reports persistently elide the reality that mining is a destructive activity that generates "significant environmental incidents".

The third theme to emerge from the analysis was an emphasis on communities. All of the firms commented on their need to maintain positive community engagement in order to gain site access and conduct operations. Indeed, 'engaging in constructive dialogues' (BHP, 2014) seemed to be a prime strategic tool to enable the mines to conduct their business and maintain their license to operate. Supporting indigenous employment and investing in community programmes emerged as main activities adopted by the four mines. In terms of employment of indigenous, RIO indicates the mining sector in Australia is 'one of the largest' private sector employer of indigenous' (RIO, 2014, p. 5). The indigenous workforce in RIO count of approximately 7.5% of the company's permanent Australian workforce and 550 indigenous contractors work on RIO's Australian mine sites. FMG, since 2011, has awarded '200 contracts and subcontracts to over 65 Aboriginal owned business and joint ventures, with a total contract value of over AU$1.8 billion' (FMG, 2013).

In terms of investment in local community, BHP in 2014 has spent over US$ 240 million worldwide (approximately 1.7% of BHP 2014 full year net profit) in community programs such as education and training, general infrastructure, environment, community support like the recent donation to the State Emergency Relief Fund for the South Australia bush fire (BHP, 2014, pg. 43). Similarly, RIO indicated to contributions of US$100 million (1.5% of RIO 2014 full year net profit) into direct community programs. However, as part of the numerical figure, no description of practices was found in the sustainability reports and supporting documents analysed. Therefore, it is unclear what activities were undertaken and what outcomes were achieved for local communities.

From the analysis, it also emerged that mines are not inclined to report potential or active conflict between the mines and communities. Only BHP reported briefly a 'community accidents' still active at their Cerro Matoso site (Colombia). However, according to Environmental Justice Atlas (http://ejatlas.org), BHP and RIO are amongst the 10 world largest mining corporations that still have active conflicts with civil society (i.e. indigenous group, NGOs, local community groups etc.) in operating sites located in Africa, South America and Papua New Guinea. A recent study conducted by Corporate Social Responsibility Initiative (CSRI) and the Centre for Social Responsibility in Mining (CSRM) in 2014 found that amongst mining companies, it is not a common procedure to 'identify, understand and aggregate the full range of costs of conflict with local communities' (Davis & Franks, 2014). It seems that more communication, transparency and real stakeholder engagement in dealing with conflict will occur only when mining firms, and their executive management, see the impact of conflict on their business bottom line.

The analysis of the four mining firms reveals a commitment to develop and implement environmental policies and plans. However, we also make the observation that CSR and its tools (e.g. sustainability report, ethics codes etc) is typically deployed as a strategic reporting device to mitigate the inevitable activity of the business, which, at core, has a permanent damaging impact on the environment and its surrounding community.

Findings

The results of the analysis suggest that the reporting of CSR activities in the Australian mining sector are focused around environmental management and community engagement. From the analysis of the definitions used by mining firms to describe their sustainability and corporate responsibility, the phrases 'sustainable development', 'stakeholder engagement' and 'license to operate' de-emphasise the ethical conduct of the firm in favour of strategies for gaining access to communities and preserving ability for the firm to achieve its business goals. Like the banking sector, the definitions used by mining firms digress from an articulation of social responsibility to an emphasis on business survival where profitability and risk mitigation feature heavily in their sustainability agenda. Again, we see Hill's (2008) observation of CSR at play in this sector.

The mining firm document their environmental management strategies and represent their core responsibilities as good intentions – by this we mean that their basic regulatory obligations are instead reported as being noble actions undertaken by choice or a will to remedy. This points to one of the core complications associated with CSR – how do we distinguish between basic compliance and "good deeds" that go above the necessities of regulatory frameworks? The movement between these two frames is clear in the way mining firms report their activities but also point towards a larger ambiguity about what we would regard as an ethically grounded CSR agenda. In this respect, the case study presented here plays out Jenkins and Obara's (2008) concern that

while multinational mining companies have 'remodelled' themselves as good corporate citizens there is little evidence as to how this recognition of the need to address sustainability issues has affected communities, and whether community development initiatives have been effective in contributing to more sustainable communities (p. 1).

The sustainability reports analysed seem to be primarily used by mining firms as a risk mitigation tool designed to detract attention away from the core business activity of extracting resources and causing environmental/social impacts in the process.

DISCUSSION AND RECOMMENDATIONS

The case studies presented here suggest two distinctly different ways in which CSR as a philosophical basis for business practice has been transformed in commercial practice. There is also evidence of an instrumental stakeholder perspective at play where the competing imperatives of stakeholder-driven CSR initiatives are mobilised against the financial goals of the firm. Table 3 summaries the principal findings that emerged from our investigations.

If we return to the key questions of how has CSR been implemented in Australia's largest industries and, secondarily, why has CSR not been more effective in transforming business practice in Australia, the two case studies enable us to start to draw some conclusions.

In the first instance, it is clear that CSR implementation in Australia has been substantively informed by the strategic intent and core business activities of the firm. The banking study shows that this sector is principally concerned with its consumer relations agenda in order to maintain profitability, thereby reflecting an instrumental stakeholder perspective. The CSR actions taken by the banks are designed to enhance consumer satisfaction, and thus, ongoing loyalty for the purposes of delivering perpetual growth. The mining study shows that the CSR agenda for this sector is designed to shed favourable light on implicitly destructive activities, preserve their so-called 'licence to operate' and mask any 'significant environmental incidents'. While the strategic intentions across these two sectors differ according to the industry requirements, the means by which the two sectors shift the CSR intent onto their own strategic terrain share several similarities.

Table 3. Summary of comparative findings across sectors

Context	CSR uptake	Drivers	CSR Activities	Effect
Banking	Reputational	• CSR as *social* responsibility • Customer satisfaction • Risk management	• Customer service • Community engagement • Company reporting • Stakeholder engagement	• Re-packaging of core business activities • Preservation of the firm
Mining	Reputational Risk mitigation	• CSR as *social* and *environmental* responsibility • Core business operations • Environmental destruction • Regulatory compliance	• Company reporting • Community engagement • Stakeholder engagement • Compliance	• Mitigation of core business effects • Preservation of the firm

Both industries have extracted the ethos of CSR and have re-cast both the language and definition attached to it. In the banking sector, the ethical specificity that underpins the CSR framework is replaced with the more ambiguous language of 'sustainability', which, once we look at the definitions in play, actually pertains to the long-term survival of the firm – not the planet or people. This discursive shift is significant in that it speaks to a certain "hollowing out" of the CSR concept where firms retain the idealism of CSR but then in-fill the concept with their own strategic purpose. The case study confirms that this strategic purpose can be self-serving rather than outwardly beneficial for society. Equally, the striking emphasis on staff training as a sustainability initiative is a further example of where core business activities are re-defined as sustainability outcomes rather than as basic business functions. It is significant to note that out of all the training reported, only ANZ undertook CSR training resulting in 2.6% of their workforce acquiring an understanding of what CSR is. The majority of the training reported pertained to technical skill acquisition in order to enhance customer satisfaction and, thus, profitability. Nowhere in the reports are ethical leadership initiatives mentioned nor do the stated company values extend beyond returning value to stakeholders. Therefore, while we can see the idea of CSR at work there is no evidence of its actual ethical impact. If we return to Jin et al's (2013) observation that CSR should, in principle, drive stronger *ethical* outcomes for business, it would appear this is not the case in the Australian banking sector.

Likewise, in the mining sector, CSR is re-cast in language that speaks of 'sustainable development' and a 'licence to operate'. As with the banking sector, this re-purposing of the CSR concept is directed towards serving the strategic needs of the firm, engaging stakeholders and meeting compliance rather than engaging in a serious agenda to improve environmental and social outcomes. In the case of mining, this typically means drawing attention away from, or masking, the core business impacts. This reflects Walker and Howard's (2002) observation that while voluntary CSR initiatives are needed in the mining sector, these initiatives are typically driven by a poor public perception of the sector – thereby requiring reputational remedy (Rae & Rouse, 2001); the force of pressure groups who has cultivated a growing awareness of mining impacts; decreased investment opportunities from a risk-adverse, corporate social performance conscious financial sector; and the perpetual need to deal with social organisations (Jenkins & Obara, 2008). In response to these pressures, a CSR agenda is staged to deal with risk, build public perception and neutralise community or lobby resistance rather than support positive or, at the minimum, responsible environmental and social effects. Thus, in both sectors, the CSR concept is effectively high jacked for its positive social connotations, and then re-aligned to aid the strategic or reputational needs of the firm in order to facilitate core business objectives.

Both the mining and banking sectors suffer from a lack of reputational capital in the Australian context. For mining, the challenge resides with a more strongly organized environmental lobby and broad base concern for climate change (Hewitt, 2015). For banking, the four main banks continue to labour under a reputation for greed, excessive fees and poor service which has seen mutuals and community credit unions make gains in the financial services sector over the last few years. In 2015, the Corporate Reputation Index ranked ANZ at 31 out of a possible 60 organisations. It was the only big four institutions to move up the index by one position. CBA, ranked 30th in 2014 slid back to 33rd in 2015. NAB was in 40 with a step back to 41st in 2015 and Westpac receded 13 positions to 52. The broad observation of this index is that the big four continue to suffer from the public view that profitability drives the agenda – often at the expense of social responsibility or customer service. The consequence of this lack of reputation capital for the mining and banking sectors alike is that they share the need to constantly work to recuperate their image, be seen to be improving their social engagement initiatives and extending their mission beyond profit seeking. CSR provides an easy framework for making the public case for social performance and enables corporations to effectively re-package their core business activities as "sustainability" or "corporate responsibility" initiatives when, as the reports show, they are simply reporting on business as usual.

So, if the findings suggest that CSR implementation in the two main Australian sectors is essentially strategic for the purposes of enhancing reputation or eliding destructive practices, this prompts the second question of why CSR has not been more successful in transforming business practice. Indeed, it also provokes larger questions about CSR uptake across global environments and whether an international comparative analysis would reveal more substantive integration of CSR. The short answer to the Australian question perhaps links to the finding that businesses do not engage with the ethical underpinning of CSR but rather elect to "cherry-pick" from the CSR framework to facilitate different strategic ends. In other words, there appears to be little evidence of an internally driven appetite in the sectors discussed to fundamentally re-evaluate the ethical dimension of business practice. In the case of mining, most environmental or social engagement initiatives have emerged as a result of external pressures from lobbyists, shifting regulatory requirements or financial backers who act as the gatekeepers to the 'license to operate'. The ethical drive has not come from within the major organisations who comply with, rather than drive, external requirements. In the case of banking, there is little pressure to fully engage in an evaluation of their ethical practice as their primary focus is consumer satisfaction, which can be achieved via refined managerial practice. This is confirmed in the reporting that emphasise staff training and development, policy and procedural development and managerial architecture as key to consumer satisfaction.

While the two case studies presented here illustrate the direction in which CSR has headed for two major sectors in Australia, it begs the larger questions of why this has occurred and what implications become apparent in a global context. The strategic appropriation of CSR, and the "emptying out" of the ethical underpinnings of CSR as it is articulated in scholarly discourse, is not constrained to the Australian environment as similar observations have been made of corporate practice in other contexts (Wagner et al., 2009), thereby reducing CSR to window-dressing (Freeman, 1984). Returning to our early discussion, we argue that the primary reason for why CSR has not effectively translated from a philosophical view of the firm to a practical, ethical agenda resides in the conceptual fragmentation that continues to characterise the CSR discourse since its inception in the 1950s. Although Lee (2007) argues that CSR has become a mainstream idea, it remains conceptually, and thus definitionally, incoherent (Dahlsrud, 2008), leading to a level of ambiguity at the level of application (Corbett & Kappagoda, 2013). This definitional, and hence, conceptual ambiguity leaves the door open to effectively deploy the CSR label to any form of reporting outside of financial performance. One of the key findings to emerge from our cases is that while the scholarly discourse may welcome a diversity of views, at the level of practice CSR is essentially open to strategic exploitation and that the lack of theoretical cohesion (that seems beneficial at the level of research) appears to be harming the effective practice of CSR.

Thus, the case studies presented here have implications both for the theoretical development and implementation of CSR. Our findings suggest that the conceptual fragmentation that has characterised our understanding of CSR to date is hindering its implementation, leaving open the door for strategic and reputational exploitation at the expense of ethical leadership. While our findings are based on the Australian context, the potential implications extend beyond national contexts prompting larger questions of what the conceptual base of CSR really means. This research suggests that greater work needs to be done for researchers and practitioners alike to begin adopting both a common language and collective sense of what is actually meant by the term CSR and what kind of organisation we are really envisaging when implementing a CSR framework. The second implication of this research is that, by working harder towards achieving a clearer sense of what is meant by the term CSR, this should drive a flow-on effect to the level of implementation. If there is a more strongly articulated meaning attached to CSR, it makes it more difficult to co-opt its framework for purely strategic or reputational purposes. It would, in turn, force the non-financial reporting of firms back into a traditional performance framework rather than representing core business activities as CSR initiatives. As such, this research seeks to extend the theoretical discourse of CSR by re-focusing our attention on its definitional and conceptual parameters while also contributing to emerging research on how CSR is actually implemented in the firm environment.

FUTURE RESEARCH DIRECTIONS

While there has been significant attention given to the shifting definitions of CSR (Valor, 2005) and the extent to which firms have taken up CSR initiatives, we are only now starting to understand the diverse purposes to which this extant framework is put and how its strategic deployment potentially detracts from its ethical intent. In undertaking this comparative analysis of two industries, we hope to shed light on the ways different industries mould CSR to their own strategic ends. However, there is substantial room for furthering research in the following ways in order to better illuminate this use of CSR.

We have looked at CSR in large-scale industries. However, it would be important to focus on smaller organisations or small to medium enterprises (SMEs) as well. The majority of literature focuses on CSR practice in large organisations since this tends to be where the greatest uptake of CSR initiatives are made visible – and the reporting that stems from these initiatives is highly accessible. However, given that for many nations, small business is a major contributor to the national economy, it is important that we do not neglect the question of how CSR is used in SMEs. According to the Australian Treasury (http://www.treasury.gov.au), small business contributed 33% of private industry value added in 2012-13 alone. If we consider the finding that the two largest sectors in Australia do not use their CSR initiatives to enhance the ethical foundations of their business but rather to report core activity or compensate for damage done, it would be useful to research whether smaller businesses engage in CSR for different reasons. This is relevant because often SMEs, being part of a supply chain, can be potentially pressured by powerful supply chain customers to adopt forms of environmentally and socially responsible actions.

Second, a further extension of the work discussed here would be to investigate how CSR has been integrated in different national contexts. CSR has been interpreted differently in different contexts and therefore needs to be viewed in relative cultural contexts across international environments. While we have shown how CSR has been appropriated in Australia, a cross-cultural comparison that takes in emerging market uses of CSR would further enrich our picture of the global uptake of CSR.

CONCLUSION

In this research, we seek to extend current knowledge on the state of CSR uptake in order to make a larger theoretical contribution to the question of what the relationship between CSR as an assemblage of ethically based concepts or definitions and its uptake as a practical business agenda is. In doing so, we visit some of the definitional ambiguities that underpin many discussions around CSR and how this ambiguity has been capitalised upon by key corporations.

Therefore, we essentially use the mining and banking cases in the Australian context as the springboard for a larger conversation regarding how the inherent conceptual ambiguities associated with CSR has led to less effective uptake and implementation. As the Australian context suggests, because CSR remains a "slippery" concept, this has enabled corporations to use CSR as a way of strategically managing some of their ethical "weak points", rather than enhance the overall ethical outlook and practice of the organisation. If we re-visit the drivers identified by Mazurkiewicz (2004), many of them apply in the Australian context and yet few of them actually speak to a core commitment to developing an ethical, sustainable business for its own sake. In all cases, the drivers are external and target a key strategic dimension that potentially affects profitability.

In conclusion, the purpose of this chapter is to scan two major industries in Australia, assess the state of the CSR field in practice via case study and draw some larger theoretical findings regarding how CSR is being utilised. In this way, we contribute to current knowledge by extending present understandings of how CSR is implemented in practice, identifying how the conceptual limitations affect practice and what the consequences or outcomes of this situation are for CSR in the future.

REFERENCES

Aguinis, H. (2011). In S. Zedeck (Ed.), *Organizational responsibility: Doing good and doing well* (Vol. 3, pp. 855–879). APA handbook of industrial and organizational psychologyWashington, DC: American Psychological Association.

Australia and New Zealand Banking Group. (2014). *Australia and New Zealand Banking Group Sustainability Review 2014*. Retrieved from www.anz.com.au

Australian Bureau of Statistic. (2014). 5204.0 - Australian System of National Accounts, 2013-14. Retrieved from http://www.abs.gov.au/AUSSTATS/abs@.nsf/MF/5204.0

Australian Centre for Corporate Social Responsibility. A. (2014). The 10th year – Progress and prospects for CSR in Australia and New Zealand. Melbourne: Australian Centre for Corporate Social Responsibility.

Australian Government Department of Employment. (2014). *Industry outlook – Mining*. Canberra: Department of Employment.

Australian Trade Commission. (2015). *Australia Benchmark Report.* Canberra" Department of Foreign Affairs and Trade. (n. d.) Retrieved from https://www.austrade.gov.au/Invest/Reports-Resources/Benchmark-Report

Balmer, J. M. T., Fukukawa, K., & Gray, E. R. (2007). The nature and management of ethical corporate identity: A commentary on corporate identity, corporate social responsibility and ethics. *Journal of Business Ethics*, *76*(1), 7–15. doi:10.1007/s10551-006-9278-z

Banerjee, S. B. (2007). *Corporate social responsibility: The good the bad and the ugly*. Cheltenham: Edward Elgar. doi:10.4337/9781847208552

Bennett, R. J., & Robson, P. J. A. (2005). The advisor-SME client relationship: Impact, satisfaction and commitment. *Small Business Economics*, *25*(3), 255–271.

Billiton, B. H. P. (2014). Value through performance. *Sustainability Report (2014).* Retrieved from www.bhpbilliton.com/society/reports/2014-bhp-billiton-sustainability-report

Bowd, R., Bowd, L., & Harris, P. (2006). Communicating corporate social responsibility: An exploratory case study of a major UK retail centre. *Journal of Public Affairs*, *6*(2), 147–155. doi:10.1002/pa.220

Bowen, H. (1953). *Social responsibilities of the businessman*. Iowa City, IA: University of Iowa Press.

Brine, M., Brown, R., & Hackett, G. (2007). Corporate social responsibility and financial performance in the Australian context. *Economic Round-Up*, Autumn, 47-58.

Buchholz, R. A., & Rosenthal, S. B. (2005). Toward a contemporary conceptual framework for stakeholder theory. *Journal of Business Ethics*, *58*(1–3), 137–148. doi:10.1007/s10551-005-1393-8

Burton, B. K., & Dunn, C. P. (1996). Feminist ethics as moral grounding for stakeholder theory. *Business Ethics Quarterly*, *6*(2), 133–148. doi:10.2307/3857619

Butterfield, K. D., Reed, R., & Lemak, D. J. (2004). An inductive model of collaboration from the stakeholder's perspective. *Business & Society*, *43*(2), 162–195. doi:10.1177/0007650304265956

Carroll, A. (1999). Corporate social responsibility. Evolution of a definitional construct. *Business & Society*, *38*(3), 268–295. doi:10.1177/000765039903800303

Carroll, A. (2008). *A history of corporate social responsibility: Concepts and practices. In The Oxford Handbook of Corporate Social Responsibility* (pp. 19–46). Oxford: Oxford University Press. doi:10.1093/oxfordhb/9780199211593.003.0002

Carroll, A. B. (1991). The pyramid of corporate social responsibility: Toward the moral management of organizational stakeholders. *Business Horizons*, *34*(4), 39–48.

Carson, T. (1993). Friedman's theory of corporate social responsibility. *Business & Professional Ethics Journal, 12*(1), 3–32. doi:10.5840/bpej199312118 PMID:11656306

Castka, P., Balzarova, M. A., Bamber, C. J., & Sharp, J. M. (2004). How can SMEs effectively implement the CSR agenda? A UK case study perspective. *Corporate Social Responsibility and Environmental Management, 11*(3), 140–149. doi:10.1002/csr.62

Cetindamar, D., & Husoy, K. (2007). Corporate social responsibility practices and environmentally responsible behavior: The case of the United Nations Global Compact. *Journal of Business Ethics, 76*(2), 163–176. doi:10.1007/s10551-006-9265-4

Chaudri, V., & Wang, J. (2007). Communicating corporate social responsibility on the internet: A case study of the top 100 information technology companies in India. *Management Communication Quarterly, 21*(2), 232–247. doi:10.1177/0893318907308746

Clark-Murphy, M., Gerrans, P., & Kristoffersen, I. (2005). The corporate social responsibility and the theory of the firm. Retrieved from http://www.business.ecu.edu.au/schools/afe/wps/papers/pdfs/wp0505ik .pdf

Clarkson, M. (1995). A stakeholder framework for analyzing and evaluating corporate social performance. *Academy of Management Review, 20*(1), 92–117.

Commonwealth Bank of Australia. (2014). *Commonwealth Bank of Australia Annual Report* 2014. Retrieved from www.commbank.com.au

Commonwealth Bank of Australia. (2014). *Sustainability Report*. Retrieved from https://www.commbank .com.au/sustainability2014/index.html

Corbett, J., & Kappagoda, M. (2013). Doing good and doing well: Corporate social responsibility in post Obamacare America. *The Journal of Law, Medicine & Ethics, 41*(1), 17–21. doi:10.1111/jlme.12032 PMID:23590734

Crane, A., McWilliams, A., Matten, D., Moon, J., & Siegel, D. (2008). The corporate social responsibility agenda. The Oxford handbook of corporate social responsibility, 3-15.

Dahlsrud, A. (2008). How corporate social responsibility is defined: An analysis of 37 definitions. *Corporate Social Responsibility and Environmental Management, 15*(1), 1–13.

Davis, R., & Franks, D. (2014). Costs of Company-Community Conflict in the Extractive Sector. *Corporate Social Responsibility Initiative Report No. 66.* Cambridge, MA: Harvard Kennedy School.

De Bakker, F. G. A., Groenewegen, P., & den Hond, F. (2005). A bibliometric analysis of 30 years of research and theory on corporate social responsibility and corporate social performance. *Business & Society, 44*(3), 283–317. doi:10.1177/0007650305278086

de Burgh-Woodman, H., Saha, A., Somasundram, K., & Torrisi, A. (2015). Sowing the Seeds for Ethical Business Leadership through Business Education.

Department of the Environment. (2014). Repealing the carbon tax. Retrieved from http://environment .gov.au/climate-change/repealing-carbon-tax.htm

Donaldson, T., & Dunfee, T. (1999). *Ties that bind.* Boston, MA: Harvard Business School Press.

Donaldson, T., & Preston, L. (1995). The stakeholder theory of the corporation: Concepts, evidence, and implications. *Academy of Management Review*, *20*(1), 70–71.

Du, S., & Vieria, E. (2012). Striving for legitimacy through corporate social responsibility: Insights from oil companies. *Journal of Business Ethics*, *110*(4), 413–427. doi:10.1007/s10551-012-1490-4

Egels-Zandén, N., & Sandberg, J. (2010). Distinctions in descriptive and instrumental stakeholder theory: A challenge for empirical research. *Business Ethics (Oxford, England)*, *19*(1), 35–49. doi:10.1111/j.1467-8608.2009.01577.x

Eisenhardt, K. (1989). Building theories from case study research. *Academy of Management Review*, *14*(4), 532–550.

Eisenhardt, K., & Graebner, M. (2007). Theory building from cases: Opportunities and challenges. *Academy of Management Journal*, *50*(1), 25–32. doi:10.5465/AMJ.2007.24160888

Fortescue Metals Group Limited. (2015). *Fortescue Metals Group Limited social responsibility reports.* Retrieved from http://fmgl.com.au/investors-media/reports/environment-reports/

Freeman, R. E. (1984). *Strategic management: A stakeholder approach.* Boston, MA: Pitman.

Galbreath, J. (2010). How does corporate social responsibility benefit firms? Evidence from Australia. *European Business Review*, *22*(4), 411–431. doi:10.1108/09555341011056186

Garriga, E., & Mele, D. (2004). Corporate social responsibility theories: Mapping the territory. *Journal of Business Ethics*, *53*(1), 51–71. doi:10.1023/B:BUSI.0000039399.90587.34

Gibbert, M., Rulgrok, W., & Wicki, B. (2008). What passes as a rigorous case study? *Strategic Management Journal*, *29*(13), 1465–1474. doi:10.1002/smj.722

Gjølberg, M. (2009). The origin of corporate social responsibility: Global forces or national legacies? *Socio-economic Review*, 17.

Golob, U., & Bartlett, J. (2007). Communicating about corporate social responsibility: A comparative study of CSR reporting in Australia and Slovenia. *Public Relations Review*, *33*(1), 1–9. doi:10.1016/j.pubrev.2006.11.001

Gustavson, R. (2009). Australia: Practices and experiences. In S. Idowu & W. Filho (Eds.), *Global practices of Corporate Social Responsibility* (pp. 463–495). Berlin, Heidelberg: Springer. doi:10.1007/978-3-540-68815-0_21

Harris, L., & Crane, A. (2002). The greening of organizational culture: Management views on the depth, degree and diffusion of change. *Journal of Organizational Change Management*, *15*(3), 214–234. doi:10.1108/09534810210429273

Hewitt, J. (2015, June 3). Big miners need to win hearts and minds in fight against environmental activism. *Australian Financial Review*. Retrieved at http://www.afr.com/opinion/columnists/big-miners-need-to-win-hearts-and-minds-in-fight-against-environmental-activism-20150603ghg1n5#ixzz3hxDI0Vb

Hills, P. (2007). The Environment. *Understanding Contemporary Asian Pacific.*

Hoejmose, S., Brammer, S., & Millington, A. (2011). Green supply chain management: The role of trust and top management in B2B and B2C markets. *Industrial Marketing Management*, *41*(4), 609–620. doi:10.1016/j.indmarman.2012.04.008

Hsieh, H.-F., & Shannon, S. E. (2005). Three approaches to qualitative content analysis. *Qualitative Health Research*, *15*(9), 1277–1288.

Isaksson, L. (2012). *Corporate social responsibility:a study of strategic management and performance in Swedish firms, PhD, ePublications@bond*. School of Business.

Ite, U. (2004). Multinationals and corporate social responsibility in developing countries: A case study of Nigeria. *Corporate Social Responsibility and Environmental Management*, *11*(1), 1–11. doi:10.1002/csr.49

Jawahar, I., & McLaughlin, G. (2001). Toward a descriptive stakeholder theory: An organizational life cycle approach. *Academy of Management Review*, *26*(3), 397–414.

Jenkins, H., & Obara, L. (2008). Corporate Social Responsibility (CSR) in the mining industry – the risk of community dependency.*Proceedings of the 2008 Centre for Resource Research Conference*. Belfast: CRRC.

Jenkins, H., & Yakovlevam, N. (2006). Corporate social responsibility in the mining industry: Exploring trends in social and environmental disclosure. *Journal of Cleaner Production*, *14*(3), 271–284. doi:10.1016/j.jclepro.2004.10.004

Jin, K., Drozdenko, R., & De Loughy, S. (2013). The role of corporate value clusters in ethics, social responsibility, and performance: A study of financial professionals and implications for the financial meltdown. *Journal of Business Ethics*, *112*(1), 15–24. doi:10.1007/s10551-012-1227-4

Jones, T. M., & Wicks, A. C. (1999). Convergent stakeholder theory. *Academy of Management Review*, *24*(2), 206–221.

Jutterström, M., & Norberg, P. (2013). 11. CSR as a management idea–discussing the contribution. *CSR as a Management Idea: Ethics in Action*, 177.

Kotler, P., & Lee, N. (2005). *Corporate social responsibility: Doing the most good for your company and your cause*. Hoboken, NJ: John Wiley & Sons, Inc.

KPMG International. (2013). *The KPMG survey of corporate responsibility reporting*. Retrieved from http://www.kpmg.com/AU/en/IssuesAndInsights/ArticlesPublications/Documents/corporateresponsibility -reporting-survey-2013.pdf

Kristoffersen, I., Gerrans, P., & Clarke-Murphy, M. (2005), *The corporate social responsibility and the theory of the firm. FIMARC Working Paper Series*. School of Accounting, Economics, and Finance Edith Cowan University: Perth.

Kunkel, J. (2014). Mining exports help underpin national growth. Canberra: Minerals Council of Australia; Retrieved from http://www.minerals.org.au/news/mining_exports_help_underpin_gdp_growth

Lazonick, W., & O'Sullivan, M. (2000). Maximizing shareholder value: A new ideology for corporate governance. *Economy and Society*, *29*(1), 13–35. doi:10.1080/030851400360541

Lee, M. (2008). A review of the theories of corporate social responsibility: Its evolutionary path and the road ahead. *International Journal of Management Reviews*, *10*(1), 53–73. doi:10.1111/j.1468-2370.2007.00226.x

Lockett, A., Moon, J., & Visser, W. (2006). Corporate social responsibility in management research: Focus, nature, salience and sources of influence. *Journal of Management Studies*, *43*(1), 115–136.

Luo, X., & Bhattacharya, C. B. (2009). The debate over doing good: Corporate social performance, strategic marketing levers, and firm-idiosyncratic risk. *Journal of Marketing*, *73*(6), 198–213.

Mallin, C. (2009). *Corporate social responsibility: A case study approach*. Glostershire: Edward Elgar.

Matten, D., Crane, A., & Chapple, W. (2003). Behind the mask: Revealing the true face of corporate citizenship. *Journal of Business Ethics*, *45*(1/ 2), 109–120. doi:10.1023/A:1024128730308

Mazurkiewicz, P. (2004). Corporate environmental responsibility: Is a common framework possible? DevComm-SDO World Bank. Retrieved from http://www-wds.worldbank.org/external/default/WDSContentServer/IW3P/IB/2008/01/22/000020953_20080122134142/Rendered/PDF/421830csrframework01PUBLIC1.pdf

McWilliams, A., & Siegel, D. (2001). Corporate social responsibility: A theory of the firm perspective. *Academy of Management Review*, *26*(1), 117–127.

McWilliams, A., Siegel, D. S., & Wright, P. M. (2006). Corporate social responsibility: Strategic implications. *Journal of Management Studies*, *43*(1), 1–18. doi:10.1111/j.1467-6486.2006.00580.x

Mole, K. F., Hart, M., Roper, S., & Saal, D. S. (2011). Broader or deeper? Exploring the most effective intervention profile for public small business support. *Environment & Planning A*, *43*(1), 87–105.

National Australian Bank. (2013). *National Australian Bank Annual review* 2013. Retrieved from www.nab.com.au

National Australian Bank. (2014). *National Australian Bank Dig Deeper paper,* 2014. Retrieved from www.nab.com.au

Newcrest Mining Limited. (2014). *Sustainability Report 2014.* Newcrest Mining Limited. Retrieved from www.newcrest.com.au

Nielsen, A., & Thomsen, C. (2009). Investigating CSR communication in SMEs: A case study among Danish middle managers. *Business Ethics (Oxford, England)*, *18*(1), 83–93. doi:10.1111/j.1467-8608.2009.01550.x

Pane-Haden, S., Oyler, J., & Humphreys, J. (2009). Historical, practical, and theoretical perspectives on green management: An exploratory analysis. *Management Decision*, *47*(7), 1041–1055. doi:10.1108/00251740910978287

Peloza, J. (2009). The challenge of measuring financial impacts from investments in corporate social performance. *Journal of Management*, *35*(6), 1518–1541. doi:10.1177/0149206309335188

Peloza, J., & Shang, J. (2011). What business leaders should know: Investing in CSR to enhance customer value. Director Notes Series. The Conference Board Governance Center, 3(3).

Pomering, A., & Dolnicar, S. (2009). Assessing the prerequisite of successful CSR implementation: Are consumers aware of CSR initiatives? *Journal of Business Ethics*, *85*(2), 285–301. doi:10.1007/s10551-008-9729-9

Porter, M. E., & Kramer, M. R. (2006). Strategy and society. The link between competitive advantage and corporate social responsibility. *Harvard Business Review*, *84*(12), 78–92. PMID:17183795

Preuss, L. (2005). Rhetoric and reality of corporate greening: A view from the supply chain management function. *Business Strategy and the Environment*, *14*(2), 123–139. doi:10.1002/bse.435

Price Waterhouse Coopers. (2014). *Mine 2014: Realigning expectations, review of global trends in the mining industry*. Toronto: PWC. Retrieved from www.pwc.com

Purser, R., Park, C., & Montuori, A. (1995). Limits to anthropocentrism: Toward an ecocentric organization paradigm? *Academy of Management Review*, *20*(4), 1053–1089. doi:10.2307/258965

Rae, M., & Rouse, A. (2001). *Mining certification evaluation project – Independent Certification of environmental and social performance in the mining sector. A WWF-Australia discussion paper*. Sydney: Resources Conservation Program, Mineral Resources Unit WWF Australia.

Rappaport, A. (1986). *Creating shareholder value: The new standard for business performance*. New York, NY: Free Press.

Reserve Bank of Australia. (2013). *Reserve Bank of Australia Annual Report, 2013*. Retrieved from www.rba.gov.au

RIO. (2013). Supporting our license to operate. *Sustainable Development, 2013*. Retrieved from www.riotinto.com

RIO. (2014). Creating mutual value for the long term. *Sustainable Development, 2014*. Retrieved from www.riotinto.com/sd2014

Shanahan, M. (2001). Globalisation in history: Issues, definitions and process identification. In K. Thorne & G. Turner (Eds.), *Global business regulation: Some research perspectives*. Sydney: Pearson Education.

Shinde, J. S., Wacker, R., Shinde, U. S., & Hou, Z. J. (2011). Superfluity and murkiness in the understanding of social responsibility: A content analysis. *Journal of Leadership, Accountability and Ethics, 8*(3).

Smith, R. (2011). Defining corporate social responsibility: A systems approach for socially responsible capitalism. (Master of Philosophy Thesis). University of Pennsylvania, USA.

Tapp, V. (2013, July 28). Australia's biggest open cut zinc mine to close. Retrieved from http://www.abc.net.au/news/2013-09-19/century-mine-closure/4969242

Trevino, L. K., & Weaver, G. R. (1999). The stakeholder research tradition: Converging theorists – not convergent theory. *Academy of Management Review*, *24*(2), 222–227. doi:10.2307/259076

Truscott, R., Bartlett, J., & Tywoniak, S. (2009). The reputation of the corporate social responsibility industry in Australia. *Australasian Marketing Journal*, *17*(2), 84–91. doi:10.1016/j.ausmj.2009.05.001

Truscott, R. A. (2007). *Corporate social responsibility in Australia: Constructing reputation.*

Tsoutsoura, M. (2004). *Corporate social responsibility and financial performance*. Berkeley, CA: University of California Berkeley.

Valor, C. (2005). Corporate social responsibility and corporate citizenship: Towards corporate accountability. *Business and Society Review*, *110*(2), 191–212. doi:10.1111/j.0045-3609.2005.00011.x

Vidal, N. G., & Kozak, R. A. (2008). Corporate responsibility practices in the forestry sector. *Journal of Corporate Citizenship*, *31*, 59–75.

Voss, C., Tsikriktsis, N., & Frohlich, M. (2002). Case research in operations management. *International Journal of Operations & Production Management*, *22*(2), 195–219. doi:10.1108/01443570210414329

Waddell, S. (2000). New institutions for the practice of corporate citizenship: Historical, intersectoral, and developmental perspectives. *Business and Society Review*, *105*(1), 107–217. doi:10.1111/0045-3609.00067

Waddock, S. (2004). Parallel universes: Companies, academics, and the progress of corporate citizenship. *Business and Society Review*, *109*(March), 5–42. doi:10.1111/j.0045-3609.2004.00002.x

Wagner, T., Lutz, R., & Weitz, B. (2009). Corporate Hypocrisy: Overcoming the Threat of Inconsistent Corporate Social Responsibility Perceptions. *Journal of Marketing*, *73*(Nov), 77–91. doi:10.1509/jmkg.73.6.77

Walker, J., & Howard, S. (2002). *Voluntary codes of conduct in the mining industry*. London: International Institute for Environmental Development.

Weber, M. (2008). The business case for corporate social responsibility: A company-level measurement approach for CSR. *European Management Journal*, *26*(4), 247–261. doi:10.1016/j.emj.2008.01.006

Westpac Banking Corporation. (2014). This is what we've delivered. *Annual Report & Sustainability Report, 2014*. Retrieved from www.westpac.com.au

Wiig, A., & Kolstad, I. (2010). Multinational corporations and host country institutions: A case study of CSR activities in Angola. *International Business Review*, *19*(2), 178–190. doi:10.1016/j.ibusrev.2009.11.006

Wood, D. J. (1991). Corporate social performance revisited. *Academy of Management Review*, *16*(4), 691–718.

World Economic Forum. (2010). 2010 *World Economic Forum The Financial Development Report*. Retrieved from www.weforum.org

Yin, R. K. (1994). *Case study research: Design and methods* (2nd ed.). Newbury Park, CA: Sage.

Zhang, Z., & Han, F. (2008). Analysis of accounting disclosure model for strengthening Corporate Social Responsibility. *International Journal of Business and Management*, *3*(9), 157–161.

Zu, L. (2009). *Corporate social responsibility, corporate restructuring and firm's performance - Empirical evidence from Chinese enterprises*. Berlin, Heidelberg: Springer-Verlag.

KEY TERMS AND DEFINITIONS

Business Ethics: Business ethics refer to the practice of organisational values or a moral code in core business operations. Business ethics should be guided by a general focus on what is right or good for the organisation and its stakeholders.

Corporate Citizenship: Corporate citizenship (CC) is sometimes conflated with CSR because of its connection with the notion of ethical conduct. Specifically, CC refers to the recognition among businesses that they operate within a stakeholder context, or a community, and that their activities need to be congruent with that larger societal context.

Corporate Social Performance: Corporate Social Performance (CSP) is a measure of the degree to which an organisation is engaged in activities that achieve positive societal outcomes, sole social problems or contribute to the community.

Environmental Sustainability: Refers to the management of the natural environment for the purposes of maintaining the long term preservation of the planet.

Organisational Ethical Competency: The conceptual, philosophical and analytical knowledge and skills derived from a commitment to CSR that develop an organisation's formal structures and support the impact of ethical practice on the organisation.

Organisational Ethical Orientation: The extent to which a firm cultivates their awareness of ethics and situates this awareness into action in their CSR strategy, policies day-to-day business practice.

Reputational Mechanism: The use of a managerial strategy, tool or operation as a means of enhancing the positive image or firm reputation among stakeholders.

Chapter 8

Determinants of Corporate Social Responsibility Disclosure in Latin American Companies:

An Analysis of the Oil and Gas Sector

Arturo Haro-de-Rosario
University of Almería, Spain

María del Mar Gálvez-Rodríguez
University of Almería, Spain

María del Carmen Caba-Pérez
University of Almería, Spain

ABSTRACT

The oil and gas sector exerts a major influence on the global economy. However, its negative impact on the environment and society has provoked increasing concerns about its activities and consumption of natural resources. Therefore, and in view of the fact that Latin America has the world's largest conventional oil reserves, the aim of this paper is to analyse the voluntary disclosure of information on the corporate social responsibility (CSR) of oil and gas companies operating in Latin America, and to study the factors that may influence the provision of this information. The results obtained show that although companies in this sector are becoming more aware of the impact of their activity, greater efforts need to be made with respect to CSR. We find that the largest, most profitable oil and gas companies tend to publish the most complete CSR reports.

DOI: 10.4018/978-1-5225-0720-8.ch008

INTRODUCTION

In recent years, there has been growing interest in better understanding the environment in which firms operate and the implications of their business activities. The concept of corporate social responsibility (CSR) is viewed as a means of reducing the negative impact of business activity on human rights and the environment (Gill et al., 2008; Paredes et al., 2010).

According to Alazzani and Wan-Hussin (2013), the oil and gas sector is a strategic area of the economy and has global repercussions. This industry faces a major handicap, namely the characteristics of the regions in which it operates, which are often geographic areas of great bioclimatic importance, or inhabited by indigenous populations, or comprised of very low income rural sectors. In consequence, as indicated by Zamora and Ramos (2009), the exploitation of oil and natural gas resources can produce negative environmental or social effects. In addition, as a result of the increased global consumption of oil and gas, the activities of these companies are having a significant adverse impact on the environment (Frynas, 2010; Durange de C. Infante et al., 2013).

In light of this situation, international organizations, governments, pressure groups and stakeholders are paying ever greater attention to the social, natural and economic consequences of oil and gas sector activities. Furthermore, companies in this sector are becoming increasingly aware of the impact of their activities, and are drawing up plans to encourage environmental and social responsibility, developing projects to minimize their environmental impact and implementing social initiatives aimed at improving living conditions in the areas in which they operate.

Vaca et al. (2007) argued that the assumption of CSR practices and standards seeks, among other goals, to acquire social legitimacy. In this context, CSR reports provide a unique opportunity to legitimize decisions and actions carried out by organizations (Gamerschlag et al., 2011; Dong et al., 2012). Ideally, these reports should comply with certain standards, and the leading guide in this respect, which has provided a major boost to this activity, is published by the Global Reporting Initiative (GRI) (AECA, 2005; Coulmont et al., 2013). In view of the crucial importance of this industry, in 2012 the GRI published its Oil and Gas Sector Supplement.

Diverse theories have been proposed to explain why organizations provide information about their performance in the field of CSR, including institutional theory (DiMaggio & Powell, 1983), legitimacy theory (Dowling & Pfeffer, 1975) and stakeholder theory (Freeman, 1984). Each of these theories sets out reasons why factors present in the economy, governance, society and the cultural environment may affect the provision of information about CSR practices and standards. In accordance with the tenets of each of these theories, it is interesting to examine which factors may influence the disclosure of CSR information by companies in the oil and gas sector.

Taking as a starting point the potential benefits to be gained from acquiring information about disclosure of CSR information in the oil and gas sector, the main objectives of this chapter are, first, to quantify the CSR information disclosed voluntarily by oil and gas companies operating in Latin America in their CSR reports (Latin American countries possess the largest conventional oil reserves in the world) and, second, to specify the factors under which oil and gas companies may or may not act in socially responsible ways.

As CSR disclosure is an important instrument in the dialog between companies in the oil and gas sector and society, the approach adopted in this study may contribute significantly to the understanding of the development of CSR strategies in the oil and gas sector. In addition, new findings may be obtained to provide a reference for the development and publication of CSR guidelines. We hope that this research will spur reflection on the benefits offered by CSR disclosure regarding actions and strategies adopted in the oil and gas sector. Thus, the present chapter makes an original contribution, filling in the lack of CSR information disclosure observed in the oil and gas sector, and extending our knowledge of the factors affecting the provision of CSR information by this sector. Therefore, the results presented may serve as a useful basis for future research.

CSR AND THE OIL AND GAS SECTOR

CSR has become increasingly important. According to the AECA (2004) definition, beyond mere compliance with legal regulations, CSR involves the voluntary commitment of companies to the development of society, to environmental preservation and to promoting responsible behavior toward the individuals and social groups with whom they interact. According to Albareda and Balaguer (2007), the main characteristics of CSR are its voluntary nature, integration, consistency and transparency.

The development of CSR has been accompanied by the emergence of evaluation standards and guidelines, which companies can adopt voluntarily, and which make it possible to quantify the extent to which an organization operates sustainably and is accountable to its stakeholders. In this respect, Larrinaga and Moneva (2002) observed that globalization, a lack of eco-efficiency and the need for comparability and reliability were the main reasons driving this standardization process.

As stated in the introduction, the most important international guidelines for the preparation of CSR reports are those published by the Global Reporting Initiative (GRI). This organization was created in 1997 to provide a global framework for the voluntary reporting of the economic, social and environmental impact of organizations (White, 1999). Since its inception, the GRI has updated its guidelines several times, most recently in the G4 document (2013). However, in addition to the GRI there are other highly reputable guides, such as Social Accountability 80, Accountability 1000, Global Compac, the Ron Brown Award for Corporate Leadership and the Gyllemhammer report.

The oil and gas industry, a major factor in the global economy, has had a very significant negative impact on society and the environment. As Carmona (1992) observed, their economic interests have led companies in this sector to operate in areas of great environmental sensitivity, without planning or concern for the preservation of natural and human values. Similarly, Zamora and Ramos (2010) argued that the production processes of this industry have had severe negative repercussions, such as soil destabilization, erosion, the loss of water sources, noise, the contamination of water, air and soil, the loss of biodiversity and the generation of harmful gases and toxic waste.

In response to growing concern about the sustainability of the oil and gas industry, a number of international conventions have been adopted, such as the 1993 Convention on Biodiversity; MARPOL 73/78; the Vienna Convention for the Protection of the Ozone Layer; the Montreal Protocol; the UN Framework Convention on Climate Change; the Kyoto Protocol to the Convention; the United Nations Framework on Climate Change; the Basel Convention on the Control of Transboundary Movements; and the Stockholm Convention on Persistent Organic Pollutants. In addition, associations have been created to promote CSR. One such association is the International Petroleum Industry Environmental Conservation Association (IPIECA), which since its founding in 1974 has published over 50 documents, reports and guides to good practice for the oil and gas sector.

The GRI believes the vitally important oil and gas industry should be working to ensure the implementation of sustainable management, that it is currently in a process of transition and that sustainable exploitation is vital for the future. Therefore, in full awareness that each sector must address specific aspects of sustainability, in 2012 the GRI published its Oil and Gas Sector Supplement. This document was produced in collaboration with IPIECA, API and OGP, among others, and considers issues that are specific to this sector, such as oil spills, the safety of installations and carbon emissions. In particular, 14 indicators were added to the G3.1 guidelines and specific comments for the sector were included in other indicators.

In view of this background, the oil and gas sector is starting to take an interest in implementing CSR policies. Accordingly, many companies in the sector are now included in prestigious international indices of sustainability such as the Dow Jones Sustainability Index (World and STOXX) and the FTSE4Good Index Series. Their inclusion in these indices is designed to provide information on compliance with certain requirements of an economic, social and environmental nature (Fernández, 2005), thus increasing social recognition and providing assurance to shareholders and potential investors that these companies represent a reliable investment in terms of CSR.

DETERMINANT FACTORS OF CSR

As commented above, various theories – institutional, legitimacy and stakeholder – have been proposed to establish a framework in which to examine and understand the strategies and actions taken by oil and gas companies to legitimize themselves, and the factors that may influence these strategies and actions.

According to the institutional theory (DiMaggio & Powell, 1983), an institutional setting, consisting of economic, political, legal, socio-cultural and technological factors, influences and determines the structures and processes adopted by organizations. Accordingly, if an organization wishes to increase its legitimacy, the actions and practices it undertakes must be considered socially appropriate or desirable (Vaca et al., 2007; Deegan & Unerman, 2011).

Evidently, this institutional theory is closely related to the concept and theory of legitimacy. According to the authors of this theory (Dowling & Pfeffer, 1975), legitimacy stems from the existence of a social contract between the company and society, and is based on the idea that companies must act within the limits of what society identifies as socially acceptable behavior. Therefore, companies tend to adapt to the social environment, i.e., the system of values established in society, in order to acquire credibility, commitment and, ultimately, legitimacy. To do so, organizations must disclose the actions performed by providing society with clear and easily accessible information. The theory of legitimacy is one of the most important frameworks available with which to explain the practice of information disclosure on sustainability and the importance of CSR reports (Pistoni & Songini, 2013).

Stakeholder theory (Freeman, 1984) is based on the premise that stakeholders can both influence and be influenced by the activities of organizations. Thus, a company's responsibility is not only that of maximizing profits for its shareholders, but also involves the creation of value for all stakeholders. This theory holds that there is no incompatibility between economic and social objectives, and therefore a company must meet its economic responsibilities by conducting socially responsible behavior and taking into account the demands of stakeholders. According to this theory, one of the key elements that a company can use to manage and enhance its relations with society is that of the CSR report.

In the context of the above theories, the literature on determinant factors of CSR asserts that the information provided on sustainability depends, among other aspects, on the applicable legislation, the activity sector and the size of the company (Cho & Patten, 2007; Chen & Bouvain, 2008; Arora &

Dharwadkar, 2011; Aguinis & Glavas, 2012; Fifka & Drabble, 2012; Pistoni & Songini, 2013). For the case at hand, the oil and gas sector, and taking into account the theoretical frameworks described above and the findings of our literature review, the following determinant factors were selected for study.

Ownership of the Company

Larrán and Giner (2002) and Cassar (2009) state that private firms are encouraged to voluntarily disclose information as they have a greater level of competition for obtaining capital than state owned companies. Focusing on CSR disclosure, Secci (2005) found that privately owned firms are the principal organizations that publish social reports as a consequence of their communication needs, in order to have better stakeholder involvement and due to management and disclosure concerns. Moreover, Wang and Dejia (2015) note that investors have a greater appreciation for the CSR reporting made by privately controlled companies than from those whose ownership structure is mainly controlled by government. This is because CSR disclosure by state owned companies is an established expectation than from those companies with a majority private ownership. Consequently, when the latter carry out CSR information disclosure, they send a strong signal to the market. Thus, benefits perceived by such organizations in this respect are greater than in the case of state owned companies. Accordingly, this study argues that companies that are entirely state owned have fewer incentives to disclose information. In view of these considerations, the first hypothesis of this study is as follows:

H1: The majority private ownership of a company in the oil and gas sector is positively associated with the amount of CSR information disclosed.

Location

Various authors like Williams (1999), Bonsón and Escobar (2004) and Leung et al. (2014) state that geographic location is a factor that affects the transparency policy of organizations, as a consequence of cultural differences in each country. Delving further into the specific issue of social responsibility Gallego-Álvarez et al, (2014) state that, practices of CSR vary because of the different social, economic and environmental concerns and the level of importance given to such issues in each region. In this line, Huang and Watson (2015) add that the information disclosure on CSR is conditioned by the CSR norms established in each geographic area and specifically, they evidence the differences between the context of the companies from the United States and those from Europe. Therefore, it seems logical to assume that the country in which an oil or gas company operates will determine, to a greater or lesser extent, the type and amount of information supplied on sustainability. Accordingly, the study hypothesis is as follows:

H2: The location of an oil or gas company influences the amount of CSR information disclosed.

Company Size

Several reasons are disclosed regarding the positive influence of companies in the CSR. To start with, many authors assert that the size of an organization is a key variable in its disclosure of information on sustainability as large organizations are more exposed to public opinion and consequently, a greater amount of information is demanded of them (Patten 1991; Deegan & Gordon, 1996; Belkaoui & Karpik,

2002; Brammer & Pavelin, 2008; Branco & Rodrigues, 2008). Moreover, Ho and Taylor (2007) argue that larger companies place greater value on the cost-benefit relation of social responsibility and can also count on greater resources to invest in social activities. Accordingly, managers are more willing to make their "social commitment" visible as part of their strategy to reinforce their competitive advantage. In addition, Giannarakis (2014) states that large companies are more incentivized to be more visible in order to meet their investors' expectations and for their greater capacity to deal with the cost of CSR disclosure. They also use CSR transparency as way to gain and retain key stakeholders such as customers and valuable employees. In line with these views, the third study hypothesis is as follows:

H3: The size of an oil or gas company positively influences the amount of CSR information disclosed.

Membership of IPIECA

Companies will be more likely to act in socially responsible ways if there are private independent organizations and social movement organizations in their environment (Campbell, 2007). In the same vein, Chih et al. (2010) suggest that those companies in countries with a presence in independent organizations will tend to be more CSR minded.

In relation to independent organizations, IPIECA is highlighted as it is the leading CSR-related association in the oil and gas industry. This organization has collaborated in the production of the Oil and Gas Sector Supplement of the GRI and has published specific reports and recommendations on sustainability for the sector.

The existence of a framework of recommendations for the preparation of CSR reports, such as IPIECA, is regarded as a minimum guarantee on issues such as the structure, content, quality and usefulness of the information supplied in these reports (Haro et al., 2012). Furthermore, since the publication of CSR reports are voluntary, not all companies prepare them in accordance with an established set of standards and guidelines. Therefore, companies that are members of IPIECA might be assumed to have developed more comprehensive CSR reports. Thus, the fourth hypothesis proposed is:

H4: Oil and gas companies that are members of IPIECA disclose more CSR information than non-members.

Profitability

As the oil and gas sector is one of the most lucrative in the world, it is particularly interesting to include variables related to profitability in this study. The positive impact of a company's profitability on CSR information disclosure has been highlighted by the literature. In particular, Hackston and Milne (1996) show that the most profitable companies, once their financial goals have been achieved, invest part of their surplus funds in activities of social interest. Furthermore, Archel and Lizarraga (2001) suggest that companies often reveal more information when financial indicators are positive. Moreover, Larrán and Giner (2002) and Marston and Polei (2004), argue that companies with positive economic results are more likely to disclose information of all kinds, including CSR information.

In short, according to many authors such as Campbell (2007), Castelo and Lima (2008), Reverte (2009) and Chivite et al. (2014), among others, companies that are more profitable have more incentives to invest in socially responsible activities. Consequently, a firm's profitability is expected to be positively related to their level of CSR (Chih et al., 2010). Furthermore, despite the fact that some authors have proposed the hypothesis of a negative impact of profitability on CSR information disclosure, they have not been able to validate it (Hamid, 2004; Pozniak et al., 2011). This negative relation is explained by the incurred competitive risk in cases of positive information disclosure. In view of these considerations, the fifth study hypothesis is as follows:

H5: The profitability of an oil or gas company positively influences the amount of CSR information disclosed.

Experience

Researchers believe that companies with more experience, credibility and reputation will disclose more and higher quality information (Larrán, 2002; Espinosa, 2004). In practice, this variable includes factors such as image, market share, know-how and relationships with stakeholders. Furthermore, it is clear that the accumulation of many years' activity by companies will be a symptom of their successful management. Thus, the age of a company is considered to be a representative measure of its experience (Scherr & Hulburt, 2001; Haro et al., 2014).

In relation to the question of age, Choi (1999) shows that company age is related to its CSR information disclosure. Other researches also reveal a positive relation between the age of a company and the level of information supplied on sustainability (Hamid, 2004; Branco & Rodrigues, 2006). In the same line, Pozniak et al. (2011) add that the company's age is linked to its involvement in CSR activities. Therefore, it is expected that oil and gas companies that have been operating for longer will publish more comprehensive CSR reports. Accordingly, the sixth study hypothesis is as follows:

H6: The acquired experience of an oil or gas company is positively associated with the amount of CSR information disclosed.

METHOD

In accordance with the study goals proposed, the research method was structured into two phases. First, a descriptive analysis was conducted, examining the CSR information published by oil and gas companies in their sustainability reports. Second, an explanatory analysis was made of the factors that may influence the sustainability information disclosed by the companies in this sector.

Descriptive Analysis

An index of responsibility (IR) was developed to analyze the content of CSR reports. This index is composed of the three dimensions of the GRI, thus constituting the following sub-indices: economic (IR_e), environmental (IR_e) and social (IR_s). The items to be included in each of these sub-indices were the main indicators recommended in the Oil and Gas Sector Supplement of the GRI, as detailed in the Annex.

In all, 72 items were used to analyze the CSR reporting behavior of the oil and gas companies. These items were scored by a dichotomous system, by which each item (ir_i) was scored as 1 if the information was available in the sustainability report and 0 otherwise. Thus, the IR was determined by the ratio of the sum of the scores for all the items ($\sum ir_i$) and the total number of items observed, as follows (the sub-indices were determined in an analogous fashion):

$$IR = \frac{\sum_{i=1}^{72} ir_i}{72} \times 100$$

Explanatory Analysis

In accordance with the second study goal, and taking into account the explanatory factors selected (see previous section), Table 1 lists the units of measurement used and the expected relationships with the index of responsibility (IR).

The degree of correlation between these determinants and the dependent variable (IR) was then analyzed. Then, after confirming that the initial hypotheses for our model (linearity, homoscedasticity, normality, independence and non-collinearity) were met, a multivariate regression analysis (multiple linear regression) was conducted. The model has the following structure:

$$IR = \alpha + \sum_{i,j=1}^{n,m} \beta_j X_{i,j} + \mu_i$$

where α is the constant term; β_j is the coefficient vector to be calculated; X_{ij} are the variables that determine the information to be disclosed; μ_i is the random error; n is the number of companies in the sample; and m is the number of independent variables.

Sample

To select the oil and gas companies to be included in the sample, the importance of these energy sources in each country was taken into account, as this industry plays an important role in the economies of the

Table 1. Determinants of CSR

Determinant	Measure	Expected Relation
Ownership	Distinguishing between: - Mainly state-owned - Mainly private-owned	Positive
Location	Country where the company is located	Positive/Negative
Size	Annual turnover (natural logarithm)	Positive
IPIECA	Membership or otherwise of IPIECA	Positive
Profitability	Ratio of operating income to net assets	Positive
Experience	Number of years the company has been active	Positive

countries in which it operates. Latin America has the highest percentage of global conventional oil reserves (10%), compared with 2.5% in North America (excluding Mexico), 9.3% in Africa, 8% in Eastern Europe, 4% in Asia and 1.6% in Western Europe.

In view of this situation, the baseline values taken were those for the Latin American oil and gas companies included in the 2014 ranking published by *América Economía*, which lists the 500 largest companies in Latin America, by turnover. Our analysis identified 29 oil and gas companies that were included in this ranking.

Between August and November 2014 we analyzed the website of each company included in the sample in search of CSR reports; however, only 20 were found. In order to increase the sample size, we then contacted the nine companies that did not make a CSR report available online, but without success. Thus, the final sample was composed of 20 CSR reports.

RESULTS

With regard to the index of responsibility (IR), composed of three sub-indices, we found that 54.44% of the items analyzed are reported in the CSR reports of companies in the oil and gas sector (see Annex). These results broadly agree with those reported by Dong et al. (2012) for the mining sector in China. These authors observed that although in recent years there had been a considerable increase in the quantity and quality of CSR information disclosed, reporting in this field was still in need of considerable improvement.

We then analyzed the economic, environmental and social sub-indices. As shown in the Annex, the area for which most information is reported is that of the economic dimension (66.28%). The social and environmental dimensions were reported by 58.49% and 53.92% of the companies, respectively. Comparison of these results with those presented by Gill et al. (2008) reveals certain differences. The latter authors found that companies reported most information concerning environmental issues, followed by economic indicators and, in last place, social ones.

In the explanatory analysis, the correlation matrix obtained shows that the only independent variables that are significantly correlated are profitability and size (Table 2). However, these correlations are not very strong and, according to Nachtsheim et al. (2004), do not pose any problem of multicollinearity that could invalidate the model. Furthermore, no significant correlations were observed between the dependent and independent variables, and so fitting the model should be straightforward.

After confirming that the conditions assumed for the model (linearity, homoscedasticity, normality, independence and non-collinearity) were met, the regression analysis was performed. The results obtained show that the model presents a moderate degree of fit (37.9%), in which three variables are statistically significant (see Table 3).

The variable state vs. private ownership of the company was found to be statistically significant, at a confidence level of 95%, and had a positive effect on the model. In other words, when the majority of the company equity is privately owned, in which case its shares are normally traded on the stock market, this fact has a positive impact on the amount of CSR information reported.

In line with the findings reported by Patten (1991) and Deegan and Gordon (1996), we observed a positive and significant (99%) relationship between the size of the company and its disclosure of information on sustainability. Therefore, the larger oil and gas companies appear to be more interested

Table 2. Matrix of Pearson correlation coefficient

	IR	Ownership	Location	Size	IPIECA	Profitability	Experience
IR	1						
Ownership	-0.122	1					
Location	-0.146	-0.021	1				
Size	0.206	0.032	0.020	1			
IPIECA	0.425	-0.257	0.188	0.157	1		
Profitability	0.236	0.028	-0.123	0.708**	0.323	1	
Experience	0.211	-0.103	-0.289	0.154	-0.020	0.260	1

Table 3. Results of the regression analysis

Modelo	Unstandardized Coefficients		Standardized Coefficients	t
	B	Std. Error	Beta	
(Constante)	0.818	0.363		2.255
Ownership	0.126	0.062	0.422	2.033**
Location	-0.034	0.021	-0.328	-1.583
Size	0.138	0.000	0.958	3.161***
IPIECA	0.147	0.107	0.296	1.378
Profitability	0.085	0.043	0.579	1.985**
Experience	-0.010	0.050	-0.043	-0.202
		R	R Square	Adj R-squared
		0.773	0.598	0.379

in supplying this information, perhaps in order to increase customer loyalty, not only by demonstrating their compliance with environmental legislation, but also by addressing society and the environment in a responsible way. These results are also consistent with those of Coulmont et al. (2013), who concluded that the CSR information disclosed by Canadian companies in the oil and gas sector largely depended on company size and the degree of exposure to the media.

The relationship between economic profitability and the index of responsibility (IR) was as expected, and presented a 95% level of significance. As noted above, the absence of information is usually considered to be a negative indicator, and so better-performing companies are more likely to make use of voluntary reporting mechanisms (Larrán & Giner, 2002; Marston & Polei, 2004), one of which is the disclosure of CSR information. Furthermore, this disclosure can enhance the company's image, and possibly enable it to raise capital at lower cost and/or increase revenues.

For the remaining independent variables analyzed (location, membership of IPIECA and experience) there is insufficient evidence to indicate the existence of a significant relationship with the index of responsibility.

DISCUSSION

In view of the results obtained, the level of visibility reached by companies in the oil and gas sector is moderate. Hence, the concern for compensating the severe impact of their activities (Zamora & Ramos, 2010) is gaining importance in the agenda of the sector. Consequently, the moderate level of visibility identified in this study supports the arguments of previous authors that pointed out the increasing interest of this industry in taking initiatives that encourage greater social commitment as well as a greater awareness in making more visible their sensitivity to social causes (Fernández, 2005). Nevertheless, the outcomes of this study add that the global vision of social responsibility has not been achieved yet. The companies disseminate more the information regarding their economic impact than that concerning their social and environmental impact, in line with the organizations that belong to the banking sector (Haro et al., 2012) and the non-profit organizations sector (Gálvez et al., 2012). This is quite surprising as, traditionally, public opinion is very critical of the environmental damage that these companies cause, and specifically in aspects such as, fauna, flora, ozone etc. (Carmona, 1992; Alazzani & Wan-Hussin, 2013).

Moreover, this study supports previous studies that assert that ownership is a powerful predictor for greater CSR disclosure (Larrán & Giner; 2002; Cassar, 2009). Thereby, while other studies state that, in general, social reporting in private companies is key for improving their competitive position in the market (Secci, 2005) and for surpassing the expectations of investors (Wang & Dejia, 2015), this study argues that this also occurs in the specific case of companies form the oil and gas sector.

Furthermore, the "size" factor is also gaining importance for explaining the drivers of social reporting in oil and gas companies. This result is in line with the literature that has analyzed the importance of this factor in other sectors such as banking (Branco & Rodrigues, 2008) or in a specific country (Brammer & Pavelin, 2008), albeit without specifically analyzing those corporations from the oil and gas sector. In this respect this study states that managers of larger companies in this industry are less reluctant to assume the cost of taking an active involvement to solve the social, economic and environmental impact of their companies as well as in being more transparent about the "best practices" concerning their social responsibility. This is in consonance with Ho and Taylor (2007) and Giannarakis (2014).

Moreover, the research supports previous authors that highlight the influence of "profitability" in CSR disclosure (Archel & Lizarraga, 2001). In this respect, it seems that social responsibility is taken into greater account when the organization feels more confident in "spending" their resources in other aspects that are not linked to the main activity of the organization (Campbell, 2007; Castelo & Lima, 2008; Reverte (2009) and Chivite et al., 2014). In addition, the oil and gas sector is often criticized for being a very profitable industry in detriment to the harm they cause to the environment. Therefore, it seems that those companies which are better placed in the market try to balance "good news" in economic terms with those related to their "good actions". To do so, they invest time and resources in social responsibility initiatives and, in turn, in developing adequate social reports that allow them to visualize their "efforts" and "responsibility" with society.

CONCLUSION

Sustainable development involves a new approach to the business outlook, one in which companies should conduct their activity taking into account not just economic aspects, but also environmental and social ones. Thus, the oil and gas sector, which has traditionally had a very negative impact on the environment, should present a more socially responsible attitude and seek to meet the needs of the present without compromising the capabilities of future generations. In this study, we contribute to understanding the sustainability policies and activities carried out by Latin American oil and gas companies, together with the factors affecting the development of their CSR practices.

The evolution that has taken place in the oil and gas sector regarding proactive CSR reporting shows that the industry is becoming more committed to sustainability, and that companies are increasingly seeking to improve their image, legitimize their actions and win the confidence and approval of society. Nevertheless, the development of CSR is still at an early stage in this sector.

Our analysis shows that the economic dimension arouses greatest concern among companies in the oil and gas industry in Latin America. Thus, information relating to the direct economic value generated is the type that is most commonly found in the reports analyzed. This may be because the information that has traditionally been published is almost exclusively financial. In any case, the differences with the other dimensions examined are not large, and so the companies in the sector can be said to address the three GRI dimensions more or less equally.

With respect to the factors affecting information disclosure on sustainability, our analysis of the results obtained raises this question: why do the largest oil and gas companies, those which are privately owned and most profitable, publish the most comprehensive sustainability reports? The answer could be; first, that these larger companies are most subject to public scrutiny, and therefore especially concerned to respond to demands of good corporate practice – demands which are made both by direct stakeholders and by society in general – as postulated by the institutional theory. On the other hand, organizations that are in private hands may behave in this socially responsible way in order to attract new investors, and so voluntary CSR disclosure would be used as part of their strategy to improve relations with the stakeholders who most directly affect the organization; this motivation would be in line with the stakeholder theory. Furthermore, the companies that are most profitable will have greater resources with which to implement mechanisms to maintain their legitimacy, and thus be viewed as companies that are beneficial to social welfare; this situation would conform with the theory of legitimacy.

Although our findings provide some new insights and contribute to a better understanding of the theories that are most commonly used to explain the motivations or reasons that lead a company to adopt socially responsible behavior – i.e., institutional theory, legitimacy theory and stakeholder theory – there remains much to learn about CSR practices in oil and gas companies.

Finally, this study has several limitations. First, the period of study is of a single year. Longitudinal studies would provide additional insights. Secondly, the sample is small, although it is comprised of all the relevant Latin American oil and gas companies. Thirdly, the determinants used have received a lot of attention in the literature for many years. Thus, even though obtaining data for Latin American companies is a complicated (and sometimes impossible), it would be interesting to add other variables related to the specificities of the oil and gas sector such as media exposure or disaster/scandal experience, among others. In any case, this chapter spotlights interesting areas for future research into the CSR information disclosure in the oil and gas sector, and also presents a valid methodology that could be transferred to studies in other regions, to sustainability studies in related energy sectors, as well as to future comparative analysis on CSR.

REFERENCES

AECA. (2004). *Marco Conceptual de la Responsabilidad Social Corporativa. Comisión de Responsabilidad Social Corporativa*. Madrid: AECA.

AECA. (2005). *Límites de la información de sostenibilidad: entidad, devengo y materialidad. Madrid, España. Asociación Española de Contabilidad y Administración de Empresas*. Madrid: AECA.

Aguinis, H., & Glavas, A. (2012). What we know and don't know about corporate social responsibility: A review and research agenda. *Journal of Management*, *38*(4), 932–968. doi:10.1177/0149206311436079

Alazzani, A., & Wan-Hussin, W. N. (2013). Global Reporting Initiative's environmental reporting: A study of oil and gas companies. *Ecological Indicators*, *32*, 19–24. doi:10.1016/j.ecolind.2013.02.019

Albareda, L. & Balaguer, M.R. (2004). La responsabilidad social de la empresa y los resultados financieros. *Contabilidad y dirección*, 11-26.

Archel, P., & Lizarraga, F. (2001). Algunos determinantes de la información medioambiental divulgada por las empresas españolas cotizadas. *Revista de Contabilidad*, *4*(7), 129–153.

Arora, P., & Dharwadkar, R. (2011). Corporate governance and corporate social responsibility (CSR): The moderating roles of attainment discrepancy and organization slack. *Corporate Governance: An International Review*, *19*(2), 136–152. doi:10.1111/j.1467-8683.2010.00843.x

Belkaoui, A., & Karpik, P. G. (2002). Determinants of the Corporate Decision to Disclose Social Information. *Accounting, Auditing & Accountability Journal*, *2*(1), 36–51.

Bonsón, E., & Escobar, T. (2004). La difusión voluntaria de información financiera en internet. Un análisis comparativo entre Estados Unidos, Europa del Este y la Unión Europea. *Revista Española de Financiación y Contabilidad*, *33*(123), 1063–1101.

Brammer, S., & Pavelin, S. (2008). Factors influencing the quality of corporate environmental disclosure. *Business Strategy and the Environment*, *17*(2), 120–136. doi:10.1002/bse.506

Branco, M., & Rodrigues, L. (2006). Communication of corporate social responsibility by Portuguese banks. *Corporate Communication: an International Journal*, *11*(3), 232–248. doi:10.1108/13563280610680821

Branco, M., & Rodrigues, L. (2008). Factors influencing social responsibility disclosure by Portuguese companies. *Journal of Business Ethics*, *83*(4), 685–701. doi:10.1007/s10551-007-9658-z

Campbell, J. L. (2007). Why Would Corporations Behave in Socially Responsible Ways? An Institutional Theory of Corporate Social Responsibility. *Academy of Management Review*, *32*(3), 946–967. doi:10.5465/AMR.2007.25275684

Carmona, M. (1992). Regulación ecológica para el sector de la energía. En: *La industria petrolera ante la regulación jurídico ecológica en México*. 485- 489. México, Universidad Nacional Autónoma de México (UNAM) y Petróleos Mexicanos (PEMEX).

Cassar, G. (2009). Financial statement and projection preparation in start-up ventures. *Accounting Review*, *84*(1), 27–51. doi:10.2308/accr.2009.84.1.27

Castelo, M., & Lima, L. (2008). Factors Influencing Social Responsibility Disclosure by Portuguese Companies. *Journal of Business Ethics*, *83*(4), 685–701. doi:10.1007/s10551-007-9658-z

Chen, S., & Bouvain, P. (2008). Is corporate responsibility converging? A comparison of corporate responsibility reporting in the USA, UK, Australia, and Germany. *Journal of Business Ethics*, *87*(Suppl. 1), 299–317. doi:10.1007/s10551-008-9794-0

Chih, H., Chih, H., & Chen, T. (2010). On the Determinants of Corporate Social Responsibility: International Evidence on the Financial Industry. *Journal of Business Ethics*, *93*(1), 115–135. doi:10.1007/s10551-009-0186-x

Chivite, M. P., Enciso, V., García, B., & Túa, J. (2014). Determinantes de la Responsabilidad Social Corporativa: La crisis y el Efecto Contagio. *CIRIEC-España, Revista de Economía Pública. Social y Cooperativa*, *81*, 127–161.

Cho, C. H., & Patten, D. M. (2007). The role environmental disclosures as tools of legitimacy: A research note. *Accounting, Organizations and Society*, *32*(7-8), 639–647. doi:10.1016/j.aos.2006.09.009

Choi, J. S. (1999). An investigation of the initial voluntary environmental disclosures made in Korean semi-annual financial reports. *Pacific Accounting Review*, *11*(1), 73–102.

Coulmont, M., Berthelot, S., & Thibault, K. (2013). Sustainability Content on Oil and Gas Company Websites. *Business and Management Research*, *2*(1), 94–103.

Deegan, C., & Gordon, B. (1996). A study of the environmental disclosure practices of Australian corporations. *Accounting and Business Review*, *26*(3), 187–199. doi:10.1080/00014788.1996.9729510

Deegan, C., & Unerman, J. (2011). *Financial Accounting Theory* (Second European ed.). Berkshire, United Kingdom: McGraw-Hill Higher Education.

Dimaggio, P. J., & Powell, W. W. (1983). The iron cage revisited: Institutional isomorphism and collective rationality in organizational fields. *American Sociological Review*, *48*(2), 146–160. doi:10.2307/2095101

Dong, S., Burritt, R., & Qian, W. (2012). *An assessment of CSR Reporting Practice in China's Mining and Minerals Industry*. Australia: Centre for Accounting, Governance and Sustainability, School of Commerce, University of South Australia.

Dowling, J., & Pfeffer, J. (1975). Organizational legitimacy: Social values and organizational behavior. *Pacific Sociological Review*, *18*(1), 122–136. doi:10.2307/1388226

Durange de C. Infante, C.E., Molica de Mendonça, F., Purcidonio, P.M. & Valle, R. (2013). Triple bottom line analysis of oil and gas industry with multicriteria decision making. *Journal of Cleaner Production*, *52*, 289–300.

Espinosa, M. (2004). *La divulgación de información en el mercado español: un análisis empírico*. España, Universidad de Alicante.

Fernández, R. (2005). *Administración de la Responsabilidad Social Corporativa*. España, Editorial Thomson.

Fifka, M. S., & Drabble, M. (2012). Focus and standardization of sustainability reporting – a comparative study of the United Kingdom and Finland. *Business Strategy and the Environment*, *21*(7), 455–474. doi:10.1002/bse.1730

Freeman, R. E. (1984). *Strategic management: a stakeholder approach*. Boston: Pitman press.

Frynas, J. G. (2010). Corporate social responsibility and societal governance: Lessons from transparency in the oil and gas sector. *Journal of Business Ethics*, *93*(Suppl. 2), 163–179. doi:10.1007/s10551-010-0559-1

Gallego-Álvarez, I., Formigoni, H., & Antunes, M. T. P. (2014). Corporate social responsibility practices in Brazilian firms. *Revista de Administração de Empresas*, *54*(1), 12–27. doi:10.1590/S0034-759020140103

Gamerschlag, R., Moller, K., & Verbeeten, F. (2011). Determinants of voluntary CSR disclosure: Empirical evidence from Germany. *Review of Managerial Science*, *2*(2-3), 233–262. doi:10.1007/s11846-010-0052-3

Giannarakis, G. (2014). Corporate governance and financial characteristic effects on the extent of corporate social responsibility disclosure. *Social Responsibility Journal*, *10*(4), 569–590. doi:10.1108/SRJ-02-2013-0008

Gill, D. L., Dickinson, S. J., & Sharl, A. (2008). Communicating sustainability: A web content analysis of North American, Asian and European firms. *Journal of Communication Management*, *12*(3), 243–262. doi:10.1108/13632540810899425

Hackston, D., & Milne, M. J. (1996). Some determinants of social environmental disclosures in New Zealand companies. *Accounting, Auditing & Accountability Journal*, *9*(1), 77–95. doi:10.1108/09513579610109987

Hamid, F. Z. A. (2004). Corporate social disclosure by banks and finance companies: Malaysian evidence. *Corporate Ownership and Control*, *1*(4), 118–130.

Haro, A., Alarcón, F., & Caba, M. (2012). Los determinantes de la divulgación de información sobre Responsabilidad Social Corporativa en el sector financiero: El caso Español. *Revista Facultad de Ciencias Económicas: Investigación y Reflexión*, *20*(1), 189–205.

Haro, A., Caba, C., & Cazorla, L. (2014). Efficiency of venture capital firms: Evidence from Spain. *Small Business Economics*, *43*(1), 229–243. doi:10.1007/s11187-014-9541-0

Ho, L. J. & Taylor, M. E. (2007). An empirical analysis of triple bottom-line reporting and its determinates: evidence from the United States and Japan. *Journal of international Financial Management and Accounting*, 18(2), 123-150.

Huang, X., & Watson, L. (2015). Corporate social responsibility research in accounting. *Journal of Accounting Literature*, *34*, 1–16. Retrieved from http://0-search.proquest.com.almirez.ual.es/docview/1675861155?accountid=14477 doi:10.1016/j.acclit.2015.03.001

Lang, M., & Lundholm, R. C. (1993). Cross-sectional determinants of analyst ratings of corporate disclosures. *Journal of Accounting Research*, *31*(2), 246–271. doi:10.2307/2491273

Larrán, M. (2002). Efectos de la divulgación de la información en el valor empresarial: Percepciones de las grandes compañías españolas. *Revista de la Asociación Española de Contabilidad y Administración de Empresas*, *60*, 37–41.

Larrán, M., & Giner, B. (2002). The Use of the Internet for Corporate Reporting by Spanish Companies. *The International Journal of Digital Accounting Research*, *2*(1), 53–82.

Larrinaga, C., & Moneva, J. (2002). Global Reporting Initiative: Contabilidad y Sostenibilidad. *Partida Doble*, *135*, 80–87.

Leung, E., & Verriest, A. (2014). Does location matter for disclosure? Evidence from geographical segment. Retrieved from http://research.chicagobooth.edu/~/media/CEBE78C71AD14878A33677E-B5C61FFB7.pdf

Marston, C. & Polei, A. (2004). Corporate reporting on the Internet by German companies. *International Journal of Accounting Standard Committee*, *5*, 285–311.

Nachtsheim, C. J., Neter, J., Kutner, M. H., & Wasserman, W. (2004). *Applied linear regression models*. Irwin, McGraw-Hill.

Paredes Gázquez, J. D., Pardo Herrasti, E., & De la Cuesta González, M. (2010). *Retos de la RSC I: Introducción a la Responsabilidad Social Corporativa. Cuaderno Red de Cátedras Telefónica*. Madrid: UNED-Telefónica.

Patten, D. M. (1991). Exposure, legitimacy, and social disclosure. *Journal of Accounting and Public Policy*, *10*(4), 297–308. doi:10.1016/0278-4254(91)90003-3

Pistoni, A., & Songini, L. (2013). Corporate Social Responsibility Determinants: The Relation with CSR Disclosure. In L. Songini, A. Pistoni & C. Herzig (Eds.), Accounting and Control for Sustainability (Vol. 26). Emerald Group Publishing Limited.

Pozniak, L., Ferauge, P., Arnone, L., & Geerts, A. (2011). Determinants of Internet Corporate Social Responsibility Communication. *Global Journal of Business Research*, *5*(4), 1–14.

Reverte, C. (2009). Determinants of Corporate Social Responsibility Disclosure Ratings by Spanish Listed Firms. *Journal of Business Ethics*, *88*(2), 351–366. doi:10.1007/s10551-008-9968-9

Scherr, F. C., & Hulburt, H. M. (2001). The debt maturity structure of small firms. *Financial Management*, *30*(Spring), 85–111. doi:10.2307/3666392

Secci, D. (2005). The Italian experience in social reporting: An empirical analysis. *Corporate Social Responsibility and Environmental Management*, *13*(3), 135–149. doi:10.1002/csr.96

Vaca, R. M., Moreno, M. J., & Riquel, F. (2007). Análisis de la responsabilidad social corporativa desde tres enfoques: stakeholders, capital intelectual y teoría institucional. In J.C. Ayala (Ed.), Conocimiento, innovación y emprendedores: camino al futuro. La Rioja: Servicio de publicaciones de la Universidad de la Rioja.

Wang, K. T., & Dejia, L. (2015). Market Reactions to the First-Time Disclosure of Corporate Social Responsibility Reports: Evidence from China. *Journal of Business Ethics*. Retrieved from http://link.springer.com/article/10.1007%2Fs10551-015-2775-1#/page-1

White, A. L. (1999). Sustainability and the Accountable Corporation. *Environment*, *41*(8), 3–43. doi:10.1080/00139159909604786

Williams, J. G. (1999). Green and social issues and the management accountant. *Management Accounting*, *1*, 64–65.

Zamora, A. C., & Ramos, J. (2010). Las actividades de la industria petrolera y el marco ambiental legal en Venezuela. Una visión crítica de su efectividad. *Revista Geográfica Venezolana*, *51*(1), 115–144.

APPENDIX

Table 4. CSR dimensions: the oil and gas sector in Latin America

	INDEX OF RESPONSIBILITY (IR)	54.44
	Economic Dimension (IR_e)	**66.28**
Code	Information to be Disclosed	%
EC1	Direct economic value generated and distributed	94.74
EC2	Financial implications and other risks and opportunities for the organization's activities due to climate change	63.16
EC3	Coverage of the organization's defined benefit plan obligations	63.16
EC4	Significant financial assistance received from government	68.42
EC6	Policy, practices, and proportion of spending on locally-based suppliers at significant locations of operation.	73.68
EC7	Procedures for local hiring and proportion of senior management hired from the local community at locations of significant operation.	78.95
EC8	Development and impact of infrastructure investments and services provided primarily for public benefit through commercial, in-kind, or pro bono engagement.	68.42
EC9	Understanding and describing significant indirect economic impacts, including the extent of impacts.	68.42
OG1	Volume and type of estimated proved reserves and production.	17.65
	Environmental Dimension (IR_e)	**53.92**
Code	Information to be Disclosed	%
EN1	Materials used by weight or volume.	68.42
EN2	Percentage of materials used that are recycled input materials.	47.37
EN3	Direct energy consumption by primary energy source.	94.74
EN4	Indirect energy consumption by primary source.	68.42
OG2	Total amount invested in renewable energy.	36.84
OG3	Total amount of renewable energy generated by source.	27.78
EN8	Total water withdrawal by source.	73.68
EN9	Water sources significantly affected by withdrawal of water.	52.63
EN11	Location and size of land owned, leased, managed in, or adjacent to, protected areas and areas of high biodiversity value outside protected areas.	78.95
EN12	Description of significant impacts of activities, products, and services on biodiversity in protected areas and areas of high biodiversity value outside protected areas.	63.16
EN14	Strategies, current actions, and future plans for managing impacts on biodiversity.	63.16
OG4	Number and percentage of significant operating sites in which biodiversity risk has been assessed and monitored.	18.75
EN16	Total direct and indirect greenhouse gas emissions by weight.	73.68
EN17	Other relevant indirect greenhouse gas emissions by weight.	57.89
EN18	Initiatives to reduce greenhouse gas emissions and reductions achieved.	55.56

continued on following page

Table 4. Continued

EN19	Emissions of ozone-depleting substances by weight.	57.89
EN20	NO, SO, and other significant air emissions by type and weight.	63.16
EN21	Total water discharge by quality and destination.	57.89
OG5	Volume and disposal of formation or produced water.	26.67
EN22	Total weight of waste by type and disposal method.	78.95
EN23	Total number and volume of significant spills.	73.68
OG6	Volume of flared and vented hydrocarbon.	22.22
OG7	Amount of drilling waste (drill mud and cuttings) and strategies for treatment and disposal.	18.75
EN26	Initiatives to mitigate environmental impacts of products and services, and extent of impact mitigation.	63.16
EN27	Percentage of products sold and their packaging materials that are reclaimed by category.	42.11
OG8	Benzene, lead and sulfur content in fuels.	12.50
EN28	Monetary value of significant fines and total number of non-monetary sanctions for noncompliance with environmental laws and regulations.	57.89
	Social Dimension (IR_s)	**58.49**
Code	Information to be Disclosed	%
LA1	Total workforce by employment type, employment contract, and region.	94.74
LA2	Total number and rate of employee turnover by age group, gender, and region.	78.95
LA4	Percentage of employees covered by collective bargaining agreements.	68.42
LA5	Minimum notice period(s) regarding operational changes, including whether it is specified in collective agreements.	47.37
LA7	Rates of injury, occupational diseases, lost days, and absenteeism, and number of work-related fatalities by region.	89.47
LA8	Education, training, counselling, prevention, and risk-control programs in place to assist workforce members, their families, or community members regarding serious diseases.	84.21
LA10	Average hours of training per year per employee by employee category.	84.21
LA13	Composition of governance bodies and breakdown of employees per category according to gender, age group, minority group membership, and other indicators of diversity.	68.42
LA14	Ratio of basic salary of men to women by employee category.	68.42
HR1	Percentage and total number of significant investment agreements that include human rights clauses or that have undergone human rights screening.	63.16
HR2	Percentage of significant suppliers and contractors that have undergone screening on human rights and actions taken.	78.95
HR3	Total hours of employee training on policies and procedures concerning aspects of human rights that are relevant to operations, including the percentage of employees trained.	52.63
HR4	Total number of incidents of discrimination and actions taken.	57.89
HR5	Operations identified in which the right to exercise freedom of association and collective bargaining may be at significant risk, and actions taken to support these rights.	78.95
HR6	Operations identified as having significant risk for incidents of child labor, and measures taken to contribute to the elimination of child labor.	78.95
HR7	Operations identified as having significant risk for incidents of forced or compulsory labour, and measures to contribute to the elimination of forced or compulsory labour.	77.78
OG9	Operations where indigenous communities are present or affected by activities and where specific engagement strategies are in place.	20.00

continued on following page

Table 4. Continued

HR10	Percentage and total number of operations that have been subject to human rights reviews and/or impact assessments.	31.58
HR 11	Number of grievances related to human rights filed, addressed, and resolved through formal grievance mechanisms.	31.58
SO1	Nature, scope, and effectiveness of any programs and practices that assess and manage the impacts of operations on communities, including entering, operating, and exiting.	89.47
SO2	Percentage and total number of business units analyzed for risks related to corruption.	57.89
SO3	Percentage of employees trained in organization's anti-corruption policies and procedures.	73.68
SO4	Actions taken in response to incidents of corruption.	68.42
SO5	Public policy positions and participation in public policy development and lobbying.	73.68
SO8	Monetary value of significant fines and total number of non-monetary sanctions for noncompliance with laws and regulations.	52.63
SO9	Operations with significant potential or actual negative impacts on local communities.	42.11
SO10	Prevention and mitigation measures implemented in operations with significant potential or actual negative impacts on local communities.	42.11
OG10	Number and description of significant disputes with local communities and indigenous peoples.	16.67
OG11	Number of sites that have been decommissioned and sites that are in the process of being decommissioned.	16.67
OG12	Operations where involuntary resettlement took place, the number of households resettled in each and how their livelihoods were affected in the process.	10.53
OG13	Number of process safety events, by business activity.	16.67
PR1	Life cycle stages in which health and safety impacts of products and services are assessed for improvement, and percentage of significant products and services categories subject to such procedures.	73.68
PR3	Type of product and service information required by procedures, and percentage of significant products and services subject to such information requirements.	73.68
PR6	Programs for adherence to laws, standards, and voluntary codes related to marketing communications, including advertising, promotion, and sponsorship.	57.89
PR9	Monetary value of significant fines for noncompliance with laws and regulations concerning the provision and use of products and services.	73.68
OG14	Volume of biofuels produced and purchased meeting sustainability criteria.	10.53

Chapter 9
Socially Responsible Mining Corporations:
Before (or in Addition to) Doing Good, Do No Harm

Nonita T. Yap
University of Guelph, Canada

Kerry E. Ground
Acorn International, LLC, USA

ABSTRACT

Mining is impact intensive regardless of commodity and scale. A socially responsible mining company, at a minimum, does not knowingly irreparably harm the community's ability to sustain itself after the mine closes. This chapter examines the mining sector in the Philippines: the public concerns, CSR responses and the challenges mining companies face in the country. Information was gathered through a review of academic and grey literature, key informant interviews and content analysis of Sustainability / CSR Reports. Many of the companies invest in the community as well as minimise their environmental impacts. A few invest in the community but appear to ignore people's right to a healthy environment. The chapter argues that mining can become an instrument for inclusive growth in the Philippines only if there is social peace, and that a streamlined and transparent mining policy regime, equitable benefits sharing and demilitarisation of mining areas will help bring this about.

INTRODUCTION

The 1990s saw a shift in the geography of metals and minerals mining to non-OECD countries, driven by the depletion of easily accessible deposits in Europe and the U.S., made possible by the development of huge ocean going vessels, and facilitated by lighter regulatory burden, the 'privatisation bonanza' of mining sector interests in many countries (OECD 2002, p. 3), and some add, the globalisation of private security (Bebbington, Hinojosa, Humphreys, Bebbington & Warnaars, 2008). More than 90 developing

DOI: 10.4018/978-1-5225-0720-8.ch009

countries revised their mining and investment code with the support of the international finance institutions (IFIs) (Bebbington et al., 2008).

The development outcomes have not been as expected. A review of World Bank projects in the extractive industries from 1990-2002 noted the following: (a) the projects tend to be in socially and environmentally sensitive areas; (b) no evidence of poverty reduction; (c) mixed benefits in terms of employment; (d) mining revenues rarely shared with impacted communities; (e) increased air pollution and environmental degradation; and (f) increased insecurity, social antagonism and conflict in mining sites (Mainhardt-Gibbs, 2003). Similar observations have been reported in other mining studies (e.g., Holden & Jacobson, 2007). Long-term negative impacts on workers' health and communities have also been reported (IIED & WBCSD, 2002). Notwithstanding this mixed economic and human development record, mining remains actively promoted as a major economic development engine (ICMM, 2012; IMF, 2012) and welcomed as such by national governments (e.g., Cabalda, Banaag, Tidalgo & Garces, 2002).

The financial outcomes on the other hand, have been more than favourable. A Price Waterhouse Cooper (2012) review of the financial performance of the world's top 40 mining companies between 2002 to 2012 showed that even during this period of decline in mining investments: (a) revenues increased 26%; (b) net profit increased 21%; (c) operating cash flows grew 34%; (d) investing cash flows grew 92% and (e) total assets remained above $1 trillion and grew a further 13%. Between 2010 and 2011 the return to shareholders increased 156% (p.1).

The financial robustness of the sector arises largely from its unique advantage over other industries. Mining outputs - processed metals and minerals, energy, construction materials, precious gems - are always needed. Furthermore, the supply chains of metals and minerals are highly stratified. Miners sell to refiners, who sell to commodity exchanges used by fabricators, who sell to wholesalers, who sell to retailers and, eventually, to the consumers (IIED & WBCSD 2002, p.18). The great 'distance' between extraction and consumption allows consumers to enjoy mined products – cars, jewelry, mobile phones, computers - without ever seeing, or needing to think of the 'holes in the ground'. Mining does suffer one major disadvantage – the resource is not transferrable. Hence the company is unavoidably vulnerable to local policy, politics and culture. CSR programs appear ideal for dealing with these constraints.

This volume is intended to highlight the variations in CSR between developing and developed countries. This chapter starts from the following positions:

1. Corporate social responsibility is a normative concept;
2. A socially responsible corporation is regulatory compliant (Snyckers, 2006), ethical (Maximiano, 2006), and does not knowingly do harm to its stakeholders; any harm done is rectified once discovered or brought to its attention (Campbell 2006); and
3. Variation in CSR practice among countries reflect less differences in level of development but "differences in national business systems" (Chapple & Moon, 2005), and the existence of independent non-state organisations and fora that monitor corporate behaviour, and institutionalized norms on what is appropriate behaviour (Campbell, 2006).

The chapter focuses on the Philippines and examines several questions: What are the major concerns about mining in the Philippines? What have been the corporate responses? Is there a difference in corporate behaviour between Filipino-owned and foreign mining companies? What are the challenges mining companies face in the Philippines? What conditions are needed that might encourage responsible mining in the country?

The Philippines is a middle income country: GDP/capita (US$2765) with a high level of inequality (GINI Coefficient of 0.40), high poverty rate (26.5%) and high corruption perception index (94/177) (Yap, 2015). It is atypical in that its literacy rate is among the highest in the world (95.4%). The country also has a dynamic social movement, the largest in Asia and the most diverse in terms of focus and alliances. The groups focusing on mining include indigenous peoples' organizations, environmental and legal rights groups and the Catholic Bishops Conference of the Philippines (Stark, Li & Terasawa, 2006). Lessons from the Philippines are potentially applicable to other developing countries with similar conditions.

METHODOLOGY

The study adopted a case study approach, combining different qualitative methods to shed light on the study questions. The approach is useful in achieving in-depth understanding of a single or small number of "cases," in this case mining companies, set in their real-world contexts (Bromley 1986, p. 1, cited in Yin, 1994).

Information on mining policy and corporate practices was gathered from a desk review of academic literature, reports of government agencies, NGO publications, and newspaper articles. This was complemented by 21 key informant interviews - 8 CEOs of mining companies and industry leaders, 5 civil servants, 5 local civil society groups, and 3 CSR scholars. The key informants were selected based on their knowledge and involvement in the sector. The civil society groups interviewed work on the ground. Interview questions included the challenges mining companies face in the Philippines, industry 'best practices', and company - civil society relationship. Both industry leaders and civil society groups were asked to identify the problems they felt need to be addressed to bridge the gap between the mining company and the host communities.

This was followed by a more targeted examination of corporate practices through content analysis of their Sustainability/CSR Reports and Annual reports. A search was done of mining company websites. Only 7 of the 27 large scale mining companies had their Reports posted online. The low number (26%) was not surprising. An examination of 50 companies with English language websites in seven Asian countries reported that only a third of companies in the Philippines posted CSR Reports with foreign owned companies one and half times more likely to disclose than Filipino-owned businesses (Chambers, Chapple, Moon & Sullivan, n.d.).

The level of social responsibility of mining firms was assessed using the grid shown in Table 1. An assessment of *High* meant the company earned Yes for 75% of the questions, *Medium* meant 50%-74%, and *Low* meant less than 50%.

The grid was developed based on research in cleaner production, environmental impact assessment centered on the processes depicted in Figure 1, influenced by Lorenzo-Molo's 'front stage'-'back stage' categories (*vide infra*) and the insights of development-oriented CSR scholars (e.g., Jenkins, 2004; Blowfield, 2005; Utting, 2005; Bannerjee, 2008). It reflects the principles underlying the Global Compact, ISO 26000, WBCSD's *Breaking New Ground*, Extractive Industries Transparency Initiative, and the IFC's sustainability framework.

The chapter unfolds as follows. The main areas of dissonance in the CSR literature are briefly reviewed to provide context to the starting positions taken and to situate the questions of interest in the comparative perspective of the book. This is followed by an overview of mining processes, their environmental implications and the Philippine regulatory responses. The context and practices of the case

Table 1. CSR assessment checklist

'INSIDE-OUT' LINKAGES (Porter & Kramer, 2006)/ 'BACK STAGE' (Lorenzo-Molo, 2008)	
1. Production and supply chain impact management	**Yes/No**
a. Solid waste	
b. Tailings pond, pipelines, siltation: operation, maintenance, and long term planning	
c. Hazardous chemicals	
d. Air emissions – NOx, SOx	
e. Water consumption and discharge	
f. Energy source and consumption	
g. Impact monitoring and management	
h. Dust and noise	
i. Risk assessment	
j. Emergency Response Programs	
k. Rehabilitation of mined areas	
l. Mine Closure Plan	
m. Replacement of depleted natural capital with other forms of capital	
n. Protection of critical ecosystem – mine free zone	
2. Employee relations and occupational health and safety	
a. Salaries and benefits	
b. Job security	
c. Occupational health and safety	
d. Gender parity	
e. Cultural diversity	
f. Child labor	
3. Accountable and democratic governance	
a. Legal compliance: environment	
b. Legal compliance: labor	
c. Provision of relevant and accurate information to stakeholders, e.g., production outputs, revenues, taxes, safety record	
d. Works with LGU	
e. Democratic decision-making	
'OUTSIDE-IN' LINKAGES (Porter & Kramer, 2006)/ 'FRONT STAGE' (Lorenzo & Molo, 2008)	
4. Community transformative and adaptive capacity	
a. Local employment	
b. Local procurement	
c. Economic livelihood diversification	
d. Health	
e. Education	
f. Transportation	
g. Community Engagement	
OVERALL (High = 75% Yes, Medium = 50-74% Yes, Low = <50% Yes)	

Figure 1. Mining operations and environmental outcomes

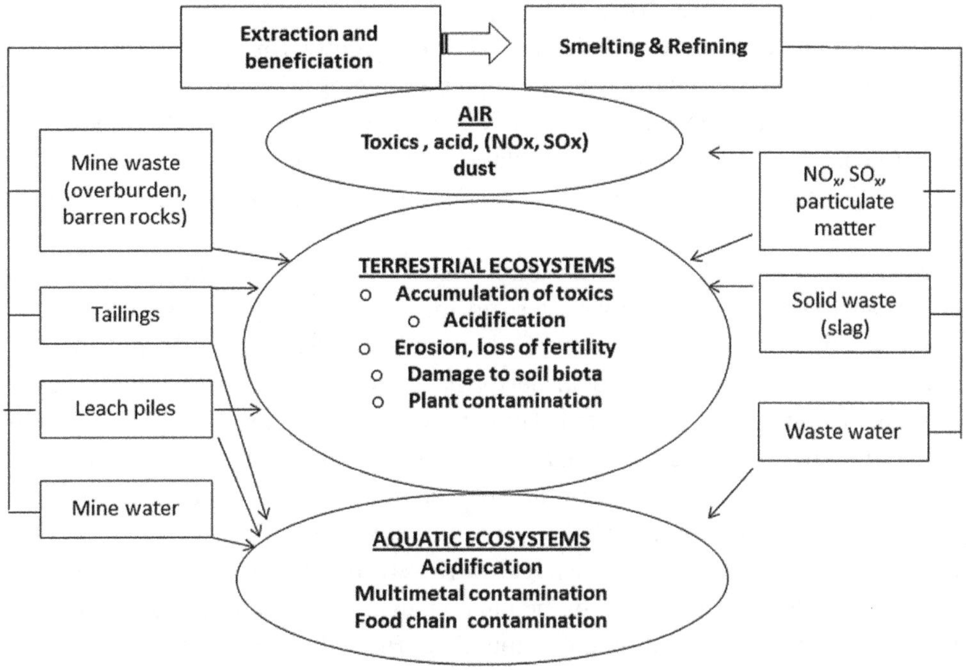

study companies are summarised. The paper closes with comments on how some of the problematic issues and controversies in the mining sector may be addressed, lessons and limitations of the study and areas that merit further investigation.

BACKGROUND

There is no universal definition of what constitutes CSR. The construct describes the relationship between business and society. Perspectives range from one that views corporations as having no social obligation other than the creation of economic rents, to one that views corporations as true development agents (Jamali, Karam & Blowfield, 2015, p.3).

The mainstream CSR literature subscribes to the win-win paradigm, implicitly assuming that the triple bottom line - economic, environmental and social sustainability - can be achieved simultaneously (e.g., Bansal, 2005). The World Business Council for Sustainable Development definition of CSR as "the *commitment* of business to contribute to sustainable economic development, working with employees, their families, the local community and society at large to improve their quality of life" (WBCSD, 2000, p. 10, italics added) captures this perspective.

Porter and Kramer (2006, p. 7) counsel companies to take a strategic approach to CSR in order to reap the biggest benefit. Rather than focusing on controlling the impacts upon society during its normal course of operation ('inside out linkages'), companies should focus on the external social conditions that significantly affect its competitive context ('outside-in linkages') (p.4). Shared value is created by building on the interrelations between the social needs in the communities where the business has interests and company assets and expertise that can help address these needs through new or expanded markets, value chains, and profitable business opportunities.

Lorenzo-Molo (2008) frames these linkages rather differently. She categories corporate activities into: (1) acts of doing good outside the regular scope of a company's core business interests, i.e., philanthropic and 'do-gooder' activities designed to elicit positive public review ('front stage'), and (2) acts directly related to core business i.e., employee relations, transparency, effects on society ('back stage'). `Back stage' activities are often not given much thought, nor synchronized with the 'front stage' activities, she notes.

Some development-oriented CSR scholars argue that CSR models (generally based on Carroll's CSR pyramid) reflect western realities, embody western norms and regulatory frameworks (e.g., Visser, 2008). Using two examples from Papua New Guinea, Gilberthorpe and Banks (2012) show how CSR practice places greater emphasis on meeting 'global performance standards' than on the specificities of the contexts in which the companies are situated. These they argue, lead to ill-conceived and inappropriate development programmes that generate inequality, fragmentation, social and economic insecurity (p.2). However, this does not necessarily represent the practice in other developing countries.

In Argentina, a study of different stakeholder perspectives on CSR practice in the mining sector concludes that CSR orientation of mining managers differs from those developed in the global headquarters. Companies negotiate economic, environmental and legal dimensions of CSR with the government, and philanthropic responsibilities with the communities. Ethical responsibilities however, are defined by the headquarters (Yakovleva & Vasquez-Brust, 2012). Vazquez-Brust and Liston-Heyes (2010) add that while companies from developed countries define their environmental obligations primarily within legal or economic domain of CSR, those from developing countries where governance is weak, tend to frame environmental issues as ethical or discretionary responsibility. Firms with poor environmental performance tend to use charitable contributions, sustainability reporting and social investment to earn social legitimacy, note Comelli, Hadad and Petz (2010).

In the Philippines, owners of the biggest businesses and industries have established foundations dedicated to CSR, focused particularly on education and community work through various kinds of philanthropy. The bequeathing of a portion of one's estate into one's foundation is considered CSR (Lorenzo-Molo, 2008). All have more than one foundation, each focusing on a specific aspect of CSR. Education programmes are directed towards students, parents and academe. In social development, the most common programmes are micro-financing for small businesses, medical missions, youth and women's empowerment, feeding programmes and disaster relief.

The emphasis on philanthropy in many developing countries is frequently explained as a (necessary and appropriate) response to the high levels of poverty, unemployment, and shortage of FDI in these contexts (Visser, 2008).

The presumed relationship between CSR practice and level of development, and the western bias of CSR were two of four hypotheses tested by Chapple and Moon (2005) in their study of CSR Reports of the top 50 companies (domestic and transnational) in each of 7 Asian countries. The seven – India, Indonesia, Malaysia, Philippines, Singapore, South Korea and Thailand are at different stages of development and diverse in terms of colonial histories, political experience and religious traditions. Their statistical analysis showed:

1. "Philanthropy as the main mode of CSR delivery" common in all seven countries;

2. Variation in CSR practice among the countries does not reflect differences in level of development but "differences in national business systems";
3. CSR modes implemented by domestic and international companies are … "broadly similar", implying that MNCs do not impose a [western] CSR model in developing countries.

These are consistent with the findings of a survey of human resource managers in the U.S., Canada, Australia, Brazil, India, China, India and Mexico. The top two priorities identified in all seven countries are "donations to local charities" and "donations to natural disasters" (SHRM, 2007). In other words, philanthropy is a top CSR priority in developing *and* developed countries. There may therefore be another explanation - charitable donations are tax deductible, and demand fairly straightforward engagement. In places like the Philippines there is a practical reason, articulated back in the early 1950s[1] by Eugenio Lopez Sr., founder patriarch of the Lopez Group of Companies, a conglomerate:

… a greater proportion of the earnings accrued from business should be returned to the people … in the form of foundations, grants, scholarships, hospitals or any other form of social welfare benefits. We consider this … a good investment which, in the long run, will pay off because it will mean more business and goodwill for the company and would minimize, if not prevent, the social unrest and disorder which are prevalent nowadays (APEC, 2012, p. 1).

Some contest the win–win paradigm. Trade-offs and conflicts between economic, environmental and social aspects in corporate management and performance represent the rule rather than the exception, argue Hahn, Figge, Pinkse and Preuss (2010). "In the extreme, sustainable development at the societal level may be best served if certain companies or sectors cease to exist" (p. 219). Campbell (2006) poses a different question:

If the raison d'être for corporations is to maximize profit and shareholder value as best they can, then it stands to reason that corporations will do whatever it takes to achieve this goal… even if that includes acting in socially irresponsible ways … However, many corporations … go to great lengths to do just the opposite … Given the wide range of corporate behaviors—both good and bad… under what conditions are corporations more likely to act in socially responsible ways than not? (p.2)

Campbell posits that the presence of independent non-state organisations and fora that monitor corporate behavior and institutionalized norms regarding appropriate corporate behavior, enhance the likelihood of socially responsible corporate behavior.

MAIN FOCUS OF THE CHAPTER

This chapter focuses on the CSR practice of large mining companies in the Philippines, one of the five most mineralised countries in the world, third in terms of gold reserves, 4th for copper, 5th for nickel and 6th for chromite (Whitmore, n. d.).

The Philippines revised its mining and investment code to attract foreign investment in the 90s. The Philippine Mining Act of 1995 (RA 7942) provides for 100% foreign-ownership and 100% repatriation of mining capital and profits for up to 50 years. It allows for the export of raw ore without value added processing (Yap, 2015).

Mining proponents must obtain an environmental compliance certificate (ECC) and show proof of social acceptability through consultation with local governments and communities. An Administrative Order under Sec 136 requires companies to allocate 1% of direct mining and milling costs on a 5-year Social Development Management Program in the host and neighbouring communities. In areas covered by ancestral domains, the Indigenous Peoples Rights Act (IPRA) of 1997 requires companies to secure the free and prior informed consent (FPIC) of the indigenous community. If an FPIC is granted, the Company must pay the indigenous community a royalty of at least 1% of the gross output. Both social acceptability and FPIC are to be renewed regularly. Local municipal councils are to be involved in the Multipartite Monitoring Committee (MMC) to monitor mining activities. Companies are also required to maintain several funds:

1. Mine Rehabilitation Fund (MRF) to rehabilitate mined areas;
2. Mine Waste and Tailings Reserve Fund (MWTRF) to deal with accumulation of the mine wastes and tailings; and
3. Final Mine Rehabilitation and Decommissioning Fund (FMRDF) to rehabilitate the mine areas after closure.

Notwithstanding the Philippines' mineral abundance and openness to FDI, mining "accounts for only a small share of the economy, exports, and government revenue" (IMF 2012, p.5), less than 1% to its GDP between 2003 to 2012, and less than 1% to national employment (GOP, 2013). In spite of the requirements of social acceptability and FPIC, the costs to the community and the environment appear to have been high. The country has several hundred abandoned mines of varying sizes and a number of highly publicized mining accidents. These accidents and the lingering legacies of abandoned mines, combined with growing public awareness of similar concerns in mining communities in other parts of the world have led to a growing and vocal constituency against large-scale mining in the Philippines.

The Chair of a fact finding mission on Philippine mining organised by the Anglican Church wrote: "I have never seen anything so systematically destructive as the mining programme in the Philippines. The environmental effects are catastrophic as are the effects on people's livelihoods" (Doyle, Wicks & Nally, 2007, p.i).

Issues, Controversies, Problems

"Contentious and ambiguous" – was how Bebbington et al (2008) describe the relationship between large-scale mining and development. "'Contentious' because of the negative social, environmental and economic effects for the many, but significant gains only for the few; 'ambiguous' because of the abiding sense, among local populations as much as development professionals, that *just maybe* mining could contribute much more" (p.887, italics in the original).

Mining is a waste intensive activity, regardless of location, commodity or scale (See Figure 1). Between 30% to 80% of the mass of the ore end up as waste in the extraction and beneficiation processes (Ripley, Redmann & Crowder, 1995). Unless appropriately managed, these wastes negatively impact the local environment and local communities, not only because of their volume but also because these are chemically reactive substances, in some cases radioactive, and many of the processes are irreversible.

Pollution burdens and landscape destruction foreclose traditional and non-market livelihoods. Conflict frequently results from competition for vital community resources like farmland, drinking water and the mineral resource itself.

Some argue that under certain conditions, mining can be sustainable (e.g., Azapagic, 2004; O'Faircheallaigh, 2010). These conditions include: (a) sharing of economic benefits with the host community; (b) compensation for the depletion of mineral resources through generation of new wealth; (c) minimal environmental impacts, and maximum recycling of used minerals and metals; and (d) discovery of new deposits, and development of new technologies to recover materials from abandoned deposits. Except for metals and minerals recycling, all these conditions are within the control of individual companies.

Major Concerns about Mining in the Philippines

The major concerns about mining in the Philippines are not very different from those reported in other countries such as Argentina (Comelli et al, 2010), Australia (Browne, Stehlik, & Buckley, 2011), Bolivia (Bebbington et al, 2008), Brazil (Tubino, Yap & Devlin, 2011), Indonesia (Welker, 2009), Peru (CARC, 2010) and South Africa (Rajak, 2006).

Environmental impacts were the most common concern of environmental and anti-mining groups. The concern assumes a sense of urgency since two thirds of mining exploration in the Philippines and half of active concessions are in seismic active zones (Whitmore, n. d.), and about 6 to 9 typhoons make landfall in the country annually. Industry informants insist that it is a matter of perception.

Most of the environmental impacts are known by now. Either the technology exists or there are ways to mitigate the problems. For most of the environmental impacts, it is more a question of perception ... People automatically believe that their water will be contaminated if a mine operates near them, which is not really an ... issue because 99.999% of the time, we can ensure the water won't get polluted... (KII 9).

Academics agree with industry informants. They identify social impacts as the most adverse consequence and inequitable revenue sharing a big concern. It was consistently pointed out that the local elite and government at all levels tend to benefit most from mining, not those on the receiving end of the most adverse impacts. "Community members told me that they understand the companies pay a lot of taxes and royalties, but they say they don't see it. It is paid to the central government, then goes to the local government, and by the time it gets to the community, it is a drop in the bucket" (KII 16). Another major concern is the displacement of indigenous peoples from their traditional territory and loss of access to traditional livelihoods. Half of staked lands are in ancestral domains.

Corporate Practices: Environmental Management, Labour, Democratic Governance and Community Engagement

CARMEN COPPER CORPORATION (a subsidiary of Atlas Consolidated Mining and Development Corporation) operates the Toledo Copper Mine (Cebu) under a Mineral Production Sharing Agreement (MPSA). The 2013 Sustainability Report (CCC, 2013) provides detailed quantitative data on key environmental parameters such as hazardous chemicals use and management, GHG emissions, WHS-associated accidents, and reforestation activities. The FMRDP describes activities planned on tailings management, air quality, biodiversity loss and landscape degradation.

Of the total workforce of 4600, 84% are local and 72% are unionised. Health insurance, housing and transportation benefits, vacation leave, sick leave, birthday leave, and retirement benefits are provided to full time employees. The entry-level wages are above the legal minimum. Employees and contractors undergo training on health and safety, code of conduct, waste and environment management, and anti-corruption. The company posts information on its outputs, revenues, tax payments, and employee profile.

The PhP40M (US$0.84M) Social Development Management Plan (SDMP) invests in transportation infrastructure, health, education, and livelihood diversification. Eighty four percent of its goods and services are procured locally.

The Toledo mine was operated by Atlas Consolidated Mining and Development Corporation from 1953 to 1994. Tagged as the 'bread and butter' of the city, ACMDC was the city's largest employer at the peak of its operations. Before its shutdown ACMDC was paying taxes of about PhP 634 million annually to the national government, out of which the city government received an annual share of PhP 11 million. Throughout these 4 decades ACMDC was a constant recipient of awards given by national safety organizations. It received the "Safest Combined Underground and Open Pit Operations" by the Philippine Mine Safety Association for 14 consecutive years. In 1994, ACMDC suspended its operations in Toledo City due to the low world market price of copper, flooding of its underground mines, and financial constraints for the necessary rehabilitation, and internal labor problems (PWGM & ESSC, 2008b).

BENGUET CORPORATION was established in 1903 and is the first and oldest mining company in the Philippines. It produces gold, nickel laterite and limestone in 11 sites. In July 2014, its Zambales subsidiary received an MGB (Mines and Geosciences Bureau) order suspending its ore extraction and future expansion areas "until a systematic mining and clean up / relocation of ore profiles to designated stockpile areas is implemented". It was one of 4 mining firms issued show-cause orders to explain why they were using the stripping method, i.e., removing large strips of soil and rock through the use of heavy equipment (Montealegre, 2015).

The company website is uninformative and poorly managed, with most of the links broken. The 2-page 2013 Sustainability Report (BC, n.d.) mentions "Environmental Protection" but provides few specifics. Under "Community Relations" it claims to provide ambulance services, medical consultations and drugs, maintenance of school grounds, daycare and scholarships in mining programs.

LEPANTO is Filipino gold producer established in 1936. It has two MPSAs and 46 mining claims, all in Benguet.

The 2014 Annual Report (LCMC, 2014) mentions establishing 40,000m^2 of fuel breaks to protect forest and critical infrastructure, solid waste dump fortification, 4-stage cyanide detoxification and filtration process, reforestation and agro-forestry program. A tailings dam (No. 5A), is described as a zoned, earth-filled catch-all dam with a twin concrete lined decanting system and a 600-meter span 4.0 x 5.0 meter concrete lined diversion tunnel. A 12-meter freeboard is maintained to handle a 600-year flood event. Wastewater is managed to comply with DENR effluent standards and water quality criteria. There is quarterly monitoring of the ambient air quality and noise levels within the residential and industrial areas of the Company. Air pollutant concentrations are reportedly well within the limits set under "Philippine Clean Air Act, and the noise level, with WHO standards. Domestic wastes are sorted by residents for re-use & recycling, and residuals disposed of in a legally compliant facility. The company is establishing a Materials Recovery Facility in partnership with the host communities and NGOs. There are oil-water separator systems. Used lead-laced crucibles and other non-useable hazardous materials are encapsulated / fixated and entombed on-site; containers of hazardous materials and wastes are cleaned and sold/disposed of in DENR-accredited Treatment, Storage and Disposal (TSD) facilities.

These mark a very significant improvement of Lepanto's previous practice. For more than half a century, Lepanto Consolidated Mining Corporation was associated with pollution of the Mangkayan-Abra River system and deforestation in the surrounding areas. Between 1960s and 1999 Lepanto saw three incidents of tailings dam collapse with serious loss of life and homes, and persistent concerns over heavy metal pollution (Stark et al, 2006).

Of its 1,107 rank-and-file employees, 83% are unionised and are provided with health and housing benefits.

The company funded community library renovation, purchased books for daycare centres, provided scholarships for college students, mining engineering students and student summer employment and sports equipment to encourage sports development. It constructed abattoirs, paved old roads and opened new ones, renovated sections of the hospital, purchased new hospital beds and constructed a chapel, schools, toilets and suspension bridges, and installed street lights and water systems. Working with government and NGOs it implements anti-rabies, anti-dengue vaccinations, undertakes medical, surgical and dental missions, and provides iodized salt and sanitation accessories. It provided training on alternative livelihood such as piggery, crafts making, *longganisa* making, bee-keeping and hair styling.

MANILA MINING CORPORATION (MMC) is an affiliate of Lepanto Consolidated Mining Company. It explores for and mines gold silver and copper. It owns 2000ha of prime mineral land in Placer (Surigao del Norte) and has applications for 4,850ha more around its mines.

MMC had three mining accidents and several recorded violations of environmental laws in two decades of operation. In July 1987, a dam failure spilled cyanide tailings causing fish kill. In September 1995, a dam foundation failed at a tailings pond due to heavier than normal rainfall. The 50,000m^3 of tailings released led to coastal pollution and loss of 12 lives. Barely 4 years later, another tailings pond failed releasing about 900 000m^3 of tailings, burying 22 houses and 51ha of croplands, coconut or nipa areas and marshlands. The company was found in violation of environmental laws – raising the elevation of a tailings pond and conducting open pit mining without ECC. Tensions with stakeholder groups developed when a university impact assessment team was denied entry by armed guards. This escalated when church-based groups barricaded roads to exploration sites. In 2001 MMC suspended its operations over "lack of funds", leaving behind unpaid real property taxes to the local government and unfulfilled commitment to post closure rehabilitation (PWGM & ESSC, 2008a). In 2011 MMC went into joint venture with Philex to resume operations.

The 14-page CSR Report covered 2011-2014 (MMC, n.d.). It claims successful rehabilitation of access roads and drill site disturbed areas and management of Acid-Mine-Drainage (AMD) from temporarily abandoned mine pits and wastes dumps. It reforested over 20ha in its mine site and is working to establish a mangrove forest. There is no information on "Employee Relations" and "Governance". In the community MMC provided medicines, built toilets, constructed a preschool classroom, repaired a daycare centre, and provided school supplies, computers and 1 university scholarship. It provided farmers rice seedlings and fertilisers, installed street lighting and water system, constructed a bridge, and supported religious and fiesta celebrations.

NICKEL ASIA CORPORATION (NAC) is the Philippines' largest producer of lateritic nickel ore, and one of the world's largest. NAC has MPSAs on 4 sites: Rio Tuba (Palawan), Taganito, (Surigao del Norte), Cagdianao (Dinagat Islands), and Hinatuan (Surigao del Norte) and has a non-operational site in Manicani Island (Eastern Samar).

The deposits in all four sites are near-surface, blanket-like layers with minimal overburden and located within 3 to 7km from the tidewater loading area. NAC employs simple open-pit mining using trucks and loaders without blasting, chemicals or complex waste handling. The Report (NAC, 2014) covers all four sites with quantitative data on all materially significant parameters - "Environmental management", "Employee relations", "Governance" and "Community relations and engagement". The data are comprehensive, but concisely structured, unambiguous and candid about where it falls short of its targets, identifying the different laws it needs to comply with. The risks assessed included climate change effects, environmental hazards such as earthquakes or landslides.

To mitigate the risks NAC conducts worker awareness and prevention programs. It also installed in the field of 340-liter tanks of potable water and make-shift sheds/shelters to protect the workers from extreme heat during warm weather and cold from sudden downpours. NAC's regular, contractual and contractor's employees reportedly enjoy medical access, free education, yearly bonuses and a "generous retirement pay."

In 2015 NAC partnered with the provincial government to build a P140-million water system to serve 10,000 households in 13 barangays in the municipality of Bataraza. The project is the third NAC CSR-related water project in Bataraza in five years (Galvez, 2015). Through rehabilitation and reforestation, NAC converted a 25-ha mined out area into one that grows papaya, grapes, *palay* and other crops. The company claims some credit for the fact that of 23 municipalities in the province, Bataraza ranks second in income, third in cash balances and fourth in assets (Kwok, 2012).

Interesting to add that there are 27 indigenous peoples (IP) clusters around the Bataraza, 11 of whom are among the impacted communities. There were protests from members of the Palawan tribe in 2011; these seem to have subsided.

This high level of responsibility does not appear to apply in NAC's other sites. Its subsidiary in Cagdianao (Cagdianao Mining Company) was among five mining companies sued by the province for refusing to pay taxes under the province's Soil Depletion Tax. Cagdianao Mining Company owed the highest - P174.8M including penalties and interest (Catoto, 2015).

The Taganito mine (Surigao del Norte) faced protests in 2009 led by the Mamanwas, one of the oldest tribes in the Philippines, over unpaid royalties, environmental degradation, desecration of sacred sites, health problems and loss of fishery resources. The NAC subsidiary and 5 other companies have operated in Taganito since the 1960s. Taganito is now known as the "red mountain" with "chocolate rivers". The mountain has been fully deforested by mining and logging operations, its rivers reportedly laden with mine waste (Scheidel, 2015). In 2010 the company agreed to pay a few years' royalties but paid it to a splinter Mamanwa group recognised by the National Commission on Indigenous People and signed an MOU with SMI. The conflict intensified in 2011, when members of the New People's Army (NPA) attacked TMC and two other facilities in town. Subsequently, the Armed Forces of the Philippines (AFP) and the mining companies entered into agreements for employing special militia (Gallardo, 2011). The conflict appears unresolved (Munson, 2013).

OCEANAGOLD CORPORATION owns and operates the open-pit high grade gold-copper Didipio mine in Nueva Vizcaya.

The 36-page 2015 Sustainability Report (OGC, 2015) covers three mining sites: Dipidio (Philippines), Macraes (El Salvador) and Reefton (NZ). The Report is rather confusing. The tabulated data are sorted out for each of three sites but the detailed discussion is sometimes specific to site, sometimes not.

The company reportedly works with the Local Government Unit (LGU) to establish a Catchment Management Organisation and with the International River Foundation to improve the water quality in the Didipio River catchment. The Didipio site achieved ISO 14001: 2004 certification. The 2014 Report described the Didipio tailings storage facility as having been "engineered to withstand a maximum category credible earthquake and typhoon" but does not provide any detail. The 2015 Report states that the amount of waste oil and waste oil in water was reduced by some 80% from 2013 and 60% decrease in oil contaminated soil through the introduction of a waste oil processing plant on site, improved maintenance of machinery and vehicles, increased operator experience and optimisation of processing and hauling activities.

Of its workforce of 1,800, 98% are Filipino nationals including more than 50% from the local communities. Didipio' earned Safest Mine Operation Award from the Philippine Mine Safety and Environment Association (PMSEA). The company reports having spent approximately US$3 million on its SDMP providing training on mining operations to community members seeking certification to work in the mining sector, and scholarships to university students.

The Didipio mine however, has been dogged with controversy and community divisions since 2009. In 2011 the Philippine Commission for Human Rights found OGC to be in violation of numerous human rights, including local peoples' Right to Residence, Adequate Housing and Property Rights; to Freedom of Movement; to Security of Person and to Manifest Culture and Identity, among others (Ayroso, 2014).

Sagittarius Mines Incorporated (SMI) has a Financial and Technical Assistance Agreement (FTAA) to develop the Tampakan mine (South Cotabato), one of the world's largest undeveloped gold-copper deposits. The $5.9B project would be the largest FDI in the Philippines and the world's largest open pit mine.

The Project occupies 4 ancestral domains of the B'laan people. Final site development requires the relocation and resettlement of over 1000 B'laan households (5000 individuals). For 8 months SMI conducted fortnightly consultations with elected representatives of affected communities on resettlement site selection, housing design, infrastructure and compensation, and separate consultations on its SDMP, the power supply and off-lease infrastructure, and community grievance mechanism put in place. It continued to face opposition from the Catholic Church and various environmental groups. The site is in a watershed that supplies water to 5 rivers in 4 provinces. The concern was that the mining operation would pollute downstream lakes and marshes, damaging farmlands and fisheries and seriously impacting the food source for the Muslim and indigenous populations. This, opponents argue, would most certainly lead to major social unrest (Godilano & Monsod, 2012). Between 2008 and 2012 Tampakan suffered several armed attacks by New Peoples' Army (NPA). In 2012 SMI's ECC application was rejected by DENR on the basis of a provincial ban on open pit mining. It was successfully appealed and ECC granted Feb 2013.

The 2012 Sustainability Report (SMI, 2012), describes outputs against set targets but no indicators. There is no information on chemicals to be used in the extraction process and how it would be detoxified. Nor does it make any reference to the environmental costs of such a huge open-pit mine. The risk mitigation measures proposed – "preventing public access" - underestimate, indeed ignore the risks from climate change.

Out of a total workforce of 377 full time (38.7% female) and 976 contractors, 41% are from host municipalities, with IPs representing 15%. It provided worker training in emergency response, security awareness, cultural awareness, ethics, values, and human rights, and environmental management.

SMI reports spending US$12M in local procurement, and US$1.5M in donations, community partnerships and sponsorships in addition to building infrastructure - school buildings, community centres, potable water systems and farm-to-market roads. It claims to have benefited more than 6200 households with income generating projects. It offers alternative livelihoods for artisanal small scale miners and provided scholarships to elementary, high school and college students, and vocational training for out-of-school youths. It supported upgrading program for teachers' skills in science and English and works with several national and local universities to enhance their mining-related courses, research capacity and training programs (Table 2).

Foreign vs. Filipino Companies: Any Difference in Practice

Industry, government and some academic researchers indicated that wholly-owned foreign companies have the added pressure of being watched by the international community. They have to ensure that they are following responsible practices, but generally have more capital and resources to reduce impacts. Security was cited as a major challenge in many Reports and responded to with the engagement of the paramilitary. Some industry informants insist communication was the best approach.

The key was just going and talking to the church. A lot of what it is in the Philippines is paying people their due respect. Some companies don't go explain and make the people comfortable, but if you do, it is much better (KII 14).

NGOs and anti-mining groups had a divided view of CSR. "CSR can only be realistic and true if it is inclusive, transparent and accountable, and participatory" (KII 12). This is missing in the Philippines, they add. Others do not see CSR as making a difference.

Since the advent of CSR codes, we have had as many problems with environmental mismanagement and conflicts with affected communities and allegations with human rights abuses as we did before...they are self-imposed and voluntary, and there are no accountability mechanisms (KII 7).

Challenges for Mining Companies in the Philippines

Opinions of the Mining Act (1995) vary among the key informants but all strongly agreed there are severe problems with the enforcement of the mining regulations. Industry stakeholders argued that the

Table 2. Key findings on CSR practice of mining companies

Company	Ownership	CSR Assessment Checklist				Level of Social Responsibility
		A	B	C	D	
Carmen Copper Corporation	Majority Filipino	H	H	H	H	High
Benguet Corporation	Majority Filipino	L	L	L	L	Low
Lepanto Consolodated Mining Company	Majority Filipino	H	H	H	H	High
Manila Mining Corporation	Majority Filipino	L	L	L	L	Low
Nickel Asia Corporation	Majority Filipino	H	H	H	H	High
OceanaGold Corporation	Foreign	M	M	L	L	Low to Medium
Sagittarius Mines INC	Foreign	L	M	L	M	Low to Medium

regulations are tight, but the implementation is a "total disaster" (KII 19). The authority granted to foreign companies to take the ore out of the country for processing elsewhere is viewed by environmental groups as very problematic.

... It is literally like cutting down the trees and taking the mountain to another country for processing ... We allow that for a mere 2% excise tax? It isn't fair. We give the permit, and then it is like everything in the land is theirs. And how can we measure how much gold they are actually taking out if they are taking the whole chunk of soil and ore? (KII 12)

...You mine for nickel, but you know there is iron there because it is like a magnet. They don't pay for the iron because they are mining the nickel, but all the metals are in the soil, so how does the government deal with that? ...We are giving a lot of what we have. (KII 13)

The Indigenous Peoples Rights Act (IPRA) of 1997 was also criticized. One company described its experience:

... we have had four different tries at it [satisfying IPRA procedures] because we have had four different regional directors, and unfortunately there has been a lot of corruption in the implementation of IPRA and many instances where IPRA approvals have been bought and sold...it has been a nightmare for mining companies to work through (KII 19)

Another challenge cited by academics and industry informants, is satisfying the constantly-changing, inconsistent procedural guidelines depending on the mine location. A good case in point is the Soil Depletion Tax enacted in Dinagat Island in 2009. It imposes a 1% tariff on gross receipts of all mineral ore "extracted and/or shipped" from the province. Mining companies complain this constitutes double taxation. Dinagat Island is a declared mineral reservation so in addition to the 2% excise tax, mining companies also pay 5% royalty based on the market value of the gross output of the minerals they extract.

Many academic researchers claimed there is much confusion as to who is responsible for what.

The Environmental Management Bureau is under the DENR, and is responsible for accepting applications for ECCs. The MGB is responsible for studying a company's proposed Social Development Program (SDP), but has nothing to do with it after the initial screening. The EMB only monitors environmental impacts, so the social impacts aren't monitored by any government body. (KII 16)

There are disputes between central and local government units over jurisdiction. "In Mindoro Oriental, a provincial board imposed a mining ban, but can't implement it, and there are still mining companies mining there because the permit was issued by the DENR" (KII 15).

One key informant from a company with operations in numerous developing countries said that while it has encountered corruption in all developing countries, the situation was worst in the Philippines. Other industry informants spoke of encountering corruption and bribery at all levels from community members to central government officials.

SOLUTIONS AND RECOMMENDATIONS

That mine workers in both developed and developing countries are among the staunchest defenders of an industry that "scars both landscapes and lungs" Bebbington et al, 2008, p. 888) indicates that benefits do flow to local communities albeit unevenly. The companies profiled in this chapter suggest that many do want to do good. How can the laggard majority be encouraged to do no harm?

Mining companies should acknowledge the finiteness of the mineral resource and vulnerability of the industry to price volatility. They should plan for closure and to leave behind stronger, less vulnerable communities. They should develop enabling 'capitals' – human (education and health programs), financial (alternative livelihoods and economic diversification), and infrastructure. Not as a gift, nor out of a sense of wanting to be good while doing good but as payment of a moral debt to future generations whom they are depriving a critical resource.

No technology is fail safe but failures can be made 'safer'. Companies should systematically assess the impacts not only of their operations on the environment but also of the environment on their operations. Take the case of tailings dams. They should be designed with the highest engineering safety standards with safeguards and response systems that accommodate uncertainties including those associated with climate change. Dams should be built to withstand 1:100 year flood at a minimum; given the severe consequences of tailings dam failure, its management should be assigned to the CEO or COO, as suggested by the Mining Association of Canada (MAC, 2012). The Philippine government should require, as part of the ECC process, assessment of climate risks to mining infrastructure, including tailings dams.

Mining companies should go beyond the legal/contractual requirement of social acceptability and work to earn their 'social license to operate'. They should take the moral high ground and not create, exploit or exacerbate community divisions. Where there is conflict with the community companies should reach out to mining opponents and help bring about more inclusive, transparent and equitable public institutions. Rather than delegitimise and devalue artisanal and small scale miners companies should work with them and help them develop sound appropriate environmental health and safety standards.

If mining is to be a driver for inclusive economic growth, there needs to be social peace. There must be a more equitable and transparent system of revenue sharing. Policy-makers could look at some successful examples of benefit sharing regimes in mining countries such as Botswana, Chile, perhaps Norway (Lindon, Canare & Mendoza, 2014). The Philippine government should rescind Executive Order 264, i.e., abolish the paramilitary arm of the Armed Forces, or at a minimum, ban their employment as mine security (Silverio, 2011). This would show tremendous good will to anti-mining groups and perhaps help win the hearts of mining communities with NPA presence.

The definition of what can and cannot constitute *force majeure* should be explicitly stated in mining licenses. Given the acknowledged increasing magnitude and ferocity of climatic and other natural shocks in the Philippines, failing to design for climate change would seem to constitute criminal negligence. Who qualifies or not qualify to receive royalties under IPRA 1997 should be clearly defined by law to prevent divide-and-rule strategy by companies and unscrupulous civil servants.

The Philippine mining policy environment has too many layers, convoluted requirements and diffused mandates. Complexity invites 'negotiation', creating opportunities for corruption and bribery. The Philippine mining regulatory environment needs to be simplified, lines of accountability streamlined, institutional mandates and boundaries clarified.

FUTURE RESEARCH DIRECTIONS

The sample of 7 companies is too small to establish the national picture or reveal the full complexities of the business-environment-community relationships in the Philippines. The CSR assessment is based on publicly available information and therefore can only be suggestive, not indicative. Six of the seven Reports examined are based on self-reported data not verified independently, raising questions regarding reliability and scope. The systematic application of the grid in Table 1 was an effort to reduce the 'apple *versus* orange' difficulty but does not eliminate the difficulty of comparing performance in the absence of standardisation of format and scope.

A mixed developed and developing country field based study of CSR practices of metals and minerals MNCs in different sites to test Campbell's (2006) hypothesis would be most instructive. One could examine the CSR practices of Xstrata (now Glencore) in Australia, Mongolia and the Philippines, Newmont in the U.S., Ghana and Peru, Sumitomo in the U.S., Canada, Chile and Peru, Vale in Canada, Brazil. Mozambique and Angola. A smaller study could look at the factors that influenced the significant improvements in Lepanto's practices, the seeming lack of improvement in MMC's, the lack of a credible impact mitigation program by SMI in relation to their use of open pit technology, and the significant differences in NAC's performance in the 3 sites.

CONCLUSION

Two of the companies rated *Low* were Filipino-owned (Benguet Corporation and MMC) but so were the three assessed *High* (Carmen Copper, Lepanto and NAC). The two foreign owned companies were ranked *Low* to *Medium*. This challenges the frequent assumption that MNCs are necessarily more responsible than local ones if only because they face stronger scrutiny and have more resources (Stark et al, 2006). The practices of Benguet Corporation and MMC are consistent with Comelli et al's (2010) observation in Argentina that firms with poor environmental performance tend to use corporate donations and social investment to earn social legitimacy.

That all seven companies reported on their environmental management and their community development programs suggests that CSR and CSR reporting is strongly influenced by the "national business system", consistent with Chapple and Moon's (2005) finding. The implementation weaknesses of the Philippine mining regulatory system specifically lack of transparency and integrity, and weak technical capacity of government personnel are countervailed, albeit not completely, by the vigilance of civil society groups. That the Chamber of Mines of the Philippines is actively promoting CSR clearly helps. These suggest that there is merit in Campbell's (2006) proposition that the presence of independent non-state organisations and fora that monitor corporate behavior and institutionalized norms regarding appropriate corporate behavior enhance the likelihood of socially responsible corporate behavior. The remarkable improvements in Lepanto's practices show that corporations can improve their performance and do no irreparable harm in addition to doing good. The challenge for CSR scholars is to understand the triggers better.

REFERENCES

APEC. (2012). *Corporate Social Responsibility in the APEC Region. Current Status and Implications.* Manila, Philippines: Asian Institute of Management RVR Center for Corporate Responsibility.

Ayroso, D. (2014, September 19). Indigenous peoples, environmentalists call for end to OceanaGold's 'mining plunder'. *Bulatlat.* Retrieved from http://bulatlat.com/main/2014/09/19/indigenous-peoples-environmentalists-call-for-end-to-oceanagolds-mining-plunder/

Azapagic, A. (2004). Developing a framework for sustainable development indicators for the mining and minerals industry. *Journal of Cleaner Production, 12*(6), 639–662. doi:10.1016/S0959-6526(03)00075-1

Banerjee, S. B. (2008). Corporate Social Responsibility: The Good, the Bad and the Ugly. *Critical Sociology, 34*(1), 51–79. doi:10.1177/0896920507084623

Bansal, P. (2005). Evolving sustainably: A longitudinal study of corporate sustainable development. *Strategic Management Journal, 26*(3), 197–218. doi:10.1002/smj.441

Bebbington, A., Hinojosa, L., Bebbington, D. H., Burneo, M. L., & Warnaars, X. (2008). Contention and Ambiguity: Mining and the Possibilities of Development. *Development and Change, 39*(6), 887–914. doi:10.1111/j.1467-7660.2008.00517.x

Benguet Corporation. (n. d.). *Moving Forward and Beyond.* Retrieved from http://benguetcorp.com/

Blowfield, M. (2005). Corporate Social Responsibility: Reinventing the meaning of development? *International Affairs, 81*(3), 515–524. doi:10.1111/j.1468-2346.2005.00466.x

Browne, A. L., Stehlik, D., & Buckley, A. (2011). Social licences to operate: For better not for worse; for richer not for poorer? The impacts of unplanned mining closure for "fence line" residential communities. *Local Environment, 16*(7), 707–725. doi:10.1080/13549839.2011.592183

Cabalda, M. M., Banaag, A. A., Tidalgo, P. N. T., & Garces, R. B. (2002). *Sustainable Development in the Philippine Minerals Industry. A baseline study. Mining Minerals and Sustainable Development Project. Report #184.* London, UK: IIED & WBCSD.

Campbell, J. L. (2006). Institutional Analysis and the Paradox of Corporate Social Responsibility. *The American Behavioral Scientist, 49*(7), 925–938. doi:10.1177/0002764205285172

Carmen Copper Corporation. (2013). *The Power to Grow. Sustainability Report 2013.* Retrieved from http://www.atlasmining.com.ph/about-atlas/carmen-copper-corporation

Catoto, R. (2015, April 24). Dinagat to sue 2 more mining firms for unpaid taxes. *Minda News,* Retrieved from http://www.mindanews.com/top-stories/2015/04/24/dinagat-to-sue-2-more-mining-firms-for-unpaid-taxes/

Centro de Análisis y Resolución de Conflitos (CARC). (2010). *Lecciones Aprendidas sobre la Defensoría para el Proyecto Camisea. Un Puente para el entendimiento* [Lessons learned from the advocacy of Project Camisea. A bridge for understanding]. Lima: Pontificia Universidad Católica del Perú.

Chambers, E. Chapple, W., Moon, J., & Sullivan, M. (n. d.). *CSR in Asia: A seven country study of CSR website reporting*. ICCR Research Paper Series. No. 09-2003. Nottingham, U.K: International Centre for Corporate Social Responsibility.

Chapple, W., & Moon, J. (2005). Corporate Social Responsibility (CSR) in Asia. A Seven-Country Study of CSR Web Site Reporting. *Business & Society*, *4*(4), 415–441. doi:10.1177/0007650305281658

Comelli, M., Hadad, M. G., & Petz, M. I. (2010). Hacia Un Desarrollo (In)Sostenible En América Latina. El Caso De La Minería A Cielo Abierto En La Argentina. Argumentos. Revista de crítica social, [Towards (Un) sustainable development in Latin America. The case of open pit mining.] *Argumentos*. Magazine of social critique)12, Octubre 2010.

Doyle, C., Wicks, C., & Nally, F. (2007). *Mining in the Philippines. Concerns and Conflicts. Report of Fact-finding Mission to the Philippines*. West Midlands, UK: Society of St. Columban.

Gallardo, F. (2011, October 3). NPA rebels attack 3 mining firms in Surigao del Norte *Minda News*. Retrieved from http://www.mindanews.com/top-stories/2011/10/03/npa-rebels-attack-3-mining-firms-in-surigao-norte/

Galvez, J. K. (2015, October 23). Nickel Asia affiliates sign Palawan water deal. *The Manila Times* Retrieved from http://www.manilatimes.net/nickel-asia-affiliates-sign-palawan-water-deal/225331/

Gilberthorpe, E., & Banks, G. (2012). Development on whose terms?: CSR discourse and social realities in Papua New Guinea's extractive industries sector. *Resources Policy*, *37*(2), 185–193. doi:10.1016/j.resourpol.2011.09.005

Godilano, E. C., & Monsod, C. S. (2012, May 31). To Mine or Not to Mine The Case of the Tampakan Copper-Gold Project: Mindanao, Philippines. *Paper presented to the Department of National Defense*, Manila, Philippines.

Government of the Philippines (GOP) Senate Economic Planning Office. (2013). *Realizing the Philippines' Mining Potential. Policy Brief. PB 3-02*. Manila, Philippines: Philippine Senate Economic Planning Office.

Hahn, T., Figge, F., Pinkse, J., & Preuss, L. (2010). Trade-offs in Corporate Sustainability. You Cannot Have Your Cake and Eat It. *Business Strategy and the Environment*, *19*(4), 217–229. doi:10.1002/bse.674

Holden, W. N., & Jacobson, D. (2007). Mining amid armed conflict: Nonferrous metals mining in the Philippines. *Canadian Geographer*, *51*(4), 475–500. doi:10.1111/j.1541-0064.2007.00193.x

ICMM. (2012). *The role of mining in national economies. Mining's contribution to sustainable development. London, UK: International Council on Mining and Metals. IIED and WBCSD (2002). Breaking New Ground. The Report of the Mining Minerals and Sustainable Development Project*. London: Earthscan Publications.

IMF. (2012). *Philippines. Reform of the Fiscal Tax Regime for Mining and Petroleum. IMF Country Report 12/219*. Washington, DC: International Monetary Fund.

Jamali, D., Karam, C., & Blowfield, M. (2015). Introduction. Corporate social responsibility in developing countries: a development-oriented approach. In D. Jamali, C. Karam & M. Blowfield (Eds.), Development-oriented Corporate Social Responsibility (Vol. 1, pp. 1-12). Sheffield, UK: Greenleaf Publishing Limited.

Jenkins, H. (2004). Corporate social responsibility and the mining industry: Conflicts and constructs. *Corporate Social Responsibility and Environmental Management*, *11*(1), 23–34. doi:10.1002/csr.50

Kwok, A. (2012, Sept 9). Nickel Asia asserts: responsible mining possible. *InterAksyon.* Retrieved from http://www.interaksyon.com/article/42681/nickel-asia-asserts-responsible-mining-possible

Lepanto Consolidated Mining Corporation. (2014). *2014 Annual Report*. Retrieved from http://www.lepantomining.com/

Lepanto Consolidated Mining Corporation. (n. d.). *Environmental Protection and Enhancement Program*. Retrieved from http://www.lepantomining.com/sustainability.html

Lepanto Consolidated Mining Corporation. (n. d.). *Social Development Management Program*. Retrieved from http://www.lepantomining.com/social_devt.html

Lindon, J. G., Canare, T. A., & Mendoza, R. (2014). Corporate governance in mining: Lessons from the Marcopper mine disaster in Marinduque, Philippines. *Asian Journal of Business Ethics*, *3*(2), 171–193. doi:10.1007/s13520-014-0038-3

Lorenzo-Molo, M. C. F. (2008). Why corporate social responsibility (CSR) remains a myth: The Case of the Philippines. *Asian Business & Management*, *8*(2), 149–168. doi:10.1057/abm.2009.2

Mainhardt-Gibbs, H. (2003). *The World Bank Extractive Industries Review. The Role of Structural Reform Programs towards Sustainable Development Outcomes*. Retrieved from http://awsassets.panda.org/downloads/2003_the_world_bank_extractive_industries_review.pdf

Manila Mining Corporation. (n. d.). *Community Development Plan (CDP), Corporate Social Responsibility (CSR) And Environmental Protection Activities Of MMC.* Retrieved from http://www.manilamining.com/aboutmmc.html

Maximiano, J. M. B. (2005, September 28–30). *The state of corporate social responsibility in the Philippine.Paper presented at theAustralian Association for Professional and Applied Ethics 12th Annual Conference*, Adelaide, Australia.

Mining Association of Canada. (2012). *TSM Assessment Protocol*. Ottawa: MAC.

Montealegre, K. A. (2015, February 20) MGB temporarily lifts suspension order vs. Benguet Corp. subsidiary. *Business World*. Retrieved from http://www.bworldonline.com/content.php?section=Corporate&title=mgb-temporarily-lifts-suspension-order-vs.-benguet-corp.-subsidiary&id=103096

Munson, J. (2013, October 27). The Philippines still a hotbed of opposition against mining. *iPolitics*. Retrieved from http://www.ipolitics.ca/2013/10/27/the-philippines-still-a-hotbed-of-opposition-to-canadian-mines-says-priest/

Nickel Asia Corporation. (2013). *2013 Sustainability Report*. Retrieved from http://www.nickelasia.com/pdf/NAC_2013_SR.pdf

Nickel Asia Corporation. (2014). *2014 Sustainability Report*. Retrieved from http://www.nickelasia.com/pdf/NAC_2014_SR.pdf

O'Faircheallaigh, C. (2010). Aboriginal-Mining Company Contractual Agreements in Australia and Canada: Implications for Political Autonomy and Community Development. *Canadian Journal of Development Studies*, *30*(1-2), 69–86.

Oceanagold Corporation. (2015). *Sustainability Report 2015. Ensuring A Better Tomorrow*. Retrieved from http://www.oceanagold.com/assets/documents/annual-reports/OceanaGold-SR-2015-FA-online.pdf

OECD. (2002, February 7-8). The Relevance of the OECD Guidelines for Multinational Enterprises to the Mining Sector and the Promotion of Sustainable Development. *Proceedings of theconference on Foreign Direct Investment and the Environment*, Paris. France.

Philippine Working Group on Mining (PWGM) & Environmental Science for Social Change. (ESSC) (2008a). 2003 Legacy Mines Visit. Manila Mining Corporation in the Surigao del Norte Mining District: Struggle with Corporate Social Responsibility at the Local. Manila: PWGM & ESSC.

Philippine Working Group on Mining (PWGM) & Environmental Science for Social Change. (ESSC) (2008b). 2003 Legacy Mines Visit. Atlas Consolidated Mining Development Corporation. Toledo City, Cebu. Environmental and Community Impact. Manila: PWGM & ESSC.

Porter, M. E., & Kramer, M. R. (2006). Strategy and Society. The link between Competitive Advantage and Corporate Social Responsibility. *Harvard Business Review*, 2006, 1–14. PMID:17183795

Price-Waterhouse Cooper. (2015, July 10). *Mine. The growing disconnect. Review of the global mining industry*. Retrieved from http://download.pwc.com/gx/mining/pwc-mine-2012.pdf

Rajak, D. (2006). The gift of CSR. Power and the Pursuit of Responsibility in the Mining Industry. In W. Visser, M. McIntosh, & C. Middleton (Eds.), *Corporate Citizenship in Africa* (pp. 190–200). Sheffield, UK: Greenleaf Publishing.

Ripley, E. A., Redmann, R. E., & Crowder, A. A. (1995). *Environmental Effects of Mining*. Florida: St. Lucie Press.

Sagittarius Mines Inc. (2012). *Tampakan Project sustainability Report*. Retrieved from http://www.smi.com.ph/EN/Publications/Pages/SustainabilityReports.aspx

Scheidel, A. (2015, June 5). Taganito Mining Corporation's Nickel Operations, Surigao del Norte, Philippines. *Environmental Justice Atlas*. Retrieved from https://ejatlas.org/conflict/taganito-mining-corporations-nickel-mine-surigao-del-nortephilippines

SHRM. (2007). *2007 Corporate Social Responsibility: United States, Australia, India, China, Canada, Mexico and Brazil. A Pilot Study*. Alexandria, VA: Society for Human Resource Management.

Silverio, I. A. R. (2011, October 14) Aquino gives go signal to deployment of CAFGUS to mining areas. *Bulatlat*. Retrieved from http://bulatlat.com/main/2011/10/14/aquino-gives-go-signal-to-deployment-of-cafgus-to-mining-areas/

Snyckers, T. (2006). Evading Corporate Social Responsibility through Tax Avoidance. In W. Visser, M. McIntosh, & C. Middleton (Eds.), Corporate Citizenship in Africa (pp. 67-79). Sheffield, UK: Greenleaf Publishing.

Stark, J., Li, J., & Terasawa, K. (2006) *Environmental Safeguards and Community Benefits in Mining: Recent Lessons from the Philippines*. USAID and Foundation for Environmental Security & Sustainability.

Tubino, D. S., Yap, N. T., & Devlin, J. F. (2011). Vale and its corporate social performance in Itabira, Brazil: Is the glass half full or half empty? *Impact Assessment and Project Appraisal*, *29*(2), 1–7. doi:10.3152/146155111X12913679730638

Utting, P. (2005). Corporate responsibility and the movement of business. *Development in Practice*, *15*(3&4), 375–388. doi:10.1080/09614520500075797

Vazquez-Brust, D. A., & Liston-Heyes, C. (2010). Environmental management intentions: An empirical investigation of Argentina's polluting firms. *Journal of Environmental Management*, *91*(5), 1111–1122. doi:10.1016/j.jenvman.2010.01.005 PMID:20110148

Visser, W. (2008). Corporate Responsibility in Developing Countries. In A. Crane, D. McWilliams, D. Matten, J. Moon, & D. Siegel (Eds.), The Oxford Handbook of Corporate Social Responsibility (pp. 473-479). Oxford, UK: Oxford University Press.

WBCSD. (2000, October 23). *Corporate Social Responsibility. Making good business sense*. Retrieved from http://www.wbcsd.org

Welker, M. A. (2009). Corporate security begins in the community. Mining, the Corporate Social Responsibility Industry and Environmental Advocacy in Indonesia. *Cultural Anthropology*, *24*(1), 142–179. doi:10.1111/j.1548-1360.2009.00029.x

Whitmore, A. (n. d.). *Philippines. Social and Environmental Impacts*. Retrieved from http://www.asienhaus.de/public/archiv/Andy_Whitmore_Philippines.pdf

Yakovleva, N., & Vasquez-Brust, D. (2012). Stakeholder Perspectives on CSR of Mining MNCs in Argentina. *Journal of Business Ethics*, *106*(2), 191–211. doi:10.1007/s10551-011-0989-4

Yap, N. T. (2015). CSR and the development deficit. Part of the solution or part of the problem. In Jamali, D., Karam, C., & Blowfield, M. (Eds.), Development Oriented Corporate Social Responsibility. (Vol. 1, pp. 134-152). Sheffield, UK: Greenfield.

Yin, R. K. (1994). *Case study research: Design and methods* (2nd ed.). Newbury Park, CA: Sage Publications.

ENDNOTE

1 The 50s in the Philippines saw the rise of peasant and labour insurgency.

Chapter 10
Leveraging CSR as a 'support-aid' for Triple Bottom-Line Development in Nigeria
Evidence from the Telecommunication Industry

Lukman Raimi
De Montfort University Leicester, UK

ABSTRACT

This book chapter focuses on the developmental-oriented perspective of CSR which views corporate involvement as a 'support-aid' for meeting triple bottom-line development in Nigeria. Arising from the literature, the stakeholder, legitimacy and social contract theories provide the required theoretical grounding for the discourse. The qualitative research method was found appropriate for this discourse. From the list of 25 registered telecommunication companies in Nigeria, a sample of 8 functional companies was selected using purposive sampling technique. The data extracted from the annual reports and websites of these companies were analysed using the content analysis. The findings indicate that the telecommunication companies are practically leveraging their CSR initiatives for social, economic and environmental wellness in Nigeria through a number of developmental programmes. The chapter explicates the fact that CSR as a private sector development model can be a potent tool for bridging governance gap environment instead of leaving all social problems to governments.

INTRODUCTION

Extant literature identified philanthropic, citizenship, instrumental, relational, normological, ethical, political and development-oriented perspectives as the prevalent modes of expressing corporate social responsibility (CSR). CSR in the developing country like Nigeria is focused on philanthropy and corporate donations to worthy cause (Amaeshi, Adi, Ogbechie and Amao, 2006). Beyond the philanthropic perspective of social responsibility, the development-oriented CSR is emerging and requires further

DOI: 10.4018/978-1-5225-0720-8.ch010

investigations. Unlike the conventional CSR, the development-oriented CSR addresses critical social issues like poverty, unemployment, diseases, infrastructural needs in the developing economies with infrastructural deficits (Frynas, 2005; Frynas, 2008; Idemudia, 2010; Sharp, 2006).

In Nigeria, corporations across different sectors of the economy focus their CSR programmes essentially on sports, sales promotion, sponsorship for the entertainment industry and donations to schools/hospitals/welfare centres. These uncoordinated CSR investments have not impacted effectively and efficiently on the social, economic and environmental development nor reduced poverty sustainably, hence this CSR strategy calls for re-examination. The CSR initiatives arising from philanthropy could at best be described as one-off effort that give momentary satisfaction and short-term benefits to the stakeholders/beneficiaries, but in the long-run such CSR investments would not address the root causes of poverty, and would not develop the capacities of the intended beneficiaries because of lack of comprehensive CSR policy or programmes (Boyle and Boguslaw (2007). A better model of CSR investment with richer theoretical foundation from what is styled a development-oriented CSR is required to meet the needs and expectations of the developing countries with weak institutional support and deteriorating governance (Adelopo, Raimi & Yekini, 2015).

The present discourse therefore attempts to fill the gap in the literature of social responsibility by leveraging CSR as a 'support-aid' for triple bottom-line development in Nigeria. In specific terms, the chapter seeks deeper understanding and application of CSR as a private sector development model (PSDM) in a poverty-ridden society with wide governence gap.

A number of studies report that socio-economic and environmental development in Nigeria is hinder by bad governance, weak institutional structures and ineffective governmental policies (Ite, 2007; Young, 1999). In a bid to redress the wrong above and promote socio-economic and environmental development in Nigeria, several attempts have been made by the governments in the past through a number of industrial policies and entrepreneurship intervention programmes (Raimi, Patel, Yekini & Fadipe, 2014), but the socio-economic impacts of these policies and interventions on the wellbeing of the people have been marginal when viewed against macro-economic indicators like unemployment, poverty rate and crime rate in the country (Raimi, Akhuemonkhan & Ogunjirin, 2015).

Retrospectively, the Nigerian government had experimented with several intervention development programmes with a view to actualizing the goals of wealth creation, technological progress and job creation. In spite of these developmental efforts, they did not produce desirable positive results; rather the rates of poverty, crime and unemployment have continued to rise over time (Raimi, Akhuemonkhan and Ogunjirin, 2015). Highlights of ineffective entrepreneurship development programmes (EDPs) in Nigeria include: the Indigenisation Policy, the Enterprises Promotion Policy, the Operation Feed the Nation (OFN), the Back-to-Land programme, the Import Substitution Strategy, the National Directorate of Employment (NDE), the Structural Adjustment Programme (SAP), the People's Bank of Nigeria (PBN), the National Economy Reconstruction Fund (NERFUND); the Community Banking Model, the Technology Business Incubation Centres (TBICs), the National Economic Empowerment and Development Strategy (NEEDS), the Bank of Industry (BOI), the Small and Medium Enterprises Development Agency of Nigeria (SMEDAN), the Small and Medium Enterprises Equity Investment Scheme (SMEEIS), the National Poverty Eradication Programme (NAPEP), the 7-Point Agenda, the Economic Transformation Programme, Youth Enterprise with Innovation in Nigeria (You Win) Programme, Subsidy Reinvestment & Empowerment Programme (SURE-P) and National Enterprise Development Programme (Njoku, Ihugba & Odii, 2014; Oghojafor, Okonji, Olayemi, & Okolie, 2011; Raimi et al., 2014).

In spite of the laudable objectives of the EDPs identified above, they have been rendered ineffective by institutionalised corruption, poor implementation, adhoc nature of the programmes and obvious bad governance (Young, 1999; Ukah, 2007; Raimi et al., 2014). Besides, the World Bank (2003) linked failure of development programmes in developing countries to two dimensions of governance gap, namely: (a) poor quality of administration in the public sector and (b) weak public accountability. The two dimensions presuppose that developing countries have low tolerance for efficient public service, rule of law, protection of property rights, quality regulations, and internal accountability, openness of political institutions and participation, respect of civil liberties, transparency of government, and press freedom (World Bank, 2003).

Analysts have therefore proposed a paradigm shift in favour of a private sector development model (PSDM). This shift entails refocusing CSR as a support-aid for socio-economic development in Nigeria judging by the positive contribution of the telecommunication industry to wealth creation, growth in national income and massive employment generation. CSR becomes development when refocused to addresses national issues like poverty, unemployment, diseases, infrastructural needs (Frynas, 2008; Adelopo et al., 2015). Latest figures show the poverty rate in Nigeria standing at 72% and the unemployment rate at 24% (National Bureau of Statistics, 2012). The country is listed among highly indebted nations (HINs) owing $44billion (Mohsin, 2013; Raimi et al., 2013). This ugly economic profile calls for proactive policy redirection, which this book chapter seeks to explore.

In the oil producing regions in Nigeria on account of intensified criticisms and indictments, multinational oil corporations adopt CSR initiatives as palliatives for improving the living conditions and wellbeing of the restive host communities (Raimi & Adeleke, 2010). These CSR initiatives have indeed improved access to basic capabilities for some privileged groups and have also impact positively on collective capabilities of the host community. However, but these initiatives have little effect on the expansion of basic capabilities for majority of the host communities (Lompo & Trani, 2013).

This chapter therefore explores CSR as a support-aid for promoting sustainable development in Nigeria where the public sector has failed woefully in its statutory obligation of meeting welfare needs of the citizens. This objective becomes expedient because of dwindling financial resources and competing priorities of the three levels of government in Nigeria (Raimi et al., 2015). The private sector intervention in the development process through CSR initiatives has started manifesting in the operations of multinational corporations (MNCs) like Microsoft, Cisco, Chevron, Gates and others which initiated developmental-oriented CSR programmes in Indonesia and the Middle East for the purpose of imbuing in the students, adults and the unemployed graduates the culture of entrepreneurship and job creation (Nelson, 2007; Jenkins, 2007).

In developing nations with governance and infrastructural deficits, there is increased involvement by MNCs in the wellbeing of host communities in the forms of community engagement (Yekini & Jallow, 2012), social entrepreneurship and corporate social entrepreneurship (Covin and Miles, 1999; Austin & Reficco, 2009), corporate citizens (Amaeshi et al., 2006) or responsible investors/responsible investment (Scholtens, 2014). Notable corporations like General Electric, IBM, Google, eBay, Johnson & Johnson, Grameen Bank & Grameen Foundation, KaBOOM, DonorsChoose, Intel, Nestlé, Unilever and Wal-Mart are using CSR as a strategic tool for promoting social wellness without losing their core economic objectives of profits and wealth creation (Kerr, 2007; Haskins, 2009; Porter & Kramer, 2011). Similarly, Aramex and Injaz corporations in Asia took over governmental role of unemployment reduction and attendant consequences like poverty, youth restiveness and hopelessness. This form of CSR initiative is developmental because it is channeled towards entrepreneurship development (Adelopo, Raimi & Yekini, 2015).

Samy, Odemilin and Bampton (2010) argue that in the contemporary times, CSR investments are not wasteful spending as many anti-CSR proponents opined, but they are social investments which are essential for corporations' sustainable survival in the competitive business environment. Therefore, making move "to isolate business from society is unrealistic and that dichotomizing economic and social objectives as distinct and competing is false" (p.203).

Based on the above, the plausibility of leveraging CSR of the Nigerian telecommunications companies as a support-aid for social, economic and environmental development is justified. The research adopts the refocusing strategy for CSR because Nigeria like of other developing African countries has a distinct CSR agenda and needs which fundamentally are different from what obtained in developed countries (Visser 2008). Implementation of CSR investments effectively and efficiently would therefore complement development gaps created by ineffective public sector in the country. More importantly, the understanding of CSR conceptualised by this chapter goes beyond the traditional expression of empathy to the society, but a development-oriented CSR which impact positively on economic, social and environmental development in developing economy like Nigeria.

Apart from the introduction Section 1 above, there are six sections in this book chapter. Section 2 focuses on conceptual issues and litereture review explore the literature. Section 3 discsusses the theoretical framework of a delopment-oriented CSR. Section 4 examines the emerging Developmental-Oriented CSR Models which provide stronger support for refocusing CSR as support-aid for triple bottom-line development. Section 5 presents the methodology and findings. Section 6 discusses the implications, conclusions and recommendations.

Conceptual Issues and Literature Review

Traditional and Developmental perspectives of CSR

Scholars have advanced different definitions for CSR from traditional and developmental perspectives in the literature. From one perspective, CSR has been defined as: (a) good neighbourliness, which means that corporations is expected to play a positive role in solving broad social problems facing the stakeholders (Eilbert & Parket, 1973). Besides, CSR is a commitment by corporations to social, economic and environmental wellness of the society beyond the minimum duties prescribed by enabling laws (Enderle & Tavis, 1998; Brønn & Vrioni, 2001). Put differently, CSR is seen as the formal and informal channels through which corporations contribute sustainably to improving "the governance, social, ethical, labour and environmental conditions of the developing countries in which they operate, while remaining sensitive to prevailing religious, historical and cultural contexts" in the operating environment (Visser, 2008:474). Also, Kotler and Lee (2005) view CSR as a commitment by corporations to improve the wellness and wellbeing of their host communities deploying organisational resources as a discretionary business policy and practice. In developing nations, where the drivers of CSR are need to bridge governance gap and pursuit of sustainable development, developmental-oriented definitions are applicable (Ite, 2007; Natufe, 2011; Dartey-Baah and Amponsah-Tawiah, 2011). Developmental side of CSR addresses national issues like poverty, unemployment, diseases, infrastructural needs in the face of governance gap (Raimi et al., 2015).

From the developmental and political viewpoints, CSR is an intervention mechanism for filling governance gap caused by markets and governance failure in developing nations (Dartey-Baah and Amponsah-Tawiah, 2011; Amaeshi et al., 2011). Scherer and Palazzo (2008) contextualized political CSR as a practice where corporations and civil society groups take on certain roles assigned to the government. Whereas, Amaeshi et al. (2011) view a political CSR perspective as the way and manner corporations as corporate citizens take-on public-sector role using their CSR investment to complement government efforts by meeting the needs and expectations of the society. Examples of development-oriented CSR abounds. Specifically, Ite (2007) identified a model of development-oriented CSR in Nigeria where Shell Petroleum Development Corporation (SPDC) is actively bridging governance gap through partnership with the Nigerian government to improve the wellbeing of the host communities in the region.

In the middle-east and north Africa (often called MENA), the wave of globalisation spurred corporations like Western Zagros Limited, HSBC, Al Muhaidib Group and SEDCO Holding to refocus their CSR programmes on economic growth and redevelopment of the local communities (Booz & Company, 2013). Another instance is the British-American Tobacco (BAT), which utilised its CSR programmes for neutralising the negative impact of its products and gaining political support thereby averting harsh tobacco regulation & control (Fooks et al., 2013). Further examples are cases of Chevron in Indonesia and Zain in Bahrain where these notable corporations fill the governance gap and elicits legitimacy in their host countries. Chevron improved national capacity and governance in Indonesia by building capacity of small local businesses and cooperatives through entrepreneurship training scheme and provision of financial support to the beneficiaries, while Zain telecommunication in Bahrain, focused community development and delivery of public goods for the citizens. Both instances are developmental-oriented CSR focused environmental issues, educational support services, youth empowerment and children-oriented support programmes, which tend to stimulate sustainable growth and development in the afore-mentioned countries (Adelopo, Raimi & Yekini, 2015).

With enriched understanding of the perspectives of CSR above, the next section provides theoretical foundation for the book.

Theoretical Foundation

The three reinforcing theories that provide grounding for CSR as a catalyst for triple-bottom line development in this discourse are: Legitimacy theory (LT), stakeholder theory (SHT) and social contract theory (SCT).

The legitimacy theory draws its basis from legal responsibility of corporations, which stipulates that while doing legitimate business, the corporations are expected to comply fully with extant laws and enabling norms in their operating environment (Raimi et al., 2015). CSR within the legitimacy theorizing is a commitment to the legal responsibility of corporations, which is one of the responsibilities, identified by Carroll (1999) several years back. According to Carroll (1999), the four social responsibilities of corporations are: economic, legal, ethical and philanthropic. CSR as a legal responsibility presupposes that corporations while fulfilling its economic responsibility in the society within the framework of extant laws must play by the rules of the game (Jamali & Mirshak, 2007). The legitimacy theory is believed to have emerged as a response to the environmental pressures and the need to avoid sanction from several stakeholders, including influential social, political and economic forces such as civil societies, NGOs, host communities, media, regulatory bodies (Jamali & Mirshak, 2006). In other words, to avoid reprimand and enjoy acceptability in the operating environment, the theory explains that corporations should look for a balance between their actions and how they are perceived by outsiders and what the society perceived as appropriate and desirable (Deegan, 2002). Whereas, Gunningham, Kagan and Thornton (2002) noted that the bottom-line of legitimacy theory is quest to earn "social licence", that is corporations seek by their CSR actions acceptability by the host communities, interest groups within the business environment and the society at large. The legitimacy theory is reinforced by the stakeholder theory.

The second theory of CSR discussed in this chapter is the stakeholder theory. Stakeholder theory explains that it is desirable for corporations to meet the needs and expectations of multiple stakeholders with varying claims and influence (Ismail, 2009; Raimi et al., 2015). From another perspective, the theory underscores the fact that corporations owe individuals and groups triple bottom-line obligations (Haskins, 2009) as well as "support, reliance, intense scrutiny and comments" (Knox & Maklan, 2004:509). The stakeholder perspective was developed by theorists to balance the diverse interests of stakeholders and reposition the corporation within a broader theory of firm (Garriga and Mele, 2004; Freeman, Wick and Parmar, 2004). Therefore, corporations are described as socially responsible when they recognise and factor stakeholders' interests into all their decision-making process (Clarkson, 1995; Donaldson & Preston, 1995; Gibson, 2000). The multiple stakeholders within the business-society relationship have been broadly categorized as the primary and secondary shareholders (Clarkson, 1995). Mitchell, Agle and Wood (1997) noted that the stakeholders of corporation are identified in terms of the power attribute (power of stakeholders to influence the decisions of corporation); the legitimacy attribute (legitimacy of the claims of stakeholders to the fortune of corporations); and the urgency attribute (urgency of the stakeholder's claim's on the corporation). From foregoing, the stakeholders are the direct (internal) and indirect (external) beneficiaries from the fortunes and miseries of corporations in any operational environment. The need for corporations to support stakeholders becomes imperative because of the scourge of poverty and worsening level of underdevelopment that threaten the operating environment and the society at large. CSR initiatives would therefore be a responsive show of empathy to mitigating myriad of social-economic and environmental challenges facing the society (Raimi et al., 2015).

The third theory is social contract theory. This theory explains the relationship between social justice and authority/responsibility in human societies from the ethical and political viewpoints. From the ethical perspective, it presumes that society will be better off, if there is strict adherence to the principles of justice, fairness and social concerns by social actors (Rawls, 1999). For clarity, Garriaga and Mele (2004) explain that social contract theory attempts to reposition the society by building the business-society relationship on sound ethical principles that right things must be done always for the purpose of creating enduring social justice in the society. When the argument above is applied to the business-society relationship, corporation's inability to fulfill the needs and expectations of people in their operational environment would engender social conflict and crisis. Therefore, the proponents of social contract perspective views CSR as tools for mitigating the social and political risk posed by corporations' inability to meet the people's expectations as well as redressing the negative effects of industrial activities in the host communities (Kytle & Ruggie, 2005; Nwadialor & Igwe, 2013; Raimi et al., 2015).

The implication of the theory is that where corporations refuse to meet the expectation of the society, it leads to violation of rights of the stakeholders (Cassel, 2001). The need to respect social contact by corporations across the globe has attracted the attention of the United Nations, which views breach of social contract as a flagrant violation of the human rights of the citizens (Garriga & Mele, 2004; UN Global Compact, 2014). According to Leisinger (2006:7), the concern for social contract and fulfillment of social obligations by corporations are the twin reasons behind the creation of the UN Global Compact with ten (10) principles which emphases need for environmental sustainability. The theory fits the present discourse because corporations can sustainably leverage CSR as intervention for social, economic and environmental development in Nigeria. In return, corporations enjoy social licence and economic licence (Gunningham, Kagan & Thornston, 2002). Whereas, flagrant disregard for "social licensers" (that is, the influential segment of the stakeholder community) have resulted in several devastating consequences like damage to corporate reputations, dwindling sales, negative brand image and loss of public trust on the products or services of disobedient corporations (Gunningham et al., 2002).

Following from the theoretical framework above the next section looks at emerging issues in CSR which justified the need for a development-oriented CSR.

Emerging Development-Oriented CSR Models

CSR because of its unending discourse has been described as having won the battle of ideas in the academic and policy circles (The Economist, 2005). Some of the developmental-oriented CSR models that explicate the triple bottom-line development in the literature which support the theme of this chapter contribution include:

Social Entrepreneurship

Social entrepreneurship emerged as an entrepreneurial activity with a social purpose of giving back to the society (Dee, 1998; Austin & Reficco, 2009). In the view of Kerr (2007), social entrepreneurship is the initiative of a number of wealthy corporate executives who conceptualised how philanthropy might work differently for the betterment of the society. Individuals and corporations that adopt social entrepreneurship mindset are called social entrepreneurs. The social entrepreneurs are useful in the development process because they sacrifice private profits for public concerns. It is therefore an interventionist investment mechanism with two interrelated results: social progress and financial returns (Kerr, 2007). Social entrepreneurs are individuals and/or corporations pioneering new products, innovative services and creative concepts that meet the aspirations, needs and desires of their immediate communities; they achieve these feats using shared value-driven business models (Porter & Kramer, 2011). Notable corporations that have adopted social entrepreneurship ideals include eBay's founders Pierre Omidyar and Jeff Skoll; Peter Hero of Community Foundation Silicon Valley; KaBOOM; DonorsChoose; Muhammad Yunus of Grameen Bank & Grameen Foundation; Google's founders Larry Page and Sergey Brin and David Green, the founder of the non-profit Project Impact. The core driving philosophy of all these neo-social entrepreneurs is social returns (Kerr, 2007).

Corporate Social Entrepreneurship

Another framework of entrepreneurship is corporate social entrepreneurship (CSE). It is a problem-solving model with the thrust of "enabling business to develop more advanced and powerful forms of Corporate Social Responsibility" (Austin & Reficco, 2009: p.2). It was developed for adoption by corporations as a template for addressing social concerns of the society. The CSE was created from three constructs, viz: entrepreneurship, corporate entrepreneurship and social entrepreneurship. It evolved to enhance the practice of CSR, especially its utilisation, for diverse ends (including enterprise development), which by current realities is ineffective in meeting the expectations of stakeholders. According to Austin and Reficco (2009), CSE is hinged on Schumpeter's creative discovery/Stevenson's redefinition of entrepreneurship, Covin and Miles's (1999) definition of corporate entrepreneurship and Dees's (1998) definition of social entrepreneurship. Austin and Reficco (2009) note that CSE was conceptualised to integrate and build on previous entrepreneurship constructs as explained above. They further explained that for the CSE framework to achieve its objective, it has to be implemented in a corporation by a Corporate Social Entrepreneur. According to Hemingway (2003), a corporate social entrepreneur is a manager with sound ethical values and passion for the welfare of the society as well as adequate capacity to drive the corporation's CSR initiatives based on altruistic motives. The theoretical foundation for CSE is therefore rooted in ethical decision making. It could be observed that the framework is designed to sensitise entrepreneurial corporations on the need to adopt better ethical strategies for dispensing with CSR initiatives in the society.

Creating Shared Value (CSV)

Another worthwhile concept of social responsibility is creating shared value (CSV), which is a practical way of engaging the society using CSR to produce the desirable impact. CSV is one out of several answers of integrating economic and non-economic goals of corporations for social engagement (Kvistgaard, 2013). In fact, Porter used the term 'philanthropy' in his earlier article on CSV to underscore the importance of this concept (Porter, Mark & Kramer, 1999). In the CSV model, philanthropy is described as donations to worthy social causes, while and CSR is perceived as good corporate citizenship and compliance with community's standards and sustainability principle. The fundamental aim of CSV is to improve the society sustainably, while at the same time creating economic value for corporation (Porter, 2011).

Furthermore, Porter and Kramer (2011) explain that the CSV is a framework for stimulating entrepreneurship growth through shared value between corporations and their suppliers within the value-chain. It extends to provision of mutually beneficial support services to vulnerable segments of the society by propelling a new wave of innovation and productivity growth in the economy. CSV when applied to corporations' activities has great prospects for improving techniques and access by small firms to better technologies and accelerate the emergence of a local cluster of small suppliers with improved efficiency, yields, product/service quality and sustainability. Other benefits of CSV are wealth creation and self-employment through collaboration. CSV is a pragmatic framework in use in the agricultural sector of the developing economy. It is a mutually rewarding experiment.

With regards to performance impact, Porter and Kramer (2011: 5) report on CSV that: "Early studies of cocoa farmers in the Côte d'Ivoire … suggest that while fair trade can increase farmers' incomes by 10% to 20%, shared value investments can raise their incomes by more than 300%." Three ways of embedding CSV by corporations in the society include: redefinition of products as well as markets by corporations; review of what really constitutes productivity in the value chain framework; and creation of an enabling environment for local suppliers and SMEs within their value-chain. With the three steps in place, it is argued that CSV would provide shared economic benefits to corporations and their host communities.

Building Business Linkages

Building Business Linkages (BBL) is a problem-solving model, which is driven by CSR programmes. BBL is premised on the presumption that poverty is not necessarily a scourge, rather the multitude living in poverty across the globe are human assets that could be economically empowered by corporations to create wealth for mutual beneficial engagements. The proponents identified four (4) forms of business linkages that could be adopted for expanding economic opportunities for the vulnerable members of the society: (a) creating inclusive benefits, (b) development of human capital, (c) building institutional capacity, (d) helping to optimise the rule of contemporary business through exposure of SMEs to regulatory, legal and policy frameworks within the business domain. An inclusive business model empowers starters and inexperienced small business owners or SMEs in the business community, while the other three forms are complementary, as they serve as intervention support services for the poor members of the society (Jenkins, 2007; Jenkins, Ishikawa, Barthes and Giacomelli, 2008; Murphy, 2010; Akhuemonkhan et al., 2012). There are several inclusive BBL models used by transnational corporations (TNCs) like Chevron, GE, Motorola, Microsoft, Vodacom etc. and localised corporations (LCs) around the world to expand economic and business opportunities for the neglected poor small businesses. Jenkins (2007) notes that building business linkages enhanced: (a) increased employment and wealth creation for local firms/vendors and the vulnerable; (b) skills, standards and capacity of SMEs/local vendors; (c) access to foreign markets; (d) diversified clients in the market; (e) access to credit; (f) reduced risk-sharing through joint funding among other SMEs in the cluster.

Corporate Social Investment (CSI)

Corporate Social Investment (CSI) from the perspective of Microsoft Corporation is the development of people as valuable human capital for sustainable economic development. There are several frameworks of CSI, but the Microsoft YouthSpark Initiative (MYSI) provides insight on how best CSR investment of corporations could be used for human capacity building. Broadly, the MYSI is aimed at stimulating the entrepreneurship drive in Africa, with a view to creating direct and indirect employment opportunities for 300 million vulnerable youth in more than 100 countries within three years (Techtalsk, 2013; Microsoft, 2013). The MYSC runs as a partnership scheme with governments and other interest groups. People are targeted in three age brackets, namely: kids (6-12 years), teens (13-18 years) and young adults (19-24) are accommodated (Microsoft, 2013). CSI in Africa is a partnership with governments, schools, SMEs advocacy groups, non-governmental organisations (NGOs) as well as other interest groups. CSI attempts to sustainably reduce poverty, youth unemployment and development crisis. It is an initiative designed to bring out young people's creativity, innovation and untapped talents so that they will be self-reliant (Aginam, 2013).

Political Corporate Social Responsibility

Political CSR is a unique social involvement where MNCs are complementing government's role in bridging governance gap. It is an emerging nuance that simply extended the understanding of role of corporations in the contemporary age of globalisation where the political processes has been widened to accommodate more actors within the corporate citizenship model of social responsibility (Edward & Willmott, 2008; Matten & Crane, 2005). The governance gap thesis, globalisation and political costs hypothesis are frameworks that provide justification for the political roles of corporations in the design and implementation of environmental regulation in their host communities/countries (Matten, 2003; Adelopo et al., 2015). In other words, political CSR emerged for several reasons – (a) globalisation pressure, (b) need for inclusiveness in governance, (c) socio-political risk management and (d) pervasive infrastructural deficits in developing nations. Conceptually, political CSR can be defined as a theory and practice whereby corporations and civil society groups take on increasingly the roles assigned to governments in a democratic milieu (Scherer & Palazzo; 2008). Political CSR as a new theorizing merely strengthens existing perspectives of CSR with regards to interventionist roles of corporations in the contemporary times (Scherer & Palazzo, 2007, 2008, 2011).

The framework of a political CSR has three actors with complementary roles in governance, namely: State, Civil Society Groups and Corporations. The role of the state is to create an enabling environment for capitalism to thrive (Porter & Kramer, 2011). The role of the civil society group is advocacy and whistle-blowing, that is, to serve as watch dog for mounting pressures on corporations to be socially responsible. The role of corporations is to complement and support government in pursuing the goal of economic growth and development (Gond & Matten, 2007; Akhuemonkhan et al., 2012). There are several cases of politically-motivated interventions by the MNCs. For instance, Shell Petroleum Development Company (SPDC) and government-owned Niger Delta Development Commission (NDDC) developed a developmental-oriented CSR aimed at boosting infrastructural facilities and empowering the environmentally-degraded host communities (Ite, 2005; Ite, 2007). The second example is the CSR programmes of the British-American Tobacco (BAT) designed as a relational instrument for lobbying and neutralising the negative impact of cigarettes thereby averting harsh tobacco regulation & control from the political elites (Fooks et al., 2013). Pathetically, in the developing countries several MNCs have negatively deployed political CSR through bribes to politicians as well as supporting oppressive governments through exports of military hardware in order to gain legitimacy and economic licence (Leigh & Evans 2009; Fooks et al., 2013).

Materials and Method

The qualitative research method was found relevant for this chapter because of its exploratory nature. The preferred data collection technique is the documentary sources, specifically extraction of information from the annual reports of the selected companies (Horn, 2010; Saunders, Lewis, Thornhill, 2012). From the sample frame of 25 telecommunications companies in Nigeria, only 13 companies are fully operational; the remaining 12 companies are at the verge of liquidation. Therefore, a sample of 8 companies was selected from the functional companies using purposive sampling technique. The sampled companies represent 61.5% of the functional companies in the industry. The qualitative data extracted from the annual reports and websites were analysed using the content analysis.

Findings and Discussions

After a critical review of the annual reports and website information, the findings on the social involvement of the 8 telecommunication companies justified the tentative presumption that CSR initiatives could be focused as a support-aid for Triple Bottom-Line Development in Nigeria. Firstly, the telecommunication companies have long-term business sustainability goal, which spurred them to establish a healthy relationship with their diverse stakeholders such as customers, employees, investors, neighbours, commercial partners and the host communities in Nigeria. Secondly, the telecommunication companies engage their stakeholders via top-bottom and bottom-up CSR approaches in three core areas of critical intervention, namely: Education, Health and Environment. In supporting these three areas of interest, the companies support school renovations, outright construction of new ones, uniforms, furniture, books and school bags to indigent students periodically. They also conduct general health check, eye screening, cardiovascular checks and weight check for both teachers and the pupils in the host communities. Furthermore, these companies provide furniture to a number of neglected schools in the turbulent Niger Delta region as well as sponsoring a variety of health intervention initiatives like the breast cancer project and National Action Committee against Aids and direct procurement/donations of state-of-the art health equipment to notable hospitals in Nigeria (Airtel, 2014; Etisalat, 2013; MTN, 2014; TechTalkAfrica.com, 2013; Visafone Communication Limited, 2013; Aginam, 2010; Zoom Mobile, 2012; Starcomms, 2013). The finding is supported by previous studies which found that CSR activities of corporations in developing countries focus more on education, health, sports, capacity building and infrastructural development in neglected host communities (Amaeshi et al., 2006; Idemudia, 2010; Ite, 2005; Ite, 2007; Osemene, 2012; Raimi & Adeleke, 2010).

CONCLUSION

This book chapter sets out exploring the practicality of refocusing CSR as a support-aid for development in Nigeria as a developing economy. This innovative idea is expedient because of infrastructural deficits in Nigeria caused by a number of institutional constraints and ineffective government policies on enterprise development. After a content analysis of the data on CSR initiatives of selected telecommunications companies in Nigeria, it was found that the 8 sampled telecommunications companies focus their CSR investments on social, economic and environmental issues which directly impact on socio-economic development of the host communities in Nigeria. The chapter has therefore justified the argument that the deteriorating business environment in Nigeria requires a boost through a private-sector led economic development. The policy implication of the paper is that it is in the interest of corporations to refocus their CSR investments as support-aid to stimulate social, economic and environmental development.

Practical Contributions and Implication for Further work

This chapter bridges the theoretical and empirical gap in the literature on the development-oriented CSR. In other words, the content analysis provided a broader and deeper appreciation of the potentials of the development side of CSR. The use of purposive sampling in the absence of a sample frame provided new insight into sampling techniques in the fields of CSR research. Thirdly, the chapter has justified the plausibility of leveraging CSR as a mechanism for triple-bottom line development where there is ineffective governence and infrastructural deficits. Finaly, adoption of three reinforcing theories provide sound grounding for the development-oriented CSR model. The implication of this study is that the CSR could be leveraged as a private sector development model (PSDM) for meeting the social, economic and environmental development in Nigeria. This will go a long way in complementing government efforts at boosting the wellness of the povery-stricken communities in Nigeria especially in places where the telecommunication companies operate. In order to provide further empirical foundation for this qualitative research, there is need to carry out a questionnaire-based survey to elicit the opinions of cross section of professionals on the impact of CSR on social, economic and environmental development in Nigeria. The present findings are exploratory, but an empirical study would provide new and richer insights.

In spite of the present limitations, this research is important for comparative work on CSR because it has reshaped the understanding of social responsibility beyond the traditional show of empathy; it has rather articulated the need for corporations to embrace development-oriented CSR which is designed to mitigate social ills such as worsening poverty, governance deficit, poor labour standards, environmental degradation, surging violence, industrial pollution as well as chronic diseases facing the host communities.

Recommendations

Since the findings from this book chapter are useful to researchers, practitioners and diverse users, the following recommendations are hereby prescribed:

1. In order to take advantage of the emergence of development-oriented CSR, there is need for sensitization on the potentials of leveraging CSR for triple-bottom line development.
2. To ensure that the benefits of CSR activities of the Nigerian telecommunications companies are impactful on the society, the management of these companies should identify and sponsor programmes and projects that add values to the lives of the communities than sports, entertainment and showbiz, which appears to be the priority of most telecommunication companies.
3. It is suggested that the government and the telecommunications companies should work together at ensuring that CSR activities are strategically targeted at supporting capacity development of disadvantaged members of the host communities, suppliers, distributors, small businesses and artisans.
4. The principle of voluntarism that drives the conventional CSR should guide the embedment of a developmental-oriented CSR in Nigeria. In other words, a development-oriented CSR should strictly be pursed as a private-sector driven model because, there is preference for private-sector led development initiatives over weak public-sector initiatives.
5. The role of the government in the process of refocusing CSR as a developmental-oriented model should be regulatory and provision of enable environment for a smooth business-society relationship. The government should encourage voluntary participation of telecommunication companies as opposed to coercive measures on CSR.
6. There is need for the civil society groups to be vigilant with regards to CSR activities that subverts national independence as well as social involvements designed as green washing to neutralise the negative impact of operations of telecommunication companies and corporate misbehaviours.

REFERENCES

Adelopo, I., Raimi, L., & Yekini, K. (2015) Bridging Governance Gap with Political CSR. In D. Jamali, C. Karam & M. Blowfield. (Eds.), CSR in Developing Countries: Towards a Development-Oriented Approach. Greenfield Publishing UK. doi:10.9774/GLEAF.9781783532445_4

Aginam, E. (2012). CSR: Multilinks Telkom donates medical equipment to UITH. *The Vanguard Newspaper Online*. Retrieved from http://www.vanguardngr.com/2010/10/csr-multilinks-telkom-donates-medical-equipment-to-uith/

Airtel Nigeria Limited. (2014) About Us – Shareholder Information. Retrieved from http://www.airtelng.com/new/shareholders.asp

Akhuemonkhan, I., Raimi, L., Ogunjirin, O. D. (2012, November 1-2). Corporate Social Responsibility and Entrepreneurship (CSRE): Antidotes to Poverty, Insecurity and Underdevelopment in Nigeria. *Presented at the international conference on Poverty, Insecurity and Development in Africa*, Universiti de Lome, Republic of Togo.

Amaeshi, K., Osuji, O. K., & Doh, J. P. (2011, May 28-29). Corporate Social Responsibility as a Market Governance Mechanism: Any implications for Corporate Governance in Emerging Economies? *Proceedings of the Corporate Governance in Emerging Markets Conference*, Seoul.

Amaeshi, K. M., Adi, B. C., Ogbechie, C., & Amao, O. O. (2006). Corporate social responsibility in Nigeria: Western mimicry or indigenous influences? *Journal of Corporate Citizenship*, *24*(24), 83–99. doi:10.9774/GLEAF.4700.2006.wi.00009

Austin, J., & Reficco, E. (2009). Corporate Social Entrepreneurship. *Harvard Business School Working Paper 09-101*. Retrieved from http://www.hbs.edu/research/pdf/09-101.pdf

Booz and Company. (2013). The Rise of Corporate Social Responsibility - A Tool for Sustainable Development in the Middle East. Retrieved from http://www.booz.com/media/file/BoozCo_The-Rise-of-Corporate-Social-Responsibility.pdf

Boyle, M., & Boguslaw, J. (2007). Business, Poverty and Corporate Citizenship Naming the Issues and Framing Solutions. *Journal of Corporate Citizenship*, Summer, 101-120.

Brønn, P. S., & Vrioni, A. B. (2001). Corporate Social Responsibility and Cause Related Marketing: An Overview. *International Journal of Advertising*, *20*(2), 207–222.

Carroll, A. (1999). 'Corporate Social Responsibility-Evolution of a Definitional Construct', Business & Society, Sage Publications. *Inc.*, *38*(3), 268–295.

Cassel, D. (2001). Human Rights Business Responsibilities in the Global Marketplace'. *Business Ethics Quarterly*, *11*(2), 261–274. doi:10.2307/3857749

Clarkson, M. (1995). A Stakeholder Framework for Analyzing and Evaluating Corporate Social Performance. *Academy of Management Review*, *20*(January), 92–117.

Covin, J. G., & Miles, M. P. (1999). Corporate entrepreneurship and the pursuit of competitive advantage'. *Entrepreneurship Theory and Practice*, *23*(3), 47–63.

Dartey-Baah, K., & Amponsah-Tawiah, K. (2011). Exploring the limits of Western Corporate Social Responsibility Theories in Africa'. *International Journal of Business and Social Science*, *2*(18), 126–137.

Deegan, C. (2002). The legitimising effect of social and environmental disclosures - a theoretical foundation. *Accounting, Auditing & Accountability Journal*, *15*(3), 282–311. doi:10.1108/09513570210435852

Dees, J. G. (1998). *The Meaning of 'Social Entrepreneurship*. Boston, MA: Harvard Business School. Comments and suggestions contributed from the Social Entrepreneurship Funders Working Group.

Donaldson, T., & Preston, L.E. (1995). The Stakeholder Theory of the Corporation: Concepts, Evidence, and Implications. *Academy of Management Review*, 20(January), 65-91.

Edward, P., & Willmott, H. (2008). Corporate citizenship: Rise or demise of a myth? *Academy of Management Review*, *33*(3), 771–773. doi:10.5465/AMR.2008.32465773

Eilbert, H., & Parket, I. R. (1973). The current status of corporate social responsibility. *Business Horizons*, *16*, 5–14.

Enderle, G., & Tavis, A. L. (1998). A balanced concept of the firm and the measurement of its long-term planning and performance. *Journal of Business Ethics*, *17*(11), 1129–1143. doi:10.1023/A:1005746212024

Etisalat. (2013). Corporate Social Responsibility. Online Resources. Retrieved from www.etisalat.com.ng/csr.php

Fooks, G., Gilmore, A., Collin, J., Holden, C., & Lee, K. (2013). The Limits of Corporate Social Responsibility: Techniques of Neutralization, Stakeholder Management and Political CSR. *Journal of Business Ethics*, *112*(2), 283–299. doi:10.1007/s10551-012-1250-5 PMID:23997379

Freeman, R. E., Wicks, A. C., & Parmar, B. (2004). Stakeholder theory and the corporate objective revisited. *Organization Science*, *15*(3), 364–369. doi:10.1287/orsc.1040.0066

Frynas, J. G. (2005). The false developmental promise of Corporate Social Responsibility: Evidence from multinational oil companies. *International Affairs*, *81*(3), 581–598. doi:10.1111/j.1468-2346.2005.00470.x

Frynas, J. G. (2008). Corporate Social Responsibility and International Development: Critical Assessment, Corporate Governance. *International Review (Steubenville, Ohio)*, *16*(4), 274–281.

Garriga, E., & Mele, D. (2004). Corporate social responsibility theories: Mapping and territory. *Journal of Business Ethics*, *53*(1/2), 51–74. doi:10.1023/B:BUSI.0000039399.90587.34

Gibson, K. (2000). The Moral Basis of Stakeholder Theory. *Journal of Business Ethics*, *26*(3), 245–257. doi:10.1023/A:1006110106408

Globacom Nigeria. (2013). Events and Sponsorships. Retrieved from http://www.gloworld.com/events_sponsorships.asp

U.N. Global Compact. (2014). Corporate Sustainability in The World Economy. UN Global Compact Office, United Nations, New York. Retrieved from http://www.unglobalcompact.org/docs/news_events/8.1/GC_brochure_FINAL.pdf

Gond, J. P., & Matten, D. (2007). Rethinking the Business-Society Interface: Beyond the Functionalist Trap. *ICCSR Research Paper series, No.47-2007.*

Gunningham, N., Kagan, R. A., & Thornton, D. (2002). *Social Licence and Environmental Protection: why businesses go beyond compliance*. London: Centre for Analysis of Risk and Regulation, London School of Economics and Political Science.

Haskins, C. (2009). Using the concept of sustainable development to encourage corporate responsibility in small enterprises (Working paper). Norwegian University of Science and Technology, Department of Industrial Economics and Technology Management Trondheim, Norway.

Hemingway, C. A., & Maclagan, P. W. (2004). Managers' personal values as drivers of corporate social responsibility. *Journal of Business Ethics*, *50*(1), 33–44. doi:10.1023/B:BUSI.0000020964.80208.c9

Horn, R. (2010). Researching and Writing Dissertations – A Complete Guide for Business and Management Students. CIPD: London.

Idemudia, U. (2010). Rethinking the role of corporate social responsibility in the Nigerian oil conflict: The limits of CSR. *Journal of International Development*, *22*(7), 833–845. doi:10.1002/jid.1644

Ismail, M. (2009). Corporate Social Responsibility and Its Role in Community Development: An International Perspective. *The Journal of International Social Research*, *2*(9), 199–209.

Ite, U. E. (2005). Poverty reduction in resource-rich developing countries: What have multinational corporations got to do with it? *Journal of International Development*, *17*(7), 913–929. doi:10.1002/jid.1177

Ite, U. E. (2007). Partnering with the state for sustainable development: Shell's experience in the Niger Delta, Nigeria. *Sustainable Development*, *15*(4), 216–228. doi:10.1002/sd.312

Jamali, D., & Mirshak, R. (2006). Corporate social responsibility (CSR): Theory and practice in a developing country context. *Journal of Business Ethics*, *72*(3), 243–262. doi:10.1007/s10551-006-9168-4

Jamali, D., & Mirshak, R. (2007). Corporate Social Responsibility (CSR): Theory and Practice in a Developing Country Context. *Journal of Business Ethics, Springer*, *72*(3), 243–262. doi:10.1007/s10551-006-9168-4

Jenkins, B. (2007) Expanding Economic opportunity: The Role of Large Firm. Corporate Social Responsibility Report No. 17. Cambridge, MA: Kennedy School of Government, Harvard University.

Jenkins, B., Ishikawa, E., Barthes, E., & Giacomelli, M. (2008, June 10-12) Supporting Entrepreneurship and the Base of the Pyramid through Business Linkages. *Report of a Roundtable Dialogue*, Rio de Jeneiro, Brazil. Washington, DC: International Finance Corporation, International Business Leaders Forum, and Kennedy School of Government, Harvard University.

Kerr, J. E. (2007) 'Sustainability Meets Profitability: The Convenient Truth of How the Business Judgment Rule Protects a Board's Decision to Engage in Social Entrepreneurship. Retrieved from http://ssrn.com/abstract=1296270

Knox, S., & Maklan, S. (2004). Corporate social responsibility: Moving beyond investment towards measuring outcomes. *European Management Journal*, *22*(5), 508–516. doi:10.1016/j.emj.2004.09.009

Kotler, P., & Lee, N. (2005). *Corporate social responsibility: Doing the most good for your company and your cause*. Hoboken, NJ: Wiley.

Kvistgaard, L. T. (2013) Creating Shared Value- A post positivistic analysis of Michael E. Porter's meta--theoretical eclecticism. Master Dissertation, Copenhagen Business School. Retrieved from http://studenttheses.cbs.dk/xmlui/bitstream/handle/10417/3549/lea_torpegaard_kvistgaard.pdf?sequence=1

Kytle, B., & Ruggie, J. G. (2005). Corporate Social Responsibility as Risk Management – A model for Multinationals. Corporate Social Responsibility Initiatives (CSRI) Working Paper No. 10. Cambridge M. A.: John F. Kennedy School of Government, Harvard University.

Leigh, D., & Evans, R. (2009, October 1). Fraud Office seeks BAE's prosecution over bribery. *The Guardian*.

Leisinger, K. M. (2006). On Corporate Responsibility for Human Rights Presentation of Special Advisor to the Secretary General on the Global Compact in Basel, April. Online Resources. Retrieved from http://www.unglobalcompact.org/docs/news_events/9.6/corpresforhr_kl.pdf

Lompo, K., & Trani, J. F. (2013). Does corporate social responsibility contribute to human development in developing countries? Evidence from Nigeria. *Journal of Human Development and Capabilities*, *14*(2), 241–265. doi:10.1080/19452829.2013.784727

Matten, D. (2003). Symbolic politics in environmental regulation: Corporate strategic responses. *Business Strategy and the Environment*, *12*(4), 215–226. doi:10.1002/bse.363

Matten, D., & Crane, A. (2005). Corporate Citizenship: Toward An Extended Theoretical Conceptualization'. *Academy of Management Review*, *30*(1), 166–179. doi:10.5465/AMR.2005.15281448

Microsoft Corporation. (2013). YouthSpark Corporate Citizenship. Retrieved from http://www.microsoft.com/about/corporatecitizenship/en-us/youthspark/youthsparkhub/default.aspx

Mitchell, R. K., Agle, B. R., & Wood, D. J. (1997). Toward a theory of stakeholder identification and salience: Defining the principle of who and what really counts. *Academy of Management Review*, *22*, 853–886.

Mohsin, M. I. A. (2013). Potential of Zakat in Eliminating Riba in and Eradicating Muslim Countries. *Islamic Management and Business*, *5*(11), 114–126.

MTN. (2014). Corporate Information. Online Resources. Retrieved from http://www.mtnonline.com/about-mtn/corporate-information

Murphy, S. (2010). Corporate Partnerships for Entrepreneurship: Building the Ecosystem in the Middle East and Southeast Asia. Corporate Social Responsibility Initiative Working Paper No. 62. Cambridge, MA: John F. Kennedy School of Government, Harvard University.

National Bureau of Statistics. (2012). Survey Report on Micro Small and Medium Enterprises (MSMEs) in Nigeria -Preliminary Report: 2010 National MSME Collaborative Survey. Retrieved from www.nigerianstat.gov.ng/pages/download/67

Natufe, O. I. (2011) Corporate Social Responsibility: Value and Strategic Intent. *Social Responsibility Review*, 2, 14-25.

Nelson, J. (2007). *Building Linkages for Competitive and Responsible Entrepreneurship: Innovative partnerships to foster small enterprise, promote economic growth, and reduce poverty in developing countries. CSR Initiative, Harvard University and United Nations Industrial Development Organization*. UNIDO.

Njoku, A. C., Ihugba, O. A., & Odii, A. (2014). Theoretical analysis of entrepreneurship challenges and prospects in Nigeria. *International Letters of Social and Humanistic Sciences*, 5, 21-34.

Nwadialor, E., & Igwe, N. N. (2013). Adapting Corporate Social Responsibility Programs to Risk Management: A Model for Multinational Organizations in Nigeria. *European Journal of Business and Management*, *5*(15), 17–24.

Oghojafor, B. E. A., Okonji, P. S., Olayemi, O. O., & Okolie, J. U. (2011, January 9-11). Fifty Years of Entrepreneurship Development in Nigeria: Challenges and Prospects. *Proceedings of the 10th International Entrepreneurship Forum*, Tamkeen, Bahrain.

Osemene, O. F. (2012). Corporate Social Responsibility Practices in Mobile Telecommunications Industry in Nigeria. *European Journal of Business and Management*, *4*(8), 149–159.

Porter, M. E. (2011, November 13). The Role of Business in Society: Creating Shared Value. *Presentation at Babson Entrepreneurship Forum*, Boston, Massachusetts. Retrieved from http://www.isc.hbs.edu/pdf/2011-1113_Babson_CSV.pdf

Porter, M.E. & Kramer. M. R. (2011). Creating Shared Value: How to reinvent capitalism—and unleash a wave of innovation and growth. *Harvard Business Review (HBR)*, January/February.

Porter, M. E., & Mark, R. Kramer. (1999). Philanthropy's New Agenda: Creating Value. *Harvard Business Review*, *77*(6), 121–130. PMID:10662001

Raimi, L., & Adeleke, I. A. (2010) Using Entrepreneurship Development and Corporate Social Responsibility as Strategies for Conflict Resolution in the Niger-Delta Region in Nigeria, Society of Petroleum Engineers - Nigeria Annual International Conference and Exhibition 2010, NAICE: 2837-846.

Raimi, L., Akhuemonkhan, I. A., & Ogunjirin, O. D. (2015). Corporate Social Responsibility and Entrepreneurship (CSRE): Antidotes to poverty, insecurity and underdevelopment in Nigeria. *Social Responsibility Journal*, *11*(1), 56–81. doi:10.1108/SRJ-11-2012-0138

Raimi, L., Patel, A., Adelopo, I., & Ajewole, T. (2013). Tackling Poverty Crisis in the Muslim Majority Nations (MMNs): The Faith-Based Model (FBM) as an Alternative Policy Option. *Advanced Journal of Business Management and Entrepreneurship*, *1*(1), 1–12.

Raimi, L., Patel, A., Yekini, K., & Fadipe, A. O. (2014). Spatio-Temporal Audit of Nigeria's Industrial Policies and Entrepreneurship Development Interventions from 1946 to 2013. *International Journal of Humanities and Social Science*, *4*(1), 294–309.

Rawls, J. (1999). *A Theory of Justice*. Cambridge, MA: Belknap Press of Harvard University Press.

Samy, M., Odemilin, G., & Bampton, R. (2010). Corporate social responsibility: A strategy for sustainable business success. An analysis of 20 selected British companies. *Corporate Governance*, *10*(2), 203–217. doi:10.1108/14720701011035710

Saunders, M., Lewis, P., & Thornhill, A. (2012). Research Methods for Business Students. Edinburgh Gate, Harlow, England: Pearson Education Limited.

Scherer, A. G., & Palazzo, G. (2007). Toward a political conception of corporate responsibility: Business and society seen from a Habermasian perspective. *Academy of Management Review*, *32*(4), 1096–1120. doi:10.5465/AMR.2007.26585837

Scherer, A. G., & Palazzo, G. (2008). Globalization and Corporate Social Responsibility. In A. Crane et al. (Eds.), *Oxford Handbook of Corporate Social Responsibility* (pp. 413–431). Oxford: Oxford University Press.

Scherer, A. G., & Palazzo, G. (2011). The New Political Role of Business in a Globalized World: A Review of a New Perspective on CSR and its Implications for the Firm, Governance, and Democracy. *Journal of Management Studies*, *48*(4), 899–931. doi:10.1111/j.1467-6486.2010.00950.x

Scholtens, B. (2014). Indicators of responsible investing. *Ecological Indicators*, *36*, 382–385. doi:10.1016/j.ecolind.2013.08.012

Sharp, J. (2006). Corporate social responsibility and development: An anthropological perspective. *Development Southern Africa*, *23*(2), 213–222. doi:10.1080/03768350600707892

Starcomms. (2013). Corporate Social Responsibility. Online Resources. Retrieved from http://www.starcomms.com/about_us/csr.aspx

TechTalkAfrica.com. (2013). Globacom Limited (GLO) – Africa's Telecoms Company. Retrieved from http://techtalkafrica.com/companies/globacom-limited-glo-africas-telecomms-company.html/

The Economist Intelligence Unit. (2005) The Importance of Corporate Responsibility. Retrieved from http://graphics.eiu.com/files/ad_pdfs/eiuoracle_corporateresponsibility_wp.pdf

Ukah, O. C. (2007). An Appraisal of the Performance of the Nigeria's National Rolling Plans in the 90's. *African Research Review*, *1*(1), 14–23.

Visafone Communications Limited. (2013). About Visafone. Retrieved from http://www.visafone.com.ng/corpmilestones2.html

Visser, W. (2008). Corporate Social Responsibility in Developing Countries. In A. Crane, A. McWilliams, D. Matten, J. Moon, & D. Siegel (Eds.), *The Oxford Handbook of Corporate Social Responsibility* (pp. 473–479). Oxford: Oxford University Press.

World Bank. (2003). Better Governance for Development in the Middle East and North Africa: Enhancing Inclusiveness and Accountability, World Bank Washington, D.C. Retrieved from http://go.worldbank.org/LGTT1USV00

Yekini, K., & Jallow, K. (2012). Corporate community involvement disclosures in annual report: A measure of corporate community development or a signal of CSR observance?' Sustainability Accounting. *Management and Policy Journal*, *3*(1), 7–32.

Young, T. (1999). The State and Politics in Africa. *Journal of Southern African Studies*, *25*(1), 149–154. doi:10.1080/030570799108803

Zoom Mobile. (2012). Retrieved from http://www.zoomnigeria.com/?page_id=4

Chapter 11
Doing Good Doing Well
Discussion of CSR in the Pulp and Paper Industry in the Asian Context

Dieu Hack-Polay
University of Lincoln, UK

Haiyan Qiu
SICEM SAGA, Italy

ABSTRACT

Corporate social responsibility (CSR) involves multi-faceted concerns and interested parties. The theoretical paper argues that pursuing CSR policies creates value for sustainable economic prosperity for the pulp and paper sector. The pulp and paper industry is one of the largest industrial sectors worldwide and plays a critical role in global development. As the fourth largest energy user and CO2 emitter, the industry is subject to the vicissitudes of global society and environment. Irresponsible pulp and paper operations are now shunned by various stakeholders, which ultimately affect their economic bottom lines. Sustainable operations bring continuity and competitiveness along with innovation, efficiency and social recognition to the industry. Using the criteria of the triple-bottom-line theory (economic, environmental and social), this paper demonstrates that a strong CSR framework and proactive initiatives add value to the pulp and paper business.

INTRODUCTION

This theoretical paper discusses how CSR brings value, though not always quantifiable, to business by employing Elkington's (1994) 'triple-bottom-line' theory and illustrates this value with reference to the pulp and paper industry with examples from the Asian context. The acknowledgement of corporate social responsibility (CSR) as a business strategy has been seen at the highest corporate levels in recent years. A number of business gurus have taken positions in favour of the incorporation of CSR into overall business strategy. "Our fundamental belief is that doing good is great for business" said Sir Richard Branson (2009: 289), the iconic entrepreneur and founder of Virgin Group. Sir Richard Branson's belief is the

DOI: 10.4018/978-1-5225-0720-8.ch011

epitome of the mutually reinforcing relationship between corporate social responsibility and business values. Industry Canada also promotes corporate social responsibility, strongly believing it will bring innovation, productivity and competitiveness to its industry in the global arena (Industry Canada, 2013).

In her speech at the '11th Chinese People's Political Consultative Conference', Helen Clark, UNDP administrator and chair of the influential UN Development Group, spoke about their work with companies incorporating corporate social responsibility in business models about the benefits from improved efficiency, cost savings, stronger branding, etc. and the adverse risk of reputational loss for not engaging in CSR (Clark, 2012).

In academia, many authors have supported a positive standpoint about the validity of corporate social responsibility as a valuable aspect of a viable contemporary business model (Davis, 1973; McWilliams et al. 2006; Buchholtz & Carroll, 2012), to name just a few. Dr Olson, director of the Pulp and Paper Center at the University of British Columbia argues in his director's message that people, especially those working in the forest industry, understand clearly about society's need for true sustainability and the equilibrium it plays with economic affluence (University of British Columbia, 2013).

This pre-eminence of corporate involvement with society has been exemplified in contemporary definitions attributed to the term. One such definition is provided by Needle who contends that corporate social responsibility or CSR with the corporation's development and management of "its relationships with various stakeholders: employees, customers, suppliers, the community, society and government. It also has a responsibility towards the sustainability of the environment" (Needle, 2010: 300). The rationality of CSR is no longer contentious. This was supported by a special report for the Economist in which only 4% of respondents thought that CSR was "a waste of time and money" (The Economist, 2008). Many business school academicians like John Ruggie of Harvard University's Kennedy School of Government concur that it is not whether there should be CSR but how corporations can best incorporate CSR to their advantage (Smith, 2003; The Economist, 2008; Rangan, Chase & Karim, 2012).

What impacts does CSR have on businesses? The impact of corporate social responsibility is multi-dimensional. "CSR enhances reputation and builds positive bridges to communities, customers and the public at large and in doing so affects the bottom line" (CSR Press Release, 2013). The point here is that CSR is not only cogent in the business context but it can bring value and sustainable corporate development. The synergistic effect of CSR between business and its social and environmental stakeholders can bring about tremendous competitive advantages in terms of efficiency, reputation and innovation.

John Elkington (in Buchholtz & Carroll, 2012) described the triple-bottom-line analysis to sustainable development as including economic, environmental and social aspects. The aim is corporate sustainability, which is to create continuing long-term shareholder value by taking responsibilities for and initiatives in respect of the economy, environment and society. As the United Nations Environmental Programme (UNEP) and the United Nations World Tourism Organization (UNWTO) agencies (2005) show in Figure 1, the aim is to ensure the balanced and long-term development for all corporate stakeholders.

According to Buchholtz and Carroll's (2012) CSR Pyramid, there are four facets of CSR, one of which is legal responsibilities. Considering that the fundamental aspect of being socially responsible germinates from abiding by laws and being responsive to regulatory changes, business would be suicidal if they only pursued the 'bottom-line'. Thus, this necessary conformity to law and regulation will not be further elaborated.

The triple-bottom-line theory will be applied to discuss in detail why and how CSR brings sustainable competitive advantages via pursing more than just the shareholder or the 'bottom-line' theory. It will also elaborate on the economic merits of proactive CSR approaches taken by pulp and paper operations

Figure 1. Sustainability through an integration of the triple bottom line
(Source: UNEP & UNWTO, 2005, p.11-12).

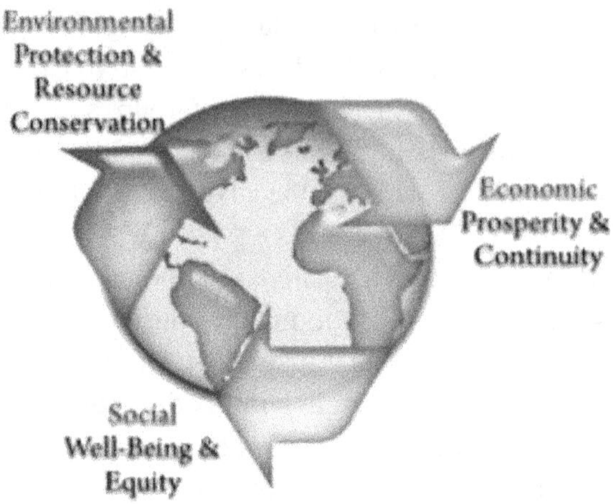

(Needle, 2010). The pulp and paper industry is one of the largest industrial sectors worldwide, and plays an important role in global economic and social development (Food and Agriculture Organization of the United Nations, 2013; WWF, 2014). However, unsustainable pulp and paper operations have caused great losses to the world's ecosystem and engendered issues like illegal logging, human rights and social conflicts. Responsible pulp and paper operations can contribute to sustainable forest plantations, world economies and employment (WWF, 2014).

This discussion will proceed in the context of the pulp and paper industry from these three interwoven constructive aspects of CSR: economic, environmental and social.

CSR and the Pulp and Paper Industry

Economic Aspects of CSR for the Pulp and Paper Industry

Being socially responsible in business brings more gain and risks little loss. Arguably, taking CSR approach is not cost free, however, the long term benefits outweigh the foreseeable costs. CSR is an inevitable socio-economic force and a proactive CSR approach can augment business's economic bottom line. According to CEPI (Confederation of European Paper Industries), the pulp and paper industry is a European strategic sector which is vital for Europe's sustainable industrial development. However, the pulp and paper sector faces strong competition from other countries as well as plastic and digital substitutes. The strategy employed by CEPI is to incorporate sustainability into the industry which contributes to reduced production costs and environmental footprints. The focus on sustainability by the European pulp and paper industry brings greater competitiveness and profitability, which is critical for the industry to adjust to tougher global competition and stricter regulations (Slaper, 2011; Sustain, 2013). Potential investors are increasingly using CSR performance as an indicator when making capital investment decisions on whether to invest in a business (Chartered Management Institute, 2012). As Figure 2 depicts, economic gain (company image, risk management and cost improvement) represents a large proportion of the reasons why companies pursue CSR.

Figure 2. Organizations' motivation for pursuing CSR (Source: Story & Price, 2006)

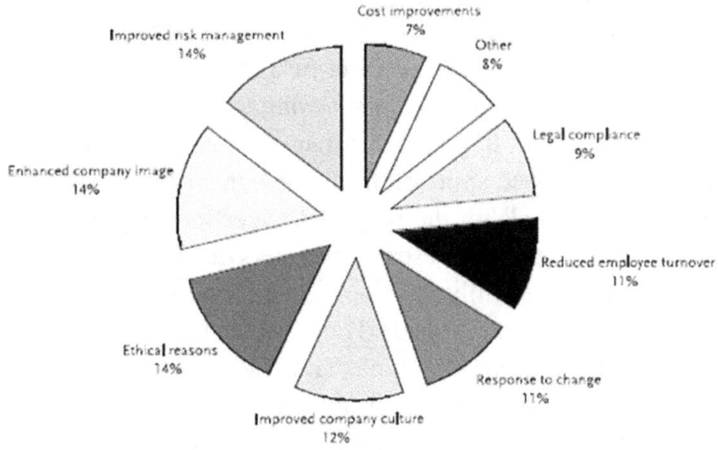

Easy and instant dissemination of news globally, reinforced by courageous whistle-blowers, leave no hiding room for unethical and unlawful corporate practices. They act as a 'yellow traffic light' warning for business operations. Irresponsible corporate behaviour dilutes the soundness of the company's reputation and eventually leads to economic anguish. The unfortunate case of the Republic of Iceland demonstrates that irresponsible and unethical corporate behaviour is powerful enough to bring down a country.

A significant number of antecedent scandals like The Gunns Limited caused investors to be stricter about a firm's responsible reputation. The Gunns, once the dominant timber corporation in Australia went into administration in 2012 due to poor financial management and relentless community campaigns against its unsustainable pulp business operations (The Sydney Morning Heralds, 2012; ABC News, 2014). With growing concerns over business sustainability, investment bodies and shareholders seek to put their money into reliable and responsible recipients. Social watchdogs and reporting venues, e.g. social auditing, CSR reporting, social performance reporting, make it impossible to attract investment and funding with an irresponsible and unsustainable social image. Stora Enso, a leading Finnish pulp and papermaking group, lost funding support from Nordea Bank and SPP due to its irresponsible and unsustainable operations in Guangxi, China. Conversely, a firm with a good CSR reputation can attract external investment and retain shareholder confidence, e.g. a responsible and sustainable image can permeate through social screening and win social responsibility investments (SRI). There is much evidence that socially responsible investment will become commonplace in mainstream investing (Widok, 2009; George, Edgerton & Berry, 2007; Robson & Wakefield, 2007).

CSR is a social force that can bring a corporation down or elevate it depending on its strategic approaches to the CSR agenda. Japanese paper industry's recycling scandal rendered the industry's reputation in tatters (D'Amato, Henderson & Florence, 2009). The scandal involving several of Japan's leading papermakers like Nippon Paper and Oji Paper, the country's biggest paper and pulp producer, have been exposed for lying about the real percentage of recycled content in their paper products. This incident affected the companies' 'bottom line' which has seen drastic drops in shares (The Guardian, 2008; Environment Graffiti, 2008). This scandalous concealment led to the realization that such white-washing approach in business operations eventually bring about fatal backlash.

Acknowledging CSR as an unavoidable duty of corporate citizenship (Verbeke, 2013) to contemporary society and instead of taking a reactive or defensive approaches, corporations can take initiatives to transfer it into unique firm specific advantages (FSAs) (Rugman, 2009) and gain first mover advantages. This strike-first-to-gain-initiative approach is a perfect fit with Machiavelli's strategic belief that knowing the inevitability of war, delaying it will only give advantages to its competitors (Clegg et al., 2012). A good example is Tralin Paper Co. Ltd., a top ten paper producer in China, and its new technology to produce pulp from wheat straw received approval from the Ministry of Environmental Protection of the People's Republic of China in 2011. With the pulp and paper industry under increasingly regulatory pressure to stop pulp making from agricultural straw and stalks due to a lack of clean technologies, Tralin took initiatives to research and successfully developed a breakthrough technology for producing pulp from agricultural by-products. The success made Tralin the forerunner for profiting from sustainable technology in the pulp and paper industry in China. Tralin's innovative technology of producing pulp from agricultural waste has not only received governmental applause as a milestone in the development of pulp and paper industry in China, but has also brought economic gains to itself and farmers supplying these resources that were left to waste in the field or were burned causing smog pollution (Ministry of Environmental Protection of the People's Republic of China, 2011; National Development and Reform Commission, 2011).

A proactive CSR brings economic returns through efficiency and innovation seeking in both operating and resource utilization, e.g. much successful entrepreneurship initiated from seeking green and alternative energy. A proactive CSR mindset keeps business responsive and innovative. For example, Siemens pursues the economic bottom line by creating portfolios of efficient energy-saving technologies like SIPAPER Reject Paper which can be beneficial to the environment and its customers in the global pulp and paper industry by reducing energy consumption and CO_2 emissions (Siemens, 2014). Furthermore, proactive CSR can create innovative ways to improve profitability, within environmental and social constraints (Chartered Management Institute, 2012). A good example in the pulp and paper industry is Ashland Water Technologies, a leading global producer of papermaking chemicals. With the objective of improving sustainability in the pulp and paper industry, Ashland endeavours to work towards practical innovations. For instance, the company's latest innovation, 'biobond technology', won the 2013 'Breakthrough Technology of the Year' award from Pulp & Paper International and made it the desirable choice for paperboard producers internationally. This technology brings efficiency and improved quality to its customers by decreasing the loss of starch and improving mechanical properties in the papermaking process. The technology also improves the sustainability of paper production by reducing water consumption and levels of COD (Chemical Oxygen Demand) (RISI, 2013). Both of these technologies generate profits and reinforce the cogency of Ashland's innovative and sustainable business models at the same time as bringing benefits to their pulp and paper customers.

Proactive CSR efforts can bring about cross-industry cooperation to create synergy for achieving business development and social sustainability. Nippon Paper Industries Co., Ltd and Coca-Cola (Japan) Co., Ltd joined forces to create benefits for their local communities. Each company has committed to social and environmental development when doing business using their respective strengths and focuses. Nippon's experience in biodiversity and Coca-Cola's in water preservation led to a collaboration which will allow the synergetic use of both companies' assets and experience to create business value and benefits to a wider community (RISI, 2013), CSR initiatives create value for sustainable economic prosperity in business beyond the level of statutory obligations.

Environmental Aspects of CSR for the Pulp and Paper Industry

Unfortunately, some solely economic bottom-line seeking opportunists advocate CSR only rhetorically to gain regulatory favour or to be on the trend wagon. Society is not ignorant and will not tolerate such 'green wash' practices. Business needs to practise what it preaches through simultaneous economic and social action in order to sustain its competitive advantage (Verbeke, 2013).

Shareholder theory or the 'bottom-line' theory contends that a corporation's ultimate goal is to augment economic profits, arguing that environmental issues are not its responsibility. In contrast, the triple-bottom-line theory sees the environment as a main stakeholder, advocating that being responsible to environment is essential to business. This perspective is supported by Needle (2010) who claims that the environment attracts the most public attention and holds the highest cost risks. Discussions here examine why corporations need to look beyond the 'bottom-line' to the economic impacts of environmental sustainability. There are studies that corroborate the existence of a positive relationship between environmental and economic performance. Unsustainable environmental performance is negatively correlated with the intangible asset values of firms, e.g. reputation, brand equity, etc. (Wagner, 2005; Konar & Cohen, 2001).

Shriveling world distances and shrinking resources put business under high-pressure for green operations. Consequently, corporate environmental activities receive increasing attention and scrutiny from the public which requires corporations to treat sustainable environment management as a priority. Indonesia's joining the Voluntary Partnership Agreement with the European Union in September 2013 highlights the importance of sustainable environment management. The Forestry products made in Indonesia had been banned from entering European markets for many years because of the country's unsustainable use of tropical forests. Without Indonesia's commitment to following sustainable operations, the European market would remain inaccessible to the country's forestry products while commitment could convey unprecedented trading opportunities for its forestry industry (Lesprom, 2013).

The pulp and paper industry has a plethora of real cases that demonstrate the above statement. Take Domtar Inc. and Resolute Forest Products Inc., two Ontario-based pulp and paper producers in Canada for example. The Ontario Provincial Court sentenced Domtar to pay 75,000 USD for violating the Fisheries Act. Following this incident, Greenpeace reported the suspension of FSC (Forest Stewardship Council) certificates for Resolute Forest Products for not following environmental and strict logging rules. The loss of the FSC certification hurt the company's image and marketability in a marketplace increasingly concerned with sustainability (RISI, 2013; Ravensbergen, 2013).

Additionally, the ever-growing influence of standards-setting bodies like the ISO (International Organization for Standardization) and FSC are significant for business. In June 2013, APRIL (Asia Pacific Resources International), the second largest Indonesian paper and pulp producer, withdrew from FSC certification trying to avoid scrutiny for violations of FSC standards (Maitar, 2013). The move marked it as a notorious pulp and paper producer and forest destroyer. It is not difficult to imagine the economic losses, considering that FSC certification is a must have in the international pulp and paper market.

Unlike APRIL, APP (Asia Pulp and Pulp), the largest pulp and paper producer in Asia, metamorphosed itself from irresponsible resources exploiter to a leader in implementing CSR (Greenpeace, 2013). Persistent campaigns by large NGOs against APP's deforestation of tropical and endangered forests caused APP to lose some major customers and also brought a negative image to APP's brand and reputation which only long-term environmental commitment could repair.

The evolution of social, economic, and global environmental issues has resulted in the environmental performance to become an inseparable component of a company's reputation which is an intangible asset that influences marketing and financial performance (Miles & Covin, 2000). APP's environmental reputation has made it a target for green pressure groups that have successfully persuaded some American companies not to buy its products and also caused obstacles to its business acquisitions in the United States and Canada (Forest Business Network, 2011).

APP learned its lessons quickly and took action involving social media to communicate its CSR commitment and carbon footprint. One prominent commitment was its introduction of the "'Zero Deforestation' policy" (Mongabay, 2013). Such a policy from APP is seen as a transformation for sustainable forest utilization in that the company's clout will force other producers to follow suit, which can lead to positive spill over effects in the industry. As part of responsible supply chain management—APP requires its suppliers to hold international certifications, e.g. FSC, PEFC (Programme for the Endorsement of Forest Certification), and strictly pursue sustainable and responsible criteria. APP's social and environmental activities are available to society on many media channels with frequent updates. Its open communication and proactive CSR approach has already started to regain confidence from social media and environmental pressure groups. However, the public remain skeptical of APP's long term commitment. APP will be under continuing and close scrutiny by environmental watchdogs. A good strategy for APP is to take long term environmental responsibility and turn the close supervision into positive promotion for itself. APP's mixed experience with Greenpeace and other environmental groups showcases the gains and losses that can occur.

Social Aspects of CSR for the Pulp and Paper Industry

As opposed to Milton Friedman's shareholder theory, business is more than just business. According to the Economist (2008), "Even capitalist Mr. Jack Welch has expressed doubts: 'on the face of it, shareholder value is the dumbest idea in the world". Admittedly, Friedman is not completely wrong about a business's goal being to maximise profit (Cadbury, 2006), which falls in the framework of the narrow and myopic shareholder theory. This discussion views it as a part of the 'triple-bottom-line' because shareholders are only one part of the business's stakeholder composition and profit-making is only one aspect of modern business. For example, the Brazilian pulp and paper industry strives for industrial competitiveness by pursuing benefits for and involvement of various economic, environmental and social stakeholders (National Confederation of Industry, 2012). As Figure 2 depicts, economic gain (company image, risk management and cost improvement), with 35%, represents a large proportion of the reasons why companies pursue CSR. However social reasons (Employee turnover, Ethical reasons, improved company culture), with 37%, have significant weight within the typology of reasons for companies to seek social responsibility actions.

An exclusive shareholder approach gives rise to a divorce between business and its community or society. "In some cases, businesses fail because of their lack of engagement with society. Involvement in social and community action has emerged as a survival tactic" (Hack-Polay, 2013: 11). This section discusses and emphasises how being responsible to social stakeholders brings value to the business, from the perspectives of human resource management (HRM), supply chain management, and China's migrant workforce in the pulp and paper industry.

According to the British Chartered Management Institute (CMI), CSR is becoming a key factor in staff recruitment and retention. Responsible human resource management brings out initiatives and commitment from employees and that, in turn, engenders sustainable staff retention and promotes their initiatives. Staff training and development is a costly and time consuming investment. It returns the investment with high staff retention; otherwise, it would be a capital cost to the firm and a gain for competitors. Treating employees ethically and responsibly is a first step towards obtaining staff commitment (Forstater et al., 2010). CSR in HRM can also add value by encouraging employees to take ownership of their work. This fosters employees' pride in being an important part of the firm by bringing personal initiatives to work. For instance, Peace River Pulp Division, a pulp producer located in Alberta, Canada, won 'the Achievers 50 Most Engaged Workplace ™ Awards' by being a top leader in engaging employees in the workplace (Pulp and Paper Canada, 2014).

Nine Dragon Paper (Holdings) Limited (ND), a worldwide leading containerboard producer, built a papermaking empire based on the visionary belief in 'no environmental protection, no papermaking'. While ND is strong in promoting environmental sustainability, it regrettably neglected the social impact of CSR. This oversight brought the corporation an unfavourable public image which generated stock speculation and employee mistrust.

On the one hand, ND was hailed for its persistent commitment and adherence to its corporate mission in environmental protection and sustainable production. Such efforts won ND many awards, e.g. Awards for China Environmentally Friendly Enterprises in 2009 and 2010 (Ifeng Finance, 2009, 2010). On the other hand, ND has been in the spot light for notorious stakeholder misconducts which have attracted governmental investigations and decreased in stock prices, etc. Such misconducts also attracted public and media attention. Some exemplary media reports were the Sweat Shop report, the Incident of Employee Suicide and the 4.12 Violence with social contractors (Ifeng Finance, 2008; Sinafinance, 2012; ChinaPaper, 2013). There are countless reports on ND's public behaviour due to its leading position in the industry, but ND has given no comment or response to these reports. Regardless of whether the allegations have any veracity, aside from the legal investigations and decreased stock prices, such negative social reports weaken ND's social image and its employer brand, employee retention and development. One escalating incident was that the S&P withdrew its rating on the company in January 2011 due to increasing concerns about the company's corporate governance and lack of response from the management. The withdrawal caused ND's shares to tumble 17% in mid-January 2011 (Cookson, 2011).

According to Davis (1973), if a business opts not to enter the arena of social responsibility it could face the wrath of its customers. Being socially responsible can earn a firm loyalty from existing customers. It is also positive for the potential to attract new customers, because recommendations from families and friends tend to be more convincing and effective than conventional corporate marketing. It is expected that 98% of consumers will be interested in sustainable lifestyles within five years, growing from the current 2%, new survey results released in September 2013 by BSR (The Business of a Better World) and Futerra.

Stakeholders, inclusive of customers in the global marketplace, are increasingly conscious of the environmental and social impacts of the products and services they buy (Chartered Management Institute, 2012; National Resources Canada, 2013). Sources such as Together for Sustainability Initiatives (TFS) and the Dow Jones Sustainability Index facilitate the dissemination of information on sustainable global suppliers. Irresponsible operators will find themselves shunned by suppliers and buyers which can cause instability in production and supply. Nippon Paper, a major Japanese paper company, was also involved in the whitewashing recycling scandal illustrated in section 2.2. Aside from a drop in share value, Nippon experienced reluctance from its retailers to sell its products and at the same time buyers withdrew business due to the tainted brand (The Guardian, 2008; Whipp, 2008). Conversely, good business operations can attract stable cooperation with external forces augmenting value from a stable and reliable supply chain.

At the macro level, going beyond pursuing sole shareholder interest, CSR brings value to the giver and benefits to the recipients. An example of a CSR approach to treat migrant workers better in China is illustrative of this point. Migrant workers in China are an underlying force generating tremendous but unrecognized wealth for national and industrial development. There are 260 million migrant workers as of 2012, according to the statistics from the National Bureau of Statistics of China (Xinhua Daily Telegraph, 2013). This workforce builds the solid foundation without which the society could collapse. Over 18% the migrant worker population operate in the construction sector and 34.5% in manufacturing. Their contributions are often underestimated and their basic needs are unmet. For example, 69.2% receive no training at all and 84.5% work over 44 hours per week (People, 2013).

Many of them are migrant parents working in factories, including those in the pulp and paper sector, and on construction sites. These migrants aspire to save money for a better life for the children they leave behind in their rural areas. There are about 61 million 'Left-Behind' Children of whom 70% show signs of mental health symptoms like depression. These left-behind children are a latent source for economic damage and societal unrest in China (Fang, 2011; Wan, 2014).

A responsible and ethical approach to treating migrant workers in China would ensure these humble and hardworking people's ready commitment to the foundation for the country and industry. Long term commitment and retention of this force would bring undeniable production sustainability. China is the world's second largest paper and paperboard producer second to none but the United States (He & Barr, 2004). Europe among many countries and regions considers China as a particular competitor in the pulp and paper industry owing to China's capacity to produce low-cost and high-quality paper products (European Commission, 2013). However, according to Zhuang, Ding and Li (n. d.), China's pulp and paper industry has not fully explored the advantage of its low-labour cost. Presently, Das and Diaye (2013) find that China is losing its edge as a low-labour-cost production base due to a shrinking labour force, resulting partially from its unsustainable labour management practices.

A virtuous cycle can be achieved from proactive CSR efforts. Training given to migrant workers can alleviate skills shortages, and care and education given to their children could free them from family worries. This in turn contributes to social stability and industrial productivity. One possibility is for China's industries to take CSR initiatives in upgrading the skills of the vast migrant workforce and develop a new skilled-labour-intensive CSA (country-specific advantage). As Jamali, Karam & Blowfield (2015: 3) argue development orientated CSR command organizational actions that are geared at tangible development outcomes for the marginalised strata in society.

The discrepancy between real CSR and social expectations is ever increasing (Buchholtz & Carroll, 2012). Levitt's (2010) argument is that it is government's responsibility, not business's. However, to narrow this gap, it requires synergistic efforts from all social actors. As part of a society, corporations need and must take responsibility for their activities.

CONCLUSION

The literature considered in our theoretical analysis of CSR and the pulp and paper industry shows that corporate economic performance and environmental and societal responsibilities are inseparable. There is no demarcation between the three bottom lines. Pulp and paper companies involved in proactive CSR strategies reap profits through increased innovation, enhanced reputation and sustained customer loyalty, etc. in the long term. A corporation taking a strategic CSR approach may not necessarily be guaranteed survival in marketplace but those that do not operate a systematic CSR agenda would be more vulnerable. Business models that pursue solely the economic bottom-line for its exclusive shareholders could restrict their level of sustainable development. The manifold value created from CSR is illustrated from the triple-bottom-line perspective. Economically, proactive CSR brings sustainable competitive advantage from efficiency and innovation seeking. Environmentally, responsible and sustainable management of natural resources gains support and economic rewards from the public and governments. Socially, one step at a time, CSR brings benefits to businesses and society. The latter, in turn, rewards such efforts with committed employees, loyal customers and a peaceful environment to operate in. Most importantly, it is only through synchronous implementation of the three bottom lines that business can harness the vast benefits of CSR.

As the fourth largest energy user and CO_2 emitter, the pulp and paper industry is subject to the vicissitudes of the global society and environment. Pulp and paper operations have caused irrevocable damage to the world's ecology and social communities. A sustainably managed pulp and paper industry can bring numerous benefits to the industry per se, e.g. sustainable raw material and industrial reputation, as well as economic gains and social recognition to individual business. Pursuing the economic bottom line should go hand in hand with responsibilities to the society and environment. The problem is not whether but how to better embed CSR into business operations and create leverage over competitors. In the pulp and paper industry, is the level of CSR commitment the same from every country? Are pulp and paper products from countries promoting CSR more competitive in terms of prices and brand image? Does the pulp and paper industry pay equal attention to its environmental and social stakeholders? Questions like these need be further investigated.

Of further interest, the world's most populous country, China, sees the largest rural migration for employment. The nation faces a plethora of problems about the massive migrant force like the working conditions, social equity and 'left-behind' children. The International Labour Organization (ILO) established the ILO Decent Work Country Programme for China focusing on reducing inequalities and improving employability for Chinese rural migrants. To obtain such grand goals, commitment and measures from both social institutions and business sectors are necessary to explore how to achieve preventive and proactive CSR. One possibility is to establish sound mechanisms for sustainable CSR composed of mandate regulations, institutional infrastructure for implementation, supervision, and evaluation as well as motivation and reward systems.

Presently, CSR is largely a discretionary option, thus more governmental enforcement and supervision from NGOs are needed. Most importantly, corporate initiatives are urgently needed to work toward a sustainable world. Taking a transparent and proactive CSR approach can bring strategic advantages *vis-à-vis* competitors that are vital to the survival of the corporation. CSR must be more than just a plaque on the wall, if its values are to be realized by business.

REFERENCES

Branson, R. (2009). *Business stripped bare*. Great Britain: Clays Ltd.

Buchholtz, K. A., & Carroll, B. A. (2012). *Business and society ethics and shareholder management*. Canada: Cengage Learning.

Cadbury, A. (2006). Twenty-first century society. *Journal of the Academy of Social Sciences*, *1*(1), 5–21.

Chartered Management Institute. (2012). Sustainable business practice. Retrieved from http://www.managers.org.uk/page/best-practice-corporate-responsibility-sustainable-business-practice

Clark, H. (2012). *Corporate social responsibility: a gateway to sustainability*. Retrieved from http://www.undp.org/content/undp/en/home/presscenter/speeches/2012/05/18/helen-clark-corporate-social-responsibility/

Clegg, S. et al.. (2012). *Strategy Theory and Practice*. Singapore: SAGE Publications Asia-Pacific Pte Ltd.

Cookson, R. (2011). S&P Withdraws Nine Dragons Paper Rating. *Financial Times*. Retrieved from http://www.ft.com/cms/s/0/ea979340-969f-11e0-baca-00144feab49a.html#axzz3zE69jU4o

CSR Press Release. (2013). Call for Entries – PR News' CSR Awards 2013. Retrieved from http://www.csrwire.com/press_releases/36220-Call-for-Entries-PR-News-CSR-Awards-2013

D'Amato, A., Henderson, S., & Florence, S. (2009). *Corporate Social Responsibility and Sustainable Business a Guide to Leadership Tasks and Functions*. Greensboro: Center for Creative Leadership.

Das, M., & Diaye, N. P. (2013). The end of cheap labor. *Finance & Development*, *50*(2), 34–37.

Davis, K. (1973). The case for and against business assumption of social responsibilities. *Academy of Management Journal*, *16*(2), 312–322. doi:10.2307/255331

Elkington, J. (1994). Towards the Sustainable Corporation: Win-win-win business strategies for sustainable development. *California Management Review*, *36*(2), 90–100. doi:10.2307/41165746

Environment Graffiti. (2008). Japanese paper industry in recycling scandal. Retrieved from http://www.environmentalgraffiti.com/businesspolitics/japanese-paper-industry-in-recycling-scandal/707#7tweH04B3AvVCrqJ.99

Fang, I. C. (2011). *Growing Up and Becoming Independent: An Ethnographic Study of New Generation Migrant workers in China* [Doctoral Thesis]. London: London School of Economics and Political Science.

Food and Agriculture Organization of the United Nations. (2014). Pulp, Paper and Wood Product Industries. Retrieved from http://www.fao.org/forestry/industries/en/

Forest Business Network. (2011). Asian paper giant sees growth opportunity in Canada. Retrieved from http://www.forestbusinessnetwork.com/3898/asian-paper-giant-sees-growth-opportunity-in-canada/

Forstater, M. et al.. (2010). *Corporate responsibility in African Development: Insights from an emerging dialogue*. Cambridge, MA: Harvard University.

George, A., Edgerton, N., & Berry, T. (2007). *Mainstreaming socially responsible investment (sri): a role for government? policy recommendations from the investment community*. Sydney: University of Technology.

Greenpeace. (2014). Asia Pulp & Paper: from confrontation to engagement. Retrieved from http://www.greenpeace.org/international/en/news/Blogs/makingwaves/asia-pulp-paper-forest-conservation-policy/blog/47162/

Hack-Polay, D. (2013). Understanding the business environment. In D. Hack-Polay & D. Davies (Eds.), Understanding Business – a Beginner's Text. Harlow: Pearson.

Ifeng Finance. (2010). 玖龙纸业再度蝉联绿色企业管理 [Nine Dragons Paper Won the Award for 'Green Management of Enterprises]. Retrieved from http://finance.ifeng.com/hk/gs/20100125/1753249.shtml

Industry Canada. (2011). Corporate Social Responsibility. Retrieved from http://www.ic.gc.ca/eic/site/csr-rse.nsf/eng/home

Konar, S., & Cohen, A. M. (2001). Does the market value environmental performance? *The Review of Economics and Statistics*, *83*(2), 281–289. doi:10.1162/00346530151143815

Lesprom. (2013). *Indonesia signs voluntary partnership agreement with EU to curb illegal ltimber trade*. Retrieved from http://www.lesprom.com/news/Indonesia_signs_Voluntary_Partnership_Agreement_with_EU_to_curb_illegal_timber_trade_58194/?lng=eng

Maitar, B. (2013). APRIL walks away from the FSC. Retrieved from http://www.greenpeace.org/international/en/news/Blogs/makingwaves/april-walks-away-from-the-fsc/blog/45634/

Miles, P. M., & Covin, J. G. (2000). Environmental marketing a source of reputational, competitive, and financial advantage. *Journal of Business Ethics*, *23*(3), 299–311. doi:10.1023/A:1006214509281

Ministry of Environmental Protection of the People Republic of China. (2011). 山东省秸秆制浆造纸技术取得重大突破领先国际先进水平 [Shandong Province achieves important breakthrough in pulp and paper making technology using straw and stalks]. Retrieved from http://www.zhb.gov.cn/zhxx/gzdt/201107/t20110705_214414.htm

Mongabay. (2013). Pulp and paper giant gets $1.8B loan from China for Indonesia's largest mill. http://news.mongabay.com/2013/1011-app-oki-pulp-mill.html

National Confederation of Industry. (2012). Forest Plantation: Opportunities and challenges for the Brazilian Pulp and Paper industry on the path of sustainability. Retrieved from www.cni.org.br

National Development and Reform Commission. (2011). 山东泉林公司依靠自主创新探索秸秆综合利用新途 [Reliant on internal initiatives and innovation, Shandong Tralin Paper explore new methods to use straw and stalks]. Retrieved from http://www.sdpc.gov.cn/hjbh/hjjsjyxsh/t20091203_317789.htm

Nature Resources Canada. (2014). Canadian forests and forest products: key sustainability questions. Retrieved from http://www.nrcan.gc.ca/forests/industry/13319

Needle, D. (2010). *Business in Context: an introduction to business and its environment*. Singapore: Cengage Learning EMEA.

A.B.C. News. (2014). The ANZ bank has sold about $200 million of debt owed to it by failed Tasmanian timber company Gunns. Retrieved from http://www.abc.net.au/news/2014-01-30/anz-offloads-debt-from-collapsed-timber-company-gunns/5227124

Paper China. (2013). 玖龙纸业违法建楼 拒付民工千万工钱 [Nine Dragons Paper refused to pay hundreds and thousands worthy of payments to migrant workers for its illegal buildings]. Retrieved from http://www.paper.com.cn/news/daynews/2013/130410085914925273.htm

Paper China. (2013). 玖龙纸业412暴力事件 受害人集体诉 [Victims' Group Petition of Nine Dragons Paper's 4.12 Incident]. Retrieved from http://www.paper.com.cn/news/daynews/2013/130416090809982380.htm

People. (2013). 统计局:2012年全国农民工总量达26万 [The National Statistics Bureau: the total number of national migrant workers reaches 262.61 million in 2012]. Retrieved from http://finance.people.com.cn/n/2013/0527/c1004-21624982.html

Pulp and Paper Canada. (2014). DMI is one of 50 best workplaces for employee engagement. Retrieved from http://www.pulpandpapercanada.com/news/dmi-is-one-of-50-best-workplaces/1002870213/?&er=NA

Rangan, K., Chase, A. L., & Karim, S. (2012, April). Why every company needs a CSR strategy and how to build it. Harvard Business School Working Paper.

Ravensbergen, J. (2013). Resolute Forest FSC certificates suspended: Greenpeace. Retrieved from http://www.montrealgazette.com/business/Resolute+Forest+certificates+suspended+Greenpeace/9278507/story.html

RISI. (2013). AkzoNobel joins together for sustainability initiative to enhance global supply chain. Retrieved from http://www.risiinfo.com/technologyarchives/environment/AkzoNobel-joins-Together-for-Sustainability-initiative.html

RISI. (2013). Ashland wins 2013 Breakthrough Technology award from PPI for improvements to sustainability and productivity for recycled paperboard manufacturers. Retrieved from http://www.risiinfo.com/technologyarchives/environment/Ashland-wins-2013-Breakthrough-Technology-award-from-PPI-for-improvements-to-sustainability-and-productivity-for-recycled-paperboard-manufacturers.html

RISI. (2013). Domtar fined $75,000 for violations to Canada Fisheries Act at Espanola, ON, mill in 2010. Retrieved from http://www.risiinfo.com/techchannels/environment/Domtar-fined-75000-for-violations-to-Canada-Fisheries-Act-at-Espanola-ON-mill-in-2010.html?source=email_cz

RISI. (2013). *Nippon Paper and Coca-Cola Japan collaborate on forest and water resources conservation.* Retrieved from http://www.risiinfo.com/technologyarchives/environment/Nippon-Paper-and-Coca-Cola-Japan-collaborate-on-forest-and-water-resources-conservation.html

Robson, A., & Wakefield, S. E. L. (2007). Socially responsible investing in "high-net-worth" asset management firms in Canada: An exploratory study. *EJBO Electronic Journal of Business Ethics and Organization Studies*, *12*(1), 29–34.

Rugman, M. A., & Collinson, S. (2009). *International business*. England: Prentice Hall.

Schermerhorn, J. R. (1999). *Management*. the United States of America: Von Hoffman Press.

Siemens. (2014) *Your expert partner for the pulp and paper industry.* Retrieved from http://www.industry.siemens.com/verticals/global/en/paper-industry/pages/default.aspx

Sinafinance. (2012). 玖龙纸业曝技改人员血案 2011财年纯利跌9.2% [Nine Dragons Paper net profit dropped 9.2% after exposure of technician's 'blood incident]. Retrieved from http://finance.sina.com.cn/stock/hkstock/ggscyd/20120217/015411396104.shtml

Slaper, T. F. (2011, Spring). The triple bottom line: what is it and how does it work? *Indiana Business Review.*

Smith, C. N. (2003, April). *Corporate social responsibility: not whether but how?* Center for Marketing, London Business School Working Papers No. 03-701.

Story, D., & Price, T. (2006). Corporate social responsibility and risk management? *Journal of Corporate Citizenship*, *22*(22), 39–51. doi:10.9774/GLEAF.4700.2006.su.00007

Sustain. (2013) *A Global player made in Europe.,* Retrieved from http://www.cepi-sustainability.eu/about-this-site-2

The Business of a Better World. (2013). *Sustainable lifestyles to Drive Sales, Market Share, and Innovation within Five Years*. Retrieved from http://www.bsr.org/en/about/press-release/sustainable-lifestyles-to-drive-sales-market-share-and-innovation-within-fi

The Economist. (2008). Special report: Corporate social responsibility: The next question. Retrieved from http://www.economist.com/printedition/specialreports?year[value][year]=2008&category=7698445

The Economist. (2008). The good company. Retrieved from http://www.economist.com/node/3555212

The Economist. (2010). *A new idolatry, the economic crisis has received the old debate about whether firms should focus most on their shareholders, their customers or their workers*. Retrieved from http://www.economist.com/node/15954434

The Guardian. (2008). Japanese paper industry in recycling scandal. Retrieved from http://www.theguardian.com/business/2008/jan/18/greenbusiness.recycling?gusrc=rss&feed=environment

The Sydney Morning Herald. (2012). Tasmania's divisive timber mill project reduced the mighty Gunns to a pulp. Retrieved from http://www.smh.com.au/federal-politics/political-opinion/tasmanias-divisive-timber-mill-project-reduced-the-mighty-gunns-to-a-pulp-20120927-26o0f.html#ixzz2rfFGYtHc

UBC. (2013). Olson J. Director's message. Retrieved from http://www.ppc.ubc.ca/about/message/

Verbeke, A. (2013). *International business strategy*. Cambridge: Cambridge University Press. doi:10.1017/CBO9781139227162

Wagner, M. (2005). How to reconcile environmental and economic performance to improve corporate sustainability: Corporate environmental strategies in the European paper industry. *Journal of Environmental Management*, *76*(2), 105–118. doi:10.1016/j.jenvman.2004.11.021 PMID:15939122

Wan, W. (2014). In China, one in five children live in rural villages without their parents. Retrieved from http://www.washingtonpost.com/world/asia_pacific/in-china-one-in-five-children-live-in-rural-villages-without-their-parents/2013/12/30/3f05a870-4b9a-11e3-9890-a1e0997fb0c0_story.html

Whipp, M. (2013). *UK paper responds to Japanese recycled content scandal.* Retrieved from http://www.printweek.com/print-week/news/1120252/uk-paper-responds-japanese-recycled-content-scandal

Widok, A. (2009). Social Sustainability: Theories, concepts, practicability. In *Environmental Informatics and industrial environmental Protection: concepts, methods and tools*. Berlin: Shaker Verlag.

WWF. (2014). *Pulp and paper.* Retrieved from http://worldwildlife.org/industries/pulp-and-paper

Xinhua Daily Telegraph. (2013). 2012年全国农民工总量2.6亿 [The total number of national migrant workers reaches 260 million in 2012]. Retrieved from http://news.xinhuanet.com/mrdx/2013-02/23/c_132187270.htm

Zhang, Zh., Ding, L. & Li, H. Zh. (n. d.). *China's pulp and paper industry: A Review*. School of Economics, Georgia Institute of Technology.

Chapter 12
Multi-Stakeholder Initiatives and Corporate Social Responsibility in Global Value Chains
Towards an Analytical Framework and a Methodology

Ahmad Hassan
Copenhagen Business School (CBS), Denmark

Peter Lund-Thomsen
Copenhagen Business School (CBS), Denmark

ABSTRACT

In this chapter, we make a contribution to the literature on corporate social responsibility in global value chains that link dispersed consumers and importers in developed countries with local manufacturers, workers, and communities in developing countries. We create an integrated analytical framework and a methodology that can guide master-level and Ph.D. students as well as practitioners on how they may map the governance processes through which multi-stakeholder initiatives (MSIs) in global value chains are formulated, implemented, monitored as well as the impact that MSI standards have on the work conditions of those laboring at the base of global value chains. We use a stylized case study of fair trade in the football manufacturing industry in Pakistan to illustrate how the framework and the methodology might be applied to the empirical analysis of MSI governance processes and their impacts on workers' conditions in export-oriented industries in the South.

DOI: 10.4018/978-1-5225-0720-8.ch012

INTRODUCTION

In the age of globalization, developing country governments often appear to lack the capacity or political will to regulate global business interests or adequately address international public goods challenges (Utting, 2015). At the same time, civil society organizations criticize the behavior of multinational corporations along their global value chains which link consumers and importers in developed countries with firms, farmers, workers, and communities in developing countries (Bair & Palpacuer, 2015). Consequently, multinational corporations are confronted with growing social and environmental demands and are asked to take responsibility for matters of public concern (Scherer, Palazzo, & Matten, 2014). As a response, a proliferation of corporate social responsibility (CSR) initiatives[1] such as the Fairtrade Labelling Organization (FLO) and the United Kingdom-based Ethical Trading Initiative have emerged, aimed at promoting voluntary governance solutions as a response to poor work conditions and high environmental pollution levels in many export-oriented industries in developing countries (Rasche & Esser, 2006).

These initiatives often involve multiple stakeholders including private sector companies, non-governmental organizations (NGOs), trade unions, social movements, and other actors. Together, they define and implement rules governing the social and environmental impact of economic activities in areas that have traditionally been under the regulatory authority of nation-states (Reed et al., 2013, Cheyns & Riisgaard, 2014). These multi-stakeholder initiatives (MSIs) do not have the political authority held by nation states in the traditional political realm. However, they have the ability to define social and environmental standards at the international level, their staff often possess skilled knowledge, and can articulate specific interests across different issue areas (Betsill & Correll 2008; Ronit, 2012). Therefore, they are widely acknowledged as an important alternative to corporate self-governance (Utting, 2015).

The regulatory influence of MSI standards in global value chains is now widely recognized (Lund-Thomsen & Lindgreen, 2014). Yet, we have less knowledge about how and why multi-stakeholder initiatives tend to differ across national contexts in the developing world (Reed et al. 2013). However, the related literature on "regulatory renaissance" suggests that public regulation – through the work of labor inspectorates and labor standards enforcement – is being revitalized in some developing countries such as Brazil and the Dominican Republic. In combination with private forms of regulation, this may help in improving the conditions of workers at the base of global value chains (see e.g., Piore & Schrank, 2008; Amengual, 2010; Locke et al., 2012).[2] However, whereas the "regulatory renaissance literature" helps us understand the interaction between public and private governance in developing countries, there is still little practical guidance in the global value chain and MSI literatures on how one can map the political processes through which MSIs evolve, and how they affect workers' conditions at the base of these value chains. In other words, how should master-level students, Ph.D. students, policy-makers, and practitioners go about analyzing the nature and impacts of these initiatives in a concrete way?

More than fifteen years ago, Kaplinsky and Morris (2001) produced a handbook for value chain research. The handbook introduced basic definitions in and the context of value chain research, key analytical constructs in this field, and a concrete methodology for engaging in value chain research. Similarly, Barrientos (2001) made a detailed step-by-step introduction to how one can map corporate codes of conduct as they travel through global value chains. Barrientos and her colleagues later followed up with an article that detailed how gender concerns might be integrated into global value chain analysis (Barrientos et al., 2003). Bolwig et al. (2010) and Riisgaard et al. (2010) subsequently created a conceptual framework, a strategic framework, and practical guide on how to integrate poverty and environmental concerns into this literature. Yet, when it comes to hands-on advice for students, academics, policy-makers, or other practitioners that are interested in mapping the political processes underpinning the development of MSIs, and the impact that MSI governance processes have on workers' conditions in developing countries, very few publications have addressed this issue.[3]

In this chapter, we make a contribution aimed at filling part of the gap in the CSR, MSI, and global value chain literatures by developing an analytical framework and a methodology that is intended to help master-level students, Ph.D. students, and practitioners in mapping the political processes through which MSIs evolve and their impact on workers' conditions at the base of global value chains.

Our line of argument is that analyzing MSI governance processes and their effects on workers at the base of global value chains cannot be meaningfully done without paying attention to the institutional contexts in which MSIs become embedded in developing countries. For this purpose, our analytical framework and methodology pay particular attention to the role that institutional contexts play in shaping such initiatives and their ultimate effects in the South. In doing so, we use a distinct MSI, the Fairtrade Labelling Organization, and its standard for fairtrade sports balls, as a stylized case study to illustrate how one might apply our analytical framework and methodology to map MSI governance processes and their effects on workers' conditions in developing countries. As fairtrade footballs are only produced in one country in the world, Pakistan (FLO 2016), this is the context that we use to illustrate our analytical framework and practical methodology.

The chapter is structured as follows. The next section elaborates our analytical framework aimed at understanding the political processes through which MSIs develop, and how these processes may have an impact upon workers' conditions in export-oriented industries in developing countries. The third section explains why this framework should be applied to the fairtrade football manufacturing industry in Pakistan. We then describe a suggested methodology for mapping (i) the political processes through which the Fairtrade standard for sports balls has evolved and (ii) its impact on workers' conditions in the football manufacturing industry of Pakistan. Next, we turn to a discussion of the wider implications that our analytical framework and methodology may have for comparative studies on MSIs and CSR in global value chains in other developing country contexts. Finally, the conclusion summarizes the main findings of our chapter.

TOWARDS AN ANALYTICAL FRAMEWORK

Multi-Stakeholder Initiatives and CSR in Global Value Chains

We start our discussion by looking at the links between collaborative governance and CSR in global value chains. The term collaborative governance refers to the emerging multi-actor and multi-layered system of global authority. In the context of CSR, a number of scholars have debated the nature of collaborative forms of governance (Gilbert & Rasche, 2008; Reed et al., 2013, Utting, 2015). Collaborative governance was previously discussed in the literature on global governance where governance was seen as multi-stakeholder processes including actors such as businesses, civil society organizations, local governments, and labor organizations that were aimed at creating consistency, order, and continuity in global political affairs (Rosenau, 1995, Rasche, 2010). Collaborative governance was here defined as arrangements that included an intentional multi-actor partnership in formulating, implementing, and monitoring guidelines or rules governing the social and environmental impact of economic activities (Lund-Thomsen, 2013a).

One perceived advantage of this kind of governance arrangement was its potential for enhancing the legitimacy of non-state regulation (Dolan & Opondo, 2005). Conventional private governance practices, such as unilaterally designed firm-specific codes of conduct, were often perceived as illegitimate because of their being Northern driven, not including sufficient local stakeholder consultation, and not considering local contextual specificities (Khan & Lund-Thomsen, 2011). Collaborative governance initiatives such as fairtrade standards aimed at alleviating these flaws, involving a range of actors in the process of standard formulation and implementation. However, this approach could be problematic if there are limitations to their inclusiveness and the kinds of discussions that can take place in such initiatives (Cheyns & Riisgaard, 2014). For instance, Gilbert and Rasche (2007) have argued that the outreach of SA 8000 as a multi-stakeholder standard was limited to some key stakeholders, ignoring supplier factories that had to implement the standard on the ground. In addition, bringing various stakeholders with different agendas and from different contexts together does not guarantee that socially and environmentally unsustainable solutions to global governance deficits are avoided (Mukherjee Reed & Reed, 2009).

Another potential advantage of collaborative governance initiatives was their increased likelihood of finding applicable solutions for governance issues by providing expert knowledge and combining resources among actors (Rein & Stott, 2009). Participants with distinct skills could in theory address social issues under the umbrella of multi-actor collaboration, particularly as various solutions were thought to need access to non-business knowledge (Utting, 2015). However, Börzel and Risse (2005) highlighted that there was no reason to believe that such initiatives that included various actors from different backgrounds were going to be more successful than other forms of regulation. They argued that this would depend on the kinds of the actors involved and the quality of their collaboration. In fact, there was a risk that these new collaborative governance arrangements might sideline some issues from the agendas of intergovernmental organizations and governments without much attention being paid to the limits of such forms of governance (Utting, 2015).

Collaborative Governance in Global Value Chains

Having outlined the potential advantages and disadvantages of MSIs as a form of collaborative governance, we now move on to considering the nature of global value chain analysis before we turn to the question of how MSI governance processes may be studied in these chains. The literature on global value chains analysis links dispersed consumers and international buyers in developed countries with local producers and workers in the developing world (Barrientos, 2015). Global value chain analysis offers a framework for exploring cross-national business activities by examining how a product from its conception, through its marketing, its distribution and final consumption is internationally connected through value chains that represent a network of actors and activities.

Gereffi (1994) originally identified three dimensions of a global value chain: (i) the input-output structure, i.e. the series of value-adding actions in the production and consumption of a product; (ii) the geographical coverage, i.e. its territoriality dispersion of participants and actions related to a global value chain; and (iii) its form of governance, i.e. the sharing of power, decision-making and authority along the global value chain. With the input-output structure and the geographical coverage being mainly descriptive considerations, global value chain analysis has since largely focused on how governance is exercised in global value chains (Gereffi & Lee, 2016). The concept of governance of global value chains is of particular significance to this chapter and will thus be discussed below.

Lund-Thomsen and Lindgreen (2014) argues that governance in global value chains refers to the ability of the global lead firms to organize value chains, defining what will be produced, where, when, how, by whom, in which quantity, and at what price. This further links to the decisions concerning what level of quality, production and perhaps distribution, standards are to be demanded of local producers in South. The notion of global value chain governance is associated with Gereffi (1994), who distinguished between two basic types of chains: producer-driven value chains (usually found in capital and technology intensive industries where chain governance is implemented by companies that control production facilities and core technologies), and buyer driven value chains (usually found in more labor intensive industries where chain governance is implemented by larger retailers and brand name companies with no direct ownership over production functions). In this form, international buyers have a central role in the governance of global value chains which permits them to implement social and environmental standards as a condition of supply. Later, Gereffi et al. (2005) expanded this understanding by developing a global value chain framework, which differentiated between five different types of global value chain governance: market mechanisms on the one hand and hierarchy on the other hand with modular, relational, and captive networks as separate buyer-supplier relationships in-between.

In short, in the global value chain literature, understanding governance has generally focused on power relations and coordination mechanisms among economic actors. More recently, this typology of global value chain governance has been extended by Neilson and Pritchard (2009, 2010). They expanded the scope of value chain analysis with respect to institutions and governance to go beyond the direct actors involved in the chain, combining *horizontal* relations (with respect to the institutional environment in producer countries) as well as *vertical* forces (with respect to the governance of global value chains). They argue that there are other important factors and players such as NGOs and the local government that may influence global value chain governance.

Of particular importance in the context of this chapter is the work of Tallontire (2007). She has contributed to our understanding of collaborative governance in global value chains by distinguishing between legislative governance (who makes standards and how?), executive governance (how are standards implemented?), and judicial governance (how are standards monitored?) in MSIs. In this chapter, we extend her work (please see Figure 1) by combining an analysis of MSI governance processes and their effects on workers' conditions at the base of global value chains that touch down in developing countries.

An Analytical Framework of MSI Governance Processes and Impacts

In terms of political processes in MSIs, legislative governance refers to the important question of whose voices, interests, and perspectives are taken into account in the process of formulating MSI standards (in our chapter, we use the FLO standard for sports balls as a stylized case study to illustrate our analytical framework). We are thus concerned with analyzing the key factors and the actors that influence the formulation process. A particular point of interest relates to whether the intended beneficiaries in particular, or developing country stakeholders more broadly, were actively involved in the decision-making processes leading to the formulation of a given MSI?

If we use the case of the fairtrade standard for sports balls in Pakistan, a key question therefore relates to whether the voices of the football workers have been heard in the process of formulating the standard for fairtrade sports balls? Have they had any particular influence on the formulation of the standard?

Figure 1. An analytical framework for understanding the political processes in MSIs and their impact on workers' conditions at the base of global value chains
(Source: Developed by the authors).

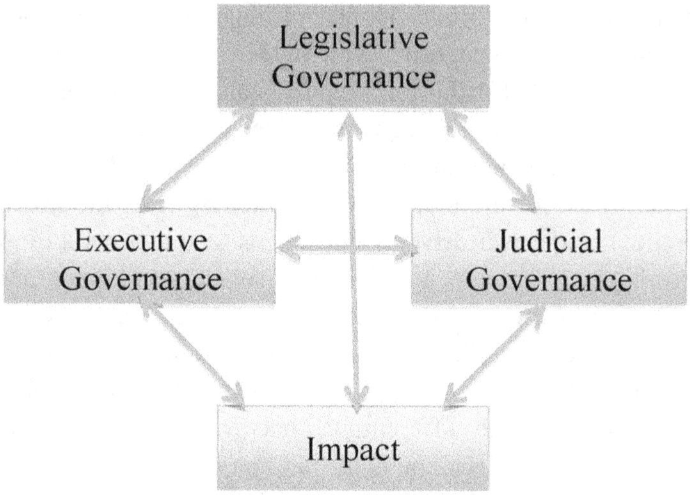

Or has the standard been formulated by actors from the 'outside' with few insights into or little on-the-ground experience of football manufacturing and the conditions under which football workers toil in this industry? Moreover, in terms of the formulation process, it would be interesting to carefully map whose perspectives and interests – in terms of the standard contents – have dominated the standard formulation process? For instance, has any attention been paid to secure living wages (however defined and measured) of football workers in this industry? Or does the standard permit local football manufacturers to produce Fairtrade footballs even if they do not pay their workers living wages?

As illustrated in Figure 1 below, we can thus draw a direct link between legislative governance and the potential impact of MSI standards on workers' conditions in developing countries. Depending upon whose voices are heard in the standard formulation process and the actor interests embodied within the standard, the standard may affect the conditions of workers at the base of global value chains in different ways. For example, in the case of the fairtrade football standard, the standard actually states that workers should receive living wages (FLO, 2016). In theory, if the standard were implemented in practice, this could result in substantially increased wages for football workers in Pakistan. However, had the living wage criteria not been included in the fairtrade sports balls standard, fairtrade football workers might have continued living in conditions of income poverty even if they were officially involved in the manufacturing of fairtade footballs.

As shown in Figure 1, legislative governance thus identifies the MSI standard criteria and principles that have to be implemented on the ground at the base of global value chains through executive governance. Executive governance here refers to the question of how MSI standards are to be implemented. It focuses on which issues are included and excluded from the implementation process. A central question is whether all of the MSI standard principles and criteria are indeed implemented on the ground or not. If we take the case of the fairtrade standard for sports balls, local manufacturers also need to be certified under the hired labor standard that requires workers to have contracts, receive living wages, have freedom of association, the right to collective bargaining, and social insurance (FLO, 2016). However, the question is whether these requirements are only implemented at factory sites or whether they are also enforced further down the football manufacturing value chain at so-called football stitching centers? Figure 2 below shows a stylized presentation of the fairtrade value chain for football manufacturing in Sialkot.

Figure 2 displays how international importers in Europe place their orders for fairtrade footballs with their suppliers based in Pakistan. These suppliers either have the footballs manufactured entirely within the factory-based premises, and then ship the finished footballs back to their European customers. Alternatively, they sometimes also outsource the most labor-intensive aspect of the football manufacturing process to village-based stitching centers. These are typically run by sub-contractors that bring the football panels and thread from the factories to the stitching centers where piece-rate workers then stitch the footballs before the subcontractors transport the finished balls back to the factories that send them off to European fairtrade importers.

If we now turn to the links between executive governance and impact displayed in figure 1 above, we can again draw a direct connection between executive governance and the potential impact of the fairtrade standard for sports balls on the conditions of workers employed at the base of the football manufacturing value chain in Pakistan. If the requirements of the FLO's hired labor standard were implemented inside the football factories themselves, we would – all other things equal – expect a direct positive impact on workers' conditions' through the provision of contracts, workers' receiving higher wages, having social insurance, and the right to collective bargaining and freedom of association at this level of the value chain. Nevertheless, if these requirements were not implemented further down the football stitching value chain, at the level of stitching centers, we would expect that there would be no impact on their

Figure 2. The fairtrade football stitching balue chain in Pakistan
Source: Adapted after Lund-Thomsen (2013b)

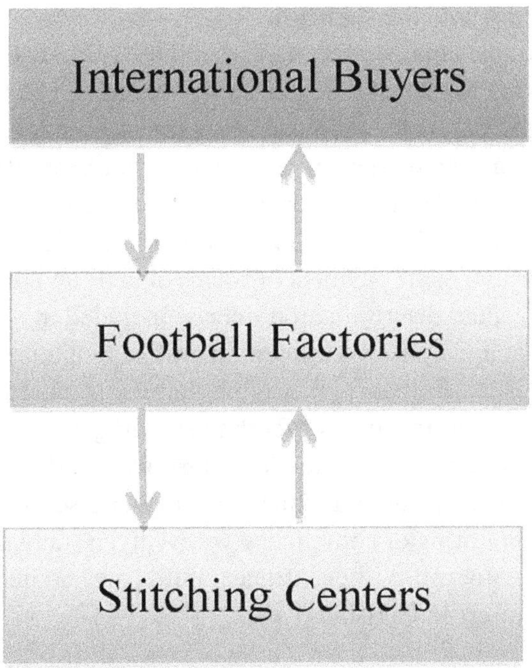

conditions at this node of the value chain. Hence, footballs stitched in these centers would still be sold under the fairtrade label although football stitchers themselves might not receive the benefits that were to accrue to them under the fairtrade sports ball standard.

Following executive governance, the next part of our framework relates to judicial governance. In other words, once the standard principles and criteria of a given MSI have been implemented, judicial governance comes into play. Judicial governance here refers to the measures that are put in place to ensure compliance with a given MSI standard. Hence, we are dealing with the question of how MSI standard implementation is monitored at the base of global value chains. In the case of the fairtrade standard for sports balls, standard implementation is checked both by 2nd party company auditors and by independent third party auditors (FLO, 2016).

Once again we find a direct link between judicial governance and the potential impact of a given MSI standard. Assuming that third party auditors carry out a thorough job of investigating compliance with the fairtrade standard for sports balls, they might be able to check whether fairtrade suppliers in Pakistan actually implement the standard. In other words, this external scrutiny can – at least in theory – pressurize these suppliers to supply football workers with the full benefits guaranteed under this standard as compliant factories will continue to be certified while non-complying factories will be disqualified from being fairtrade suppliers of footballs. In other words, judicial governance could positively affect the conditions of workers at the base of the global football value chain in Pakistan. However, if Pakistani fairtrade suppliers are able to "cheat the auditors" by coaching workers to provide the right answers to auditors questions, if they can falsify worker records to provide the right types of information that auditors seek, and if factory owners can threaten workers that they lose their jobs if they criticize factory management during 3rd party auditor visits, it is unlikely that the Fairtrade standard for sports balls will have any direct impact on the conditions of football workers in this industry. Instead it will be possible for local manufacturers to continue selling footballs under the fairtrade label to their international buyers although they might not comply with the standard.

Finally, in our analytical framework, we speculate that there is likely to be continuous feedback from the impact part of our framework to each of the three above-mentioned factors: legislative, executive, and judicial governance. In other words, once an impact assessment is undertaken of a given MSI standard, this is likely to directly affect all three types of governance. For example, the results of an impact assessment might reveal that important criteria or principles are not included in the standard. For instance, it may be that the standard does not pay sufficient attention to gender discrimination (in this case the Fairtrade standard for sports balls) in the payment of wages of male and female football stitchers. Hence, additional criteria related to gender discrimination may be included in the fairtrade standard for sports balls. Moreover, it may be that an impact assessment identifies loopholes in the implementation of the fairtrade standard for sports balls. In theory, it may be that the standard is only implemented fully at the level of factories, not as much as the level of football stitching centers. This could lead to a revision of executive governance procedures to ensure that the Fairtrade standard for sports balls is fully implemented at the level of stitching centers as well. Finally, an impact assessment could also reveal that there is a need for tightening the monitoring of compliance with a given standard. This would in turn imply a change in judicial governance procedures. For instance, third party audits might become more frequent at Fairtrade football manufacturers in Pakistan.

The Football Manufacturing Industry and Fairtrade in Pakistan

In the last section, we outlined an analytical framework that combined considerations regarding the political processes through which legislative, executive, and judicial aspects of MSI governance evolve over time. This framework also considered how the evolution of these different MSI governance processes might result in 'on-the-ground' changes in the work conditions of football stitchers in Pakistan[4]. In this section, we explain why the football manufacturing industry is particularly important for the study of MSI governance processes and their impacts on workers' conditions at the base of global value chains.

First, football is acknowledged to be the most popular sport in the world and football manufacturing is a billion US$ industry. It is a major global industry with its leading international clubs, and star players, watched and followed across the globe (Nadvi, 2011). However, minor attention is paid by fans to know about how the ball itself, the very heart of the game, is produced. In Pakistan, football production is a vital source of foreign currency earnings. Footballs exports amounted to $ 151.5 million (52% of the total sporting goods exports) in 2012-13 (The Trade Development Authority of Pakistan, 2015). The industry is located in the town of Sialkot, Punjab province, Pakistan. It provides jobs to approximately 20.000 football stitchers whose families partly depend upon the income generated from footballs stitching. The industry has approximately 390 producers and is highly export-oriented. Most of the manufacturers are small and medium enterprises (SMEs) while the industry is also home to a handful of large firms. The Pakistani producers sell footballs to a range of international brands including Nike, Adidas, Puma, Mitre, and Select Sports. As explained above, they have traditionally subcontracted most of the labor-intensive aspect of manufacturing, football stitching, to stitching centers in the villages surrounding Sialkot (Lund-Thomsen, 2013b).

Secondly, the industry is interesting, because it faces substantial international pressures to comply with the corporate codes of conduct of international sports brands such as Nike and Adidas (Lund-Thomsen & Nadvi, 2010). Industry wages are often below the government's minimum rates and the stitchers associated with the industry are amongst the most marginalized. Their privileges are precarious, and unionization is a rare phenomenon (Nadvi, 2011).

Fairtrade initiatives aim to alleviate these flaws and football was the first non-food product to be certified by the FLO in 2002. FLO defines fairtrade as:

a trading partnership, based on dialogue, transparency and respect, which seeks greater equity in international trade. It contributes to sustainable development by offering better trading conditions to, and securing the rights of, marginalized producers and workers – especially in the South. Fairtrade Organizations, backed by consumers, are engaged actively in supporting producers, awareness raising and in campaigning for changes in the rules and practice of conventional international trade (Fairtrade International Organization, 2009).

At present however, we do not know; (i) whether the fairtrade standard for sports balls is indeed able to live up to their promise of being more inclusive in terms of stakeholder participation, and legitimate forms of social and environmental standards setting; and (ii) whether the governance processes, through which the fairtrade standard for sports balls was formulated, implemented, and monitored have contributed to or undermined the work conditions of football stitchers in this industry in Pakistan.

TOWARDS A METHODOLOGY FOR MAPPING MSI GOVERNANCE PROCESSES AND IMPACTS

In the previous section, we tried to explain why it is important to focus on the governance processes and the impacts of the fairtrade standard for sports balls on workers in the football manufacturing industry in Pakistan. This section focuses on a methodology that could be used to empirically investigate the governance processes and the impact of the fairtrade standard for sports balls on workers in football manufacturing industry of Pakistan.

A comparative, multiple case study design (Eisenhardt & Graebner, 2007) might be helpful in applying our analytical framework outlined above to map the FLO governance processes and the impact of the fairtrade standard on sports balls in the global value chain for football manufacturing that touches down in Sialkot, Pakistan. This design would be useful in establishing how similar and different factors are likely to affect the successful/unsuccessful formulation, implementation, and monitoring of fairtrade sports balls standard in the football manufacturing industry of Pakistan. The study might be based on a mixed methods approach including three types of investigations which could be combined in the analysis in order to acquire a deeper appreciation of how different stakeholders in the fairtrade football manufacturing value chain facilitate or constrain the implementation of the standard.

The three types of investigation could be: (i) explorative, (ii) qualitative, and (iii) quantitative. In the explorative part, the authors suggest to undertake a detailed literature review for assessing what we know about the field of MSI governance, CSR, and global value chains. The qualitative part should take a bottom-up approach by interviewing workers, suppliers, civil society organizations, international buyers, and standard setting organizations about their understanding of the governance process, through which the fairtrade sports balls standard was formulated, implemented, and monitored. The quantitative part should assess the impact of the sports balls standard through standardized, survey-style interviews with local suppliers and workers.

Data Collection Methods

For such a study, we suggest that it would be useful to follow rigorous data collection methods and coding ethics as suggested by Eisenhardt (1989) and Yin (2013). Data analysis should use software such as NVivo for the development and condensation of codes. Both primary and secondary sources might be helpful for data collection. Major sources for collecting primary data could be based on semi-structured in-depth interviews, a mixture of surveys, and in-depth focus group interviews. The sampling size could be; around 5-6 Fairtrade buyers; Fairtrade International Organization (FLO); all 6 FLO suppliers in Pakistan, (Ali Trading Company (Pvt) Ltd., Anwar Khawaja Industries (Pvt.) Ltd., Leatherware (Pvt.) Ltd., Talon Sports, Tramondi Pakistan, and Vision Technologies Corporation (Pvt) Ltd.; around 5-6 local labor contractors in Pakistan; the civil society organization (such as Baidarie, which is actively working in the Pakistani football industry), local government agencies, and around 100 workers in the Fairtrade production network in Pakistan. With reference to the background of the case for this study; secondary data could be collected from the FLO homepage, annual reports, other written information regarding standards and sustainability reports.

Within this broader research, it is possible to develop a methodology for mapping the links between MSI governance processes and their effects on workers' conditions in the football manufacturing industry through two consecutive steps. These include the analysis of (i) legislative, executive, and judicial governance, and (ii) an initial assessment of the impact of the FLO sports balls standard on workers' conditions within the industry.

Step 1: *Legislative, executive, and judicial governance - How was the fairtrade standard for sports balls formulated, implemented, and monitored in football manufacturing industry in Sialkot, Pakistan?* In terms of legislative governance, interviews could be undertaken with the FLO representatives, local suppliers and workers in Pakistan, a mixture of the intergovernmental, private sector, and civil society stakeholders involved in the formulation of the FLO standard for sports balls, asking them about the key factors leading to the formulation of the FLO standard for sports balls, and what the main challenges in formulating the standard were. In addition, it would be important to probe whether there was any involvement of local suppliers and workers in this process. If affirmed, it could be investigated how they have been involved, what their main interests were in this process, and whether they felt that their concerns were taken into account, and if not, why they were not been involved.

In terms of executive governance, it would be possible to map the fairtrade football value chain, and the inclusion/exclusion of particular suppliers form this chain due to the (non)implementation of the fairtrade standard for sports balls. It would be important to interview the fairtrade suppliers, asking about the challenges they face in this process of implementation, how they work together to establish a fairtrade value chain, and what they perceived as the strengths and weaknesses of the fairtrade standard for sports balls versus conventional football production in Pakistan.

In terms of judicial governance, an assessment could be made of how the FLO monitors compliance with its standard for sports balls, what protective mechanisms exist to ensure the compliance with the standard, and what sanctions exist in the case of non-compliance with the standard. This assessment could focus on understanding how the FLO-Cert (the independent auditing section of the FLO) conducts audits to confirm compliance with the fairtrade standard for sports balls, how it decides to issue the fairtrade certificates, and how it deals with the complaints regarding the implementation of the fairtrade standard for sports balls.

Step 2: *What impact does the fairtrade standard for sports balls have on work conditions in the football manufacturing industry?* In Pakistan, an initial assessment could be made of impact of the fairtrade sports ball standard on conditions of football workers in the industry. A maximum variation case study sampling could be employed. Together with a control group of suppliers and workers connected to conventional football manufacturing industry, these could be intentionally selected to give a sense of the likely range of the work conditions within football factories and stitching centers in the fairtrade football stitching value chain of Sialkot vis-à-vis the control group.

In terms of the economic impact, local suppliers and workers could be asked about any changes observed after the implementation of fairtrade sports ball standard relating to their monthly income, monthly expenditures, possible savings, support for children's schooling, etc. In terms of social conditions, workers could be asked about any changes observed after the implementation of the fairtrade standard for sports balls in areas such as forced labor, eradication of child labor, freedom from discrimination, occupational health and safety, conditions of employment, etc.

Implications for Comparative CSR studies in Other Developing Countries

In the preceding sections, we outlined an analytical framework for studying the interaction between MSI governance processes and their impact on workers' conditions at the base of global value chains. We also introduced a short, stylized methodology for assessing the impact of MSI governance processes using the fairtrade standard for sports balls as a case example. In light of the overall theme of this book, we might then wonder what the implications are of using this particular analytical framework and its associated methodology for studying MSI governance processes and their effects in other developing country contexts?

On the one hand, we believe that the analytical framework can be used to map MSI governance processes and their effects on workers' conditions in other developing country contexts beyond Pakistan. Most MSIs are likely to involve some form of standard formulation, implementation, and compliance monitoring even if the terminology used for describing these processes will differ between MSIs. Similarly, in relation to MSIs that become embedded in other developing country contexts, we would expect similar feedback loops between the legislative, executive, and judicial forms of governance described in our analytical framework. Moreover, it seems reasonable to assume that each of these different types of MSI governance is likely to directly affect workers' conditions at the base of global value chains. Moreover, if impact assessments are conducted of different MSIs in other developing country contexts, we would argue that they are likely to result in refinements of various aspects of legislative, executive, and judicial MSI governance as described in our analytical framework.

On the other hand, there are some aspects related to the particular case of football manufacturing which are context specific to Pakistan. First, at present, there are only six locations in the world that are active as significant sourcing locations for footballs. These include India, Pakistan, China, Thailand, Indonesia, and Vietnam (Fayyaz et al., 2015). Moreover, at present, it is only in Pakistan that we find manufacturers that are certified as fairtrade football producers (FLO, 2016). Hence, in the particular case of Fairtrade football manufacturing, the suggested methodology for assessing the impact of Fairtrade footballs will only be possible to implement in the case of Pakistan. Hence, for other industries and countries where fairtrade standards or other MSIs are being implemented, the exact methodology for assessing the impact of MSI governance processes on workers' conditions will have to be adjusted to the developing country context and the value chain in question.

In short, we suggest that our analytical framework for mapping MSI governance processes and their effects on workers is likely to be helpful for master-level students, Ph.D. students, and practitioners across a range of industries and developing country contexts. However, we would also like to emphasize that students, academics, and practitioners would need to tailor the methodology to take into account the specificities of other MSIs, value chains, and country contexts in the South in order to achieve an appropriate fit between the analytical framework and its associated methodology.

CONCLUSION

In this chapter, an analytical framework was outlined combining two types of analysis: (i) the governance processes through which multi-stakeholder initiatives are formulated, implemented, and monitored; and (ii) the impact that these processes have on the conditions of workers in export-oriented industries in developing countries. Furthermore, a methodology was developed to explain how this theoretical framework could be employed to empirically investigate the effects of MSI governance processes on workers' conditions within a given value chain (the fairtrade football value chain). Finally, we suggested that the analytical framework outlined in this chapter could be used to analyze other MSIs in different developing country contexts whereas the methodology would need to be adapted in order to achieve a suitable fit between the MSI, the value chain, and the country context which is being analyzed.

Analytically, the framework brings together insights from an expanded approach to the analysis of the MSI initiatives in global value chains. This framework links two different strands which have rarely been combined; (i) the governance processes through which MSIs initiatives are formulated, implemented, and monitored; and (ii) the impact that these MSI governance processes have on the conditions of workers in export-oriented industries in developing countries. Empirically, we sought to apply this framework to the context of the fairtrade standards in the football manufacturing industry of Pakistan, and the public, private and NGO actors involved in this MSI. We welcome any feedback from students, policy-makers, and practitioner on our analytical framework and its accompanying methodology.

REFERENCES

Amengual, M. (2010). Complementary labour regulation: The uncoordinated combination of state and private regulators in the Dominican Republic. *World Development*, *38*(3), 405–414. doi:10.1016/j.worlddev.2009.09.007

Bair, J., & Palpacuer, F. (2015). CSR beyond the corporation: Contested governance in global value chains. *Global Networks*, *15*(1), 1–19. doi:10.1111/glob.12085

Barrientos, S. (2002). Mapping codes through the value chain: from researcher to detective. In R. Jenkins, R. Pearson, & G. Seyfang (Eds.), *Corporate Social Responsibility and Labor Rights: Codes of Conduct in the Global Economy* (pp. 113–124). London: Earthscan.

Barrientos, S., Dolan, C., & Tallontire, A. (2003). A gendered value chain approach to codes of conduct in African horticulture. *World Development*, *31*(9), 1511–1526. doi:10.1016/S0305-750X(03)00110-4

Betsill, M. M., & Corell, E. (2008). *NGO diplomacy: The influence of nongovernmental organizations in international environmental negotiations*. MIT Press.

Bolwig, S., Ponte, S., Du Toit, A., Riisgaard, L., & Halberg, N. (2010). Integrating poverty and environmental concerns into value-chain analysis: A conceptual framework. *Development Policy Review*, *28*(2), 173–194. doi:10.1111/j.1467-7679.2010.00480.x

Börzel, T. A., & Risse, T. (2005). Public-Private Partnerships: Effective and legitimate tools of international governance. In E. Grande & L. W. Pauly (Eds.), *Complex Sovereignty: Reconstructing Political Authority in the Twenty First Century* (pp. 195–216). Toronto: University of Toronto Press.

Cheyns, E., & Riisgaard, L. (2014). Introduction to the Symposium. *Agriculture and Human Values*, *31*(3), 409–423. doi:10.1007/s10460-014-9508-4

Coslovsky, S. V. (2014). Flying Under the Radar? The State and the Enforcement of Labor Standards in Brazil. *Oxford Development Studies*, *42*(2), 190–216. doi:10.1080/13600818.2013.875135

Dolan, C., & Opondo, M. (2005). Seeking Common Ground. *Journal of Corporate Citizenship*, *18*(18), 87–98. doi:10.9774/GLEAF.4700.2005.su.000012

Eisenhardt, K. (1989). Building theories from case study research. *Academy of Management Review*, *14*(4), 532–550.

Eisenhardt, K. M., & Graebner, M. A. (2007). Theory Building from Cases: Opportunities and Challenges. *Academy of Management Journal*, *50*(1), 25–32. doi:10.5465/AMJ.2007.24160888

Fairtrade International Organization (FLO). (2009). *Making the Difference: A new global strategy for Fairtrade*. Bonn, Germany.

Fairtrade Labelling Organization (FLO). (2016). Fairtade Customer Search. Retrieved from http://www.flocert.net/fairtrade-services/fairtrade-certification/fairtrade-customer-search/

Fayyaz, A., Lund-Thomsen, P., & Lindgreen, A. (2015). Industrial clusters and CSR in developing countries: the role of international donor funding. *Journal of Business Ethics*.

Gereffi, G. (1994). The organization of buyer-driven global commodity chains: how US retailers shape overseas production networks. In G. Gereffi & M. Korzeniewicz (Eds.), *Commodity Chains and Global Capitalism* (pp. 95–123). CT: Praeger.

Gereffi, G., Humphrey, J., & Sturgeon, T. (2005). The governance of global value chains. *Review of International Political Economy*, *12*(1), 78–104. doi:10.1080/09692290500049805

Gereffi, G., & Lee, J. (2016). Economic and social upgrading in global value chains and industrial clusters: Why governance matters. *Journal of Business Ethics*, *133*(1), 25–38. doi:10.1007/s10551-014-2373-7

Gilbert, D. U., & Rasche, A. (2007). Discourse ethics and social accountability: The ethics of SA 8000. *Business Ethics Quarterly*, *17*(02), 187–216. doi:10.5840/beq200717230

Gilbert, D. U., & Rasche, A. (2008). Opportunities and problems of standardized ethics initiatives: A stakeholder theory perspective. *Journal of Business Ethics*, *82*(3), 755–773. doi:10.1007/s10551-007-9591-1

Jamali, D., Lund-Thomsen, P., & Khara, N. (2015). *CSR institutionalized myths in developing countries: an imminent threat of selective decoupling, Business & Society*. Online First.

Kaplinsky, R., & Morris, M. (2001). *A Handbook for Value Chain Research*. Ottawa: International Development Research Center.

Khan, F. R., & Lund-Thomsen, P. (2011). CSR as imperialism: Towards a phenomenological approach to CSR in the developing world. *Journal of Change Management*, *11*(1), 73–90. doi:10.1080/14697017.2011.548943

Knorringa, P., & Nadvi, K. (2016). Rising power clusters and the challenges of local and global standards. *Journal of Business Ethics*, *133*(1), 55–72. doi:10.1007/s10551-014-2374-6

Locke, R. M., Rissing, B. A., & Pal, T. (2012). Complements or substitutes? Private codes, state regulation, and the enforcement of labor standards in global supply chains. *British Journal of Industrial Relations*, *51*(3), 519–552. doi:10.1111/bjir.12003

Lund-Thomsen, P. (2004). Towards a Critical Framework on Corporate Social and Environmental Responsibility in the South: The Case of Pakistan. *Development*, *47*(3), 106–113. doi:10.1057/palgrave.development.1100059

Lund-Thomsen, P. (2013a). Multi-stakeholder Initiatives in Cotton Value Chains: Towards a Theoretical Framework and a Methodology. In A. Lindgreen, F. Maon, J. Vanhamme, & S. Sen (Eds.), *Sustainable Value Chain Management: A Research Anthology* (pp. 257–270). Farnham: Gower Publishing Ltd.

Lund-Thomsen, P. (2013b). Labor agency in the football manufacturing industry of Sialkot, Pakistan. *Geoforum*, *44*(1), 71–81. doi:10.1016/j.geoforum.2012.04.007

Lund-Thomsen, P., & Lindgreen, A. (2014). Corporate social responsibility in global value chains: Where are we now and where are we going? *Journal of Business Ethics*, *123*(1), 11–22. doi:10.1007/s10551-013-1796-x

Lund-Thomsen, P., & Nadvi, K. (2010). Global value chains, local collective action and corporate social responsibility: A review of empirical evidence. *Business Strategy and the Environment*, *19*(1), 1–13. doi:10.1002/bse.670

Mukherjee-Reed, A., & Reed, D. (2009). Partnerships for development: Four models of business involvement. *Journal of Business Ethics*, *90*(S1), 3–37. doi:10.1007/s10551-008-9913-y

Nadvi, K. (2011). Labour standards and technological upgrading: Competitive challenges in the global football industry. *International Journal of Technological Learning. Innovation and Development*, *4*(1-3), 235–257.

Neilson, J., & Pritchard, B. (2009). Value Chain struggles: Institutions and Governance in the Plantations of South India. Wiley-Blackwell, Gloucester. doi:10.1002/9781444308723

Neilson, J., & Pritchard, B. (2010). Fairness and ethicality in their place—The regional dynamics of fair trade and ethical sourcing agendas in the plantation districts of south India. *Environment & Planning A*, *42*(8), 1833–1851. doi:10.1068/a4260

Piore, M. J., & Schrank, A. (2008). Toward managed flexibility: The revival of labour inspection in the Latin world. *International Labour Review*, *147*(1), 1–23. doi:10.1111/j.1564-913X.2008.00021.x

Posthuma, A., & Bignami, R. (2014). 'Bridging the Gap'? Public and private regulation of labour standards in the apparel value chains in Brazil. *Competition and Change*, *18*(4), 345–364. doi:10.1179/1024529414Z.00000000065

Pyke, F., & Lund-Thomsen, P. (2016). Social upgrading in developing country clusters: A reflection on the literature. *Competition and Change*, *20*(1), 53–68. doi:10.1177/1024529415611265

Rasche, A. (2010). Collaborative Governance 2.0. *Corporate Governance: The International Journal of Business in Society*, *10*(4), 500–511. doi:10.1108/14720701011069713

Rasche, A., & Esser, D. E. (2006). From stakeholder management to stakeholder accountability. *Journal of Business Ethics*, *65*(3), 251–267. doi:10.1007/s10551-005-5355-y

Reed, D. Utting, P., & Reed, A.M. (Eds.), (2013). Business Regulation and Non-state Actors. Whose Actors? Whose Development? London: Routledge.

Rein, L., & Stott, L. (2009). Working together: Critical perspectives on six cross-sector partnerships in Southern Africa. *Journal of Business Ethics*, *90*(3), 79–89. doi:10.1007/s10551-008-9915-9

Riisgaard, L., Bolwig, S., Ponte, S., Du Toit, A., Halberg, N., & Matose, F. (2010). Integrating poverty and environmental concerns into value-chain analysis: A strategic framework and practical guide. *Development Policy Review*, *28*(2), 195–216. doi:10.1111/j.1467-7679.2010.00481.x

Ronit, K. (2012). Global Strategies and Policy Arrangements: Institutional Drivers for Innovation in the Wind Turbine Industry. In Innovation Policy and Governance in High-Tech Industries (pp. 201-217). Berlin Heidelberg: Springer.

Rosenau, J. N. (1995). Governance in the twenty-first century. *Global Governance*, 1995, 13–43.

Scherer, A. G., Palazzo, G., & Matten, D. (2014). The business firm as a political actor a new theory of the firm for a globalized world. *Business & Society*, *53*(2), 143–156. doi:10.1177/0007650313511778

Tallontire, A. (2007). CSR and regulation: Towards a framework for understanding private standards initiatives in the agri-food chain. *Third World Quarterly*, *28*(4), 775–791. doi:10.1080/01436590701336648

The Trade Development Authority of Pakistan. (2015). Statistics. Retrieved from http://tdap.gov.pk

Utting, P. (2015). Corporate accountability, fair trade, and multi-stakeholder regulation. In L. Raynolds & E. A. Bennett (Eds.), *Handbook of Research on Fair Trade*. Cheltenham, UK: Edwar Elgar. doi:10.4337/9781783474622.00013

Yin, R. K. (2013). *Case Study Research: Design and methods*. London: Sage publications.

ENDNOTES

1. Corporate social responsibility is here defined as companies integrating economic, social, and environmental concerns into their core business processes (Lund-Thomsen, 2004).
2. According to Knorringa and Nadvi (2016, p. 59), a lot depends on the 'social contract' between the public sector, the private sector, and civil society organizations in any given society. The social contract includes "the formal and informal institutional arrangements, rules and norms in a society, and refers among others to historically and culturally shaped expectations concerning (minimally) acceptable social and environmental behaviour by various actors". In the case of India for example, the social contract appears not to be geared towards encouraging small and medium-sized firms (SMEs) to comply with labor standards as the state prioritizes economic development over social and environmental protection policies (Pyke and Lund-Thomsen, 2016). In contrast, the enforcement of labor legislation amongst SMEs in Brazil seems to be more widespread with recent studies pointing towards innovative forms of public and private regulation interacting, sometimes in unintentional ways, to raise the bar regarding labor standards enforcement in the country (Coslovsky, 2014, Posthuma and Bignami, 2014). At the same time, Knorringa and Nadvi (2016) argue that China may illustrate an intermediate situation where national and local governments compete to

attract investments and jobs in ways that do not permit them to completely ignore labor standards enforcement as is sometimes the case in India, but where actual enforcement is seen to be more negotiable than in Brazil.

3 A possible exception may be Lund-Thomsen (2013) who also sought to develop an analytical framework and a practical methodology for the study of MSIs and their impacts at the base of global value chains in developing countries. However, Lund-Thomsen mainly did this on the context of sustainable cotton production and had a broader concern with the impact of MSIs on farmer incomes, environmental pollution levels at cotton farms, on the conditions of on-farm workers.

4 See Jamali et al. (2015) for a consideration of how such processes play out in the Indian football manufacturing industry where an MSI has also been implemented.

Chapter 13
CSR in China
The Road to New Sustainable Business Models

Ruth Wolf
Bar-Ilan University, Israel

Monica Thiel
Guangdong University of Foreign Studies, China

ABSTRACT

This chapter presents challenges in China's governance outlook within a Corporate Social Responsibility (CSR) analysis of China's social, environmental and economic resources and potential impacts in other countries. The purpose of this article sheds light of how CSR in China is emerging as a doorway to a) promote understanding of changes in firm governance for general managers through state and corporate socially responsible practices and b) to explain that preserving the environment and preventing pollution is necessary if China would like to trade with the West and enter global markets with other countries that place importance of governance and CSR principles.

INTRODUCTION

Governments worldwide are steering Corporate Social Responsibility (CSR) nationally and globally through varying roles in public-private collaborations and in sustainability programs (Dentchev et al., 2015). Likewise, other countries within the continent of Africa are also seeking the value of CSR into their national and business strategies, and often focus on corruption and governance issues and concerns (Kolk & Tulder, 2010). India has known the value of social responsibility from the Vedic periods to CSR practices within Indian corporations today, with an emphasis in cultural and religious traditions such as *dharma* as a *moral and economic driver of CSR in India* (Dhanesh, 2015). However, values, ethics, regulations, and broad variance of CSR constructs across countries may contradict current CSR strategies and practices in each country, thereby increasing tension and widening gaps in CSR globally. Moreover, some local acts, and regulations in local areas of emerging and developing countries often

DOI: 10.4018/978-1-5225-0720-8.ch013

lack adequate regulatory capacity and NGO engagement, despite sufficient labor and environmental laws (Jamali, Lund-Thomsen & Jeppesen, 2015). Although CSR practices are growing in emerging economies, there is less specific information about sociocultural practices and traditions that could drive CSR (Dhanesh, 2015), China can play a key role in how governments can shape CSR business models within emerging and developing countries.

This chapter will focus on the development of CSR in China among government departments, large and small firms with a strong focus on the political role in CSR (Scherer & Palazzo, 2011) and instrumental and ethical theories of CSR (Garriga & Mele, 2004) between public and private sectors in China and worldwide. The chapter will shed light about how CSR in China is emerging as a doorway to promote understanding of changes in firm governance for general managers through state and corporate socially responsible practices and behavior by decreasing poor corporate and state governance, and to demonstrate that preserving the environment and preventing pollution is necessary if China would like to trade with the West and enter global markets with other countries that place importance of governance and CSR principles.

BACKGROUND

Although CSR initiatives and strategies are fairly new in China and could be considered to be in the infancy stage (Chi, 2011), the Chinese government has embraced CSR as a tool to help address social and environmental issues resulting from a turbulent economic transition. For example, many Chinese companies have joined the United Nations Global Compact, a global public policy network to promote ten universal principles in the areas of human rights, labor standards, environmental protection, and anti-corruption. China's vast local networks in the United Nations Global Compact address global governance issues and gaps with other member countries worldwide. The Chinese economy is profoundly influenced by the state. Similar to China, the Government of Kerala in India is promoting CSR and sustainable development. Oommen Chandy, Chief Minister of the Kerala Government proposed greater understanding between the centers of the states will strengthen the confidence of the people (World Economic Forum, 2011). Further to this, a statement from the Minister of State in New Delhi describes sustainable development as having different meanings for different contexts. For instance, while developed countries are grappling with lifestyle sustainability, the developing countries are tackling issues of livelihood sustainability (INDIA CSR News Network, 2012). Thus, could strong traditional societal practices of social and environmental protection in developing countries become a driver of CSR for weak states? Giving rights to the states to enhance environmental policies is crucial to sustainable development. Although Indian States have had very little power to implement environmental policies, decentralization from the Central Government has proven successful for industrial policies in Kerala while prohibiting sustainable environmental policies. Therefore, government endorsement of CSR performance standards, ratings, and indexes is a primary factor in determining competitive advantage (National Chamber Foundation, Asia-United States Chamber of Commerce, 2012). Responsible conduct requires every general manager, organization and company to have a system of rules and regulations in order to maintain the responsibilities of companies and enterprises to protect the environment. Generally, most companies seek to become the most responsible company to increase and sustain profits and to drive local, regional, and national operations for competitive and comparative advantage. Furthermore, the Chinese government does not directly control general management, but has strong oversight of a firm's operations. Therefore, the Chinese government plays an integral role in a Chinese firm's capacity to sustain growth.

Today, wide-reaching agreement exists regarding the social responsibility of corporations and enterprises to protect the natural environment and guard it as "public property" resources such as air, earth, water and other natural resources in society's domain. For example, Chinese citizens are demanding responsible corporate practices. At the same time, Chinese business leaders and managers are embracing CSR to compete and meet international standards of responsibility as part of their global business strategies in global markets (National Chamber Foundation, Asia-United States Chamber of Commerce, 2012). The 2008 economic crisis challenged political and regulatory CSR theories moving broadly between "underlying changes in political and economic theory" (Kemper & Martin, 2010, p. 236). Furthermore, 2008 economic crisis opened the door to increasing state control, new CSR strategies, stronger stakeholder management, business and societal impacts, and doing well by doing good (Kemper & Martin, 2010). Consequently, this chapter examines how China can become a world leader in CSR through changes in firm governance and environmental protection.

China produces and exports significant amounts of products globally, resulting in approximately 50 percent of all products in demand worldwide (Bongiorni, 2007). It is an emerging nation with significant economic advancement. However, the lack of laws and regulations to prevent and decrease pollution is a deterrent to China's economic success. China's weakness in CSR stems from inadequate responsibility for environmental and social resources. The country is continually developing reforms for business and environmental strategies (Haley, U.C. & Haley G.T., 2013). Nevertheless, a more embedded and comparative CSR approach from general management and business leaders is vital for China to succeed as a nation capable of successful business and economic trade and to manage conduct globally.

The Western press continually reports about China's severe transgressions in the field of environmental preservation. The exposure of corruption in Chinese manufacturing and design provides additional difficult details about the exploitation of air pollution, water pollution and other natural resources in China that often occur in the name of necessary economic development, tarnishing China's reputation and entry into the circle of emerging and developing countries in the world. Providing social stability, decreasing corruption, and protecting social and environmental resources is a primary and continuing strategy of China and for all countries. (Darigan & Post, 2009; Wolf, 2010, 2015). Similar to many developing and emerging global economies, there are changes in consumer, corporate, and government governance and behavior. Western standards of excellence can provide emerging countries such as China guidance for improving corporate citizenship (Darigan & Post, 2009). Nevertheless, changes in Chinese firm governance require Chinese standards of excellence. Likewise, other emerging and developing countries will require evaluating national, regional and local social responsibility standards of excellence.

It seems, therefore, that Chinese CSR is essential not only to the Chinese, but to wide-scale populations throughout the world as China continues to expand Chinese business operations globally. China's social, environmental and economic resources and its capacity and potential to lead to changes in firm governance will play a role in how advanced, emerging, and developing countries practice and reciprocate CSR. *Consequently, this will require China to implement and manage CSR within multiple levels because it is shaped collectively by country-level, industry-level and firm-level factors* (Lattemann, et al., 2009, p. 438). Chinese and non-Chinese general management with operations in China will be scrutinized by other countries for their social, economic and environmental performance, and to demonstrate that business leaders and management in China are responding and engaging in China's national CSR priorities.

These include green growth, livelihood improvement, outward development into the West, and a general integration of Chinese businesses into global markets. At the same time, as China's influence in international markets and on the global policy stage increases, active engagement in CSR offers an opportunity to influence one of the most powerful forces shaping the landscape for global business and sustainable development (National Chamber Foundation, Asia-United States Chamber of Commerce, 2012, p. 6).

CSR IN CHINA

CSR in China has become a national strategy for social, environmental and economic development in multiple ownership enterprises and in state-owned firms to improve and strengthen CSR in China and worldwide (Chinese Academy of Social Sciences (CASS) Blue Book on Corporate Responsibility, 2013). China is in a unique position to become a global CSR world leader in the 21st Century. This has implications not only on for the diverse concept of CSR, but also for other countries and general management approaches and strategies of CSR to advance national, global, and firm competitive and comparative advantage. Many Chinese scholars employ different origins of CSR in China, and share a similar general shareholder and stakeholder theory of CSR with the West (Zhang & Liang, 2013). It is interesting to note that Chinese scholars share a consensus of CSR as responsibility, but disagree whether it is a moral or legal theory (Zhang-Liang, 2013). Despite the use and wording of 'Corporate' in CSR, the government plays a strong role in supporting and sustaining social, economic and environmental CSR strategies in companies (Thiel, 2010; Moon & Vogel, 2008; Aguilera et al., 2007, Barnett, 2007; Waldman, et. al., 2006; Moon, 2004). Thus, CSR requires government enforcement and intervention (Thiel, 2010). However, many corporations are playing the role of government (Scherer & Palazzo, 2011) due to inadequate and weak governmental agencies (Margolis & Walsh, 2003). Gaps in social, economic, and environmental performance of government agencies combined with diverse global legal frameworks provide opportunities for corporations to meet increasing needs and demands from stakeholders. Furthermore, as Chinese companies are increasingly entering global markets, Chinese CSR frameworks will require greater social, environmental and economic governance reforms for sustainable global competitiveness.

In China, it is clear that the government plays a primary role. Adding to the complexity of broad and varying CSR theories and practices for business and state management is differing CSR strategies from firms. Some global companies educate stakeholders for improving and increasing socially responsible behavior, while other companies' foster voluntary social responsibility from stakeholders. Hung, et. al, (2013) found

Contrary to common criticism that mandatory CSR disclosure lacks credibility and is simply window dressing in emerging markets such as China. Mandatory CSR disclosure reduces the information disadvantages of investors that are less informed about firms' CSR activities by helping these investors assess firms' political or social risk and by increasing analyst following (p.85).

Who can adequately govern CSR among government, business and civil society relationships? The government is increasingly looking to business for help in addressing these challenges. Therefore, CSR is a tool for social and environmental protection that speaks to a company's needs of gaining political recognition and to mobilize state support (Zhao, 2012).

MAIN FOCUS OF THE CHAPTER

China as a Global Power

Today, China negotiates economically with many countries in the world. The distinguishing factor in China's development of ties with the West is related to several events. First, the visit of United States President Nixon in 1972 in Shanghai, second, the subsequent renewal of ties with the Communist regime, and third, Shanghai's declaration in February 1972, which led to improved relations between the China and the United States.

With the death of Mao Zedong in 1976, China developed a wider opening to the West and, starting in 1978, tried to advance commercial ties on a basis similar to *Laissez-Faire*. It should be noted that the move from a planned economy to a market economy brought with it many reforms in China. The reforms were put in place gradually and led to China's introduction to the West. While the Chinese government has previously taken measures to implement reforms in the ecological arena, they were insufficient due to increasing pollution and environmental damage and detriments of public health and safety. Moreover, China still does not meet CSR standards in the global economy, as demonstrated by the many news articles regarding the defective manner in which China produces and supplies its products, which are flooding the market (Wolf, 2010; 2011; Johnston & Hao, 1995; Leavy et al., 2008; Birkin et al., 2009). Indeed, scholars emphasize that corruption in Chinese organizations within the ecological and social dimensions are frequent, and there is no doubt that this will lead to significant damage to the Chinese economy in the future.

It is worth mentioning that according to data provided by the Chinese Office of Trade, China's annual growth was approximately 10% for 20 years (until 2008) (GDP). Today, China is a very powerful country and its power is recognized throughout the world. Nevertheless, there is a great deal of criticism about the country's ethical conduct in the field of environmental preservation. It seems that China permits pollution in the country's natural treasures to foster economic development and agricultural strengthening, endangering not only its territory and inhabitants, but the entire world as well.

Factors and Reasons for the Existence of Transgressions in the Field of Ecology in Chinese Factories and Firms

As for the reason why CSR is not well established in China as in the West, it should be noted that the management structure of organizations and companies in the East is different from management structures in the West. This determines the nature of general management and its perception of ethics. For example, western general management utilizes division of roles, including a chairman and a CEO who usually manage the project alongside independent directors. However, Asian companies in the East are often found in which there is ownership with limited partnership, occasionally family partnership, and a small group of independent directors at its side (Wolf, 2010).

The familial nature of Asian companies demands a different approach for general management in which there is not always a clear ethical critique. In practice, there is continuous mutual cover-up and bailing out of one another, which sometimes enables people to shut their eyes to the severe ecological transgressions taking place in family-owned factories and their assembly lines. In those firms, there is no significant critique between managers and senior rankings are managed like a pyramid. It was found that, in general, there is a dominant and leading member of the family who pulls the strings and the others generally listen to and obey him. Of course, even familial interests require economic processes and it is not always possible to establish ethical insights and customs concerning environmental preservation within this management structure in the same way that organizations and enterprises do (Wolf, 2010).

China is a relation-based society in comparison to rule-based societies in Western Europe and North America. *When a rule-based MNC sets up operations in a relation-based country, it may be difficult for it to uphold its CSR standards in the host country due to the macro institutional environment that does not favor or facilitate a high level of CSR practices* (Lattemann, et al., 2009, p. 437). For these reasons, general management should create partnerships with the Chinese government to avoid spillovers of perceived irresponsible conduct and decreasing reputation management among managers and business leaders. "Thus the impact of these connections on issuing CSR reports may be particularly important for privately controlled firms, as responding to policy signals may be one of the few ways they can show their commitment to government initiatives" (Marquis & Qian, 2014, p. 132).

In these relation-based management structures, preferential treatment and preservation of family interests are important principles that may also draw from Confucianism, which emphasizes the added value of relationships with others, especially the value of family (Wolf, 2010.) It seems that such a familial structure is concerned with preventing outsiders from criticizing the firms, and that in many instances there is an incentive to utilize the company's resources for the sake of the controlling family so that outsiders will not be involved in the company and will not attempt to assert control over it. Furthermore, in order to raise the bar of CSR reporting standards, it is crucial for general management in firms and government leaders to acknowledge and understand how governance is associated with culture (Bae, et. al., 2012), thereby requiring organizational, local, regional and national cultural contexts into the role of corporate and state governance in CSR.

Likewise, it should be noted that some manufacturers still have not internalized the idea of personal responsibility on the part of a general manager or enterprise owner for all of the processes that take place under her or his supervision. This concept of responsibility is well expressed in the American 'Sarbanes-Oxley Act' (2002), which emphasizes the manager's personal responsibility over everything that happens in his factory. Therefore, it becomes clear that proper teaching of this economic outlook can foster optimal responsible behavior. Sometimes, there is environmental pollution caused by assembly lines in small factories or family run factories that demand profits at any cost, proving that China has not yet met standards for enforcement of laws and norms. It is clear that this is not only due to a lack of legislation, but also to a lack of proper law enforcement among the broad manufacturing population, especially small manufacturers.

The Phenomenon of Pollution in China

China's behavior in the preservation of nature is very problematic. The Western media often report about air and water pollution in China (Business Insider, 2014). Recently, China and the United States agreed to limit greenhouse gases. According to a United States Newspaper:

"China's announcement is the culmination of years of change in attitudes among Chinese now fed up with dire levels of pollution that a study in the British medical journal the Lancet blamed for 1.2 million premature deaths in 2010 alone. China has cap-and-trade pilot programs in five provinces and eight cities. It is also the world's largest investor in solar and wind energy". However, "China completes a new coal plant every eight to 10 days, and while its economic growth has slowed, it is still expanding at a brisk rate of over 7 percent" (The Washington Post, November 12, 2014).

It is clear that a competitive economy should also consider different constraints, such as those related to preserving a green environment. China, in its race for technological and industrial development, often disregard preservation of the environment and endanger its inhabitants. In addition, the Chinese government does not pay attention to ecological problems. Such behavior is reminiscent in the following Chinese proverb: *Xing xing zhi hur ke yi liar yuan* (A spark can start a fire that burns the entire prairie). Consequently, some of China's growth and development has been achieved at the expense of its natural resource base as described in the following examples:

- Increasing and widespread degradation of grasslands; a high ratio of actual to potential desertified land, and significant water erosion problems worldwide.
- Declining forests and ecosystems for over 50 years, despite efforts to reverse rapid deforestation.
- Continual substantial stress on biodiversity, despite the establishment of a national system of nature reserves.
- Decreasing water availability and quality, especially in the rivers north of the Yangtze that require technical progress and improvements in institutional, administrative and regulatory arrangements.

Western newspapers, such as The Telegraph, refer to China's air and water pollution problem due to rapid economic development (October 2, 2009). China's accelerated economic development brings with it wealth and economic prosperity. There are those who wish to achieve this wealth at any cost, raising the question of how it is possible to help Chinese workers achieve integrity, social responsibility, social decency and behavior. Kohlberg referred to this behavior as the highest level of moral judgment. The following excerpt appeared in a New York Times article about the danger of pollution in China.

Foreign workers in Beijing are also becoming much less willing to tolerate the toxic air. That was reflected in an annual survey released on March 19 by the American Chamber of Commerce in China. Almost half of the 365 companies in the survey, most of them in the Beijing area, said they had problems recruiting or retaining senior executives because of the poor air. That figure was only 19 percent in the chamber's 2008 survey.

As a result, some companies are now offering bonuses or higher salaries to fill openings in China, which foreign workers are calling pollution pay — and a few are even announcing the policy publicly, as Panasonic, the electronics maker, did in mid-March.

On Tuesday, the World Health Organization announced that air pollution, both indoors and outdoors, contributed to seven million deaths worldwide in 2012. More than one-third of those occurred in fast-developing nations in Asia, including China and India. In both those countries, nearly the entire population is exposed to fine particles in the air known as PM 2.5, which can penetrate deep into the lungs and enter the bloodstream, researchers reported on Wednesday in an article posted on Scientific American's website. They wrote that a recent global environmental index showed that China and India ranked worst in terms of populations affected by poor air (New York Times, 2014).

The passion for profit and the desire to become rich that are emphasized in China, are sources of immorality that open the door to economic violations. Sometimes, it permits environmental damage for the sake of economic profit. There is no doubt that the situation is not only connected to problematic manufacturing, but also to the rampant corruption amongst the officials that do not enforce laws related to nature preservation. The recent ecological scandals in China and their exposure in the global press has caused the Chinese government to deal more severely with economic-related corruption within the ecological realm and the demand for preserving natural resources, such as air, water, and land. The recent media storms forced the Chinese government to deal more seriously with law enforcement and to prevent criminal offenses that can endanger the Chinese economy and reputation. Clearly, new business models are urgently needed in China (Birkin, et al., 2007). Furthermore, public policy processes require governmental agencies to develop CSR frameworks within local, regional and national policy priorities (The World Bank, 2002).

Justifying Responsible Nature Preservation

Desjardins (1999) recommends that the moral imperatives about the preservation of nature and ecology be applied from the point of view that natural resources should not only be used out of concern for man himself because natural resources are liable to dwindle and disappear. As a result, there is a need to take care of others in order for everyone to benefit from nature. For example, carmakers should be advised to think about future generations, which will be harmed by continued environmental damage from fuel. Therefore, it is worthwhile for them to consider using solar energy for cars instead of fuel.

In order to engage in forward thinking, it is important to work diligently on product development and on developing an economic vision that takes into account what is good for everyone in the present and in the future. This approach calls for considering the benefits for man, both immediate and long-term (future generations). Sen (2002) also claims that there are "public goods", which are not private or exclusive, and that are used by everyone, such as the air we breathe, land, water and so forth. The preservation of these goods is important because they refer to common betterment and not personal profit. For example, the preservation of the natural environment can prevent disease. In other words, people should not always be motivated by personal interest. People should pay attention not only to the safeguarding of his or her own interests, but also to *establishing a need for the use of non-profit values. Particularly social concerns in private decisions* (Sen, 2002, p. 249).

According to Sen (2002), a person needs to take into account not only the decisions regarding personal profit in business, but the values that are unrelated to profit as well. Sen (2002) emphasizes that people need to move from a win-lose situation to a win-win situation. In other words, management should not strive towards profit for the company or organization at the expense of others. Rather, management should strive towards gains for everyone. Both the individual and the organization need to take into account the existence of the interest of others. This does not refer to the capitalistic exploitation of others, but rather to moral behavior that brings about betterment for everyone.

Sen (2002) proposes the economic world needs to be motivated by ethical laws and norms on the global level, and should not deal solely with the interests of profit maximization. Profit does not always indicate betterment. For instance, a factory that pumps industrial waste and pollutes the ground water does not bring about benefit in the end. Rather, it causes great damage to the environment and by the time this damage is realized, it is likely to be irreversible.

Preserving the Environment in the Framework of CSR Activities in the West

The change that companies and general management undergo today in order to contribute to the community and the environment is also connected to the change in perception of green ecology. Just as the idea of preserving a clean environment from the outset has been espoused by many companies around the world, so has the concept of contributing to the community. For instance, the company, General Electric, went from polluting the Hudson River in New York to serving as a leader of the electric car industry when it purchased tens of thousands of cars that do not emit smoke. Companies today discuss "doing good", the need to reduce costs, and the strategy that takes the Earth into account. Protecting the environment has therefore, become a value which general managers and companies have to present an opinion. Furthermore, companies must strategically manage and influence beyond doing good to gaining political legitimacy with the Chinese State and other Chinese institutions to "investigate the political contextualization and the political outcome of CSR activities as mechanisms of CSR–performance relationship, particularly in transitional economies" (Zhao, 2012, p. 457). Moreover, developing and emerging Asian countries can benefit from Buddhist economics because it has the potential to provide Asian managers a moral and relational Asian framework between society and business to promote higher governance principles beyond compliance for preserving the environment and public benefits (Abeysuriya, Mitchell & White, 2006). Overall, many companies include protection of the natural environment in the framework of CSR as well.

Chinese, and Western Relations in CSR

In China there is a widespread difficulty in perceptions of CSR toward the community and environment, which is more common in the West, but not in the East. Watsi (2003) highlights the importance of organizations' and companies' contribution to the community. And, indeed, the article by Shafer, Fukukawa & Lee (2006) emphasizes the idea of social responsibility and the development of community assistance in the United States and China. The above-mentioned authors note that Chinese society views CSR differently in how CSR is practiced and defined. Do the differences in CSR limit or enhance CSR in organizations nationally and globally? In China, a more conservative society, personal ties are cultivated and invested in while responsibility to society at large is diminished. In contrast, the idea of social responsibility in the United States was developed along with general economic factors. This situation leads to a lack of sufficient financial resources and attention even in the framework of CSR, in contrast to those found in companies and organizations in the West that contribute to the preservation of the environment and the prevention of pollution. Although a large proportion of India's population resides in rural areas, CSR in an India context has strong roots in corporate philanthropy, public-private partnerships, and in preserving the natural environment (Shah, 2012). Further to this, many family-owned companies and *Public Sector Units (PSUs) provide social welfare to the local communities and society at large* (Shah, 2012, p.57).

It is important to note that there are several ways to help the community. Assistance can be provided through housing, education, training and so on. There is no doubt that less established companies can also take on a donor approach. Contributions do not necessarily have to be expressed with money. For instance, the United States fast-food restaurant chain, McDonalds promoted the idea of a green and natural environment. It is among the largest companies that purchases agricultural produce in the United States and in the world. McDonalds set a number of requirements for its suppliers regarding growing produce under conditions that will not harm animals and the soil. In effect, this company garnered a lot of sympathy by setting these rules, which serve as a guiding principle for Chinese and non-Chinese companies operating in China. McDonalds acts with principles and values of giving, which are not related to finance that serve as an example for other firms as well.

It is crucial that the subject of corporate responsibility becomes an integral part of general management and firms' shared activities. It is preferable for companies to appoint a reliable manager to this issue, and for a company's business activities to be examined through this prism. It should be noted that reports regarding corporate responsibility in many countries, including China are still not compulsory, and companies sometimes publicize these activities only at their own initiative. It is preferable for countries to introduce a requirement to report on corporate responsibility as an essential and integral part of public companies' financial reports. The information should be made available to the public and revealed to the media. Perhaps in this way, companies will be of greater benefit to the environment and the community, as well as to the firm, which will win public sympathy.

Solutions for Fighting the Widespread Pollution in China

Indeed, China's government is making an effort to reduce energy and improve the situation of pollution in the country. The question is whether or not these efforts are sufficient. It is important to note that in his annual speech in Parliament in March 2011, China's Premier, Wen Jiabao, referred to the goals that China placed for itself in the field of ecology and environmental preservation. The goals include reduction of carbon emissions and the reduction of pollutant emissions. It should be noted that China's carbon emissions are one of the largest in the world and increased by 32.5% between 2006-2009 (The Marker, March 8, 2011).

Nevertheless, Chinese companies are supposed to tailor themselves to the values of global companies. For instance, today there are expectations of them in terms of social responsibility and social involvement. In fact, a company's reputation today is also tied to activities related to preserving the earth, which are not sufficiently developed in Chinese companies as compared to those in the West. It should be noted that the phenomenon of China's economic growth demands its increased use of energy. However, in light of the nuclear tragedy in Japan, China must reduce its energy pollution. Indeed the magazine, The Telegraph, reported on the efforts made by the Chinese government to reduce energy:

The Government announced in the 11th Five Year Economic Plan (2005-2010) that in order to make progress on this issue, China is committing itself to increase energy conservation through the application of more efficient use of power in industrial ad economic processes. Its aim is to secure a 20% reduction in energy consumption by these efficiency savings alone. Given the scale of China's energy appetite, this will not mean feat and represents a very serious and very ambitious policy objective for the government to achieve (Telegraph, 2009).

Accounting work and economic analysis are connected to the task of preventing pollution through an examination of different expenses. These include expenses that result from mishaps in the work, not only of accountants, but also of general managers in the organization or enterprise who are not always strict about following environmental regulations and laws. However, the emphasis for accountants, economists, and general managers requires understanding economic ethics, and understanding that economic principles, both personal and rational may contradict one another, but continue to exist together. On the one hand, there is a demand for immediate economic growth and even short-term growth, and on the other hand, there is both short and long-term damage to the environment. Therefore, this association emphasizes that the correct ethical position is to attempt to mediate between these two principles, which demands the responsibility of economists and general management. Thus, the association between ecology and the economic spheres raises questions. What is the limit of the responsibility of enterprises and companies that cause environmental damage? What is the magnitude of the damage? How can it be evaluated? In addition, can norms and principles to preserve the quality of the environment be enforced with respect to limited and valuable natural resources?

Chen and Fang (2000) found that higher education and international commerce contribute greatly to economic development in China. There is no doubt that this development can expand if ethical studies about a green environment are incorporated into higher education in China. Such lessons should be delivered within group classes, universities, and technical colleges that teach subjects in economics and finance (accounting, economics, business administration, etc.). Instruction should be directed toward manufacturers, craftsmen, the common manufacturing worker, the consumer citizen, and the general managers for product distribution. Indeed, ethical instruction has already existed for a decade in Chinese universities and colleges that train students in management and engineering, but this is not enough. Today's focus should be education for the small manufacturers and the general population, and should cover the prevention of pollution as well as economics and a wide range of professional positions. Moreover, similar to many countries, CSR principles and activities require strict enforcement and credible tools for strengthening and improving performance. For these reasons, moving China to a global world leader in CSR principles of governance necessitates governance components and success criteria for successful initiation of a sustainability governance framework, which include sustainability vision, sustainability targets, governance principles, sustainability actions, sustainable impacts, and organization (Smith & Wiek, 2012). Furthermore, specific governance principles to generate new sustainable business models with collaboration among governments, business and society require *social learning, integrative, consensual decision making, adaptive capacity, openness to creativity and innovation, and accountability and transparency*. (Smith & Wiek, 2012, pp. 433-434). Likewise, a linear sustainability phase model by Benn, Dunphy and Griffiths (2014) offers some guidance for general management to move an organization from rejection, non-response, compliance, efficiency, proactivity to sustainability, and to new sustainable business models revealing actions for increasing governance, social and environmental practices among countries worldwide.

It seems to the authors that such guidelines regarding ecological preservation and implementation of moral training are possible and can be implemented as long as education is emphasized. As Tony Blair stated in his speech at the Labor Party conference on October 1, 1996 stated, *Ask me my three main priorities for government, and I tell you: education, education and education.* It is clear that China is unable to fight pollution. Indeed, newspapers have reported on China's obstacles to pollution reduction.

So what is the solution? One possibility is to shut down all the sources of pollution. But this would create more problems such as unemployment at home and economic crisis around the world. Development clearly has to continue but it has to be sustainable, and investment in environmental infrastructure is an essential part of this (Telegraph, 2009).

This excerpt testifies to the fact that preservation of the environment and ecology must be done simultaneous within economic growth. It is impossible to halt economic advancement, but solutions must be found to prevent subsequent pollution at any price. Economists are supposed to apply their knowledge to computing financial reports of costs related to environmental protection and public health, and not just to computing economic gains. Nevertheless, sometimes cost and profit analysis of organizations and enterprises overshadow the calculations that deal with concern for environmental quality. This association emphasizes that the personal economic model generally considers a person's happiness. Rational decision-making also entails taking into account considerations regarding environmental quality. It is clear that economic profitability sometimes clashes with environmental quality principles.

DISCUSSION

The Chinese government should slowly adopt international standards of CSR for learning and constructing China's CSR framework (National Chamber Foundation, Asia-United States Chamber of Commerce, 2012). Consequently, China should create its own CSR practices for Chinese society and share international and comparative CSR practices with the West in global markets for trade. There are gaps among the social, economic and environmental dimensions that promote uncertainty of the practical application of CSR in general management CSR decisions. Nevertheless, "Despite an obviously low starting point and its current inadequacies we see gradual increases in CSR by China Top 100 Firms CSR Indices through recent years, improvement on CSR reporting and environmental information disclosure, and more and more enterprises beginning to practice CSR" (Zhang & Liang, 2013, p. 250). Therefore, CSR reporting would help general management and large and small firms to identify the politically contextualized strategy of managing the business and government relationship through comparative CSR practices (Zhao, 2012). Moving towards a stronger and sustainable platform of CSR as a national priority in China requires increasing public participation and an evaluation and supervision system of information disclosure (Sun, 2008), for the mobilization of resources within and across agencies, for the exchange of experiences and best practices among Environmental Protection Boards (EPBs), for strengthening the legal status (also vis-à-vis other regulations) of environmental information disclosure, and for the enforcement of polluting firms (Mol, et al., 2011).

Comparative CSR provides general management and government oversight and monitoring in CSR that could result in higher rates of implementation of labor provisions (Dobbin et al., 2009), environmental self-regulation (Short & Toffel, 2010), and corporate governance codes that are easier to monitor (Okhmatovskiy & David, 2012; Marquis & Qian, 2014). However, firms *may evolve hybridized responses entailing compliance or conformity with some aspects of CSR, and buffering or avoidance in relation to others. This hybridized response model may help account for how institutional decoupling is often sustained in the developing world, although it carries with it risk of detection, shaming, or the loss of legitimacy* (Jamali, et al., 2015, p. 24).

Similar to China, the government in India plays a key role on how CSR is governed by multiple stakeholders. However, the United States and other Western countries implement CSR in differing economic, social, cultural and environmental contexts. As a result, global government oversight should encompass a holistic evaluation framework describing CSR in emerging and developed countries contexts for *mandating, facilitating, partnering, endorsing and enforcing* (Atale & Helge, 2014, p. 80). Although State governance in China plays a critical role in shaping ethical and corporate socially responsible behavior in Chinese business and government, China requires greater understanding of global comparative CSR practices to better address international CSR gaps and practices. Clearly, new global and national sustainable business models are inadequate without political support from China and other countries. Furthermore, effective sustainable business models will require a strong understanding of the social domain to adequately gauge governance levels (Thiel, 2015). Therefore, changes in Chinese firm governance is politically contextual and interdependent within harmonious relationships among business leaders, government, and civil society, and require greater understanding of comparative CSR to effectively decrease CSR gaps worldwide.

According to the OECD, China is expected to lead above the EU and United States in science and technology spending by 2019 (OECD, November 12, 2014), paving the way for China to reduce pollution and potentially become a global world leader in CSR. New sustainable business models require consistency, traceability, and strategies of internal and external firm implementations beyond governance within a legal structure, and require broad understanding of CSR contexts for China to influence CSR globally. This chapter demonstrates that the Chinese government plays an integral role in a Chinese firm's capacity to sustain growth. As the world's second largest economy, China's role and impact in CSR is significant. Similar to the US, China must evaluate differing institutional contexts and emerging business models globally to sustain global trade in markets and non-markets. Future comparative research on CSR should examine national, regional, and local contexts with an emphasis on social and environmental protection within the development strategies of the One Belt and One Road national initiative and Pilot Free Trade zones in Guangdong, Fujian, Shanghai, and Tianjin provinces.

In conclusion, firms can create, deliver and capture value for the company and the state that will lead to a continual value chain embedded within Chinese society, and create behavioral spillovers into other countries with Chinese business operations. Although CSR is more prominent in the West, Chinese business leaders and general management should study comparative CSR practices for global market share and competitiveness while simultaneously developing a Chinese brand of CSR for new sustainable business governance models in China and worldwide.

REFERENCES

Abeysuriya, K., Mitchell, C., & White, S. (2006). Can corporate social responsibility resolve the sanitation question in developing countries? *Ecological Economics*, *62*(1), 174–181. doi:10.1016/j.ecolecon.2006.06.003

Aguilera, R. V., Rupp, D. E., Williams, C. A., & Ganapathi, J. (2007). Putting the S back in corporate social responsibility: A multilevel theory of social change in organizations. *Academy of Management Review*, *32*(3), 836–863. doi:10.5465/AMR.2007.25275678

Atale, N., & Helge, E. J. (2014). Proposed Framework for Government of India to Effectively Monitor Mandatory CSR Initiatives of Public Sector Enterprises in India. *Journal of Human Values*, *20*(1), 75–83. doi:10.1177/0971685813515594

Bae, S. C., Chang, K., & Kang, E. (2012). Culture, corporate governance, and dividend policy: International evidence. *Journal of Financial Research*, *35*(2), 289–316. doi:10.1111/j.1475-6803.2012.01318.x

Barnett, M. L. (2007). Stakeholder influence capacity and the variability of financial returns to corporate social responsibility. *Academy of Management Review*, *32*(3), 794–816. doi:10.5465/AMR.2007.25275520

Benn, S., Dunphy, D., & Griffiths, A. (2014). *Organizational change for corporate sustainability*. Routledge.

Birkin, F., Cashman, A., Koh, S. C. L., & Liu, Z. (2009). New Sustainable Business Models in China. *Business Strategy and the Environment*, *18*(1), 64–77. doi:10.1002/bse.568

Bongiorni, S. (2007). *A Year Without 'Made in China': One Family's True Life Adventure in the Global Economy*. Hoboken, NJ: John Wiley and Sons, Inc.

Insider, B. (2014, January 21). *Pollution From China Is Hitting America's West Coast.* Retrieved from www.businessinsider.com

Chen, B., & Feng, Y. (2000). Determinants of economic growth in China: Private enterprise, education and openness. *China Economic Review*, *11*(1), 1–15. doi:10.1016/S1043-951X(99)00014-0

Chi, T. (2011). Building a sustainable supply chain: An analysis of corporate social responsibility (CSR) practices in the Chinese textile and apparel industry. *Journal of the Textile Institute*, *102*(10), 837–848. doi:10.1080/00405000.2010.524361

Chinese Academy of Social Sciences (CASS). (November 15, 2013). Blue Book on Corporate Responsibility. Retrieved from www.globaltimes.cn

Cleaner Production in China. (n. d.). *Cleaner Production/Pollution Prevention Organizations in China.* Retrieved from http://www.chinacp.org.cn/eng/cp_organizations.html

Darigan, K. H., & Post, J. E. (2009). Corporate citizenship in China. *Journal of Corporate Citizenship*, (35), 39–53. doi:10.9774/GLEAF.4700.2009.au.00005

Dentchev, N. A., Haezendonck, E., & van Balen, M. (2015). The Role of Governments in the Business and Society Debate. *Business & Society*. doi:10.1177/0007650315586179

Desjardins, J. R. (1999). Businesses' environmental responsibility. In: E.R. Freedrick (Ed.). A Companion to Business Ethics (pp. 280-289). Bentley College, Blackwell Publishers.

Dhanesh, G. S. (2015). Why Corporate Social Responsibility? An Analysis of Drivers of CSR in India. *Management Communication Quarterly*, *29*(1), 114–129. doi:10.1177/0893318914545496

Dobbin, F., Schrage, D., & Kalev, A. (2009). *Someone to watch over me: Coupling, decoupling, and unintended consequences in corporate equal opportunity* (Working paper). Harvard University, Cambridge, MA.

Fan, S., & Zhang, X. (2004). Infrastructure and regional economic development in rural China. *China Economic Review*, *15*(2), 203–214. doi:10.1016/j.chieco.2004.03.001

Fox, T., Ward, H., & Howard, B. (n. d). Corporate Responsibility for Environment and Development Programme. *International Institute for Environment and Development (IIED).* Retrieved from http://eldis.org/go/homeandid=12031

Garriga, E., & Mele, E. (2004). Corporate Social Responsibility Theories: Mapping the Territory. *Journal of Business Ethics*, *53*(1/2), 51–71. doi:10.1023/B:BUSI.0000039399.90587.34

Haley, U. C., & Haley, G. T. (2013). *Subsidies to Chinese industry: State capitalism, business strategy, and trade policy*. Oxford University Press. doi:10.1093/acprof:oso/9780199773749.001.0001

Hung, M., Shi, J., & Wang, Y. (2013). The Effect of Mandatory CSR Disclosure on Information Asymmetry: Evidence from a Quasi-natural Experiment in China (Working paper).

Indian CSR News Network. (2012). *Mega CSR Conference in Mumbai*. Retrieved from www.indiacsr.in

Jamali, D., Lund-Thomsen, R., & Jeppesen, S. (2015). SMEs and CSR in developing countries. *Business and Society*, 1-12. doi:10.1177/0007650315571258

Jamali, D., Lund-Thomsen, P., & Khara, N. (2015). CSR Institutionalized Myths in Developing Countries: An Imminent Threat of Selective Decoupling. *Business & Society*. doi:10.1177/0007650315584303

Johnston, M., & Hao, Y. (1995). China's surge of corruption. *Journal of Democracy*, *6*(4), 80–94. doi:10.1353/jod.1995.0068

Kemper, A., & Martin, R. L. (2010). After the fall: The global financial crisis as a test of corporate social responsibility theories. *European Management Review*, *7*(4), 229–239. doi:10.1057/emr.2010.18

Kolk, A., & van Tulder, R. (2010). International business, Corporate Social Responsibility and sustainable development. *International Business Review*, *19*(1), 1–14.

K'ung-fu-tzu. (1996). *The Wise Man Said* (Trans. Ofek Bina). Tel Aviv: Ofarim [Hebrew].

Lattemann, C., Fetscherin, M., Alon, I., Li, S., & Schneider, A. M. (2009). CSR Communication Intensity in Chinese and Indian Multinational Companies. *Corporate Governance: An International Review*, *17*(4), 426–442. doi:10.1111/j.1467-8683.2009.00758.x

Lavie, Y. (2006). Stealing organs from death-row inmates for transplants in China – a call to end Israeli cooperation in the process (in Hebrew). *Harefua*, *145*, 749–753.

Leavy, G. D., Lam, J., & Hr, S. S. M. (2008). Does East meet West in business ethics?: An introduction to the special issue. *Journal of Business Ethics*, *79*(1-2), 1–8. doi:10.1007/s10551-007-9384-6

Lu, X. (2009). A Chinese perspective: Business ethics in China now and in the future. *Journal of Business Ethics*, *86*(4), 451–461. doi:10.1007/s10551-008-9857-2

Margolis, J. D., & Walsh, J. P. (2003). Misery loves companies: Rethinking social initiatives by business. *Administrative Science Quarterly*, *48*(2), 68–305. doi:10.2307/3556659

Marquis, C., & Qian, C. (2014). Corporate Social Responsibility reporting in China: Symbol or substance? *Organization Science*, *25*(1), 127–148. doi:10.1287/orsc.2013.0837

Mol, A. P., He, G., & Zhang, L. (2011). Information Disclosure in Environmental Risk Management: Developments in China. *Journal of Current Chinese Affairs*, *40*(3), 163–192.

Moon, J. (2004). *Government as a driver of corporate social responsibility: The UK in comparative perspective. International Centre for Corporate Social Responsibility research paper no. 20*. Nottingham: Nottingham University Business School.

Moon, J., & Vogel, D. (2008). Corporate responsibility, government and civil society. In A. Crane, A. McWilliams, D. Matten, J. Moon, & D.S. Siegel (Eds.), Oxford handbook of corporate social responsibility. Oxford: Oxford University Press. doi:10.1093/oxfordhb/9780199211593.003.0013

National Chamber Foundation (NCF). (2012). *Corporate Responsibility and Sustainable Economic Development in China: Implications for Business.* Asia United States Chamber of Commerce. Retrieved from www.uschamber.com

New York Times. (2014, March 27). *Most Chinese Cities Fail Minimum Air Quality Standards, Study Says*. Retrieved from www.nytimes.com

OECD Newsroom. (2014, November 12). *China headed to overtake EU, United States in science and technology spending, OECD says*. Retrieved from www.oecd.org

Okhmatovskiy, I., & David, R. J. (2012). Setting your own standards: Internal corporate governance codes as a response to institutional pressure. *Organization Science*, *23*(1), 155–176. doi:10.1287/orsc.1100.0642

Pan, J. (2009, October 2). Development as China's environmental solution. *Telegraph*.

Shafer, W., Fukukawa, K., & Lee, G. M. (2006). Values and perceived importance of ethics and social responsibility: The United States versus China. *Journal of Business Ethics*, *70*(3), 265–284. doi:10.1007/s10551-006-9110-9

Scherer, A.G., & Palazzo, G. (2011, June). The New Political Role of Business in a Globalized World: A Review of a New Perspective on CSR and its Implications for the Firm, Governance and Democracy. *Journal of Management Studies, 48*(4), 899-931.

Sen, A. (2002). Does business ethics make economic sense? In T. Donaldson, P.H. Werhane, & M. Cording (Eds.). Ethical Issues in Business – A Philosophical Approach (pp. 244-251). New Jersey: Prentice Hall.

Shah, S. (2012). Proposing a welfare framework for the society and local community stakeholders: A mixed method study. *Journal of Human Values*, *18*(1), 53–71. doi:10.1177/097168581101800105

Short, J. L., & Toffel, M. W. (2010). Making self-regulation more than merely symbolic: The critical role of the legal environment. *Administrative Science Quarterly*, *55*(3), 361–396. doi:10.2189/asqu.2010.55.3.361

Smith, R., & Wiek, A. (2012). Achievements and opportunities in initiating governance for urban sustainability. *Environment and Planning. C, Government & Policy*, *30*(3), 429–447. doi:10.1068/c10158

Snell, R. S., & Tseng, C. (2001). Commentary: Ethical dilemmas of relationship building in China. *Thunderbird International Business Review*, *43*(2), 171–201. doi:10.1002/tie.1

Sun, Y. (2008). Woguo zhengfu huanjing xinxi gongkai shenji de sikao [Audit Environmental Information Disclosure]. Green Finance and Accounting, 6, 30-32.

Telegraph. (October 2, 2009). *Development as China's Environmental Solution*. Retrieved from http://www.telegraph.co.uk

The EcoGateway Link Center. (n. d.). *Pollution Prevention – Federal Agencies and Programs.* Retrieved from http://www.ecoiq.com/onlineresources/center/prevention/fed.html

The EcoGateway Link Center, Pollution Prevention- *United States Nonprofit Organizations*. Retrieved from http://www.ecoiq.com/onlineresources/center/prevention/nonprofit.html

The World Bank. (2002). *Public Sector Roles in Strengthening Corporate Social Responsibility: A Baseline Study.*

Fox, T., Ward, H. and Howard, B. (n. d.). Corporate Responsibility for Environment and Development Programme International Institute for Environment and Development (IIED). Retrieved from http://eldis.org/go/homeandid=12031and type=Document

Thiel, M. (2015). *The Social Domain in Corporate Social Responsibility and Sustainability*. Farham, UK: Gower Publishing Limited.

Thiel, M. (2010). Innovations in Corporate Social Responsibility from global business leaders at Panasonic, Thomson Reuters and Nanyang Business School. *American Journal of Economics and Business Administration*, *2*(2), 194–200. doi:10.3844/ajebasp.2010.194.200

Waldman, D. A., Sully de Luque, M., Washburn, N., House, R. J., Adetoun, B., Barrasa, A., & Wilderom, C. P. M. et al. (2006). Cultural and leadership predictors of corporate social responsibility values of top management: A global study of 15 countries. *Journal of International Business Studies*, *37*(6), 823–837. doi:10.1057/palgrave.jibs.8400230

Wolf, R. (2008). *Ethics is Good for Business* (in Hebrew). Jerusalem; Reuven Mass.

Wolf, R., & Kantor, J. (2006). *Sarbanes-Oxley's Code of Ethics: An Attempt to deter 21th Century Wrongdoings With Financial Implications. Absolute Standards in an Age of Relativity*. Torea and Science, Proceedings.

Wolf, R. (2015a). Corporate Social Responsibility – Contribution to All. In R. Wolf, T. Issa, & M. Thiel (Eds.), Empowering organizations through corporate social responsibility, (pp. 255- 264). Hershey, PA: IGI Global.

Wolf, R. (2015b). Corporate Social Responsibility in the West (United States and West Europe) vs. East (China). In R. Wolf & T. Issa (Eds.), International business ethics and growth opportunities, (pp. 97-112). Hershey, PA: IGI Global.

Wolf, R. (2015c). Self-Awareness: A Way to Promote Ethical Management. In R. Wolf, & T. Issa (Eds.), International Business Ethics and Growth Opportunities, (pp. 147-157). Hershey, PA: IGI Global. doi:10.4018/978-1-4666-7419-6.ch007

World Economic Forum. (2011). *State and Central Government Cooperation.* Retrieved from www.webforum.org

Wright, P. C., Szeto, W. F., & Lee, S. K. (2003). Ethical perceptions in China: The reality of business ethics in an international context. *Management Decision*, *41*(2), 180–189. doi:10.1108/00251740310457623

Zhang, M., & Liang, X. (2013). Advances Among Debates: Research On and Practice of Corporate Social Responsibility from the Legal Perspective in China. *Fordham Environmental Law Review*, *XXV*, 191–250.

Zhao, M. (2012). CSR-based political legitimacy strategy: Managing the state by doing good in China and Russia. *Journal of Business Ethics*, *11*(4), 439–460. doi:10.1007/s10551-012-1209-6

KEY TERMS AND DEFINITIONS

Beijing: The north eastern capital city of the People's Republic of China.
Biodiversity: Diverse life in an ecosystem or habitat.
Familial: Family members.
Kerala: A south western State in India.
New Delhi: The Northern capital city of India.
Spillovers: Something that spreads into another area.
Yangtze: The longest river of Asia that flows from Tibet to the Shanghai East China Sea.

Chapter 14
The Call for Global Responsible Inter-Generational Leadership:
The Quest of an Integration of Inter-Generational Equity in Corporate Social Responsibility (CSR) Models

Julia Puaschunder
The New School, USA

ABSTRACT

Global systemic risks of climate change, over-indebtedness in the aftermath of the 2008/09 World Financial Crisis and the need for pension reform in the wake of an aging Western world population, currently raise attention for inter-generational fairness. Pressing social dilemmas beyond the control of singular nation states call for corporate social activities to back governmental regulation in crisis mitigation. The following chapter therefore promotes the idea of inter-generational equity in the corporate world to find an inclusive solution comprised by the public and private sectors. In the given literature on global responsible leadership in the corporate sector and contemporary Corporate Social Responsibility (CSR) models, inter-generational equity appears to have been neglected. While the notion of sustainability has been integrated in CSR models, inter-generational equity has hardly been touched on as for being a more legal case for codifying the triple bottom line. Advocating for integrating inter-generational equity concerns in CSR models in academia and practice holds untapped advantages of economically influential corporate entities, corporate adaptability and independence from voting cycles. Integrating a temporal dimension in contemporary CSR helps imbuing a longer-term perspective into the corporate world alongside advancing tax ethics and global governance crises prevention. Practical implications for the financing of an inter-generational harmonious solution on climate change burden sharing are proposed. Future research avenues comprise of investigating situational factors influencing inter-generational leadership in the international arena in order to advance the idea of corporations tackling the most pressing contemporary challenges of mankind.

DOI: 10.4018/978-1-5225-0720-8.ch014

INTRODUCTION

Globalization leveraged pressure on contemporary society. Unprecedented interdependency of massive global systems causes systemic risks to increase exponentially creating pressing social dilemmas beyond the control of singular nation states (Centeno et al, 2013). Global challenges of climate change, over-indebtedness in the aftermath of the 2008/09 World Financial Crisis and the need for pension reform in the wake of an aging Western world population, currently raise attention to transnational intertemporal fairness (Puaschunder, 2012, 2015). While classic economic models portrayed balancing the interests of different generations as ethical problem of competitive markets and state governance and some economists even opposed discounting of future utilities in the past (Allais, 1947; Harrod, 1948; Ramsey, 1928). inter-generational equity nowadays has come into public scrutiny entering the academic and practical discourse in the public and private sector (Puaschunder, 2012, 2015).

Since the 2008/09 World Financial Crisis pervaded societal demand to increase the socio-ethical commitments of corporations. Social awareness due to mass media reporting heightened stakeholder pressure exerting influence on corporate decision makers for ethicality. Therefore, today's most pressing societal long-term downfalls call for corporate social activities to back governmental regulation to steer inter-generational justice (Puaschunder, 2015). In the implementation of inter-generational equity, the age of globalization shifted the influence of national governments and their policies as a predominant force in the economy to international governance of the corporate sector. Since decisions in one country can directly impact on the interest of citizens of other societies in a whole new range of trans-boundary problems, the range of influence and efficacy of national democracy got challenged. National economic autonomy and sovereignty are vanishing due to increased international interdependence. With a trend towards the constitutionalization of free trade and capital movements through bi- and multilateral agreements to protect free markets around the world, corporatism grew (Panitch & Gindin, 2012). Holding widespread access to vital economic resources and markets, today multinationals have become quasi-global governance institutions that leveraged into implicit legal and political authorities to regulate economic activity in the architecture of the world economy.

Today's most pressing societal long-term downfalls call for corporate social activities to back governmental regulation on sustainable development (Puaschunder, 2015). Sustainable development goals pay attention to the conservation of natural resources, environmental protection and societal well-being. Holding widespread access to vital economic resources and markets, contemporary multinationals have become quasi-global governance institutions and implicit political authorities to regulate economic activity in the architecture of the world economy. With respect to UN estimates on population growth ranging from 10 to 10.5 billion by 2050 and assuming that everyone has to be brought to the minimum living standard (including inflation price effects) by 2050, contemporary CSR notions (including economic development as a dimension) and inter-generational equity concerns (including continued population problem as a consideration) are challenged and arise to the most pressing demand of our time.

The following paper promotes the idea of inter-generational equity in the corporate world as an alternative to national governance and novel extension of contemporary Corporate Social Responsibility (CSR) models. Inter-generational equity – as the economic balance between generations – and inter-generational fairness, as the justice between generations, but also inter-generational social conscientiousness account for the main foundations of inter-generational CSR leadership (see Figure 1).

Inter-generationally responsible leadership is built on the idea that corporate executives have an obligation to incorporate needs of far-ranging constituents, including future generations. In the eye of

Figure 1. Inter-generational CSR leadership

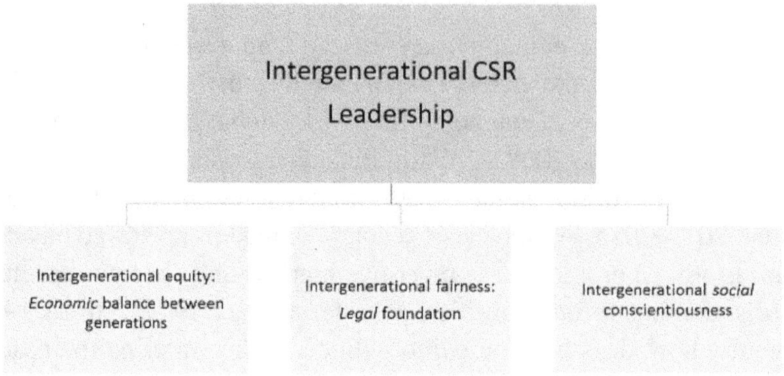

a current pressing demand for attention to inter-generational equity in the domains of climate justice, austerity and pension reform needs in an aging Western world population, the following paper theoretically highlights the corporate world's potential to alleviate current inter-generational equity imbalances and explores inter-generational justice implementation strategies of the corporate world.

Current Quest of an Integration of Inter-Generational Equity Considerations in CSR Models

Globalization lowered the range of opportunities of what contemporary nation states can autonomously do by rising dependence on each other (Panitch & Gindin, 2012). The role of states in maintaining property rights, overseeing contracts, stabilizing currencies and reproducing class relations has gradually deteriorated since the beginning of internationalization. International interdependence limits national sovereignty and economic autonomy (Held & McGrew, 2007). In the wake of global capitalism, the power and political authority have been diffused away from local state ruling to global governance. The classic ideal of the command and control state was displaced by a philosophy of global economic hegemony (Held & McGrew, 2007).

While industrialization has weakened the power of local governance and national control, globalization has also lead to unprecedented problems of climate change, overindebtedness in the aftermath of the 2008/09 World Financial Crisis and pension reform needs of an aging Western world population (Puaschunder, 2012). National governments' inter-generational equity implementation has shifted to international governance solutions in the corporate world (Panitch & Gindin, 2012). Nowadays pressing dilemmas beyond the control of singular nation states call for attention for inter-generational fairness and corporate social activities to back governmental crisis mitigation (Centeno et al., 2013). As multilayered economic system are structured by the strategic coordination of international corporate entities, corporate multinationals have turned to solve global societal crisis beyond the control of singular nation states.

In the light of growing socio-political and environmental challenges, heightened stakeholder concern has risen attention of global stakeholders on corporate ethical conduct in the inter-generational domain. Today's inter-generational imbalances become more visible through information provided to stakeholders by heightened transparency in the digital age that makes corporate conduct and governmental actions visible to a broad range of constituents. Inter-generational equity deficiencies subsequently became tackled in bottom up approaches to shed light on the rights of upcoming youth, voice the needs of unborn not being present in courtrooms and lobby for favorable future conditions (Puaschunder, 2011).

International trade, global capitalism and economic hegemony of corporations has led to a strategic coordination of public and private actors in addressing inter-generational imbalances (Binder, Kriebaum, Marboe, Nowak, Reinisch & Wittich, 2014). With growing socio-political and environmental challenges around the world in the domains of financial social irresponsibility, environmental resource consumption and growing costs for an aging populace, there is increasing pressure from stakeholders – among them governments, local communities, NGOs, and society at large – that corporations and their leaders contribute to societally-attentive business practices. Access to information law revolutions in the Western World have steered attention to corporate ethicality. Corporate social reporting and the engagement of stakeholders have led to the adoption of a variety of global ethical standards, which may directly impact on the propensity to engage in inter-generational equity implementations of the corporate world. Local communities, customers, employees, and NGOs as well as shareholders are increasingly monitoring ethical behavior in the digital age featuring greater transparency, accessibility and reachability of corporate conduct. Especially in the aftermath of the 2008/09 World Financial Crisis, corporations have become under scrutiny for societal contributions and corporate board managers increasingly respected for corporate social conduct with stakeholders playing a conspicuous role in influencing the interaction between governments and business. The corporate world is nowadays more than ever urged to consider the needs of a wider range of stakeholders in their decision-making, go beyond ethical requirements and outperform responsibility expectations within the surge of a positive organizational scholarship movement. In the age of heightened shareholder and stakeholder activism towards corporate social endeavors, the time is ripe to investigate the potential of corporate activities to engage on inter-generational equity in the aftermath of the 2008/09 World Financial Crisis.

In the international arena, the United Nations (UN) plays a key role in advancing inter-generational equity. The United Nations Global Compact (UNGC) initiative is an entry point for corporations to engage in social partnership projects featuring operational flexibility and focus on pragmatic solutions. The UN Global Compact has raised over 10,000 members 2000, including over 7,000 businesses in 145 countries around the world (Puaschunder, 2010). In addition, the UNGC secretariat promotes CSR to the corporate world as a competitive advantage and PPP-administered social responsibility as a corporate success factor beyond the boundaries of legal compliance and philanthropy. Pro-active CSR reporting gains public recognition for sustainable development. In networking events, public and private partners are brought together to find a consensus on social responsibility. A fruitful dialogue of UNGC partners and stakeholders guideline a successful implementation of CSR partnerships on inter-generational concerns. International conferences serve as CSR vision councils in which governmental representatives, business executives, financial professionals, NGO representatives and academics share insights on CSR success factors to advance PPPs. Summits produce a constant stream of literature on PPP best practices that must be made accessible on the internet to further CSR in PPPs. Increasing and expanding CSR initiatives indicate that more and more business leaders commit their companies to contribute to the "triple bottom line" to harmoniously consider social, environmental, and economic sustainability in every day corporate decision making (Elkington, 1997). Respect for 'people, planet, and profits' has become a corporate necessity and industrial imperative. Corporate sustainability and social responsibility has thus emerged to unprecedented momentum in academia and practitioners' discourse. Today business leaders tend to contribute to the creation of economic and societal progress in a globally responsible and sustainable way by means as never before experienced. The corporate sector backs international organizations on inter-generational concerns. Global governance entities create a partnership-enhancing institutional, political and judicial infrastructure. Legislative frameworks aim at corporate social value creation. International public policy makers ratify social responsibility declarations that are in sync with societal goals and advocate for the adoption of social responsibility policies.

Given the pressing demand for attention to climate change mitigation and overindebtedness soft landing demands in the aftermath of the 2008/09 World Financial Crisis, the need for an introduction of inter-generational equity conscientiousness in the corporate world is rising. In a climate of corporate governance and global challenges beyond the control of singular nation states, the idea of promoting inter-generational equity in the corporate world has reached unprecedented momentum. Departing from narrow-minded, outdated views of responsibilities of corporations only adherent to making profit for shareholders and abiding by the law (Friedman, 1970); corporate executives nowadays are more prone to act responsibly in meeting the needs of a wide range of constituents. Apart from avoiding unethical societally harmful behavior, such as bribery, fraud and employment discrimination, corporate executives currently pro-actively engage in corporate governance practice with a wider constituency outlook, including the needs of future generations.

Advocating for integrating inter-generational concerns in CSR models in academia and practice holds untapped advantages of economically influential corporate entities contributing to sustainable development. Integrating a political dimension in contemporary sustainable development helps imbuing a longer-term perspective into the corporate and finance world alongside advancing international development and global governance crises prevention by directing corporate assets and financial towards activities that foster sustainable development.

Apart from the social value created, PPPs engage multiple stakeholders in the policy dialogue and mobilize resources for societal welfare. Governments create a CSR-fostering environment and assist the coordination of multi-stakeholder CSR partnerships. Based on international regulations, governments build PPPs frameworks to mitigate social, environmental and political risks in the implementation of CSR. Governmental officials advocate for the adoption of socially responsible corporate practices and encourage responsible leadership. Governmental initiatives inform corporate leaders about societal challenges and nurture an understanding of governmental priorities throughout the stakeholder community. Corporate executives' motivation is enhanced by information on the positive economic, social and environmental advantages of CSR. Partnerships are networking forums in which multiple stakeholders discuss topics of social concern in an atmosphere of trust and confidentiality.

The future conceptualization of sustainable and responsible managerial behavior may therefore embrace the wider constituency range and stretch the concept of corporate responsibility to voluntary sustainability for future generations. An extended stakeholder view considers a broader set of constituencies, including future generations, in corporate decision making with impact on the social performance and long-term viability of their organizations. A broader, social contract between business and future society may be enacted by discretionary activities that are not expected of corporations and their leaders in a moral or legal sense but directly contribute to societal welfare and the wellbeing of future generations. This suggests that there is a need for a broader definition of corporate responsibility that goes beyond compliance and encompasses the obligation to contribute to societal progress in a responsible and sustainable way.

Inter-generationally responsible leadership is called for that steers intentional corporate executive actions to benefit the stakeholders of the company as well as the larger society including future generations. Inter-generational corporate leadership imbues s*hould-do* care for future generations alongside concerns about future society. Not simply considering to avoid unethical behavior, such as bribery, fraud and employment discrimination, but also adopting a positive and pro-active ethics lens, inter-generationally responsible leadership is an uber-ethical drive to consider the interests of a wider range of stakeholders (Puaschunder, 2015). Inter-generational justice concerns of the corporate world thereby directly reach out to future world inhabitants. Surpassing state-of-the-art ethical corporate leadership quests on ethically compliant behavior and avoidance of unethical corporate conduct, incorporating inter-generational equity into contemporary CSR models may extend the idea of 'positive CSR' – that is outdoing legal and ethical expectations – with respect for future constituents. Going beyond mere compliance involves actions that pro-actively promote social good, beyond what is required by law, inter-generational corporate responsibility extends CSR as a broader social contract between business and society over time. Inter-generational equity leadership of the corporate sector defines social responsibility beyond compliance and encompasses the wider obligation to contribute to societal progress in a responsible and sustainable way to ensure the long-term viability of society.

Corporate leaders thereby pro-actively outperform legal and ethical expectations regarding the rights and needs of future generations. This positive CSR drive refers to an uber-ethical enhancement of societal welfare beyond the narrow scope of the current generation. As a broader definition of corporate responsibility beyond avoidance of negative downfalls, the call for inter-generational responsible leadership in the corporate world encompasses the obligation to contribute to societal progress with respect for the needs of future generations. Defining novel responsibilities with a broader social contract between business and society embraces discretionary activities that contribute to sustainable societal welfare and thereby provides a broad range of corporate, social and societal advantages.

Inter-Generational CSR Advantages

In the given literature on global responsible leadership in the corporate sector and contemporary CSR models, inter-generational equity appears to have widely been neglected. While the notion of sustainability has been integrated in CSR models (Steurer, Martinuzzi & Margula, 2012), inter-generational equity has hardly been touched on as inter-generational fairness differs from sustainability as for being a more legal case for codifying the triple bottom line, which pays attention to a balance of social, economic and environmental obligations of corporations to the wider constituency.

Since 2008 the International Law Commission of the United Nations has been promoting inter-generational equity as the most unified consensus primarily on global governance issues – such as climate change awareness, over-indebtedness and pension reform – to the public sector (Puaschunder, 2015). The implementation of inter-generational equity in this domain, though, seems to be slowed by an ongoing discussion of whether international law can overrule nation states' sovereignty. The debate has just recently started and may not come to a satisfactory end in the foreseeable future.

Integrating inter-generational equity in CSR models in academia and practice appears as advantageous alternative given the enormous untapped potential of transnational Corporations and Multinational Enterprises (TC&MEs) to implement equity. Nowadays, international trade is driven by transnational corporations. As corporate entities with economic influence beyond the borders of nation states holding subsidiaries in various nations of the world (Binder et al., 2014), TC&MEs are acknowledged as international legal entities and must therefore abide by international law standards and fulfill international court laws (e.g., ICSID and UNCITRAL). As a consequence, TC&MEs should, like nation states, consider adopting concern for inter-generational equity.

There are several advantages of TC&MEs implementing inter-generational equity as a CSR means. TC&MEs hold enormous economic power, with the largest multi-national corporations having revenues larger than many nation states. In their corporate governance, TC&MEs leadership decision making quickly adapts to market demands without having to reach international consensus – contrary to stakeholder engagement and international negation demands of classic global governance entities such as the United National, International Monetary Fund and the World Bank.

In addition, TC&MEs are not dependent on voters – such as governmental officials – and can thus address inter-generational concerns faster and more flexibly than governmental technocrats. Further TC&ME leadership may be more stable than governmental officials enacted through voting cycles – that is global corporate leaders are likely to stay longer in 'office' than their governmental counterparts. Governments, being unsure to be re-elected, are inherently short-sighted and may not fully take into account the longer term implications of deficits.

If the corporate world adopts inter-generational equity in current CSR endeavors, it could help governmental officials in very many different ways ranging from tax ethics to first-aid global governance support. For society, acknowledging inter-generational equity in the CSR practices promises to alleviate currently-pressing societal predicaments of over-indebtedness, social welfare reform needs and environmental threats in the wake of climate change. Investigating the possibilities to integrate a temporal dimension in contemporary CSR thus innovatively guides the implementation of financial social responsibility, environmental protection education and social welfare. Corporate attention to inter-generational concerns would thereby embrace future crisis prevention in the eye of the societal costs and negative externalities of corporate misconduct and financial collapse resulting in economic downturns, unemployment and pension saving losses. Besides averting negative impacts of managerial unethical corporate conduct, corporate inter-generational ethicality would also build business reputation attracting talent, raise customer confidence as well as sustainable employee and citizenry welfare. Within academia integrating the notion of inter-generational fairness in corporate governance models fills an up-to-date undiscovered research gap that spearheads interdisciplinary behavioral law and economic models.

Overall, enhancing inter-generational social conscientiousness in the corporate world is an innovative way to unprecedentedly leverage untapped potentials to implement social welfare and environmental protection through future-oriented and socially responsible economic market approaches. Thereby averting future predictable economic, social and environmental crises serves the greater goal to ensure a future sustainable and temporally-harmonious mankind.

Inter-Generational Equity Implementation

The outlined inter-generational equity constraints are complex and their solution interdependent. The current world economy opens possibilities but also threatens future generations. This unprecedented inter-generational kink heralds an overall call for inter-generational equity to address justice over time. As an implicit contract and transfer inbetween living and future generations, inter-generational equity not only reduces unfairness for future world inhabitants who are born in less favorable condition than their parents. Inter-generational equity also ensures future infrastructure, equal opportunities over time and constant access to social welfare for the youth. Inter-generational equity avoids discriminating against future generations on the basis of remoteness of the time at which they will live. Thereby inter-generational equity grants a favorable climate between generations, ensures climate stability and averts frictions arising from austerity plans and diminishing social welfare standards.

The Economics of Climate Stability: Climate Burden Sharing with Bonds

Climate change accounts for one of the most pressing problems in the age of globalization as for exacerbating more risks than ever before in terms of water crises, food shortages, constrained economic growth, weaker social cohesion and increased security risks (Centeno & Tham, 2012; The World Economic Forum Report, 2015). The implementation of climate stability accounts for the most challenging contemporary global governance predicament that seems to pit today's generation against future world inhabitants in a trade-off of economic growth versus sustainability. Current climate stability policies (e.g., cap & trade, carbon tax, green energy) outline that the burden of climate change aversion – including the cost of mitigation and adaptation – is unevenly distributed by falling mostly on the current generation. The excess burden for current generations has also been implicit in the work of the typical Integrated Assessment Model, IAM, (Nordhaus, 2008), contemporary threshold as well as other mitigation and adaptation models, e.g., social cost of carbon. Innovative intertemporal fiscal policy approaches (e.g., of Jeffrey Sachs, 2014) guide the development of a basic framework to study how an efficient and fair allocation of efforts towards mitigation and adaptation can be achieved.

In standard neo-classical economic models, climate change abatement is perceived as trading off from economic growth as for cost cutting behavior. While classic economics portrayed balancing the interests of different generations as ethical problem of competitive markets requiring governance for inter-generational transfers and some economists even opposed discounting of future utilities (Allais, 1947; Harrod, 1948; Ramsey, 1928); climate change has leveraged inter-generational equity as contemporary challenge of modern democracy and temporal justice an ethical obligation for posterity.

In general, resources are balanced across generations by social discounting to weight the well-being of future generations relative to those alive today. Regarding climate justice, current generations are called upon to make sacrifices today for future generations by mobilizing low-carbon energy to cut carbon emissions to avert global warming (Sachs, 2014). Climate change mitigation at the expense of lowered economic growth seems to pit the current generation against future ones. Costly climate change abatement prospects are thus hindering currently necessary action on climate change given a shrinking time window prior to reaching tipping points that make global warming irreversible (Oppenheimer, O'Neill, Webster & Agrawal, 2011).

As a novel alternative to ensure climate justice, Sachs (2014) proposes to fund today's climate mitigation through intertemporal fiscal policies funded by climate bonds financed through taxation faced by future generations. Climate stability bonds are introduced as a means of inter-generational climate change burden sharing strategy to elicit future-oriented climate stability for posterity. The current generation mitigates climate change and provides infrastructure against climate risk financed through climate bonds to be paid by future generations. Since for future generations the currently created externalities from economic activities – the effects of $C0_2$ emissions – are removed, this entails that the current generations remain financially as well off as without mitigation while improving environmental well-being of future generations. As Sachs (2014) shows, this inter-generational tax-and-transfer policy turns climate change mitigation and adaptation policy into a Pareto improving strategy. In particular, consumers are not anymore obliged to curb their consumption in order to reduce resource utilization for nonexistent future stakeholders. This model also interprets inter-generational equity as a whole-rounded transfer of assets and liabilities in an implicit contract of overlapping generations over time. Sachs' (2014) inter-generational burden sharing idea presents a 3-model climate change burden sharing through fiscal policy (with bond issuing) and reflects the implementation regarding contemporary finance and growth models with respect for maximizing utility of the model. The current generation thereby mitigates climate change financed through bonds to remain financially as well off as without mitigation while improving environmental well-being of future generations. The Sachs' (2014) approach would also ensure an at least as minimum standard of living if not an improvement of the living conditions of future generations that will enjoy a stable climate without incurred costs of curbed consumption. This model also appears relevant given a predicted overall world population rise and thus a higher human body to pay back debts incurred for climate stability.

Overall, Jeffrey Sachs (2014) novel angle towards climate justice elicits future-oriented loss aversion, which lead to a fairer solution across generations. Shifting the costs for climate abatement to the recipients of the benefits of climate stability appears as novel, feasible and easily-implementable solution to nudge many overlapping generations towards future-oriented loss aversion in the sustainability domain. This powerful strategy instigates immediate climate change mitigation in an overall Pareto improving crisis management for all generations. While inter-generational burden sharing on climate change is a novel economically superior strategy and real-world relevant emergent risk prevention means (Centeno et al., 2013); we currently lack information on the impact of climate mitigation through debt on economic growth and the model's sustainability over time. Testing for the feasibility and sustainability will provide real-world relevant means how to implement climate stability on a long-term scale. Studying the types of bonds issuing that would achieve such goals will help exploring the more complicated bond issuing practices involved. In this context, it should also be investigated if the climate change debt adjusted growth model stays within the bounds of a sustainable fiscal policy. This elementary but very innovative model by Sachs (2014) can be integrated in contemporary growth and economic climate models. Yet unknown remains how climate bonds can actually be phased into climate policies to obtain socially optimal solutions. Future research should also analyze micro- and macroeconomic insights on the well-balanced harmonization of climate change mitigation and adaptation in order to provide public policy recommendations.

Overall climate stability bonds offer to lead a well-balanced climate mitigation and adaptation public policy mix guided by macroeconomic analysis results. Shifting the costs for climate abatement to the recipients of the benefits of climate stability appears as novel, feasible and easily-implementable solution to nudge overlapping generations towards future-oriented loss aversion. Adding onto the contemporary idea and practice of climate bonds alongside providing incentives to channel funds into climate stability, research in this area will also retrieve information on the harmonious interplay of climate change mitigation and adaptation in the public policy domain for ensuring a sustainable mankind.

Future Perspectives

Globalization has placed social and environmental concerns on managerial agendas to an increased extent while more and more managers operate in a global environment. Multidisciplinary and multilevel research approaches may therefore investigate the comparative and cross-national dimensions of inter-generational equity and their implications for leadership decision making and behavior in the global arena. Interdisciplinary and multilevel research approaches could feature scientific collaborations with researchers based in different countries to investigate the comparative and cross-national dimensions of inter-generationally responsible managerial behavior representing different disciplinary backgrounds (economics, business, psychology, etc.), research fields (e.g., strategy, organizational behavior, and international and cross-cultural management within the field of business), methodological approaches (both qualitative and quantitative), and regional expertise (in-depth knowledge of North-American, European, and Asian business systems and institutional environments). International studies of inter-generational equity should be targeted at deriving a sophisticated conceptualization of 'responsible behavior' in the inter-generational domain that is applicable to all cultural groups and stakeholders.

International research on inter-generational equity could unravel drivers of inter-generationally responsible managerial behavior. Cross-national, multi-level analyses could thereby retrieve influence factors on the adoption of globally responsible inter-generational leadership and corporate practices. Knowledge of contextual factors that promote inter-generational managerial decision-making with regard to corporate sustainability and social responsibility could include favorable characteristics of the organization and aspects of the broader institutional and cultural contexts in which firms are embedded that automatically trigger inter-generational concern. Thereby the antecedents of sustainable and responsible management at multiple levels (individual, group, organization, national context, supranational bodies) but also the interlinkages among variables should be investigated.

Institutional contexts within which companies and their managers operate determine executives' responsible choices. Differences in corporate governance and legal contexts but also the nature of regulation and the likelihood of enforcement shape business ethics as well as expectations of what is considered good governance and ethical conduct in a country. Managers' responsible leadership may therefore vary across institutional contexts in the international arena. What may be considered as inter-generational practice in one part of the world may not be ethical state-of-the-art in another. As a consequence, corporate leaders embedded in different national systems may exhibit different inter-generational ethics. Cross-national variations in socially responsible practices could be captured in order to derive implications for organizational decision-makers on their corporate responsibility. Adopted CSR strategies may be scrutinized for globally standardized, locally adapted, and transnational factors to delineate globally consistent as well as locally-oriented inter-generational equity CSR approaches with attention to inter-generational equity.

With the underlying premises of exhibited behavior being a function of both the person and the environment in which that behavior takes place, future research may also unravel ethical decision-making under situational constraints that the broader cultural and institutional environment impose on the adoption of sustainable and socially responsible practices. Cross-culturally operating institutions may face challenges for inter-generational equity implementation stemming from local differences in corporate practices and social ethical norms as well as differing thresholds to sustainable behavior. For instance, challenges arise if corporations or even nation states of the industrialized world outsource inter-generational practices (e.g., environmental pollution) into territories with weaker law enforcement and public scrutiny. These findings emphasize the need for sensitivity to local conditions, transparency along the production and value chains as well as stakeholder expectations monitoring when conducting business in different contexts. Future research may also address ethical dilemmas facing managers in the global arena and their coping strategies in order to enhance research outcomes are leaders' potential operating in the global arena to balance global and local considerations in making responsible decisions. As an implication, inter-generational CSR practices should be locally-oriented and emphasize sensitivity to local conditions when conducting business in different cultural contexts. Corporate executives with foreign subsidiaries should gain training to adapt to specific needs and circumstances of local CSR inter-generational equity customs.

The role of supranational factors that influence responsible leader behavior provide further insight into the propensity to engage in inter-generational equity. With supranational institutions – such as the

UN – having turned to the codification of the triple bottom line in the UN Global Compact, managers are increasingly respected for their accountability and responsibility. Insights on the influence of supra-national regulatory measures and institutions (e.g., NGO activism and the enactment of the UN Global Compact) on inter-generationally-responsible managerial behavior may shed light on success factors in the adoption of inter-generationally socially responsible corporate practices in the global arena. International institutions should set priorities on the corporate inter-generational equity implementation agenda. Quantitative metrics based on standardized evaluation frameworks will coordinate a global monitoring and impact assessment of the role of corporations in the inter-generational equity implementation. Indices of local, national, regional and global corporate inter-generational equity endeavor will help build public private partnership synergies but also shed light on positive and negative externalities and trade-offs. Independent governance institutional evaluation frameworks will help streamline social, economic and environment goals through cost-benefit analysis, life cycle cost discounting and social equality programs. Public private partnerships will aid adaptability and flexibility in collaborations between governments, the private sector and academia. International organizations' emergent risk and crises prevention frameworks will help reform CSR endeavors to imbue an inter-generational equity focus.

Academic research can aid to spearhead temporal perspectives in contemporary CSR research. In particular, a macroeconomic model of global inter-generational equity could study intertemporal transfers between generations with special attention to public and private sector contributions as well as benefit and burden sharing (Puaschunder, 2015). Based on the inter-generational equity dimensions of social responsibility and future orientation, public and private sector inter-generational benefit transfers and burden sharing will thereby capture social, environmental and economic inter-generational contribution potentials of the corporate world. Cross-cultural differences could be outlined by cross-sectional regression analyses on a global scale.

A wider conceptualization of inter-generational equity leadership based on comparative cross-cultural research will help detect inter-generational equity antecedents. Interdisciplinary, multilevel research will detect drivers of inter-generational responsibility and situational influence factors on inter-generational conscientiousness in the international arena. Avenues of future research could also enhance our understanding of how companies and other stakeholders can effectively promote socially responsible behavior for future generations. The organizational-, situational-, societal, and supranational-level determinants of responsible managerial behavior can be influenced by top management teams, policy makers, educators, and external regulators. Best practice studies in this area could shed light on how companies can systematically design and utilize human resource management practices and leadership development programs to promote responsible managerial behavior. Prospective findings may thus enhance our understanding of how companies and other stakeholders can effectively prevent, manage and control the corporate risks associated with unethical conduct of leaders. Capturing the impact of external factors on inter-generational equitable decision making and coping with the ethical dilemmas in leadership challenges may serve as a basis for training and development activities. The implementation of inter-generational equity could further be solicited through building corporate cultures that enhance an ethical climate.

On the corporate incentive level, inter-generational equity may be implemented through performance management and reward systems to hold managers accountable for irresponsible behavior as well as creating psychological incentives to think about future consequences of current corporate conduct. Best practices studies on inter-generational equity in the corporate world will serve as corporate risk management tool to help build a culture of inter-generational CSR and foster a corporate design that pays tribute to inter-generational leadership. In building a cadre of inter-generational equity corporate leaders through corporate trainings and team building development but also corporate inter-generational performance measurement and inter-generational equity reward systems, inter-generational leadership in the corporate sector will be advanced.

At the organizational level, when recruiting, selecting and promoting managers, it is essential for organizations to understand how individual-level variables such as personality traits, motives and values may predict managers' propensity to engage in ethical behavior. For example, firms can use personality tests and integrity tests, along with interviews and assessment centers, to help determine which employees might be more likely to act irresponsibly. They can also assess applicants' attitudes and values to decide whether they will match the corporate culture, with the assumption that candidates' formal qualifications and job-related skills may not be the best predictors of responsible behavior on the job. Studying personality traits but also motives and values that steer managers' propensity to engage in inter-generational equity will allow to set up assessment centers that reveal which individuals are more likely to act irresponsibly and if the managerial ethics will likely match the corporate culture on the inter-generational equity scale.

Inter-generational equity can also be imbued in corporate activities by creating and enforcing company policies and codes of conduct, supporting training and development initiatives which are aimed at increasing moral awareness regarding future generations. Once the individual has joined the organization, induction programs, individual coaching by the supervisor, training and development programs, and other socialization practices could ensure that newcomers learn values, expected behaviors, and social knowledge that are necessary to become inter-generationally conscientious managerial leaders. In terms of communication and control systems, top management teams and governmental officials may actively promote responsible behavior and discourage irresponsible behavior by communicating ethical integrity messages. Implementing performance management and reward systems to hold managers accountable for irresponsible behavior could in addition create a psychologically favorable situation for inter-generational ethicality (Crane & Matten, 2007).

CONCLUSION

The age of globalization heralded the call for inter-generational responsible leadership. With internationalization trends imposing significant challenges regarding sustainability of climate stability, indebtedness and social welfare for an aging Western world population, the need for inter-generationally responsible leadership has leveraged into an international concern. Adopting inter-generational equity in the corporate world underlines the legal case for codifying inter-generational fairness on a global basis. Contributing to interdisciplinary behavioral law and economic models in inter-generational leadership may help alleviating current intertemporal predicaments and future predictable economic, social and environmental crises. The quest for an integration of inter-generational equity in contemporary CSR models of capitalism in the 21st century is targeted at strengthening socially responsible economic market approaches. Acknowledging the untapped potential of corporate entities to address global challenges beyond the reach of singular nation states, calls for the integration of inter-generational equity into contemporary CSR models with attention to differing societal cultural values and institutional aspects related to social responsibility and ethics. Differences in business systems, legal context, the nature of regulation and the likelihood of enforcement and punishment modes therefore have to be scrutinized when shaping inter-generational business ethics in the global arena. The proposed research promises to connect the individual experience to social responsibility in order to unravel ethicality nudges. Common goal compliance is hoped to be modeled by contexts that automatically nudge corporate decision makers in an inter-generational equitable direction. Public and private sector discourse on inter-generational imbalances will help fortify the codification of inter-generational fairness on a global scale. Internationally validated inter-generational equity models will elucidate intercultural, national and regional differences on social responsibility in the inter-generational domain. Findings will help imbue efficiency measures on inter-generational equity implementation through real-world relevant means. CSR advocates advanced with inter-generational conscientiousness will lead to fruitful corporate contributions for a sustainable mankind alongside fostering a harmonious corporate-citizen relation. Cross-national sustainability solutions and interculturally-sensitive inter-generationally equitable business practices may help imbue inter-generational equity in corporate conduct in the global arena with direct implications for today's and tomorrow's society.

REFERENCES

Allais, M. (1947). *Economie et intérét* [Economy and interest]. Paris: Imprimerie Nationale.

Binder, Ch., Kriebaum, U., Marboe, I., Nowak, M., Reinisch, A., & Wittich, St. (2014). *Völkerrecht* [International law]. Vienna: University of Vienna Juridicum.

Centeno, M. A., Cinlar, E., Cloud, D., Creager, A. N., DiMaggio, P. J., Dixit, A. K., . . . Shapiro, J. N. (2013, April). *Global systemic risk*. Princeton Institute for International and Regional Studies, Princeton University.

Centeno, M. A., & Tham, A. (2012). *The emergence of risk in the global system* (working paper). Princeton University.

Crane, A., & Matten, D. (2007). *Corporate Social Responsibility*. London: Sage. doi:10.4135/9781446261194

Elkington, J. (1997). *Cannibals with forks: The triple bottom line of twenty-first century business*. Oxford: Capstone.

Friedman, M. (1970, September 13). The social responsibility of business is to increase its profits. *The New York Times*.

Harrod, R. F. (1948). *Towards a dynamic economics*. London: Macmillan.

Held, D., & McGrew, A. G. (2007). *A new world economic order? Global markets and state power: Beyond globalization/anti-globalization: Beyond the great divide*. New York: Polity.

Nordhaus, W. D. (2008). *A question of balance: Weighting the options on global warming*. New Haven: Yale University Press.

Oppenheimer, M., O'Neill, B. C., Webster, M., & Agrawal, S. (2011). Climate change: The limits of consensus. *Science*, *317*(5844), 1505–1506. doi:10.1126/science.1144831 PMID:17872430

Panitch, L., & Gindin, S. (2012). *The making of global capitalism: The political economy of American empire*. New York: Verso.

Puaschunder, J. M. (2010). On corporate and financial social responsibility [Unpublished doctoral thesis]. University of Vienna, Vienna.

Puaschunder, J. M. (2011). Inter-generational equity as a natural behavioral law. *Library of Congress United States of America Copyright Office.*

Puaschunder, J. M. (2012). On the social representations of inter-generational equity. *Oxford Journal of Finance and Risk Perspectives, 4*(4), 78–99.

Puaschunder, J. M. (2015). On eternal equity in the fin-de-millénaire (Unpublished manuscript). The New School, New York.

Ramsey, F. P. (1928). A mathematical theory of saving. *The Economic Journal, 38*(152), 543–559. doi:10.2307/2224098

Sachs, J. D. (2014). Climate change and inter-generational well-being. In L. Bernard & W. Semmler (Eds.), *The Oxford Handbook of the Macroeconomics of Global Warming*. Oxford: Oxford University Press.

Steurer, R., Martinuzzi, R.-A., & Margula, S. (2012). Public policies on CSR in Europe: Themes, instruments and regional differences. *Corporate Social Responsibility and Environmental Management, 19*(4), 206–227. doi:10.1002/csr.264

World Economic Forum. (2015). Report.

Chapter 15
Teaching Business Ethics Post GFC:
A Corporate Social Responsibility of Universities

Theodora Issa
Curtin University, Australia

David Pick
Curtin University, Australia

ABSTRACT

Following the recent downfall of several high ranking executives, not only in the business world, but also in governments, attention is directed to the teaching of ethics in business schools. More specifically, attention is drawn to these schools' purposes, values, methods, research, partnerships and dialogues in terms of their responsibilities regarding management education. In the current academic environment, business ethics are recognized as an important element in curriculum, but these topics have not yet become fully and successfully embedded in the mainstream business education. Consequently, business schools worldwide are adapting their curricula, research, teaching methodologies and institutional strategies to become better aligned with new challenges and opportunities. However, there is a need for research that will provide theoretical underpinnings for such changes to curricula in terms of pedagogy and content. This chapter examines a method of teaching business ethics. The results of this research were conducted on undergraduate students in their final year study.

INTRODUCTION AND BACKGROUND

The global ramifications of the 2008 Global Financial Crisis (GFC) are extraordinary. Undeniably, the 21st century has become infamous for failure of governance, but what needs to be done to elevate these ramifications? Weitzner and Peridis (2011) posit that investigations into the 2008 GFC have concluded that failures of corporate governance in many financial institutions, financial services firms, credit rat-

DOI: 10.4018/978-1-5225-0720-8.ch015

ing agencies, and government-sponsored entities, were a key cause of the crisis. Weitzner and Darroch (2010) offer a practical framework for managers to approach ethical problems at the heart of many failures. They believe that most of the practising managers are all too aware of issues of corporate responsibility and ethics, but do not receive sufficient guidance on how to discuss or explore the issues, let alone resolve them. Weitzner and Peridis (2011) go on to argue that faith displayed in public policy lulled many sophisticated players in the financial sector who should have known better. Unfortunately, managers have dropped their guard and that resulted in a lapse in the critical scrutiny of recent financial innovations despite earlier governance and ethical failures and the subsequent collapse of companies at the vanguard of financial product innovations.

Though, and as Scott (2014) posits the financial crises are not a new marvel, but they have grown more common, and the financial flows involved have become loftier and more explosive in the past twenty years as indicated by Eichengreen, Andrew and Wypolosz (1995). Scott (2014) states this passé corresponds generally with the era of "economic opening" in emerging markets, a time when most of the Latin American countries, the former Soviet republics, and several Asian countries theatrically reduced their barriers against foreign company undertakings such as imports, foreign direct investment, and foreign portfolio investment. Scott concludes, although, financial crisis origin can encompass a variation of elements, this assignment has focused on three countries and their journey through a corrosive period that have written history. However, and following the 2007-2009 GFC calls for investigation at more than one level have been initiated, especially into business schools, policy makers and accreditation agencies such as The Association to Advance Collegiate Schools of Business (AACSB International) and The European Quality Improvement System (EQUIS) to name a few. As Benson (2004) argues, business education has become a big affair over the last century, and these schools need to respond to market demands and change their way of doing business in its commercial and professional manner.

In an attempt to find solutions to the problems facing business schools, Swanson, Piper, Fort, Gentile, Shreve, Hartman and Margolis (2007) propose solutions for these schools that might move them forward to become an integral part of the recovery. They suggest an outline business schools may adopt, which highlights the need to teach students narratives from the real world, and incorporate ethics in business and business in ethics. Indeed, Sawnson et al., (2007) do not envisage accreditation as one way of solving the problem, but rather the teaching of business ethics in these business schools as a major issue that needs to be considered to solve such problems. In this respect, Lowrie and Willmott (2009) note that the mission-linked approach, underpinned by peer-review, has been good for AACSB International's growth but has, they suggest, been restrictive and unhealthy for business education that does not fit its seemingly flexible and accommodating mould. Further, Lowrie and Willmott (2009) elaborate on this contending that the attention is directed to the educationally unhealthy consequences of an established regional mode of accreditation becoming an international benchmark for business education consumption. At the heart of the AACSB International's mission-linked approach is an evacuation of core content from business education. The change to a mission-linked architecture was originally motivated; it is argued, primarily by expansionist, rather than pedagogical, considerations.

In response to these issues, as well as feedback from students, the business ethics curriculum at Curtin University's Business School has been reviewed. This review was accomplished prior to the school's endeavours for AACSB International's accreditation, which are currently still undergoing the process. This review aimed at the development and facilitation of units at the undergraduate level that aims to equip students to have an understanding of different ethical perspectives to assist them generate their own perception when faced with challenging, demanding, and uncertain and ever-changing business environment that they are part of. Indeed, the curriculum development was particularly focused on the areas of assessment feedback, workload and development of learning activities. As a result, the unit was re-organised. The unit has been given a unifying conceptual theme based around Seeing, Talking, Acting and Reflecting (S.T.A.R.). Thus during the process of teaching this unit, the students would be able to see the ethical dimensions, take an ethical position and communicate that position, act on one's ethical position and reflect on that action. At the time this is an individual effort by educators, rather than adherence to accreditation agencies (e.g. AACSB International, EQUIS) requirements that recognize The United Nations Principles of Responsible Management 'Six Principles' (PRiME 2011), which has been described by Bendel (2007) as the latest illustration of a trend in management education that appears to be responding to criticism of business schools from business, students and wider society during the first years of the 21st century. This chapter derives from data collected through the Curtin University student evaluation system of both the unit and the teaching staff (N = 2215). This chapter provides evidence of teaching business ethics post global financial crisis. Thus, this chapter is an Australian viewpoint outlining the impact of teaching business ethics at the undergraduate level.

LITERATURE REVIEW

Business Ethics Teaching

With regards to teaching business ethics, Krohn (1985 p. 60) contends that scholarly enquiry has concentrated on questions such as (1) who should teach business ethics, (2) what should be taught in business ethics component or course, (3) where or in what courses should business ethics be taught, and, (4) when would business ethics education be of greatest value to the student. Deriving from Garaventa (1998), Krohn provides some indicators in this respect pointing to the results of such scholarly inquiries: Firstly, no one single type of instructor is best qualified to teach business ethics; neither the philosopher nor the theologian is sufficiently familiar with widespread business practices. The business practitioner is usually unfamiliar with ethical theory. Secondly, the content of business ethics courses should relate as closely as possible to the students' own life experiences. Thirdly, business ethics should be integrated into all business courses and not left to a single course often taught by those unfamiliar with the broad spectrum of business activities. And, fourthly, values are learned at a very early age; thus, it is most desirable that business ethics instruction commence as early as possible in the business student's career. Cragg's (1997) considers traditional ways fail to recognize that a principal function of ethics is to facilitate cooperation.

Despite this, Garaventa (1998) argues that the concept of business ethics has continued to remain a major item on the agenda of corporations for the last twenty years. Regrettably, this longevity of interest has not been matched by equal attention given to the pedagogical methods and techniques used to address these issues. The mode of teaching business ethics then generally involved reliance on 'war stories', 'case studies', and 'seminars'. Garaventa (1998) contends that today's dynamic environment creates pressures for higher levels of ethical behaviour by business, whereas many ethical challenges faced by contemporary managers are not easily resolved by existing guidelines and require managers to expand their scope of analysis in attempting to arrive at satisfactory resolutions. Nonetheless, Brinkmann and Sims (2001) suggest that literature be an alternative source of insights, as authors are able to highlight behaviours that may not be available from traditional sources. Thus, the non-traditional approach to teaching business ethics enhances the ability to relate to the increasingly complex ethical issues facing the individual and the organization. Early in the 21st century, especially following the aftermath of the GFC, business ethics and its teaching at business schools have become paramount. In this respect, Brinkmann and Sims (2001p. 174) argue that the teaching of a well-established, well-intended and designed business ethics unit can still have little effect. Brinkmann and Sims (2001) elaborate such views in a systematic fashion and formulate a list of thirteen premises and nine recommendations in thesis format. From these premises: Firstly, 'Business ethics is not the only subject students are taught. This means that business ethics competes with other subjects for limited student working time and attention, and that business ethics is perceived selectively with mindsets which may be acquired in other courses'. Secondly, 'Superficial like or dislike of business ethics teaching, passive resistance against it or repressive tolerance of it is understandable, if faculty and students have not had the opportunity to discuss goals or to participate in curriculum design decisions' (Brinkmann and Sims 2001p. 187).

In their report on the inclusion of business ethics in the curriculum, Philips et al. (2004) contend that while many schools have initiated new ethics instructions, cannot be assumed that the majority of students are adequately prepared to meet the ethical challenges of the modern workplace, concluding that more work is still needed. They consider that accreditation (e.g. AACSB International) might be one of the avenues to ensure that this is being done, as AACSB International identify a need to ascertain whether or not business schools demonstrate their ongoing commitment to ethics which is considered essential in the delivery of quality business education. However, Durand and McGuire (2005) argue that legitimating accreditation organizations face selection pressures to both maintain their legitimacy among their constituents, and to expand the domain of their activities. In this respect, Durand and McGuire (2005) raise three important issues: firstly, the factors that lead legitimating agencies to expand their domain; secondly, the need to maintain legitimacy among existing constituents; and thirdly, the establishment of legitimacy in the new domain. They use the domain expansion of the AACSB International to develop propositions relevant to these three research issues. They conclude that quality concerns, process vs. content strategy, and institutional entrepreneurship are the main factors that impact on the effectiveness of legitimating agencies. Thus, it is our belief that business schools should not only incorporate business ethics in their curriculum for the sake of accreditation, but this addition to the curriculum should aim at teaching students about business ethics. These business schools need to start with their mission which calls for graduating business students, the future employees, managers and leaders the opportunity to learn and be equipped with knowledge that will assist them to recognise, critically examine, reflect and solve issues relating to ethical dilemmas before embarking on their careers.

An increased effort has been made to incorporate business ethics, and terms such as *sustainability*, *corporate social responsibility* and *corporate governance* in the curricula offered to undergraduate and postgraduate students at several universities worldwide. For example, Harris (2008) argues that the 'case study' provides a basis for considering the purpose of business ethics teaching. Brinkmann and Henriksen (2010) suggest vocational ethics as a legitimate sub-specialty for business ethics research and development. In a recent study from the Middle East on the importance of ethics in the teaching of accounting, Bogharian and El-Cheikh (2012) provide evidence from students and faculty members that the teaching of ethics is essential, and that universities at the highest level should do more to instil ethics into its programmes. Espinosa and Porter (2011) and Viswanathan (2012) call for the inclusion of sustainability in the MBA curriculum in an attempt to enhance the understanding of students that business has concerns other than profit. Although the calls for change are insistent, some academics have highlighted the complexity of management in organizations and doubted the organizations' ability to implement sustainability in their day-to-day activities (Whitla 2011). Further, Whitla (2011) examines the process of integrating ethics into the teaching of international business within the Greater China region, presenting a modified 'learning outcomes based' framework for such integration with practical suggestions and advice on how such a course can be introduced.

In their review of the AACSB International-accredited business school courses to determine compliance with the standards set by AACSB International, Heller, and Heller (2011) contend that business ethics is not a separate moral standard, but the study of how the business environment poses its own unique challenges for the moral person who acts as an agent for business. Further, and in their recent paper, Trapnell and Boxx (2011) describe some of the essential outcomes that business schools need to achieve to secure AACSB International's accreditation (a process our school is currently undergoing). This module is intended to achieve this outcome: it exposes students to the need to engage with internal and external stakeholders at personal and social levels as well as professionally. This requires a high level of engagement, strong student learning, and a relevant curriculum.

However, Corcoran (2007) argues that the adoption of more flexible mission-linked standards make accreditation a doable proposition for many unaccredited business programs. In this respect, Fancisco, Noland and Sinclair (2008) argue that the AACSB International needs to reconsider its mission and divide accredited institutions into tiers or classes based on criteria such as the types of degrees granted, research productivity, and financial resources. Lowrie and Willmot (2009) question the value of accreditation of business schools as merely satisfying a need for a 'seal of approval on what they do' which they might use since 'when it comes to recruiting of students and of faculty, it is a critical additional affirmation that we are a place worth coming to.' (Lowrie and Willmott 2009p. 412). These are serious issues that must be addressed.

Responding to the events at the start of the 21st century, the UN principles for Responsible Management Education (UN PRiME) were launched in Geneva in July 2007 (United Nations 2007). These principles call for the incorporation of universal values in curricula and research, and are offered as a guiding framework for academic institutions to advance the broader cause of corporate social responsibility. The Principles have been developed by an international task force of 60 deans, university presidents and official representatives of leading business schools. The institutions that contributed to its development are from the higher learning sector. They are involved in the education of current and future managers who would voluntarily commit to the ongoing improvement of the principles and purpose of higher education incorporating values, educational frameworks and method, partnership with corporations, and conduct dialogue with other stakeholders such as businesses and governments. Furthermore, they would provide ongoing reports on progress to all the stakeholders and exchange effective practices with other academic institutions (Solitander et al. 2011). Although commitment to the six principles (UN PRiME) initiative continues to be 'voluntary' in nature, it has been co-convened by the United Nations Global Compact, the AACSB International, the European Foundation for Management Development (EFMD), the Aspen Institute's Business and Society Program (AIBSB), the Globally Responsible Leadership Initiative (GRLI) and Net Impact (NI), which might enhance its legitimisation and authority, but might be insufficient in the long run.

There is limited literature on teaching business ethics in Australia; however, some of what was published would be either in the form of books or journal articles. For example, and back in 1997 Milton-Smith and following an extensive survey and literature review, stated that then there seemed to have been a widespread awareness of the need for reform in many areas of public administration, corporate governance and professional behaviour. However, a continuing cause for concern was the lack of leadership in identifying and addressing complex ethical dilemmas, particularly in the areas of conflict of interest and disclosure. Milton-Smith goes on to state that feedback from professional bodies, industry associations and university business schools indicated slow but uneven progress in ethics education. While several ethic centres and prominent individual ethicists have introduced innovative programs and given ethical issues greater prominence in the media, narrow vocationalism continued to take place precedence over personal values in the business and management curriculum.

Further, Grace (1998) published a book that sets out in plain language ethical questions of direct relevance to business with expanded range of issues covered including a chapter on international business ethics, drawing extensively from Asian examples. Examining these cases, it can be noticed that the teaching of business ethics in Australia places on corporate social responsibility and sustainability. More recently, the discussion in relation to ethics and business schools have taken another view, whereas a study by Brimble and Stevenson-Clarke (2005) confirmed the significance of the issue of academic dishonesty within the Australian tertiary sector, indicating considerable divergence between students and staff in terms of perceptions of the seriousness and prevalence of student academic misconduct. Brimble and Stevenson-Clarke (2005) concluded by suggesting that university administrators need to examine this issue closely in order to develop mechanisms for managing and curtailing the level of academic misconduct, since a failure to do so may lead to a further undermining of the academic integrity of the Australian tertiary sector.

Moreover, it is worthwhile to note here that Australia is really a unique country with the increased number of international students, who bring with them their own cultural understanding of how they deal with ethical issues, thus, this is a vast topic to discuss however, Jonson, McGuire and O'Neill (2015) and in their study trying to respond to the question how ethics is best taught to undergraduate business students in Australia found that culture is important especially with the presence of high number of international students in Australia, which in their opinion is more important than gender.

Finally, in their examination of the teaching of business ethics (BE567) in Australia to postgraduate students, Issa and Pick (2008) concluded that while the design of the unit is important, the attitudes and skills of the teaching staff have a significant impact on student engagement and learning. The evidence from the literature, combined with the findings of Issa and Pick's (2008) research, support the idea that business ethics should become a compulsory unit in the business curriculum regardless of accreditation requirements, but this needs to be supported by the appointment of competent and enthusiastic teaching staff.

METHODOLOGY

The methodology used in the development of this chapter was mainly a mix of quantitative and qualitative techniques. The main vehicle was the 'eVALUate' survey. According to Oliver et al. (2011), 'eVALUate' prompts students to reflect on what helps their achievement of unit learning outcomes, and to report their levels of motivation, engagement and overall satisfaction with a semester-long course or unit of study.

This study is based on data collected over the period 2009 to 2015 from Curtin University's 'eVALUate' student feedback system which is divided into two sections: (i) the unit, and, (ii) the teaching staff. Tables 1 and 2 provide the aspects that students are asked to comment upon in relation to the unit and the teaching staff.

In addition to the quantitative data provided in response to these eleven aspects, the students were given the opportunity to add comments on: (1) the most helpful aspects of Business Ethics Unit (course)

Table 1. 'eVALUate' students' learning aspects examined

Aspect #	Students' Learning Aspects Examined Via 'eVALUate' Survey on Unit
1	The learning outcomes in this unit are clearly identified
2	The learning experiences in this unit help me to achieve the learning outcomes
3	The learning resources in this unit help me to achieve the learning outcomes
4	The assessment tasks in this unit evaluate my achieve the learning outcomes
5	Feedback on my work in this unit helps me to achieve the learning outcomes
6	The workload in this unit is appropriate to the achievements of the learning outcomes
7	The quality of teaching in this unit helps me to achieve the learning outcomes
8	I am motivated to achieve the learning outcomes in this unit
9	I make best use of the learning experiences in this unit.
10	I think about how I can learn more effectively in this unit
11	Overall, I am satisfied with this unit

Table 2. 'eVALUate' survey on teaching staff

Aspect #	Students' 'eVALUate' Survey on Teaching Staff
1	Is well organized
2	Communicates clearly
3	Is approachable
4	Provides useful feedback
5	Appears knowledgeable in this subject area
6	Is enthusiastic in teaching this unit
7	Is an effective teacher

(BE300) and, (2) how they think (BE300) might be improved. Students were limited to 600 characters per comment under these two sections. In addition, the responses provided by the students in 2010 on what are the pluses, minuses and the interesting aspects (PMI) of the newly-designed unit.

Further, this chapter advances a study conducted by Issa and Pick (2010) who reported on the development of a new business ethics curriculum for undergraduates (BE300), and the eVALUate data up to 2009. In introducing a new teaching model (Seeing, Talking, Acting and Reflecting – 'S.T.A.R.'), various resources, activities and assessment tasks were adopted to encourage critical thinking, creativity and imagination in ethical decision making, and to stimulate a depth of learning that students could transfer to their workplaces. Dickie, Pick and Issa (2011) reported on a cohort of approximately 100 undergraduate business ethics students who responded to the PMI survey asking them to state the pluses, minuses and interesting aspects of the newly-designed unit. The student cohort was extremely diverse in terms of age, education and workplace or business experience. In this study which compared two PMI results, Dickie, Pick and Issa (2011) concluded that at the end of semester, university-wide eVALUate results indicated that the development of new approaches can leverage the learning experiences of students to result in a greater level of student engagement. The results also provided an indication of the changing levels of engagement as the students' learning experiences cumulatively developed through the implementation of the S.T.A.R. model. These results also indicated the satisfaction with the academic staff.

Sample and Analysis

Between 2009 and 2015, 2,215 students enrolled in the unit (course). Of these, 825 (38%) responded to the 'eVALUate' survey. Response rates varied between a low of 27% in Semester 1, 2012 and a high of 49% in Semester 2, 2010. These 'eVALUate' surveys include students studying at partner institutions and campuses in offshore locations (e.g. Singapore, Malaysia, and Mauritius) and other Australian cities (e.g. Sydney) (Table 3).

Issa and Pick (2010) posed the question 'Is business ethics worth teaching?', providing evidence from their teaching of a business ethics unit (BE300) that, if students study business ethics, this makes a difference and has the potential to encourage a shift from the conventional 'business mindset' or perspective students seem to acquire in their studies to a more critical and reflective perspective. The results clearly suggest that this unit (BE300) has a positive effect on students' learning about business ethics. This confirms the research suggesting that the moral reasoning of individuals can be advanced by carefully designed training. However, it seems that although the design of the unit is important, the attitudes and skills of the teaching staff have a significant impact on how well the students learn – so it appears that students do not just 'learn the subject'; they also 'learn the lecturer'. This has significant implications for the delivery of the unit in locations away from the main campus where the unit coordinator has limited control, which is a shortcoming that is being addressed on the highest levels at the university. The extent to which this is unique to the teaching of business ethics is an issue that requires further research.

Table 3. Number of business ethics Students (onshore and offshore) 2009-2015 and their responses rates to eVALUate

Brief eVALUAte Statistics Business Ethics Undergraduate unit 'BE300' (2009-2015)			
Semester/year	**# Students**	**# Responses**	**Percentages**
Semester 1, 2009	122	55	45%
Semester 2, 2009	333	141	42%
Semester 1, 2010	100	38	38%
Semester 2, 2010	131	64	49%
Semester 1, 2011	119	47	39%
Semester 2, 2011	428	139	33%
Semester 1, 2012	181	48	27%
Semester 2, 2012	246	87	35%
Semester 1, 2014	150	52	35%
Semester 2, 2014	263	105	40%
Semester 1, 2015	142	53	37%
Total	**2215**	**829**	**38%**

In this follow-on research, further evidence is provided on the importance of the calibre of the teaching staff and their enthusiasm for the teaching of business ethics. In commenting on the most helpful aspects of the unit, students would without hesitation include the names of those lecturers who were the most helpful.

The format of the lectures made them challenging and enjoyable. This is one of the few units I have taken in which I felt that the lecturer had a genuine interest in the understanding of content that was developed by students. The directed discussions were very valuable in both learning the precepts of the topic and learning to apply them to case studies (eVALUate)

[Lecturer] was excellent. The case studies also helped (eVALUate)

[Lecturer's] enthusiasm and involvement with the class really aided my understanding of Business Ethics. Lecturer was always patient and made sure we understood the concepts (eVALUate)

[Lecturer] was clearly passionate and knowledgeable about the topics and business ethics in general. This helped in motivation and my personal understanding. I feel like the open book exam was a very appropriate addition to the unit as there were a lot of theories to learn and understand. It would be unreasonable to expect students to memorize so many. The learning outcomes were clear and weighted appropriately. This helped to consolidate my learning. (eVALUate)

[Lecturer] was brilliant at communicating with us - the students. (eVALUate).

[Lecturer] was brilliant at constantly communicated and letting it known what is expected. It was very helpful that she was providing feedback that was personal which aided in my learning and completing other assessments. [Lecturer] was a fantastic tutor and really added to my experience in learning. (eVALUate).

I really enjoyed studying this unit. It has helped explain some of the incidences that I have observed in the workplace. I believe that the knowledge that I gained from studying this unit will assist me in my current role at work. I found that the workshops facilitated by [Lecturer] were very effective in achieving the learning outcomes. (eVALUate).

[Lecturer] was a great Tutor, very passionate about business ethics and was a great teacher to learn from. I found the background notes that were provided for each topic very helpful in assisting me to gain a quick understanding of the topic which enabled me to then complete further research. Overall is good. (eVALUate)

[Lecturer] was very good at explaining the theory and what was expected. [Lecturer] responded to individual questions and issues quickly, but the results for assignments where slow to be released. The tutorials were helpful in assisting our learning, particularly applying knowledge to case studies. (eVALUate)

I loved this unit!! I think it is fabulous we are learning this and I think it should be a pre-requisite for ALL degrees!! [Lecturer] was wonderful, very enthusiastic. The lectures were great. I think the tutori-

als were fabulous, [Lecturer] clearly explained theories with examples and made it easy to understand. Selected journal articles were fabulous too! (eVALUate).

I really liked how [Lecturer] recapped the topics each week, which was really helpful for learning the new materials. (eVALUate)

[Lecturer] is the most helpful aspect of the unit, and her mind maps each week were a big help to follow and to understand the concepts. (eVALUate)

Engaging and inspirational teaching staff, helps the class to feel motivated to prepare, participate and excel within the unit. Overall, a very well structured and engaging unit, that I have thoroughly enjoyed. (eVALUate).

The best aspect of BE300 was the tutorials, hands down. I attended almost every one because they were so helpful. It was great being able to discuss ethical dilemmas and ideas in such a supportive environment. It really improved my learning and gave me a far better understanding of all the coursework. [Lecturer] was particularly helpful in explaining difficult concepts and the differences between some of them. The coursework and the tutorials have given me a solid foundation from which to make ethical decisions for the future. (Semester 1, 2014)

This unit helped me to understand in relation to many ethics concepts. [Lecturer] a is being patient enough to teach us in all those concepts and gave us task every single week in our tutorial class in order to let us to have more understanding about all those concepts. (eVALUate)

This was also evident in the survey conducted with that same cohort, asking them to comment on the 'pluses, minuses and interesting (PMI)' aspects of this unit. They made statements such as:

Good, positive and interactive lecturer (PMI)

Lecturer always encourages students to express their thoughts and always "dig" deeper towards their thinking (PMI)

However, and due to changes in the teaching staff, a new cadre was established between semesters. Although the design and the material continued to be the same, the students' comments were:

I did not like my tutor [name of tutor] at all. Class was very boring. I even started to miss out on classes sometimes and study on my own (eVALUate)

Choose better lecturer (eVALUate)

Change tutor (eVALUate)

It is evident here that the design of the unit, although important, must be supported by competent academics to teach the unit. Further, the approach was unique for Curtin University (fewer PowerPoint slides, fewer notes, and more class activities), which was not the norm in other units at the school. This led to negative comments from the students:

Lecture slides could be a bonus, but that is also where this unit separates itself from other regurgitation type units (eVALUate)

More notes need to be given maybe every week notes should be given as to what was discussed in the unit (eVALUate)

[It is] hard to study with few notes, or lecture notes. Also the concepts are hard to grasp so maybe a page full of definitions at the end of semester would be good (eVALUate)

On the other hand, there were students who appreciated the new method of teaching, including the concept maps, the peer-reviewed journal articles, the debates and discussions about the current news linking theory to practice, and the unit or the course (BE300) as a whole that attracted positive comments from the students. For example:

It is a fun unit to learn. (eVALUate)

BE300 has been a surprisingly interesting unit. It has encouraged in-class discussion and debate that has been really helpful to my learning experience. It has also achieved its goal of helping me think ethically in decision making, and also to go back over past experiences and assess how they went. (eVALUate).

The mind maps are amazing! Best tool for helping work through concepts. Great help with all the relevant case studies provided each week. (Semester 1, 2014).

This unit helped me realised that there is more to be learn about ethics than we think. Same time, it taught me to reflect on my behaviour in general as a student, stakeholder and as a good citizen. I learnt a lot and this unit is very valuable for life lesson not just for business related matter but also for life as well. Keep up the good work. (eVALUate).

This course has helped me to understand the basic norms, or values that distinguish between what is good and bad or right and wrong. it focuses on examining conduct and policies and promoting appropriate conduct and policies within the context of commercial enterprise, both at the individual and the organizational level. It has also helped to identify major ethical concerns of businesses and proposing solutions to them through ethical theory, and also examining case studies that shed light on ethical dilemma. (eVALUate)

There is consistency in the module throughout the teaching weeks. Furthermore, the tasks allocated to us in the different seminars allow us to get familiar with the concepts and we do not have to try hard to remember them. All the learning outcomes in the different seminars are interlinked. Business Ethics allows us to question ourselves on our behaviour in our everyday life as well. It allows us to have a broader perspective on everything. (eVALUate)

Ethics is not only interesting but also very helpful in decision-making. I have learned a lot from this unit and I know that I will not judge people on their behavior or decisions because we should look at things from different perspectives. What is right for me is not right for other people and that is the most important consideration if we need to leave in our globalised world. (eVALUate)

Almost hoping I fail so I can do this unit again - it has changed the way I look at business and think about theories in my other units. (eVALUate)

Indeed, students are used to different styles of teaching by other lecturers of different units at the same business school; thus, if a new, unique and novel approach is to be adopted for the teaching of business ethics, it must have faculty support at the highest level. It will require a major re-shaping of the delivery of all units, enabling students to concentrate on the topics rather than the method of delivery and the allocation of participation marks. In this chapter, we suggest a framework that highlights issues involved in the enhancement of university reputation other than accreditation for a successful business school as illustrated in Figure 1.

At the centre of this Figure 1 we can see the core of the University's mission that should concentrate on students' character building, which can only be achieved through understanding of ethical perspectives, theories and training on how best to take an ethical decision in their own life and their future business life. This will eventually improve the reputation of the university both locally and internationally. To assist the University achieve and comply with this mission, there are some requirements, and these

Figure 1. Issues involved in the enhancement of university reputation – other than accreditation

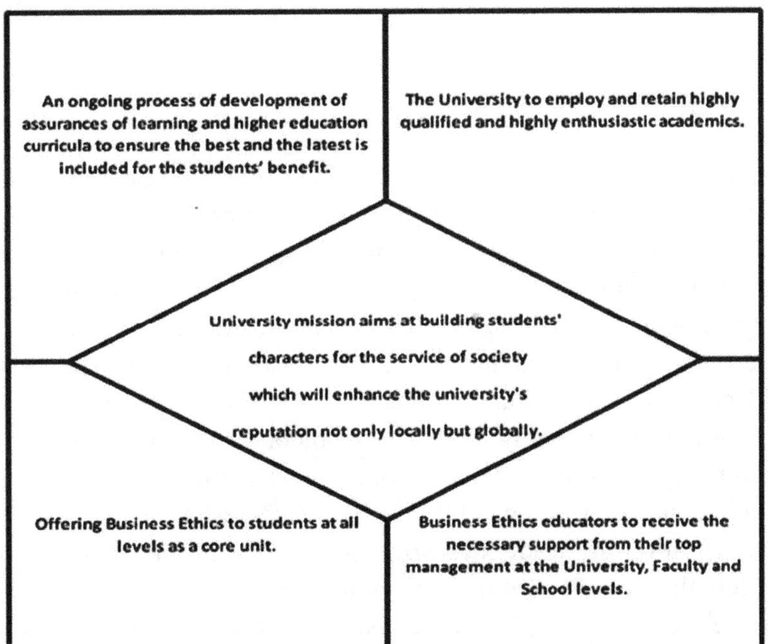

would be the ongoing development of the higher education curricula for the students' benefits and the building of their character, this cannot be achieved without the presence of the highly qualified and enthusiastic academics and those academics who are keen to teach business ethics be given the necessary support from top management at the university and faculty levels to ensure that they can achieve their goals of changing the mindsets of students ensuring that taking an ethical decision comes as a second nature of these students. Finally, having business ethics taught as one topic within a unit, would never be sufficient to ensure long term positive results, but, what is needed to have these students, and at all levels, especially when they commence their university journey to be exposed to the basics of business ethics and this should be given as a core unit rather than an elective unit. Therefore, these four issues combined if dealt with properly might assist universities to enhance their reputation by concentrating on building the students' character rather than only ensuring that students have the technical and discipline knowledge only. This is not an easy task, especially when we notice that government funding is not as high to those specialising in business ethics than any other field in the social studies.

Certainly, business schools need to ensure the teaching of business ethics is embedded in the curriculum as a core unit, coupled with standardised assessment and the employment of highly qualified and competent academic staff who are assured of faculty support in teaching a business ethics unit. This is aligned with the university's mission to build the students' character, thus enhancing the university's reputation not only locally but globally. Further, the University needs to ensure the ongoing development of not only the curriculum but rather the assurances of learning aiming at the benefit of students. Such actions need to be supported by the employment and retention of highly qualified and highly enthusiastic academics who would receive the university, the faculty and the school's ultimate support, which must ultimately and surely enhance the university's reputation regardless of any type of accreditation. It is with great pleasure to state here, that due to the ongoing process of accreditation at our school, these have been implemented and the ethical understanding and ethical sensitivity are part of what is being assessed at all levels.

Limitations and Significance

Despite the fact that this chapter derives from data obtained from only one University in Australia, yet, this chapter provided a brief discussion about the benefits of investing in the development and teaching of business ethics at all levels at the University. However, this can only be achieved with the involvement of enthusiastic and well-informed, knowledgeable lecturers, who are keen to engage in discussions with the students regarding issues of ethical nature. This needs to be coupled with the involvement of industry to allow the students have direct insights from industry on the latest in relation to the managerial significance of learning and understanding business ethics, and how such an understanding would improve the business as a whole, not only limited to the theoretical understanding. While this might be difficult to achieve, as not every business would be ready to share their business secrets, but there is need to increase collaboration and cooperation between University education and business for the benefit of the students, whereas whatever the academics would teach if the business culture dictates ignoring the ethical issues, definitely the work done at the University level would be lost in the jungle of mere what is referred to as 'business decisions' that in some cases are differentiated from 'ethical decisions'.

Indeed, those who would be developing and teaching business ethics to the University students should themselves maintain an ethical mindset (Issa, 2009). Ethical mindsets are '...an appreciation of and reflection on any situation through the filter of personal beliefs and values such as honesty, integrity, harmony, balance, truth seeking, making a difference, and demonstrating professionalism, deriving from the strength rooted in individual's inner-self'. (Issa, 2009, p. 163). As a result of Issa (2009) ethical mindsets have some eight components (a) Aesthetic spirituality, (b) Religious spirituality, (3) Optimism, (4) Harmony and Balance, (5) Truth seeking, (6) Pursuit of joy, peace and beauty, (7) Making a difference, and (8) Professionalism. Therefore, those involved in developing and teaching business ethics need at least to maintain these components in their mindsets, enlightened by spirituality, optimistic, eager to make a difference, always perusing joy, peace and beauty, keen to establish harmony and balance, truth seeker, and continuously acting in a professional manner. These might be too difficult to find in an individual, but training might assist to develop these, and co-teaching and team work in the development and delivery of teaching business ethics might assist achieve this.

CONCLUSION

The main aim of this chapter was to provide a background on the teaching of business ethics, providing evidence from Australia on the business ethics curriculum. While the findings apply to only one University in Australia, they indicate that if engaging content and pedagogies coupled with enthusiastic and well-versed academic staff, are provided, student learning about business ethics is enhanced and their ideas about the role of business and the practice of management becomes more sophisticated, and they adopt a more critical and reflective attitude. This is extremely important following the recent transgressions which have led to attention being directed to business schools, and more specifically to their purposes, values, methods, researches, partnerships and dialogues in relation to their responsible management education.

Certainly, the six principles established by the United Nations are supported by several organisations responsible for accrediting business schools (e.g. EFMD, EABIS, AACSB, etc.) in order to inspire and champion responsible management education, research and thought leadership globally (PRiME 2011), but questions emerge regarding the effectiveness or otherwise of these initiatives. In the current academic environment, business ethics, corporate governance, corporate responsibility and sustainability have been recognised as important elements in the curricula, but have hitherto not fully and successfully been embedded in the mainstream of business education. As a result, business schools and universities worldwide are now gradually adapting their curricula, research, teaching methodologies and institutional strategies to the new business challenges and opportunities.

These are long-term goals which might be achieved only by concentrating on the core university mission that focuses on graduating students of solid character who aim to serve their community and society. This can be achieved by employing highly qualified and highly passionate academics with ethical mindsets supported by the faculty and the university, who are prepared to commit to the ongoing development of business curriculum to meet the relentless challenges of the 21st century, which might be achieved in collaboration and co-operation with industry. Indeed, embedding business ethics in the curricula, hiring better quality teaching staff, ensuring the ongoing development of the assurances of learning and curricula, and most importantly, the retention of experienced business ethics lecturers for the teaching of such a unit, would foster a more responsible management education. This might prove to be challenging, especially given the ongoing changes to higher education funding in the Western world, but needs to be done. The reputation of business schools may be improved if they focus on issues beyond that of merely seeking accreditation such as AACSB International or EFMD.

REFERENCES

Bendell, J. (2007). World Review: A synopsis of the key strategic developments in corporate responsibility around the globe over the last quarter. *JCC,* July-September, 4-14.

Benson, P. G. (2004, September 14). The Evolution of Business Education in the U.S. *Decision Line*, September, 17-20.

Brimble, M. & Stevenson-Clarke, P. (2005). Perceptions of the Prevalence and Seriousness of Academic Dishonesty in Australian Universities. *The Australian Educational Researcher*, 32(3), 19-44.

Brinkmann, J., & Henriksen, A. M. (2008). Vocational Ethics as a Subspecialty of Business Ethics - Structuring a Research and Teaching Field. *Journal of Business Ethics*, *81*(3), 623–634. doi:10.1007/s10551-007-9536-8

Brinkmann, J. & Sims, RR. (2001). Stakeholder-Sensitive Business Ethics Teaching. *Teaching Business Ethics*, 5(2), 171-193.

Corcoran, C.P. (2007). Distinctions Among Accreditation Agencies For Business Programs. *Journal of College Teaching and Learning*, 4(9), 27-30.

Dickie, C., Pick, D. & Issa, T. (2011). Leveraging Learning Experiences to Promote Student Engagement in a Business Ethics Class. *Practice and Evidence of Scholarship of Teaching and Learning in Higher Education (PESTLHE)*, 6 (3), 214-231.

Durand, R., & McGuire, J. (2005). Legitimating Agencies in the Face of Selection: The Case of AACSB. *Organization Studies*, 26(2), 165-196.

Eichengreen, B., Andrew, R., & Wypolosz, C. (1995). Exchange market mayhem: The antecedents and aftermath of speculative attacks. *Economic Policy*, *10*(October), 249–312. doi:10.2307/1344591

Espinosa, A., & Porter, T. (2011). Sustainability, complexity and learning; insights from complex systems approaches. *The Learning Organization*, 18(1), 54-72.

Francisco, W., Noland, T.G. & Sinclair, D. (2008). AACSB Accreditation: Symbol of Excellene or March Toward Mediocrity? *Journal of College Teaching and Learning*, 5(5), 25-30.

Frank, G., Ofobike, E., & Gradisher, S. (2010). Teaching Business Ethics: A Quandary for Accounting Educators. *Journal of Education for Business*, 85,132–138.

Garaventa, E. (1998). DRAMA: A Tool for Teaching Business Ethics. *Business Ethics Quarterly*, 8(3), 535-545.

Grace, D. (1998). *Business Ethics: Australian Problems and Cases*. Oxford University Press.

Heller, N.A., & Heller, V.L. (2011). Business Ethics Education: Are Business Schools Teaching to the AACSB Ethics Education Task Force Recommendations? *International Journal of Business and Social Science*. 2(20), 30-38.

Issa, T. (2009). Ethical mindsets, aesthetics and spirituality: A mixed-methods approach analysis of the Australian services sector. Available online through. Perth: School of Management, Curtin Business School, Curtin University of Technology. Retrieved from http://espace.library.curtin.edu.au/R/?func=dbin-jump-full&object_id=131986&local_base=GEN01-ERA02

Issa, T., & Pick, D. (2010) Is business ethics worth teaching? An Australian higher education experience. *Paper read at European Business Ethics Network Conference*, Queen Mary University, London.

Jonson, E. P., McGuire, L.M. & O'Neill, D. (2015). Teaching Ethics to Undergraduate Business Students in Australia: Comparison of Integrated and Stand-alone Approaches. *Journal of Business Ethics*, 132(2), 477-491.

Krohn, F.B. (1985). A General Semantics Approach to Teaching Business Ethics. *The Journal of Business Communication*, 22(3), 59-66.

Lowrie, A. & Willmott, H. (2009). Accreditation Sickness in the Consumption of Business Education: The Vacuum in AACSB Standard Setting. *Management Learning*, 40(4), 411-420.

Milton-Smith, J. (1997). Business Ethics in Australia and New Zealand. *Teaching Business Ethics*, 16(14), 1485-1497.

Oliver, B., Tucker, B., Gupta, R. & Yeo, S. (2008). eVALUate: an evaluation instrument for measuring students' perceptions of their engagement and learning outcomes. *Assessment and Evaluation in Higher Education,* 33(6), 619-630.

Philips, S. M., Blood, M., Bosland, N., Burke, L., Conrad, C. F., Fernandes, J., et al. (2004). Ethics Education in Business Schools. AACSB International.

Scott, K. D. (2014). "Global Financial Crises" The SelectedWorks of Kimberly D Scott. Retrieved from http://works.bepress.com/kimberly_scott/1

Solitander, Nikodemus; Martin; Fougere, Sobczak, A., & Herlin, H. (2011). We Are the Champions: Organizational Learning and Change for Responsible Management Education. *Journal of Management Education*, *36*(3), 337–360.

Swanson, D., Piper, T. R., Fort, T., Gentile, M. C., Shreve, R. S., Hartman, E., & Margolis, J. (2007). *Shaping Tomorrow's Business Leaders: Principles and Practices for a Model Business Ethics Program.* USA: Business Roundtable.

Trapnell, J. & Boxx, W.R. (2011). Attributes of excellence. *BizEd,* 411, 50-54.

United Nations. (2007) *The Principles for Responsible Management Education.* Retrieved from www.unglobalcompact.com/HowToParticipate/academic_network/index.html#bus_ed

Viswanathan, M. (2012). Curricular Innovations on Sustainability and Subsistence Marketplaces: Philosophical, Substantive, and Methodological Orientations. *Journal of Management Education,* 36(3), 389-427.

Weitzner, D. & Darroch, J. (2010). The Limits of Strategic Rationality: Ethics, Enterprise Risk Management, and Governance. *Journal of Business Ethics*, 92(3), 361-372.

Weitzner, D. & Peridis, T. (2011). Corporate Governance as Part of the Strategic Process: Rethinking the Role of the Board. *Journal of Business Ethics*, 102(1), 33-42.

Whitla, P. (2011). Integrating Ethics into International Business Teaching: Challenges and Methodologies in the Greater China Context. *Journal of Teaching in International Business*, *22*(3), 168–184. doi :10.1080/08975930.2011.653745

ADDITIONAL READING

Martin, K., & Parmar, B. (2012). Assumption in Decision Making Scholarship: Implications for Business Ethics Research. *Journal of Business Ethics*, *105*(3), 289–306. doi:10.1007/s10551-011-0965-z

McDonald, G.M. (2005). A Case Example: Integrating Ethics into the Academic Business Curriculum. *Journal of Business Ethics*, 54(4), 371-384.

Morris, D. (2001). Business Ethics Assessment Criteria: Business V. Philosophy - Survey Results. *Business Ethics Quarterly*, 11(4), 623-650.

Saat, M.M., Porter, S., & Woodbine, G. (2010). The effect of ethics courses on the ethical judgment-making ability of Malaysian accounting students. *Journal of Financial Reporting and Accounting*, 8(2), 92-109.

Sims, R.R. (2004). Business Ethics Teaching: Using Conversational Learning to Build an Effective Classroom Learning Environment. *Journal of Business Ethics,* 49(2), 201-211.

Sims, R.R., & Brinkmann, J. (2003). Business Ethics Curriculum Design: Suggestions and Illustrations. *Teaching Business Ethics,* 7(1), 69-86.

Sims, R.R., & Felton, E.L., Jr. (2006). Designing and Delivering Business Ethics Teaching and Learning. *Journal of Business Ethics,* 63(3), 297-312.

Stiles, P., Jameson, A., & Lord, A. (1993). Teaching Business Ethics: an Open Learning Approach. *Management Learning,* 24(3), 246-261.

Vega, G. (2003). Teaching Business Ethics for Effective Learning, by Ronald R. Sims. *Academy of Management Learning & Education*, December,426–427.

Weber, J., & Glyptis, S.M. (2000). Measuring the impact of business ethics course and community service experience on students' values and opinions. *Teaching Business Ethics,* 4(4), 341-358.

KEY TERMS AND DEFINITIONS

AACSB: Stands for the Association to Advance Collegiate Schools of Business and is the benchmark of quality for business education worldwide. Earning and maintaining AACSB accreditation is a comprehensive, demanding process.

EFMD: Stands for European Foundation for Management Development which is an international not-for-profit association, based in Brussels, Belgium.

EQUIS: Stands for European Quality Improvement System which is the world's leading international accreditation for business schools.

eVALUate: Linguistically it means to judge or determine the significance, worth, or quality of; assess: to evaluate the results of an experiment. In this chapter, it refers to a system that is in use by Curtin University to collect judgements from students regarding their learning journey.

GFC: Stands for Global Financial Crisis that affected the world during 2007-2009.

PRiME: As indicated on the Sustainable Teaching and Learning website, the mission of the Principles for Responsible Management Education (PRME) initiative is to inspire and champion responsible management education, research and thought leadership globally. The PRiME are inspired by internationally accepted values such as the principles of the United Nations Global Compact. They seek to establish a process of continuous improvement among institutions of management education in order to develop a new generation of business leaders capable of managing the complex challenges faced by business and society in the 21st century.

Compilation of References

A.B.C. News. (2014). The ANZ bank has sold about $200 million of debt owed to it by failed Tasmanian timber company Gunns. Retrieved from http://www.abc.net.au/news/2014-01-30/anz-offloads-debt-from-collapsed-timber-company-gunns/5227124

Aaronson, S. A. (2003). Corporate Responsibility in the Global Village: The British Role Model and the American Laggard. *Business and Society Review*, *108*(3), 309–338. doi:10.1111/1467-8594.00167

Abdullah, S. N., & Nasir, N. M. (2004). Accrual management and the independence of the boards of directors and audit committees. *International Journal of Economics, Management and Accounting, 12*(1).

Abeysuriya, K., Mitchell, C., & White, S. (2006). Can corporate social responsibility resolve the sanitation question in developing countries? *Ecological Economics*, *62*(1), 174–181. doi:10.1016/j.ecolecon.2006.06.003

Abu-Baker, N., & Naser, K. (2000). Empirical Evidence on Corporate Social Disclosure (CSD) practices in Jordan. *International Journal of Commerce and Management*, *10*(3/4), 18–34. doi:10.1108/eb047406

Adam, A., Kammas, P., & Lapatinas, A. (2015). Income inequality and the tax structure: Evidence from developed and developing countries. *Journal of Comparative Economics*, *43*(1), 138–154.

Adams, C. A., & Larrinaga-González, C. (2007). Engaging with organisations in pursuit of improved sustainability accounting and performance. *Accounting, Auditing & Accountability Journal*, *20*(3), 333–355. doi:10.1108/09513570710748535

Adams, C. A., & McNicholas, P. (2007). Making a difference: Sustainability reporting, accountability and organisational change. *Accounting, Auditing & Accountability Journal*, *20*(3), 382–402. doi:10.1108/09513570710748553

Adams, C., Coutts, A., & Harte, G. (1995). Corporate Equal Opportunities (non-) Disclosure. *The British Accounting Review*, *27*(2), 87–108. doi:10.1006/bare.1994.0005

Adams, C., & Frost, G. (2004). *The Development of Corporate Web-sites and Implications for Ethical, Social and Environmental Reporting Through these Media*. Edinburgh, UK: The Institute of Chartered Accountants of Scotland.

Adams, C., Hill, Y., & Roberts, C. (1998). Corporate Social Reporting Practices in Western Europe: Legitimating Corporate Behavior? *The British Accounting Review*, *30*(1), 1–21. doi:10.1006/bare.1997.0060

Adelopo, I., Raimi, L., & Yekini, K. (2015) Bridging Governance Gap with Political CSR. In D. Jamali, C. Karam & M. Blowfield. (Eds.), CSR in Developing Countries: Towards a Development-Oriented Approach. Greenfield Publishing UK. doi:10.9774/GLEAF.9781783532445_4

AECA. (2004). *Marco Conceptual de la Responsabilidad Social Corporativa. Comisión de Responsabilidad Social Corporativa*. Madrid: AECA.

AECA. (2005). *Límites de la información de sostenibilidad: entidad, devengo y materialidad. Madrid, España. Asociación Española de Contabilidad y Administración de Empresas*. Madrid: AECA.

Aginam, E. (2012). CSR: Multilinks Telkom donates medical equipment to UITH. *The Vanguard Newspaper Online*. Retrieved from http://www.vanguardngr.com/2010/10/csr-multilinks-telkom-donates-medical-equipment-to-uith/

Agle, B. R., & Van Buren, H. J. (1999). God and Mammon: The modern relationship. *Business Ethics Quarterly*, *9*(4), 563–582. doi:10.2307/3857935

Aguilera, R. V., Rupp, D. E., Williams, C. A., & Ganapathi, J. (2007). Putting the S back in corporate social responsibility: A multilevel theory of social change in organizations. *Academy of Management Review*, *32*(3), 836–863. doi:10.5465/AMR.2007.25275678

Aguinis, H. (2011). In S. Zedeck (Ed.), *Organizational responsibility: Doing good and doing well* (Vol. 3, pp. 855–879). APA handbook of industrial and organizational psychologyWashington, DC: American Psychological Association.

Aguinis, H., & Glavas, A. (2012). What we know and don't know about corporate social responsibility: A review and research agenda. *Journal of Management*, *38*(4), 932–968. doi:10.1177/0149206311436079

Airtel Nigeria Limited. (2014) About Us – Shareholder Information. Retrieved from http://www.airtelng.com/new/shareholders.asp

Akhuemonkhan, I., Raimi, L., Ogunjirin, O. D. (2012, November 1-2). Corporate Social Responsibility and Entrepreneurship (CSRE): Antidotes to Poverty, Insecurity and Underdevelopment in Nigeria. *Presented at the international conference on Poverty, Insecurity and Development in Africa*, Universiti de Lome, Republic of Togo.

Alazzani, A., & Wan-Hussin, W. N. (2013). Global Reporting Initiative's environmental reporting: A study of oil and gas companies. *Ecological Indicators*, *32*, 19–24. doi:10.1016/j.ecolind.2013.02.019

Albareda, L. & Balaguer, M.R. (2004). La responsabilidad social de la empresa y los resultados financieros. *Contabilidad y dirección*, 11-26.

Allais, M. (1947). *Economie et intérêt* [Economy and interest]. Paris: Imprimerie Nationale.

Al-Qaradawi, Y. (1985). *The Lawful and The Prohibited in Islam*. Kuala Lumpur: Islamic Book Trust.

Amaeshi, K., Adi, B., Ogbechie, C., & Amao, O. (2006). *Corporate Social Responsibility (CSR) in Nigeria: western mimicry or indigenous influences?* International Centre for Corporate Social Responsibility (ICCSR), Nottingham University Business School, Nottingham, UK. Retrieved from http://www.nottingham.ac.uk/business/ICCSR/assets/researchpapers/39-2006.pdf

Amaeshi, K., Osuji, O. K., & Doh, J. P. (2011, May 28-29). Corporate Social Responsibility as a Market Governance Mechanism: Any implications for Corporate Governance in Emerging Economies? *Proceedings of the Corporate Governance in Emerging Markets Conference*, Seoul.

Amaeshi, K. M., & Adi, B. (2007). Reconstructing the corporate social responsibility construct in *Utlish. Business Ethics (Oxford, England)*, *16*(1), 3–18. doi:10.1111/j.1467-8608.2006.00465.x

Amaeshi, K. M., Adi, B. C., Ogbechie, C., & Amao, O. O. (2006). Corporate social responsibility in Nigeria: Western mimicry or indigenous influences? *Journal of Corporate Citizenship*, *24*(24), 83–99. doi:10.9774/GLEAF.4700.2006.wi.00009

Amaeshi, K., Adegbite, E., & Rajwani, T. (2016). Corporate social responsibility in challenging and non-enabling institutional contexts: Do institutional voids matter? *Journal of Business Ethics*, *134*(1), 135–153. doi:10.1007/s10551-014-2420-4

Amazon.com. (n. d.) *Amazon and the Planet*. Retrieved from http://www.amazon.com/p/feature/tdfn6a3sn2bg5xg?ref_=aa_bx_7&pf_rd_r=18RQAVEGVEVFC5SZDZT8&pf_rd_p=d4e53df4-3f1f-4d63-b9c4-eb3f5a5db605

Amengual, M. (2010). Complementary labour regulation: The uncoordinated combination of state and private regulators in the Dominican Republic. *World Development*, *38*(3), 405–414. doi:10.1016/j.worlddev.2009.09.007

Anderson, R. C., Mansi, S. A., & Reeb, D. M. (2004). Board characteristics, accounting report integrity, and the cost of debt. *Journal of Accounting and Economics*, *37*(3), 315–342. doi:10.1016/j.jacceco.2004.01.004

Andrew, B., Gul, F., Guthrie, J., & Teoh, H. (1989). A Note on Corporate Social Disclosure Practices in Developing Countries: The Case of Malaysia and Singapore. *The British Accounting Review*, *21*(4), 371–376. doi:10.1016/0890-8389(89)90034-6

Anheuser-Busch. (2014). *Bringing People Together for a Better World*. Anheuser-Busch InBev /2014 Global Citizenship Report. Retrieved from http://www.ab-inbev.com/content/dam/universaltemplate/abinbev/pdf/media/press-kit/2014/ABInBev_AR_14_EN_Narrative.pdf

Antolin-Lopez, R., Delgado-Ceballos, J., & Montiel, I. (2016). (Forthcoming). Deconstructing Corporate Sustainability: A Review of Stakeholder Metrics. *Journal of Cleaner Production*. doi:10.1016/j.jclepro.2016.01.111

APEC. (2012). *Corporate Social Responsibility in the APEC Region. Current Status and Implications*. Manila, Philippines: Asian Institute of Management RVR Center for Corporate Responsibility.

Ararat, M. & C. Gocenoglu (2006). Drivers for sustainable corporate responsibility: Case of Turkey. *Report for MDF 5*.

Archel, P., & Lizarraga, F. (2001). Algunos determinantes de la información medioambiental divulgada por las empresas españolas cotizadas. *Revista de Contabilidad*, *4*(7), 129–153.

Aribi, Z., & Gao, S. (2010). Corporate Social Responsibility Disclosure: A Comparison between Islamic and Conventional Financial Institutions. *Journal of Financial Reporting and Accounting*, *8*(2), 72–91. doi:10.1108/19852511011088352

Arora, P., & Dharwadkar, R. (2011). Corporate governance and corporate social responsibility (CSR): The moderating roles of attainment discrepancy and organization slack. *Corporate Governance: An International Review*, *19*(2), 136–152. doi:10.1111/j.1467-8683.2010.00843.x

Asahi, (2012) *Asahi Group CSR activities*. Retrieved from http://www.asahigroup-holdings.com/en/csr/pdf/summary12_e_all.pdf

Aspen Institute Center for Business Education. (2008). Where Will They Lead.

Atale, N., & Helge, E. J. (2014). Proposed Framework for Government of India to Effectively Monitor Mandatory CSR Initiatives of Public Sector Enterprises in India. *Journal of Human Values*, *20*(1), 75–83. doi:10.1177/0971685813515594

Athanasopoulou, A., & Selsky, J. W. (2015). The social context of corporate social responsibility: Enriching research with multiple perspectives and multiple levels. *Business & Society*, *54*(3), 322–364. doi:10.1177/0007650312449260

Attig, N., & Brockman, P. (2015). The local roots of corporate social responsibility. *Journal of Business Ethics*. doi:10.1007/s10551-015-2757-3

Austin, J., & Reficco, E. (2009). Corporate Social Entrepreneurship. *Harvard Business School Working Paper 09-101*. Retrieved from http://www.hbs.edu/research/pdf/09-101.pdf

Australia and New Zealand Banking Group. (2014). *Australia and New Zealand Banking Group Sustainability Review 2014*. Retrieved from www.anz.com.au

Australian Bureau of Statistic. (2014). 5204.0 - Australian System of National Accounts, 2013-14. Retrieved from http://www.abs.gov.au/AUSSTATS/abs@.nsf/MF/5204.0

Australian Centre for Corporate Social Responsibility. A. (2014). The 10th year – Progress and prospects for CSR in Australia and New Zealand. Melbourne: Australian Centre for Corporate Social Responsibility.

Australian Government Department of Employment. (2014). *Industry outlook – Mining*. Canberra: Department of Employment.

Australian Trade Commission. (2015). *Australia Benchmark Report*. Canberra" Department of Foreign Affairs and Trade. (n. d.) Retrieved from https://www.austrade.gov.au/Invest/Reports-Resources/Benchmark-Report

Ayroso, D. (2014, September 19). Indigenous peoples, environmentalists call for end to OceanaGold's 'mining plunder'. *Bulatlat*. Retrieved from http://bulatlat.com/main/2014/09/19/indigenous-peoples-environmentalists-call-for-end-to-oceanagolds-mining-plunder/

Ayuso, S., & Argandona, A. (2009). Responsible corporate governance: Towards a stakeholder board of directors? *Corporate Ownership & Control*, *6*(4), 9–19.

Azapagic, A. (2004). Developing a framework for sustainable development indicators for the mining and minerals industry. *Journal of Cleaner Production*, *12*(6), 639–662. doi:10.1016/S0959-6526(03)00075-1

Bae, S. C., Chang, K., & Kang, E. (2012). Culture, corporate governance, and dividend policy: International evidence. *Journal of Financial Research*, *35*(2), 289–316. doi:10.1111/j.1475-6803.2012.01318.x

Bair, J., & Palpacuer, F. (2015). CSR beyond the corporation: Contested governance in global value chains. *Global Networks*, *15*(1), 1–19. doi:10.1111/glob.12085

Balfour, F. (2008) *China's Li Ning Toe-to-Toe Against Nike and Adidas* Bloomberg Business, Retrieved from http://www.bloomberg.com/bw/stories/2008-04-30/chinas-li-ning-toe-to-toe-against-nike-and-adidas

Balmer, J. M. T., Fukukawa, K., & Gray, E. R. (2007). The nature and management of ethical corporate identity: A commentary on corporate identity, corporate social responsibility and ethics. *Journal of Business Ethics*, *76*(1), 7–15. doi:10.1007/s10551-006-9278-z

Banerjee, S. B. (2007). *Corporate social responsibility: The good the bad and the ugly*. Cheltenham: Edward Elgar. doi:10.4337/9781847208552

Banerjee, S. B. (2008). Corporate Social Responsibility: The Good, the Bad and the Ugly. *Critical Sociology*, *34*(1), 51–79. doi:10.1177/0896920507084623

Bansal, P. (2005). Evolving sustainably: A longitudinal study of corporate sustainable development. *Strategic Management Journal*, *26*(3), 197–218. doi:10.1002/smj.441

Barako, D. G., & Brown, A. M. (2008). Corporate social reporting and board representation: Evidence from the Kenyan banking sector. *Journal of Management & Governance*, *12*(4), 309–324. doi:10.1007/s10997-008-9053-x

Barboza, D., & Buckley, C. (2013). China plan cuts the state's role in the economy. *The New York Times*, May 25, p. A1.

Bardy, R., Drew, S., & Kennedy, T. F. (2012). Foreign investment and ethics: How to contribute to social responsibility by doing business in less-developed countries. *Journal of Business Ethics*, *106*(3), 267–282. doi:10.1007/s10551-011-0994-7

Barkemeyer, R. (2011). Corporate perceptions of sustainability challenges in developed and developing countries: Constituting a CSR divide? *Social Responsibility Journal*, *7*(2), 257–281. doi:10.1108/1747111111141521

Barnett, M. L. (2007). Stakeholder influence capacity and the variability of financial returns to corporate social responsibility. *Academy of Management Review*, *32*(3), 794–816. doi:10.5465/AMR.2007.25275520

Barrick, (2013) *Responsible Mining. Responsibility report 2013*. Retrieved fro: http://www.barrick.com/files/responsibility-report/2013/Barrick-2013-Corporate-Responsibility-Report.pdf

Barrientos, S. (2002). Mapping codes through the value chain: from researcher to detective. In R. Jenkins, R. Pearson, & G. Seyfang (Eds.), *Corporate Social Responsibility and Labor Rights: Codes of Conduct in the Global Economy* (pp. 113–124). London: Earthscan.

Barrientos, S., Dolan, C., & Tallontire, A. (2003). A gendered value chain approach to codes of conduct in African horticulture. *World Development*, *31*(9), 1511–1526. doi:10.1016/S0305-750X(03)00110-4

Basar, A.B. & M. Basar (2006). Social Responsibility Reporting: The Case of Turkey. *Sosyal Bilimler Dergisi*, 2.

Baughn, C. C., Bodie, N. L., & McIntosh, J. C. (2007). Corporate Social and Environmental Responsibility in Asian Countries and Other Geographical Regions. *Corporate Social Responsibility and Environmental Management*, *14*, 189–205. doi:10.1002/csr.160

Baur, D., & Palazzo, G. (2011). The moral legitimacy of NGOs as partners of corporations. *Business Ethics Quarterly*, *21*(4), 579–604. doi:10.5840/beq201121437

Baxi, C.V. (2013). *Corporate social responsibility, the Indian experience.*

Beach, S. (2013). Challenged in China. *Committee to Protect Journalists*, March 11.

Bear, S., Rahman, N., & Post, C. (2010). The impact of board diversity and gender composition on corporate social responsibility and firm reputation. *Journal of Business Ethics*, *97*(2), 207–221. doi:10.1007/s10551-010-0505-2

Beasley, M. (2015). Dysfunctional equivalence: Why the OECD Anti-Bribery Convention provides insufficient guidance in the era of multinational corporations. *The George Washington International Law Review*, *47*(1), 191–231.

Bebbington, A., Hinojosa, L., Bebbington, D. H., Burneo, M. L., & Warnaars, X. (2008). Contention and Ambiguity: Mining and the Possibilities of Development. *Development and Change*, *39*(6), 887–914. doi:10.1111/j.1467-7660.2008.00517.x

Bechtel, R. B., Verdugo, V. C., & de Queiroz Pinheiro, J. (1999). Environmental Belief Systems United States, Brazil, and Mexico. *Journal of Cross-Cultural Psychology*, *30*(1), 122–128. doi:10.1177/0022022199030001008

Beckman, Z. (2013). *7 ways Western and Eastern business relationships differ*. Hyrax International, LLC.

Belal, A. (2001). A Study of Corporate Social Disclosures in Bangladesh. *Managerial Auditing Journal*, *16*(5), 274–289. doi:10.1108/02686900110392922

Belal, A., Cooper, S., & Roberts, R. (2013). Vulnerable and Exploitable: The Need For Organizational Accountability and Transparency in Emerging Less Developed Economies. *Accounting Forum*, *37*(2), 81–91. doi:10.1016/j.accfor.2013.04.001

Belal, A., & Momin, M. (2009). Corporate Social Reporting (CSR) in Emerging Economies: A Review and Future Directions. *Research in Accounting in Emerging Economies.*, *9*, 119–143.

Belhaj, M., & Damak-Ayadi, S. (2011). Financial performance, environmental performance and environmental disclosure: The case of Tunisian firms. *Afro-Asian Journal of Finance and Accounting*, *2*(3), 248–269. doi:10.1504/AAJFA.2011.041632

Belkaoui, A., & Karpik, P. G. (2002). Determinants of the Corporate Decision to Disclose Social Information. *Accounting, Auditing & Accountability Journal*, *2*(1), 36–51.

Belke, A., & Wernet, A. (2015). Poverty reduction through growth and redistribution policies—a panel analysis for 59 developing countries. *Review of Development Economics*, *19*(1), 143–162. doi:10.1111/rode.12131

Bendell, J. (2007). World Review: A synopsis of the key strategic developments in corporate responsibility around the globe over the last quarter. *JCC,* July-September, 4-14.

Benguet Corporation. (n. d.). *Moving Forward and Beyond.* Retrieved from http://benguetcorp.com/

Bennedsen, M., Feldmann, S. E., & Lassen, D. D. (2011, June 28). Lobbying and bribes - A survey-based analysis of the demand for influence and corruption. CESifo Working Paper Series No. 3496. Retrieved from http://ssrn.com/abstract=1873891

Bennett, R. J., & Robson, P. J. A. (2005). The advisor-SME client relationship: Impact, satisfaction and commitment. *Small Business Economics*, *25*(3), 255–271.

Benn, S., Dunphy, D., & Griffiths, A. (2014). *Organizational change for corporate sustainability.* Routledge.

Benson, P. G. (2004, September 14). The Evolution of Business Education in the U.S. *Decision Line*, September, 17-20.

Bergman, M. M., Leisinger, K. M., Bergman, Z., & Berger, L. (2015). An analysis of the conceptual landscape of corporate responsibility in academia. *Business & Professional Ethics Journal*, *34*(2), 165–193. doi:10.5840/bpej20157728

Bernardi, R. A., Bosco, S. M., & Vassill, K. M. (2006). Does Female Representation on Boards of Directors Associate With Fortune's "100 Best Companies to Work For" List? *Business & Society*, *45*(2), 235–248. doi:10.1177/0007650305283332

Betsill, M. M., & Corell, E. (2008). *NGO diplomacy: The influence of nongovernmental organizations in international environmental negotiations*. MIT Press.

Billiton, B. H. P. (2014). Value through performance. *Sustainability Report (2014).* Retrieved from www.bhpbilliton.com/society/reports/2014-bhp-billiton-sustainability-report

Binder, Ch., Kriebaum, U., Marboe, I., Nowak, M., Reinisch, A., & Wittich, St. (2014). *Völkerrecht* [International law]. Vienna: University of Vienna Juridicum.

Birdsall, N. (2015). Does the rise of the middle class lock in good government in the developing world? *European Journal of Development Research*, *27*(2), 217–229. doi:10.1057/ejdr.2015.6

Birkin, F., Cashman, A., Koh, S. C. L., & Liu, Z. (2009). New Sustainable Business Models in China. *Business Strategy and the Environment*, *18*(1), 64–77. doi:10.1002/bse.568

Blindheim, B. T. (2015). Institutional models of corporate social responsibility: A proposed refinement of the explicit-implicit framework. *Business & Society*, *54*(1), 52–88. doi:10.1177/0007650312443961

Blowfield, M. (2005). Corporate Social Responsibility: Reinventing the meaning of development? *International Affairs*, *81*(3), 515–524. doi:10.1111/j.1468-2346.2005.00466.x

Bolwig, S., Ponte, S., Du Toit, A., Riisgaard, L., & Halberg, N. (2010). Integrating poverty and environmental concerns into value-chain analysis: A conceptual framework. *Development Policy Review*, *28*(2), 173–194. doi:10.1111/j.1467-7679.2010.00480.x

Bondy, K., Matten, D., & Moon, J. (2004). The Adoption of Voluntary Codes of Conduct in MNCs: A Three-Country Comparative Study. *Business and Society Review*, *109*(4), 449–477. doi:10.1111/j.0045-3609.2004.00205.x

Bondy, K., Moon, J., & Matten, D. (2012). An institution of corporate social responsibility (CSR) in multi-national corporations (MNCs): Form and implications. *Journal of Business Ethics*, *111*(2), 281–299. doi:10.1007/s10551-012-1208-7

Bondy, K., & Starkey, K. (2014). The dilemmas of internationalization: Corporate social responsibility in the multinational corporation. *British Journal of Management*, *25*(1), 4–22. doi:10.1111/j.1467-8551.2012.00840.x

Bongiorni, S. (2007). *A Year Without 'Made in China': One Family's True Life Adventure in the Global Economy*. Hoboken, NJ: John Wiley and Sons, Inc.

Bonsón, E., & Escobar, T. (2004). La difusión voluntaria de información financiera en internet. Un análisis comparativo entre Estados Unidos, Europa del Este y la Unión Europea. *Revista Española de Financiación y Contabilidad*, *33*(123), 1063–1101.

Booz and Company. (2013). The Rise of Corporate Social Responsibility - A Tool for Sustainable Development in the Middle East. Retrieved from http://www.booz.com/media/file/BoozCo_The-Rise-of-Corporate-Social-Responsibility.pdf

Börzel, T. A., & Risse, T. (2005). Public-Private Partnerships: Effective and legitimate tools of international governance. In E. Grande & L. W. Pauly (Eds.), *Complex Sovereignty: Reconstructing Political Authority in the Twenty First Century* (pp. 195–216). Toronto: University of Toronto Press.

Bouvain, P., Baumann, C., & Lundmark, E. (2013). Corporate social responsibility in financial services: A comparison of Chinese and East Asian banks *vis-à-vis* American banks. *International Journal of Bank Marketing*, *31*(6), 420–439. doi:10.1108/IJBM-05-2012-0054

Bowd, R., Bowd, L., & Harris, P. (2006). Communicating corporate social responsibility: An exploratory case study of a major UK retail centre. *Journal of Public Affairs*, *6*(2), 147–155. doi:10.1002/pa.220

Bowen, H. (1953). *Social responsibilities of the businessman*. Iowa City, IA: University of Iowa Press.

Bowen, H. R. (1953). *Social Responsibility of the Businessman*. New York: Harper & Row.

Boyle, M., & Boguslaw, J. (2007). Business, Poverty and Corporate Citizenship Naming the Issues and Framing Solutions. *Journal of Corporate Citizenship*, Summer, 101-120.

Brammer, S., & Millington, A. (2006). Firm size, organizational visibility and corporate philanthropy: An empirical analysis. *Business Ethics (Oxford, England)*, *15*(1), 6–18. doi:10.1111/j.1467-8608.2006.00424.x

Brammer, S., & Pavelin, S. (2008). Factors influencing the quality of corporate environmental disclosure. *Business Strategy and the Environment*, *17*(2), 120–136. doi:10.1002/bse.506

Branco, M., & Rodrigues, L. (2006). Communication of Corporate Social Responsibility by Portuguese Banks. *Corporate Communication: An International Journal*, *11*(3), 232–248. doi:10.1108/13563280610680821

Branco, M., & Rodrigues, L. (2008). Factors influencing social responsibility disclosure by Portuguese companies. *Journal of Business Ethics*, *83*(4), 685–701. doi:10.1007/s10551-007-9658-z

Branco, M., & Rodrigues, L. (2008). Social Responsibility Disclosure: A Study of Proxies for the public Visibility of Portuguese Banks. *The British Accounting Review*, *49*(2), 161–181. doi:10.1016/j.bar.2008.02.004

Branson, R. (2009). *Business stripped bare*. Great Britain: Clays Ltd.

Brimble, M. & Stevenson-Clarke, P. (2005). Perceptions of the Prevalence and Seriousness of Academic Dishonesty in Australian Universities. *The Australian Educational Researcher*, 32(3), 19-44.

Brine, M., Brown, R., & Hackett, G. (2007). Corporate social responsibility and financial performance in the Australian context. *Economic Round-Up*, Autumn, 47-58.

Brinkmann, J. & Sims, RR. (2001). Stakeholder-Sensitive Business Ethics Teaching. *Teaching Business Ethics*, 5(2), 171-193.

Brinkmann, J., & Henriksen, A. M. (2008). Vocational Ethics as a Subspecialty of Business Ethics - Structuring a Research and Teaching Field. *Journal of Business Ethics*, *81*(3), 623–634. doi:10.1007/s10551-007-9536-8

Brønn, P. S., & Vrioni, A. B. (2001). Corporate Social Responsibility and Cause Related Marketing: An Overview. *International Journal of Advertising*, *20*(2), 207–222.

Brown, J. (2013, March 13). Art, China, and censorship according to Ai Weiwei (Television program). *PBS Newshour*.

Browne, A. L., Stehlik, D., & Buckley, A. (2011). Social licences to operate: For better not for worse; for richer not for poorer? The impacts of unplanned mining closure for "fence line" residential communities. *Local Environment*, *16*(7), 707–725. doi:10.1080/13549839.2011.592183

Brundenius, P. (2005). *China's emerging civil society: the autonomy of NGOs in China*. Department of Political Science, Lund University.

Bruton, G. D., Ahlstrom, D., & Puky, T. (2009). Institutional differences and the development of entrepreneurial ventures: A comparison of the venture capital industries in Latin American and Asia. *Journal of International Business Studies*, *40*(5), 762–778. doi:10.1057/jibs.2009.3

Bryan, H., Jamali, D., & Saffar, W. (forthcoming). Near and dear? The role of location in CSR engagement. *Strategic Management Journal*.

Buchholtz, K. A., & Carroll, B. A. (2012). *Business and society ethics and shareholder management*. Canada: Cengage Learning.

Buchholz, R. A., & Rosenthal, S. B. (2005). Toward a contemporary conceptual framework for stakeholder theory. *Journal of Business Ethics*, *58*(1–3), 137–148. doi:10.1007/s10551-005-1393-8

Buckley, P. J., & Ghauri, P. N. (2004). Globalisation, economic geography and the strategy of multinational enterprises. *Journal of International Business Studies*, *35*(3), 81–98. doi:10.1057/palgrave.jibs.8400076

Buckley, P. J., & Strange, R. (2015). The governance of the global factory: Location and control of world economic activity. *Academy of Management Perspectives*, *29*(2), 237–249. doi:10.5465/amp.2013.0113

Bunch, R., Yang, D., & Qi, D. (2008), Where will they lead: China 2008 MBA student attitudes about business & society. The Aspen Institute Centre for Business Education.

Burton, B. K., & Dunn, C. P. (1996). Feminist ethics as moral grounding for stakeholder theory. *Business Ethics Quarterly*, *6*(2), 133–148. doi:10.2307/3857619

Butterfield, K. D., Reed, R., & Lemak, D. J. (2004). An inductive model of collaboration from the stakeholder's perspective. *Business & Society*, *43*(2), 162–195. doi:10.1177/0007650304265956

Cabalda, M. M., Banaag, A. A., Tidalgo, P. N. T., & Garces, R. B. (2002). *Sustainable Development in the Philippine Minerals Industry. A baseline study. Mining Minerals and Sustainable Development Project. Report #184*. London, UK: IIED & WBCSD.

Cadbury, A. (2006). Twenty-first century society. *Journal of the Academy of Social Sciences*, *1*(1), 5–21.

Campbell, D. (2000). Legitimacy Theory or Mangerial Reality Construction? Corporate Social Disclosure in Marks and Spencer Plc Corporate Reports 1969 - 1997. *Accounting Forum*, *24*(1), 80–100. doi:10.1111/1467-6303.00030

Campbell, D., & Beck, A. (2004). Answering Allegations: The Use of The Corporate Websites for Restorative Ethical and Social Disclosure. *Business Ethics: European Review*, *13*(2/3), 100–116. doi:10.1111/j.1467-8608.2004.00357.x

Campbell, J. L. (2004). *Institutional change and globalization*. Princeton, NJ: Princeton University Press.

Campbell, J. L. (2006). Institutional Analysis and the Paradox of Corporate Social Responsibility. *The American Behavioral Scientist*, *49*(7), 925–938. doi:10.1177/0002764205285172

Campbell, J. L. (2007). Why Would Corporations Behave in Socially Responsible Ways? An Institutional Theory of Corporate Social Responsibility. *Academy of Management Review*, *32*(3), 946–967. doi:10.5465/AMR.2007.25275684

Campos, N. F., & Giovannoni, F. (2007). Lobbying, corruption and political influence. *Public Choice*, *131*(1), 1–12. doi:10.1007/s11127-006-9102-4

Carmen Copper Corporation. (2013). *The Power to Grow. Sustainability Report 2013*. Retrieved from http://www.atlas-mining.com.ph/about-atlas/carmen-copper-corporation

Carmona, M. (1992). Regulación ecológica para el sector de la energía. En: *La industria petrolera ante la regulación jurídico ecológica en México*. 485- 489. México, Universidad Nacional Autónoma de México (UNAM) y Petróleos Mexicanos (PEMEX).

Carnogurska, M. (1998). Original ontological roots of ancient Chinese philosophy. *Asian Philosophy*, *8*(3), 203–213. doi:10.1080/09552369808575484

Carothers, T., & Brandt, W. (1999). Civil society. *Foreign Policy*, *117*(117), 18–24, 26–29. doi:10.2307/1149558

Carroll, A. (1999). 'Corporate Social Responsibility-Evolution of a Definitional Construct', Business & Society, Sage Publications. *Inc.*, *38*(3), 268–295.

Carroll, A. (1999). Corporate social responsibility. Evolution of a definitional construct. *Business & Society*, *38*(3), 268–295. doi:10.1177/000765039903800303

Carroll, A. (2008). *A history of corporate social responsibility: Concepts and practices. In The Oxford Handbook of Corporate Social Responsibility* (pp. 19–46). Oxford: Oxford University Press. doi:10.1093/oxfordhb/9780199211593.003.0002

Carroll, A. B. (1979). A Three-Dimensional Conceptual Model of Corporate Performance. *Academy of Management Review*, *4*(4), 497–505.

Carroll, A. B. (1991). The pyramid of corporate social responsibility: Toward the moral management of organizational stakeholders. *Business Horizons*, *34*(4), 39–48. doi:10.1016/0007-6813(91)90005-G

Carroll, A. B. (2015). Corporate social responsibility: The centerpiece of competing and complementary frameworks. *Organizational Dynamics*, *44*(2), 87–96. doi:10.1016/j.orgdyn.2015.02.002

Carson, T. (1993). Friedman's theory of corporate social responsibility. *Business & Professional Ethics Journal*, *12*(1), 3–32. doi:10.5840/bpej199312118 PMID:11656306

Cassar, G. (2009). Financial statement and projection preparation in start-up ventures. *Accounting Review*, *84*(1), 27–51. doi:10.2308/accr.2009.84.1.27

Cassel, D. (2001). Human Rights Business Responsibilities in the Global Marketplace'. *Business Ethics Quarterly*, *11*(2), 261–274. doi:10.2307/3857749

Castka, P., Balzarova, M. A., Bamber, C. J., & Sharp, J. M. (2004). How can SMEs effectively implement the CSR agenda? A UK case study perspective. *Corporate Social Responsibility and Environmental Management*, *11*(3), 140–149. doi:10.1002/csr.62

Catoto, R. (2015, April 24). Dinagat to sue 2 more mining firms for unpaid taxes. *Minda News,* Retrieved from http://www.mindanews.com/top-stories/2015/04/24/dinagat-to-sue-2-more-mining-firms-for-unpaid-taxes/

Centeno, M. A., & Tham, A. (2012). *The emergence of risk in the global system* (working paper). Princeton University.

Centeno, M. A., Cinlar, E., Cloud, D., Creager, A. N., DiMaggio, P. J., Dixit, A. K., . . . Shapiro, J. N. (2013, April). *Global systemic risk.* Princeton Institute for International and Regional Studies, Princeton University.

Centro de Análisis y Resolución de Conflitos (CARC). (2010). *Lecciones Aprendidas sobre la Defensoría para el Proyecto Camisea. Un Puente para el entendimiento* [Lessons learned from the advocacy of Project Camisea. A bridge for understanding]. Lima: Pontificia Universidad Católica del Perú.

Cerbioni, F., & Parbonetti, A. (2007). Exploring the effects of corporate governance on intellectual capital disclosure: An analysis of European biotechnology companies. *European Accounting Review*, *16*(4), 791–826. doi:10.1080/09638180701707011

Cetindamar, D., & Husoy, K. (2007). Corporate social responsibility practices and environmentally responsible behavior: The case of the United Nations Global Compact. *Journal of Business Ethics*, *76*(2), 163–176. doi:10.1007/s10551-006-9265-4

Chambers, E. Chapple, W., Moon, J., & Sullivan, M. (n. d.). *CSR in Asia: A seven country study of CSR website reporting*. ICCR Research Paper Series. No. 09-2003. Nottingham, U.K: International Centre for Corporate Social Responsibility.

Chan, A. (1995). The emerging patterns of industrial relations in China and the rise of two new labor movements. China Information, 9(4).

Chao, L. (2012, June 3). Google tips off users in China. *The Wall Street Journal.*

Chapple, W., & Moon, J. (2005). Corporate social responsibility (CSR) in Asia: A seven-country study of CSR web site reporting. *Business & Society*, *44*(4), 415–441. doi:10.1177/0007650305281658

Chartered Management Institute. (2012). Sustainable business practice. Retrieved from http://www.managers.org.uk/page/best-practice-corporate-responsibility-sustainable-business-practice

Chaudhri, V., & Wang, J. (2007). Communicating Corporate Social Responsibility on the Internet A Case Study of the Top 100 Information Technology Companies in India. *Management Communication Quarterly*, *21*(2), 232–247. doi:10.1177/0893318907308746

Chauvey, J. N., Giordano-Spring, S., Cho, C. H., & Patten, D. M. (2015). The Normativity and Legitimacy of CSR Disclosure: Evidence from France. *Journal of Business Ethics*, *130*(4), 789–803. doi:10.1007/s10551-014-2114-y

Chen, B., & Feng, Y. (2000). Determinants of economic growth in China: Private enterprise, education and openness. *China Economic Review*, *11*(1), 1–15. doi:10.1016/S1043-951X(99)00014-0

Chen, S., & Bouvain, P. (2008). Is corporate responsibility converging? A comparison of corporate responsibility reporting in the USA, UK, Australia, and Germany. *Journal of Business Ethics*, *87*(Suppl. 1), 299–317. doi:10.1007/s10551-008-9794-0

Cheyns, E., & Riisgaard, L. (2014). Introduction to the Symposium. *Agriculture and Human Values*, *31*(3), 409–423. doi:10.1007/s10460-014-9508-4

Chidozie, F. C., Odunayo, L. P., & Olutosin, A. O. (2015). Deregulation of the Nigerian telecommunication sector: Interrogating the nexus between imperialism and development. *Academic Journal of Interdisciplinary Studies, 4*(1), 173-184. Retrieved from http://www.mcser.org/journal/index.php/ajis/article/view/5968/5739

Chih, H., Chih, H., & Chen, T. (2010). On the Determinants of Corporate Social Responsibility: International Evidence on the Financial Industry. *Journal of Business Ethics, 93*(1), 115–135. doi:10.1007/s10551-009-0186-x

Chinese Academy of Social Sciences (CASS). (November 15, 2013). Blue Book on Corporate Responsibility. Retrieved from www.globaltimes.cn

Chi, T. (2011). Building a sustainable supply chain: An analysis of corporate social responsibility (CSR) practices in the Chinese textile and apparel industry. *Journal of the Textile Institute, 102*(10), 837–848. doi:10.1080/00405000.2010.524361

Chivite, M. P., Enciso, V., García, B., & Túa, J. (2014). Determinantes de la Responsabilidad Social Corporativa: La crisis y el Efecto Contagio. *CIRIEC-España, Revista de Economía Pública. Social y Cooperativa, 81*, 127–161.

Cho, C. H., & Patten, D. M. (2007). The role of environmental disclosures as tools of legitimacy: A research note. *Accounting, Organizations and Society, 32*(7), 639–647. doi:10.1016/j.aos.2006.09.009

Choi, J. S. (1999). An investigation of the initial voluntary environmental disclosures made in Korean semi-annual financial reports. *Pacific Accounting Review, 11*(1), 73–102.

Chu, K. (2013), A billion strong but short on workers. *The Wall Street Journal*, May 2, p. B 1.

Chung, K. Y., Eichenseher, J., & Taniguchi, T. (2008). Ethical perceptions of business students: Differences between East Asia and the USA and among "Confucian" cultures. *Journal of Business Ethics, 79*(1-2), 121–132. doi:10.1007/s10551-007-9391-7

CIA. (2012). World Factbook. Retrieved from http://www.photius.com/rankings/economy/gdp_per_capita_2012_0.html

CIA. (2015). Fact Book. Retrieved from https://www.cia.gov/library/publications/the-world-factbook/geos/eg.html

CIA. (n. d.) Retrieved from www.cia.gov

Clark, H. (2012). *Corporate social responsibility: a gateway to sustainability.* Retrieved from http://www.undp.org/content/undp/en/home/presscenter/speeches/2012/05/18/helen-clark-corporate-social-responsibility/

Clark-Murphy, M., Gerrans, P., & Kristoffersen, I. (2005). The corporate social responsibility and the theory of the firm. Retrieved from http://www.business.ecu.edu.au/schools/afe/wps/papers/pdfs/wp0505ik .pdf

Clarkson, M. (1995). A Stakeholder Framework for Analyzing and Evaluating Corporate Social Performance. *Academy of Management Review, 20*(January), 92–117.

Clarkson, M. (1995). A stakeholder framework for analyzing and evaluating corporate social performance. *Academy of Management Review, 20*(1), 92–117.

Cleaner Production in China. (n. d.). *Cleaner Production/Pollution Prevention Organizations in China.* Retrieved from http://www.chinacp.org.cn/eng/cp_organizations.html

Clegg, S. et al.. (2012). *Strategy Theory and Practice.* Singapore: SAGE Publications Asia-Pacific Pte Ltd.

Coffey, B. S., & Wang, J. (1998). Board diversity and managerial control as predictors of corporate social performance. *Journal of Business Ethics, 17*(14), 1595–1603. doi:10.1023/A:1005748230228

Comelli, M., Hadad, M. G., & Petz, M. I. (2010). Hacia Un Desarrollo (In)Sostenible En América Latina. El Caso De La Minería A Cielo Abierto En La Argentina. Argumentos. Revista de crítica social, [Towards (Un) sustainable development in Latin America. The case of open pit mining.] *Argumentos*. Magazine of social critique)12, Octubre 2010.

Commonwealth Bank of Australia. (2014). *Commonwealth Bank of Australia Annual Report* 2014. Retrieved from www.commbank.com.au

Commonwealth Bank of Australia. (2014). *Sustainability Report*. Retrieved from https://www.commbank .com.au/sustainability2014/index.html

Cookson, R. (2011). S&P Withdraws Nine Dragons Paper Rating. *Financial Times*. Retrieved from http://www.ft.com/cms/s/0/ea979340-969f-11e0-baca-00144feab49a.html#axzz3zE69jU4o

Cooper, S. (2003). Stakeholder Communication and The Internet in UK Electricity Companies. *Managerial Auditing Journal*, *18*(3), 232–243. doi:10.1108/02686900310469925

Corbett, J., & Kappagoda, M. (2013). Doing good and doing well: Corporate social responsibility in post Obamacare America. *The Journal of Law, Medicine & Ethics*, *41*(1), 17–21. doi:10.1111/jlme.12032 PMID:23590734

Corcoran, C.P. (2007). Distinctions Among Accreditation Agencies For Business Programs. *Journal of College Teaching and Learning*, 4(9), 27-30.

Coslovsky, S. V. (2014). Flying Under the Radar? The State and the Enforcement of Labor Standards in Brazil. *Oxford Development Studies*, *42*(2), 190–216. doi:10.1080/13600818.2013.875135

Costello, T., Smith, B. & Brecher, J. (2007). Labor rights in China. *Post-Autistic Economics Review*, issue 41, 34-38.

Coulmont, M., Berthelot, S., & Thibault, K. (2013). Sustainability Content on Oil and Gas Company Websites. *Business and Management Research*, *2*(1), 94–103.

Coupland, C. (2006). Corporate Social and Environmental Responsibility in Web-based Reports: Currency in the banking sector? *Critical Perspectives on Accounting*, *17*(7), 865–881. doi:10.1016/j.cpa.2005.01.001

Covin, J. G., & Miles, M. P. (1999). Corporate entrepreneurship and the pursuit of competitive advantage'. *Entrepreneurship Theory and Practice*, *23*(3), 47–63.

Cowen, S. S., Ferreri, L. B., & Parker, L. D. (1987). The impact of corporate characteristics on social responsibility disclosure: A typology and frequency-based analysis. *Accounting, Organizations and Society*, *12*(2), 111–122. doi:10.1016/0361-3682(87)90001-8

Crane, A., McWilliams, A., Matten, D., Moon, J., & Siegel, D. (2008). The corporate social responsibility agenda. The Oxford handbook of corporate social responsibility, 3-15.

Crane, A., & Matten, D. (2007). *Corporate Social Responsibility*. London: Sage. doi:10.4135/9781446261194

Crifo, P., & Forget, V. D. (2015). The economics of corporate social responsibility: A firm-level perspective survey. *Journal of Economic Surveys*, *29*(1), 112–130. doi:10.1111/joes.12055

CSR Press Release. (2013). Call for Entries – PR News' CSR Awards 2013. Retrieved from http://www.csrwire.com/press_releases/36220-Call-for-Entries-PR-News-CSR-Awards-2013

D'Amato, A., Henderson, S., & Florence, S. (2009). *Corporate Social Responsibility and Sustainable Business a Guide to Leadership Tasks and Functions*. Greensboro: Center for Creative Leadership.

Dahawy, K., Merino, B., & Conovort, T. (2002). The Conflict between IAS Disclosure Requirements and The Secretive Culture in Egypt. *Advances in International Accounting*, *15*, 203–228. doi:10.1016/S0897-3660(02)15024-0

Dahlsrud, A. (2008). How corporate social responsibility is defined: An analysis of 37 definitions. *Corporate Social Responsibility and Environmental Management*, *15*(1), 1–13.

Darigan, K. H., & Post, J. E. (2009). Corporate citizenship in China. *Journal of Corporate Citizenship*, (35), 39–53. doi:10.9774/GLEAF.4700.2009.au.00005

Dartey-Baah, K., & Amponsah-Tawiah, K. (2011). Exploring the limits of Western Corporate Social Responsibility Theories in Africa'. *International Journal of Business and Social Science*, *2*(18), 126–137.

Das, M., & Diaye, N. P. (2013). The end of cheap labor. *Finance & Development*, *50*(2), 34–37.

Davidson, D. K. (2011), The importance of context in understanding CSR: China's lab conditions as a case study. *Paper presented at the annual meeting of the International Association for Business and Society.*

Davis, R., & Franks, D. (2014). Costs of Company-Community Conflict in the Extractive Sector. *Corporate Social Responsibility Initiative Report No. 66.* Cambridge, MA: Harvard Kennedy School.

Davis, D. D. (2004). The Tao of leadership in virtual teams. *Organizational Dynamics*, *33*(1), 47–62. doi:10.1016/j.orgdyn.2003.11.004

Davis, K. (1973). The case for and against business assumption of social responsibilities. *Academy of Management Journal*, *16*(2), 312–322. doi:10.2307/255331

Dawson, T. C. (2003, March 14). *Globalization, the Transition Economies, and the IMF.* International Monetary Fund. Retrieved from https://www.imf.org/external/np/speeches/2003/031403.htm

Day, R., & Woodward, T. (2009). CSR Reporting and the UK Financial Services Sector. *Journal of Applied Accounting Reserach*, *10*(3), 159–175. doi:10.1108/09675420911006398

De Bakker, F. G. A., Groenewegen, P., & den Hond, F. (2005). A bibliometric analysis of 30 years of research and theory on corporate social responsibility and corporate social performance. *Business & Society*, *44*(3), 283–317. doi:10.1177/0007650305278086

de Burgh-Woodman, H., Saha, A., Somasundram, K., & Torrisi, A. (2015). Sowing the Seeds for Ethical Business Leadership through Business Education.

de Jong, G., & van Houten, J. (2014). The impact of MNE cultural diversity on the internationalization-performance relationship: Theory and evidence from European multinational enterprises. *International Business Review*, *23*(1), 313–326. doi:10.1016/j.ibusrev.2013.05.005

De Neve, G. (2014). Fordism, flexible specialization and CSR: How Indian garment workers critique neoliberal labour regimes. *Ethnography*, *15*(2), 184–207. doi:10.1177/1466138112463801

Deegan, C. (2002). The legitimising effect of social and environmental disclosures - a theoretical foundation. *Accounting, Auditing & Accountability Journal*, *15*(3), 282–311. doi:10.1108/09513570210435852

Deegan, C., & Gordon, B. (1996). A study of the environmental disclosure practices of Australian corporations. *Accounting and Business Review*, *26*(3), 187–199. doi:10.1080/00014788.1996.9729510

Deegan, C., Rankin, M., & Vought, P. (2000). Firms' Disclosure Reactions to Major Social Incidents: Australian Evidence. *Accounting Forum*, *24*(1), 101–130. doi:10.1111/1467-6303.00031

Deegan, C., & Unerman, J. (2011). *Financial Accounting Theory* (Second European ed.). Berkshire, United Kingdom: McGraw-Hill Higher Education.

Dees, J. G. (1998). *The Meaning of 'Social Entrepreneurship*. Boston, MA: Harvard Business School. Comments and suggestions contributed from the Social Entrepreneurship Funders Working Group.

Dell, (2015). *An annual update of our 2020 Legacy of Good Plan. FY15 Corporate Social Responsibility Report*. Retrieved from http://i.dell.com/sites/doccontent/corporate/corp-comm/en/Documents/fy15-cr-report.pdf

Dentchev, N. A., Haezendonck, E., & van Balen, M. (2015). The Role of Governments in the Business and Society Debate. *Business & Society*. doi:10.1177/0007650315586179

Denyer, S., & Gu, J. (2015). The end of an era for journalism in China. *The Washington Post*, January 11, A10.

Department of the Environment. (2014). Repealing the carbon tax. Retrieved from http://environment .gov.au/climate-change/repealing-carbon-tax.htm

Desjardins, J. R. (1999). Businesses' environmental responsibility. In: E.R. Freedrick (Ed.). A Companion to Business Ethics (pp. 280-289). Bentley College, Blackwell Publishers.

Dhanesh, G. S. (2015). Why Corporate Social Responsibility? An Analysis of Drivers of CSR in India. *Management Communication Quarterly*, *29*(1), 114–129. doi:10.1177/0893318914545496

Dhouibi, R., & Mamoghli, C. (2013). Determinants of voluntary disclosure in Tunisian bank's reports. *Research Journal of Finance and Accounting*, *4*(5), 80–94.

Dickie, C., Pick, D. & Issa, T. (2011). Leveraging Learning Experiences to Promote Student Engagement in a Business Ethics Class. *Practice and Evidence of Scholarship of Teaching and Learning in Higher Education (PESTLHE)*, 6 (3), 214-231.

Dimaggio, P. J., & Powell, W. W. (1983). The iron cage revisited: Institutional isomorphism and collective rationality in organizational fields. *American Sociological Review*, *48*(2), 146–160. doi:10.2307/2095101

Dobbin, F., Schrage, D., & Kalev, A. (2009). *Someone to watch over me: Coupling, decoupling, and unintended consequences in corporate equal opportunity* (Working paper). Harvard University, Cambridge, MA.

Dolan, C., & Opondo, M. (2005). Seeking Common Ground. *Journal of Corporate Citizenship*, *18*(18), 87–98. doi:10.9774/GLEAF.4700.2005.su.000012

Donaldson, T., & Preston, L.E. (1995). The Stakeholder Theory of the Corporation: Concepts, Evidence, and Implications. *Academy of Management Review*, 20(January), 65-91.

Donaldson, L., & Davis, J. H. (1991). Stewardship theory or agency theory: CEO governance and shareholder returns. *Australian. Journal of Management*, *16*(1), 49–64.

Donaldson, T., & Dunfee, T. (1999). *Ties that bind*. Boston, MA: Harvard Business School Press.

Donaldson, T., & Preston, L. (1995). The stakeholder theory of the corporation: Concepts, evidence, and implications. *Academy of Management Review*, *20*(1), 70–71.

Dong, S., Burritt, R., & Qian, W. (2012). *An assessment of CSR Reporting Practice in China's Mining and Minerals Industry*. Australia: Centre for Accounting, Governance and Sustainability, School of Commerce, University of South Australia.

Douglas, A., Doris, J., & Johnson, B. (2004). Corporate Social Reporting In Irish Financial Institutions. *The TQM Magazine*, *16*(6), 387–395. doi:10.1108/09544780410563301

Dowling, J., & Pfeffer, J. (1975). Organizational legitimacy: Social values and organizational behavior. *Pacific Sociological Review*, *18*(1), 122–136. doi:10.2307/1388226

Doyle, C., Wicks, C., & Nally, F. (2007). *Mining in the Philippines. Concerns and Conflicts. Report of Fact-finding Mission to the Philippines*. West Midlands, UK: Society of St. Columban.

Dunning, J. H. (1979). Explaining changing patterns of international production: In defense of the eclectic theory. *Oxford Bulletin of Economics and Statistics*, *41*(4), 269–295. doi:10.1111/j.1468-0084.1979.mp41004003.x

Dunn, P., & Sainty, B. (2009). The relationship among board of director characteristics, corporate social performance and corporate financial performance. *International Journal of Managerial Finance*, *5*(4), 407–423. doi:10.1108/17439130910987558

Durand, R., & McGuire, J. (2005). Legitimating Agencies in the Face of Selection: The Case of AACSB. *Organization Studies*, 26(2), 165-196.

Durange de C. Infante, C.E., Molica de Mendonça, F., Purcidonio, P.M. & Valle, R. (2013). Triple bottom line analysis of oil and gas industry with multicriteria decision making. *Journal of Cleaner Production*, *52*, 289–300.

Du, S., & Vieria, E. (2012). Striving for legitimacy through corporate social responsibility: Insights from oil companies. *Journal of Business Ethics*, *110*(4), 413–427. doi:10.1007/s10551-012-1490-4

Ebrahim, M., & Joo, T. (2001). Islamic Banking in Brunei. *International Journal of Social Economics*, *28*(4), 314–337. doi:10.1108/03068290110357708

Edward, P., & Willmott, H. (2008). Corporate citizenship: Rise or demise of a myth? *Academy of Management Review*, *33*(3), 771–773. doi:10.5465/AMR.2008.32465773

Egels-Zandén, N., & Sandberg, J. (2010). Distinctions in descriptive and instrumental stakeholder theory: A challenge for empirical research. *Business Ethics (Oxford, England)*, *19*(1), 35–49. doi:10.1111/j.1467-8608.2009.01577.x

Eichengreen, B., Andrew, R., & Wypolosz, C. (1995). Exchange market mayhem: The antecedents and aftermath of speculative attacks. *Economic Policy*, *10*(October), 249–312. doi:10.2307/1344591

Eilbert, H., & Parket, I. R. (1973). The current status of corporate social responsibility. *Business Horizons*, *16*, 5–14.

Eisenhardt, K. (1989). Building theories from case study research. *Academy of Management Review*, *14*(4), 532–550.

Eisenhardt, K., & Graebner, M. (2007). Theory building from cases: Opportunities and challenges. *Academy of Management Journal*, *50*(1), 25–32. doi:10.5465/AMJ.2007.24160888

Elkington, J. (1994). Towards the Sustainable Corporation: Win-win-win business strategies for sustainable development. *California Management Review*, *36*(2), 90–100. doi:10.2307/41165746

Elkington, J. (1997). *Cannibals with forks: The triple bottom line of twenty-first century business*. Oxford: Capstone.

Elliott, R. K., & Jacobson, P. D. (1994). Costs and Benefits of Business information. *Accounting Horizons*, *8*(4), 80–96.

Enderle, G., & Tavis, A. L. (1998). A balanced concept of the firm and the measurement of its long-term planning and performance. *Journal of Business Ethics*, *17*(11), 1129–1143. doi:10.1023/A:1005746212024

Eng, L. L., & Mak, Y. T. (2003). Corporate governance and voluntary disclosure. *Journal of Accounting and Public Policy*, *22*(4), 325–345. doi:10.1016/S0278-4254(03)00037-1

Environment Graffiti. (2008). Japanese paper industry in recycling scandal. Retrieved from http://www.environmentalgraffiti.com/businesspolitics/japanese-paper-industry-in-recycling-scandal/707#7tweH04B3AvVCrqJ.99

Epstein, M.J. (1993). The Fall of Corporate Charitable Contributions. *Public RelationsQuarterly*, 1993, 37-39.

Espinosa, A., & Porter, T. (2011). Sustainability, complexity and learning; insights from complex systems approaches. *The Learning Organization*, 18(1), 54-72.

Espinosa, M. (2004). *La divulgación de información en el mercado español: un análisis empírico.* España, Universidad de Alicante.

Esrock, S. L., & Leichty, G. B. (1998). Corporate World Wide Web pages: Serving the news media and other publics. *Journalism & Mass Communication Quarterly*, *76*(3), 456–467. doi:10.1177/107769909907600304

Esrock, S., & Leichty, G. (2000). Organization of Corporate Web Pages: Publics and Functions. *Public Relations Review*, *26*(3), 327–344. doi:10.1016/S0363-8111(00)00051-5

Etisalat. (2013). Corporate Social Responsibility. Online Resources. Retrieved from www.etisalat.com.ng/csr.php

Etzion, D., & Ferraro, F. (2010). The role of analogy in the institutionalization of sustainability reporting. *Organization Science*, *21*(5), 1092–1107. doi:10.1287/orsc.1090.0494

European Commission. (2011, October 25). *Communication from the Commission to the European Parliament, the Council, the European Economic and Social Committee and the Committee of the Regions: A renewed EU strategy 2011-14 for Corporate Social Responsibility*. Retrieved from http://ec.europa.eu/enterprise/policies/sustainable-business/files/csr/new-csr/act_en.pdf

Ezat, A., & El-Masry, A. (2008). The impact of corporate governance on the timeliness of corporate internet reporting by Egyptian listed companies. *Managerial Finance*, *34*(12), 848–867. doi:10.1108/03074350810915815

Fairtrade International Organization (FLO). (2009). *Making the Difference: A new global strategy for Fairtrade*. Bonn, Germany.

Fairtrade Labelling Organization (FLO). (2016). Fairtade Customer Search. Retrieved from http://www.flocert.net/fairtrade-services/fairtrade-certification/fairtrade-customer-search/

Fang, I. C. (2011). *Growing Up and Becoming Independent: An Ethnographic Study of New Generation Migrant workers in China* [Doctoral Thesis]. London: London School of Economics and Political Science.

Fan, S., & Zhang, X. (2004). Infrastructure and regional economic development in rural China. *China Economic Review*, *15*(2), 203–214. doi:10.1016/j.chieco.2004.03.001

Fayyaz, A., Lund-Thomsen, P., & Lindgreen, A. (2015). Industrial clusters and CSR in developing countries: the role of international donor funding. *Journal of Business Ethics*.

Fernandez-Feijoo, B., Romero, S., & Ruiz, S. (2012). Does board gender composition affect corporate social responsibility reporting. *International Journal of Business and Social Science*, *3*(1), 31–38.

Fernández, R. (2005). *Administración de la Responsabilidad Social Corporativa*. España, Editorial Thomson.

Fields, M. A., & Keys, P. Y. (2003). The emergence of corporate governance from Wall St. to Main St.: Outside directors, board diversity, earnings management, and managerial incentives to bear risk. *Financial Review*, *38*(1), 1–24. doi:10.1111/1540-6288.00032

Fifka, M. (2013). Corporate Responsibility Reporting and Its Determinants in Comparative Perspective: A Review of the Empirical Literature and a Meta-analysis. *Business Strategy and the Environment*, *22*(1), 1–35. doi:10.1002/bse.729

Fifka, M. S., & Drabble, M. (2012). Focus and standardization of sustainability reporting – a comparative study of the United Kingdom and Finland. *Business Strategy and the Environment*, *21*(7), 455–474. doi:10.1002/bse.1730

Filatotchev, I., & Stahl, G. K. (2015). Towards transnational CSR: Corporate social responsibility approaches and governance solutions for multinational corporations. *Organizational Dynamics*, *44*(2), 121–129. doi:10.1016/j.orgdyn.2015.02.006

Flextronics. (2013). Corporate Sustainability Report 2012-13. Retrieved from http://www.flextronics.com/sites/default/files/component_b2/FLEXTRONICS%2520Corporate-Sustainability-Report-2012-2013.pdf

Flory, L. (2014). How 5 companies used Kaizen effectively. Effex Management Solutions Blog. Retrieved from http://blog.effexms.com/how-5-companies-used-kaizen-effectively

Fombrun, C. J. (2005). Building Corporate Reputation through CSR Initiatives: Evolving Standards. *Corporate Reputation Review*, *8*(1), 7–11. doi:10.1057/palgrave.crr.1540235

Food and Agriculture Organization of the United Nations. (2014). Pulp, Paper and Wood Product Industries. Retrieved from http://www.fao.org/forestry/industries/en/

Fooks, G., Gilmore, A., Collin, J., Holden, C., & Lee, K. (2013). The Limits of Corporate Social Responsibility: Techniques of Neutralization, Stakeholder Management and Political CSR. *Journal of Business Ethics*, *112*(2), 283–299. doi:10.1007/s10551-012-1250-5 PMID:23997379

Ford. (2014). *Go Further. Sustainability Report 2013/14.* Retrieved from http://corporate.ford.com/microsites/sustainability-report-2013-14/doc/sr13.pdf

Forest Business Network. (2011). Asian paper giant sees growth opportunity in Canada. Retrieved from http://www.forestbusinessnetwork.com/3898/asian-paper-giant-sees-growth-opportunity-in-canada/

Forker, J. J. (1992). Corporate governance and disclosure quality. *Accounting and Business Review*, *22*(86), 111–124. doi:10.1080/00014788.1992.9729426

Forstater, M. et al.. (2010). *Corporate responsibility in African Development: Insights from an emerging dialogue.* Cambridge, MA: Harvard University.

Fortescue Metals Group Limited. (2015). *Fortescue Metals Group Limited social responsibility reports.* Retrieved from http://fmgl.com.au/investors-media/reports/environment-reports/

Fox, T., Ward, H. and Howard, B. (n. d.). Corporate Responsibility for Environment and Development Programme International Institute for Environment and Development (IIED). Retrieved from http://eldis.org/go/homeandid=12031and type=Document

Fox, T., Ward, H., & Howard, B. (n. d). Corporate Responsibility for Environment and Development Programme. *International Institute for Environment and Development (IIED).* Retrieved from http://eldis.org/go/homeandid=12031

Foxconn. (2014). Social and Environmental Sustainability Report. Retrieved from http://www.foxconn.com/Files/index/Foxconn_SER_Report_EN.pdf

Francisco, W., Noland, T.G. & Sinclair, D. (2008). AACSB Accreditation: Symbol of Excellene or March Toward Mediocrity? *Journal of College Teaching and Learning*, 5(5), 25-30.

Frank, G., Ofobike, E., & Gradisher, S. (2010). Teaching Business Ethics: A Quandary for Accounting Educators. *Journal of Education for Business*, 85,132–138.

Fransen, L. (2013). The embeddedness of responsible business practice: Exploring the interaction between national-institutional environments and corporate social responsibility. *Journal of Business Ethics, 115*(2), 213–227. doi:10.1007/s10551-012-1395-2

Freeman, R. E. (1984). *Strategic management: A stakeholder approach*. Boston, MA: Pitman.

Freeman, R. E. (1984). *Strategic management: a stakeholder approach*. Boston: Pitman press.

Freeman, R. E. (1984). *Strategic Management: A Stakeholder Approach*. Boston: Pitman.

Freeman, R. E., Wicks, A. C., & Parmar, B. (2004). Stakeholder theory and the corporate objective revisited. *Organization Science, 15*(3), 364–369. doi:10.1287/orsc.1040.0066

Friedman, M. (1970, September 13). The social responsibility of business is to increase its profits. *The New York Times*.

Frynas, J. G. (2005). The false developmental promise of Corporate Social Responsibility: Evidence from multinational oil companies. *International Affairs, 81*(3), 581–598. doi:10.1111/j.1468-2346.2005.00470.x

Frynas, J. G. (2008). Corporate Social Responsibility and International Development: Critical Assessment, Corporate Governance. *International Review (Steubenville, Ohio), 16*(4), 274–281.

Frynas, J. G. (2010). Corporate social responsibility and societal governance: Lessons from transparency in the oil and gas sector. *Journal of Business Ethics, 93*(Suppl. 2), 163–179. doi:10.1007/s10551-010-0559-1

Fukukawa, K., & Moon, J. (2004). A Japanese model of corporate social responsibility: A study of website reporting. *Journal of Corporate Citizenship, 16*(16), 45–59. doi:10.9774/GLEAF.4700.2004.wi.00008

Galbreath, J. (2010). How does corporate social responsibility benefit firms? Evidence from Australia. *European Business Review, 22*(4), 411–431. doi:10.1108/09555341011056186

Gallardo, F. (2011, October 3). NPA rebels attack 3 mining firms in Surigao del Norte *Minda News*. Retrieved from http://www.mindanews.com/top-stories/2011/10/03/npa-rebels-attack-3-mining-firms-in-surigao-norte/

Gallego-Álvarez, I., Formigoni, H., & Antunes, M. T. P. (2014). Corporate social responsibility practices in Brazilian firms. *Revista de Administração de Empresas, 54*(1), 12–27. doi:10.1590/S0034-759020140103

Galvez, J. K. (2015, October 23). Nickel Asia affiliates sign Palawan water deal. *The Manila Times* Retrieved from http://www.manilatimes.net/nickel-asia-affiliates-sign-palawan-water-deal/225331/

Gamerschlag, R., Moller, K., & Verbeeten, F. (2011). Determinants of voluntary CSR disclosure: Empirical evidence from Germany. *Review of Managerial Science, 2*(2-3), 233–262. doi:10.1007/s11846-010-0052-3

Gao, H. (2013). A press renaissance? The legacy of China's "Southern Weekend.". *Atlantic (Boston, Mass.)*, (January): 13.

Garaventa, E. (1998). DRAMA: A Tool for Teaching Business Ethics. *Business Ethics Quarterly*, 8(3), 535-545.

Garcia, J. L., Maldonado, A., Alvarado, A., & Rivera, D. (2014). Human critical success factors for kaizen and its impacts in industrial performance. *International Journal of Advanced Manufacturing Technology, 70*(9-12), 2187–2198. doi:10.1007/s00170-013-5445-4

García-Rodríguez, F. J., García-Rodríguez, J. L., Castilla-Gutiérrez, C., & Major, S. A. (2013). Corporate social responsibility of oil companies in developing countries: From altruism to business strategy. *Corporate Social Responsibility and Environmental Management, 20*(6), 371–384. doi:10.1002/csr.1320

Garriga, E., & Mele, D. (2004). Corporate social responsibility theories: Mapping the territory. *Journal of Business Ethics, 53*(1/2), 51–71. doi:10.1023/B:BUSI.0000039399.90587.34

George, A., Edgerton, N., & Berry, T. (2007). *Mainstreaming socially responsible investment (sri): a role for government? policy recommendations from the investment community*. Sydney: University of Technology.

George, O. J., Kuye, O. L., & Onokala, U. C. (2012). Corporate social irresponsibility (CSI) a catalyst to the Niger Delta crisis: The case of Nigerian oil multinational companies versus the militants of Niger Delta Region of Nigeria. *Journal of Management Research*, *4*(2), 205–215. doi:10.5296/jmr.v4i2.1186

Geppert, M., & Dörrenbächer, C. (2014). Politics and power within multinational corporations: Mainstream studies, emerging critical approaches and suggestions for future research. *International Journal of Management Reviews*, *16*(2), 226–244. doi:10.1111/ijmr.12018

Gerard, G. (2014). Rethinking management scholarship. *Academy of Management Journal*, *57*(1), 1–6. doi:10.5465/amj.2014.4001

Gereffi, G. (1994). The organization of buyer-driven global commodity chains: how US retailers shape overseas production networks. In G. Gereffi & M. Korzeniewicz (Eds.), *Commodity Chains and Global Capitalism* (pp. 95–123). CT: Praeger.

Gereffi, G., Humphrey, J., & Sturgeon, T. (2005). The governance of global value chains. *Review of International Political Economy*, *12*(1), 78–104. doi:10.1080/09692290500049805

Gereffi, G., & Lee, J. (2016). Economic and social upgrading in global value chains and industrial clusters: Why governance matters. *Journal of Business Ethics*, *133*(1), 25–38. doi:10.1007/s10551-014-2373-7

Ghosh, S. (2015). Is corporate social responsibility in India still in a confused state?—A study of the participation of the private sector companies of India in corporate social responsibility activities. *Global Business Review*, *16*(1), 151–181. doi:10.1177/0972150914553528

Giannarakis, G. (2014). Corporate governance and financial characteristic effects on the extent of corporate social responsibility disclosure. *Social Responsibility Journal*, *10*(4), 569–590. doi:10.1108/SRJ-02-2013-0008

Gibbert, M., Rulgrok, W., & Wicki, B. (2008). What passes as a rigorous case study? *Strategic Management Journal*, *29*(13), 1465–1474. doi:10.1002/smj.722

Gibson, K. (2000). The Moral Basis of Stakeholder Theory. *Journal of Business Ethics*, *26*(3), 245–257. doi:10.1023/A:1006110106408

Gilbert, D. U., & Rasche, A. (2007). Discourse ethics and social accountability: The ethics of SA 8000. *Business Ethics Quarterly*, *17*(02), 187–216. doi:10.5840/beq200717230

Gilbert, D. U., & Rasche, A. (2008). Opportunities and problems of standardized ethics initiatives: A stakeholder theory perspective. *Journal of Business Ethics*, *82*(3), 755–773. doi:10.1007/s10551-007-9591-1

Gilberthorpe, E., & Banks, G. (2012). Development on whose terms?: CSR discourse and social realities in Papua New Guinea's extractive industries sector. *Resources Policy*, *37*(2), 185–193. doi:10.1016/j.resourpol.2011.09.005

Gildea, R.L. (1995). Consumer Survey Confirms Corporate Social Action Affects Buying Decisions. *Public Relations Quarterly,* 1995, 20-21.

Gill, D. L., Dickinson, S. J., & Sharl, A. (2008). Communicating sustainability: A web content analysis of North American, Asian and European firms. *Journal of Communication Management*, *12*(3), 243–262. doi:10.1108/13632540810899425

Gilligan, C. (1982). *In a different voice*. Cambridge, MA: Harvard University Press.

Giuliani, E., & Macchi, C. (2014). Multinational corporations' economic and human rights impacts on developing countries: A review and research agenda. *Cambridge Journal of Economics*, *38*(2), 479–517. doi:10.1093/cje/bet060

Gjolberg, M. (2009). Measuring the immeasurable?: Constructing an index of CSR practices and CSR performance in 20 countries. *Scandinavian Journal of Management*, *25*(1), 1, 10–22. doi:10.1016/j.scaman.2008.10.003

Gjølberg, M. (2009). The origin of corporate social responsibility: Global forces or national legacies? *Socio-economic Review*, 17.

Globacom Nigeria. (2013). Events and Sponsorships. Retrieved from http://www.gloworld.com/events_sponsorships.asp

Godfrey, P. C., & Hatch, N. W. (2006). Researching corporate social responsibility: An agenda for the 21st century. *Journal of Business Ethics*, *70*(1), 87–98. doi:10.1007/s10551-006-9080-y

Godilano, E. C., & Monsod, C. S. (2012, May 31). To Mine or Not to Mine The Case of the Tampakan Copper-Gold Project: Mindanao, Philippines. *Paper presented to the Department of National Defense*, Manila, Philippines.

Godinez, J. R., & Liu, L. (2015). Corruption distance and FDI flows into Latin America. *International Business Review*, *24*(1), 33–42. doi:10.1016/j.ibusrev.2014.05.006

Golob, U., & Bartlett, J. (2007). Communicating about corporate social responsibility: A comparative study of CSR reporting in Australia and Slovenia. *Public Relations Review*, *33*(1), 1–9. doi:10.1016/j.pubrev.2006.11.001

Gond, J. P., & Matten, D. (2007). Rethinking the Business-Society Interface: Beyond the Functionalist Trap. *ICCSR Research Paper series, No.47-2007.*

Google. (2013, April). Public Data: China. Retrieved from http://www.google.com/publicdata/explore?ds=d5bncppjof8f9_&met_y=ny_gdp_mktp_cd&idim=country:CHN&dl=en&hl=en&q=gdp%20china

Government of the Philippines (GOP) Senate Economic Planning Office. (2013). *Realizing the Philippines' Mining Potential. Policy Brief. PB 3-02*. Manila, Philippines: Philippine Senate Economic Planning Office.

Graafland, J., Mazereuw, C., & Yahia, A. (2006). Islam and Socially Responsible Business Conduct: An Empirical Study of Dutch Entrepreneurs. *Business Ethics (Oxford, England)*, *15*(4), 390–406. doi:10.1111/j.1467-8608.2006.00458.x

Grace, D. (1998). *Business Ethics: Australian Problems and Cases*. Oxford University Press.

Gray, R., Javad, M., Power, D. M., & Sinclair, C. D. (2001). Social and environmental disclosure and corporate characteristics: A research note and extension. *Journal of Business Finance & Accounting*, *28*(3-4), 327–356. doi:10.1111/1468-5957.00376

Gray, R., Owen, D., & Maunders, K. (1987). *Accounting and Accountability: Changes and Challenges in Corporate Social and Environmental Reporting*. London, UK: Prentice Hall.

Gray, R., Owen, D., & Maunders, K. (1987). *Corporate Social Reporting - Accounting & Accountability*. Hemel Hempstead: Prentice-Hall.

Gray, R., Walters, D., Bebbington, J., & Thompson, I. (1995). The greening of enterprise: An exploration of the (non) role of environmental accounting and environmental accountants in organizational change. *Critical Perspectives on Accounting*, *6*(3), 211–239. doi:10.1006/cpac.1995.1021

Greenpeace. (2014). Asia Pulp & Paper: from confrontation to engagement. Retrieved from http://www.greenpeace.org/international/en/news/Blogs/makingwaves/asia-pulp-paper-forest-conservation-policy/blog/47162/

Gugler, P., & Shi, J. Y. J. (2009). Corporate social responsibility for developing country multinational corporations: Lost war in pertaining global competitiveness? *Journal of Business Ethics*, *87*(S1), 3–24. doi:10.1007/s10551-008-9801-5

Gul, F. A., & Leung, S. (2004). Board leadership, outside directors' expertise and voluntary corporate disclosures. *Journal of Accounting and Public Policy*, *23*(5), 351–379. doi:10.1016/j.jaccpubpol.2004.07.001

Gunningham, N., Kagan, R. A., & Thornton, D. (2002). *Social Licence and Environmental Protection: why businesses go beyond compliance*. London: Centre for Analysis of Risk and Regulation, London School of Economics and Political Science.

Gupta, S., & Shapiro, D. (2014). Building and transforming an emerging market global enterprise: Lessons from the Infosys journey. *Business Horizons*, *57*(2), 169–179. doi:10.1016/j.bushor.2013.10.007

Gustavson, R. (2009). Australia: Practices and experiences. In S. Idowu & W. Filho (Eds.), *Global practices of Corporate Social Responsibility* (pp. 463–495). Berlin, Heidelberg: Springer. doi:10.1007/978-3-540-68815-0_21

Guthrie, J., & Parker, L. (1990). Corporate Social Disclosure Practice: A Comparative International Analysis. *Advances in Public Interest Accounting*, *3*, 251–176.

Hack-Polay, D. (2013). Understanding the business environment. In D. Hack-Polay & D. Davies (Eds.), Understanding Business – a Beginner's Text. Harlow: Pearson.

Hackston, D., & Milne, M. J. (1996). Some determinants of social and environmental disclosures in New Zealand companies. *Accounting, Auditing & Accountability Journal*, *9*(1), 77–108. doi:10.1108/09513579610109987

Hafsi, T., & Farashahi, M. (2005). Applicability of Management Theories to Developing Countries: A Synthesis. *Management International Review*, *45*(4), 483–511.

Hah, K., & Freeman, S. (2014). Multinational enterprise subsidiaries and their CSR: A conceptual framework of the management of CSR in smaller emerging economies. *Journal of Business Ethics*, *122*(1), 125–136. doi:10.1007/s10551-013-1753-8

Hahn, T., Figge, F., Pinkse, J., & Preuss, L. (2010). Trade-offs in Corporate Sustainability. You Cannot Have Your Cake and Eat It. *Business Strategy and the Environment*, *19*(4), 217–229. doi:10.1002/bse.674

Hair, J. F., Black, W. C., Babin, B. J., Anderson, R. E., & Tatham, R. L. (2006). *Multivariate data analysis* (Vol. 6). Upper Saddle River, NJ: Pearson Prentice Hall.

Haley, U. C., & Haley, G. T. (2013). *Subsidies to Chinese industry: State capitalism, business strategy, and trade policy*. Oxford University Press. doi:10.1093/acprof:oso/9780199773749.001.0001

Hamid, F. (2004). Corporate Social Disclosure by Banks and Finance Companies: Malaysian Evidence. *Corporate Ownership and Control*, *1*(4), 118–130.

Hamid, F. Z. A. (2004). Corporate social disclosure by banks and finance companies: Malaysian evidence. *Corporate Ownership and Control*, *1*(4), 118–130.

Hamid, S., Craig, R., & Clarke, F. (1993). Religion: A Confounding Cultural Element In The International Harmonization of Accounting? *Abacus*, *29*(2), 131–148. doi:10.1111/j.1467-6281.1993.tb00427.x

Haniffa, R. M., & Cooke, T. E. (2005). The impact of culture and governance on corporate social reporting. *Journal of Accounting and Public Policy*, *24*(5), 391–430. doi:10.1016/j.jaccpubpol.2005.06.001

Hardt, M. (1995). The withering of civil society. *Social Text*, (45): 27–44. doi:10.2307/466673

Haro, A., Alarcón, F., & Caba, M. (2012). Los determinantes de la divulgación de información sobre Responsabilidad Social Corporativa en el sector financiero: El caso Español. *Revista Facultad de Ciencias Económicas: Investigación y Reflexión*, *20*(1), 189–205.

Haro, A., Caba, C., & Cazorla, L. (2014). Efficiency of venture capital firms: Evidence from Spain. *Small Business Economics*, *43*(1), 229–243. doi:10.1007/s11187-014-9541-0

Harris, L., & Crane, A. (2002). The greening of organizational culture: Management views on the depth, degree and diffusion of change. *Journal of Organizational Change Management*, *15*(3), 214–234. doi:10.1108/09534810210429273

Harrod, R. F. (1948). *Towards a dynamic economics*. London: Macmillan.

Harstad, B., & Svensson, J. (2011). Bribes, lobbying and development. *The American Political Science Review*, *105*(1), 46–63. doi:10.1017/S0003055410000523

Hart, S., & Milstein, M. (2003). Creating sustainable value. *The Academy of Management Executive*, *17*(2), 56–67. doi:10.5465/AME.2003.10025194

Haskins, C. (2009). Using the concept of sustainable development to encourage corporate responsibility in small enterprises (Working paper). Norwegian University of Science and Technology, Department of Industrial Economics and Technology Management Trondheim, Norway.

Heakal, R. (2015, December 8). *What Is An Emerging Market Economy?* Retrieved from http://www.investopedia.com/articles/03/073003.asp

Held, D., & McGrew, A. G. (2007). *A new world economic order? Global markets and state power: Beyond globalization/anti-globalization: Beyond the great divide*. New York: Polity.

Heller, N.A., & Heller, V.L. (2011). Business Ethics Education: Are Business Schools Teaching to the AACSB Ethics Education Task Force Recommendations? *International Journal of Business and Social Science*. 2(20), 30-38.

Hemingway, C. A., & Maclagan, P. W. (2004). Managers' personal values as drivers of corporate social responsibility. *Journal of Business Ethics*, *50*(1), 33–44. doi:10.1023/B:BUSI.0000020964.80208.c9

Hewitt, J. (2015, June 3). Big miners need to win hearts and minds in fight against environmental activism. *Australian Financial Review*. Retrieved at http://www.afr.com/opinion/columnists/big-miners-need-to-win-hearts-and-minds-in-fight-against-environmental-activism-20150603ghg1n5#ixzz3hxDI0Vb

Hills, P. (2007). The Environment. *Understanding Contemporary Asian Pacific*.

Hilson, G. (2012). Corporate Social Responsibility in the extractive industries: Experiences from developing countries. *Resources Policy*, *37*(2), 131–137. doi:10.1016/j.resourpol.2012.01.002

Ho, L. J. & Taylor, M. E. (2007). An empirical analysis of triple bottom-line reporting and its determinates: evidence from the United States and Japan. *Journal of international Financial Management and Accounting*, 18(2), 123-150.

Hoejmose, S., Brammer, S., & Millington, A. (2011). Green supply chain management: The role of trust and top management in B2B and B2C markets. *Industrial Marketing Management*, *41*(4), 609–620. doi:10.1016/j.indmarman.2012.04.008

Hofstede Centre. (2015). Retrieved from http://geert-hofstede.com/

Hofstede, G. (1983). The cultural relativity of organizational practices and theories. *Journal of International Business Studies*, 1983, 75–89.

Hofstede, G. (1984). *Culture's consequences: International differences in work-related values* (Vol. 5). Sage publications.

Holden, W. N., & Jacobson, D. (2007). Mining amid armed conflict: Nonferrous metals mining in the Philippines. *Canadian Geographer*, *51*(4), 475–500. doi:10.1111/j.1541-0064.2007.00193.x

Hooghiemstra, R. (2000). Corporate communication and impression management-new perspectives why companies engage in corporate social reporting. *Journal of Business Ethics*, *27*(1/2), 55–68. doi:10.1023/A:1006400707757

Horn, R. (2010). Researching and Writing Dissertations – A Complete Guide for Business and Management Students. CIPD: London.

Ho, S. S., & Wong, K. S. (2001). A study of the relationship between corporate governance structures and the extent of voluntary disclosure. *Journal of International Accounting, Auditing & Taxation*, *10*(2), 139–156. doi:10.1016/S1061-9518(01)00041-6

Hoskisson, R. E., Eden, L., Lau, C. M., & Wright, M. (2000). Strategy in emerging economies. *Academy of Management Journal*, *43*(3), 249–267. doi:10.2307/1556394

Hsieh, H.-F., & Shannon, S. E. (2005). Three approaches to qualitative content analysis. *Qualitative Health Research*, *15*(9), 1277–1288.

Htay, S. N. N., Rashid, H. M. A., Adnan, M. A., & Meera, A. K. M. (2012). Impact of corporate governance on social and environmental information disclosure of Malaysian listed banks: Panel data analysis. *Asian Journal of Finance & Accounting*, *4*(1), 1–24. doi:10.5296/ajfa.v4i1.810

Huafang, X., & Jianguo, Y. (2007). Ownership structure, board composition and corporate voluntary disclosure: Evidence from listed companies in China. *Managerial Auditing Journal*, *22*(6), 604–619. doi:10.1108/02686900710759406

Huang, X., & Watson, L. (2015). Corporate social responsibility research in accounting. *Journal of Accounting Literature*, *34*, 1–16. Retrieved from http://0-search.proquest.com.almirez.ual.es/docview/1675861155?accountid=14477 doi:10.1016/j.acclit.2015.03.001

Huijser, M., Stück, J. M., & Tanaka, L. S. (2002). *Cross-cultural management education in China: from Marx to markets*. CMC/Global Associates/AER.

Hung, M., Shi, J., & Wang, Y. (2013). The Effect of Mandatory CSR Disclosure on Information Asymmetry: Evidence from a Quasi-natural Experiment in China (Working paper).

Hunter, T., & Bansal, P. (2007). How standard is standardized MNC global environmental communication? *Journal of Business Ethics*, *71*(2), 135–147. doi:10.1007/s10551-006-9130-5

Hvidt, M. (2013). Economic Diversification in GCC countries: Past Record and Future Trends. Kuwait Programme on Development, Governance and Globalization in The Gulf States.

Ibrahim, N. A., & Angelidis, J. P. (1995). The corporate social responsiveness orientation of board members: Are there differences between inside and outside directors? *Journal of Business Ethics*, *14*(5), 405–410. doi:10.1007/BF00872102

Ibrahim, N. A., & Angelidis, J. P. (2011). Effect of board members' gender on corporate social responsiveness orientation. *Journal of Applied Business Research*, *10*(1), 35–40. doi:10.19030/jabr.v10i1.5961

ICMM. (2012). *The role of mining in national economies. Mining's contribution to sustainable development. London, UK: International Council on Mining and Metals. IIED and WBCSD (2002). Breaking New Ground. The Report of the Mining Minerals and Sustainable Development Project*. London: Earthscan Publications.

Idemudia, U. (2010). Rethinking the role of corporate social responsibility in the Nigerian oil conflict: The limits of CSR. *Journal of International Development*, *22*(7), 833–845. doi:10.1002/jid.1644

Idemudia, U. (2011). Corporate social responsibility and developing countries: Moving the critical CSR research agenda in Africa forward. *Progress in Development Studies*, *11*(1), 1–18. doi:10.1177/146499341001100101

Ifeng Finance. (2010). 玖龙纸业再度蝉联绿色企业管理 [Nine Dragons Paper Won the Award for 'Green Management of Enterprises]. Retrieved from http://finance.ifeng.com/hk/gs/20100125/1753249.shtml

IFRS UAE. (2015). *IFRS Jurisdictional profile*. United Arab Emirates: IFRS Foundation.

IMF. (2012). *Philippines. Reform of the Fiscal Tax Regime for Mining and Petroleum. IMF Country Report 12/219*. Washington, DC: International Monetary Fund.

Indexmundi. (n. d.). Retrieved from www.indexmundi.com/china/gdp_per_capita_(ppp).html

Indian CSR News Network. (2012). *Mega CSR Conference in Mumbai*. Retrieved from www.indiacsr.in

Industry Canada. (2011). Corporate Social Responsibility. Retrieved from http://www.ic.gc.ca/eic/site/csr-rse.nsf/eng/home

Infosys. (2013). *Rethinking Corporate Social Responsibility (CSR) in Financial Services: Making business sense of sustainable CSR*. Bangalore, India: White Paper. Retrieved from http://www.infosys.com/industries/financial-services/white-papers/Documents/corporate-social-responsibility.pdf

Insider, B. (2014, January 21). *Pollution From China Is Hitting America's West Coast*. Retrieved from www.businessinsider.com

Ip, P. K. (2002). The Weizhi group of Xi'an: A Chinese virtuous corporation. *Journal of Business Ethics*, *35*(1), 15–26. doi:10.1023/A:1012619405545

Isaksson, L. (2012). *Corporate social responsibility:a study of strategic management and performance in Swedish firms, PhD, ePublications@bond*. School of Business.

Ismail, M. (2009). Corporate Social Responsibility and Its Role in Community Development: An International Perspective. *The Journal of International Social Research*, *2*(9), 199–209.

Issa, T. (2009). Ethical mindsets, aesthetics and spirituality: A mixed-methods approach analysis of the Australian services sector. Available online through. Perth: School of Management, Curtin Business School, Curtin University of Technology. Retrieved from http://espace.library.curtin.edu.au/R/?func=dbin-jump-full&object_id=131986&local_base=GEN01-ERA02

Issa, T., & Pick, D. (2010) Is business ethics worth teaching? An Australian higher education experience. *Paper read at European Business Ethics Network Conference*, Queen Mary University, London.

Ite, U. (2004). Multinationals and corporate social responsibility in developing countries: A case study of Nigeria. *Corporate Social Responsibility and Environmental Management*, *11*(1), 1–11. doi:10.1002/csr.49

Ite, U. E. (2005). Poverty reduction in resource-rich developing countries: What have multinational corporations got to do with it? *Journal of International Development*, *17*(7), 913–929. doi:10.1002/jid.1177

Ite, U. E. (2007). Partnering with the state for sustainable development: Shell's experience in the Niger Delta, Nigeria. *Sustainable Development*, *15*(4), 216–228. doi:10.1002/sd.312

Jacobs, A. (2013, May 4). Plans to harness Chinese river's power threatens a region. *The New York Times*.

Jamali, D., Karam, C., & Blowfield, M. (2015). Development Oriented CSR. London: Greenfield Press.

Jamali, D., Karam, C., & Blowfield, M. (2015). Introduction. Corporate social responsibility in developing countries: a development-oriented approach. In D. Jamali, C. Karam & M. Blowfield (Eds.), Development-oriented Corporate Social Responsibility (Vol. 1, pp. 1-12). Sheffield, UK: Greenleaf Publishing Limited.

Jamali, D., Lund-Thomsen, P., & Khara, N. (2015). CSR institutionalized myths in developing countries: An imminent threat of selective decoupling. *Business & Society*. doi:10.1177/0007650315584303

Jamali, D. (2010). The CSR of MNC subsidiaries in developing countries: Global, local, substantive or diluted? *Journal of Business Ethics*, *93*(Suppl. 2), 181–200. doi:10.1007/s10551-010-0560-8

Jamali, D., & Karam, C. (forthcoming). CSR in developing countries as an emerging field of study. *International Journal of Management Reviews*.

Jamali, D., Lund-Thomsen, P., & Khara, N. (2015). *CSR institutionalized myths in developing countries: an imminent threat of selective decoupling, Business & Society*. Online First.

Jamali, D., Lund-Thomsen, R., & Jeppesen, S. (2015). SMEs and CSR in developing countries. *Business and Society*, 1-12. doi:10.1177/0007650315571258

Jamali, D., & Mirshak, R. (2006). Corporate Social Responsibility (CSR): Theory and Practice in a Developing Country Context. *Journal of Business Ethics*, *72*(3), 243–262. doi:10.1007/s10551-006-9168-4

Jamali, D., & Neville, B. (2011). Convergence versus divergence in CSR in developing countries: An embedded multi-layered institutional lens. *Journal of Business Ethics*, *102*(4), 599–621. doi:10.1007/s10551-011-0830-0

Jamali, D., & Sidani, Y. (2011). Is CSR counterproductive in developing countries: The unheard voices of change. *Journal of Change Management*, *11*(1), 69–71. doi:10.1080/14697017.2011.548940

Jamali, D., Sidani, Y., & El-Asmar, K. (2009). A three country comparative analysis of managerial CSR perspectives: Insights from Lebanon, Syria and Jordan. *Journal of Business Ethics*, *85*(2), 173–192. doi:10.1007/s10551-008-9755-7

Jamali, K., Karam, C., & Blowfield, M. (2015). *Development-Oriented Corporate Social Responsibility*. Sheffield: Greenleaf Publishing.

Jawahar, I., & McLaughlin, G. (2001). Toward a descriptive stakeholder theory: An organizational life cycle approach. *Academy of Management Review*, *26*(3), 397–414.

Jenkins, B. (2007) Expanding Economic opportunity: The Role of Large Firm. Corporate Social Responsibility Report No. 17. Cambridge, MA: Kennedy School of Government, Harvard University.

Jenkins, B., Ishikawa, E., Barthes, E., & Giacomelli, M. (2008, June 10-12) Supporting Entrepreneurship and the Base of the Pyramid through Business Linkages. *Report of a Roundtable Dialogue*, Rio de Jeneiro, Brazil. Washington, DC: International Finance Corporation, International Business Leaders Forum, and Kennedy School of Government, Harvard University.

Jenkins, H. (2004). Corporate social responsibility and the mining industry: Conflicts and constructs. *Corporate Social Responsibility and Environmental Management*, *11*(1), 23–34. doi:10.1002/csr.50

Jenkins, H., & Obara, L. (2008). Corporate Social Responsibility (CSR) in the mining industry – the risk of community dependency.*Proceedings of the 2008 Centre for Resource Research Conference.*Belfast: CRRC.

Jenkins, H., & Yakovlevam, N. (2006). Corporate social responsibility in the mining industry: Exploring trends in social and environmental disclosure. *Journal of Cleaner Production*, *14*(3), 271–284. doi:10.1016/j.jclepro.2004.10.004

Jenkins, R. (2005). Globalization, corporate social responsibility and poverty. *International Affairs*, *81*(3), 525–540. doi:10.1111/j.1468-2346.2005.00467.x

Jenkins, R., & Newell, P. (2013). CSR, tax and development. *Third World Quarterly*, *34*(3), 378–396. doi:10.1080/01436597.2013.784596

Jensen, M. C. (1993). The modern industrial revolution, exit, and the failure of internal control systems. *the Journal of Finance, 48*(3), 831-880.

Jensen, M. C., & Meckling, W. H. (1976). Theory of the firm: Managerial behavior, agency costs and ownership structure. *Journal of Financial Economics, 3*(4), 305–360. doi:10.1016/0304-405X(76)90026-X

Jensen, N. M., Li, Q., & Rahman, A. (2010). Understanding corruption and firm responses in cross-national firm-level surveys. *Journal of International Business Studies, 41*(9), 1481–1504. doi:10.1057/jibs.2010.8

Jeucken, M., & Bouma, J. (1999). The Changing Environment of Banks. *Greener Management International, 27*, 21–35.

Jin, K., Drozdenko, R., & De Loughy, S. (2013). The role of corporate value clusters in ethics, social responsibility, and performance: A study of financial professionals and implications for the financial meltdown. *Journal of Business Ethics, 112*(1), 15–24. doi:10.1007/s10551-012-1227-4

Jo, H., & Harjoto, M. A. (2011). Corporate governance and firm value: The impact of corporate social responsibility. *Journal of Business Ethics, 103*(3), 351–383. doi:10.1007/s10551-011-0869-y

Johnson, R. A., & Greening, D. W. (1999). The effects of corporate governance and institutional ownership types on corporate social performance. *Academy of Management Journal, 42*(5), 564–576. doi:10.2307/256977

Johnston, M., & Hao, Y. (1995). China's surge of corruption. *Journal of Democracy, 6*(4), 80–94. doi:10.1353/jod.1995.0068

Jones Christensen, L., Siemsen, E., & Balasubramanian, S. (2015). Consumer behavior change at the base of the pyramid: Bridging the gap between for-profit and social responsibility strategies. *Strategic Management Journal, 36*(2), 307–317.

Jones, T. M., & Wicks, A. C. (1999). Convergent stakeholder theory. *Academy of Management Review, 24*(2), 206–221.

Jonson, E. P., McGuire, L.M. & O'Neill, D. (2015). Teaching Ethics to Undergraduate Business Students in Australia: Comparison of Integrated and Stand-alone Approaches. *Journal of Business Ethics*, 132(2), 477-491.

Jose, A., & Lee, S. M. (2007). Environmental Reporting of Global Corporations: A Content Analysis based on Website Disclosures. *Journal of Business Ethics, 72*(4), 307–321. doi:10.1007/s10551-006-9172-8

Jutterström, M., & Norberg, P. (2013). 11. CSR as a management idea–discussing the contribution. *CSR as a Management Idea: Ethics in Action*, 177.

Kamla, R. (2007). Critically Appreciating Social Accounting and Reporting in The Arab Middle East: A Postcolonial Perspective. *Advances in International Accounting, 20*, 105–177. doi:10.1016/S0897-3660(07)20005-4

Kamla, R., Gallhofer, S., & Haslam, J. (2006). Islam, Nature and Accounting: Islamic Principles and the Notion of Accounting for The Environment. *Accounting Forum, 39*(3), 245–265. doi:10.1016/j.accfor.2006.05.003

Kang, N., & Moon, J. (2012). Institutional complementarity between corporate governance and corporate social responsibility: A comparative analysis of three capitalisms. *Socio-economic Review, 10*(1), 85–108. doi:10.1093/ser/mwr025

Kaplinsky, R., & Morris, M. (2001). *A Handbook for Value Chain Research*. Ottawa: International Development Research Center.

Katsioloudes, M., & Brodtkorb, T. (2007). Corporate Social Responsibility: An Exploratory Study in The United Arab Emirates. *SAM Advanced Management Journal*, Autumn, 9-20.

Kaufmann, D., & Vicente, P. C. (2011). Legal corruption. *Economics and Politics, 23*(2), 195–219. doi:10.1111/j.1468-0343.2010.00377.x

Kaymak, T., & Bektas, E. (2008). East meets west? Board characteristics in an emerging market: Evidence from Turkish banks. *Corporate Governance: An International Review*, *16*(6), 550–561. doi:10.1111/j.1467-8683.2008.00713.x

Keig, D. L., Brouthers, L. E., & Marshall, V. B. (2015). Formal and informal corruption environments and multinational enterprise social irresponsibility. *Journal of Management Studies*, *52*(1), 89–116. doi:10.1111/joms.12102

Kemper, A., & Martin, R. L. (2010). After the fall: The global financial crisis as a test of corporate social responsibility theories. *European Management Review*, *7*(4), 229–239. doi:10.1057/emr.2010.18

Kerr, J. E. (2007) 'Sustainability Meets Profitability: The Convenient Truth of How the Business Judgment Rule Protects a Board's Decision to Engage in Social Entrepreneurship. Retrieved from http://ssrn.com/abstract=1296270

Khan, F. R., & Lund-Thomsen, P. (2011). CSR as imperialism: Towards a phenomenological approach to CSR in the developing world. *Journal of Change Management*, *11*(1), 73–90. doi:10.1080/14697017.2011.548943

Khan, M. (2010). The Effect of Corporate Governance Elements on Corporate Social Responsibility (CSR) Reporting. *International Journal of Commerce and Management*, *52*(2), 82–109.

Khojastehpour, M. (2015). How does corporate social responsibility avoid the incidence of corruption in international expansion? *European Business Review*, *27*(3), 334–342. doi:10.1108/EBR-01-2015-0002

Kiel, G. C., & Nicholson, G. J. (2003). Board composition and corporate performance: How the Australian experience informs contrasting theories of corporate governance. *Corporate Governance: An International Review*, *11*(3), 189–205. doi:10.1111/1467-8683.00318

Kim, J., & Jeon, Y. (2015). Dividend policy and corporate social responsibility: A comparative analysis of multinational enterprise subsidiaries and domestic firms in Korea. *Emerging Markets Finance and Trade*, *51*(2), 306–319. doi:10.1080/1540496X.2015.1021605

Knorringa, P., & Nadvi, K. (2016). Rising power clusters and the challenges of local and global standards. *Journal of Business Ethics*, *133*(1), 55–72. doi:10.1007/s10551-014-2374-6

Knox, S., & Maklan, S. (2004). Corporate social responsibility: Moving beyond investment towards measuring outcomes. *European Management Journal*, *22*(5), 508–516. doi:10.1016/j.emj.2004.09.009

Knudsen, J. S., Moon, J., & Slager, R. (2015). Government policies for corporate social responsibility in Europe: A comparative analysis of institutionalisation. *Policy and Politics*, *43*(1), 81–99. doi:10.1332/030557312X656016

Koleva, P., & Gherib, J. (2012). La responsabilité sociale des entreprises en Tunisie: Une lecture institutionnaliste. *Revue Tiers Monde*, *212*(4), 83–99. doi:10.3917/rtm.212.0083

Kolk, A. (2003). Trends in sustainability reporting by the Fortune Global 250. *Business Strategy and the Environment*, *12*(5), 279–291. doi:10.1002/bse.370

Kolk, A. (2005). Environmental reporting by multinationals from the Triad: Convergence or divergence? *Management International Review*, 2005, 145–166.

Kolk, A., & Lenfant, F. (2013). Multinationals, CSR and partnerships in Central African conflict countries. *Corporate Social Responsibility and Environmental Management*, *20*(1), 43–54. doi:10.1002/csr.1277

Kolk, A., & van Tulder, R. (2010). International business, Corporate Social Responsibility and sustainable development. *International Business Review*, *19*(1), 1–14.

Konar, S., & Cohen, A. M. (2001). Does the market value environmental performance? *The Review of Economics and Statistics*, *83*(2), 281–289. doi:10.1162/00346530151143815

Kotilainen, J., Prokhorova, E., Sairinen, R., & Tiainen, H. (2015). Corporate social responsibility of mining companies in Kyrgyzstan and Tajikistan. *Resources Policy*, *45*, 202–209. doi:10.1016/j.resourpol.2015.06.001

Kotler, P., & Lee, N. (2005). *Corporate Social Responsibility: Doing the Most Good for Your Company and Cause*. New Jersey: John Wiley & Sons.

Kotler, P., & Lee, N. (2005). *Corporate social responsibility: Doing the most good for your company and your cause*. Hoboken, NJ: John Wiley & Sons, Inc.

KPMG International. (2013). *The KPMG survey of corporate responsibility reporting*. Retrieved from http://www.kpmg.com/AU/en/IssuesAndInsights/ArticlesPublications/Documents/corporateresponsibility -reporting-survey-2013.pdf

KPMG. (1999). *The KPMG Survey of Corporate Responsibility Reporting 1999*. Netherlands: KPMG International.

Kristoffersen, I., Gerrans, P., & Clarke-Murphy, M. (2005), *The corporate social responsibility and the theory of the firm. FIMARC Working Paper Series*. School of Accounting, Economics, and Finance Edith Cowan University: Perth.

Krohn, F.B. (1985). A General Semantics Approach to Teaching Business Ethics. *The Journal of Business Communication*, 22(3), 59-66.

Krüger, P. (2009). *Corporate social responsibility and the board of directors. Job Market Paper*. France: Toulouse School of Economics.

K'ung-fu-tzu. (1996). *The Wise Man Said* (Trans. Ofek Bina). Tel Aviv: Ofarim [Hebrew].

Kunkel, J. (2014). Mining exports help underpin national growth. Canberra: Minerals Council of Australia; Retrieved from http://www.minerals.org.au/news/mining_exports_help_underpin_gdp_growth

Kusku, F., & Frazer, A. Z. (2004). An Empirical Investigation of Corporate Citizenship in Australia and Turkey. *British Journal of Management*, *15*(1), 57–72. doi:10.1111/j.1467-8551.2004.t01-1-00400.x

Kvistgaard, L. T. (2013) Creating Shared Value- A post positivistic analysis of Michael E. Porter's meta--theoretical eclecticism. Master Dissertation, Copenhagen Business School. Retrieved from http://studenttheses.cbs.dk/xmlui/bitstream/handle/10417/3549/lea_torpegaard_kvistgaard.pdf?sequence=1

Kwok, A. (2012, Sept 9). Nickel Asia asserts: responsible mining possible. *InterAksyon*. Retrieved from http://www.interaksyon.com/article/42681/nickel-asia-asserts-responsible-mining-possible

Kytle, B., & Ruggie, J. G. (2005). Corporate Social Responsibility as Risk Management – A model for Multinationals. Corporate Social Responsibility Initiatives (CSRI) Working Paper No. 10. Cambridge M. A.: John F. Kennedy School of Government, Harvard University.

Lang, M., & Lundholm, R. C. (1993). Cross-sectional determinants of analyst ratings of corporate disclosures. *Journal of Accounting Research*, *31*(2), 246–271. doi:10.2307/2491273

Larrán, M. (2002). Efectos de la divulgación de la información en el valor empresarial: Percepciones de las grandes compañías españolas. *Revista de la Asociación Española de Contabilidad y Administración de Empresas*, *60*, 37–41.

Larrán, M., & Giner, B. (2002). The Use of the Internet for Corporate Reporting by Spanish Companies. *The International Journal of Digital Accounting Research*, *2*(1), 53–82.

Larrinaga, C., & Moneva, J. (2002). Global Reporting Initiative: Contabilidad y Sostenibilidad. *Partida Doble*, *135*, 80–87.

Lattemann, C., Fetscherin, M., Alon, I., Li, S., & Schneider, A. M. (2009). CSR Communication Intensity in Chinese and Indian Multinational Companies. *Corporate Governance: An International Review, 17*(4), 426–442. doi:10.1111/j.1467-8683.2009.00758.x

Lau, D.-C. (1979). *Analects*. London: Penguin.

Lau, D.-C. (2001). *Tao Te Ching*. Hong Kong: Chinese University Press.

Lavie, Y. (2006). Stealing organs from death-row inmates for transplants in China – a call to end Israeli cooperation in the process (in Hebrew). *Harefua, 145*, 749–753.

Lazonick, W., & O'Sullivan, M. (2000). Maximizing shareholder value: A new ideology for corporate governance. *Economy and Society, 29*(1), 13–35. doi:10.1080/030851400360541

Leavy, G. D., Lam, J., & Hr, S. S. M. (2008). Does East meet West in business ethics?: An introduction to the special issue. *Journal of Business Ethics, 79*(1-2), 1–8. doi:10.1007/s10551-007-9384-6

LeBeau, P. (2013, April 18). New study finds China manufacturing costs rising to US level. *CNBC*.

Lee, C. K. (2007). *Against the law: labor protests in China's rustbelt and sunbelt*. Berkeley: University of California Press.

Lee, M. (2008). A review of the theories of corporate social responsibility: Its evolutionary path and the road ahead. *International Journal of Management Reviews, 10*(1), 53–73. doi:10.1111/j.1468-2370.2007.00226.x

Leigh, D., & Evans, R. (2009, October 1). Fraud Office seeks BAE's prosecution over bribery. *The Guardian*.

Leisinger, K. M. (2006). On Corporate Responsibility for Human Rights Presentation of Special Advisor to the Secretary General on the Global Compact in Basel, April. Online Resources. Retrieved from http://www.unglobalcompact.org/docs/news_events/9.6/corpresforhr_kl.pdf

Lepanto Consolidated Mining Corporation. (2014). *2014 Annual Report*. Retrieved from http://www.lepantomining.com/

Lepanto Consolidated Mining Corporation. (n. d.). *Environmental Protection and Enhancement Program*. Retrieved from http://www.lepantomining.com/sustainability.html

Lepanto Consolidated Mining Corporation. (n. d.). *Social Development Management Program*. Retrieved from http://www.lepantomining.com/social_devt.html

Lesprom. (2013). *Indonesia signs voluntary partnership agreement with EU to curb illegal ltimber trade*. Retrieved from http://www.lesprom.com/news/Indonesia_signs_Voluntary_Partnership_Agreement_with_EU_to_curb_illegal_timber_trade_58194/?lng=eng

Leung, E., & Verriest, A. (2014). Does location matter for disclosure? Evidence from geographical segment. Retrieved from http://research.chicagobooth.edu/~/media/CEBE78C71AD14878A33677EB5C61FFB7.pdf

Lewis, M. (2001). Islam and Accounting. *Accounting Forum, 25*(2), 103–127. doi:10.1111/1467-6303.00058

LG. (2015). *Life's Good with LG. 2014-2015 LG Electronics Sustainability Report*. Retrieved from http://www.lg.com/global/sustainability/communications/sustainability-reports

Li Ning. (2014). *Environmental, Social and Governance Report. Li Ning Company Limited 2014*. Retrieved from http://ir.lining.com/eng/csr/csr_reports/csr_report_2014.pdf

Lindgreen, A., Swaen, V., & Johnston, W. J. (2008). Corporate Social Responsibility: An Empirical Investigation of U.S. Organizations. *Journal of Business Ethics, 85*(Suppl. 2), 303–323. doi:10.1007/s10551-008-9738-8

Lindon, J. G., Canare, T. A., & Mendoza, R. (2014). Corporate governance in mining: Lessons from the Marcopper mine disaster in Marinduque, Philippines. *Asian Journal of Business Ethics*, *3*(2), 171–193. doi:10.1007/s13520-014-0038-3

Lin, L. H., Ho, Y., & Lin, W. E. (2013). Confucian and Taoist work values: An exploratory study of the Chinese transformational leadership behavior. *Journal of Business Ethics*, *113*(1), 91–103. doi:10.1007/s10551-012-1284-8

Lin, L.-W. (2010). Corporate social responsibility in China: Window dressing or structural change? *Berkeley Journal of International Law*, *28*(1), 64–100.

Lin, N. (2011, March). Capitalism in China: A centrally managed capitalism (CMC) and its future. *Management and Organization Review*.

Locke, R. M., Rissing, B. A., & Pal, T. (2012). Complements or substitutes? Private codes, state regulation, and the enforcement of labor standards in global supply chains. *British Journal of Industrial Relations*, *51*(3), 519–552. doi:10.1111/bjir.12003

Lockett, A., Moon, J., & Visser, W. (2006). Corporate social responsibility in management research: Focus, nature, salience and sources of influence. *Journal of Management Studies*, *43*(1), 115–135. doi:10.1111/j.1467-6486.2006.00585.x

Lompo, K., & Trani, J. F. (2013). Does corporate social responsibility contribute to human development in developing countries? Evidence from Nigeria. *Journal of Human Development and Capabilities*, *14*(2), 241–265. doi:10.1080/19452829.2013.784727

Lorenzo-Molo, M. C. F. (2008). Why corporate social responsibility (CSR) remains a myth: The Case of the Philippines. *Asian Business & Management*, *8*(2), 149–168. doi:10.1057/abm.2009.2

Lowrie, A. & Willmott, H. (2009). Accreditation Sickness in the Consumption of Business Education: The Vacuum in AACSB Standard Setting. *Management Learning*, 40(4), 411-420.

Luetkenhorst, W. (2004). Corporate social responsibility and the development agenda: The case for actively involving small and medium enterprises. *Inter Economics*, *39*(3), 157–166. doi:10.1007/BF02933583

Lund-Thomsen, P. (2004). Towards a Critical Framework on Corporate Social and Environmental Responsibility in the South: The Case of Pakistan. *Development*, *47*(3), 106–113. doi:10.1057/palgrave.development.1100059

Lund-Thomsen, P. (2013a). Multi-stakeholder Initiatives in Cotton Value Chains: Towards a Theoretical Framework and a Methodology. In A. Lindgreen, F. Maon, J. Vanhamme, & S. Sen (Eds.), *Sustainable Value Chain Management: A Research Anthology* (pp. 257–270). Farnham: Gower Publishing Ltd.

Lund-Thomsen, P. (2013b). Labor agency in the football manufacturing industry of Sialkot, Pakistan. *Geoforum*, *44*(1), 71–81. doi:10.1016/j.geoforum.2012.04.007

Lund-Thomsen, P., & Lindgreen, A. (2014). Corporate social responsibility in global value chains: Where are we now and where are we going? *Journal of Business Ethics*, *123*(1), 11–22. doi:10.1007/s10551-013-1796-x

Lund-Thomsen, P., & Nadvi, K. (2010). Global value chains, local collective action and corporate social responsibility: A review of empirical evidence. *Business Strategy and the Environment*, *19*(1), 1–13. doi:10.1002/bse.670

Lund-Thomsen, P., & Wad, P. (2014). Global value chains, local economic organization and corporate social responsibility in the BRICS countries. *Competition & Change*, *18*(4), 281–290. doi:10.1179/1024529414Z.00000000061

Luo, J. (2005). Particularistic trust and general trust: A network analysis in Chinese organizations. *Management and Organization Review*, *1*(3), 437–458. doi:10.1111/j.1740-8784.2005.00022.x

Luo, X., & Bhattacharya, C. B. (2009). The debate over doing good: Corporate social performance, strategic marketing levers, and firm-idiosyncratic risk. *Journal of Marketing*, *73*(6), 198–213.

Lu, X. (2009). A Chinese perspective: Business ethics in China now and in the future. *Journal of Business Ethics*, *86*(4), 451–461. doi:10.1007/s10551-008-9857-2

Lu, X. (2010). *Business ethics: a Chinese approach.* Shanghai Academy of Social Sciences Press.

Maignan, I., & Ralston, D. A. (2002). Corporate Social Responsibility in Europe and the US: Insights from businesses' self-presentations. *Journal of International Business Studies*, *33*(3), 497–514. doi:10.1057/palgrave.jibs.8491028

Mainhardt-Gibbs, H. (2003). *The World Bank Extractive Industries Review. The Role of Structural Reform Programs towards Sustainable Development Outcomes.* Retrieved from http://awsassets.panda.org/downloads/2003_the_world_bank_extractive_industries_review.pdf

Maitar, B. (2013). APRIL walks away from the FSC. Retrieved from http://www.greenpeace.org/international/en/news/Blogs/makingwaves/april-walks-away-from-the-fsc/blog/45634/

Makower, J. (2014). Kara Hurst named Amazon's first sustainability executive. Retrieved from http://www.greenbiz.com/blog/2014/08/15/kara-hurst-named-amazons-first-sustainability-executive

Mallin, C. (2009). *Corporate social responsibility: A case study approach.* Glostershire: Edward Elgar.

Manila Mining Corporation. (n. d.). *Community Development Plan (CDP), Corporate Social Responsibility (CSR) And Environmental Protection Activities Of MMC.* Retrieved from http://www.manilamining.com/aboutmmc.html

Ma, Q. (2002). The Governance of NGOs in China since 1978: How much autonomy? *Nonprofit and Voluntary Sector Quarterly*, *31*(3), 305–328. doi:10.1177/0899764002313001

Marano, V., & Kostova, T. (2015). Unpacking the institutional complexity in adoption of CSR practices in multinational enterprises.[online ahead of print]. *Journal of Management Studies.* doi:10.1111/joms.12124

Margolis, J. D., & Walsh, J. P. (2003). Misery loves companies: Rethinking social initiatives by business. *Administrative Science Quarterly*, *48*(2), 68–305. doi:10.2307/3556659

Markarian, G., Parbonetti, A., & Previts, G. J. (2007). The Convergence of Disclosure and Governance Practices in the World's Largest Firms. *Corporate Governance: An International Review*, *15*(2), 294–310. doi:10.1111/j.1467-8683.2007.00561.x

Marques, J. C., & Mintzberg, H. (2015). Why corporate social responsibility isn't a piece of cake. *MIT. Sloan Management Review*, *56*(4), 8–11.

Marquis, C., & Qian, C. (2014). Corporate Social Responsibility Reporting in China: Symbol or Substance? *Organization Science*, *25*(1), 127–148. doi:10.1287/orsc.2013.0837

Marston, C. & Polei, A. (2004). Corporate reporting on the Internet by German companies. *International Journal of Accounting Standard Committee*, *5*, 285–311.

Mathews, M. (1993). *Socially Responsible Accounting.* London: Chapman & Hall.

Matoussi, H., Karaa, A., & Maghraoui, R. (2004). Information asymmetry, disclosure level and securities liquidity in the BVMT. *Finance India*, *18*, 547–558.

Matten, D. (2003). Symbolic politics in environmental regulation: Corporate strategic responses. *Business Strategy and the Environment*, *12*(4), 215–226. doi:10.1002/bse.363

Matten, D., & Crane, A. (2005). Corporate Citizenship: Toward An Extended Theoretical Conceptualization'. *Academy of Management Review*, *30*(1), 166–179. doi:10.5465/AMR.2005.15281448

Matten, D., Crane, A., & Chapple, W. (2003). Behind the mask: Revealing the true face of corporate citizenship. *Journal of Business Ethics*, *45*(1/ 2), 109–120. doi:10.1023/A:1024128730308

Matten, D., & Moon, J. (2008). "Implicit" and "explicit" CSR: A conceptual framework for an understanding of corporate social responsibility. *Academy of Management Review*, *33*(2), 404–424. doi:10.5465/AMR.2008.31193458

Maximiano, J. M. B. (2005, September 28–30). *The state of corporate social responsibility in the Philippine.Paper presented at theAustralian Association for Professional and Applied Ethics 12th Annual Conference*, Adelaide, Australia.

Mazurkiewicz, P. (2004). Corporate environmental responsibility: Is a common framework possible? DevComm-SDO World Bank. Retrieved from http://www-wds.worldbank.org/external/default/WDSContentServer/IW3P/IB/2008/01/22/000020953_20080122134142/Rendered/PDF/421830csrframework01PUBLIC1.pdf

Mckee, D., Garner, D., & Mckee, Y. (1999). *Accounting Services, The Islamic Middle East and The Global Economy*. Westport, CT: Quorum Books.

McWilliams, A., & Siegel, D. (2001). Corporate social responsibility: A theory of the firm perspective. *Academy of Management Review*, *26*(1), 117–127.

McWilliams, A., Siegel, D. S., & Wright, P. M. (2006). Corporate social responsibility: Strategic implications. *Journal of Management Studies*, *43*(1), 1–18. doi:10.1111/j.1467-6486.2006.00580.x

Menassa, E. (2010). Corporate Social Responsibility: An Exploration Study of the Quality and Extent of Social Disclosures by Lebanese Commercial Banks. *Journal ofAppliedAccounting Research*, *11*(1), 4–23. doi:10.1108/09675421011050009

Microsoft Corporation. (2013). YouthSpark Corporate Citizenship. Retrieved from http://www.microsoft.com/about/corporatecitizenship/en-us/youthspark/youthsparkhub/default.aspx

Midttun, A., Gjølberg, M., Kourula, A., Sweet, S., & Vallentin, S. (2015). Public policies for corporate social responsibility in four Nordic countries: Harmony of goals and conflict of means. *Business & Society*, *54*(4), 464–500. doi:10.1177/0007650312450848

Miles, M. (1987). *Managing the Corporate Social Environment*. NJ, USA: Prentice- Hall.

Miles, P. M., & Covin, J. G. (2000). Environmental marketing a source of reputational, competitive, and financial advantage. *Journal of Business Ethics*, *23*(3), 299–311. doi:10.1023/A:1006214509281

Miller, J. (2013). Authenticity, sincerity and spontaneity: The mutual implication of nature and religion in China and the West. *Method & Theory in the Study of Religion*, *25*(3), 283–307. doi:10.1163/15700682-12341259

Millner, A., & Dietz, S. (2015). Adaptation to climate change and economic growth in developing countries. *Environment and Development Economics*, *20*(3), 380–406. doi:10.1017/S1355770X14000692

Milne, M. J., & Adler, R. W. (1999). Exploring the reliability of social and environmental disclosures content analysis. *Accounting, Auditing & Accountability Journal*, *12*(2), 237–256. doi:10.1108/09513579910270138

Milton-Smith, J. (1997). Business Ethics in Australia and New Zealand. *Teaching Business Ethics*, 16(14), 1485-1497.

Mining Association of Canada. (2012). *TSM Assessment Protocol*. Ottawa: MAC.

Ministry of Environmental Protection of the People Republic of China. (2011). 山东省秸秆制浆造纸技术取得重大突破领先国际先进水平 [Shandong Province achieves important breakthrough in pulp and paper making technology using straw and stalks]. Retrieved from http://www.zhb.gov.cn/zhxx/gzdt/201107/t20110705_214414.htm

Mitchell, R. K., Agle, B. R., & Wood, D. J. (1997). Toward a theory of stakeholder identification and salience: Defining the principle of who and what really counts. *Academy of Management Review*, *22*, 853–886.

Mohsin, M. I. A. (2013). Potential of Zakat in Eliminating Riba in and Eradicating Muslim Countries. *Islamic Management and Business*, *5*(11), 114–126.

Mol, A. P., He, G., & Zhang, L. (2011). Information Disclosure in Environmental Risk Management: Developments in China. *Journal of Current Chinese Affairs*, *40*(3), 163–192.

Mole, K. F., Hart, M., Roper, S., & Saal, D. S. (2011). Broader or deeper? Exploring the most effective intervention profile for public small business support. *Environment & Planning A*, *43*(1), 87–105.

Mongabay. (2013). Pulp and paper giant gets $1.8B loan from China for Indonesia's largest mill. http://news.mongabay.com/2013/1011-app-oki-pulp-mill.html

Montealegre, K. A. (2015, February 20) MGB temporarily lifts suspension order vs. Benguet Corp. subsidiary. *Business World*. Retrieved from http://www.bworldonline.com/content.php?section=Corporate&title=mgb-temporarily-lifts-suspension-order-vs.-benguet-corp.-subsidiary&id=103096

Montiel, I. (2008). Corporate social responsibility and corporate sustainability: Separate pasts, common futures. *Organization & Environment*, *21*(2), 245–269. doi:10.1177/1086026608321329

Montiel, I., & Delgado-Ceballos, J. (2014). Defining and measuring corporate sustainability: Are we there yet? *Organization & Environment*, *27*(2), 113–139. doi:10.1177/1086026614526413

Moon, J., & Vogel, D. (2008). Corporate responsibility, government and civil society. In A. Crane, A. McWilliams, D. Matten, J. Moon, & D.S. Siegel (Eds.), Oxford handbook of corporate social responsibility. Oxford: Oxford University Press. doi:10.1093/oxfordhb/9780199211593.003.0013

Moon, J. (2004). *Government as a driver of corporate social responsibility: The UK in comparative perspective. International Centre for Corporate Social Responsibility research paper no. 20*. Nottingham: Nottingham University Business School.

Moon, J., & Shen, X. (2010). CSR in China research: Salience, focus and nature. *Journal of Business Ethics*, *94*(4), 613–629. doi:10.1007/s10551-009-0341-4

Morsing, M., & Schultz, M. (2006). Corporate Social Responsibility Communication: Stakeholder Information, Response and Involvement Strategies. *Business Ethics (Oxford, England)*, *15*(4), 323–338. doi:10.1111/j.1467-8608.2006.00460.x

MTN. (2014). Corporate Information. Online Resources. Retrieved from http://www.mtnonline.com/about-mtn/corporate-information

Mufson, S. (2013, May 12). In China, pollution resists change. *The Washington Post*, p. A12.

Mukherjee-Reed, A., & Reed, D. (2009). Partnerships for development: Four models of business involvement. *Journal of Business Ethics*, *90*(S1), 3–37. doi:10.1007/s10551-008-9913-y

Mullich, J. (2011). Corporate social responsibility emerges in China. *The Wall Street Journal*.

Munson, J. (2013, October 27). The Philippines still a hotbed of opposition against mining. *iPolitics*. Retrieved from http://www.ipolitics.ca/2013/10/27/the-philippines-still-a-hotbed-of-opposition-to-canadian-mines-says-priest/

Murphy, S. (2010). Corporate Partnerships for Entrepreneurship: Building the Ecosystem in the Middle East and Southeast Asia. Corporate Social Responsibility Initiative Working Paper No. 62. Cambridge, MA: John F. Kennedy School of Government, Harvard University.

Nachtsheim, C. J., Neter, J., Kutner, M. H., & Wasserman, W. (2004). *Applied linear regression models*. Irwin, McGraw-Hill.

Nadvi, K. (2011). Labour standards and technological upgrading: Competitive challenges in the global football industry. *International Journal of Technological Learning. Innovation and Development*, *4*(1-3), 235–257.

Nahar Abdullah, S. (2006). Board structure and ownership in Malaysia: the case of distressed listed companies. Corporate Governance: *The international journal of business in society, 6*(5), 582-594.

Nasrullah, N. M., & Rahim, M. A. (2013). *CSR in private enterprises in developing countries: Evidences from the ready-made garments industry in Bangladesh*. Heidelberg, Germany: Springer.

National Australian Bank. (2013). *National Australian Bank Annual review* 2013. Retrieved from www.nab.com.au

National Australian Bank. (2014). *National Australian Bank Dig Deeper paper,* 2014. Retrieved from www.nab.com.au

National Bureau of Statistics. (2012). Survey Report on Micro Small and Medium Enterprises (MSMEs) in Nigeria -Preliminary Report: 2010 National MSME Collaborative Survey. Retrieved from www.nigerianstat.gov.ng/pages/download/67

National Chamber Foundation (NCF). (2012). *Corporate Responsibility and Sustainable Economic Development in China: Implications for Business.* Asia United States Chamber of Commerce. Retrieved from www.uschamber.com

National Confederation of Industry. (2012). Forest Plantation: Opportunities and challenges for the Brazilian Pulp and Paper industry on the path of sustainability. Retrieved from www.cni.org.br

National Development and Reform Commission. (2011). 山东泉林公司依靠自主创新探索秸秆综合利用新途 [Reliant on internal initiatives and innovation, Shandong Tralin Paper explore new methods to use straw and stalks]. Retrieved from http://www.sdpc.gov.cn/hjbh/hjjsjyxsh/t20091203_317789.htm

Natufe, O. I. (2011) Corporate Social Responsibility: Value and Strategic Intent. *Social Responsibility Review*, 2, 14-25.

Nature Resources Canada. (2014). Canadian forests and forest products: key sustainability questions. Retrieved from http://www.nrcan.gc.ca/forests/industry/13319

Needle, D. (2010). *Business in Context: an introduction to business and its environment*. Singapore: Cengage Learning EMEA.

Neilson, J., & Pritchard, B. (2009). Value Chain struggles: Institutions and Governance in the Plantations of South India. Wiley-Blackwell, Gloucester. doi:10.1002/9781444308723

Neilson, J., & Pritchard, B. (2010). Fairness and ethicality in their place—The regional dynamics of fair trade and ethical sourcing agendas in the plantation districts of south India. *Environment & Planning A*, *42*(8), 1833–1851. doi:10.1068/a4260

Nekhili, M., & Fakhfakh, I. (2006). Les relations entre les mécanismes de gouvernement et l'indice de divulgation volontaire d'informations: étude clinique de deux entreprises tunisiennes. *Paper presented at the 27th conference of AFC on Comptabilité, Contrôle*, Audit et Institution(s). Tunis, Tunisia.

Nelson, J. (2007). *Building Linkages for Competitive and Responsible Entrepreneurship: Innovative partnerships to foster small enterprise, promote economic growth, and reduce poverty in developing countries. CSR Initiative, Harvard University and United Nations Industrial Development Organization*. UNIDO.

New York Times. (2014, March 27). *Most Chinese Cities Fail Minimum Air Quality Standards, Study Says*. Retrieved from www.nytimes.com

Newcrest Mining Limited. (2014). *Sustainability Report 2014*. Newcrest Mining Limited. Retrieved from www.newcrest.com.au

Nguyen, Q. T. K. (2014). The regional strategies of British multinational subsidiaries in South East Asia. *British Journal of Management*, *25*(Suppl. 1), S60–S76. doi:10.1111/1467-8551.12006

Nickel Asia Corporation. (2013). *2013 Sustainability Report*. Retrieved from http://www.nickelasia.com/pdf/NAC_2013_SR.pdf

Nickel Asia Corporation. (2014). *2014 Sustainability Report*. Retrieved from http://www.nickelasia.com/pdf/NAC_2014_SR.pdf

Nielsen, A., & Thomsen, C. (2009). Investigating CSR communication in SMEs: A case study among Danish middle managers. *Business Ethics (Oxford, England)*, *18*(1), 83–93. doi:10.1111/j.1467-8608.2009.01550.x

Nielsen, M. E. J., & Frederiksen, C. S. (2015). Political institutions and corporate social responsibility: A Nordic welfare state perspective from Denmark. In S. O. Idowu, R. Schmidpeter, & M. S. Fifka (Eds.), *Corporate social responsibility in Europe* (pp. 197–208). Cham, Switzerland: Springer International Publishing. doi:10.1007/978-3-319-13566-3_11

Nike. (2013). *Sustainable Business Performance Summary. Nike, Inc. FY12/13*. Retrieved from http://www.nikeresponsibility.com/report/uploads/files/FY12-13_NIKE_Inc_CR_Report.pdf

Nissan. (2015). *Nissan Sustainability Report, 2015*. Retrieved from http://www.nissan-global.com/EN/CSR/SR/2015/

Njoku, A. C., Ihugba, O. A., & Odii, A. (2014). Theoretical analysis of entrepreneurship challenges and prospects in Nigeria. *International Letters of Social and Humanistic Sciences*, 5, 21-34.

Nordhaus, W. D. (2008). *A question of balance: Weighting the options on global warming*. New Haven: Yale University Press.

Nwadialor, E., & Igwe, N. N. (2013). Adapting Corporate Social Responsibility Programs to Risk Management: A Model for Multinational Organizations in Nigeria. *European Journal of Business and Management*, *5*(15), 17–24.

O'Faircheallaigh, C. (2010). Aboriginal-Mining Company Contractual Agreements in Australia and Canada: Implications for Political Autonomy and Community Development. *Canadian Journal of Development Studies*, *30*(1-2), 69–86.

Oceanagold Corporation. (2015). *Sustainability Report 2015. Ensuring A Better Tomorrow*. Retrieved from http://www.oceanagold.com/assets/documents/annual-reports/OceanaGold-SR-2015-FA-online.pdf

OECD Newsroom. (2014, November 12). *China headed to overtake EU, United States in science and technology spending, OECD says*. Retrieved from www.oecd.org

OECD. (2002, February 7-8). The Relevance of the OECD Guidelines for Multinational Enterprises to the Mining Sector and the Promotion of Sustainable Development. *Proceedings of theconference on Foreign Direct Investment and the Environment*, Paris. France.

Oghojafor, B. E. A., Okonji, P. S., Olayemi, O. O., & Okolie, J. U. (2011, January 9-11). Fifty Years of Entrepreneurship Development in Nigeria: Challenges and Prospects. *Proceedings of the 10th International Entrepreneurship Forum*, Tamkeen, Bahrain.

Okhmatovskiy, I., & David, R. J. (2012). Setting your own standards: Internal corporate governance codes as a response to institutional pressure. *Organization Science*, *23*(1), 155–176. doi:10.1287/orsc.1100.0642

Oliver, B., Tucker, B., Gupta, R. & Yeo, S. (2008). eVALUate: an evaluation instrument for measuring students' perceptions of their engagement and learning outcomes. *Assessment and Evaluation in Higher Education,* 33(6), 619-630.

Olsen, B. E., & Sorensen, K. E. (2014). Strengthening the enforcement of CSR guidelines: Finding a new balance between hard law and soft law. *Legal Issues of Economic Integration*, *41*(1), 9–35.

Oppenheimer, M., O'Neill, B. C., Webster, M., & Agrawal, S. (2011). Climate change: The limits of consensus. *Science*, *317*(5844), 1505–1506. doi:10.1126/science.1144831 PMID:17872430

Orij, R. (2010). Corporate social disclosures in the context of national cultures and stakeholder theory. *Accounting, Auditing & Accountability Journal*, *23*(7), 868–889. doi:10.1108/09513571011080162

Osemene, O. F. (2012). Corporate Social Responsibility Practices in Mobile Telecommunications Industry in Nigeria. *European Journal of Business and Management*, *4*(8), 149–159.

Osman, M. (2013). *Corporate Social Responsibility (CSR) of Egyptian Banking Sector: A Critical and Postcolonial Perspective* [PhD Thesis]. Queen Mary, University of London, UK.

Ozuem, W., Howell, K., & Lancaster, G. (2014). Corporate social responsibility: Towards a context-specific perspective in developing countries. *Social Responsibility Journal*, *10*(3), 399–415. doi:10.1108/SRJ-04-2012-0086

Pagliusi, S., Leite, L. C., Datla, M., Makhoana, M., Gao, Y., Suhardono, M., & Homma, A. (2013). Developing countries vaccine manufacturers network: Doing good by making high-quality vaccines affordable for all. *Vaccine*, *31*, B176–B183. doi:10.1016/j.vaccine.2012.11.060 PMID:23598479

Pan, J. (2009, October 2). Development as China's environmental solution. *Telegraph*.

Pane-Haden, S., Oyler, J., & Humphreys, J. (2009). Historical, practical, and theoretical perspectives on green management: An exploratory analysis. *Management Decision*, *47*(7), 1041–1055. doi:10.1108/00251740910978287

Panitch, L., & Gindin, S. (2012). *The making of global capitalism: The political economy of American empire*. New York: Verso.

Paper China. (2013). 玖龙纸业412暴力事件 受害人集体诉 [Victims' Group Petition of Nine Dragons Paper's 4.12 Incident]. Retrieved from http://www.paper.com.cn/news/daynews/2013/130416090809982380.htm

Paper China. (2013). 玖龙纸业违法建楼 拒付民工千万工钱 [Nine Dragons Paper refused to pay hundreds and thousands worthy of payments to migrant workers for its illegal buildings]. Retrieved from http://www.paper.com.cn/news/daynews/2013/130410085914925273.htm

Paredes Gázquez, J. D., Pardo Herrasti, E., & De la Cuesta González, M. (2010). *Retos de la RSC I: Introducción a la Responsabilidad Social Corporativa. Cuaderno Red de Cátedras Telefónica*. Madrid: UNED-Telefónica.

Parinduri, R., & Paul, S. (2015, January). *Investors are unwilling to pay for corporate social responsibility activities: Evidence from India's Companies Act 2013*. Nottingham University Business School, University of Nottingham, Malaysia Campus, MPRA Paper No. 61360. Retrieved from http://mpra.ub.uni-muenchen.de/61360/

Parker, L. D. (2005). Social and environmental accountability research: A view from the commentary box. *Accounting, Auditing & Accountability Journal*, *18*(6), 842–860. doi:10.1108/09513570510627739

Park, Y. R., Song, S., Choe, S., & Baik, Y. (2015). Corporate social responsibility in international business: Illustrations from Korean and Japanese electronics MNEs in Indonesia. *Journal of Business Ethics*, *129*(3), 747–761. doi:10.1007/s10551-014-2212-x

Patten, D. (2002). Give or Take on the Internet: An Examination of the Disclosure Practices of Insurance Firm Web Innovators. *Journal of Business Ethics*, *36*(3), 247–259. doi:10.1023/A:1014009229437

Patten, D. M. (1991). Exposure, legitimacy, and social disclosure. *Journal of Accounting and Public Policy*, *10*(4), 297–308. doi:10.1016/0278-4254(91)90003-3

Paul, K. (2008). Corporate Sustainability, Citizenship and Social Responsibility Reporting. *Journal of Corporate Citizenship*, *32*(32), 63–78. doi:10.9774/GLEAF.4700.2008.wi.00007

Pedersen, E. R. G., & Gwozdz, W. (2014). From resistance to opportunity-seeking: Strategic responses to institutional pressures for corporate social responsibility in the Nordic fashion industry. *Journal of Business Ethics*, *119*(2), 245–264. doi:10.1007/s10551-013-1630-5

Peloza, J., & Shang, J. (2011). What business leaders should know: Investing in CSR to enhance customer value. Director Notes Series. The Conference Board Governance Center, 3(3).

Peloza, J. (2009). The challenge of measuring financial impacts from investments in corporate social performance. *Journal of Management*, *35*(6), 1518–1541. doi:10.1177/0149206309335188

People. (2013). 统计局:2012年全国农民工总量达26万 [The National Statistics Bureau: the total number of national migrant workers reaches 262.61 million in 2012]. Retrieved from http://finance.people.com.cn/n/2013/0527/c1004-21624982.html

Perera, M., & Mathews, M. (1990). The Cultural Relativity of Accounting and International Patterns of Social Accounting. *Advances in International Accounting*, *13*, 215–251.

Peterson, H. (2014). *The Key Differences Between Alibaba and Amazon in One Chart.* Retrieved fromwww.businessinsider.com/alibaba-versus-amazon-2014-9

Petra, S. T. (2005). Do outside independent directors strengthen corporate boards?. *Corporate Governance: The international journal of business in society, 5*(1), 55-64.

Philippine Working Group on Mining (PWGM) & Environmental Science for Social Change. (ESSC) (2008a). 2003 Legacy Mines Visit. Manila Mining Corporation in the Surigao del Norte Mining District: Struggle with Corporate Social Responsibility at the Local. Manila: PWGM & ESSC.

Philippine Working Group on Mining (PWGM) & Environmental Science for Social Change. (ESSC) (2008b). 2003 Legacy Mines Visit. Atlas Consolidated Mining Development Corporation. Toledo City, Cebu. Environmental and Community Impact. Manila: PWGM & ESSC.

Philips, S. M., Blood, M., Bosland, N., Burke, L., Conrad, C. F., Fernandes, J., et al. (2004). Ethics Education in Business Schools. AACSB International.

Piore, M. J., & Schrank, A. (2008). Toward managed flexibility: The revival of labour inspection in the Latin world. *International Labour Review*, *147*(1), 1–23. doi:10.1111/j.1564-913X.2008.00021.x

Pistoni, A., & Songini, L. (2013). Corporate Social Responsibility Determinants: The Relation with CSR Disclosure. In L. Songini, A. Pistoni & C. Herzig (Eds.), Accounting and Control for Sustainability (Vol. 26). Emerald Group Publishing Limited.

Pomering, A., & Dolnicar, S. (2009). Assessing the prerequisite of successful CSR implementation: Are consumers aware of CSR initiatives? *Journal of Business Ethics*, *85*(2), 285–301. doi:10.1007/s10551-008-9729-9

Porter, M. E. (2011, November 13). The Role of Business in Society: Creating Shared Value. *Presentation at Babson Entrepreneurship Forum*, Boston, Massachusetts. Retrieved from http://www.isc.hbs.edu/pdf/2011-1113_Babson_CSV.pdf

Porter, M.E. & Kramer. M. R. (2011). Creating Shared Value: How to reinvent capitalism—and unleash a wave of innovation and growth. *Harvard Business Review (HBR)*, January/February.

Porter, M. E., & Kramer, M. R. (2006). Strategy and Society. The link between Competitive Advantage and Corporate Social Responsibility. *Harvard Business Review*, 2006, 1–14. PMID:17183795

Porter, M. E., & Kramer, M. R. (2006). Strategy and society. The link between competitive advantage and corporate social responsibility. *Harvard Business Review*, *84*(12), 78–92. PMID:17183795

Porter, M. E., & Mark, R. Kramer. (1999). Philanthropy's New Agenda: Creating Value. *Harvard Business Review*, *77*(6), 121–130. PMID:10662001

Post, C., Rahman, N., & Rubow, E. (2011). Green governance: Boards of directors' composition and environmental corporate social responsibility. *Business & Society*, *50*(1), 189–223. doi:10.1177/0007650310394642

Posthuma, A., & Bignami, R. (2014). 'Bridging the Gap'? Public and private regulation of labour standards in the apparel value chains in Brazil. *Competition and Change*, *18*(4), 345–364. doi:10.1179/1024529414Z.00000000065

Pozniak, L., Ferauge, P., Arnone, L., & Geerts, A. (2011). Determinants of Internet Corporate Social Responsibility Communication. *Global Journal of Business Research*, *5*(4), 1–14.

Preuss, L. (2005). Rhetoric and reality of corporate greening: A view from the supply chain management function. *Business Strategy and the Environment*, *14*(2), 123–139. doi:10.1002/bse.435

Price Waterhouse Coopers. (2014). *Mine 2014: Realigning expectations, review of global trends in the mining industry.* Toronto: PWC. Retrieved from www.pwc.com

Price-Waterhouse Cooper. (2015, July 10). *Mine. The growing disconnect. Review of the global mining industry.* Retrieved from http://download.pwc.com/gx/mining/pwc-mine-2012.pdf

Puaschunder, J. M. (2010). On corporate and financial social responsibility [Unpublished doctoral thesis]. University of Vienna, Vienna.

Puaschunder, J. M. (2011). Inter-generational equity as a natural behavioral law. *Library of Congress United States of America Copyright Office.*

Puaschunder, J. M. (2015). On eternal equity in the fin-de-millénaire (Unpublished manuscript). The New School, New York.

Puaschunder, J. M. (2012). On the social representations of inter-generational equity. *Oxford Journal of Finance and Risk Perspectives*, *4*(4), 78–99.

Pulp and Paper Canada. (2014). DMI is one of 50 best workplaces for employee engagement. Retrieved from http://www.pulpandpapercanada.com/news/dmi-is-one-of-50-best-workplaces/1002870213/?&er=NA

Purser, R., Park, C., & Montuori, A. (1995). Limits to anthropocentrism: Toward an ecocentric organization paradigm? *Academy of Management Review*, *20*(4), 1053–1089. doi:10.2307/258965

Pyke, F., & Lund-Thomsen, P. (2016). Social upgrading in developing country clusters: A reflection on the literature. *Competition and Change*, *20*(1), 53–68. doi:10.1177/1024529415611265

Quan, K. (2011, March 18). Presented at the 17th annual Symposium on Corporate Social Responsibility, Mount St. Mary's University.

Rae, M., & Rouse, A. (2001). *Mining certification evaluation project – Independent Certification of environmental and social performance in the mining sector. A WWF-Australia discussion paper.* Sydney: Resources Conservation Program, Mineral Resources Unit WWF Australia.

Rahim, M. M. (2013). A meta-regulation approach to laws to incorporate CSR principles in corporate self-regulation. In *Legal Regulation of Corporate Social Responsibility* (pp. 129–177). Heidelberg, Germany: Springer. doi:10.1007/978-3-642-40400-9_5

Rahim, M. M., & Wisuttisak, P. (2013). Corporate social responsibility–oriented compliances and SMEs access to global market: Evidence from Bangladesh. *Journal of Asia-Pacific Business, 14*(1), 58–83. doi:10.1080/10599231.2013.741417

Raimi, L., & Adeleke, I. A. (2010) Using Entrepreneurship Development and Corporate Social Responsibility as Strategies for Conflict Resolution in the Niger-Delta Region in Nigeria, Society of Petroleum Engineers - Nigeria Annual International Conference and Exhibition 2010, NAICE: 2837-846.

Raimi, L., Akhuemonkhan, I. A., & Ogunjirin, O. D. (2015). Corporate Social Responsibility and Entrepreneurship (CSRE): Antidotes to poverty, insecurity and underdevelopment in Nigeria. *Social Responsibility Journal, 11*(1), 56–81. doi:10.1108/SRJ-11-2012-0138

Raimi, L., Patel, A., Adelopo, I., & Ajewole, T. (2013). Tackling Poverty Crisis in the Muslim Majority Nations (MMNs): The Faith-Based Model (FBM) as an Alternative Policy Option. *Advanced Journal of Business Management and Entrepreneurship, 1*(1), 1–12.

Raimi, L., Patel, A., Yekini, K., & Fadipe, A. O. (2014). Spatio-Temporal Audit of Nigeria's Industrial Policies and Entrepreneurship Development Interventions from 1946 to 2013. *International Journal of Humanities and Social Science, 4*(1), 294–309.

Rajak, D. (2006). The gift of CSR. Power and the Pursuit of Responsibility in the Mining Industry. In W. Visser, M. McIntosh, & C. Middleton (Eds.), *Corporate Citizenship in Africa* (pp. 190–200). Sheffield, UK: Greenleaf Publishing.

Ramasastry, A. (2015). Corporate social responsibility versus business and human rights: Bridging the gap between responsibility and accountability. *Journal of Human Rights, 14*(2), 237–259. doi:10.1080/14754835.2015.1037953

Ramsey, F. P. (1928). A mathematical theory of saving. *The Economic Journal, 38*(152), 543–559. doi:10.2307/2224098

Rangan, K., Chase, A. L., & Karim, S. (2012, April). Why every company needs a CSR strategy and how to build it. Harvard Business School Working Paper.

Rappaport, A. (1986). *Creating shareholder value: The new standard for business performance.* New York, NY: Free Press.

Rasche, A. (2010). Collaborative Governance 2.0. *Corporate Governance: The International Journal of Business in Society, 10*(4), 500–511. doi:10.1108/14720701011069713

Rasche, A., & Esser, D. E. (2006). From stakeholder management to stakeholder accountability. *Journal of Business Ethics, 65*(3), 251–267. doi:10.1007/s10551-005-5355-y

Ravensbergen, J. (2013). Resolute Forest FSC certificates suspended: Greenpeace. Retrieved from http://www.montreal-gazette.com/business/Resolute+Forest+certificates+suspended+Greenpeace/9278507/story.html

Rawls, J. (1999). *A Theory of Justice.* Cambridge, MA: Belknap Press of Harvard University Press.

Reed, D. Utting, P., & Reed, A.M. (Eds.), (2013). Business Regulation and Non-state Actors. Whose Actors? Whose Development? London: Routledge.

Rein, L., & Stott, L. (2009). Working together: Critical perspectives on six cross-sector partnerships in Southern Africa. *Journal of Business Ethics*, *90*(3), 79–89. doi:10.1007/s10551-008-9915-9

Reserve Bank of Australia. (2013). *Reserve Bank of Australia Annual Report, 2013.* Retrieved from www.rba.gov.au

Reverte, C. (2009). Determinants of Corporate Social Responsibility Disclosure Ratings by Spanish Listed Firms. *Journal of Business Ethics*, *88*(2), 351–366. doi:10.1007/s10551-008-9968-9

Rice, G. (1999). Islamic Ethics and the Implications for Business. *Journal of Business Ethics*, *18*(4), 345–358. doi:10.1023/A:1005711414306

Riisgaard, L., Bolwig, S., Ponte, S., Du Toit, A., Halberg, N., & Matose, F. (2010). Integrating poverty and environmental concerns into value-chain analysis: A strategic framework and practical guide. *Development Policy Review*, *28*(2), 195–216. doi:10.1111/j.1467-7679.2010.00481.x

Rikhardsson, P., Andersen, A., & Bang, H. (2002). Sustainability Reporting on the Internet: A Study of Global Fortune 500. *Greener Management International,* Winter, 57-75.

RIO. (2013). Supporting our license to operate. *Sustainable Development*, *2013*, •••. Retrieved from www.riotinto.com

RIO. (2014). Creating mutual value for the long term. *Sustainable Development*, *2014*, •••. Retrieved from www.riotinto.com/sd2014

Ripley, E. A., Redmann, R. E., & Crowder, A. A. (1995). *Environmental Effects of Mining*. Florida: St. Lucie Press.

RISI. (2013). AkzoNobel joins together for sustainability initiative to enhance global supply chain. Retrieved from http://www.risiinfo.com/technologyarchives/environment/AkzoNobel-joins-Together-for-Sustainability-initiative.html

RISI. (2013). Ashland wins 2013 Breakthrough Technology award from PPI for improvements to sustainability and productivity for recycled paperboard manufacturers. Retrieved from http://www.risiinfo.com/technologyarchives/environment/Ashland-wins-2013-Breakthrough-Technology-award-from-PPI-for-improvements-to-sustainability-and-productivity-for-recycled-paperboard-manufacturers.html

RISI. (2013). Domtar fined $75,000 for violations to Canada Fisheries Act at Espanola, ON, mill in 2010. Retrieved from http://www.risiinfo.com/techchannels/environment/Domtar-fined-75000-for-violations-to-Canada-Fisheries-Act-at-Espanola-ON-mill-in-2010.html?source=email_cz

RISI. (2013). *Nippon Paper and Coca-Cola Japan collaborate on forest and water resources conservation.* Retrieved from http://www.risiinfo.com/technologyarchives/environment/Nippon-Paper-and-Coca-Cola-Japan-collaborate-on-forest-and-water-resources-conservation.html

Rivoli, P., & Waddock, S. (2011). "First They Ignore You…": The time-context dynamic and corporate responsibility. *California Management Review*, *53*(2), 87–104. doi:10.1525/cmr.2011.53.2.87

Rizk, R., Dixon, R., & Woodhead, A. (2008). Corporate social and environmental reporting: A survey of disclosure practices in Egypt. *Social Responsibility Journal*, *4*(3), 306–323. doi:10.1108/17471110810892839

Roberts, C. (1991). Environmental Disclosure: A Note on Reporting Practices in Mainland Europe. *Accounting, Auditing & Accountability Journal*, *4*(3), 62–71. doi:10.1108/09513579110005536

Robertson, D. C. (2009). Corporate Social Responsibility and Different Stages of Economic Development: Singapore, Turkey, & Ethiopia. *Journal of Business Ethics*, *88*(Suppl. 4), 617–633. doi:10.1007/s10551-009-0311-x

Robson, A., & Wakefield, S. E. L. (2007). Socially responsible investing in "high-net-worth" asset management firms in Canada: An exploratory study. *EJBO Electronic Journal of Business Ethics and Organization Studies*, *12*(1), 29–34.

Rodriguez, P., Siegel, D. S., Hillman, A., & Eden, L. (2006). Three lenses on the MNE: Politics, corruption and corporate social responsibility. *Journal of International Business Studies*, *37*(6), 733–746. doi:10.1057/palgrave.jibs.8400229

Rolland, S. E. (2007). Developing country coalitions at the WTO: In search of legal support. *Harvard International Law Journal*, *48*(2), 483–551.

Ronit, K. (2012). Global Strategies and Policy Arrangements: Institutional Drivers for Innovation in the Wind Turbine Industry. In Innovation Policy and Governance in High-Tech Industries (pp. 201-217). Berlin Heidelberg: Springer.

Rose-Ackerman, S. (2002). "Grand" corruption and the ethics of global business. *Journal of Banking & Finance*, *26*(9), 1889–1918. doi:10.1016/S0378-4266(02)00197-8

Rosenau, J. N. (1995). Governance in the twenty-first century. *Global Governance*, 1995, 13–43.

Rugman, M. A., & Collinson, S. (2009). *International business*. England: Prentice Hall.

Rupp, D. E., & Mallory, D. B. (2015). Corporate social responsibility: Psychological, person-centric, and progressing. *Annual Review of Organizational Psychology and Organizational Behavior*, *2*(1), 211–236. doi:10.1146/annurev-orgpsych-032414-111505

Rupp, D. E., Wright, P. M., Aryee, S., & Luo, Y. (2015). Organizational justice, behavioral ethics, and corporate social responsibility: Finally the three shall merge. *Management and Organization Review*, *11*(1), 15–24. doi:10.1017/mor.2015.8

Sachs, J. D. (2014). Climate change and inter-generational well-being. In L. Bernard & W. Semmler (Eds.), *The Oxford Handbook of the Macroeconomics of Global Warming*. Oxford: Oxford University Press.

Saeidi, S. P., Sofian, S., Saeidi, P., Saeidi, S. P., & Saaeidi, S. A. (2015). How does corporate social responsibility contribute to firm financial performance? The mediating role of competitive advantage, reputation, and customer satisfaction. *Journal of Business Research*, *68*(2), 341–350. doi:10.1016/j.jbusres.2014.06.024

Sagittarius Mines Inc. (2012). *Tampakan Project sustainability Report*. Retrieved from http://www.smi.com.ph/EN/Publications/Pages/SustainabilityReports.aspx

Salama, A. (2009). Egypt: Social responsibility disclosure practices. In S. O. Idowu & W. L. Filho (Eds.), *Global Practices of Corporate Social Responsibility* (pp. 325–342). Berlin, Heidelberg: Springer. doi:10.1007/978-3-540-68815-0_16

Saleh Al Arussi, A., Hisyam Selamat, M., & Mohd Hanefah, M. (2009). Determinants of financial and environmental disclosures through the internet by Malaysian companies. *Asian Review of Accounting*, *17*(1), 59–76. doi:10.1108/13217340910956513

Samaha, K., & Dahawy, K. (2010). An empirical analysis of corporate governance structures and voluntary corporate disclosure in volatile capital markets: The Egyptian experience. *International Journal of Accounting. Auditing and Performance Evaluation*, *7*(1-2), 61–93.

Samuels, J., & Oliga, J. (1982). Accounting Standards in Developing Countries. *The International Journal of Accounting*, *18*(1), 69–88.

Samy, M., Odemilin, G., & Bampton, R. (2010). Corporate social responsibility: A strategy for sustainable business success. An analysis of 20 selected British companies. *Corporate Governance*, *10*(2), 203–217. doi:10.1108/14720701011035710

Saunders, M., Lewis, P., & Thornhill, A. (2012). Research Methods for Business Students. Edinburgh Gate, Harlow, England: Pearson Education Limited.

Scheidel, A. (2015, June 5). Taganito Mining Corporation's Nickel Operations, Surigao del Norte, Philippines. *Environmental Justice Atlas*. Retrieved from https://ejatlas.org/conflict/taganito-mining-corporations-nickel-mine-surigao-del-nortephilippines

Scherer, A.G., & Palazzo, G. (2011, June). The New Political Role of Business in a Globalized World: A Review of a New Perspective on CSR and its Implications for the Firm, Governance and Democracy. *Journal of Management Studies, 48*(4), 899-931.

Scherer, A. G., & Palazzo, G. (2007). Toward a political conception of corporate responsibility: Business and society seen from a Habermasian perspective. *Academy of Management Review*, *32*(4), 1096–1120. doi:10.5465/AMR.2007.26585837

Scherer, A. G., & Palazzo, G. (2008). Globalization and Corporate Social Responsibility. In A. Crane et al. (Eds.), *Oxford Handbook of Corporate Social Responsibility* (pp. 413–431). Oxford: Oxford University Press.

Scherer, A. G., & Palazzo, G. (2011). The new political role of business in a globalized world: A review of a new perspective on CSR and its implications for the firm, governance, and democracy. *Journal of Management Studies*, *48*(4), 899–931. doi:10.1111/j.1467-6486.2010.00950.x

Scherer, A. G., Palazzo, G., & Matten, D. (2014). The business firm as a political actor: A new theory of the firm for a globalized world. *Business & Society*, *53*(2), 143–156. doi:10.1177/0007650313511778

Scherer, A. G., Palazzo, G., & Seidl, D. (2013). Managing legitimacy in complex and heterogeneous environments: Sustainable development in a globalized world. *Journal of Management Studies*, *50*(2), 259–284. doi:10.1111/joms.12014

Schermerhorn, J. R. (1999). *Management*. the United States of America: Von Hoffman Press.

Scherr, F. C., & Hulburt, H. M. (2001). The debt maturity structure of small firms. *Financial Management*, *30*(Spring), 85–111. doi:10.2307/3666392

Schmitz, J., & Schrader, J. (2015). Corporate social responsibility: A microeconomic review of the literature. *Journal of Economic Surveys*, *29*(1), 27–45. doi:10.1111/joes.12043

Schnittfeld, N. L., & Busch, T. (2016). Sustainability management within supply chains – A resource dependence view. *Business Strategy and the Environment*, 25(5), 337-354. doi:10.1002/bse.1876

Scholtens, B. (2014). Indicators of responsible investing. *Ecological Indicators*, *36*, 382–385. doi:10.1016/j.ecolind.2013.08.012

Schwartz, S. H., & Bardi, A. (2001). Value hierarchies across cultures taking a similarities perspective. *Journal of Cross-Cultural Psychology*, *32*(3), 268–290. doi:10.1177/0022022101032003002

Scott, K. D. (2014). "Global Financial Crises" The SelectedWorks of Kimberly D Scott. Retrieved from http://works.bepress.com/kimberly_scott/1

Secci, D. (2005). The Italian experience in social reporting: An empirical analysis. *Corporate Social Responsibility and Environmental Management*, *13*(3), 135–149. doi:10.1002/csr.96

See, G. (2009). Harmonious society and Chinese CSR: Is there really a link? *Journal of Business Ethics*, *89*(1), 1–22. doi:10.1007/s10551-008-9981-z

Sen, A. (2002). Does business ethics make economic sense? In T. Donaldson, P.H. Werhane, & M. Cording (Eds.). Ethical Issues in Business – A Philosophical Approach (pp. 244-251). New Jersey: Prentice Hall.

Shafer, W. E., Fukukawa, K., & Lee, G. M. (2007). Values and the perceived importance of ethics and social responsibility: The U.S. versus China. *Journal of Business Ethics*, *70*(3), 265–284. doi:10.1007/s10551-006-9110-9

Shah, S. (2012). Proposing a welfare framework for the society and local community stakeholders: A mixed method study. *Journal of Human Values*, *18*(1), 53–71. doi:10.1177/097168581101800105

Shanahan, M. (2001). Globalisation in history: Issues, definitions and process identification. In K. Thorne & G. Turner (Eds.), *Global business regulation: Some research perspectives*. Sydney: Pearson Education.

Sharp, J. (2006). Corporate social responsibility and development: An anthropological perspective. *Development Southern Africa*, *23*(2), 213–222. doi:10.1080/03768350600707892

Shenuah. (2012). *CSR Report 2012*. Retrieved from http://www.shenhuachina.com/cs/sh_china_en/PAGE1382683238892/sh_china_en_ED.html

Shen, Z. Y., Liu, X. G., & Zhou, X. H. (2008). Research on state-owned enterprise reform: In view of social responsibility[in Chinese]. *China Industrial Economics*, *9*, 141–149.

Shinde, J. S., Wacker, R., Shinde, U. S., & Hou, Z. J. (2011). Superfluity and murkiness in the understanding of social responsibility: A content analysis. *Journal of Leadership, Accountability and Ethics*, *8*(3).

Shin, J. Y., Jung, M., Khoe, K. I., & Chae, M. S. (2015). Effects of government involvement in corporate social responsibility: An analysis of the Indian Companies Act, 2013. *Emerging Markets Finance and Trade*, *51*(2), 377–390. doi:10.1080/1540496X.2015.1021600

Shleifer, A., & Vishny, R. W. (1997). A survey of corporate governance. *The Journal of Finance*, *52*(2), 737–783. doi:10.1111/j.1540-6261.1997.tb04820.x

Short, J. L., & Toffel, M. W. (2010). Making self-regulation more than merely symbolic: The critical role of the legal environment. *Administrative Science Quarterly*, *55*(3), 361–396. doi:10.2189/asqu.2010.55.3.361

SHRM. (2007). *2007 Corporate Social Responsibility: United States, Australia, India, China, Canada, Mexico and Brazil. A Pilot Study*. Alexandria, VA: Society for Human Resource Management.

Siciliano, J. I. (1996). The relationship of board member diversity to organizational performance. *Journal of Business Ethics*, *15*(12), 1313–1320. doi:10.1007/BF00411816

Siemens. (2014) *Your expert partner for the pulp and paper industry*. Retrieved from http://www.industry.siemens.com/verticals/global/en/paper-industry/pages/default.aspx

Silverio, I. A. R. (2011, October 14) Aquino gives go signal to deployment of CAFGUS to mining areas. *Bulatlat*. Retrieved from http://bulatlat.com/main/2011/10/14/aquino-gives-go-signal-to-deployment-of-cafgus-to-mining-areas/

Simpson, W., & Kohers, T. (2002). the Link between Corporate Social and Financial Performance: Evidence from the Banking Industry. *Journal of Business Ethics*, *35*(2), 97–109. doi:10.1023/A:1013082525900

Sinafinance. (2012). 玖龙纸业曝技改人员血案 2011财年纯利跌9.2% [Nine Dragons Paper net profit dropped 9.2% after exposure of technician's 'blood incident]. Retrieved from http://finance.sina.com.cn/stock/hkstock/ggscyd/20120217/015411396104.shtml

SIS. (2015). State Information Service, Egypt. Retrieved from http://www.sis.gov.eg/en/

Slack, K. (2012). Mission impossible?: Adopting a CSR-based business model for extractive industries in developing countries. *Resources Policy*, *37*(2), 179–184. doi:10.1016/j.resourpol.2011.02.003

Slaper, T. F. (2011, Spring). The triple bottom line: what is it and how does it work? *Indiana Business Review*.

Smith, C. N. (2003, April). *Corporate social responsibility: not whether but how?* Center for Marketing, London Business School Working Papers No. 03-701.

Smith, R. (2011). Defining corporate social responsibility: A systems approach for socially responsible capitalism. (Master of Philosophy Thesis). University of Pennsylvania, USA.

Smith, N., & Thomas, E. (2015). Determinants of Russia's informal economy: The impact of corruption and multinational firms. *Journal of East-West Business*, *21*(2), 102–128. doi:10.1080/10669868.2015.1004148

Smith, R., & Wiek, A. (2012). Achievements and opportunities in initiating governance for urban sustainability. *Environment and Planning. C, Government & Policy*, *30*(3), 429–447. doi:10.1068/c10158

Snell, R. S., & Tseng, C. (2001). Commentary: Ethical dilemmas of relationship building in China. *Thunderbird International Business Review*, *43*(2), 171–201. doi:10.1002/tie.1

Snell, R. S., & Tseng, C. S. (2003). Images of the virtuous employee in China's transitional economy. *Asia Pacific Journal of Management*, *20*(3), 307–331. doi:10.1023/A:1024045415888

Snyckers, T. (2006). Evading Corporate Social Responsibility through Tax Avoidance. In W. Visser, M. McIntosh, & C. Middleton (Eds.), Corporate Citizenship in Africa (pp. 67-79). Sheffield, UK: Greenleaf Publishing.

Solitander, Nikodemus; Martin; Fougere, Sobczak, A., & Herlin, H. (2011). We Are the Champions: Organizational Learning and Change for Responsible Management Education. *Journal of Management Education*, *36*(3), 337–360.

Spegele, B. (2013, May 6). Chinese protest plans for industrial plants, *The Wall Street Journal*, p. A8.

Spence, L. J. (2007). CSR and small business in a European policy context: The five "C"s of CSR and small business research agenda 2007. *Business and Society Review*, *112*(4), 533–552. doi:10.1111/j.1467-8594.2007.00308.x

Srisuphaolarn, P. (2013). From altruistic to strategic CSR: How social value affected CSR development – a case study of Thailand. *Social Responsibility Journal*, *9*(1), 56–77. doi:10.1108/17471111311307813

Stanwick, P.A. & S.D. Stanwick (2001). The Determinants of Corporate Social Performance: An Empirical Examination. *American Business Review*, 2001, 86-93.

Stanwick, P. A., & Stanwick, S. D. (1998). The determinants of corporate social performance: An empirical examination. *American Business Review*, *16*(1), 86.

Starcomms. (2013). Corporate Social Responsibility. Online Resources. Retrieved from http://www.starcomms.com/about_us/csr.aspx

Stark, J., Li, J., & Terasawa, K. (2006) *Environmental Safeguards and Community Benefits in Mining: Recent Lessons from the Philippines.* USAID and Foundation for Environmental Security & Sustainability.

Steurer, R. (2010). The role of governments in corporate social responsibility: Characterising public policies on CSR in Europe. *Policy Sciences*, *43*(1), 49–72. doi:10.1007/s11077-009-9084-4

Steurer, R., Martinuzzi, R.-A., & Margula, S. (2012). Public policies on CSR in Europe: Themes, instruments and regional differences. *Corporate Social Responsibility and Environmental Management*, *19*(4), 206–227. doi:10.1002/csr.264

Story, D., & Price, T. (2006). Corporate social responsibility and risk management? *Journal of Corporate Citizenship*, *22*(22), 39–51. doi:10.9774/GLEAF.4700.2006.su.00007

Strand, R., Freeman, R. E., & Hockerts, K. (2015). Corporate social responsibility and sustainability in Scandinavia: An overview. *Journal of Business Ethics*, *127*(1), 1–15. doi:10.1007/s10551-014-2224-6

Strike, V., Gao, J., & Bansal, P. (2006). Being good while being bad: Social responsibility and the international diversification of U.S. firms. *Journal of International Business Studies*, *37*(6), 850–862. doi:10.1057/palgrave.jibs.8400226

Sun, Y. (2008). Woguo zhengfu huanjing xinxi gongkai shenji de sikao [Audit Environmental Information Disclosure]. Green Finance and Accounting, 6, 30-32.

Sustain. (2013) *A Global player made in Europe.,* Retrieved from http://www.cepi-sustainability.eu/about-this-site-2

Svensson, J. (2003). Who must pay bribes and how much? Evidence from a cross section of firms. *The Quarterly Journal of Economics*, *118*(1), 207–230. doi:10.1162/00335530360535180

Swanson, D., Piper, T. R., Fort, T., Gentile, M. C., Shreve, R. S., Hartman, E., & Margolis, J. (2007). *Shaping Tomorrow's Business Leaders: Principles and Practices for a Model Business Ethics Program.* USA: Business Roundtable.

SynTao. (2015). A Journey to Discover Values: A Study on sustainability reporting in China. Retrieved from http://www.syntao.com

Tabachnick, B. G., & Fidell, L. S. (2001). *Using multivariate analysis. California State University Northridge.* Harper Collins College Publishers.

Tallontire, A. (2007). CSR and regulation: Towards a framework for understanding private standards initiatives in the agri-food chain. *Third World Quarterly*, *28*(4), 775–791. doi:10.1080/01436590701336648

Tapp, V. (2013, July 28). Australia's biggest open cut zinc mine to close. Retrieved from http://www.abc.net.au/news/2013-09-19/century-mine-closure/4969242

TechTalkAfrica.com. (2013). Globacom Limited (GLO) – Africa's Telecoms Company. Retrieved from http://techtalkafrica.com/companies/globacom-limited-glo-africas-telecomms-company.html/

Telecom, S. K. (2013). *Partner for New Possibilities.*www. SK*Telecom Annual Report 2013.* Retrieved from http://www.sktelecom.com/en/social/list_persist_report.do

Telegraph. (October 2, 2009). *Development as China's Environmental Solution.* Retrieved from http://www.telegraph.co.uk

Tepper, R. (2012). *World's Most Popular Beers: 'The Drinks Business' Names Top 10 Biggest Brands Of 2011* Retrieved from http://www.huffingtonpost.com/2012/09/26/worlds-most-popular-beer_n_1914327.html

The Business of a Better World. (2013). *Sustainable lifestyles to Drive Sales, Market Share, and Innovation within Five Years.* Retrieved from http://www.bsr.org/en/about/press-release/sustainable-lifestyles-to-drive-sales-market-share-and-innovation-within-fi

The EcoGateway Link Center, Pollution Prevention- *United States Nonprofit Organizations.* Retrieved from http://www.ecoiq.com/onlineresources/center/prevention/nonprofit.html

The EcoGateway Link Center. (n. d.). *Pollution Prevention – Federal Agencies and Programs.* Retrieved from http://www.ecoiq.com/onlineresources/center/prevention/fed.html

The Economist Intelligence Unit. (2005) The Importance of Corporate Responsibility. Retrieved from http://graphics.eiu.com/files/ad_pdfs/eiuoracle_corporateresponsibility_wp.pdf

The Economist. (2008). Special report: Corporate social responsibility: The next question. Retrieved from http://www.economist.com/printedition/specialreports?year[value][year]=2008&category=7698445

The Economist. (2008). The good company. Retrieved from http://www.economist.com/node/3555212

The Economist. (2010). *A new idolatry, the economic crisis has received the old debate about whether firms should focus most on their shareholders, their customers or their workers*. Retrieved from http://www.economist.com/node/15954434

The Guardian. (2008). Japanese paper industry in recycling scandal. Retrieved from http://www.theguardian.com/business/2008/jan/18/greenbusiness.recycling?gusrc=rss&feed=environment

The Sydney Morning Herald. (2012). Tasmania's divisive timber mill project reduced the mighty Gunns to a pulp. Retrieved from http://www.smh.com.au/federal-politics/political-opinion/tasmanias-divisive-timber-mill-project-reduced-the-mighty-gunns-to-a-pulp-20120927-26o0f.html#ixzz2rfFGYtHc

The Trade Development Authority of Pakistan. (2015). Statistics. Retrieved from http://tdap.gov.pk

The World Bank. (2002). *Public Sector Roles in Strengthening Corporate Social Responsibility: A Baseline Study*.

Thiel, M. (2010). Innovations in Corporate Social Responsibility from global business leaders at Panasonic, Thomson Reuters and Nanyang Business School. *American Journal of Economics and Business Administration*, *2*(2), 194–200. doi:10.3844/ajebasp.2010.194.200

Thiel, M. (2015). *The Social Domain in Corporate Social Responsibility and Sustainability*. Farham, UK: Gower Publishing Limited.

Thompson, P., & Zakariya, Z. (2004). Corporate Social Responsibility Reporting in Malaysia: Progress and Prospects. *Journal of Corporate Citizenship*, *13*(Spring), 125–136. doi:10.9774/GLEAF.4700.2004.sp.000014

Toto. (2014). *Toto Corporate Report 2014*. Retrieved from http://www.toto.co.jp/company/profile/library/pdf/report2014_en.pdf

Trapnell, J. & Boxx, W.R. (2011). Attributes of excellence. *BizEd,* 411, 50-54.

Trevino, L. K., & Weaver, G. R. (1999). The stakeholder research tradition: Converging theorists – not convergent theory. *Academy of Management Review*, *24*(2), 222–227. doi:10.2307/259076

Tricker, R. I. (1984). *Corporate governance: Practices, procedures, and powers in British companies and their boards of directors*. Aldershot: Gower Pub Co.

Truscott, R. A. (2007). *Corporate social responsibility in Australia: Constructing reputation*.

Truscott, R., Bartlett, J., & Tywoniak, S. (2009). The reputation of the corporate social responsibility industry in Australia. *Australasian Marketing Journal*, *17*(2), 84–91. doi:10.1016/j.ausmj.2009.05.001

Tschopp, D., & Nastanski, M. (2014). The Harmonization and Convergence of Corporate Social Responsibility Reporting Standards. *Journal of Business Ethics*, *125*(1), 147–162. doi:10.1007/s10551-013-1906-9

Tsoutsoura, M. (2004). *Corporate social responsibility and financial performance*. Berkeley, CA: University of California Berkeley.

Tubino, D. S., Yap, N. T., & Devlin, J. F. (2011). Vale and its corporate social performance in Itabira, Brazil: Is the glass half full or half empty? *Impact Assessment and Project Appraisal*, *29*(2), 1–7. doi:10.3152/146155111X12913679730638

U.N. Global Compact. (2014). Corporate Sustainability in The World Economy. UN Global Compact Office, United Nations, New York. Retrieved from http://www.unglobalcompact.org/docs/news_events/8.1/GC_brochure_FINAL.pdf

UBC. (2013). Olson J. Director's message. Retrieved from http://www.ppc.ubc.ca/about/message/

Ukah, O. C. (2007). An Appraisal of the Performance of the Nigeria's National Rolling Plans in the 90's. *African Research Review*, *1*(1), 14–23.

UNDP. (2009). Arab Human Development Report: Challenges to Human Security in The Arab Countries. New York, USA: United Nations Development Programme: Regional Bureau for Arab States.

UNDP. (2010). *Youth in Egypt: Building our Future*. Egypt: United Nations Development Programme & the Institute of National Planning.

UNDP. (2012). *Assessment of Development Results: Evaluation of UNDP Contribution in Egypt*. Egypt: United Nations Development Programme.

Unerman, J. (1999). A Critique of Content Analysis as A Research Method for Corporate Social Reporting. *Paper presented atCritical Perspectives on Accounting Conference*.

Unerman, J. (2000). Methodological issues-reflections on quantification in corporate social reporting content analysis. *Accounting, Auditing & Accountability Journal*, *13*(5), 667–681. doi:10.1108/09513570010353756

United Nations Department of Economic and Social Affairs. (2007, February). *CSR and Developing Countries: What scope for government action?* Sustainable Development Innovation Briefs. Retrieved from http://www.un.org/esa/sustdev/publications/innovationbriefs/no1.pdf

United Nations. (2007) *The Principles for Responsible Management Education*. Retrieved from www.unglobalcompact.com/HowToParticipate/academic_network/index.html#bus_ed

Utting, P. (2005). Corporate responsibility and the movement of business. *Development in Practice*, *15*(3&4), 375–388. doi:10.1080/09614520500075797

Utting, P. (2015). Corporate accountability, fair trade, and multi-stakeholder regulation. In L. Raynolds & E. A. Bennett (Eds.), *Handbook of Research on Fair Trade*. Cheltenham, UK: Edwar Elgar. doi:10.4337/9781783474622.00013

Vaca, R. M., Moreno, M. J., & Riquel, F. (2007). Análisis de la responsabilidad social corporativa desde tres enfoques: stakeholders, capital intelectual y teoría institucional. In J.C. Ayala (Ed.), Conocimiento, innovación y emprendedores: camino al futuro. La Rioja: Servicio de publicaciones de la Universidad de la Rioja.

Vaccaro, A., & Palazzo, G. (2015). Values against violence: Institutional change in societies dominated by organized crime. *Academy of Management Journal*, 58(4), 1075-1101. doi:10.5465/amj.2012.0865

Vachon, S. (2010). International operations and sustainable development: Should national culture matter? *Sustainable Development*, *18*(6), 350–361. doi:10.1002/sd.398

Valor, C. (2005). Corporate social responsibility and corporate citizenship: Towards corporate accountability. *Business and Society Review*, *110*(2), 191–212. doi:10.1111/j.0045-3609.2005.00011.x

van Beveren, I. (2007). Footloose multinationals in Belgium? *Review of World Economics. Weltwirtschaftliches Archiv*, *143*(3), 483–507.

Van der Laan Smith, J., Adhikari, A., & Tondkar, R. H. (2005). Exploring differences in social disclosures internationally: A stakeholder perspective. *Journal of Accounting and Public Policy*, *24*(2), 123–151. doi:10.1016/j.jaccpubpol.2004.12.007

Vazquez-Brust, D. A., & Liston-Heyes, C. (2010). Environmental management intentions: An empirical investigation of Argentina's polluting firms. *Journal of Environmental Management*, *91*(5), 1111–1122. doi:10.1016/j.jenvman.2010.01.005 PMID:20110148

Verbeke, A. (2013). *International business strategy*. Cambridge: Cambridge University Press. doi:10.1017/CBO9781139227162

Vidal, J. (2014, June 11). Soco halts oil exploration in Africa's Virunga national park: British oil company bows to pressure and abandons drilling in volatile and biodiverse region of Democratic Republic of Congo. Retrieved from http://www.theguardian.com/environment/2014/jun/11/soco-oil-virunga-national-park-congo-wwf

Vidal, N. G., & Kozak, R. A. (2008). Corporate responsibility practices in the forestry sector. *Journal of Corporate Citizenship*, *31*, 59–75.

Vigneau, L., & Humphreys, M. (2014, January). Embedding CSR in an MNE: A process model of translation of complex institutional pressures. In Academy of Management Proceedings (Vol. 2014, No. 1, p. 15883). doi:10.5465/AMBPP.2014.15883abstract

Visafone Communications Limited. (2013). About Visafone. Retrieved from http://www.visafone.com.ng/corpmilestones2.html

Visser, W. (2008). Corporate Responsibility in Developing Countries. In A. Crane, D. McWilliams, D. Matten, J. Moon, & D. Siegel (Eds.), The Oxford Handbook of Corporate Social Responsibility (pp. 473-479). Oxford, UK: Oxford University Press.

Visser, W. (2011b, December 8). Myths about CSR in developing countries: "Glocality" - the act of thinking globally, acting locally - may be the antidote to CSR myths. Retrieved from http://www.csrwire.com/blog/posts/238-myths-about-csr-in-developing-countries

Visser, W. (2008). *"Corporate Social Responsibility in developing countries", The Oxford Handbook of Corporate Social Responsibility* (pp. 473–499). Oxford University Press.

Visser, W. (2008). Corporate social responsibility in developing countries. In A. Crane, A. McWilliams, D. Matten, J. Moon, & D. Siegel (Eds.), *The Oxford handbook of corporate social responsibility* (pp. 473–479). Oxford, UK: Oxford University Press.

Visser, W. (2008). Corporate Social Responsibility in Developing Countries. In A. Crane, A. McWilliams, D. Matten, J. Moon, & D. Siegel (Eds.), *The Oxford Handbook of Corporate Social Responsibility* (pp. 473–479). Oxford: Oxford University Press.

Visser, W. (2011a). *The age of responsibility: CSR 2.0 and the new DNA of business*. New York: Wiley.

Visser, W. (2013). *CSR 2.0: Transforming corporate sustainability and responsibility*. New York: Springer.

Viswanathan, M. (2012). Curricular Innovations on Sustainability and Subsistence Marketplaces: Philosophical, Substantive, and Methodological Orientations. *Journal of Management Education,* 36(3), 389-427.

Vogel, D. (2007). *The market for virtue: The potential and limits of corporate social responsibility*. Washington, DC: Brookings Institution Press.

Voss, C., Tsikriktsis, N., & Frohlich, M. (2002). Case research in operations management. *International Journal of Operations & Production Management*, *22*(2), 195–219. doi:10.1108/01443570210414329

Waddell, S. (2000). New institutions for the practice of corporate citizenship: Historical, intersectoral, and developmental perspectives. *Business and Society Review*, *105*(1), 107–217. doi:10.1111/0045-3609.00067

Waddock, S. (2004). Parallel universes: Companies, academics, and the progress of corporate citizenship. *Business and Society Review*, *109*(March), 5–42. doi:10.1111/j.0045-3609.2004.00002.x

Wagner, M. (2005). How to reconcile environmental and economic performance to improve corporate sustainability: Corporate environmental strategies in the European paper industry. *Journal of Environmental Management*, *76*(2), 105–118. doi:10.1016/j.jenvman.2004.11.021 PMID:15939122

Wagner, S. M., & Anastasiadis, S. (2014). Do multinational enterprises contribute to sustainable development by engaging in lobbying? The automotive industry and environmental regulations. In R. Van Tulder, A. Verbeke, & R. Strange (Eds.), *International business and sustainable development* (pp. 173–202). Bingley, UK: Emerald Group Publishing Limited. doi:10.1108/S1745-8862(2013)0000008013

Wagner, T., Lutz, R., & Weitz, B. (2009). Corporate Hypocrisy: Overcoming the Threat of Inconsistent Corporate Social Responsibility Perceptions. *Journal of Marketing*, *73*(Nov), 77–91. doi:10.1509/jmkg.73.6.77

Waldman, D. A., de Luque, M. S., Washburn, N., House, R. J., Adetoun, B., Barrasa, A., & Wilderom, C. P. (2006). Cultural and leadership predictors of corporate social responsibility values of top management: A GLOBE study of 15 countries. *Journal of International Business Studies*, *37*(6), 823–837. doi:10.1057/palgrave.jibs.8400230

Walker, J., & Howard, S. (2002). *Voluntary codes of conduct in the mining industry*. London: International Institute for Environmental Development.

Wan, W. (2014). In China, one in five children live in rural villages without their parents. Retrieved from http://www.washingtonpost.com/world/asia_pacific/in-china-one-in-five-children-live-in-rural-villages-without-their-parents/2013/12/30/3f05a870-4b9a-11e3-9890-a1e0997fb0c0_story.html

Wanderley, L. S. O., Rafael, L., Francisca, F., & Sousa Filho, J. M. (2008). CSR Information Disclosure on the Web: A Context-Based Approach Analyzing the Influence of Country of Origin and Industry Sector. *Journal of Business Ethics*, *82*(2), 369–378. doi:10.1007/s10551-008-9892-z

Wang, K. T., & Dejia, L. (2015). Market Reactions to the First-Time Disclosure of Corporate Social Responsibility Reports: Evidence from China. *Journal of Business Ethics*. Retrieved from http://link.springer.com/article/10.1007%2Fs10551-015-2775-1#/page-1

Wang, L., & Juslin, H. (2009). The impact of Chinese culture on corporate social responsibility: The harmony approach. *Journal of Business Ethics*, *88*(S3), 433–451. doi:10.1007/s10551-009-0306-7

WBCSD. (2000, October 23). *Corporate Social Responsibility. Making good business sense*. Retrieved from http://www.wbcsd.org

Weber, M. (2008). The business case for corporate social responsibility: A company-level measurement approach for CSR. *European Management Journal*, *26*(4), 247–261. doi:10.1016/j.emj.2008.01.006

Weber, R. (1988). *Basic Content Analysis*. Beverly Hills, CA: Sage Publications.

Weitzner, D. & Darroch, J. (2010). The Limits of Strategic Rationality: Ethics, Enterprise Risk Management, and Governance. *Journal of Business Ethics*, 92(3), 361-372.

Weitzner, D. & Peridis, T. (2011). Corporate Governance as Part of the Strategic Process: Rethinking the Role of the Board. *Journal of Business Ethics*, 102(1), 33-42.

Welford, R. (2004). Corporate Social Responsibility in Europe and Asia: Critical Elements and Best Practice. *Journal of Corporate Citizenship*, *13*(13), 31–47. doi:10.9774/GLEAF.4700.2004.sp.00007

Welford, R. (2005). Corporate Social Responsibility in Europe, North America and Asia: 2004 Survey Results. *Journal of Corporate Citizenship*, *17*(17), 33–52. doi:10.9774/GLEAF.4700.2005.sp.00007

Welker, M. A. (2009). Corporate security begins in the community. Mining, the Corporate Social Responsibility Industry and Environmental Advocacy in Indonesia. *Cultural Anthropology*, *24*(1), 142–179. doi:10.1111/j.1548-1360.2009.00029.x

West, J. (2013). Social Media Ignited the Arab Spring. In M. Haerens & L. Zott (Eds.), *The Arab Spring*. USA: Greenhaven Press.

Westpac Banking Corporation. (2014). This is what we've delivered. *Annual Report & Sustainability Report, 2014.* Retrieved from www.westpac.com.au

Whipp, M. (2013). *UK paper responds to Japanese recycled content scandal.* Retrieved from http://www.printweek.com/print-week/news/1120252/uk-paper-responds-japanese-recycled-content-scandal

Whitcomb, L. L., Erdener, C. B., & Li, C. (1998). Business ethical values in China and the U.S. *Journal of Business Ethics*, *17*(8), 839–852. doi:10.1023/A:1005793424492

White, A. L. (1999). Sustainability and the Accountable Corporation. *Environment*, *41*(8), 3–43. doi:10.1080/00139159909604786

Whitla, P. (2011). Integrating Ethics into International Business Teaching: Challenges and Methodologies in the Greater China Context. *Journal of Teaching in International Business*, *22*(3), 168–184. doi:10.1080/08975930.2011.653745

Whitmore, A. (n. d.). *Philippines. Social and Environmental Impacts.* Retrieved from http://www.asienhaus.de/public/archiv/Andy_Whitmore_Philippines.pdf

Widok, A. (2009). Social Sustainability: Theories, concepts, practicability. In *Environmental Informatics and industrial environmental Protection: concepts, methods and tools*. Berlin: Shaker Verlag.

Wiedemann-Goiran, T., Perier, F., Lépineux, F., & Tiberghien, F. (2003). *Développement durable et gouvernement d'entreprise: un dialogue prometteur*. Paris: Éditions d'Organisation.

Wiig, A., & Kolstad, I. (2010). Multinational corporations and host country institutions: A case study of CSR activities in Angola. *International Business Review*, *19*(2), 178–190. doi:10.1016/j.ibusrev.2009.11.006

Williams, J. G. (1999). Green and social issues and the management accountant. *Management Accounting*, *1*, 64–65.

Williams, R. J. (2003). Women on corporate boards of directors and their influence on corporate philanthropy. *Journal of Business Ethics*, *42*(1), 1–10. doi:10.1023/A:1021626024014

Windsor, D. (2007). Toward a global theory of cross-border and multilevel corporate political activity. *Business & Society*, *46*(2), 253–278. doi:10.1177/0007650307301387

Windsor, D. (2013). Corporate social responsibility and irresponsibility: A positive theory approach. *Journal of Business Research*, *66*(10), 1937–1944. doi:10.1016/j.jbusres.2013.02.016

Wolf, R. (2008). *Ethics is Good for Business* (in Hebrew). Jerusalem; Reuven Mass.

Wolf, R. (2015a). Corporate Social Responsibility – Contribution to All. In R. Wolf, T. Issa, & M. Thiel (Eds.), Empowering organizations through corporate social responsibility, (pp. 255- 264). Hershey, PA: IGI Global.

Wolf, R. (2015b). Corporate Social Responsibility in the West (United States and West Europe) vs. East (China). In R. Wolf & T. Issa (Eds.), International business ethics and growth opportunities, (pp. 97-112). Hershey, PA: IGI Global.

Wolf, R. (2015c). Self-Awareness: A Way to Promote Ethical Management. In R. Wolf, & T. Issa (Eds.), International Business Ethics and Growth Opportunities, (pp. 147-157). Hershey, PA: IGI Global. doi:10.4018/978-1-4666-7419-6.ch007

Wolf, R., & Kantor, J. (2006). *Sarbanes-Oxley's Code of Ethics: An Attempt to deter 21th Century Wrongdoings With Financial Implications. Absolute Standards in an Age of Relativity.* Torea and Science, Proceedings.

Wood, D. J. (1991). Corporate social performance revisited. *Academy of Management Review*, *16*(4), 691–718.

World Bank. (2003). Better Governance for Development in the Middle East and North Africa: Enhancing Inclusiveness and Accountability, World Bank Washington, D.C. Retrieved from http://go.worldbank.org/LGTT1USV00

World Bank. (n. d.) Retrieved from: www.google.com/publicdata/explore

World Economic Forum. (2010). 2010 *World Economic Forum The Financial Development Report.* Retrieved from www.weforum.org

World Economic Forum. (2011). *State and Central Government Cooperation.* Retrieved from www.webforum.org

World Economic Forum. (2015). Report.

Wright, P. C., Szeto, W. F., & Lee, S. K. (2003). Ethical perceptions in China: The reality of business ethics in an international context. *Management Decision*, *41*(2), 180–189. doi:10.1108/00251740310457623

WWF. (2014). *Pulp and paper.* Retrieved from http://worldwildlife.org/industries/pulp-and-paper

Xinhua Daily Telegraph. (2013). 2012年全国农民工总量2.6亿 [The total number of national migrant workers reaches 260 million in 2012]. Retrieved from http://news.xinhuanet.com/mrdx/2013-02/23/c_132187270.htm

Xinhua News. (2006). The decisions on the key problems in building socialist harmonious society by Chinese communist party central committee. Retrieved from http://cpc.people.com.cn/GB/64093/64094/4932424.html

Xu, S., & Yang, R. (2010). Indigenous characteristics of Chinese corporate social responsibility conceptual paradigm. *Journal of Business Ethics*, *93*(2), 321–333. doi:10.1007/s10551-009-0224-8

Yakovleva, N., & Vasquez-Brust, D. (2012). Stakeholder Perspectives on CSR of Mining MNCs in Argentina. *Journal of Business Ethics*, *106*(2), 191–211. doi:10.1007/s10551-011-0989-4

Yap, N. T. (2015). CSR and the development deficit. Part of the solution or part of the problem. In Jamali, D., Karam, C., & Blowfield, M. (Eds.), Development Oriented Corporate Social Responsibility. (Vol. 1, pp. 134-152). Sheffield, UK: Greenfield.

Yekini, K., & Jallow, K. (2012). Corporate community involvement disclosures in annual report: A measure of corporate community development or a signal of CSR observance?' Sustainability Accounting. *Management and Policy Journal*, *3*(1), 7–32.

Yin, J. (2015). Institutional Drivers for Corporate Social Responsibility in an Emerging Economy A Mixed-Method Study of Chinese Business Executives. *Business & Society*.

Yin, J., & Zhang, Y. (2012). Institutional dynamics and corporate social responsibility (CSR) in an emerging country context: Evidence from China. *Journal of Business Ethics*, *111*(2), 301–316. doi:10.1007/s10551-012-1243-4

Yin, R. K. (1994). *Case study research: Design and methods* (2nd ed.). Newbury Park, CA: Sage.

Yin, R. K. (2013). *Case Study Research: Design and methods*. London: Sage publications.

Young, T. (1999). The State and Politics in Africa. *Journal of Southern African Studies*, *25*(1), 149–154. doi:10.1080/030570799108803

Zadek, S., & Wickerham, J. (2009). Managerial survey on corporate responsibility: China's CSR change makers. *Fortune China*. Retrieved from http://www.accountability.org/home.aspx

Zamora, A. C., & Ramos, J. (2010). Las actividades de la industria petrolera y el marco ambiental legal en Venezuela. Una visi6n crítica de su efectividad. *Revista Geográfica Venezolana*, *51*(1), 115–144.

Zander, I., McDougall-Covin, P., & Rose, E. L. (2015). Born globals and international business: Evolution of a field of research. *Journal of International Business Studies*, *46*(1), 27–35. doi:10.1057/jibs.2014.60

Zhang, Y. (2003, June). China's emerging civil society. Center for Northeast Asian Policy Studies, Brookings Institution.

Zhang, Zh., Ding, L. & Li, H. Zh. (n. d.). *China's pulp and paper industry: A Review*. School of Economics, Georgia Institute of Technology.

Zhang, M., & Liang, X. (2013). Advances Among Debates: Research On and Practice of Corporate Social Responsibility from the Legal Perspective in China. *Fordham Environmental Law Review*, *XXV*, 191–250.

Zhang, Z., & Han, F. (2008). Analysis of accounting disclosure model for strengthening Corporate Social Responsibility. *International Journal of Business and Management*, *3*(9), 157–161.

Zhao, M. (2012). CSR-based political legitimacy strategy: Managing the state by doing good in China and Russia. *Journal of Business Ethics*, *11*(4), 439–460. doi:10.1007/s10551-012-1209-6

Zhou, Z. (2008). Business ethics education in China's MBA curriculum. *Journal of Business Ethics Education*, *5*, 261–266.

Zhou, Z., Nakano, C., & Luo, B. N. (2011). Business ethics as field of training, teaching, and research in East Asia. *Journal of Business Ethics*, *104*(Suppl. 1), 19–27. doi:10.1007/s10551-012-1259-9

Zhou, Z., Ou, P., & Enderle, G. (2009). Business ethics education for MBA students in China. *Journal of Business Ethics Education*, *6*, 103–118.

Zoom Mobile. (2012). Retrieved from http://www.zoomnigeria.com/?page_id=4

Zu, L. (2009). *Corporate social responsibility, corporate restructuring and firm's performance - Empirical evidence from Chinese enterprises*. Berlin, Heidelberg: Springer-Verlag.

About the Contributors

Alessandro Bressan is a lecturer in the School of Business at the University of Notre Dame Sydney campus. Alessandro is a specialist in the fields of CSR and sustainability with additional interest in the relationships between sustainability, innovation and business environments. Alessandro has published extensively in these areas and supervises a number of postgraduate projects.

D. Kirk Davidson earned his BA degree from Princeton University, his MBA from Harvard University, and his PhD from Golden Gate University. He has had extensive careers in both business and academia.

María del Carmen Caba-Perez is an Assistant Professor in the Public Management Sector at the University of Almeria and Vice Dean in the Economics and Business Faculty. Her research is concerning to online transparency of public administration; nonprofit organizations and Venture Capital sectors. Dr. Caba's strong research and teaching activity has led to her being accredited as a Full Professor by ANECA, Spain's National Agency for Quality Assessment and Accreditation. She is author of several articles published in JCR publications including The American Review of Public Administration, International Review of Administrative Science, Online Information Review, Government Information Quarterly, Voluntas, Latin American Research Review or Public Administration and Development, Public Relations Review, Information Development, etc. Also, she has written more than 15 book chapters (Kluwer Academic Publishers; IGI Global, Springer, Cappelen Akademisk Forlag).

María del Mar Gálvez-Rodríguez is a lecturer of Management at the Economics and Business Faculty at the University of Almería (Spain). Her line of research is focused on online transparency, accountability and social media. She has published JCR articles in VOLUNTAS, Latin American Research, Review Public Relations Review, Information Development and Online Information Review.

Kerry E. Ground has been with Houston-based Acorn International, LLC since 2013 as an environmental and social risk management consultant. In particular, Kerry's work focuses on EIAs, EHS risk assessment and management, and social performance in the extractive industry worldwide. Kerry holds a Master of Science in International Planning and Development from the University of Guelph Canada.

Dieu Hack-Polay has worked in NGOs, Local Government and universities in the United Kingdom, Canada and China. He is currently Programme Leader and Senior Lecturer in Organisational Behaviour & Management at the University of Lincoln, UK and Executive President of the Institute of International Education Canada (IEC), Canada. Dieu has a Doctorate in Education (EdD) and a PhD in Sociology. He is a Fellow of the Higher Education Academy, UK.

Arturo Haro-de-Rosario is a lecturer at the Department of Economics and Business at the University of Almería (Spain). His research interests are focused on the financial information disclosures on the Web (e-government) and on the management system and communication in the federal and local governments. He is author of numerous articles in national and international journals, including *Small Business Economics, Social Science Computer Review, Transforming Government: People, Process and Policy, Local Government Studies* and so on. Also, he has written some book chapters (IGI Global and Springer).

Ahmad Hassan is an external lecturer at the Copenhagen Business School, Denmark. His research focuses on Corporate Social Responsibility (CSR) in developing countries, and political roles of business. Particularly, he is interested in exploring the governance processes and impact of Multi-stakeholder Initiatives in Global Value Chains.

Theodora Issa is a Senior Lecturer at Curtin University, Australia. Theodora's PhD thesis on ethical mindsets was the recipient of the 2010 EFMD/Emerald Outstanding Doctoral research award. Theodora also holds three Masters Degrees in Business Administration, Electronic Commerce and Management Research. In August 2011, Theodora was awarded 'The New Researcher of the Year' prize of the Curtin Business School, Australia. In 2013 Theodora was awarded the prize for Highest Return on Performance Index points for Early Career Researcher in Curtin Business School. Theodora is journals' associate editor. Theodora had published and continues to publish several peer-reviewed journals, books, edited books and book chapters. Theodora is a member of the World Council of Churches Central Committee, Geneva, Switzerland, and a member of the Education and Ecumenical Formation Commission, Geneva, Switzerland. Theodora is a member of the editorial committee of Noohro http://noohro.cjb.net and the church's community website http://soca.cjb.net.

Jensena Kaplan received her MBA from Loyola Marymount University in Marketing focusing on Corporate Social Responsibility, and holds a Bachelor of Science in Apparel Design from Oregon State University. She continues her work combining fiber science and sustainability working towards an executive management career in the U.S apparel market.

Peter Lund-Thomsen is Associate Professor at the Copenhagen Business School, Denmark. His research focuses on the linkages between global value chains, local economic development, and corporate social responsibility in developing countries.

Ivan Montiel is an Associate Professor of Management at Baruch College, City University of New York. His research interests include corporate social responsibility and sustainability strategies with a focus in emerging economies. He holds a Ph.D. from the Bren School of Environmental Science and Management at University of California, Santa Barbara. His research has been published in Strategic Management Journal, Journal of International Business Studies, Journal of Policy Analysis and Management, Journal of Economics & Management Strategy, Journal of Business Ethics, Business & Society and Organization & Environment among others.

Mohamed Nagy Osman is a lecturer in accounting, faculty of commerce, Benha University (Egypt). He holds PhD and master degrees from Queen Mary University of London and Dundee University (UK). Furthermore, He is an associate fellow in Higher Education Academy (UK). His research focuses on social, environmental and sustainability reporting in the Arab Middle East Countries (AMEC), transparency and governance.

David Pick is an Associate Professor in Management at Curtin University. His primary research focus is the study of change and identity in organizations. He has a particular interest in exploring public sector work and has published work on higher education, nursing and public sector managers. His ongoing research interests include applying literary theory to examining and understanding organization.

Julia M. Puaschunder graduated from the University of Vienna (2003 Master of Philosophy/Psychology, 2010 Doctor of Natural Sciences), Vienna University of Economics and Business (2006 Doctor of Social and Economic Sciences, 2007 Master of Business Administration), and the Maxwell School (2008 Master of Public Administration). She currently studies Law and Economics at the University of Vienna and The New School Department of Economics. Julia launched and administered research projects on four continents. She was invited to present her research at Harvard, Princeton, Columbia, Oxford and Cambridge as well as The Academic Council on the United Nations System. As a current Prize Fellow in the Inter-University Consortium of New York, she supports the Economics of Climate Change Project Speaker Series hosted at The Schwartz Center for Economic Policy Analysis. At The New School, her research investigates western world intergenerational equity constraints in the domains of environmental sustainability, over indebtedness, and demographic aging.

Haiyan Qiu is currently China Country Manager for European pulp producer SICEM-SAGA s.p.a, dealing with business development, marketing and contracts and customer relations in the pulp and paper industry. Petrel tutored in management at the Xi'an Jiaotong-Liverpool University. She holds a degree in English Language and a Masters in Management and is TESOL certified.

Lukman Raimi is a Senior Lecturer, Mentor & Economist at the Centre for Entrepreneurship Development, (CED), Yaba College of Technology Yaba Lagos, Nigeria. He has over fifteen years of management, research and lecturing experience in the academia. His research interests include: Corporate Social Responsibility, Economics of Development, Entrepreneurship and Human Resources Management. His research orientation is multidisciplinary with focus on developmental issues and economic growth.

Wajdi Ben Rejeb is an Assistant Professor at National Institute of Applied Sciences and Technology, University of Carthage, Tunisia. Dr. Ben Rejeb research fields cover topics in relation with corporate governance, corporate social responsibility and business ethics.

Monica Thiel is a member of the Academy of Management and the European Group for Organizational Studies. Her research articles and case studies have been published in the American Journal of Economics and Business Administration, International Journal of Business and Globalization, Asian Journal of Business and Management Cases, Procedia: Social and Behavioral Sciences, and the International Journal of Entrepreneurship and Innovation. Prior to her pursuit of a PhD in Social Science at the

Tilburg School of Social and Behavioral Sciences, she worked in multinational corporations, non-profit organizations, government, military and small–medium enterprises in business management and social responsibility initiatives. Her current research interests include corporate social responsibility, sustainability, competitiveness, strategic management and innovation.

Angela Torrisi holds a Bachelor of Public Relations & Marketing from the University of Notre Dame and has continued her work in CSR into a PhD. Her area of interest focuses on the strategic integration of CSR into business models and the ethical impacts that this has on business activity.

Duane Windsor, PhD (Harvard University), is Lynette S. Autrey Professor of Management in the Jesse H. Jones Graduate School of Business, Rice University. His work focuses on corporate social responsibility and stakeholder theory. He has published a number of books and in various academic journals.

Ruth Wolf (PhD) is an expert in ethics and business administration at Bar-Ilan University in Israel and also taught at The Hebrew University. To date, she has authored about 80 publications. The most recent books,' International Business Ethics and Growth Opportunities' (2015, IGI) and 'Empowering Organizations through Corporate Social Responsibility' (2015, IGI). Both books were Published by the University of Pennsylvania/ IGI. The topics she writes about include: Legislation of ethics, training for ethics conduct employee-employer relations, CSR, leadership, and business administration. She is also credited with a theory that she composed regarding ethical and moral training and education. In addition, she is a mediator and has taught mediation to generations of students in the academy as part of the management outlook that promotes" managing from the heart".

Hélène de Burgh-Woodman is Associate Dean – Research and Academic Development and Postgraduate Co-ordinator at The University of Notre Dame Sydney School of Business. Hélène has published extensively in several top-tier journals and is a respected scholar in the field of consumer research. Hélène currently supervises numerous postgraduate projects in management and marketing. She has been the recipient of an Endeavour Research Fellowship, chaired various research committees and been a member of ERA review panels. She has also held positions in industry as a senior marketing manager and a marketing/management consultant.

Nonita T. Yap is Professor at the University of Guelph, Canada. She holds a PhD in Chemistry and Masters in Environmental Studies. She has worked in nearly 20 developing countries in Asia, Africa, the Middle East, and Latin America on waste management, cleaner production and environmental impact assessment.

Juelin Yin is an Associate Professor of Management at the International Business School Suzhou in Xi'an Jiaotong-Liverpool University, Suzhou China. She has taught and researched on corporate social responsibility, with a particular interest in the CSR strategies in emerging country contexts. She holds a PhD from Nankai University and did her postdoctoral research in Harvard University. She has published over ten articles in journals including Journal of Business Ethics, Long Range Planning, and Business & Society.

Index

P

R

S

T

U

V

W

Y

www.ingramcontent.com/pod-product-compliance
Lightning Source LLC
LaVergne TN
LVHW060411300926
849162LV00006B/1397

9781522507208